HANDBOOK
TO LIFE
IN THE ANCIENT
MAYA WORLD

LYNN V. FOSTER

Facts On File, Inc.

Handbook to Life in the Ancient Maya World

Facts On File, Inc.
132 West 31st Street
New York NY 10001

Library of Congress Cataloging-in-Publication Data
Foster, Lynn V.
    Handbook to life in the Ancient Maya world / Lynn V. Foster.
       p. cm.
    Includes bibliographical references and index.
    ISBN 0-8160-4148-2
    1. Mayas—History. 2. Mayas—Social life and customs. I. Title.

F1435 .F676 2001

2001023924

Facts On File books are available at special discounts when purchased in bulk quantities for businesses, associations, institutions, or sales promotions. Please call our Special Sales Department in New York at (212) 967-8800 or (800) 322-8755.

You can find Facts On File on the World Wide Web at http://www.factsonfile.com

Text design by Cathy Rincon
Cover design by Semadar Megged
Graphics research by Peter Selverstone
Illustrations on chapter openers courtesy of John Montgomery

Printed in the United States of America

VB Hermitage 10 9 8 7 6 5 4

This book is printed on acid-free paper.

CONTENTS

To the collaborative spirit, intellectual generosity,
and friendships that have been fostered by the
Maya Meetings at Texas,
founded by Linda Schele.

ACKNOWLEDGMENTS

Writing this book has demonstrated to me the incomparable kindness of Maya scholars and friends. Peter Selverstone undertook the daunting task of organizing the numerous illustrations in the *Handbook* and preparing them for publication, forsaking many weekends and evenings in the process. Kaylee Spencer-Ahrens and Linnea H. Wren braved snowstorms and Ruth Krochock left her hospital bed in order to meet manuscript deadlines. Peter Mathews set aside his own scholarship demands to carefully review the manuscript. Ian Graham, Justin Kerr, John Montgomery, David Schele, and Cherra Wyllie generously granted permission to reproduce many photographs and drawings to improve the pages of this book, and Nikolai Grube, Peter Keeler, Barbara MacLeod, Dorie Reentz-Budet, Peter Foster and Naomi Smith readily offered contributions. I am forever grateful to them all.

FOREWORD

When one thinks about the Maya civilization of southern Mexico and northern Central America, the adjective *mysterious* inevitably comes to mind. *The mysterious Maya* has been an epithet for this great people for the past two centuries at least. Early Spanish expeditions found the remains of great ruined cities and speculated that they were evidence of the lost tribes of Israel. Nineteenth-century travel writers explored the cities and echoed the same sentiments or brought the lost continent of Atlantis into the equation; only a few travelers such as John Lloyd Stephens maintained that the cities and temples were built by the ancestors of the very people whose villages and towns they passed through on their journeys: the Maya. Even in the middle of the 20th century—when virtually all scholars agreed that the ruined cities in the jungle were built by ancient Maya—there was considerable debate about the origin and nature of Maya civilization.

By the early 1950s most scholars believed that what we now recognize as Maya cities were "vacant ceremonial centers," inhabited only by a few calendar-priests and their retainers and used as places of ritual for the surrounding hamlets of peasant-farmers. This view held that the Maya did not have cities, and according to some scholars, if the Maya had a complex society it could only have been introduced from outside: the Maya area was too impoverished, with its tropical forest and poor soils and lack of resources, to sustain "civilization." Moreover, Maya hieroglyphic inscriptions were all astrological mumbo-jumbo: to write of history and kings and individual exploits would have been sacrilegious.

This view of the ancient Maya began to change in the late 1950s and 1960s. On the archaeological front, excavations were being made, not just in temples and ceremonial precincts, but also in surrounding mounds, where evidence of houses and household activities was discovered. The "vacant ceremonial centers" were not vacant after all: some ancient Maya cities were inhabited by tens of thousands of Maya. On the hieroglyphic front, major discoveries between 1958 and 1964 led to the discovery of the names of historical individuals and of the cities they ruled. These cities were governed by dynasties of kings, and the magnificent stone stelae, altars, and lintels recorded their exploits—their births and deaths, their conquests and ceremonies.

Thus over the past 40 years or so, and especially over the past 20 years, the popular view of the ancient Maya has been radically transformed. The earlier view of a strange society unlike any other in Earth's history has yielded to one that has much more in common with other world civilizations. Finally, the Maya have become less mysterious—and more human—with human strengths and foibles.

There has not been any single great breakthrough in the study of the Maya that has been responsible for this progress, although breakthroughs there have certainly been. Rather, the advances have been similar to those in most other fields of endeavour; they are the result of patient and painstaking work by dozens of scholars working in a variety of disciplines to find yet one more piece of the puzzle. And while the puzzle still has many missing pieces, both the "big picture" and many of its details are now clear and in focus.

The recent advances in our knowledge of the ancient Maya have been the result of research in many fields—archaeology, epigraphy, ethnohistory—and the result of learning from the contemporary Maya.

From archaeology we have come to learn about the dating of ancient Maya civilization and the various stages in its development. We now know that large public buildings were being built in the Maya area several centuries before Christ, and by the time of Christ huge cities existed in the central part of the Yucatán Peninsula. From trenches and tunnels excavated into major architectural complexes at sites like Tikal in northern Guatemala and Copán in Honduras, we know that Maya ceremonial precincts were built and rebuilt above long-sacred localities. In some cases, the resulting seventh- or eighth-century C.E. temples cover dozens of earlier building phases stretching back more than 1,000 years earlier.

Inside temple-pyramids, archaeologists have excavated royal tombs that reveal sumptuous burial offerings of jade, shell, and pottery. Other excavations in more humble structures have shown how the other 85 percent or so of Maya lived and died: skeletal remains have been analyzed for evidence of disease, nutrition, and dietary patterns.

Archaeology has also revealed much about the ancient Maya environment—from the damage that was done to the forest through centuries of overclearing during the first millennium C.E. to studies of plaster making, stone quarrying, and water-storage management. Analyses of pottery and stone tools have led to a greater understanding of Maya trade.

Still other studies by scholars in different fields—from art historians who study the wonderful art left by the Maya to linguists who have been able to reconstruct the ancient forms of their languages—have elucidated other aspects of the ancient Maya.

Some of the greatest advances in our understanding of the ancient Maya have come from the decipherment of Maya hieroglyphic writing. The process of decipherment has now reached the point where the content of most inscriptions is now well understood, and most texts can be translated fairly completely. Debate over the glyphs has now reached the level of debate over grammatical forms and the finer details of glyphic spelling.

The Maya have long been famed for their mathematical and astronomical knowledge, for their use of zero and place-value notation, and their knowledge of eclipses and the cycles of Venus. Maya hieroglyphs also reveal the names of Maya kings and the nature of ceremonies over which they presided. We know of the gods who presided over their spiritual world and of the companion spirits of the Maya kings and lords that enabled them to travel into and communicate with the Otherworld. We know about Maya social structure and political organization and the almost endemic warfare between the Maya kingdoms: kings could gain great power and prestige (and wealth through tribute) through victory in battle, but they could also lose, quite literally, their heads.

A great source of our knowledge of the ancient Maya is the wealth of "ethnohistorical" data that survives about the Maya. From the Quiché Maya of highland Guatemala we have their great epic the *Popol Vuh*, which includes one of humankind's great creation stories. From northern Yucatán we have the *Books of the Chilam Balam*, with their mixture of prophecy and arcane astrological knowledge, and a book of medical incantations, the *Ritual of the Bacabs*—to name just a few.

It is a great irony that the early Spaniards, who did so much to destroy the traditional ways of the 16th-century Maya, have also been responsible for preserving myriad details on all aspects of ancient Maya life. The first Spanish friars in the Maya area realized early on that the only way they could hope to proselytize the Maya was to do it in the various Mayan languages. Accordingly, they compiled various dictionaries and wrote grammars and other works in many of the Mayan languages. These works have come to be important tools for scholars working with the hieroglyphic inscriptions. They are also invaluable for the wealth of information that they contain on the lifeways of the 16th-century Maya, from small dictionary entries that shed some light on an ancient Maya ritual to full ethnographies such as Diego de Landa's lengthy treatise *An Account of the Things of Yucatán*.

One of the great advantages in our understanding of the ancient Maya is the fact that the Maya are still very much alive. The contemporary Maya number in the millions, and there are still two dozen Mayan languages spoken today. In some cases the Maya are still practicing traditions that are thousands of years old. Our ability to learn from the contemporary Maya about their ancient forebears is in stark contrast to some other ancient civilizations, such as that of Sumer and ancient Egypt.

The first three chapters of this book introduce the ancient Maya and their great civilization. The first gives an overview of the history of research into the ancient Maya and of the recent advances that have made Classic Maya civilization so much more understandable.

The second and third chapters concern the history and geography of Maya civilization, respectively. Chapter 2 summarizes the development and growth of Maya civilization using the time periods into which Mayanists have conventionally divided Maya history. This overview concentrates on the three subphases of the Classic Period (250–1000 C.E.)—the peak of ancient Maya cultural achievement.

Chapter 3 is ostensibly about the geography of the Maya area but is in fact far more: it also covers climate and climate change, cultivars and natural resources, and the location of Maya settlement. It concludes with a brief description of more than 50 sites in the Maya area, including the most important of the Classic Maya cities.

In the remaining chapters of the book the authors present details of various aspects of ancient Maya life, from ancient Maya society and rulership (Chapter 4) to warfare (Chapter 5), from religion and the afterlife (Chapters 6 and 7) to Maya architecture and construction (Chapter 8). Chapter 9 deals with Maya calendrics and astronomy, and Chapter 12 with Maya hieroglyphic writing; Chapter 11 concerns Maya economy and trade.

The final chapter deals with the daily life of the ancient Maya. As with the information in the preceding chapters, much of the information on Maya daily life is gleaned from Spanish and Maya descriptions dating from the 16th century. Increasingly, however, information comes also from archaeology and epigraphy—from such diverse analyses as osteological analysis, for our understanding of ancient

Maya diet and nutrition, to analyses of art and hieroglyphic texts, for our understanding of Maya ritual, dancing and banquets.

In the process of reading these chapters, you will find that Maya civilization is both exotic and human. Their ancient beliefs and practices may in some instances seem strange to us. But their shortcomings are all too familiar, and some aspects of their history—such as the widespread environmental destruction that they had wreaked upon much of their landscape by the end of the Classic period—has a dark lesson for us today when so much of the Maya area is again under threat, as are tropical forests everywhere. In other words, the adjectives used to describe the ancient Maya have changed. The Maya are no longer so *mysterious*. Precocious they certainly were, and esoteric perhaps, but above all, they come across from history and from the pages of this book as *human*, with all the greatness and foibles of civilizations around the world.

The authors of this book have done a masterful job in amassing information about Maya civilization from a wide variety of sources and from some reports that are so recent that they have not yet been published. This is no mean task, considering the huge amount of ink that is now expended on the ancient Maya each year and the wide array of professional journals and other publications through which that ink is spread. In a field where new information emerges almost daily, and major discoveries still occur several times each year, the authors are impressively current in the information they provide. Lynn Foster has been responsible for most of the text, but she has been ably assisted by Kaylee Spencer-Ahrens and Linnea H. Wren (Chapters 6 and 9) and Ruth Krochock (Chapter 10). They have collaborated well: this book is an easy-to-read and most up-to-date account of ancient Maya civilization.

In March 2001, tens of thousands of Maya Zapatistas and their supporters poured into the Zócalo, the main square in Mexico City (and the heart of the former Aztec capital Tenochtitlan). The symbolism of this act is hard to underestimate. The Zapatistas are a popular army of Maya who are fighting in Chiapas, southern Mexico, for indigenous rights. The fact that they successfully completed a 3,000-kilometer journey from their jungle base to the Mexican capital, to be greeted there by thousands of supporters and sympathizers, shows what a potent force the Maya still are in the area of their ancestral homeland.

Upon reading this book, then, you will find that the ancient Maya are not nearly so "mysterious" as they used to be. While there is still much to discover about the Maya, this book shows how much is now known about this remarkable ancient civilization.

—Peter Mathews

INTRODUCTION

In just the last few decades, great strides—quantum leaps, in fact—in our knowledge of Maya civilization have been made. As the results from excavations and regional surveys have been reported, the sheer volume of new archaeological evidence has collapsed old theories and forced a reevaluation of virtually every aspect of the ancient Maya world. The sudden and fast-paced decipherment of Maya hieroglyphic writing has humanized the Maya, providing names for rulers, their spouses, and their children and exposing their political intrigues and wars of conquest. Studies of Maya art have revealed world creation myths and royal bloodletting rituals.

These different areas of expertise—archaeology; epigraphy, or the decipherment of the hieroglyphs; and iconography—have joined together to create a multidisciplinary field that has achieved a level of understanding of the ancient Maya world that was once thought impossible. Greater understanding has also prompted energetic debate about some of the most fundamental aspects of Maya civilization. There is every reason to expect yet new surprises will be forthcoming from ongoing investigations. In the year 2000, one of the longest hieroglyphic texts known from the Classic Maya world was discovered at the site of Piedras Negras in Chiapas, Mexico. The discovery of the palace of a Palenque king in 1999 threw new light on what was considered one of the best-known Maya cities. Paleobotanical studies are just now illuminating the agricultural foundations of Maya civilization. Ceramic paste analyses are permitting archaeologists to pinpoint where a looted vase was made and the point of origin of widely traded wares.

Maya studies remains a dynamic field, subject to new discoveries and even revolutionary changes in perspective. This *Handbook to Life in the Ancient Maya World* will draw on this basic truth, presenting the contrasts between old and new theories and providing the background for understanding ongoing debates. It is hoped that the reader, understanding the process of discovery and the give-and-take of scientific discussion, will become engaged in the intellectual excitement that pervades the field.

A Note on Orthography

There are different spellings of Maya place-names used in the literature. The *Handbook* has followed spellings that coincide most closely with how these place-names are spelled in their country of origin: Yucatán, for example, not Yukatan. And their spelling includes accent marks to help the reader pronounce these place-names as they are in Mayan languages, with emphasis placed on the last syllable. Following current linguistic practice, many Mayan words are spelled with apostrophes to indicate where they are pronounced with glottalized consonants. Nahuatl place-names, such as Teotihuacan, are pronounced with emphasis on the penultimate syllable, unlike Mayan words; they are rendered in the text without diacritical marks.

LIST OF MAPS

LIST OF ILLUSTRATIONS

LIST OF TABLES

1

MAYA CIVILIZATION AND ARCHAEOLOGY

Pre-Columbian Maya civilization spans a period of nearly 2,000 years. Well before all the salient features of this civilization were completely developed, the Maya were building monumental ceremonial and civic centers. This urban tradition endured from 600 B.C.E. until 1524, when the Spanish Conquest of the Maya began. Maya civilization began to evolve in the Middle Preclassic Period (1000 B.C.E.–300 C.E.), flourished in the Classic Period (250–900 C.E.), which many archaeologists and art historians consider its apogee, and redefined itself during the Postclassic Period (900–1524) to overcome regional wars, droughts, and even cultural collapse, persisting in new ways for two millennia. Maya civilization is admired for more than its endurance, however. It is among the most sophisticated pre-Columbian cultures in the New World and is renowned for its artistry and achievements in astronomy and hieroglyphic writing.

The ancient Maya inhabited the region that is now divided among the Mexican states of Yucatán, Quintana Roo, Campeche, Chiapas, and Tabasco and the modern-day nations of Guatemala, Belize, western Honduras, and El Salvador. Here they built their cities and erected stone monuments to their rulers and their gods. The *Handbook* focuses on the development of Maya culture during the 2,000 years that it was an urban civilization. The Maya, however, have occupied the region far longer than these remarkable centuries of their ancient civilization. Millions of Mayas live in the region today, and many continue to live by traditions that regulated the lives of their distant ancestors. Before the rise of the monumental architecture and stone carving that are the hallmarks of pre-Columbian civilization, the Maya lived here in simple villages. Even before agriculture was introduced to the region around 2000 B.C.E., they lived in fishing settlements constructed of perishable materials along the rivers and marshes. By 1550 B.C.E., pottery was being used in the southern region, and by 1200 B.C.E. the presence of pottery and earthen constructions was quite widespread. Jade deposits were worked in the Motagua Valley by at least 900 B.C.E., and from the same period, a ritual bloodletter for self-sacrifice was found at the lowland site of Seibal. For more than 4,000 years, then, the Maya have occupied the region.

Maya civilization evolved, flourished, and declined over the millennia, but it consistently remained distinctively Maya. Its fluid art style and portraiture contrast with that of most contemporary cultures in neighboring areas of Middle America. There is considerable unity across the Maya region: The art of highland Guatemala in the Late Preclassic Period (300 B.C.E.–250 C.E.), for example, can be strikingly similar to that of northern Yucatán. Also, the same type of architecture and ritual and elite goods are found across Maya regions. Yet this cultural unity never resulted in a single Maya empire but resulted instead in many nation states.

As distinctive and artistically homogenous as Maya civilization seems on first impression, there are regional and local differences. Maya cities exhibit unusual variety in their setting and size, in their longevity and political authority, and even in their artistic preferences. Artistic preferences varied from city to city, most favoring low-relief sculpture, some preferring stucco reliefs, and a few tending toward sculpture in the round. The Maya themselves spoke several mutually unintelligible languages during the apogee of their civilization, and the number increased as the culture fragmented over time. (There were 31 Mayan languages documented by the Spaniards at the time of the conquest.) Despite such diversity, Maya culture remained remarkably homogenous throughout the lowlands, from the Petén to the Yucatán Peninsula.

Map 1. *Mesoamerica. The ancient Maya civilization was an integral part of what archaeologists call* Mesoamerica. *Mesoamerica did not coincide with any modern nation or single people, but rather encompassed most of Mexico, all of Guatemala, Belize, El Salvador, and parts of Honduras, Nicaragua, and Costa Rica.*

Maya civilization developed as part of a broader and older cultural area called Mesoamerica. Mesoamerica encompassed much of Mexico and extended south, at times all the way into parts of Nicaragua and Costa Rica. The first pottery, the first cities, and even the first known instances of hieroglyphic writing had their origin in Mesoamerica in the millennium before the rise of Maya civilization. Although the Maya region accounted for one-third of the territory, Mesoamerica included other important cultures, such as the Olmec and the Aztec, and Maya civilization developed through constant interaction with these other Mesoamerican cultures. All these cultures traded with each other and shared mythologies and a sacred calendar. Also, they all built massive cities and created exceptional art with an astonishingly limited technology: They had no wheel for pottery, no pack animals or carts for transport, and no metal tools until the last centuries before the Spanish Conquest—even then, the tools were only copper blades and fishing hooks, not bronze or steel hatchets.

DEVELOPMENTS IN MAYA ARCHAEOLOGY

The Lost Maya

Knowledge of Maya civilization is relatively recent, and archaeological investigations, even more so. Until the early 19th century, antiquarians were unaware that Classic Period Maya civilization had ever existed. Although they were familiar with artifacts that later turned out to be Maya, the few Maya codices, or painted manuscripts, that made their way to Europe were initially identified as Aztec, the

culture best known from the Spanish Conquest. Historical circumstances prevented scholars from understanding the origin of these artifacts. At the time of the conquest, the Classic Period of Maya civilization had been over for more than 500 years, and the Petén, the heartland of this ancient culture, had reverted to tropical forest. By the time conquistador Hernán Cortés cut his way through the Petén in 1525, the ancient cities were hidden under centuries of forest growth. Although 16th-century Spanish missionaries working in the Yucatán Peninsula and highland Guatemala wrote about the Maya and their preconquest cities, the reports of these religious men gathered dust in European archives, and any clues they held to the Maya past were forgotten. During the three centuries of Spanish colonial rule, the Classic Period ruins and their relationship to other Mesoamerican cultures remained almost unknown.

Early Explorers

Once Mexico and Central America gained their independence from Spain in the early 19th century, explorers traveled through the Maya region in search of the lost cities and recorded what they found. Such explorations were charged with romantic excitement: Here was the discovery of a civilization that had developed far from the influences of Old World civilizations. The American lawyer John Lloyd Stephens and the English artist Frederick Catherwood brought the forgotten civilization to the world's attention in well-illustrated, best-selling volumes describing their travels through the Maya lowlands in 1839 and 1842. Other explorers made important contributions in the late 19th century; foremost among them was the Englishman Alfred P. Maudslay, who traveled through the Maya region for 13 years,

ical and calendrical system of the ancient Maya. Once the Long Count Calendar was understood (see page 255), the Classic Period could be dated. The importance of the Long Count for not just Maya but Mesoamerican archaeology cannot be overemphasized. Once correlated with our Gregorian calendar, the Maya Long Count yields absolute dates, such as May 10, 810 C.E. Radiocarbon (also called carbon 14 or RC) and other modern dating methods are accurate only within a range of 100 or more years; stratigraphic and other analyses result in a relative chronology of earlier and later but cannot yield absolute dates by themselves. The exactitude of the Long Count dates in combination with carbon-14 dates, as well as shared pottery and other artifacts, have allowed archaeologists to cross-date events in the rest of Mesoamerica as well. Unfortunately, however, most Long Count dates survive only from the Classic Period.

Excavations and Technology

The first large-scale investigation of a Maya site took place in the 1890s at Copán (in present-day Honduras) and was sponsored by the Peabody Museum of Harvard University. In the decades between World Wars I and II, other long-term projects were initiated: For example, Uaxactún, excavated from 1926 to 1937, was the first site closely studied in the Maya heartland of the Petén; and work at Chichén Itzá from 1924 to 1946 in northern Yucatán provided information on the transition from the Late Classic to the Postclassic Period. At the same time, less ambitious projects were undertaken at smaller sites.

Excavations often were (and still are) conducted under difficult circumstances. Since the abandonment of many Maya city-states in the

1.1   A carved Maya stela depicting a ruler of Copán, Honduras, Late Classic Period.   (Lithograph Frederick Catherwood, 1844)

photographing and carefully recording the hieroglyphic inscriptions, the art, and the architecture of such great Maya cities as Copán, Yaxchilán, Palenque, and Chichén Itzá.

The publication of these early studies, especially Maudslay's eight-volume scholarly work, finally enabled the correct identification of the writing system of the codices found in libraries in Paris, Madrid, and Dresden as the same as the hieroglyphs on Maya monuments. The enlarged corpus of hieroglyphs also laid the foundation for the decipherment of the numer-

tropical lowlands in the ninth and 10th centuries C.E., trees and vines have ripped at stone buildings, rain has decomposed perishable materials such as wood carvings, cloth, and paper books, and acidic soils have eaten away at bones. Yet these archaeological materials are often the best evidence for reconstructing the past. Dense vegetation similarly has hampered surveys of the region, but new sites have been identified and continue to be rediscovered to this day. In the past, *chicleros*, or workers for chewing gum companies who tapped trees in some of the remotest regions, often were the trailblazers for archaeologists; today, radar photography and a disappearing forest canopy have made the job of Mayanists easier.

In the late 1950s, the University Museum of the University of Pennsylvania undertook the long-term investigation of the great Petén city of Tikal, located in Guatemala. These excavations began a cycle of field studies throughout the Maya region that eventually culminated in a fuller understanding of the evolution of the civilization that took root there. In the early 20th century, archaeologists thought Maya civilization began around 300 C.E. based on the then-known Long Count dates. Archaeological remains of earlier monuments were difficult to detect; many were embedded inside later ones, much like nested tables, or they were destroyed and recycled into rubble fill for new construction. But today, findings from excavations of an increasing number of sites with clearer and longer stratigraphic deposits (the layers of cultural debris; the most recent deposits are on the surface, the oldest are most deeply buried and are often found atop bedrock) have pushed back the beginnings of Maya urban civilization to at least 600 B.C.E. Ruined Preclassic Maya cities, such as Nakbé (c. 600 B.C.E.–250 C.E.), which were discovered late in the 20th century, are treasure troves of early monuments with no subsequent construction preventing their study. And at Copán, recent excavators have used new technology to reveal early structures without collapsing the later buildings that still encase them.

Settlement Surveys

Archaeologists have discovered more than stone monuments commemorating the feats of Maya nobility. Settlement surveys have revealed details about farming techniques and the lives of the supporting population. Technology has facilitated this work: Electronic distance meters (EDM) and video cameras permit sophisticated computer mapping of sites; airborne radar sensing has been used to detect preconquest farm systems of artificially raised fields. Simpler devices, such as flotation machines and fine-mesh sieves, retrieve fossilized seeds, faunal remains, and other materials for laboratory analysis. These seeds, phytoliths (plant traces), bones, and charcoal have revealed much about the environment and diet of the ancient Maya, about the causes of death, and even, based on radiocarbon analysis and stratigraphy, about the timeframe in which such events occurred. These studies have forced archaeologists to revise their former beliefs about when the Maya first occupied the lowlands and about the population levels of Classic Maya cities, as well as agricultural practices needed to support such dense populations (see Chapter 2).

Epigraphy

Improvements in technology and in the sheer volume of the archaeological record of the ancient Maya have been accompanied in recent decades by the decipherment of Maya hieroglyphic writing. Material remains have now combined with the literary record to revolutionize the understanding of pre-Columbian Maya civilization. From the late 19th century until the mid-20th century, scholars believed the Maya writing system was basically undecipherable except for calendrical notations and astronomical observations, which were all that could be understood at the time. In the 1950s, however, linguists, art historians, and epigraphers, or those who study ancient writing systems, started deciphering texts and revealed a world of Maya politics and dynastic history (see Chapter 10). No longer can scholars believe peaceful priest-astronomers, concerned only with measuring time and honoring the gods, ruled Maya cities when the decoded texts tell the war stories of all-powerful secular rulers. These pre-Columbian histories, however, are basically limited to the Classic Period (250–900 C.E.), when Maya rulers carved their dynastic boasts into stone monuments that could survive the erosion of time.

Multidisciplined Approaches

Technology, epigraphy, and the great increase in the number of excavated sites have enabled archaeologists to reconstruct many aspects of the development of Maya civilization. Although our understanding of two millennia of ancient Maya civilization has reached new levels of complexity, much remains to be learned. The most formative periods still are not well understood, for example, nor is there a scientific consensus on the cause of such a momentous event as the ninth-century collapse of the Petén cities—despite the existence of hieroglyphic texts from that period. The exact nature of the relationships between Maya cities and central Mexican ones remains controversial as well.

Some day, perhaps, a technique for reconstructing the decomposed books buried in rulers' tombs will open new pages to the past. Oxygen isotope analysis may clarify the nature of climatic changes during the Classic Period collapse. And skeletal remains may prove adequate to provide strontium-90 studies and DNA clues as to dynastic relationships between various states. But even without new technologies, the interdisciplinary study of the Maya past involving art historians, linguists, and epigraphers, as well as archaeologists, has brought about a level of understanding that was not thought possible a few decades ago. Each new excavation and newly deciphered text will only add to this understanding—and challenge it, if the past few decades are any guide. Maya archaeology remains an ongoing process.

SOURCE MATERIALS

The types of material available for understanding the pre-Columbian Maya range greatly, from modern archaeological techniques to the artifacts and books produced by the Maya themselves.

Monuments

Entire ruined cities built of stone have been recovered. Quite a number have been excavated, and some have been partially restored for tourism, such as Tikal in the Guatemala lowlands of the Petén, Copán in western Honduras, and Chichén Itzá in Yucatán. The architecture and sculpture found at these sites vary with location and time period, but most Maya cities were constructed around massive political and ceremonial centers, with lesser struc-

1.2   The palace at the ruined eighth-century city of Palenque, in Mexico.   (Photo courtesy Lawrence Foster)

tures and simple houses or huts built on the periphery. Raised and plastered roads sometimes joined sections of cities, and occasionally, they joined cities: The longest known *sacbe*, or road, links the Mexican site of Cobá with Yaxuná, 100 kilometers (62 miles) away.

City centers at Maya sites usually include palace structures, ritual ball courts, dance platforms, and pyramid-temples (flat-topped pyramids with temples constructed atop them). Royal tombs have been excavated in the base of some pyramids and under elite residences; steam baths have been found near both religious buildings and residential ones. Stucco masks often decorate early buildings,

and bas-reliefs and hieroglyphic texts are often carved on lintels and facades, as well as on free-standing stone monuments, called stelae. These monumental and urban legacies of the Maya enable archaeologists and art historians to reconstruct religious and political practices, social hierarchies, and settlement patterns. Moats and defensive walls indicate warfare. Stone canals and plastered reservoirs are evidence of agricultural and water-management practices. The carvings on monuments can provide a wealth of information on far less complex matters: The pattern woven into a woman's skirt and the feather design of a nobleman's headdress may have been made of perishable materials but are forever preserved in stone.

Pottery and Painting

Pottery is one of the most effective archaeological tools for reconstructing and dating the past. Pottery existed before the rise of stone buildings and urban architecture and represents traces of cultural evolution from early village life dating back to at least 1600 B.C.E. in the southern Maya region up to the abandonment of urban centers at the time of the Spanish Conquest. Pottery styles can define temporal periods, and layers of potsherds can define the duration of a site, once carbon 14 or the Maya Long Count has provided each phase with an absolute date. Also, shared pottery between regions indicates cultural interaction, whether direct or indirect, among various peoples, such as was the case with the Ocós villages on the Pacific coast of Guatemala and the Olmec villages along the Gulf coast of Mexico. In addition, Classic Period Maya ceramics exhibits some of the finest work of Maya artists. Maya polychrome vases, painted with courtly scenes as well as mythological ones and often accompanied by glyphic texts, present some of the most detailed and intimate glimpses into the ancient Maya world. Valued in pre-Columbian times, these vases were buried with the dead and have been preserved in tombs. The Maya painted walls as well. Murals such as those that cover three rooms at Bonampak, Mexico, depict war, autosacrifice, and palace scenes; cave paintings such as those at Naj Tunich in the Petén depict erotic rituals. Unlike the vases, few murals have survived the elements, but the use of infrared photography promises to facilitate the reconstruction of some of these lost works of art.

Precious Objects and Artifacts

Many types of objects have been recovered from tombs, household mounds, and dedicatory caches in buildings and sacred wells. Jade, serpentine, and, by the end of the Classic Period, turquoise were among the most precious materials to the Maya. Stingray spines, used by royalty as bloodletters, orange-red *Spondylus* shells, and pearls were also items precious enough to accompany wealthy Maya in death. Many of these items were carved into ornaments and made into jewelry. Obsidian, iron ores, and gold were polished into mirrors, probably used for divination and visions as well as for more mundane purposes. Gold and copper objects are found primarily after 800 C.E.; gold was shaped into luxury items, but copper was also made into practical ones, such as fishhooks and needles. When these items accompany burials, they usually indicate wealth and status. They also tell us about Maya dress, Maya social classes, and mortuary rituals and religious beliefs. Furthermore, they indicate trade among pre-Columbian peoples: Turquoise, for example, was traded from what is now the Southwest of the United States.

There are many other materials retrieved from excavations, among them are cinnabar, obsidian, chert, mica, and crocodile hides, as well as the rarely surviving pieces of wooden sculptures or fabric. Carved animal bones—and carved human ones, perhaps kept as relics of a famous ancestor or a trophy of a war victory—are also found in graves. Although obsidian could be carved into elaborate objects worthy of a tomb, it was also used for razor-sharp tools. Many such artifacts, shaped and formed and treasured by the Maya, can be carefully identified through various techniques—X-ray flourescence spectronomy (XRF) and

1.3 Examples of Classic and Postclassic trade ceramics from the Maya region. Early Classic Period (top row): stucco-covered bowl with lid from Tikal, painted with a deity in the style of Teotihua-can; molded effigy pot of a water bird with a fish in its beak and tetrapod legs. Late Classic Period (middle row): molded Puuc slateware bowl from Yucatán; detail of polychrome cylinder drinking vessel with hieroglyphs painted for the word kakawa, *or "chocolate," made in the Guatemala highlands. Postclassic Period (bottom row): molded Plumbate animal effigy vessel made on the Pacific coast of Guatemala; Mayapán-style effigy censer of a diving god from Yucatán* (Photos courtesy Peter Selverstone)

atomic absorption spectronomy (AAS), for example. Such techniques can identify the origin of materials such as obsidian, providing further evidence of trade patterns among the Maya and their neighbors; some techniques, such as obsidian hydration, can assist in dating the artifacts. Even when technology cannot reveal the source of materials—or date them—careful excavation often can. Most tools were made of chert and flint, and debris from these materials may indicate artisan workshops and worker specialization; Colhá, located near a source of chert, was an important Preclassic city.

Hieroglyphic Texts

Hieroglyphic texts carved into stone and jade or painted onto pottery are found as early as the Preclassic Period, and the number of texts increases over time until the end of the Classic Period. The earliest known Maya glyphlike carvings are from El Portón in the northwestern highlands of Guatemala and date from c. 400 B C.E. These texts continue until c. 1000 C.E. Despite this great time span in which hieroglyphic texts appear, the texts are most characteristic of the Classic Period. It once was an archaeological tradition to date the Classic Period from 292 C.E., the Long Count date (see Chapter 8) on a monument found in situ at Tikal, and to end the period with 909 C.E., the Long Count date on a monument from Toniná in Chiapas, Mexico. Although securely dated inscriptions occur before and after the Classic Period, most are concentrated within this time frame. Not only is the Long Count closely associated with the Classic Period, but so are most surviving glyphic texts. The history of the ancient Maya rulers that is now being reconstructed primarily concerns the 600 years or so of this epoch;

earlier periods of Mesoamerican civilization remain prehistoric, and the understanding of them must rely more heavily on archaeological reconstruction of material deposits.

Later periods, however, have been at least partially illuminated by written materials, including Spanish eyewitness accounts of the culture. After the Classic Period, the Maya did not revert to illiteracy; they simply stopped writing their dynastic histories and mythologies onto nonperishable materials. The Spanish conquistadores and missionaries described Maya books and Maya writing in the 16th century, and one priest in Yucatán claimed to have burned all the books he could find in order to destroy their pagan content. Only four Maya hieroglyphic manuscripts, called codices, survive today. All were compiled, written, and recopied in the centuries before the conquest. All four are devoted to astronomical and astrological topics, and each is a great resource for understanding Maya mathematics and astronomy as well as ritual and divinatory practices based on the calendar.

Postconquest Maya Books

Maya scribes adapted the Spaniards' Roman alphabet to their own needs, and continued writing books in Mayan languages after the conquest, but no longer in hieroglyphs. In the 17th and 18th centuries, a number of these secretly kept manuscripts came to light. The manuscripts seem to include material from a variety of sources: Some material apparently was recopied from preconquest hieroglyphic texts, other manuscripts are written in the cadence of what may have once been orally preserved histories and myths, and yet other texts contain postconquest materials. The most famous of these books is the *Popol Vuh*, originally written in Quiché Mayan, a language used in highland Guatemala. It records the Quiché's view of

1.4 A page from the Dresden Codex, *Postclassic Period. This page was painted with Maya hieroglyphic writing and shows scenes of deities performing rituals.* (Drawing Cyrus Thomas, 1882)

world creation as well as the history of the Quiché and their lineages from the dawn of the world until the middle of the 16th century. Father Francisco Ximénez found the manuscript early in the 18th century and copied it; his transcription of the Quiché manuscript is the only copy now known. Several other books have been preserved from Yucatán, such as the *Book of the Chilam Balam of Chumayel.* Maintained over the centuries, many of these books were written in Yucatec Mayan by priestly scribes known as the Chilam Balam. Some of the books tell the history of various Yucatecan peoples, such as the Xiu of Chumayel, from the founding of their territories in the mythic past. The language is often esoteric, and the story is related in the cyclical format of the ancient Maya *k'atun* calendar (see page 257). Difficult to understand, such postconquest Maya books are nonetheless important sources about creation myths and religion (the 18th-century *The Ritual of the Bacabs* mentions more than 150 deities) and about the history of certain Postclassic sites, such as Chichén Itzá. Combined with archaeological evidence and readings of the hieroglyphs, these works have proven invaluable to the reconstruction of the past.

Ethnologies and Ethnohistorical Documents

Books and letters written by Spanish conquistadores and 16th-century missionaries and administrators provide eyewitness descriptions of Mesoamerican civilization. Some missionaries devoted themselves to compiling information on this American culture, interviewing Mesoamerican leaders about their books, their origins and history, and their religious beliefs. The resultant chronicles provide the most detailed information about Mesoamerican civilization at the time of contact. Father Bernardino de Sahagún's 22-volume study of the Aztecs is a case in point. Although there was no missionary-"ethnohistorian" of Sahagun's stature in the Maya region, valuable studies were produced. The most important 16th-century chronicle of the Maya was written by Bishop Diego de Landa of Yucatán, whose compilation of a Maya "alphabet" led to the eventual decipherment of the hieroglyphs. Landa described Maya religious festivals that have been correlated with earlier, more cryptic descriptions, such as those in the *Dresden Codex.* Spain administered formal questionnaires to the populace that serve as another source of information on native practices and beliefs, as do the many legal documents submitted to Spanish officials by indigenous peoples entangled in land disputes. Recent ethnologies and ethnohistories have enriched our understanding not only of the contemporary Maya but also of the pre-Columbian worldview and rituals, and linguistic studies have led to the publication of dictionaries of many Mayan languages that assist in the decipherment of the hieroglyphs.

READING

See also "Reading" for Chapters 2, 9, and 10.

Culbert 1998: changing views of Maya civilization; Sabloff 1990: new developments in Maya archaeology; Scarre 1999: technological innovations Deuel 1974, Maudslay 1889–1902, Stephens 1962 and 1963 reprints: early descriptions of Maya ruins; Willey and Sabloff 1974: history of American archaeology; Love 1994: correlations between the codices and ethnohistories; Zeuner 1970: dating techniques.

2

EVOLUTION OF
MAYA CIVILIZATION

The evolution of Maya civilization was not a straightforward, progressive development from simple villages to great empires. Instead it today reads as an archaeological drama of fabulous attainments, tumultuous collapses, and renewal. Different areas of the Maya region rose to prominence during the unfolding of this drama. In the Archaic Period (7000–1200 B.C.E.), the southern region (the Pacific littoral and the Guatemala highlands) was the most precocious, for example. But in the Classic Period (250–900 C.E.), the south became peripheral to cultural developments in the lowlands, particularly in the Petén region of Guatemala, which is often called the heartland of Maya civilization. At the end of the Classic Period, most cities in the heartland were abandoned, but ones in northern Yucatán flourished into the Postclassic Period (900–1524 C.E.). And just before the arrival of the Spanish conquistadores, Maya civilization was most prominent in the peripheral areas around the heartland, in the southern region, along the Caribbean coast, and in northern Yucatán.

This chapter on the evolution of Maya civilization describes the different cultural periods recognized by archaeologists and the developments that distinguish each period. Before concentrating on Maya civilization, there is a brief introduction to the Lithic Period (c. 12,500–7000 B.C.E.) and the Archaic Period (7000–1200 B.C.E.), the periods when the Americas were first peopled and settled. The Early Preclassic Period (1200–1000 B.C.E.) is examined more fully because Mesoamerican civilization developed during this period, laying the foundation for Maya culture. In the Middle Preclassic Period (1000–300 B.C.E.) a distinctive Maya culture first appeared, stimulated by contacts with the rest of Mesoamerica. Maya culture becomes adequately complex to be defined as a civilization during the Late Preclassic Period (300 B.C.E.–250 C.E.), and it flourished at many sites in the lowlands during the Classic Period (250–900 C.E.). During the Postclassic Period (900 to the Spanish Conquest), the Maya region gradually became a less powerful part of Mesoamerica, particularly after the rise of the Aztecs in the 14th century.

SUMMARY OF MAJOR PERIODS

Lithic (c. 12,000–7000 B.C.E.)
Peopling of the Americas.

Archaic (c. 7000–1200)
Permanent settlements and plant domestication lead to more populous, socially stratified, and pottery-producing villages sustained by maize agriculture. By 1400 B.C.E., an Isthmian culture was shared from the Pacific coast of the Maya region to the Gulf coast of southern Veracruz.

Early Preclassic (c. 1200–1000)
Foundation of Mesoamerican civilization through evolution of Isthmian culture into Olmec culture, the first civilization of Mesoamerica.

Middle Preclassic (c. 1000–300)
A distinctive Maya culture evolves; Olmec civilization flourishes, then declines.

Late Preclassic (ca. 300 B.C.E.–250 C.E.)
The Izapán, or Epi-Olmec, horizon in the southern Maya area ushers in the stela cult with hieroglyphic texts and the earliest known Long Count date (31 B.C.E.). Maya urban civilization assumes its characteristic traits in the central and southern lowlands, or "heartland"; population

levels peak in settlements on the Pacific coast and in the Guatemala highlands.

Early Classic (c. 250–600)
Maya lowland cities flourish while ones on the Pacific coast decline or are abandoned; glyphic texts are carved on public monuments proclaiming feats of dynastic rulers; there is contact with the central Mexican city of Teotihuacan.

Late Classic (c. 600–900)
Maya lowland cities proliferate; number of public hieroglyphic texts increases. The culture reaches its artistic zenith. As the population peaks in the heartland, widespread warfare precedes the collapse of most southern lowland cities.

Terminal Classic (c. 800–1000)
A period that overlaps the Classic and Postclassic in order to focus on the transition from the decline of the Petén cities to the rise of a pan-Mesoamerican culture in northern Yucatán. By the end of the period, public monuments no longer are inscribed with texts and Long Count dates.

Early Postclassic (c. 900–1200)
Maya cities in the northern lowlands, particularly the great city of Chichén Itzá, are part of far-flung trade networks. Pan-Mesoamerican influences on the Maya art style typify the period, and the culture is less concerned with ruler glorification.

Late Postclassic (c. 1200–1521)
Maya rulers continue to govern cities on the periphery of the Maya region, especially in the Yucatán, along the Caribbean coast, and in fortified hill towns of highland Guatemala. Fortified cities typify the period, and the northern region is less invested in public monuments than in commerce. The Aztec Empire in central Mexico increasingly influences the Maya region and receives tribute from kingdoms in the Guatemala highlands.

Post-conquest (1521–2000)
Pre-Columbian Maya civilization ends with the Spanish conquest of Mesoamerica, which begins with the defeat of the Aztecs in 1521 and continues into the southern Maya region in 1524 and Yucatán in 1542. The Maya persevere; today approximately 10 million Maya live in the area.

LITHIC PERIOD (C. 12,000–7000 B.C.E.)

The first Americans arrived from Asia, traveling from Siberia to the North American continent by small shore-hugging boats or over an Ice Age land bridge that crossed the Bering Strait. The beginning date of this momentous event for the Americas is currently a matter of considerable debate among paleontologists, but there is agreement that these small hunting bands arrived during the Pleistocene, or Late Ice Age (40,000–7000 B.C.E.). A massive mammoth kill in central Mexico associated with human skeletal remains and fluted stone projectile points similar to 11,500-year-old Clovis points found in New Mexico date the arrival of these elephant hunters in Mesoamerica. Radiocarbon (RC) dates place Clovis hunters in the Maya region no later than 9000–8000 B.C.E. There may have been earlier migrations, but evidence for such migrations is not easily recovered: Along the coasts, traces of human presence have been submerged by rising sea levels, and in the highlands, volcanic eruptions may have buried evidence under thick layers of ash. While only a few scientists argue for an arrival as early as 40,000 B.C.E., all agree that humans arrived by at least 12,000 B.C.E. and not much later than 7000 B.C.E. Ten thousand years ago, a climatic change melted the polar ice caps until the Bering land bridge was submerged for the last time. The first peoples and their game were left to evolve on the American continents.

During the Pleistocene, there may have been different waves of migration from different parts of Asia: Evidence from Monte Verde, Chile, indicates the use of a tool kit different from the Clovis big-game hunters at least a thousand years before Clovis. However, the best-documented peoples—and the only ones currently documented for the region of Mesoamerica—are the big-game hunters from c. 11,500 years ago. These "Clovis" hunters followed the bison, mastodons, and hairy mammoths, or elephants that were 4 meters (13 feet) tall, across the 1,000-mile-wide tundra of the Bering land mass into what is now Alaska. Successive generations eventually made their way down an ice-free corridor along the edge of the Rocky Mountains into Mexico and Central America. The climatic changes at the end of the Ice Age forced these nomadic hunters to adapt to a different environment. Less rain and shrinking grasslands—and perhaps overexploitation of big game—led to the extinction of these animals, including the giant armadillo and the Ice Age horse. But in what is now Mexico and Central America, the absence of the vast grasslands of the Great Plains probably made big-game hunting a somewhat unreliable food source from the beginning. Toward the end of the Lithic Period, the descendants of the Clovis hunters came to subsist on smaller game, such as deer, rabbits, and wildcats and even lizards, mice, and locusts. The daily hunt for food included wild plants and seeds and, when feasible, fishing in the shallows of bays, estuaries, and lakes.

The selection and modification of wild plants led to the early domestication of a few species: The 10,000-year-old seeds of domesticated squash have been identified in a Oaxacan cave in Mexico, and domesticated squash and chiles are relatively widespread in Mesoamerica by 7000 B.C.E. But these cultivars accounted for no more than 5 percent of the diet and did little to change the nomadic lifestyle of Americans. They remained hunters (meat constituted 54 percent of the diet of highland peoples) and foragers.

The quality of Amerindian existence depended on the environment, of course, but all these New World peoples exploited seasonal econiches and, when possible, lived in naturally protective shelters or caves. In highland regions, where hunter-gatherers would have had more difficulty foraging for food during the dry season than those in coastal regions, population levels were low. And in somewhat marginal areas of the highlands, their number could be very low: Human deposits from caves in the Tehuacan Valley indicate that only three family bands made up of 12 to 24 individuals each occupied the central Mexican region.

ARCHAIC PERIOD (C. 7000–1200 B.C.E.)

The hunter-gatherers who occupied the Americas began to live in more permanent settlements during the Archaic Period, and by 1400 B.C.E., many of these settlements had evolved into socially stratified pottery-producing villages sustained by agriculture. These settlements, whose year-round stable food resources and sedentary lifestyle permitted increased populations, were the foundation of the Mesoamerican civilization that soon followed.

The trend toward sedentarism was well under way by 5000 B.C.E. In highland areas,

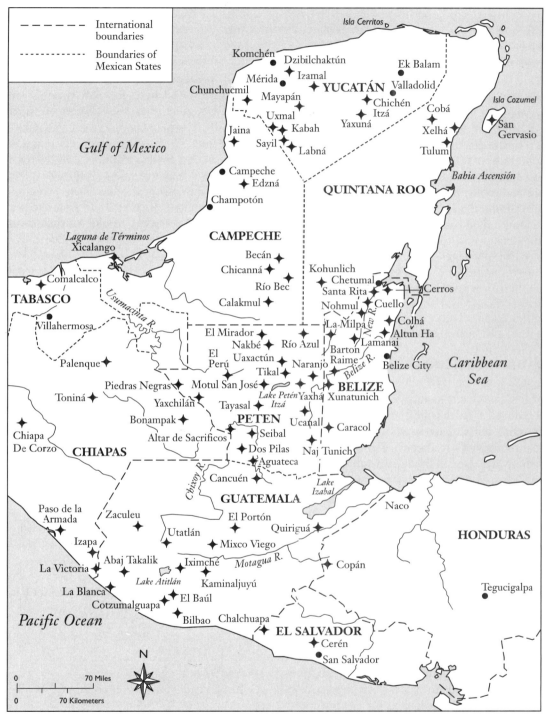

Map 2. *Major Maya Sites 1000 B.C.E.–1524.*

20

such as the Central Basin of Mexico, permanent settlements were limited to lakeshores and river valleys. In the lowlands, however, where wetlands and coastal zones permitted a steady food source of fish and shellfish, such dispersed settlements were already widespread. Hunting for rabbits and small game continued—and continues today—at the same time that gardening for fruits and crops increased. By 4000 to 3000 B.C.E., these early Amerindians could supplement their fish and game and wild plants and fruits with an increasing number of domesticated crops. Domesticated roots crops, such as manioc and sweet potatoes, which required little labor, sustained many of the earliest villages in the New World; these drought-resistant tubers added nourishment to the diet along with cultivated squash, chile peppers, beans, and, increasingly, maize.

Domesticated Maize

Around 3000 B.C.E. domesticated maize was introduced into the diet, and within the next thousand years, maize was being cultivated in most regions of Mesoamerica, including much of the Maya area. The cultivation of maize—the New World equivalent to rice and wheat—held the key to the development of more complex Mesoamerican society. Maize could be harvested and stored in such quantity that it provided sustenance year-round in both the highlands and lowlands. As maize agriculture encouraged more peoples to settle in permanent villages, it also sustained larger populations and created food surpluses. More complex societies resulted. No longer did everyone need to produce food for group survival, and material possessions no longer were limited by a nomadic lifestyle. Social functions could lead to specialization; pottery could replace lighter-weight baskets, and

well-made thatched houses on earthen platforms were more comfortable than the temporary shelter of caves.

By at least 2000 B.C.E., maize was being cultivated in most of the Maya region, although some highland areas such as the Antigua Valley in Guatemala, with its volcanic eruptions and layers of ash rather than soil, were too geologically unstable to attract settlers for another thousand years. Maize did not completely supplant earlier food-gathering strategies, however, but as the plant became more productive, there was heavier reliance on it. Before the end of the Archaic Period, maize cultivation was widespread in Mesoamerica, and farm crops accounted for an increasing percentage of the diet. In the Tehuacan Valley, for example, cultivated foods grew from 5 percent of the diet in c. 5500 B.C.E. to 35 percent by 1500 B.C.E.—and by 600 C.E., they would constitute 75 percent. Enough corn could be grown, harvested, dried, and stored during the rainy season to sustain people during the dry season, which lasted half the year in much of the Mesoamerican region.

Complex societies evolved, especially in the wetland areas. The earliest evidence for sophisticated villages is from the Pacific coast lowlands and southern Veracruz in Mexico. These exceptionally fertile and well-watered regions could produce two crops a year and sometimes three, and their maize harvest simply added to the bounty of fish and tropical fruits.

Isthmian Culture: Pottery and Social Complexity

BARRA PHASE

In the Maya region, precocious settlements evolved along the Pacific coast of Chiapas in the Mazatán area, where some of the earliest

Mesoamerican pottery—and certainly the earliest refined pottery—appeared during the Barra Phase (c. 1600 B.C.E.). Similar ceramics have recently been discovered in coastal Honduras, which suggests the Barra Phase may have been more widespread than previously thought. This pottery was shaped into neckless jars, called *tecomates*, and inspired by gourds and deep bowls; it was grooved and incised before being decorated with up to three colors. The pottery was so thin walled that it could not be used for cooking. Archaeologists believe it served as containers for foods or liquids (an intoxicating brew made from maize was probably one such liquid) consumed during ceremonial feasts or given as offerings. Food for daily consumption, however, was probably prepared and stored in waterproof baskets or gourds until around 1400 B.C.E., when there is evidence of more common household pottery. Clay figurines, some hollow and most of women, appear around the same time as the pottery and continue as part of the cultural complex of the region through the Maya Preclassic Period. The figurine cult persisted in central Mexico into Aztec times when it was part of a fertility cult.

LOCONA PHASE

By 1400 B.C.E., the Barra Phase had evolved into the Locona Phase, the first culture that is known to have diffused over a significant geographic area of Mesoamerica. The Locona Phase evolved into the more socially stratified villages of the Ocós Phase by c. 1250 B.C.E. Based on the similarity of pottery and figurines among villages, it is clear that many were trading goods and exchanging ideas by at least 1400 B.C.E. The Locona horizon extended geographically along the Pacific coast from El Salvador up to the Isthmus of Tehuantepec and across the 200 kilometers (124 miles) of the isthmus to include the Gulf coast regions of Veracruz and Tabasco in Mexico. From El Salvador, the route extended to the Caribbean coast of Honduras (see Map 1, page 4 and Map 8, page 320). The contacts may have been even more far flung if some archaeologists are correct in suggesting that pottery was introduced from the Guayaquil area of Ecuador, where pottery making had a longer tradition. Indeed, the iridescent pink slip and the designs of some Locona ceramics are somewhat similar to those in Ecuador, and seasonal trade winds could have encouraged occasional canoe contacts between the two areas of the Pacific coast, although such contacts have yet to be adequately demonstrated. It is just as possible that the technique, along with rocker stamping and other decorative devices that appeared at this time, were locally inspired.

Some villages participating in this lowland Isthmian culture—30 have been archaeologically identified along the Pacific—show evidence of the first ranked societies on the order of petty chiefdoms, in which clusters of hamlets were ruled by a capital village. In one such capital, Paso de la Amada, excavators discovered the clay foundations of a large structure of 122 square meters (1,313 square feet), a public or ritual building that could have been the residence of a chief. Another large clay building set upon a clay foundation 1 meter (3.3 feet) in height was oriented toward a local volcano, suggesting the worship of sacred mountains (see Chapter 6) already occurred in this early period.

OCÓS PHASE

During the Ocós Phase, more than 42 archaeologically identified villages along the Pacific coast shared an even more sophisticated culture. Capital villages in the Mazatán area of Chiapas and on the nearby Guatemalan coast had quite sizable populations of about 1,000, and the concentration of obsidian in these capitals, such as Paso de la Amada and La Victoria, suggests their growth and power came from control of this valuable trade commodity. The interaction sphere expanded beyond that of the Locona Phase to include the Caribbean coast of Honduras. Ocós-style pottery and figurines were elaborate enough to have required a class of artisan specialists, and ceramic ear spools, an ornament that would be favored by Mesoamericans until the Spanish Conquest, were manufactured for the first time during this phase. Figurines depicting fat males seated on stools (a well-known posture for shamans in parts of Central America even today) were introduced, and the more wealthy burials included polished shaman mirrors. In one capital village on the Pacific coast, an infant was buried, covered with red cinnabar and a mirror on his forehead, probably a sign of shamanistic power, which, in this case, must have been inherited.

The thatched-roof houses of the Ocós-period villages, some of which were apsidal in shape, much like Yucatec Maya homes of today, were situated near the coast or slightly inland near seasonal lakes and wetlands that permitted extra harvests in the dry season. These villages are the earliest socially complex cultures presently known for the Maya region. Whether the villagers were Mayan speaking is difficult to determine, but linguists suggest that Proto-Mayan, the original Mayan language before it splintered into many different ones, existed before 2000 B.C.E. and was probably already spoken in the Guatemala highlands and Pacific littoral of the southern Maya region. Mixe-Zoquean speakers may have resided in the Isthmian region of Chiapas as well as along the Gulf coast, just as they did in the 20th century. The cultural homogeneity of the Isthmian horizon could simply have disguised the ethnic diversity, both Maya and Mixe-Zoque, that would normally be found over such a wide geographic range.

Whatever the ethnicity of particular Pacific coast villages, the unprecedented Ocós cul-

ture was facilitated by the fertility of the volcanic-enriched soils of the Pacific corridor, and it was stimulated by interaction among Isthmian villages. Such interaction meant that the agricultural surplus could be spent on exotic items that were controlled by an emerging elite, some of whom may have bolstered their status by claiming shamanistic powers. In Gulf coast villages, where Ocós-style pottery underlies later urban centers, this elite class produced the first civilization of Mesoamerica, that of the Olmec.

EARLY PRECLASSIC PERIOD (C. 1200–1000 B.C.E.)

The first civilization of Mesoamerica blossomed during the early formative period. This Olmec civilization flourished in the tropical wetlands of the Gulf coast and diffused through Mesoamerica. By the end of the period, the most defining characteristics of Mesoamerican civilization had evolved. The exact nature of the process that led to a pan-Mesoamerican culture is still disputed, but that there was interaction among the various regions is uncontested. Perhaps trade occurred directly at regional markets or through itinerant merchants. Perhaps goods were exchanged indirectly through intermediaries along a down-the-line long-distance trade route. Culture may have diffused through religious cults, trade pacts, or even conquest. Probably all these forms of interaction were involved in the formation of a Mesoamerican culture, and each region contributed to its formation. However, one region—that of the Gulf coast the homeland of the Olmec—rose to unprecedented cultural and political levels during the Early Preclassic Period.

Ocós and Olmec

Until about 1150 B.C.E., the Ocós culture continued to develop in the southern Maya region. More settlements increased in population and constructed more elaborate villages; for example, former hamlets in the mango forests on the southeastern Pacific coast of Guatemala grew into towns with as many as 22 large structures, not simply one or two. Even during this early phase of the formative period, cultural and economic interaction expanded, affecting more regions of Mesoamerica: Obsidian from the Basin of Mexico is found in the Gulf coast lowlands by 1200 B.C.E., and ceramics from San Lorenzo Tenochtitlan on the Gulf coast are found as far away as the Honduran Caribbean.

Mesoamerican Interaction

After 1150 B.C.E., the Olmec horizon supplanted Ocós culture, a shift that is clearly reflected in the material remains at Los Alvarez, in Chiapas, where an Olmec platform 4 meters (13 feet) high was constructed over Ocós fill. Even if not usually so completely and dramatically as at Los Alvarez, Olmec culture spread throughout Mesoamerica for the following 600 years. Political capitals and ranked societies evolved outside the Gulf coast area, from the central Mexican and Oaxacan highlands to the lowlands of Guatemala and the Yucatán Peninsula (see Map 1, page 4). Rapid change and intense regional interaction make it difficult for archaeologists to determine which culture did what first, but not all developments originated in the Olmec heartland of southern Veracruz and Tabasco. The Ocós-sphere village of Paso de la Amada on the Pacific coast of Chiapas, for example, constructed an earthen ball court by 1400 B.C.E. that consisted of two parallel structures 79 meters (260 feet) in length with a playing surface between them. Located amid elite residences, this structure indicates that some form of the ritual ball game, thought to have originated in the Olmec period, derives from the earlier Ocós culture. In addition, stone building facades appear first in Guerrero, not Veracruz, and the protowriting that appears on Olmec monuments during the Middle Preclassic Period may have been preceded by calendrical notations found in Oaxaca. Not everything Mesoamerican originated within the Olmec realm. For such reasons, some archaeologists have argued that the term Olmec should refer to a cultural-interaction sphere, an Olmec horizon, rather than to the ethnic group that occupied the so-called Gulf heartland. Recent excavations, however, demonstrate that the political and social complexity, as well as the artistic innovations at Olmec cities on the Gulf coast, far exceeded those in other regions of Mesoamerica and merit special attention.

Olmec Culture

In the Gulf region, the homeland of Olmec culture, the Olmecs constructed monumental public buildings and carved immense stone sculptures, including 20-ton ruler portraits that outstripped in size and artistry anything found elsewhere in Mesoamerica at the time. The Olmecs were the first sculptors of Mesoamerica. Their art created new symbols of political authority and gave coherence to a religious worldview that would persist throughout the millennia of Mesoamerican civilization. Olmec trade items and political symbols are found at most important contemporary sites in Mesoamerica, and Olmec artifacts have been found in such concentration in such areas as Chiapas, Guerrero, and Morelos that disputes have arisen over whether Olmec colonies may have been established in these regions. The elaborate central Mexican religious shrine carved into the mountain above Chalcatzingo, Morelos (1100–500 B.C.E.), was an Olmec pilgrimage site. Monumental sculptures in quintessential Olmec style at such farflung settlements as Pijijiapán, Chiapas, and Chalchuapa, El Salvador, as well as the city of Teopantecuanitlan, in western Mexico, have led a few archaeologists to argue for the existence of an Olmec empire. Olmec accomplishments stand out as extraordinary for the time, and their diffusion laid the foundation for all subsequent Mesoamerican civilization.

SAN LORENZO TENOCHTITLAN

The Olmec people who occupied the Gulf coast were probably the ancestors of contemporary Mixe and Zoque speakers who still live in lowland areas of southern Veracruz. The Olmecs constructed their cities along the Coatzacoalcos, Tonalá, and Papaloapan Rivers in the Mexican states of Veracruz and Tabasco, and this region is still considered to be the homeland of Olmec culture. San Lorenzo Tenochtitlan (1200–900 B.C.E.), the earliest Olmec urban center, dominated trade and traffic from its hilltop site overlooking the Coatzacoalcos River basin. A planned city, San Lorenzo was organized along a north-south axis and built on a massive platform, 606 meters wide (almost 2,000 feet) by 909 meters long (3,000 feet). On top of the platform were more than 200 earthen structures, both residential and ceremonial; the largest residence, the Red Palace, had basalt columns and basalt-covered steps. An underground aqueduct of basalt blocks provided drinking water to different areas of San Lorenzo from artificial ponds. Monolithic stone sculptures were carefully arranged in relation to some of the public buildings and palaces to create ceremonial spaces. The more than 70 sculptures excavated at San Lorenzo included 50-ton thrones depicting the shaman-ruler in front of the cave entrance to the otherworld, immense statues of mythic creatures with both human and animal features as well as of feathered serpents and avian-jaguar beings that can be identified as deities in later Mesoamerican cultures, and basalt boulders shaped into powerful ruler portraits.

Some archaeologists have argued that the helmets on the monolithic ruler portraits indicate the ruler was depicted as a ballplayer, especially given that the Olmecs exported rubber (made from sap of the *Castilla elastica* tree that is native to Veracruz) and that rubber balls, used in the traditional Mesoamerican ball game, were excavated at El Manatí, a sacred shrine across the Coatzacoalcos River from San Lorenzo. Others have suggested that the helmets indicate warrior-rulers, but there is no evidence that the Olmecs achieved their cultural and economic dominance by conquest. Two colossal heads from San Lorenzo are known to have been recycled from former thrones, suggesting that all portrait heads may have been made from earlier monuments and venerated after a ruler's death. Such a practice would indicate that Mesoamerican ancestor worship originated by at least the Early Preclassic Period. Ruler portraiture continued as a characteristic of Maya civilization, but monolithic heads such as these ended with the Olmec culture.

URBAN CONSTRUCTION

Covering an area of almost 7 square kilometers (3 square miles), San Lorenzo Tenochtitlan was the largest city in Mesoamerica during the Early Preclassic Period and was the first great capital of Olmec civilization. The construction of such a large urban center required enormous resources and unprecedented organization of labor: For example, the source for basalt—the volcanic stone carved into colossal sculptures and shaped into grinding stones for maize, called *metates*—was the Tuxtla Mountains, 30 miles from San Lorenzo and 60 miles from the later Olmec site of La Venta. Another Olmec center, Laguna de los Cerros was established near the quarry to acquire and transport these massive boulders (for the most party by river rafts, although the process is not fully understood) to other Olmec centers. Archaeologists estimate that up to 1,000 laborers might have been required in the transport of some of the largest boulders. The control of such valuable material was most likely in the hands of the ruler; at San Lorenzo, basalt columns adorn the largest palace, and nearby is a basalt workshop. The time and effort required to carve the basalt with a stone tool kit (all that was available to Mesoamerica until just before the Spanish Conquest) suggest a class of full-time artisans.

OTHER URBAN CENTERS

Many Olmec settlements, ranging from substantial towns with monumental sculptures and farming hamlets to shrines at sacred places such as springs and mountain summits, developed in the heartland. Many of these settlements were apparently under the economic control of San Lorenzo until its decline around 900 B.C.E., when La Venta (1100–300 B.C.E.) rose to power. La Venta and urban centers outside the heartland, such as Teopantecuanitlan (1200–500 B.C.E.), did not reach their apogee until the Middle Preclassic Period, however. Like San Lorenzo, these important cities were both sacred religious centers and regional economic powers that straddled important trade routes. La Venta had an estimated population of 18,000,

2.1 *A 7-foot-tall Olmec colossal head (1200–900 B.C.E.) in the Museo de Antropología de Jalapa in Veracruz, Mexico. Seventeen of these colossal ruler portraits have been discovered on the Gulf coast, almost all of them from the regional capitals of San Lorenzo and La Venta. These heads never had bodies.* (Photo by Michael Edwards)

a veritable metropolis for this period in world history, not simply for formative Mesoamerican development. Not as large as the heartland cities, Teopantecuanitlan nonetheless occupied an impressive site in Guerrero (see Map 1, page 4) that was 1.6 square kilometers (a half square mile) in size and included massive building complexes—some faced with stone—and monolithic sculptures—some weighing 2 tons. An irrigation system with a dam and stone canal (c. 700–500 B.C.E.) is the earliest known for Mesoamerica.

LA VENTA

The people of La Venta constructed a 100-foot-high pyramid (its final phase was completed c. 400 B.C.E.) and organized the city in a series of plazas surrounded by buildings, an urban plan that later became prevalent in Mesoamerican cities, including those of the Maya. The ceremonial center was designed to be a microcosm of all that was sacred in the Olmec universe: The pyramid represented the mountain where maize was created, for example, and the ball court recalled the place in Mesoamerican mythology where the evil gods were defeated so that this world could be born.

La Venta rulers were buried with precious jades (including jade bloodletters for autosacrifice), a tradition continued by the Maya, and great quantities of imported goods were buried 7.5 meters (25 feet) below the surface, perhaps as offerings to underworld gods. One burial contained more than 3,000 pieces of polished jade; another, 1,000 tons of serpentine blocks imported from Guerrero; and four burials, immense deity masks measuring 5 by 6 meters (16.5 by 20 feet). The amount of trade necessary to acquire vast quantities of imported jade and serpentine is a testament to Olmec wealth and economic organization.

SOCIAL AND ECONOMIC COMPLEXITY

Olmec society had a growing number of specialists: traders, farmers, and artisans, including sculptors, potters, jade workers, builders, and stonecutters. The elaborate religious iconography on San Lorenzo sculptures and symbolism in La Venta's urban plan suggest that the Olmecs had a priestly class too. Society was increasingly complex and, based on items found in burials, stratified into several different classes. At the summit was the ruler in his palace. In between were other members of the nobility; some may have been priests and others rulers of smaller dependent towns. Traders, artisans, and architects followed, and at the bottom were the commoners living in thatched-roof huts.

San Lorenzo and La Venta, the two largest regional capitals of the Olmec horizon, reached a level of such economic complexity and political hegemony that they were incipient states. Based on carvings from Olmec thrones and caves, Olmec rulers legitimized their power by claims of shamanistic communication with the supernatural. But the rulers had material advantages as well. They probably descended from wealthy lineages that controlled the economic resources of the city, its local trade in basalt and agricultural products, and long-distance trade to other Mesoamerican regions.

The Olmecs traded many kinds of materials, among them such essential items as salt, chert, basalt, and obsidian and other materials for tools and grinding stones. It was also feasible to trade agricultural surpluses at the local level. Many such perishables were involved in the trade, not the least of which was prestige. As complex societies began to emerge, rulers and other members of the nouveau riche looked for ways to properly demonstrate their special status. The sophisticated Olmecs provided them. The so-called flame-eyebrow and jaguar paw–and–wing designs, each a symbol of two Olmec deities, are found as lineage emblems on precious artifacts from Oaxaca to Honduras. Rubber for a ritual ball game came from the Gulf coast; scepters and jaguar pelts were traded as badges of ruling authority; and polished jades were valued as far away as Costa Rica. In return, the Olmecs received obsidian from the Mexican and

Guatemalan highlands, iron ore from Oaxaca to polish into mirrors, and serpentine from Guerrero and jade from the Motagua Valley in Guatemala, both of which they carved and polished into amulets, pendants, and celts that were so valued by others that they were cherished as heirlooms hundreds of years later. Cotton and cacao (chocolate beans) most likely came from the southern Maya region, shells from the Pacific, and quetzal and other feathers from the rain and cloud forests were all part of the trade. All these precious items—jade, exotic feathers and shells, cacao beans, finely woven cotton textiles, obsidian, rubber—were demanded as tribute payment by the Mesoamerican elite for the next few millennia; at the time of the Spanish Conquest, they were still being demanded and received by the Aztec emperor, Moctezuma.

Mesoamerican Traits

With the Olmec culture, Mesoamerica had its first civilization in which a wealthy elite class, based in urban centers, dominated regional economies and controlled long distance trade. The Olmec interaction sphere, from highland Mexico to Costa Rica, basically delineated the borders of what would be Mesoamerica in the following millennia, save for the occasional contraction or expansion along the frontiers. Through exchange and interaction, all Mesoamerican regions achieved greater political complexity and ranked societies.

Interaction also consolidated a worldview that was shaped by new symbols and given expression by new art forms. This worldview, or cosmogony, was reflected in the site orientations, paintings, and sculpture of Olmec cities. Creation myths existed at least by the Early Preclassic Period, when they were given artistic form, and these myths were elaborated throughout Mesoamerican civilization and persisted into his-

torical times in Maya books, such as the *Popol Vuh*. The central gods of Mesoamerican religion, like the maize and rain gods and the feathered serpent creator god, already were depicted in Olmec sculpture. Ancestor worship, especially of powerful individuals, is indicated by archaeological evidence, and ritual human sacrifice was depicted in the art.

The concept of Mesoamerica originated with archaeologist Paul Kirchhoff, who listed a set of characteristics that differentiated Mesoamerica from its neighbors. The list included the following traits.

- Urbanism: Mesoamerica is one of the seven world areas where cities were invented.
- Monumental stone buildings built on stepped platforms—some pyramidal in height—arranged around public plazas, and associated with freestanding sculpture.
- Agriculture based on maize, beans, and squash.
- Hieroglyphic or pictographic writing; books folded like a screen and made of bark paper or deerskin.
- A 260-day ritual calendar and other calendrical calculations.
- Astronomical knowledge.
- A rubber ball game played in earthen or masonry courts.
- Human sacrifice and autosacrifice by drawing blood from the penis, tongue, or ears.
- A quadripartite world in which the earth is horizontally ordered in four directions and centered by a fifth in the middle of them; each direction was associated with colors, plants, animals, deities, and rituals. This ordered world was symbolized by cruciform shapes and the quincunx in which the center was indicated along with the four directions.
- A tripartite vertical division of the universe into the earth, multilayered heavens, and the Underworld; communication between these levels was through the center, or fifth direc-

tion, that of the vertical axis or world tree. The shaman ruler often represented this conduit between the realms of the cosmos.

- A pantheon of gods.

By the end of the Early Preclassic Period, practically all these traits were in place, if not with all their future Mesoamerican detail. Evidence for the Mesoamerican calendrical and writing systems, however, would not appear until later formative times. Kirchhoff's delineation of Mesoamerican traits has often been criticized as inadequate, but the geographical and cultural concept of Mesoamerica has proved too useful to be abandoned. Archaeologists have basically limited themselves to insisting on the addition of other traits, such as long-distance trade in elite goods and the shared creation myths that reflect an integrated Mesoamerican worldview. These, too, existed by the Early Preclassic Period.

MIDDLE PRECLASSIC PERIOD (C. 1000–300 B.C.E.)

Olmec cultural and economic influence, under the auspices of La Venta, reached its peak in the beginning of the Middle Preclassic Period. Although Olmec influence in the Maya region was most pervasive along the Pacific littoral, the first and most monumental Maya cities arose in the central lowland region where, based on current evidence, there was more limited artifact exchange with the Olmecs. At the same time that these lowland Maya cities emerged around 700 to 500 B.C.E., Olmec influence persisted in

the Isthmian zone, or southern Maya region. Although the Middle Preclassic Period represents the most widespread adaptation of the Olmec style, the period ended with the abandonment of many heartland Olmec cities and the growth of urban centers in the central Mexican and Maya regions.

Urban planning and monumental architecture, including ball courts and pyramids, typified an increasing number of settlements. La Venta's preference for low-relief sculpture created a Mesoamerican artistic shift away from San Lorenzo–style sculpture in the round, although pot-bellied, full-figured sculptures persisted through the Late Preclassic along the Pacific coast. As cultures outside the Olmec heartland became more complex, they modified the prevailing Gulf coast culture to create their own symbols of authority, just as they took control of valuable resources to benefit themselves from trade. The Maya, more than any culture, would continue Olmec traditions of ruler veneration, realistic portraiture, and narrative art, and they, too, would create a complex culture in the heart of the tropical lowlands. Yet a distinctive Maya culture emerged during the Middle Preclassic Period.

Southern Maya Region

Maya settlements on the Pacific coast and in the highlands of Chiapas and Guatemala indicate close contact with the Olmecs during the first half of this period. La Venta's desire for jade and obsidian moved its traders along the Pacific coast and into the Guatemalan highlands. Cacao may account for the strong Olmec influence at this time in the fertile Soconusco region shared by coastal Chiapas and Guatemala. Pijijiapán and Izapa in Chiapas, Abaj Takalik, La Blanca, and Monte Alto in Guatemala, and Chalchuapa in El Salvador are significant sites found along this trade route, and all shared much of the material culture of the Olmecs, if not the monumental size of Olmec cities.

LA VENTA INFLUENCE

Olmec figurines and black and gray ceramics replaced those of the Ocós sphere at many sites. Inhabitants of San Isidro in Chiapas buried jade objects in the manner, but not in the quantity, of La Venta; at Copán, near the jade sources of the Río Motagua Valley, more than 300 pieces of jade accompanied the burial of an individual skull in c. 1000 B.C.E. An increasing number of settlements were configured like the plaza-and-pyramid urban plans found at La Venta. La Venta–style sculptures in low relief may have accompanied potbellied sculptures in the round that were more typical of the Guatemalan coastal region, although the dating of these figures might be later. Some urban centers constructed massive complexes between 850 and 650 B.C.E. A pyramid at La Blanca rose 25 meters (83 feet) high; another pyramid was built at Chalchuapa. And some Chiapan sites featured platforms that were 100 meters (330 feet) in length and 3 meters (10 feet) high. All these settlements were located at points along the trade route.

CHALCHUAPA

Although numerous sites on the Pacific slopes exhibited increasing wealth and social complexity, few are currently known to have constructed massive structures by this time. Chalchuapa, however, was a major exception. Chalchuapa—or El Trapiche and La Victoria, which are parts of the site dating from the Preclassic Period—was an important trading center with a strategic location near highland sources of obsidian, a material that attracted Olmec traders judging from the monumental boulder discovered at the Salvadoran site but carved in the pure Gulf-coast style. Commerce in manufactured obsidian

enabled Chalchuapa to construct a conical pyramid 20 meters (66 feet) high by 600 B.C.E., an exceptional undertaking considering that La Venta's pyramid may not have reached a greater height until a few hundred years later. A similar feat was only achieved in La Blanca. Chalchuapa remained an important center throughout the Late Preclassic Period.

KAMINALJUYÚ

New centers emerged in the central Guatemala highlands at this period, probably because the flat plateaus became more habitable due to diminishing volcanic activity. All these new settlements were well situated for trade. Kaminaljuyú in the Valley of Guatemala, for example, could control nearby obsidian sources, but it was also in an enviable position to command trade between the Caribbean and the Pacific coast through the river routes in the Motagua Valley, and through the highland pass down to the Pacific. Cacao, obsidian, and jade

2.2 *Monument 12, Chalchuapa, El Salvador (900–500 B.C.E.). One of four Olmec-style low reliefs that were incised into a basalt boulder above the site of Chalchuapa.* (Drawing after Sharer and Sheets, 1978)

were part of the valuable trade that would expand in the Late Preclassic, making Kaminaljuyú flourish into one of the most important cities of that period. By 700 B.C.E., Kaminaljuyú already had constructed a major irrigation canal, and by 500 B.C.E., it began carving freestanding stone slabs called stelae.

EL PORTÓN AND PROTOWRITING

Early Preclassic sites in the northern highlands were more common than in the central valley of Guatemala. The Salamá Valley typified the attractions of the region; it straddled river routes between the Petén and highlands and could access nearby sources of blue-green quetzal feathers and jade. The Salamá settlements exhibited only minor Olmec influences, but between 800 and 500 B.C.E., they constructed elite residences, earthen platforms for thatched-roof temples, and elaborate tombs. At Los Mangales, one stone-lined tomb contained an individual adorned with jades and shells and accompanied by three trophy heads and 12 retainers, the latter apparently sacrificed to accompany him in the otherworld. At El Portón, stelae were carved and carefully placed in front of altars, a sculptural arrangement that spread in the Late Preclassic Period and typified the lowland Maya during the Classic Period. Other Mesoamerican sites combined carved stelae with altars, but at this early date only one other site, in Oaxaca, also featured what appear to be hieroglyphs carved on stelae. Best described as protowriting, the texts would become the hallmark of Maya civilization in the lowlands. In Oaxaca (500–400 B.C.E.) these texts are currently believed to predate the Maya ones, but those at El Portón, dating to 400 B.C.E., are the earliest Maya protoglyphs currently known. The El Portón texts seem to employ the bar-and-dot numerical system that was in use until the conquest in both the Oaxaca and Maya regions.

The Lowlands

Until recently, the lowlands of the Maya region during the Preclassic Period were less understood than even the southern area, so much so that they were once thought to have been practically uninhabited until c. 1000 B.C.E., when the first pottery appeared. However, recent evidence indicates a much earlier date for the settlement of the lowlands. Paleobotanists have demonstrated that there was drastic deforestation in northern Belize and other wetland areas by as early as 2500 B.C.E. and that by 1000 B.C.E. elaborate agricultural drainage and perhaps raised field systems already were constructed in the lowlands (see Chapters 3 and 11). In the 1990s, the discovery of Nakbé, a site that turned out to be the largest known Maya settlement for the Middle Preclassic Period, reminded archaeologists of how little they knew about the lowlands during the formative years of Maya civilization.

EARLIEST TRACES

Just as trade stimulated settlements along the Pacific littoral, it created complex centers in the lowlands where formerly there had been only small agricultural villages. From 1000 to 700 B.C.E., many of these agricultural villages seem to have been relatively egalitarian, but this impression could very well be due to insufficient information, as later construction has covered and obscured this early period of occupation at most sites.

Gradually the pole-and-thatch houses, often in the same aspsidal, or oval, shape used by many Maya today, mingled with platform and plaza groups, which probably supported religious buildings as well as elite housing. The plastered platform at Cuello in Belize, constructed by 1000 B.C.E., is the earliest securely dated public architecture currently known for the lowlands, but other early buildings are being found, such as the nearly 4-meter- (13-foot-) high platform on a ceremonial plaza at Altar de Sacrificios. At sites such as Nakbé and Uaxactún, archaeologists have discovered early but less easily detected constructions of flat stones, layered without mortar and with roughly plastered floors. The number of known sites will probably increase as archaeologists intensify their search for these formative structures.

Burials have been found as well. At Seibal, a simple farming village in the Guatemalan Petén, a La Venta–style cache of jade and pottery, laid out in a cruciform arrangement, was discovered. An even more impressive cache of 20 jades, dated to La Venta culture, was found in northern Yucatán.

PUBLIC WORKS C. 700 B.C.E.

By 700 B.C.E., major transformations were taking place in the lowlands. Like the southern Maya region, the lowlands were experiencing population growth and extensive trade, especially in areas with sufficient water resources to supply settlements during the four-month-long dry season. Population growth or perhaps a demand for export crops, such as cacao, explains the development of intensive agriculture in the swampy Río Hondo region of Belize by 1000 B.C.E. Other Middle Preclassic settlements grew next to rivers along ridges overlooking shallow ponds, or wetlands, or next to natural limestone wells, called cenotes.

Ridged and drained fields were not the only great public projects as monumental building complexes began to define important lowland centers. Unlike in the southern region, however, the lowlands had readily available sources of limestone, so plastered buildings and masonry construction spread to Maya lowland towns in this early period. Small buildings of crude masonry blocks are found after 700 B.C.E. throughout the lowlands—even in the dry, riverless region of northern Yucatán where many hamlets, such as Dzibilchaltún, developed next to cenotes.

TRADE AND THE MAMOM HORIZON

As in the Isthmian area, lowland centers flourished from trade. Nakbé was located at an important juncture for portage between rivers in what is now northern Guatemala, and Lamanai in Belize had a river dock by the seventh century B.C.E. Colhá, situated next to an important source of chert in northern Belize, manufactured and traded stone tools. Komchén, a sizable center in northern Yucatán, arose near valuable salt flats even though the surrounding land could not agriculturally sustain its population. Excavations indicate other valuable commodities were available in the Petén during this period: *Strombus* shell (conch) ornaments from the Gulf of Mexico or Caribbean; cotton, perhaps from Yucatán; and cinnabar from the Guatemalan highlands. The location of important early lowland centers was chosen with trade in mind, not simply agriculture. In their attempt to control and transport valuable resources, these Maya cities, like those of their central Mexican counterparts, may have eventually undermined the Olmec economy.

The role of trade in the transformation of the lowlands at this time is indisputable. Yet Olmec artifacts, such as those found at Seibal, have not been detected in great numbers, and only one Olmec sculpture—the Xoc cliff carving in Chiapas along the western periphery of the Maya lowlands—has been recovered. There is some evidence, however, for greater exchange between La Venta and the Gulf coast region of Yucatán. The Olmec civilization certainly stimulated trade and development even if it did not have the direct impact on the lowlands that occurred along the Pacific. With or without Olmec control of the routes, trade existed and explains the unified Mamom

Ceramic Complex (700–400 B.C.E.) that spread across the lowlands, replacing earlier diverse traditions such as Xé (Pasión River area), Swasey (northern Belize), and Eb (Tikal and northeastern Petén). Mamom ceramics share certain features with earlier Isthmian traditions, but they are also distinctively Maya with their burnished reds and oranges in contrast to the gray and black wares of the Olmec horizon.

NAKBÉ AND MASONRY ARCHITECTURE

The most impressive changes during the Mamom ceramic phase were in architecture, particularly at Nakbé and Wakná in the northeastern Petén, where numerous monumental stone-building projects were completed by 600 B.C.E. Like Chalchuapa, Nakbé constructed a massive pyramidal platform, but the 18-meter- (59-feet-) high pyramid was only one of many enormous undertakings. A neighboring pyramid platform in the East Group rose 14 meters (46 feet); and in the West Group, platforms, ranging in height from 3 to 8 meters (10 to 26 feet), covered up to 40,000 square meters (430,400 square feet) and provided the foundations for planned arrangements of temples and range-style buildings around open patios.

Architectural forms at Nakbé were not only monumental but also distinctive in many ways from constructions at La Venta and even those in the Maya region to the south, so much so, in fact, that some archaeologists believe much of the development of lowland Maya public and residential buildings was locally conceived. Nakbé's orientation, for example, was east to west rather than north to south. And many innovations, including quarried building stones, apron moldings, and limestone-plastered floors and walls that characterize Classic Period Maya masonry architecture, are already present. Other typical Maya structures existed in this formative period at Nakbé: *sacbeob*, or raised and plastered roads linking sections of the site; ritual building clusters, such as the E-groups (see page 235); and radial platforms with stairways on all four sides. Round platforms also were introduced into many Maya centers at this time, although they were previously thought to be an invention of Postclassic central Mexico. Ball courts appeared in the Middle Preclassic Period, indicating a connection with the Isthmian ball game tradition, and these courts continued to be constructed throughout the remaining millennia of Maya civilization.

Olmec Decline

Most Olmec cities were abandoned by 400 B.C.E., although La Venta probably continued for a while with greatly diminished powers and other centers, such as Tres Zapotes in Veracruz, persisted. The reason for the decline is not known, but it has been suggested that San Martín Pajapan, the sacred volcano near the Olmec basalt sources, was active throughout the Olmec horizon and may have finally erupted with devastating consequences. Or the Olmecs may simply have lost control of the trade routes to those who had formerly been dependent on them.

By the end of the Middle Preclassic Period, there were Mesoamerican urban centers—including Maya ones like Chalchuapa, Kaminaljuyú, and Nakbé—that were clearly growing in economic power and political complexity. Recent excavations at La Blanca suggest it may have been one of the largest Middle Preclassic centers in Mesoamerica, although this material is not yet well understood. Masonry architecture in the lowlands already had many characteristics distinctive of Maya civilization, and the Mamom Ceramic Complex indicated a cultural unity and trade network in the lowlands that had not been seen before. At the very time the Olmec heartland cities were being abandoned, substantial settlements were appearing throughout the Maya region. The Olmec heartland gave birth to the first civilization of Mesoamerica, but other regions were ready to match and even outstrip the once great Gulf-coast culture.

LATE PRECLASSIC PERIOD (300 B.C.E.–250 C.E.)

The Late Preclassic was a period of dynamic growth and development. Well before the end of the period, the defining traits of Maya civilization were already present, from monumental stone cities and vaulted buildings to stelae and altar complexes that were carved with short hieroglyphic texts and with the first Long Count dates (see page 255). Mythological themes about the creation of the Maya world are identifiable in the art of this period and sophisticated polychrome ceramics already exist. Although it was not until the Classic Period that Maya hieroglyphic inscriptions became lengthier and polychrome ceramics developed into a narrative style rivaling that of the ancient Greeks, the Preclassic Period accomplishments were tremendous. The Late Preclassic Maya world—its level of social, political, and cultural complexity—is now considered equivalent to that of the Classic Period in all but name.

The entire Maya region, even in areas away from rivers and other natural water resources, experienced population growth. Both highland and lowland cities emerged, building monumental pyramidal platforms and creating elaborate burials filled with exotic goods obtained by extensive trade networks. Usulután ceramics—the cream-on-red resistware manufactured in El Salvador, probably at Chalchuapa—are found in elite burials from the southern area to the northern lowlands, from Chiapa de Corzo (Chiapas) to Costa Rica, and are diagnostic of the Late Preclassic Period. The largest cities from the period are Kaminaljuyú in the Guatemalan highlands; Chalchuapa in the Salvadoran highlands; Izapa and La Blanca along the Pacific slope; Tikal, Uaxactún, and Nakbé in the Petén; and Calakmul, Becán, and Edzná to the north of the Petén in Campeche, Mexico; Komchén in northern Yucatán; and Cuello, Lamanai, Caracol, and Cerros in Belize. No city, however, matched the northern Petén city of El Mirador for sheer architectural monumentality—nor would any Maya city match it in later times.

The figurine cult that had begun in the Early Preclassic Period in the Pacific region was confined to households by the end of the period and disappeared entirely from some sites, suggesting that the emerging state substituted its own ceremonies in new monumental plazas decorated with sculptures. Facade decorations on the temples and stelae carvings found in the great new plazas suggest that cosmological symbolism and human sacrifice were involved in these ceremonies and were used to legitimize the increasingly centralized authority of rulers.

After this period of extraordinary accomplishment in architecture, art, and writing, there was a hiatus in which many Maya cities were depopulated and some were totally abandoned. The eruption of Ilopango Volcano in El Salvador c. 250 C.E., but perhaps as much as a century later, made a large area of the southern region uninhabitable, but there may have been other reasons for the hiatus, especially in the lowlands. By the beginning of the Classic Period, there was a major adjustment in the Maya world in which the lowlands emerged as the heartland of Maya civilization, greatly eclipsing the southern region and rendering it peripheral despite its fertile lands enriched by volcanic ash and lava.

Southern Region

The first recognizably Maya-style carved stelae made their appearance not in the Petén, which would become the heartland of Maya civilization in the Classic Period, but rather in the southern area along the Pacific coast, in the Guatemala highlands, and in the region of the old Isthmian culture. In the course of the development of the stela-and-altar complex, hieroglyphic texts with the first Maya Long Count dates were carved onto the stelae at many sites. Three-dimensional sculptures were also common in the southern region; these include the so-called mushroom stones, whose function is not known, and the potbellied human figures with puffy faces that probably derived from the Early Preclassic Olmec tradition. This latter sculptural tradition ended with the Preclassic Period.

It is the stelae and altars, hieroglyphic writing on public monuments, and a curvilinear, narrative art style that are considered among the most salient features of Classic Period Maya civilization. The fact that these features evolved in the southern area is particularly interesting because they ceased being produced there in the Classic Period, just as they were being embellished in the lowlands. For this reason, the southern area is often considered atypical and "peripheral" to Maya civilization,

despite its central importance in the Late Pre-classic Period.

THE STELA CULT

In the Late Preclassic Period, a stela cult swept through the southern region but appeared only rarely in the lowlands. These freestanding stone monuments were carved in a curvilinear two-dimensional style that can be found from southeastern Guatemala into the Gulf-coast region and remaining Olmec sites of the period, such as Tres Zapotes. For this reason, the style has been called Epi-Olmec. It is far more prevalent, however, in the southern Maya region along the Pacific coast and also in the highlands, from Toniná in Chiapas and Kaminaljuyú in central Guatemala to Chalchuapa in El Salvador. It is even found occasionally in the lowlands and as far north as Yucatán. The style has also been called Izapan after the site of Izapa on the Pacific slope where 38 carved stelae were recovered in addition to 51 uncarved ones. Izapa may have been inhabited by ancestors of Mixe-Zoque rather than Mayan speakers, although this remains a controversial issue. Yet the so-called Izapa style was found at Maya sites and has been used to define the naturalistic low-relief sculptural style that became the hallmark of Maya culture in the Late Preclassic and Classic Periods from the southern to the northern areas.

Mythological Scenes Many Izapan-style stelae depict mythological scenes in which deities enact events that led to the creation of the Maya world. Art historians have been able to identify some of these scenes by their similarity to those described in the 17th-century *Popol Vuh*, the book of creation of the Quiché Maya. Maya gods well known from the Classic and Postclassic Periods, such as the long-lipped lightening-and-rain god, Chak, and the serpent-footed God K of Maya royal lineages, also can be identified in Izapan art at this early time (see Chapter 6). But in the Late Preclassic, the deity most often associated with rulership was Vuqub Caquix (Seven Macaw), known also as the Principal Bird Deity, who ruled as the sun in a prior creation, as related in the Maya Hero Twin myth in the *Popol Vuh*. His image is found on stelae not just at Izapa but at other sites as well, on pottery, and, in the Maya lowlands, on facade sculptures.

Historical Scenes   Other stelae are carved with historical scenes that depict a single individual in profile, probably a ruler, elaborately attired and often wearing a trophy head on his belt. Some scenes depict such elite individuals involved in human decapitation. Others show them accompanied by incense-burning braziers, standing on the monster mask of the earth deity—the entrance to the Underworld—with a sky deity emerging from a swirl of cloud scrolls above them. Such symbolism suggests these rulers were at the center of the cosmos and could perform rituals to communicate with the Maya otherworld. Yet other stelae depict two such individuals facing each other in a manner suggesting the transfer of power to a ruler.

Ruler Cult   The stelae were lined up in front of important public buildings and were often paired with what became known as altars that may have actually served as thrones. These stelae probably served to legitimize the power of rulers by associating them with rituals and cosmic forces that could protect the community. Like earlier shaman chiefs, Maya rulers gained legitimacy by claiming access to supernatural forces. Trophy heads and sacrificial scenes indicate that prowess in war was also important to a ruler's authority. The stela cult of the Late Preclassic Period was the beginning of what would become the dynastic ruler cult of the Classic Period.

2.3   Jade-and-shell mosaic pendant, Late Classic Period. Jade and exotic shells were treasured throughout the millennia of Mesoamerican civilization. This Maya pendant combines both materials in a mosaic portrait.   (Photo courtesy Peter Selverstone)

WRITING AND LONG COUNT CALENDAR

Hieroglyphic writing and Long Count dating appeared with the stela cult and were incorporated into the bas-relief sculptures. The spread of the stela cult and writing was uneven during the Late Preclassic Period, however. At Izapa, the site so well known for its many stelae that it has given its name to the sculptural style, there is no known example of writing dating from this early period. At Kaminaljuyú, where relatively extensive texts have been recovered from this period, no Long Count dates have been found. Yet dated stelae appear at some smaller Pacific slope sites, such as Abaj Takalik and El Baúl, and fragmentary calendrical glyphs have been recovered at Chalchuapa in El Salvador. In highland Verapaz and the Salamá Valley, the reliefs on stelae have occasional glyphic elements incorporated into them, but no text. In the lowlands, the stela cult was not quickly adopted. These sculptures are found only at a few sites (Nakbé, El Mirador, and Cerros) and even less often with glyphic texts (El Mirador); a few stucco sculptures and small portable

2.4 El Baúl Stela 1. This Izapa-period stela depicts a ruler communicating with an ancestor in a cloud of scrolls above him. The monument is incised with the earliest known Maya Long Count date (37 C.E.). (Drawing by Linda Schele, copyright David Schele)

objects, however, are incised with glyphic elements, but not Long Count dates.

Origin of Writing and Long Count Protowriting on numerous stela-like monuments is detected from as early as c. 500 to 400 B.C.E. in Oaxaca. A few carvings found in the Olmec heartland suggest the Long Count Calendar was first developed by Mixe-Zoque peoples, not the Maya. The earliest known Long Count dates appear on monuments at Chiapa de Corzo in Chiapas, Mexico (December 7, 36 B.C.E., in our calendar) which may have been occupied by the Mixe-Zoque at the time, and at Tres Zapotes in Veracruz (31 B.C.E.), which definitely was not Maya. Although one Middle Preclassic monument with hieroglyphs has been found in the Maya region in the Salamá Valley, further examples are not found until several centuries later in that region or elsewhere. The earliest Maya monuments dated in the Long Count Calendar are at sites along the Pacific slopes, such as El Baúl (Stela 1, 37 C.E.) and Abaj Takalik (first century C.E.).

The origin of writing and the origin of the Long Count Calendar, then, probably occurred outside the Maya area. Archaeological understanding of the development of writing and the Long Count Calendar is limited, however, and the border between the Mixe-Zoque groups and the Maya in this period is difficult to delineate. The texts often are not yet decipherable; those that have been recovered are few in number and often badly eroded. Much has been lost, particularly in the destructive environment of the tropical lowlands. Based on the evidence currently available, however, two writing systems developed in the Isthmian region at this time, one in Mixe-Zoque and the other in Mayan.

Maya Hieroglyphs The Maya hieroglyphic monuments that have been recovered present an already well developed Maya symbolic system and a version of Long Count dating with an introductory glyph that is idiosyncratic to the Maya. Obviously the Maya writing system had been evolving before it was inscribed in stone. More needs to be understood about the origins and development of Mesoamerican writing, but even if the Maya initially derived their writing system from others, which appears likely based on the current evidence, they eventually developed the most complex hieroglyphic writing system and calendrical notations in the New World.

KAMINALJUYÚ

Kaminaljuyú grew from a small center in the Valley of Guatemala in 500 B.C.E. to a capital city dominating the valley by the terminal Preclassic Period. Although the sprawl of modern Guatemala City has destroyed much of the ancient site and made a careful reconstruction of its development impossible, Kaminaljuyú in its final phase (Early Classic) was a city of more than 200 earthen and adobe-plastered mounds in contrast to approximately 80 at Izapa. The majority of the mounds dated to the Late Preclassic Period. Some were 20 meters (66 feet) high and once supported adobe or wooden temples with thatched roofs. One massive structure, judging from the rich tombs it contained, must have been an ancestor shrine dedicated to deceased rulers. An artificial canal, built c. 400 B.C.E. to replace one from the Middle Preclassic Period, fed a vast irrigation system. Great platforms with temples and what may have been a palace courtyard complex were constructed; stelae, some almost 2 meters (6 feet) tall, were carved in low relief, with hieroglyphic inscriptions.

Kaminaljuyú was more powerful and wealthier than any other city in the southern region during this period. Kaminaljuyú influence can be seen at other highland sites and from the Salamá Valley to El Baúl and Chalchuapa. Although population estimates for Kaminaljuyú cannot be made because of the destruction of the site, tens of thousands of laborers, probably drawn from all over the valley, were necessary to construct and maintain the city.

Many archaeologists believe that the centralized power required to organize such public works would have been beyond that of a mere chiefdom. And the stela cult probably served to glorify the rulers of such an incipient state. One tomb—Burial C in Structure E-III-3—is the richest yet discovered anywhere in the Maya realm for the Late Preclassic Period. Its more than 300 artifacts—jade, obsidian, quartz crystals, entire sheets of mica, stingray spines (known to be used by Maya royalty for autosacrifice), fish teeth, and, of course, ceramics including Usulután-ware—certainly suggest that its occupant, accompanied by four sacrificed individuals, was a Kaminaljuyú king. The burial contents also demonstrate the extensive trade and wealth of this strategically located city.

Maya Lowlands

If the southern region was precocious in writing and the stela cult, the Petén was inventive in masonry architecture, stucco decorations, and the mythic religious symbolism associated with these arts. In fact, many of the same themes discovered in the southern area are also found expressed in these other, more monumental forms in the Petén and Belize lowlands. Triadic architectural arrangements may have associated the ruler—often buried within—with cosmic forces, such as the Maya Three-Stone-Place of creation (see Chapter 6). The earliest evidence of lowland use of the Long Count Calendar occurs 200 years after that on the Pacific slopes, but the lowland Maya were marking time long before they carved Long

Count dates in stone: In the Middle Preclassic Period, they were building solar observatories in stone complexes known as E-groups, and these complexes spread during the Late Preclassic Period (see Chapter 8).

Around 300 B.C.E. there was an enormous cultural shift in the lowlands. Stucco sculptures covered masonry facades. The corbeled arch was introduced and spread in the lowlands from masonry tomb construction to residential and temple architecture by the end of the period. The most monumental building projects of Maya civilization are accompanied by a new ceramic style as well: the Chicanel. The Chicanel Ceramic Complex, which included Usulután-ware, marks a period of increasing population growth, the development of new urban centers, and political complexity in the lowlands.

URBAN GROWTH

Although urbanism, monumental masonry architecture, and intensive agricultural production existed during the Middle Preclassic Period, these characteristics of Maya settlements in the lowlands became more common and more impressive in size. Urban centers that had existed in the previous phase underwent enormous growth, and population levels must have ranged from several thousand to tens of thousands. Small villages—such as Calakmul in southern Campeche, Mexico; Cerros situated on the Bay of Chetumal; and Caracol in western Belize—became ceremonial centers complete with all the architectural pretentions associated with the new ruling class. Cerros, a modest-size center, probably paid for its grand building projects through trade alliances; its port facilities, including a canoe basin and dock, must have been used by more important cities, such as El Mirador and nearby Lamanai, to trade around the Yucatán Peninsula to places such as Komchén, which produced salt for export. Edzná constructed a system of canals for intensive agriculture that was large enough to sustain boat travel from the far end of the fields to the ceremonial center. Cacao and other produce of such an agricultural system may very well have been for export as well as for local subsistence. Such public works both displayed and reinforced the religious and economic power of the ruling class.

Massive Construction Projects There is considerable evidence for the development of a new political order akin to that occurring in the southern area. Large construction projects of huge blocks of quarried stone demonstrate the rulers' abilities to command and organize labor and resources (see Chapter 8). The Lost World Complex at Tikal measured 80 meters (264 feet) on each side of its base and rose 20 meters (66 feet) in height. Lamanai constructed a pyramid platform that was 33 meters (more than 100 feet) high—almost twice the size of the largest pyramids built during the Middle Preclassic Period. El Mirador, however, undertook a building program that outstripped all other cities in the Preclassic Period—or the Classic Period, for that matter—in its massiveness. Its El Tigre complex covered the equivalent of three football fields and rose 55 meters (181 feet) in height. Although the Structure II complex at Calakmul matched El Tigre in size, El Mirador also had the resources to build the Danta Complex, which was even more monumental, rising 70 meters (231 feet) high. Although not an edifice, Edzná's vast canal system covered more than 23 kilometers (14 miles) and was one of the largest public undertakings in the Maya world.

EMBLEMS OF RULERSHIP

As in the southern area during the Late Preclassic Period, lowland art associated rulers with cosmic forces and the mythic gods of creation. Instead of stelae, however, the lowland

Maya created massive stucco deity masks and attached them to building facades. These stucco sculptures of various deities, particularly creation deities such as Vuqub Caquix and the sun, are found at many sites during this period, including Uaxactún in the central Petén, Nakbé in the Mirador Basin, Edzná in Campeche, and Kohunlich in Quintana Roo. From Cerros in Belize to Mirador in the Petén, these great stucco sculptures flanked the stairways leading up to triadic complexes associated with rulership. At Nakbé, the stucco masks of the Vuqub Caquix, or the Principal Bird Deity, were almost 5 meters (16 feet) tall and 10 meters (34 feet) wide.

Ruler as Cosmic Center   The significance of these monumental buildings and sculptural complexes to rulership is clearest from the excavations at Cerros. The terraced pyramid adorned with masks was located at the most northern point of the site, the Maya location for the sky and ancestral deities. With the Bay of Chetumal at its back, the sculpted 22-meter (72.5-foot) pyramid dominated the town and looked toward the ball court situated to the south, the Maya location of the Underworld. The stucco masks flanking the staircase on the east represented the rising sun and the morning star; and on the west, the setting sun and evening star. The temples on top of these pyramids gradually grew from a single one at the first phase of the pyramid to a triadic complex with royal tombs. A ruler performing rituals on the top of the pyramid would be seen as essential to the cosmic order and its continuation, symbolized by the daily passage of the sun. (See also "The Structure of Cosmic Space" in Chapter 6.)

Trade   Exotic goods and art both were used to elevate the Late Preclassic Period ruler. Depictions of the rulers themselves were rare in the lowlands, and some archaeologists have argued that the rulers themselves were not yet the objects of veneration that they were in the stela cult found along the Pacific slopes. In fact, royal tomb contents in the lowlands are more modest compared to their southern counterparts, even though the earliest corbeled vaults were used for such tombs. There are surviving traces of murals from a temple at Tikal, a few stelae in the Mirador Basin, and a bas-relief carving at Loltún in northern Yucatán. Although these few surviving works depict rulers in the naturalistic style of the southern area, these rulers are adorned with new low-

2.5   Stucco sun god mask, Kohunlich, Quintana Roo, Mexico. This giant mask is one of four that flanked the stairway of a Late Preclassic pyramid platform.   (Photo courtesy Peter Selverstone)

land insignia of rulership, such as the distinctive tripartite jade headband that symbolizes sprouting maize.

Exotic trade items that first appear in the lowlands at this time, such as coral-colored thorny oyster (*Spondylus*) shells, symbolized the ruler's economic ties with faraway places on the Pacific, perhaps as distant as Ecuador through trade with Costa Rica or the north coast of Mexico. Objects like *Spondylus* shells, stingray spines for autosacrifice, and jade ornaments, symbolized rulership, not simply personal power, and they are repeatedly found in lowland tombs. They persisted as royal symbols in the Classic Period. Most remarkable perhaps is the absence of sacrificed retainers in royal tombs during the Late Preclassic Period.

MIRADOR BASIN

The Mirador Basin in the northwestern Petén experienced exceptional development in the lowlands during this period. The urban centers with the most massive constructions congregated here at Nakbé, Wakná, and Tintal, as well as the largest of any city at the time, El Mirador. Just to the north, the city of Calakmul constructed the pyramidal complex, Structure II, from the top of which El Mirador's soaring buildings could be seen more than 35 kilometers (22 miles) away. El Mirador spread over an area 2 kilometers (1.2 miles) wide, approximately the same as Tikal, Edzná, and Komchén at the time, but the massive buildings at El Mirador dwarfed these settlements and all others in the lowlands. The population that constructed and maintained El Mirador must have also exceeded that at other sites. Kaminaljuyú is said to have called upon tens of thousands for its support; El Mirador certainly was sustained by even larger a population. If size indicates power, there must have been a hierarchy of sites with El Mirador alone at the apex.

The extent and nature of El Mirador's political power is hard to determine from the archaeological record in most instances, but its dominant role in the northern Petén is unusually clear. Causeways radiated from the center of El Mirador, connecting not only various sections of the city but also neighboring cities in the Mirador Basin, one as far away as 23 kilometers (14 miles). A 13-kilometer (8-mile) *sacbe*, or road, connected the important city of Nakbé with El Mirador. These causeways suggest a regional alliance, or perhaps a kingdom, with its capital at El Mirador. Strategically situated between the Caribbean coast and the southern area, El Mirador probably achieved its dominance through trade. Far-ranging contacts, from Cuello to Kaminaljuyú, are in evidence in the artifacts at the site. El Mirador is one of the few lowland sites with stelae, and one of the rare ones with a Kaminaljuyú-style hieroglyphic text. When the hiatus occurred, it affected all these sites that apparently were partners in trade.

Late Preclassic Hiatus

Maya civilization developed and flourished during the Late Preclassic Period, but as the period came to a close, c. 150 to 250 C.E., many cities that had experienced the most dynamic growth collapsed or at least shriveled in size, and this phenomenon occurred from the Pacific to northern Yucatán. The archaeological record indicates that most cities on the Pacific littoral were abandoned by 250 C.E., as was Komchén in northern Yucatán, Altar de Sacrificios on the Río Pasión, and Cerros in northern Belize. The great cities of the Mirador Basin and Kaminaljuyú in the highlands were seriously depopulated but not abandoned. This hiatus in Maya cultural development has received considerable scrutiny because it occurs at a critical period: the onset of Classic Period civilization and the shift of Maya power into the lowlands.

TEOTIHUACAN

Despite the importance of the hiatus, the reasons for such demographic and cultural shifts are not well understood, giving rise to considerable speculation about the causes, which have ranged from warfare to ecological disaster. Some archaeologists have argued that the rise of the great central Mexican city of Teotihuacan (c. 100 B.C.E.–c. 650 C.E.) disrupted valuable Maya trade routes in cacao, cotton, jade, salt, and exotic feathers and shells. Although some green obsidian from central Mexico does appear in the archaeological record for this time period, it is difficult to imagine that Teotihuacan could have wreaked havoc on the entire Maya region simultaneously. Teotihuacan's push into the region is now believed to have come in the Early Classic Period, after trade connections had been disrupted by the abandonment of some Maya cities.

FORTIFICATIONS

War between Maya cities competing to control resources may have caused the hiatus, and there is some evidence for this hypothesis. Stelae depict trophy heads, signs of warfare, and at the close of the Preclassic Period, sites such as Cuello depict rulers in war regalia. The archaeological records suggest warfare as well: The palace at Chiapa de Corzo was deliberately destroyed, and when the site revived, it was occupied by people using different ceramics. Competing cities may have vied for control of the lowlands. El Mirador, for example, was greatly eclipsed by Tikal by the end of the period; the shift in powers may have affected other cities, such as Cuello, because of the disruption in trade alliances. The first fortifications—or, more neutrally stated, barriers—at

Maya sites appear at some sites at this time, including a moat at Becán and perhaps Cuello. An encircling wall was constructed at El Mirador. A fortified ditch separated Tikal and Uaxactún, and decipherments of the texts from those two cities suggest conflict between them into the Early Classic Period. Populations became less dispersed and were concentrated instead in the fortified city centers.

NATURAL DISASTERS

Paleoclimatic studies provide another view of the Maya Preclassic hiatus. Droughts and volcanic eruptions occurred during this period and could have caused the social displacement and political upheaval that explain the increase in fortifications at this time. Studies suggest that a drying trend reached its climax by 100 C.E. The drier climate, exacerbated by deforestation and dense populations in the Mirador Basin, turned wet marshlands into *bajos*, or seasonal swamps, and transformed rich earth into hard-to-farm clays. The combination destroyed the elaborate gardens and wetland agriculture of dykes and artificial fields (see Chapter 3) that had sustained large Preclassic populations in the lowlands. The Maya built reservoirs and dug wells to support their cities during the dry season, but populations nonetheless contracted after the Preclassic Period. The situation is less clear at Komchén, but the northern Yucatán has always been more subject to drought than the Petén, and a drying trend would have exacerbated climatic conditions there. The same climatic changes that affected the lowlands caused the small lakes at Kaminaljuyú to dry up, destroying the canal irrigation system there and forcing the populace to rely on a system of wells instead. Depopulation was the result.

In the southern Maya area, the impact of drought was compounded by the eruption of the Ilopango volcano (c. 200–250 C.E.) in central El Salvador. Chalchuapa, manufacturer of obsidian blades and the Usulután ceramics that were valued items in Maya trade, had to be abandoned. Not until the Late Classic Period (600–900) could the soil be farmed again. The eruption affected more than the Chalchuapa region, however. Ash-clogged rivers flooded the southeastern Pacific littoral and caused the rivers to change course.

SHIFT OF POWER

These natural catastrophes destroyed some cities and disrupted both agriculture and trade. From Chalchuapa to western Guatemala, many cities were abandoned for the next few centuries. The devastation of the southern area resulted in a massive political and economic readjustment. War may have broken out. Teotihuacan may eventually have tried to take advantage, although the first to take advantage of the devastation were the Maya themselves.

EARLY CLASSIC PERIOD (C. 250–600)

The heartland of Maya culture shifted to the central area, away from the southern coast and highlands. The abandonment of most cities along the Pacific littoral permitted the lowlands to dominate the Maya region during the Classic Period. But even within the lowlands, there was a major shift in power. El Mirador declined, while others cities rose to prominence, and judging from the introduction of stelae carved with hieroglyphs and new building projects, the most prominent among them

were Tikal in the central Petén, Caracol in western Belize, and Calakmul in southern Campeche. Maya cities flourished, and they developed throughout the lowlands: Piedras Negras and Yaxchilán, for example, in the Usumacinta region; Altar de Sacrificios on the Pasión River; Copán and Quiriguá in the Motagua Valley region; and Edzná, Oxkintok, Yaxuná, Ek Balam, and Cobá in the northern lowlands. The stela cult was less prevalent in the north, however, and written texts were quite rare during this period.

Along with the political shifts of the period, the ruler cult that had already evolved in the Pacific slopes and highlands of Guatemala was adopted by lowland cities during the Early Classic Period. Lowland rulers adorned themselves with the emblems of office used in the Late Preclassic Period, but in the Early Classic they added the stela cult to the lowland program and extolled themselves and their ancestors in hieroglyphic texts that were dated with the exactitude of the Long Count Calendar. Royal tombs reflected this personality cult, too: Sacrificed individuals were buried with the king, as were an increasing number of exotic goods. The personality cult reinforced the more abstract but monumental message of rulership already existing in Late Preclassic Period architecture. In architecture, in portraiture, and in writing, Early Classic Maya rulers were the subjects. They became more than the facilitators between the gods and the people; they themselves were venerated.

By the fourth century, the art began to portray the ruler in a new specialized costume, that of the warrior. The details of this ritual dress were borrowed from the central Mexican city of Teotihuacan. The new symbols of the warrior-ruler were accompanied by a new weapon: The atlatl, or spear-thrower, also introduced from central Mexico. The now-deciphered Early Classic hieroglyphic texts confirm the political presence of Teotihuacan in the Maya lowlands. These texts, despite their paucity and uneven distribution, provide the earliest history of the Maya. The history is only a skeletal one, but it nonetheless reveals wars and shifting alliances among the Maya as they developed into many separate archaic states controlled by the centralized authority of dynastic rulers. In the 1990s, decipherment of these texts revealed the startling information that Tikal had accomplished its hegemony under a dynasty installed by Teotihuacan.

Tikal

Beginning c. 200 C.E., Tikal attempted to seize control of the Petén, replacing El Mirador as the most powerful city. Tikal and its residential suburbs covered an area of 60 square kilometers (23 square miles), but the city fortifications defended an area of 123 square kilometers (47.5 square miles). By the end of the Early Classic Period, its population probably numbered 60,000.

Tikal successfully extended its territory by absorbing smaller neighboring cities, such as Bejucal to the south, and fighting the substantial city of Uaxactún to the north. Based on artifacts found at lowland sites, Tikal probably disrupted El Mirador's trade routes, too, replacing the port at Cerros with new ones along the Belizean coast, such as Santa Rita, and directing trade further south into the Petén. Based on Tikal's domination of Río Azul and Nakum, both located by rivers, Tikal probably controlled the portage between rivers that branched into the Petén from the Caribbean and Gulf of Mexico. From the decipherment of the glyphs and trade items, Tikal also appears to have gradually installed its dynastic allies at other cities such as Copán in Honduras, Oxkintok in Yucatán, and for a few years, at Caracol in Belize.

FIRST LOWLAND STELA

Tikal, the political giant in the Early Classic Period, also was the first lowland state to carve Long Count dates on its stelae. Although El Mirador had erected a stela inscribed with text in the Late Preclassic Period, it was atypical of that period in the lowlands. The widespread adoption of the stela cult in the lowlands begins at Tikal with the erection of Stela 29 in 292 C.E. No earlier dated monument is known, but later Tikal stelae refer back in time to the founder of the first Tikal dynasty c. 100. Other lowland cities did not begin boasting of their dynastic founders until 100 years later, and the erection of stelae was basically confined to the central Petén region around Tikal until the middle of the fifth century. Although stelae are notoriously subject to erosion and destruction (century-long dynastic gaps are not unusual among those that have been recovered), it now appears that the powerful city of Tikal was initially the source of inspiration for the ruler cult in the lowlands.

Based on the contents of its Early Classic Period tombs and ritual caches, Tikal used its political power to expand its long-distance trade and to amass considerable wealth. In the early fifth century, under the rule of Yax Ain (379–420), or First Crocodile, better known as Curl Nose, there were unprecedented amounts of imported materials: obsidian from both central Mexico and the Guatemalan highlands, jade from the Motagua Valley, shells from the Pacific and the Caribbean, and ceramic vessels influenced by Teotihuacan in central Mexico. Curl Nose's tomb, painted with Maya hieroglyphs and astronomical symbols, was filled with all these imported riches as well as other exotic materials, including a variety of bird feathers, two turtle carapaces, and the body of a crocodile, his namesake and spirit companion, or *way* (see Chapter 6).

2.6   *Tikal Complex Q, plaza with stelae and altars. The stela–and–altar cult spread into the lowlands in the third century and persisted until the Terminal Classic Period collapse.*   (Photo courtesy Cherra Wyllie)

Cultural Shifts

RULER CULT

With the introduction of the stela cult, the portrayal of deities in giant stucco panels was eclipsed by ruler portraiture. Those stucco friezes that were made in the Early Classic Period depicted the ruler dressed as a deity, such as one on a panel said to be from near Calakmul, in southern Campeche. Smaller stucco decorations were more common, however, and persisted on friezes and corner decorations of buildings; they depicted both rulers and gods. Mural art from this time period, although much destroyed, has survived better and with greater variety of colors than the few fragments remaining from the Late Preclassic Period. Some paintings are naturalistic, showing festivals and local buildings, such as those

at a palace in Uaxactún, but tomb murals are most often painterly renditions of glyphs.

ARCHITECTURE

The Maya increasingly used the corbeled arch to construct stone temples, elite tombs, and palaces. Despite this architectural advancement, the massive complexes and the huge quarried stones of the Late Preclassic Period became less fashionable—or less feasible. The deforestation that occurred during the Preclassic Period due to both farming and urbanization—even plaster required trees for fuel to burn the limestone—may have imposed more conservative building techniques on the Maya. The Preclassic Danta complex at El Mirador alone consumed more than 2 million cubic meters (70.6 million cubic feet) of quarried limestone and stucco and was so massive that it could have covered the central plaza and two towering pyramids of Classic Period Tikal. Early Classic complexes were less ambitious but nonetheless monumental. They were also built more efficiently, with more finely worked stone veneer that saved on both quarrying costs and the need for thick layers of plaster.

CERAMICS

The ceramic complex changed too. With the eruption of Ilopango Volcano, there was disruption in the production and distribution of Usulután-ware. When it was revived, it was as part of the Copador ceramic complex found at Copán but not in the remainder of the lowlands, reinforcing the fact that Salvadoran sites, like most of those on the Pacific littoral, were only on the fringe of Classic Period Maya civilization. Those Preclassic cities that survived into the Early Classic Period, such as Kaminaljuyú and coastal Tiquisate, employed new ceramic forms, many of them imported or inspired by the central Mexican city of Teotihuacan. Thin orange effigy vessels were actually imported from Teotihuacan, but central Mexican slab-legged tripod pots painted with Maya scenes may have been locally manufactured. These central Mexican–style ceramics were found in burials throughout the Maya region. The Maya continued to manufacture their characteristic polychrome ware as well but in a new style called Tzakol. Some of this complex is characterized by wide bowls decorated with stylized birds and human figures.

Teotihuacan Influences

Teotihuacan, located 40 kilometers (25 miles) from modern Mexico City, intensified its trade in the Maya region during the Early Classic Period. The introduction of Teotihuacan spear-throwers and warrior symbolism sug-

gests the trade was not always voluntary, but the exact nature of this central Mexican exchange with the Maya has long perplexed Mesoamericanists.

During its fifth-century apogee, Teotihuacan was one of the largest cities in the world with a population estimated to have ranged from 100,000 to 200,000. The city dominated central Mexico politically and economically and controlled rich veins of green obsidian that it traded throughout Mesoamerica. Its twin pyramids were awesome features in the Valley of Mexico; the Pyramid of the Sun, greater in volume than Egypt's Pyramid of Khufu (but smaller than El Mirador's Danta complex), was constructed over a sacred spring and was the site of major pilgrimages. Wealthy, sacred, and enormous, Teotihuacan was probably both revered and feared by most Mesoamericans.

In the fourth century, Teotihuacan attempted to revive and control trade in the southern Maya area in order to obtain jade, tropical bird feathers, jaguar pelts, and other prestige items. Traders, or warrior-traders, established a base at Kaminaljuyú c. 400, building an enclave there in an architectural style characteristic of Teotihuacan, manufacturing tripod pots similar to those from central Mexico, and burying their dead in tombs containing many central Mexican artifacts. Teotihuacan's cultural and economic influence in the southern Maya area left the region with a central Mexican imprint distinctive from that in the lowlands.

Although it was long thought that Teotihuacan used its base at Kaminaljuyú to spread its influence in the lowlands, particularly at Tikal, recently recovered evidence demonstrates that it was already present at Tikal by 378. At Tikal, there is a small Teotihuacan-style structure, as well as sculptures and ceramics executed in the central Mexican style. Stelae also begin depicting Maya warrior-rulers dressed in costumes marked by Teotihuacan symbols. Stela 31 at

Tikal even showed its ruler flanked by a figure dressed like a Teotihuacano.

Many archaeologists have concluded from such evidence that Teotihuacan actually conquered Maya cities such as Tikal and controlled trade in the region. Teotihuacan influences are found from the Pacific coast and the highlands to Tikal and Yucatecan sites such as Becán. But Maya influences are also present at Teotihuacan, and Maya residential complexes, the so-called traders' enclaves that were decorated in the lowland art style, existed at the central Mexican city. The cultural interaction between the two regions could have been the result of intensive trade and mutual admiration. Maya adoption of the more lethal weaponry of the central Mexican city was an outcome of such contact. It has been difficult to decide the exact nature of Teotihuacan's presence in the Maya region based solely on such archaeological artifacts.

GLYPHIC EVIDENCE FOR CONQUEST

In 1983, new sculptures were found at Tikal. In the style of Teotihuacan, these monuments were nonetheless inscribed with Maya texts. Their decipherment provided compelling evidence about the militant nature of Teotihuacan's role in the politics of the lowlands. Based on the texts, Siyah K'ak (known as Smoking Frog) arrived at Tikal from the west, the direction of Teotihuacan, and on that same day of January 31, 378, Tikal's king Chak Tok Ich'aak I (better known as Jaguar Paw) died. Tikal and Uaxactún were subjugated by Smoking Frog. Tikal's new king, Yax Ain, or Curl Nose, was not the son of Jaguar Paw nor did he claim the throne as the legitimate heir of the Tikal dynasty. Rather he arrived at Tikal with Smoking Frog from Teotihuacan and may have been the son of that eminent city's ruler. It now is believed that it is Curl Nose who appears dressed as a Teotihuacano on the sides of Tikal

2.7 *Tikal Stela 31, 439 C.E. The two side panels depict a Teotihuacano warrior, now known to be the Tikal ruler Curl Nose. The goggle-eyed figure on the shield is the Teotihuacan storm and war god Tlaloc. The god's characteristic ringed eyes became common elements on Maya war costumes, and the spear-thrower, held in the warrior's right hand, became part of the standard weaponry of war. Stela 31 is the accession stela of Tikal's ruler Siyah Chan K'awil, better known as Stormy Sky, who is depicted in the center. The two side panels depict his Teotihuacano father. Despite the declaration of dynastic ties with the central Mexican city, the sculpture of Stormy Sky is purely Maya in form and style; the hieroglyphic text on the reverse is the longest Maya inscription surviving from the Early Classic Period.* (Drawings courtesy John Montgomery)

Stela 31, the accession monument of Curl Nose's son, Stormy Sky.

COPÁN

Recent glyphic evidence from other sites suggests that the foreign dynasty at Tikal installed Yax K'uk Mo as ruler of Copán in 426. Yax K'uk

Mo, like Curl Nose, arrived at Copán from another region and was buried in a tomb with central Mexican architectural traits. Yet there are fewer traces of central Mexican influence at Copán than at Tikal and Kaminaljuyú. Strontium-90 analysis of Yax K'uk Mo's remains suggests, however, he spent most of his youth in the Petén before arriving at Copán. Rather than being a Teotihuacano, the Copán founder appears to have been a Maya ally of that powerful city and its new dynasty at Tikal. He was also installed as king of nearby Quiriguá.

TEOTIHUACAN'S CONTROL

There can be little doubt that Teotihuacan propelled Tikal into the greatest Early Classic power in the lowlands and that it installed rulers of its choice at Tikal, Uaxactún, Copán, and Quiriguá. Although there are no hieroglyphic texts at Kaminaljuyú to record Teotihuacan's takeover of its dynasty, the archaeological record there demonstrates even greater control and dominance by the Mexicans. Some archaeologists have suggested that the rulers who arrived in the lowlands from Teotihuacan may have been Maya nobles who had been residing in the central Mexican traders' enclaves. Based on future DNA and strontium-90 analyses of human remains, such refinements in the history of the period may one day be possible.

Teotihuacan used its might to establish dynasties in a few of the most powerful Early Classic cities of the Maya region. Once it was guaranteed the political loyalty and trade of these lowland cities, it seems to have left the Maya alone culturally: Tikal and Copán remained quintessentially Maya, unlike Kaminaljuyú, which no longer erected stelae. The ruler cult flourished in the Maya lowlands in contrast to Teotihuacan, where there was nothing comparable: no portraiture, no hieroglyphic writing, and no Long Count Calendar.

Teotihuacan's cultural imprints in the lowlands are actually quite few: the rulers' warrior costume, transformed into a very Maya costume (see figure 5.2, page 144); a scattering of buildings in the central Mexican style; and certain fashions in pottery, including the somewhat abstract Teotihuacan-style deity designs (see figure 1.3 upper left, page 11). While Maya civilization continued to develop in the lowlands, some Maya cities became part of the central Mexican long-distance trade network, and the riches from such trade appeared in the burials like that of Curl Nose at Tikal during the Early Classic Period. In return, Teotihuacan received its supply of exotic tropical commodities and jade.

Tikal Defeated

In backing Tikal's hegemony in the central Maya area, Teotihuacan must have alienated the losers—as did Tikal. The introduction of the central Mexican war spear-thrower into the lowlands escalated the level of warfare at the very time there was an increasing number of powerful cities. Despite its dominance, Tikal had its rivals during the Early Classic Period. Calakmul, to the north, was impressive in size and well fortified, and Caracol in western Belize was expanding rapidly. These cities wrote about their dynasties and wars on stone monuments, and one altar found at Caracol boasted that its ruler, Lord Muluc, had defeated Tikal in 562. At that time, many of Tikal's stelae were broken and upended, including those of the Teotihuacanos Curl Nose and Stormy Sky. This defeat led to the subjugation of that city for 130 years. During this hiatus, no carved monuments were erected at Tikal, and the riches once found in its caches and burials disappeared. Its population built their homes close to the central city for security. Tikal's allies and dependencies suffered too: Building ceased at Uaxactún, and a hiatus occurred in the hieroglyphic record at Río Azul.

LATE CLASSIC PERIOD (C. 600–900)

The Late Classic Period was initiated with profound cultural and political changes. Tikal, encircled by its rivals and isolated from trade, would not become a political force again until late in the seventh century. Teotihuacan declined as a power in Mesoamerica, and c. 700, its sacred center was sacked and burned. Kaminaljuyú also declined. Yet, this was not a period of decline in the Maya world, perhaps because the Maya were free of foreign interference. The Late Classic Period witnessed enormous growth in population, in the number of Maya polities, in the power of the elite class, and in the sophistication of artistic expression. Hieroglyphic texts, more numerous than before, displayed the virtuosity of Maya scribes and recorded the ingenuity of Maya calendrics and astronomical knowledge.

From Palenque in the west and Copán in the east to Uxmal in the north and Dos Pilas in the south of the Petén heartland, Maya cities flourished, leaving a legacy that would define Maya civilization. Preclassic cities, like Becán, revived, and Early Classic ones, like Caracol, grew exponentially; furthermore, entirely new ones such as Dos Pilas became powerful in the Petexbatún area. Maya artistic influence spread outside the Maya area and extended into central Mexico, Xochicalco and Cacaxtla, cities that rose into prominence after the fall of Teotihuacan.

At the end of the period, a revived Tikal and its enemy Calakmul may have attempted to become Maya superpowers, forging a loose confederation of states. Warfare was prevalent and devastating to the Maya heartland, setting the stage for the collapse that was completed in the southern lowlands during the Terminal Classic Period.

Proliferation of Cities

Calakmul and Caracol continued their ascendency during the seventh century. Caracol probably installed a member of its own nobility on the Tikal throne in order to control that once powerful kingdom, located 70 kilometers (43 miles) away, and to guarantee tribute payments. But during the Late Classic Period, other Maya city-states also built great ceremonial complexes and controlled territories that included secondary, tertiary, and quaternary towns as well as ports, agricultural, and military outposts. Many of these cities carved long dynastic histories into stone, establishing their legitimacy in the mythic past when deities ruled and founding their lineage in the Early Classic Period before such texts were inscribed. The lineage of Palenque's great seventh-century king, Hanab Pakal (615–683), was commemorated on a stone-carved tablet 96 glyphs in length; an eighth-century successor required 200 glyphs to assert his legitimacy. Yaxchilán's dynastic record spanned 500 years; Copán's dynasty asserted its greatness in a hieroglyphic staircase composed of 2,200 glyphs. Stelae appeared in the usually silent northern lowlands as well: Cobá erected 23 carved stelae, and Edzná's monuments covered a 200-year period.

In 800, there were an estimated 40 to 60 cities in the Maya region, based on emblem glyphs, or titles that include the place-name. Hundreds more are suggested by their archaeological remains. Altun Há, for example, was a town in northern Belize with a population of only 3,000, few stone inscriptions, and no emblem glyphs. Yet its burials were filled with riches, including a jade carving that weighs 4.4 kilograms (almost 10 pounds) and a decomposed Maya-style book. Northern lowland cities, even the largest ones, rarely used emblem glyphs. The number of cities now known is too great for individual descriptions of their evolution or dynasties. An overview of general trends and political developments among the more powerful city

states follows. (See also "Place-Names" in Chapter 3.)

SIZE OF CITY-STATES

The political relationships among the various cities, whether they were capitals or dependencies within a political state at a given time period, remain a subject of inquiry (see Chapter 4). The decipherment of the hieroglyphs has clarified some of these hierarchical relationships, but in most areas, such as the northern lowlands and the Belize River valley, the texts are too few to make such political relationships explicit. Mapping and extensive settlement sur-

2.8   *Tikal Central Plaza, with the towering Temple I, Late Classic Period. In addition to the ruler stela cult, Maya rulers constructed pyramid temples in the sacred center as funerary monuments to themselves.*

The Palenque Dynasty*

	Accession	Death	Comments
K'uk' B'alam	431	?	Founder
"Casper"	435	487	52-year reign
Sak Chik	487	?	
Akul Anab I	501	524	
K'an Hoy Chitam I	529	565	
Akul Anab II	565	570	
Kan B'alam I	572	583	
Lady Olnal	583	604	First woman Maya ruler
Ah Ne Ol Mat	605	612	
Lady Sak K'uk'	612	640	Mother and regent of Hanab Pakal
Hanab Pakal	615	683	Only 12 when he acceded
Kan B'alam II	684	702	Hanab Pakal's son
K'an Hoy Chitam II	702	?	Hanab Pakal's son; captured in 711 and sacrificed later at Toniná; death not recorded at Palenque
Akul Anab III	722	736	Grandson (?) of Hanab Pakal
Hanab Pakal II	?	?	Great-grandson of Hanab Pakal; an event during his rule was recorded in 742
K'uk' B'alam II	764	c. 783	
6-Kimi Hanab Pakal	799		Last recorded date at city

* From decipherments and reconstructions as presented in Mathews and Schele 1974, Mathews and Robertson 1985, Schele 1991, Schele and Mathews 1998, and David Stuart 1999a. The earlier rulers are known primarily from the dynastic statements of their Late Classic Period descendants.

veys, when they have been performed, provide information that the written texts cannot, especially in regard to population levels and territorial extent. Population estimates routinely range from 3,000 to 25,000 for most Maya cities with monumental architecture, but estimates of 50,000 to 125,000 are the norm for about 20 of the very largest ones and their surrounding areas. By the end of the period, Tikal's population had grown to an estimated 125,000—double that of the Early Classic Period.

Population estimates of entire states, however, have rarely been attempted because of the difficulties of establishing borders and surveying such large areas. But the kingdoms ruled by the capital cities of Tikal and Calakmul have been estimated at more than 400,000, and the population of the southern and northern lowlands combined was somewhere between 8 and 10 million c. 800. The territories overseen by capital cities can, in fact, be surprisingly vast even for regional states less famous than Tikal or Calakmul. Cobá, for example, was connected by a 100-kilometer (62-mile) raised causeway to its dependency, Yaxuná, and its population ranged from 70,000 to 125,000. Dzibilchaltún was a sprawling kingdom surrounded by 100 square kilometers (38 square miles) of settlement and agricultural fields.

ALLIANCES

Despite the proliferation of cities and the extent of their political domain, the central area remained the most populous and powerful Maya region for much of the Late Classic Period. Study of Maya politics has also been focused on that region because that is where Maya cities and hieroglyphic texts both are most abundant. The texts mention lineage and ruler accession, rituals, and wars, and many of these events coincide with astronomical events such as eclipses and the position of Jupiter or Venus. These texts also mention other cities and dynasties, the diplomatic visits between them, and marriage alliances, as well as warfare. Alliances among polities became more common in the seventh and early eighth centuries, or at least they were written about more frequently than before. These alliances crisscrossed the lowlands and included large cities in the northern lowlands, such as Cobá and Dzibilchaltún, that participated in the trade and culture of the southern lowland cities.

Not all alliances were voluntary, nor were they between equal polities: The small site of Pomoná was not simply an ally of Palenque; it was also part of the Palenque kingdom. And Quiriguá was a colony of Copán—until it rebelled in 738. The density of cities in southern Campeche was impressive and included Río Bec, Chicanná, Becán, and many others, but these cities did not erect stelae or write about their dynasties or allies. Archaeologists can therefore only speculate about whether they were subjugated by nearby Calakmul,

which alone erected 100 stelae in the Late Classic Period.

Calakmul Calakmul was something of a mystery site until the 1980s. It had been discovered in 1931, but its great size was not known and its glyphic name (emblem glyph) was not identified until more recent excavations. With more than 6,200 buildings in a core area of 30 square kilometers (11.5 square miles), Calakmul was more densely built up than Tikal, and it had more palace-style buildings and stelae (115) than any other Maya city. As excavations continue into the new millennium, the role of Calakmul in Maya lowland politics will continually be reassessed, but it is now recognized as one of the largest Classic Period cities. Unfortunately, its stelae are often so badly eroded that the texts cannot be easily deciphered, but efforts to retrieve its history are ongoing. Much can be reconstructed from mention of the site at other cities, now that its name is recognized, and based on the hieroglyphic texts for the period, it clearly was one of the major powers in Late Classic politics.

Caracol Some Mayanists argue that Caracol defeated and subjugated Tikal with the backing of Calakmul. After that momentous sixth-century war, Caracol may have become a dependency of Calakmul given the repeated mention of Calakmul in the hieroglyphic texts at Caracol, including that of a marriage alliance between the two cities. If so, the power of Calakmul must have been formidable because Caracol itself was a vast metropolis in the seventh century, with a population estimated at more than 120,000—the largest for any Mesoamerican city during the late seventh century. Calakmul's core population has been estimated at half that number, but the kingdom that that capital city oversaw was much larger, covering a territory of 8,000 square kilometers (3,088 square miles).

Tikal   Although no Long Count texts are inscribed on monuments at Tikal during the hiatus (562–692), other cities do recount events that affected Tikal. Its isolation was guaranteed by Calakmul and Caracol, who encircled it by either defeating other Petén polities (Caracol conquered Naranjo in 631), demanding their allegiance and tribute (Dos Pilas and El Perú recognized Calakmul as overlord) or forming a friendly trade alliance (Cancuén with Calakmul). Even faraway polities allied with Tikal were subject to the power of these cities as evidenced by Calakmul's attacks on Palenque, 227 kilometers (150 miles) away, in 599 and 611. Tikal also seems to have been abandoned by a disgruntled branch of its nobility. In 645, Balah Chan K'awil, the founder of a dynasty at the twin cities of Dos Pilas and Aguateca, erected a carved and dated monument that identified his domain with the same emblem glyph used by Tikal, 105 kilometers (65 miles) away. Apparently Balah Chan K'awil represented a splinter group from the royal lineage at Tikal and rose to power under the auspices of Calakmul.

Century of Greatness

The 100 years beginning around 672 witnessed the flowering of many great cities, including some outside the Petén. The absence of powerful central Mexican cities like Teotihuacan enabled the Maya to control more trade routes and to concentrate greater quantities of wealth in their own region during this century. Population pressures also contributed to the growing number of cities as well as an increase in the size of the elite class. Competition among these Maya cities fueled more wars and demand for tribute; wealth generated building booms and increased production of luxury goods. The result was a period fraught with political tension and warfare but also one in which artistic production culminated in the greatest works of Maya civilization.

GREAT RULERS

There may have been many great rulers in other periods, but few of them are known by name. More than in any other period, the eighth-century rulers commemorated their accomplishments in hieroglyphic inscriptions carved for eternity into stone. They claimed to be great patrons of the arts, commissioning buildings, sculptures, and paintings, and they presented themselves as powerful warriors and politicians. Among them was Yukom Yich'ak K'ak (686–695?), or Jaguar Paw Smoke, who dominated the southern lowlands from Calakmul during his brief rule. Hanab Pakal (615–683) and his son Kan B'alam (684–702) governed the beautiful city of Palenque; Shield Jaguar the Great (681–742) and Bird Jaguar the Great (752–768?) brought Yaxchilán into prominence. Balah Chan K'awil (c. 645–698) founded Dos Pilas, and his daughter, Lady Six Sky, reestablished the Naranjo dynasty in 682. Hasaw Chan K'awil (682–734) revived Tikal after its long hiatus. Cauac Sky (724–785) defeated the great ruler of Copán, Waxaklahun U'bah K'awil, better known as 18 Rabbit (695–738), and created a moment of splendor at Quiriguá. And there were many others, all who contributed to the Maya history that was so richly recorded during this period.

POLITICAL REVERSALS

During this period, Caracol experienced a reversal of fortune, going into a decline during which it did not erect any carved stelae for more than 100 years. At the time it began its fall from power, the cities it had subjugated in the central Petén reemerged as major powers. Naranjo shook off its subjugation in 680, when it dared to raid Caracol, and in 682, when it formed a marriage alliance with Dos Pilas. Lady Six Sky, a princess from Dos Pilas, was sent to give prestige to the Naranjo dynasty; within a few years, she was ruling as regent for her five-year-old son. Under her rule, Naranjo repeatedly raided Ucanal, a city not far from Caracol. While Naranjo attacked the Caracol polity, Tikal was reviving too and initiating new building projects. In 695, Hasaw Chan K'awil, Tikal's greatest ruler, defeated the king of Calakmul, Jaguar Paw Smoke, ending Tikal's decades of humiliation. As the seventh century came to a close, the politics of the southern lowlands shifted, but the wars were far from over.

Petexbatún Kingdom The decline of Caracol and humiliating defeat of Calakmul perhaps gave Dos Pilas the opportunity to carve out the powerful Petexbatún kingdom. Beginning with the reign of Balah Chan K'awil's son, Itzamná K'awil in 698, the Dos Pilas–Aguateca polity rapidly expanded into the Pasíon region, making alliances and conquests with such cities as Tamarindito, La Amelia, and Itzán. The kingdom was also extended through marriage with the royal lineage at Cancuén, a large trading center on the Pasíon River near the foothills of highland Guatemala. In 735, the Petexbatún kingdom subjugated the venerable city of Seibal, capturing its king and sacrificing him at Dos Pilas. By 741, the Petexbatún region controlled an area of 4,000 square kilometers (1,544 square miles), including trade routes into the highlands and along the Pasíon to the Usumacinta.

SUPERPOWERS: TIKAL AND CALAKMUL

War between Tikal and Calakmul intensified after Tikal's defeat of Jaguar Paw Smoke at the end of the seventh century. By the middle of the eighth century, the wars had weakened Calakmul considerably. But until 800, Tikal and Calakmul were exceptionally powerful,

2.9   *War scene (detail), Bonampak mural, Room 2, c. 790. This detail from the Bonampak mural provides the fullest depiction of Maya warfare surviving from the pre-Columbian era, but it is only one of many artistic monuments dedicated to warfare themes during the Late Classic Period.* (Watercolor copy by Antonio Tejada, 1955)

and they used their power against each other. They were the talk of other cities, based on the frequent mentions of them in the texts. Calakmul and the large Petexbatún kingdom were clearly allies in the seventh century, for example, and the inscriptions at Dos Pilas mention the Calakmul kings. More refined readings of the glyphs have revealed that numerous rulers acceded to the throne of other polities under the auspices of the rulers of Tikal and Calakmul, and that monuments erected at some cities were dedicated by administrators for Tikal or Calakmul, not independent rulers (see Chapter 4). During the seventh century, Calakmul seemed to control far more cities than Tikal, and a new royal title was employed in the inscriptions at Calakmul that effectively elevated that city's rulers to the stature of emperors above ordinary kings.

There is little doubt that Calakmul and Tikal were exceptionally powerful rival states. There is glyphic evidence that Calakmul and its allies attacked Tikal four or five times during the Late Classic Period. Tikal retaliated and warfare spread through each great city's allies and dependencies. Tikal, for example, defeated El Perú (743) and Naranjo (744); Calakmul encouraged Quiriguá to rebel against Tikal's ally Copán (738). These cities also expanded their domains elsewhere through both alliances and conquest.

Trade Routes Tikal and Calakmul were more than political rivals; they were probably also economic competitors. Both were well positioned to control the transshipment of goods across the base of the Yucatán Peninsula from the Caribbean and the Gulf of Mexico and also from the northern lowlands into the Guatemalan highlands. Both had allies in the Motagua Valley, in Belize, and along the Usumacinta and in the north. Such wide-ranging alliances were strategically located for trade—and tribute.

The wealth of royal tombs at Calakmul is testament to its economic success: One contained more than 2,000 pieces of worked jade, the largest jade cache known from the ancient Maya world. Another tomb included not one but three exquisite jade mosaic masks of the type found in the richest royal burials. At Tikal, jades and exquisitely painted cylindrical vases accompanied burials, but the wealth, and probably tribute labor as well, was also dedicated to rebuilding the sacred center of that capital city. Now in ruins, the city nonetheless continues to awe visitors with its six towering pyramid-tem-

ples rising above the forest canopy (see figure 2.8, page 50).

Maya Cultural Apogee

In the midst of such political maneuvering—and the instability it caused—Maya art reached what many consider its highest level of achievement. With so many cities, the number of royal families and their increasingly ostentatious elite and priestly supporters required more exotic artifacts to define their position. Perhaps this fueled the greatest artistic period of Maya civilization.

Although there is considerable diversity, there is a distinctive Maya style that persists through the Late Classic Period. The alliances, the elite visits, and exchanges spread an ideology across the Maya lowlands that produced shared religious and political symbolism and considerable artistic homogeneity. The hieroglyphs and the kinds of events they describe vary only marginally; regional preferences exist, but the commitment to portraiture and narrative scenes in painting and sculpture and to certain types of buildings and their mode of construction is almost unvarying.

Most art was in the service of the ruler cult. Rulers were not just war captains but also patrons of the arts: Lady Six Sky and her son, Smoking Squirrel of Naranjo, for example, sponsored a school of painting that produced some of the most exquisite versions of mythological scenes on ceramic vessels; Lord Hanab Pakal and Lord Kan B'alam of Palenque supported architects who invented complex vaulting and constructed some of the most elegant Maya temples; K'ak' Tiliw Chan Yoaat, known as Cauac Sky, of Quiriguá oversaw the elaborate carving of zoomorphic thrones, a sculptural form unique to his city. Judging from the inscriptions, astronomy was in the service of the rulers as well; they fought their wars under the signs of Venus and predicted eclipses and other astronomical events to coincide with royal rituals.

RULER GLORIFICATION

The rulers did not just commission art, however; they used it to glorify themselves. Painters portrayed their powerful patrons, sitting enthroned and receiving tribute. Funerary pyramid-temples dedicated to the commemoration and worship of deceased rulers were constructed for the first time in the sacred centers of cities in the seventh century, and their temples were adorned with roof combs emblazoned with stucco sculptures of the king. Palace-style buildings multiplied and acropolises grew grander (see figures 1.2, page 9, and 8.5, page 232). The few surviving mural cycles, such as the famous one at Bonampak, recorded the palace retinue around the king and his war captives (see figures 2.9, page 54, and 5.5, page 150). An increasing number of hieroglyphic inscriptions, the lengthiest and most numerous from any period, extolled the feats of the rulers and linked them to astronomical events and the mythic gods of creation. (See also Chapters 6, 9, and 10.)

DIVERSITY

The diversity of sculptural and architectural styles of the period may have been part of the dynastic ruler cult, specifically an attempt by each city-state to make itself distinctive from its competitors. Such styles, whether in architecture or sculpture, may have also identified regional alliances. The mosaic facades of the Chenes and Río Bec region of Campeche and Quintana Roo, for example, spread only in the northern lowlands. The mosaic style evolved into geometric designs that defined the later Puuc style, which was prevalent in a cluster of cities dominated by Uxmal (see Chapter 8 for more on architectural styles). Style might also have identified enemies: The city of Toniná exhibited a sculpture of a captured Palenque king that, based on its technique, was carved by Palenque's artists and must have been demanded as a particularly humiliating form of tribute by Toniná.

Local materials and traditions influenced style as well. Palenque produced some of the finest Maya portraiture in stucco, partially because the appropriate stone was not available for the carving and erecting of stelae. Copán and Quiriguá, however, easily could carve the local stone, transforming it into ornate, practically freestanding sculpture (see figure 1.1, page 6). Subject matter was not as variable as the carving technique and material, but there were some variations. Some sites such as Piedras Negras produced many multifigured scenes of the royal court (see figure 4.1, page 120) similar to those in the murals and polychrome vases of the time, while other sites, such as Tikal and Seibal, preferred to depict the king alone (see figure 2.12, page 62, for example). Few sites depicted women on their stelae, but that should not be surprising since only four women are known to have ruled Maya cities: Olnal (583–604) and Sak K'uk' (612–620?) both ruled Palenque, Six Sky (688–?) ruled Naranjo, and the Lady of Tikal (511–527?) became the titular ruler of Tikal at the age of six. Yet Calakmul paired its stelae, erecting one portraying the king and another, his spouse. In a more narrative format, the sculpture of Yaxchilán prominently featured women participating in rituals with the king. Whatever the cause of such differences in technique, style, and subject matter, the result was an exceptionally rich artistic legacy that remained thoroughly Maya.

Political Fragmentation

In the latter half of the eighth century, the Maya kingdoms appear to splinter, breaking off into many smaller states.

2.10 Yaxchilán Lintel 26, Late Classic Period. Lady Xoc, holding a jaguar war helmet, helps her husband, Shield Jaguar the Great, dress for battle. (Photo courtesy Peter Selverstone)

PETEXBATÚN WARS

The fragmentation of large polities was most dramatic in the Petexbatún region. In 761, the modest city of Tamarindito attacked its overlord at Dos Pilas and began erecting monuments to its own royal lineage. Wars in the region intensified, and Dos Pilas was forced to dismantle its most sacred buildings in order to build stone barricades, but to no avail. The elite of war-ravaged Dos Pilas fled to Aguateca, where a steep ravine, 61 meters (200 feet) deep, made it more easily defensible. The warfare was so fierce that no one had time to gather up valuables from the palaces at Dos Pilas—or to loot them. War led the Petexbatún cities to invest in palisades and other fortifications rather than in royal monuments. Punta de Chimino, a port on Lake Petexbatún, was protected by three rings of moats and palisades; nonetheless it, too, fell. In 790, the last dated monument was erected at Aguateca. By 800, the Petexbatún kingdom had disappeared.

SMALL CITIES

Although the intensity and destructiveness of Petexbatún warfare was not matched elsewhere in the region, the process of balkanization was. Pomoná, long part of Palenque, failed to mention its overlord in 771 when it erected monuments to its own dynasty and with its own emblem glyph. Many other small cities asserted their independence through art and glyphic proclamations. These included some that had been under Calakmul and Tikal: Oxpemul and Nakum, for example. Also, cities that had not erected their own monuments for centuries, began doing so again, including Tikal's former dependencies of Uaxactún and Río Azul. Small polities in the Belize River valley that had never erected stelae began to do so, and inscriptions gradually gained currency in the northern lowlands as well. At the same time, the hieroglyphic inscriptions no longer spoke of alliances or diplomatic visits. This fragmentation of the lowlands may indicate that the powerful dynasties were too weak to control their political challengers.

THE GROWING ELITE

Many developments caused the balkanization of the central area; the increasing wealth and power of the elite certainly was one of them. The elite, representative of the expanding bureaucracy and commerce of the many states, multiplied in number during the Late Classic Period. The number of palace-style buildings and the number of tombs with exotic goods increased with the growing elite. Although the stela cult remained reserved for royal proclamations, sculptural decoration on elite residences was not. Other arts, such as carved jade and shell ornaments and polychrome pottery, had an increasingly wide distribution. Caracol grew so wealthy from war that rich burials, many with vaulted tombs normally reserved for royalty, were constructed in outlying residential neighborhoods. At Copán, elaborate residences, such as the House of the Bacabs, mimicked royal palaces with sculptural and textual adornments.

The importance of the elite can also be deduced from their portrayal in the art of the period, mostly in painting but also occasionally in sculpture and ceramic figurines. Painting permitted more multifigured, naturalistic scenes than sculpture did, and eighth-century polychrome cylindrical vases took full advantage of the medium. These exceptional vases—actually they were used by the elite as drinking vessels, often for chocolate drinks—reveal much about court life and include scenes of enthroned individuals surrounded by lesser officials, scribes, and women. Many polychrome vessels were preserved in the tombs of the privileged.

ELITE POWER

Archaeologists believe the elite class, which had grown substantially by this period, probably put increasing demands on the state to satisfy its interests. There is evidence for an increase in elite involvement in governance (see Chapter 4). Council buildings (*popol nah*), where the king met with the heads of other lineages and his officials at secondary sites, are found most often during this period. Texts, previously reserved for royal proclamations, increasingly mention those who were officers of the king, and some were even carved into the walls of elaborate residences for nonroyal lineages. It is possible that the use of emblem glyphs and dynastic pretences of subservient cities may have been permitted by kings in order to keep the peace. If so, the once great Maya dynasts seem to have been forced to share their insignia of power—and probably their political power as well—with their elite

2.11   Late Classic Maya polychrome cylinder vase. A lord of the modest Petén site of Motul San José, one of many Maya cities c. 800, is depicted on his throne. (Photo copyright Justin Kerr, file K2573)

supporters. If the Petexbatún is an indicator of conditions in the heartland, the centralized authority of capital cities was, in fact, being successfully challenged.

CLASS RIGIDITY

At the end of the eighth century, the elite increasingly settled in the center of cities. Residential-style buildings, with inward-looking patios and limited public access, became more numerous than temple constructions. This new residential pattern was accompanied by a decrease in rich burials on the periphery. The concentration of wealth in the sacred centers suggests a more rigidly stratified society that must have excluded those who had formerly enjoyed the sacred center as an arena for the entire populace. At Caracol, rituals that outlying areas had once shared with the center no longer were practiced. This lack of participation in the prestigious rituals in the sacred center may have meant there were growing obstacles to upward mobility.

Overpopulation

The Late Classic Period witnessed exceptional growth, both in population and in the size of cities. For example, it is estimated that Caracol's population of 19,000 in the sixth century grew to over 120,000 a century later. Paved causeways led from its ceremonial core to outlying residences that covered an area of 168 square kilometers (65 square miles). Urban sprawl and population growth typified the period. Land that once had been farmed and forests that had been hunted for deer and peccary disappeared.

The remaining terrain surrounding the great cities often could no longer agriculturally sustain the populace. There is considerable evidence that the heartland cities encouraged the cultivation of crops in peripheral areas. In western El Salvador and northern Belize, the lack of population pressures permitted the production of export crops. At settlements like K'axob on the Pulltrouser Swamp, where plentiful Belizean wetlands permitted the construction of dams,

canals, and artificial terraces for intensive agriculture, the population peaked c. 800, and more crops were produced at these sites than could have been consumed locally.

Not all agricultural undertakings, however, were for basic foodstuffs; the elite engaged in conspicuous consumption regardless of the agricultural crisis. New settlements, such as Pechtún Há, appeared in southern Belize at the end of the Late Classic Period for the purpose of producing cacao. The presence of Peténstyle artifacts at these Sibun River settlements suggests this prestigious commodity was being imported to the heartland for elite feasts. Whether the heartland cities actually controlled production or received tribute through intimidation is unclear. But K'axob and Pechtún Há were abandoned with the Classic Period collapse, unlike many other Belizean settlements.

Summary of Late Classic Period

For two centuries, the Maya participated in a period of extraordinary wealth and artistic accomplishment. Although warfare and environmental degradation plagued the southern lowlands, the Maya were able to build massive cities of stone and adorn them with exquisite sculpture. They forged confederacies and participated in long-distance trade routes. They carved their shared myths and distinctive dynastic histories into stone for perpetuity, and recorded events with the exactitude of the Long Count Calendar and astrological flourish from their astronomical charts (see Chapter 9). Yet these accomplishments of Maya civilization would soon take another direction.

Terminal Classic Period (c. 800–1000)

The southern lowland cities, despite clear signs of stress, began the ninth century at the peak of their cultural development. Yet from 800 to 1000, the shift of Maya civilization out of the heartland was so thorough that it is known as the Classic Period collapse. The collapse did not occur in a single year or with a single event, but evolved during the Terminal Classic Period. At the same time, the northern lowlands emerged as the new center of Maya power. Chichén Itzá, not Calakmul or Tikal, became the capital of trade in the Maya lowlands; Uxmal, not Palenque or Copán, the great artistic center. Most southern lowland cities were abandoned, and after 909, not one Long Count text was inscribed again in the central Maya region.

The Collapse

Over a period of more than 100 years, one city after another was abandoned in the central area. The decline was accompanied by the cessation of dated stone monuments. The Usumacinta cities, such as Palenque, Piedras Negras, and Yaxchilán, stopped inscribing texts into stone between 795 and 810, and they were soon joined by other cities, including Calakmul (810). The last monument at Naranjo was dedicated in 820; Copán, in 822; Caracol, in 849; Tikal, in 869; Uaxactún and Seibal, in 889. Toniná carved the final Long Count date into stone on January 15, 909. The dynastic ruler cult had collapsed. Some sites continued to be occupied through the Terminal Classic Period, but the great ceremonial cities no longer were used; no stela commemorated a king or ritual, and no monumental complexes were built. Poor squatters apparently occupied Tikal's Central Acropolis, the former residence of kings. By the end of the Terminal Classic Period, the southern and central lowlands were abandoned except for coastal and riverine sites in Belize and Campeche. Trade routes bypassed the transshipment route of the once powerful Petén. The region never revived and has remained sparsely populated up to the present day.

DYNASTIES FALL

The southern lowland dynasties ceased to exist. The rulers no longer gained the favor of the gods, as drought and too few crops demonstrated to their subjects. Monumental sacred temples failed to bring blessings to the community. Warfare did not guarantee tribute or secure peace. In the face of such devastating failure, the cult of the semidivine ruler was abandoned. Maya civilization thrived in the northern lowlands, but even there examples of the stela cult in honor of the once boastful dynasties were unusual. Stelae were no longer carved with texts, sculptures no longer featured the solitary ruler, and elaborate burials disappeared. Court scenes on murals and pottery ceased as well. Polychrome pottery was replaced by fine paste slatewares. (See figure 1.3, page 11.)

Causes of the Collapse

There have been many attempted explanations, from invasions to epidemics, of the collapse of the great cities of the southern lowlands. But the collapse was not a single, catastrophic event, and the cause, or causes, that culminated in the end of centralized authority and dynastic rule took various forms from city to city. There is no evidence of a pandemic sweeping the region, nor of global warfare: The Petexbatún cities may have annihilated each other, for example, but there is no sign of violence accompanying Tikal's abandonment, and at Cancuén, warfare is not even mentioned in the hieroglyphic texts. There may have been different reasons for the failure of individual polities. Nonetheless, the lowland cities were interdependent, and the collapse was a regional phenomenon demanding explanation. The following is a review of the most convincing theories for the collapse and their acceptability in light of recent studies.

INVASION

Noting that the first cities to cease inscribing texts into stone were along the western frontier, many Mayanists have argued that there was an invasion of foreigners who traveled from the Gulf coast and along the Usumacinta River into the southern lowlands. These invaders caused the collapse of the Petexbatún polity and eventually cut off the heartland cities that were the last to fall, such as Tikal. Other evidence appears to support this theory, including the appearance at Seibal and other central lowland sites of fine paste ceramics from the Gulf area. But the most compelling support comes from the appearance of non-Maya-looking rulers in the art of Seibal and Machaquila. These rulers, however, apparently accepted Maya traditions and even had themselves portrayed on stelae inscribed with Maya hieroglyphic texts.

There have been numerous theories about the identity of these invaders. At one point they were believed to be Toltecs from the central Mexican city of Tula, but that city was not constructed until the tenth century, after the Maya collapse. The most prevalent theory identifies the invaders with the Chontal-speaking Putún Maya, who lived in what is now the Mexican state of Tabasco on the Gulf coast, an area where it is speculated that both central Mexican and Maya traditions possibly merged. However, there is currently no archaeologically known ninth-century Chontal city. The Itzá Maya, rulers of Chichén Itzá (see "Early Postclassic Period") and sometimes identified by archaeologists with the Putún also have been assigned this role of invaders.

Criticisms Criticisms of the invasion theory have been mounting, although it still has many proponents. Even accepting the evidence of its proponents, it is hard to understand how an invasion of Seibal and Machaquila, the only two sites with portrayals of the so-called outsiders, could have caused the collapse of more powerful cities such as Calakmul or Tikal. Also, the stelae depicting the so-called Putún invaders were erected in 849, after the great dynasties at Calakmul had ceased to inscribe their own texts and when the heartland was already collapsing.

The evidence for an invasion has also been questioned. More careful analysis of the distribution of fine paste pottery and clay sources demonstrates that much of this new ceramicware was being produced within the heartland itself; the new ceramics may have had more to do with trade than with an invasion. Furthermore, the now deciphered texts at Seibal reveal that the allegedly non-Maya ruler was functioning under the auspices of the heartland city of Ucanal. Rather than a foreign invasion, the establishment of a new dynasty at Seibal resulted from the ongoing territorial warfare occurring in the southern lowlands. In the Late Classic, cities such as

2.12   Seibal Stela 10, 849. Ruler Ah-Bolon-Abte appears on this stela without the deformed sloping forehead favored by the Maya but dressed in a royal Maya costume. The mustache adds to his unusual appearance. For this reason, some scholars have argued that he was a foreigner who invaded the Maya heartland and conquered Seibal. The decipherment of the inscriptions at Seibal, however, has shown this "foreign" individual is the same ruler portrayed on other Seibal stelae where he appears as a Classic Period Maya king with a sloping forehead. Also, mustaches appear on other Maya kings, if only rarely. These stelae were erected when most heartland cities were in collapse, and they may represent a change in the concept of nobility during the ninth century. In northern Yucatán, Maya elite were also depicted without sloping foreheads, especially at Chichén Itzá. During this period, cultural attributes of other parts of Mesoamerica are often displayed alongside Maya ones, and such evidence has been used to argue for various theories, including invasion and new central Mexican trade alliances. (Drawing courtesy John Montgomery; photo Herbert J. Spinden 1913)

Seibal and Ucanal had been dependencies of Dos Pilas and Caracol, respectively, but by the ninth century, these smaller states were taking advantage of the political turbulence: Seibal's new dynasty was installed in 830, just after the destruction of the Petexbatún polity. Based on the accumulating evidence, it currently seems quite likely that Seibal's rulers were Maya who assumed some of the cultural and artistic preferences of trading partners outside the heartland.

DROUGHT

Paleoecological studies of lake sediments have demonstrated that during the Terminal Classic Period rainfall reached its lowest levels in 3,500 years. This drought affected all the Maya lowlands. The Petén, basically without rivers, was dependent on rainfall that filled its reservoirs and seasonal swamps. The reservoirs at Tikal, for example, held enough water to sustain the central city during a four-month-long dry season. But a prolonged drought could have extended the dry season and diminished the rainy season so that the reservoirs were not sufficiently replenished to carry Tikal, and other cities like it in the heartland, through the year. Only cities near more reliable sources of water, such as rivers and springs, could survive. Although drought must have created hardships, few archaeologists believe that it alone caused the collapse; in fact, the more arid northern Yucatán experienced the same drought, yet flourished.

OVERPOPULATION

By the Terminal Classic, the lowland regions reached their maximum population. Even some rural areas in the Petén had almost 200 persons per square kilometer (124 per square mile), making the heartland as densely populated as preindustrial 19th-century China. The Petén must have been practically continuous settlement. The amount of maize pollen recovered from this period by isotopic analysis suggests less corn was being grown at the same time the population was peaking. Although many cities imported maize from less populous regions, this strategy must have been compromised by intense competition for this subsistence crop. Skeletal analyses have indicated malnutrition during the final phases of occupation at some cities, such as Copán, but the results have been less compelling for the Pasión region.

UPRISINGS AND COUPS

It has been suggested that the failure of dynastic rulers to adequately sustain their subjects may have caused uprisings. Also, the expanding elite class intensified competition for both commodities and political power. At Caracol, there is evidence for such an internal rebellion, although hunger does not seem to have been the cause. Luxury items that had been distributed throughout the vast site earlier in the Classic Period were concentrated in the urban center after 800. This sudden inequity appears to have provoked an uprising against the city's ruling class. The sacred center was burned and abandoned c. 890, but 25 percent of outlying residential districts remained occupied and well maintained for another 150 years. At Copán, one building apparently was destroyed by fire, and some tombs were ransacked, perhaps during the ninth century, but outlying residences remained occupied after the abandonment of the ceremonial center. Whether this constituted a peasant revolt or an elite coup is unclear. Other cities, such as Altun Há, suffered desecration of royal tombs, but the actors in such events are unknown.

For most cities, including Tikal and Calakmul, such traces of upheaval are absent. Even if peasant rebellions or coups by the nobility did not cause a widespread collapse, overpopulation created enormous stress on the environmental resources of the region and could have weakened support for the ruling dynasties. Drought would have exacerbated the situation, undermining any efforts by rulers to supply their subjects.

WAR

The Late Classic hieroglyphic texts relate a history of intensifying warfare in the southern lowlands, but war did not involve all cities or kingdoms equally. Mayanists recently claimed that there is no evidence the city of Cancuén ever engaged in warfare, unlike its allies in the Petexbatún region that experienced the most devastating wars in the Maya lowlands. And just to the east of the Petexbatún region, the city of Seibal revived during the Terminal Classic Period, perhaps as the result of the fall of its neighbors. Although the hieroglyphic inscriptions mention many wars, it seems that most of these did not result in the actual destruction of cities, based on the few traces of violence retrieved from the archaeological remains. Also, the fortifications found in the Late Preclassic Period do not reappear at this time in the central area. Many sites located along rivers and in coastal Belize were never abandoned, although they did become disconnected from long-distance trade routes until the Postclassic.

MULTIPLE CAUSES

Many Mayanists would argue that multiple factors were involved in the political collapse and eventual abandonment of the central Maya area. Rulers were forced to share power with a growing elite class, and political fragmentation of the largest polities undermined trade alliances, while it also increased warfare. At this time of crisis, Maya dynasts were sapped of the authority needed to unify their people and rule effectively. Added to the political turmoil, the central Maya region suffered from overpopulation, drought, food shortages, and environmental degradation. Suffering from so many internal stresses, the Maya in the Classic Period heartland were in no position to prevent other regions from taking advantage of their weakening prestige and lessening economic clout within Mesoamerica. The central Maya region was eventually cut off from the new trade routes and the cultural horizon that replaced it. Whether the heartland suffered invasion or simply had trade with bearers of a new culture remains unclear. Seibal, well situated for trade with the Gulf coast, collapsed, but late, probably because there were no cities to make trade in the region profitable.

Northern Lowlands Flourish

Maya civilization did not end when the central area collapsed but rather shifted geographically. Northern cities, many of which had existed since the Late Preclassic Period, such as Dzibilchaltún and Edzná, and others that were settled during the Late Classic Period, such as Uxmal, reached their peak population levels. All these cities were transformed by a new architectural style and new trade connections. In the Puuc Hills, Uxmal dominated a large, populous region that included a cluster of cities, each one with palaces and quadrangle complexes finished with the most refined mosaic veneer masonry known in the Maya world (see figures 8.1, page 215, and 8.4, page 225). In the center of the northern lowlands, Chichén Itzá grew into one of the powerful polities of Mesoamerica, and it, too, defined new artistic forms with great inventiveness and skill.

WRITING

The majority of dated stone monuments from the late ninth century are from the northern lowlands: Chichén Itzá, Ek Balam, and such Puuc cities as Uxmal, Sayil, and Kabah. But the north had never been as verbose on stone as the south had, and the inscriptions are brief statements about dedications, rituals, and the like (see "Terminal Classic Inscriptions," Chapter 10). Although many northern monuments were dated, they were dated in the abbreviated, more ambiguous *k'atun* system, or Short Count (see "Short Count: *K'atun* Endings," Chapter 9), not with the more exact Long Count Calendar. Most dates were carved on house lintels or ball-court markers; few inscriptions are found on ruler stelae. The ruler cult gradually ended with the tenth century, even in the north. For example, Dzibilchaltún, Edzná, and Cobá—

2.13 *Sea trade (mural detail), Temple of the Warriors, Chichén Itzá, Terminal Classic Period.*
(Drawing after Ann Axtell Morris, 1931)

trading partners with southern lowland cities during the Classic Period—did not collapse, but they, too, stopped erecting stelae. The last stelae erected at Uxmal has been interpreted as dating to 909.

TRADE

By 800, a new Mesoamerican trade network was well under way. In central Mexico, cities like Xochicalco, Cholula, and Cacaxtla in the highlands and El Tajín in northern Veracruz, took control after the fall of Teotihuacan. In the Maya region, trade and power shifted to the periphery—Yucatán and coastal Belize and Honduras as well as along the Pacific coast. This maritime trade around the Yucatán Peninsula had existed since the Preclassic Period, but during the Terminal Classic, it rose in importance, particularly in the northern lowlands.

Many of the northern cities were not port cities, but the most important ones nonetheless established ties with coastal villages. Uxmal probably exchanged goods with ports on the Campeche coast, such as Uaymil, 90 kilometers (56 miles) to the north; Chunchucmil was partially linked to its port of Punta Canbalam by a 2-kilometer (1.2 mile) sacbe, and in Quintana Roo, Cobá had allied itself with the nearby port of Xel Há earlier in the Classic Period. Chichén Itzá was the most ambitious, however; it constructed docks and a harbor protective wall at its own port of Isla Cerritos, an island off the northern tip of the peninsula, and it controlled the nearby port of Emal, located next to the finest salt flats in Mesoamerica. To guarantee the safe passage of its goods, Chichén Itzá established secondary centers every 20 kilometers (12 miles) along the 120 kilometers (74 miles) between the port and the capital.

Northern Yucatán traded salted fish, cotton, hemp rope, and honey, but above all, it traded high-quality white salt. These commodities could be produced in the hot, dry climate of that peninsula, and they were highly valued in highland Mexico. In return, the northern lowlands received obsidian, volcanic ash (a temper for clay), cacao beans, and other precious items. These peninsular commodities were bulky—Chichén Itzá apparently exported 3,000 to 5,000 metric tons (3,300 to 5,500 tons) of salt annually—and thus more easily transported in canoes than overland.

The trade did not end at the coast of northern Yucatán, however. It stimulated increased settlement on the island of Cozumel, where obsidian may have been stored for transshipment. The route continued south along the Belizean coast, where the fine paste slatewares of northern Yucatán were widely traded. Many villages in Belize thrived, producing salt or cotton, and probably cacao, for trade. Inland cities such as Lamanai and Colhá continued to function because they, too, traded by canoes, but on rivers; the influence of the northern lowlands on this trade is most clearly demonstrated at Nohmul where Chichén Itzá–style buildings have been excavated.

The maritime trade continued into Honduras and El Salvador, where cacao was being grown; in fact, at this time, parts of the southern Maya area revived at cities such as Tazumal (formerly Chalchuapa) in El Salvador and El Baúl and Cotzumalguapa on Guatemala's Pacific slope. Tazumal had traditional trade ties with the Motagua Valley, where Quiriguá remained a vital center during the Terminal Classic Period. The cacao, obsidian, and fashionable Tohil Plumbate ceramics (see figure 1.3, page 11) exported by cities from the southern Maya region could have linked with the maritime trade in the Bay of Honduras via the Motagua River (see Map 8, page 320).

Terminal Classic trading canoes traveled from Honduras around the Yucatán Peninsula to the Gulf coast of northern Veracruz. As the heartland weakened, the periphery grew stronger, and eventually coastal trade predominated over the Classic Period portage route. The maritime trade extended during the period, reaching into Costa Rica and Panama for gold, copper, and silver. Terminal Classic cities found opportunities through coastal trading to exchange their foodstuffs, obsidian, textiles, and precious cacao, while cutting off the heartland—and they did.

PAN-MESOAMERICAN CULTURE

The successful Maya cities of the Terminal Classic Period continued many of the ritual and artistic traditions of the Classic Period. They built with the corbeled arch and veneer masonry and organized their cities like their southern lowland predecessors (see Chapter 8). They also inscribed stone monuments with hieroglyphic texts and reenacted the myths of creation through their art and in the ritual spaces of their cities.

These cities also introduced pan-Mesoamerican symbols into their artistic repertoire, reflecting their trade alliances with cities outside the Maya region—and central Mexicans cities borrowed Maya motifs. The nobility of these suddenly powerful new cities needed to establish their prestige, and they did so by emphasizing their control of long-distance trade. The art of the period boasted of their foreign connections and ability to deliver luxury items.

The successful Maya cities of the Terminal Classic Period were pan-Mesoamerican ones with trade alliances that extended beyond the Maya world. At Chichén Itzá, for example, as much obsidian was traded from central Mexico as from the Maya highlands in Guatemala, and its art reflected these multi-ethnic connections. The emphasis on ties with other parts of Mesoamerica was far from new. In the Preclassic, Olmec symbols of prestige had given rise to early Maya civilization. In the Early Classic, central Mexican influences from Teotihuacan had permeated Maya trade and culture. Even in the Late Classic, the Maya were actively involved in pan-Mesoamerican trade, judging by the Bonampak-style murals found in the central Mexican city of Cacaxtla and the hieroglyphic writing found on Gulf coast ceramics. Such trade and cultural exchange were occurring throughout the Late Classic Period, but it was not until the Terminal Classic that these Mesoamerican relationships were once again emphasized by Maya cities.

This Mesoamerican focus resulted in an art style that was as "international" as it was Maya. Images of a feathered serpent god, called Kukulcán in Yucatec Mayan but better known by the central Mexican name of Quetzalcoatl (literally meaning "plumed serpent") decorated sacred buildings in Xochicalco in highland Mexico as well as in northern Yucatán. A religious cult associated with Quetzalcoatl, a creator god, may have been spread by traders at this time; by the Spanish Conquest, Quetzalcoatl also was a patron deity of long-distance traders. Such universal signs must have facilitated trade among diverse ethnic groups and may explain why universally recognizable pictographs were also carved on public buildings in the ceremonial center at Chichén Itzá, but not the more local Maya hieroglyphs. Hieroglyphs were reserved for elite Maya residences, where they were carved on lintels and door

2.14   Feathered serpent column, Chichén Itzá. (Photo Alfred P. Maudslay, 1889–1902)

jambs, not stelae. For this pan-Mesoamerican horizon, the old cults extolling local rulers were no longer seen as promoting the new economic prosperity.

POLITICAL INCLUSIVENESS

At Chichén Itzá, Kabah, Edzná, and other northern lowland sites, sculpture was increasingly devoted to narrative scenes involving many individuals in processions and rituals, as opposed to previous static portrayals of a single ruler. Such narrative scenes could also be found at sites along the Gulf coast, such as El Tajín, as well as at Cotzumalguapa in southern Guatemala. Although pyramid-temples were constructed, they were few and may have originated in the Late Classic Period. Colonnaded administrative buildings that permitted gatherings of large groups (see figure 3.2, page 96) and range-style elite compounds were more common.

The Terminal Classic centers appear to have embraced many groups, not just the royal few. Throughout northern Yucatán, on the Pacific littoral in Guatemala, and along the coast of the Gulf of Mexico, the ball game evolved to symbolize this new inclusiveness. The importance of the ball court during this period is demonstrated by the presence of 17 courts at El Tajín, in Veracruz, and at least 13 at Chichén Itzá and by the introduction of ball courts at cities in the northern lowlands where previously there were none. Ethnohistoric sources indicate that ball-court rituals often consecrated alliances. The existence of ball courts in residential areas outside the sacred ceremonial center may indicate the new ball-court ritual also reinforced alliances among different lineage groups living within a city. However, the Chichén Itzá sacred ball court (see figure 8.6, page 233), continued the Maya tradition of representing one of the most ancient Maya creation myths, that of the birth of the maize god (see Chapter 6).

Transition to the Postclassic

The Terminal Classic Period witnessed the gradual but nonetheless dramatic shift from the Maya culture of the southern lowlands to the more pan-Mesoamerican culture of northern Yucatán and central Mexico. New artistic and religious traditions accompanied the political and economic changes. This transitional period, focusing on these regional shifts, has been defined to overlap the Classic and Postclassic Periods. By 900, however, the Early Postclassic Period was well rooted in the northern lowlands, and the southern lowlands had been eclipsed, if not yet entirely abandoned. There may have been a shift among the pan-Mesoamerican trade cities, with a consolidation of power at Cholula, El Tajín, Tula, and Chichén Itzá. These cities may have led to the decline of El Baúl in the Cotzumalguapa region of Guatemala, Uxmal in the Puuc area, and Xochicalco and Cacaxtla in central Mexico after 900.

EARLY POSTCLASSIC PERIOD (C. 900–1200)

The Early Postclassic Period originally was delineated as the period in which the Toltecs of Tula in central Mexico conquered the Maya region and established their capital at Chichén Itzá in northern Yucatán. It is a view of the northern lowlands that has been seriously challenged by the wealth of new evidence now available from excavations in both central Mexico and the Maya region. It is likely that the Early Postclassic Period is just a temporal extension of the internationalism of the Terminal Classic Period and more properly ends with the collapse of Chichén Itzá. For this reason, archaeologists increasingly favor use of the Terminal Classic label even for what has been called the Early Postclassic Period. Whichever label is used, archaeologists agree that in the northern lowlands this period was dominated by the city of Chichén Itzá and that Chichén Itzá maintained its dominance through a pan-Mesoamerican network of trade and cultural exchange. Chichén Itzá was the last truly monumental city of Maya civilization.

The Toltec Connection

The confusing postconquest cyclical histories that make up the *Books of the Chilam Balam* (see Chapter 10) suggest that foreigners arrived in northern Yucatán toward the end of the first millennium and introduced new cultural traits to the region. Based on some striking architectural and artistic similarities between Tula and Chichén Itzá, Mayanists in the first half of the 20th century believed the central Mexicans defeated the Maya in 987 and built their Toltec capital at Chichén Itzá, amid the earlier Maya city. These Toltecs, the ethnohistories suggest, introduced warfare and rituals of human sacrifice into the Maya realm as well as the cult of Quetzalcoatl, or the feathered serpent god.

Archaeologists now know that the Maya practiced human sacrifice and engaged in warfare from the beginning of their civilization in the Preclassic Period. And more careful excavations have revealed that the so-called Toltec traits are not a late, intrusive development at Chichén Itzá, but rather they overlapped and even coincided with the Maya phase in the early ninth century. Artistic styles that seemed Toltec, it is now argued, resulted from the pan-Mesoamericanism of the Terminal Classic Period. Based on ceramics and trade items found at the two sites, it now appears that Chichén Itzá had already constructed monumental "Toltec" edifices and sculpted "Toltec" feathered serpents almost 100 years before the introduction of such artifacts at Tula between 900 and 1000.

A MAYA CITY

Under the revised, non-Toltec view, Chichén Itzá constructed a sacred center that fused Maya and non-Maya symbols (especially those from the fallen but once powerful city of Teotihuacan) into a distinctive pan-Mesoamerican code that extolled the city's far-flung commercial connections. Among the new artistic forms were the monolithic feathered serpent columns, carvings of warriors in processions, and *chac mools* (see figure 2.15) that also are found later at Tula. But Chichén Itzá was also an intensely Maya city. In the artistic symbolism carved into its Great Ball Court and in the manner in which it framed hundreds of column sculptures, Chichén Itzá displayed a continued faith in Maya creation myths and cosmic order.

Outside the cosmopolitan center, the palaces and elite residential quarters were even more traditionally Maya in their architecture

and sculptural adornments, albeit with so-called Toltec, or central Mexican, elements interspersed. Chichén Itzá's use of *sacbeob* to link its suburbs with the center also was distinctively Maya. And in the great Classic Maya tradition, Chichén Itzá continued to carve dated hieroglyphic texts, the most found at any northern lowland site, until the late ninth century and, perhaps, as late as 998, depending on how one badly eroded inscription is interpreted. The decipherment of these inscriptions at Chichén Itzá has revealed the ritual activities of many individuals—all with Maya names—including that of the important ruler K'ak'upakal (or Fire-His-Shield in Yucatec Mayan).

CONTROVERSY

Given its early ninth-century founding and its extraordinary wealth and might, Chichén Itzá now is believed to have been a greater city than its central Mexican cousin, Tula. Perhaps Tula copied the cultural innovations of Chichén Itzá, not vice versa. Although the Toltec invasion hypothesis has been seriously undermined by the new chronology, there are scholars who continue to entertain some modified version of it or some other theory about an earlier influx of outsiders, particularly Maya ones. A Putún Maya invasion from the Gulf coast remains the foremost among these because of some similarities between the art style of Chichén Itzá and Seibal, although a more recent view argues that Maya escaping from the southern heartland settled here and created this northern capital.

Whatever the origin of the Chichén Itzá's founders—Putún, the Usumacinta region, or the Petén, depending on the theory—they were Maya and were known as the Itzá. Some scholars argue that the city was built by the Maya of northern Yucatán. The name of Chichén Itzá, which means either "the mouth of the well of the witches" or "of the Itzá Maya" in Yucatec Mayan, most likely dates from the Late Postclassic

Period when the well had become a sacred pilgrimage site. According to the native chronicles, in the ninth century the city was known as Uucil Abnal; the names Ah Abnal and Yabnal have also been identified in the inscriptions at the site.

Apart from the issue of the identity of Chichén Itzá's founders, most scholars agree that Mexican Tula, controlling highland obsidian sources, and Maya Chichén Itzá, controlling salt production and probably cotton as well, were two important cities at the northern and southern extremes of the pan-Mesoamerican trade network some time after 900, and that their striking similarities resulted from this interaction, not from invasion or warfare. Although the decipherment of the inscriptions at the Yucatecan city can be interpreted in various ways, leaving the controversy surrounding the founding of the city unresolved, studies of the material remains in both central Mexico and Yucatán continue in the hope of clarifying this enigmatic period of Mesoamerican development.

Chichén Itzá

What is not controversial is that Chichén Itzá was the most powerful Maya state and one of the great polities in all Mesoamerica by the middle of the ninth century. The duration of its hegemony is less certain, but it probably lasted until the 12th century. This city controlled much of the maritime trade in Yucatán and beyond. Judging from artifacts dredged from its sacred well, Chichén Itzá commanded goods from the farthest reaches of the Mesoamerican trade network. The wealth preserved in the well of Chichén Itzá is truly astonishing: gold discs and jewelry from Panama and Costa Rica—the earliest significant gold cache in all of Mesoamerica—copper from western Mexico, turquoise from what is now Cerritos in the modern state of New Mex-

2.15 Chac mool *sculpture, entrance to the Temple of the Warriors, Chichén Itzá. These life-size sculptures, called* chac mools, *were installed at the entrances to temples and ritual spaces, with their heads turned to face the public stairways and plazas. Art historian Mary Ellen Miller has convincingly argued that they represent war captives holding offering plates, perhaps for human hearts, on their stomachs.*

ico, and carved jades from Classic Period southern lowland cities, such as Palenque, that may have been looted or demanded in tribute.

Although excavations in northern Yucatán are just beginning to reveal the extent of the polity governed by Chichén Itzá, the most densely occupied part of the city had a population estimated at 50,000. Its best-mapped causeways extended to outlying districts such as Yulá, 5 kilometers (3 miles) away. The city depicted itself a military power in its sculpture and murals; the latter show battalions of canoes setting fire to villages, for example, and the hundreds of piers and columns are carved with warriors armed with atlatls, or spear-throwers (see figure 5.3, page 146). The city's exploits were recounted centuries later in the *Books of the Chilam Balam*, the native Maya chronicles compiled well after the Spanish Conquest. Although these mytho-historic accounts are confusing in regard to details, they never fail to leave the impression that Chichén Itzá was intimidating.

Chichén Itzá thrived during the ninth and 10th centuries, but how much longer it dominated Yucatán is not certain. The last dated Maya stone monument is from Chichén Itzá and most likely records the date of 998. The *Books of the Chilam Balam* suggest that Chichén Itzá survived as a great capital until the rise of Mayapán c. 1200. These examples of postconquest literature, however, are written in a formulaic cyclical manner in which the dates of events are often altered to conform to the prophecies of a 20-year calendrical cycle. Archaeologists suggest that Chichén Itzá may have been declined much earlier, between 1000 and 1100. Whenever its hegemony ended, Chichén Itzá was never forgotten in Mesoamerica. Its artistic innovations—*chac mool* sculptures, feathered serpent architectural decorations, and colonnaded buildings, among them—became symbols of prestige and authority and were copied by later great states, including that of the Aztecs.

Power Struggles in Yucatán

In recent decades, proof of alliances and military conflict has been excavated at some Yucatecan sites. Surveys of the region between Chichén Itzá and its two ports on the north coast, Isla Cerritos and Emal, indicate that the great city reorganized earlier Classic Period cities into the Itzá polity. Whether this was done peacefully is unknown, but these cities share Chichén Itzá's sculpture, architectural styles, and ceramics.

UXMAL

A relationship, the nature of which is still unclear, existed between Uxmal and Chichén Itzá. One hieroglyphic text at Uxmal mentions Chichén Itzá's ninth-century ruler, K'ak'upakal; sculptural motifs of feathered serpents suggest participation in the same pan-Mesoamerican trade sphere. At Uxmal, excavators have found a Chichén Itzá–style round structure and Tohil Plumbate trade ceramics that were imported by Chichén Itzá from Guatemala. The evidence suggests the two great cities were engaged in joint rituals and direct trade at the very least; some archaeologists believe that Chichén Itzá eventually took over Uxmal and caused its decline in the 10th century. Chichén Itzá's interest could have been in the region's agricultural potential: The fertile soils around the Puuc region may have permitted it to function somewhat as a breadbasket for the agriculturally poor but densely populated cities further to the north, where half the land is bare bedrock.

WAR

Unlike Uxmal, some cities suffered devastation from warfare. Although there are almost no defensive structures built at this time in the northern lowlands, a handful of cities were sufficiently threatened to be exceptions. Fortifications and hastily constructed barricades testify to conflicts at these few cities. Chunchucmil, the important trade center in northeastern Yucatán, was apparently so completely destroyed that it never revived enough to remove the barricades across the city's main entrance. Ek Balam, located to the north of Chichén Itzá, constructed a substantial defensive system but was nonetheless destroyed. Yaxuná, the boundary town of the immense polity ruled by Cobá, built a fort to protect any approach from the north—the side vulnerable to Chichén Itzá. The fort was demolished, and Yaxuná itself, destroyed.

There is reason to suspect that Chichén Itzá was the victor in these battles, making sure that it dominated the areas once controlled by earlier Classic Period cities. Chunchucmil and Cobá were probably Chichén Itzá's greatest competitors in maritime trade, for example. Native Maya chronicles from the 17th and 18th centuries mention many conquests by a war captain named K'ak'upakal; his name is also mentioned repeatedly in the ninth-century inscriptions at Chichén Itzá. In addition, the chronicles mention a "visit" by Chichén Itzá to Yaxuná. These battles may have occurred at different periods: Chunchucmil and Yaxuná may have fallen in the ninth century, but Ek Balam may have been a vibrant city until c. 1000.

Northern Decay

The great Mesoamerican trade alliance collapsed by the end of the Early Postclassic Period and probably even earlier. Many cities in the northern lowlands contracted in size or were actually abandoned c. 1100, and Chichén Itzá declined as well. A similar collapse occurred at the central Mexican cities of Tula and El Tajín. Even if these cities continued to be occupied, massive building projects ceased. No great power immediately rose up to replace these powerful Early Postclassic states. Feuds among the various Yucatecan lineages are mentioned in the *Books of the Chilam Balam* in regard to the fall of Chichén Itzá, but these accounts remain far from clear and may relate to Mayapán instead.

DROUGHT

The prolonged drought already noted for the southern lowland collapse may have finally brought the arid northern lowlands into a crisis situation. Excavations suggest that the densest populations—200 to 300 inhabitants per square kilometer (124 to 186 per square mile)—were living in the regions that had poor agricultural potential and that required imported foodstuffs. Drought could have caused shortages in the interior of Yucatán even where low population levels and fertile lands had formerly permitted surpluses. In the Puuc region, population density probably was greater than the carrying capacity of the land by the 10th century; always an arid region, without any natural year-round supplies of water, the Puuc would have been particularly affected by a drought.

A MESOAMERICAN ISSUE

The decline was not just a Yucatecan one, however. If a drought indeed caused food shortages, canoes could have carried foodstuffs from wetland areas in Belize and even the Petén lake region, where there were no longer any population pressures. Much more needs to be understood about what was happening during the 11th and 12th centuries throughout Mesoamerica before the fall of Chichén Itzá can be understood. Currently, it seems that the causes of the collapse in the southern lowlands, environmental stresses, and warfare disrupted the northern lowlands, too. But unlike the southern lowlands, the northern and peripheral regions were not abandoned. Maya culture persisted.

LATE POSTCLASSIC PERIOD (C. 1200–1524)

The Late Postclassic Period was distinguished by the rise of a more commercial, less elite-oriented Maya culture than had previously existed,

2.16   *Tulum, Quintana Roo, Mexico, Late Postclassic Period. On the Caribbean coast, Tulum was strategically located for maritime trade.*

particularly in the lowlands. There were few large dominating political states apart from Mayapán in the Yucatán in the early part of the Late Postclassic Period and the Quiché confederacy in highland Guatemala during the terminal part of the period. The Late Postclassic Period is believed by many Mayanists to represent a shift toward a more inclusive form of government, called *multepal* (Yucatec Mayan for "joint rule") that permitted various nonroyal but elite members to take a more active and recognized role in government (see Chapter 4).

The political landscape of this final phase of Maya civilization was marked by decentralization and warfare among many competing petty states. Defensive features characterize Postclassic cities. Mayapán and Tulum were surrounded by ramparts, and Utatlán and other

cities in the Guatemalan highlands were defensively located on hilltops. On the Pacific coast as well, villages on the open plain were abandoned for settlements on defensible hilltops, where they remain to this day.

The period is also notable for the relative absence of the immense cities that had previously defined Maya urban civilization, and it represents a further reorganization of state resources away from the glorification of the ruler. Although Mayapán modeled itself on Chichén Itzá and was the last lowland Maya city built with any ambitions of grandeur, it was an inferior imitation of Chichén Itzá. In the southern Maya region, fortified hill towns became common; though more impressive than those in the lowlands, they were limited in size by their location. Murals, on both building interiors and facades, and incense burners shaped into effigies of the gods, replaced the grander sculptural programs of earlier periods. For these reasons, the art of the period, particularly in the north, has been called decadent.

Northern Area

The Maya area was densely populated and commercially active throughout this period. Coastal towns and a few along Belizean rivers participated in a maritime trade that circumnavigated the entire Yucatán Peninsula, from Campeche and Tabasco on the Gulf of Mexico to Belize and Honduras on the Caribbean. These towns increased in number as the period progressed. There were some 150 coastal sites at the time of the conquest, and the Spaniards reported that some of these towns were substantial in size, such as Santa Rita and Tulum on the Caribbean, Naco near the Bay of Honduras, and Xicalango in Tabasco. The maritime trade reinvigorated some cities that had survived from the Classic Period: Cobá with its port at Xel Há had just such a revival, with Postclassic-style temples constructed atop older pyramids, and Lamanai in Belize remained active as well. All these cities were in contact with each other, as demonstrated by their shared ceramics.

COMMERCIALISM AND TRADE

Excavations have shown a more entrepreneurial society that was interested in profits, not kingly displays. Not only were there few investments in large public projects, but there was a flattening of social distinctions. Obsidian, shell ornaments, and copper jewelry were distributed throughout a site rather than being restricted to elite residences. It appears that commoners and nobility all participated in maritime trade, some producing honey, salt, or salted fish, others growing cacao and cotton, and yet others harvesting marine shells. Some sites, such as Naco in Honduras, were transshipment centers for obsidian and quetzal plumes from the Guatemalan highlands and gold and other metals from Costa Rica and Panama. Xicalango on the Gulf coast was probably a transshipment center for items such as obsidian coming from the central Mexican highlands. Probably only the nobility had the money to invest in canoes and undertake major trade expeditions, but the trade benefited commoners as well.

MAYAPÁN

Despite the coastal nature of trade, Mayapán dominated the region until c. 1450 from its location some 40 kilometers (25 miles) from the coast. It controlled most of the northern cities in the Yucatán through a confederacy called the League of Mayapán, and it heavily influenced the independent nations that flourished along the coast, such as Tulum. Mayapán was the last centralized state in the northern lowlands. It symbolized the transition in Maya civilization between the Classic and Postclassic Periods. Although the most important city in the lowlands during this period (c. 1220 to c. 1450), Mayapán's population was only 15,000, and it covered an area of only 4.2 square kilometers (1.6 square miles), whereas nearby Dzibilchaltún had been 12 times larger in the Late Classic Period. Nonetheless, Mayapán was fortified, and its encircling wall constrained the area it occupied, as a result it had one of the densest populations known for a Maya city.

Mayapán copied some of the architectural forms of Chichén Itzá, including colonnaded buildings and feathered serpent columns, but the city's four-sided pyramid was an inferior imitation in both size and craftsmanship. Traditional Maya vaulting was used in the construction of some buildings, but the corbeled

2.17   Mayapán-style effigy censers, Late Postclassic Period. Called idols by the Spanish conquistadores, these ceramic images of gods were used by the Maya for burning incense.   (Photo Thomas Gann, 1900)

arches were shoddily constructed, and the buildings subsequently collapsed. A few stelae were erected but they seem to have been carved only with a *k'atun* date, suggesting they were part of a Maya calendrical ritual and not the Classic Period ruler cult. In fact, plain pillarlike stones and, occasionally, dated stelae were erected in calendrical ceremonies throughout the Yucatán at the time of the conquest.

Cultural Changes   There was no ball court at Mayapán, but there was a ceremonial core with substantial buildings. Throughout the city, there were many small shrines containing effigy censers, or ceramic vessels in the shapes of various gods, for burning incense. These shrines were found in many residential complexes, and some have argued they indicate a decentralization of state authority over religion. These Mayapán-style ceramics and shrines are the hallmark of the period and are found throughout the region of maritime trade, suggesting instead a new form for Maya religious practice, probably that of ancestor worship, that may have been controlled by the state (see Chapter 7). The fact that the effigy censers were assembled from mass-produced parts made them cheaper to produce in quantity, and they were therefore available to commoners, not just the elite. Another popular practice during this period, ritual offerings of smashed ceramics, may indicate just how efficient ceramic production had become.

Destruction of Mayapán Native accounts state that an alliance of Yucatec rulers formed the League of Mayapán c. 1250, after the fall of Chichén Itzá. But this league may not have been voluntary because the native chronicles also complain that the Cocom, one of the Itzá lineages named in the inscriptions at Chichén Itzá, hired foreign mercenaries to enforce the alliance. Nobles were forced to live within the defensive walls of the site so that their kingdoms remained loyal to the confederacy. With no farms either inside or outside the fortified walls, Mayapán lived off the foodstuffs paid in tribute to the city and from the subjects of the captive nobility. Around 1450, the nobility, led by the Xiu lineage, rebelled and burned Mayapán.

FRAGMENTATION

The Yucatán region fragmented into at least 16 petty states with the fall of Mayapán. Ruled by the noble lineages freed from the League of Mayapán, few of the capital cities had monumental architecture or other symbols of elite culture that could compare well with that of Mayapán. The Xiu, the most powerful lineage in northern Yucatán, had their capital at Maní, a town that failed to impress the Spaniards. The Itzá retreated to the Petén to the island kingdom of Tayasal (Spanish corruption of the Maya name Tah Itzá), near modern Flores on Lake Petén Itzá, where some of their predecessors from Chichén Itzá may already have established themselves. Tayasal represented a renewal of the Petén region, if a relatively isolated one. From their inland location, the Itzá maintained trade connections with ports in Quintana Roo and Belize, and according to the native chronicles, they continued to exert considerable influence on trade and even received tribute from a number of towns.

Some of the noble lineages established their capitals amid the more monumental buildings of Classic Period cities. The Cupul, for example, lived at the abandoned site of Chichén Itzá; most of the sacred center had reverted to forest, but the Cupul maintained the largest plaza area and the sacred cenote (natural well) for ceremonies. Other Yucatec kingdoms made pilgrimages to the cenote as well. Tulum is the best known of the Late Postclassic cities on the Caribbean coast. Its sacred center was constructed in the style initiated by Chichén Itzá, with feathered serpent columns, but the diminished size is quite striking: The Castillo at Chichén Itzá, at 23 meters (75 feet), is three times the height of Tulum's, at 7.5 meters (25 feet). Perhaps 500 people lived in the ceremonial center itself, although the site was larger and extended beyond the fortified area.

PILGRIMAGE SITES AND TRADE

Despite the feuds and battles between the many Yucatec kingdoms, commerce continued until the Spanish Conquest. One issue is how trade was regulated without a centralized authority like Mayapán. One theory states that religious pilgrimage zones were neutral trading zones, where the various factions could peacefully engage in commerce. The Spaniards recorded that such neutrality was the usual custom for pilgrimages to the cenote at Chichén Itzá. And archaeologists have argued that San Gervasio on the island of Cozumel was just such a protected zone for sea traders. A shrine to the moon goddess at San Gervasio was constructed with a false rear wall, apparently so that a priest could make the statue appear to speak for the goddess Ix Chel, an important deity along the Caribbean coast. This oracle was the religious pretense under which trade could be conducted peacefully, even between enemies; in fact, Cozumel was one of the few places the Spaniards were not attacked in the Maya region.

Guatemalan Highlands: The Quiché

The native chronicles recount the founding of the Quiché confederacy. In the 14th century, the Quiché Maya, under their legendary leader K'ucumatz (Feathered Serpent), who is said to have ruled from 1375 until 1425, waged a series of wars to control the central highlands of Guatemala. His son Qik'ab (d. 1475), with Cakchiquel and Tzutujil allies, extended the Quiché kingdom; by the late 15th century, the Quiché controlled the Guatemalan highlands from the frontier of modern El Salvador on the east to Chiapas on the west, and included the Pacific coast well into Chiapas. From their sacred capital of Utatlán (or K'umarcaaj in Quiché Mayan), the Quiché appointed governors to conquered cities and demanded tribute from others in a realm that covered 67,358 square kilometers (26,000 square miles) and included an estimated 1 million Maya.

They consolidated their hold on the region through intermarriages and the joint performances of important rituals. They established themselves as a capital of learning, producing sacred books and history recorded with Long Count dates. These books were seen by 16th-century Spaniards but subsequently disappeared. And the Quiché Maya controlled trade in highland obsidian and lowland cacao production. At the time of the Spanish Conquest, it is estimated that 50,000 Quiché lived in the province around the capital of Utatlán.

QUICHÉ ORIGINS

There has been much speculation about the origin of the Quiché. The change in settle-ments from the valley to hilltops and the use of architectural elements associated with Chichén Itzá and other pan-Mesoamerican cities have made archaeologists speculate whether the highlands were invaded and conquered by outsiders. The legends of the Quiché people, who include both the Cakchiquel and Tzutujil Maya, suggest that their founding lineages arrived in Guatemala from a legendary place of origin; some of the myths indicate the place of origin was to the west. These native chronicles have led archaeologists and ethnohistorians to believe that the Quiché were either Toltecs from Postclassic Period central Mexico or Terminal Classic Period Putún Maya from the Gulf coast, for many of the same reasons already discussed under Chichén Itzá and the Classic Period collapse. The most recent version of the theory holds that the Quiché were a splinter lineage of the Putún Maya, believed to have occupied both Seibal and Chichén Itzá (see "Terminal Classic Period" above).

However, the late chronology required by the invasion theories has not correlated with the data provided by excavations of Quiché sites, casting doubt on both the Toltec and Putún hypotheses. The Quiché Maya apparently already were living in the highlands as early as the Preclassic Period. To confuse matters more, in the *Popol Vuh*, the Quiché myth states that the founders came from the east, perhaps the Motagua Valley, not the west. Maya origin myths provided legitimacy to the ruling lineages, but they may have been purely legendary and may have changed over time to associate the ruling elite with the most dominant Mesoamericans in any given period. Architecture and art styles often changed to reflect alliances with the most powerful states, and in fact the Quiché cities copied central Mexican styles in the period before the Spanish Conquest. To date, archaeology has not been able to substantiate the foreign origin myths. The view that the Quiché arrived in the region after 800, however, permeates much of the literature for that culture.

FORTIFICATIONS

The Quiché wars took their toll and continued until the arrival of the Spaniards. In the 14th century, 1,000-year-old Maya settlements in the fertile valleys were abandoned for more easily defended hilltops. These citadels were much like medieval castles in Europe. Surrounded by steep, moatlike ravines, the cities were also fortified with ramparts and guard gates. At Utatlán, the part of the causeway ascending to the city could be dismantled, making the city impregnable. Farmers cultivating the fields and others working in the valleys could flee to safety when endangered. Three other citadels protected Utatlán, and the four fortresses could have accommodated much of the Quiché population. There were other fortresses located throughout the Quiché kingdom. The Spaniards described Utatlán as so strong and dangerous that they had to destroy it, and they did.

SACRED CENTERS

Although the hilltop location of these late cities prevented them from approaching the monumentality of earlier lowland cities, they were well built, and Utatlán was large enough to accommodate 15,000 people. Unlike northern settlements of this late period, the highland citadels represented a substantial public investment, and the sacred centers included important civic and religious buildings. Utatlán had 140 buildings, including noble lineage houses, a royal palace, a ball court, and four temples representing the four major lineages and the quadripartite Maya cosmos. It was a place of elite culture and learning, and Spaniards reported seeing hieroglyphic books at the city. The greatest temple, dedicated to Tohil, the royal lineage god of Utatlán, was covered with murals and built atop a steep pyramid base that was 404.6 square meters (4,356 square feet) and probably exceeded 18 meters (60 feet) in height. Another temple had a shrine with an oracle stone, and the palace was 90 meters (297 feet) in length and almost as wide. Although stylistically these highland centers, including Iximché and Mixco Viejo, copied many features from central Mexico, the sacred center, with its quadripartite cosmos and lineage worship, was as old as Maya civilization.

FRAGMENTATION

In 1475, the Cakchiquel Maya rebelled against their former Quiché allies and successfully established an independent kingdom at Iximché. Their success was followed by other rebellions, including that of the Tzutujil Maya who lived on Lake Atitlán. The wars among the highland groups persisted right up to the arrival of the conquistador Pedro de Alvarado and his army in 1524. The highland Maya had built exceptional fortresses and sacred centers; the Quiché had briefly forged the largest confederate state known in the highlands. History would make it their last.

Eve of Conquest: The Aztecs

The Maya region was commercially vigorous but increasingly politically decentralized as it entered the 16th century. In political clout and prestige, the Maya were eclipsed by the powerful Aztecs, or Mexica, as they called themselves, in central Mexico. Aztec tastes defined the new fashions and art styles, even in the Maya region, where central Mexican painting styles were used to depict traditional Maya themes, from Utatlán in Guatemala to Tulum and Santa Rita on the Caribbean. Highland

2.18   Mixco Viejo, a Maya citadel in the Guatemala highlands, Late Postclassic Period.   (Photo by John Montgomery)

cities—Iximché, Zaculeu, Mixco Viejo, and others—even copied architectural features of Tenochtitlan, the Aztec capital. At Utatlán, the nobility also learned to speak the Aztec language, Nahuatl. The wealthy Aztec Empire, with its great consumption of luxury items, was the engine that drove much of Maya trade in the 15th century.

The Aztecs were traders, but their merchants were also military spies. When it benefited the empire, the Aztecs conquered regions and demanded tribute in return, not simply reciprocal trade agreements. In 1500, the Aztecs fought with the Quiché over the cacao-rich Soconusco region and incorporated what is present-day Chiapas into its empire. By 1510, they were receiving tribute payments from the Quiché kingdom. The

Aztecs seemed to have set their sights on the Yucatán as well, the land of cotton, salt, and honey with a maritime route to Costa Rican and Panamanian gold. Aztec presence was unmistakable, if not yet fully in control: The Spaniards said Nahuatl was the lingua franca at ports. The Aztec encroachment on the Maya region, however, was soon replaced by that of the Europeans.

When the Spaniards first started exploring Mesoamerica early in the 16th century, the Aztec emperor, Moctezuma, suggested to the highland Maya that they consolidate their forces against the Europeans. The Quiché apparently agreed, but the first struggles occurred in central Mexico and the Aztecs were defeated, their capital of Tenochtitlan destroyed.

THE SPANISH CONQUEST TO THE PRESENT

Conquest Period

Soon after Hernán Cortés defeated the Aztec capital in 1521, the Spaniards spread out over Mesoamerica, following the tribute trail of the Aztec. Diseases such as malaria and measles spread wherever the Spaniards went, and the infections preceded them into every corner of the New World, killing and debilitating the Indians who had no natural immunity to them. As early as 1521, a smallpox plague killed one-third of the population of highland Guatemala. An earlier plague had killed many in the Yucatán. By the time the conquistadores advanced, the Maya were already greatly weakened.

GUATEMALAN HIGHLANDS

The Quiché ruler made a plea to the neighboring Maya to fight together against the Spaniards, but the Cakchiquel had already made an agreement to help the Spaniards against their traditional enemies, and they did. In 1524, Pedro de Alvarado—one of Cortés's most notoriously brutal captains—his Spanish soldiers, and central Mexican Indian allies advanced on Guatemala. The Quiché mounted 30,000 troops, according to Alvarado, but his calvary charges, guns, and steel swords were sufficient to force their surrender in the first battle. In a later battle, however, he needed the assistance of the Cakchiquel to definitively defeat the Quiché. After his victory, Alvarado was welcomed at Iximché, which he made the first Spanish capital of Guatemala, but the Spaniards found themselves starving and iso-

lated in the citadel, as the Cakchiquel soon rebelled against them and deserted the hilltop city. The Spanish capital was relocated to the area of what is now known as Antigua. Although the Cakchiquel continued guerrilla warfare until 1530, the southern Maya region had become a Spanish possession even before their surrender.

YUCATÁN

The Yucatec Maya were the first Mesoamericans to encounter the Spaniards. A Maya trading canoe was stopped by Christopher Columbus in 1502 in the Bay of Honduras and, after a brief exchange, released. Then in 1511, the few survivors of a Spanish ship washed ashore near Tulum and were enslaved by the Maya. The Hernández de Córdova expedition in 1517 reported seeing Tulum from the sea and thought it as grand as Seville, Spain. Cortés himself camped on Cozumel in 1519 before continuing around the peninsula and discovering the far wealthier Aztec Empire. The Yucatec Maya, however, would be the last conquered in Mesoamerica. Well aware of what had happened to their neighbors, they were more familiar with Spanish tactics. Their determined resistance made the conquest of their region unusually difficult for the Spaniards.

Not until 1527 did the first conquest attempt begin. Francisco de Montejo, another of Cortés's captains, landed on the peninsula along the Quintana Roo coast before setting out to explore and conquer. At Aké, near modern Tizimin, the Spaniards killed more than 1,000 Maya in a single battle and gained the surrender of nearby towns. But in future action along the Caribbean coast, the Maya managed to separate the Spanish troops and ambush them, and in 1528, the remaining conquistadores, fewer than 100 in number, withdrew.

Montejo tried again in 1530, this time establishing troops at Campeche on the Gulf of

Mexico, the Bay of Chetumal on the Caribbean coast, and the interior where he sent his son, also named Francisco. Montejo the Younger established a base at Chichén Itzá. Despite this multipronged Spanish attack, the Maya coordinated their strategies, and the Spaniards were once again forced to retreat, first from Chetumal and then from Chichén Itzá. By 1535, the Yucatán again belonged to the Maya. When Montejo the Younger returned in 1541, however, the two most powerful lineages in northern Yucatán, the Xiu and Cocom, were once again at war. The Xiu allied themselves with Montejo, thereby guaranteeing the victory of the Spaniards. In 1542, the first permanent Spanish town, Mérida, was founded on the Maya city of Tiho, symbolizing the end of the conquest. The Maya repeatedly rebelled, however, and in one fierce uprising in 1546, they attacked not only the Spaniards themselves but also uprooted the European plants they had seeded in the Yucatán. The Yucatec Maya nonetheless were defeated, and the age of the conquest was over.

2.19   The 1524 conquest of the highland Guatemalan town now known as Santiago Atitlán. The Lienzo, the work of a central Mexican Tlaxcalan Indian, depicts a mounted and armored Spaniard defeating the Maya with his Tlaxcalan allies.   (Copy of the 16th-century Lienzo de Tlaxcala by Diodoro Serrano, from Chavero, 1892)

DEVASTATION

The conquest devastated the Maya population. War, disease, and enslavement killed an estimated 90 percent of the population. The conquistadores represented the most brutal attack on Maya culture, but another assault was soon to follow. Catholic missionaries came to the New World in the 16th century intent on saving the Maya from their heathen beliefs and converting them to Catholicism. For the most part, they were protective of the Maya against the worst abuses of the conquistadores and settlers, and some, such as Bartolomé de las Casas, were responsible for the passage of laws that prevented the enslavement of the Indians. Yet the friars were engaged in a spiritual conquest of the Maya and attempted to destroy the Maya belief system, smashing images of deities and burning books. Through much of the 16th century, the sense of cultural dislocation was so severe that Catholic missionaries reported that in some instances, Indians refused to have children. The Maya, however, endured.

Early Colonial Period

Spain ruled what had once been Mesoamerica as its colony of New Spain. Initially, the Spaniards were too few to rule without the assistance of the Maya, so they substituted themselves for the Maya nobility at the top of the governmental hierarchy and left the rest of the political hierarchy basically intact. Maya lineage chiefs collected tribute for the Spaniards in the form of food, labor, clothing, and, in the Guatemala highlands, gold panning. In return, the Maya governors were permitted to dress like Spanish gentlemen, ride horses, and even carry arms—and, of course, continue to collect their own tribute and own their personal slaves.

The commerce of the early colonial period also relied on Maya—and Mesoamerican—trade routes, Maya human carriers, and Maya cacao beans for currency. Although the art styles changed with the conquest, the Maya were the builders of the Spanish colonial world: Their tribute labor constructed roads, churches, and palaces, and they were the stonemasons, sculptors, and fresco painters. Gradually, Spanish artisan guilds replaced the Maya, and the Spaniards created their own trade networks for European goods of wheat and cattle, not maize and turkeys.

Frontier Maya Settlements

Some Maya escaped from New Spain and continued their pre-Columbian traditions in areas distant from Spanish settlements. Quintana Roo, the eastern half of the Yucatán Peninsula, remained free of Spaniards, and runaway Maya settled there. Others fled to established settlements in the Petén and Belize interior, such as Tah Itzá (Tayasal) and Tipú. These towns occupied some of the most fertile regions of the interior, including the Petén lakes and the western Belize River valley where settlements had once supplied Classic Period cities with its agricultural surplus and cacao beans. The ceramics and tools at these sites remained identical to those in earlier centuries except that they were mixed with European cups and steel axes.

These frontier regions were basically unexplored during the conquest period and remained remote for most of the 300 years of the Spanish colony. During the conquest, however, Hernán Cortés took what he thought

would be a shortcut across the Petén on his way to put down a rebellion by his captain in Honduras. In 1525, he did not find continuous settlement and the great white plastered cities of the Classic Period but instead nearly died attempting to find a route through the rugged rain forest that had grown from the time of the collapse. Cortés came upon, and probably was even directed to, the substantial Itzá capital city of Tayasal in this remote region. Cortés's visit would be the last by a Spaniard for almost 100 years, when two Franciscan priests attempted and failed to convert the Itzá. When the Spaniards finally decided to dislodge the Itzá from Lake Petén Itzá and captured the ruler Kan Ek' in 1697, it represented the end of pre-Columbian Maya civilization. Until that year, the Maya at Tayasal had lived much as they had in ancient times, carving stone sculptures to their gods, worshiping under the guidance of noble priests and practicing human sacrifice, trading cacao with other Maya settlements on the frontier, and wearing gold ornaments and tatooing their bodies. They also wrote books in hieroglyphs, an art that was lost with the conquest of Tayasal.

Although the capital at Tayasal was destroyed, and along with it much of Maya elite culture, many Maya continued to live in relative isolation from Spanish communities. The Lacandón Maya moved into the Usumacinta region around Bonampak, where they managed to elude foreigners until mahogany loggers encountered them in the 20th century. Many Maya lived in independent communities in the eastern half of the Yucatán Peninsula for centuries; in 1847, the European encroachment on these settlements provoked an uprising, known as the Caste War of Yucatán, that nearly caused the evacuation of every European from the peninsula. The evacuation was halted only when the Europeans realized the Maya had abandoned the fight in order to plant their maize fields. In Chiapas, too, an increasing number of Spanish settlements led to a violent upheaval in 1869. As the frontier contracted, however, the Maya managed to persist.

Maya Cultural Survival

CONDITIONS OF SURVIVAL

Maya traditions survived in both settled regions and remote ones. Although many Maya were enslaved and assimilated, significant numbers of Maya were basically left alone as long as they paid their tribute. The Maya often lived in their own settlements surrounded by their own lands and governed by their traditional leaders on matters of village concern. This was possible for centuries after the conquest because the Maya region never had the rich gold mines to attract large numbers of Europeans. Guatemala and the Yucatán remained sparsely settled.

NATIVE CATHOLICISM

Although Catholic missionaries and priests often lived in Maya villages, they were always too few to have a dominating presence. They usually permitted the Maya to raise money and manage the religious processions surrounding the various *cofradías*, or cults of the saints. These *cofradías* became infused with pre-Columbian beliefs and created what has been called native Catholicism. In this syncretic religion, Catholic saints fused with ancient Maya gods, Christian resurrection became inseparable from the pre-Columbian maize god's sacrifice and rebirth, and the ritual calendars combined to celebrate Catholic holidays and native celebrations, such as was the case with All Saints' Day, which merged with the honoring of ancestors in Day of the Dead ceremonies. The religious synthesis constantly adapted to new challenges; as late as the 19th-

century, the Caste War rebels living in eastern Yucatán reinterpreted a Christian cross into a Maya oracle known as the Speaking Cross, thereby continuing the tradition of oracular shrines that had been established in the area for centuries before the Spanish Conquest.

NATIVE CHRONICLES

During the three centuries of the colonial period, some Maya were able to maintain their ancient books about the creation of the Maya world their ancient history, and their calendrical prophecies. They were written in Mayan languages but in the less cumbersome Roman script learned from the 16th-century Spanish missionaries. Most of the native literature, such as the Yucatec *Book of the Chilam Balam of Chumayel* and the Quiché *Popol Vuh*, were discovered in the late 17th and early 18th centuries. Even when literacy disappeared through increasing Spanish neglect, the myths and sacred calendar were maintained by oral traditions (see Chapter 10).

POSTINDEPENDENCE

In 1810, the colony of New Spain declared its independence. The modern governments that replaced the colony changed the laws and conditions under which the Maya culture had survived. The modern states eliminated the protective laws that had enabled the Maya to maintain their distinct rules of self-government and land use. The Maya were forced to struggle against attempts to assimilate them in both Mexico and Guatemala. They fought outsiders who attempted to control village affairs, they fought forced labor on commercial plantations that would have taken them from their traditional lands and practically enslaved them, and they fought legal battles to keep their communal lands from coffee *finca* owners and sugar plantations—often to no avail. These struggles, in new guises, continue today.

MAYA CULTURAL AUTONOMY

Yet the Maya have survived these nearly 500 years of cultural challenges since the Spanish Conquest. Thirty-one Mayan languages still are spoken and many Maya continue to wear traditional dress, often woven with designs of ancient origin, that identify their village. Today there are Maya daykeepers, or shaman priests, who maintain the sacred calendar, divining the fate of their people as Maya priests have done for millennia and dictating the rhythm of daily life with its rituals and festivals. The centered quadripartite world still defines the Maya cosmos and infuses everyday acts, such as planting cornfields. The village, with its sacred landscape of ancestral mountains, caves, and cenotes and led by its traditional civic leaders and shaman priests, still shapes the identity of millions of Maya.

Living Maya

There are approximately 10 million living Maya at the beginning of the 21st century. They live primarily in the periphery of the Classic Period Maya domain, in Guatemala, Honduras, Belize, and the Mexican states of

2.20   *Maya children in the Mérida market, Yucatán, Mexico.*   (Photo courtesy Peter Foster)

Chiapas, Tabasco, Campeche, Yucatán, and Quintana Roo. As the population has increased, land has become increasingly scarce, and once again Mayas are settling the Petén.

Land shortages and poverty afflict most Maya who live in traditional villages and farm their village lands, but many Maya are clamoring for change. In 1994, Mexicans were shocked by the armed uprising of 2,000 Maya in Chiapas. As members of the Zapatista Army of National Liberation, they demanded more land, better resources, and more constitutional protections—demands they are still struggling to achieve in a more peaceful manner. In the 1990s, Mopán Maya in Belize protested against a multinational corporation's logging of mahogany on their lands and negotiated a nature preserve with the government. Yucatec Maya have found both employment opportunities and land pressures from tourist development along the Caribbean coast, and the most traditional among them prophesy the Feathered Serpent at Chichén Itzá will inflict destruction on those who no longer revere the gods.

While only limited violence has accompanied the on-going Zapatista movement in Chiapas, a holocaust occurred in Guatemala. Highland Maya civilians were the victims of a 36-year civil war in which 900,000 of them were displaced from their lands, many of them becoming refugees in Mexico, Belize, and the United States, and another 166,000 were killed or "disappeared." By the time a cease-fire was declared in 1996, the Maya constituted 83 percent of the war dead. A United Nations study stated that Guatemala's war policies had been tantamount to Maya genocide.

MAYA REVIVAL

Out of the violence and turmoil of recent decades, Maya revivalist movements emerged. Before the end of the Guatemalan civil war, Rigoberta Menchú Tum, a Quiché woman, wrote *I, Rigoberta Menchú: An Indian Woman in Guatemala*, a book about the Maya experience during the civil war and for which she received the Nobel Peace Prize in 1992. Her book brought world pressure on Guatemala to end the war. Out of the shared experience of the war, some Guatemalan Maya have transcended their village identity to form a pan-Maya political movement, demanding educational and legal rights for the Maya, who constitute more than half the population of Guatemala.

There is a cultural revival as well. Maya in Guatemala and Yucatán are studying the hieroglyphs and learning to decipher them from epigraphers; in the highlands, Maya shaman priests travel to the most traditional villages to learn ancient customs from the daykeepers. The Maya's knowledge of their own languages and culture may lead to new understandings of the ancient texts and native documents. And the political determination of contemporary Maya, in both Chiapas and Guatemala, may put them in the center of the Maya world once again.

READING

See also "Reading" for Chapters 5, 7, 8, and 9.

Lithic and Archaic Periods

Adams 1991: Lithic and Archaic Periods; Blake, et al. 1995, Clark 1991, Joyce and Henderson 2001: Isthmian cultural horizon; MacNeish 1967, MacNeish and Nelken-Terner 1983, Mangelsdorf 1974: domestication of maize and preceramic settlements; Dixon 2000, Meltzer and Sabloff 1995: Ice Age peoples of the Americas; Andrews V 1990, Lowe 1977: discussion of ethnic identity in Isthmian and Maya regions.

Early Preclassic Period

OLMEC CULTURE

Coe and Diehl 1980, Cyphers 1996: excavations at San Lorenzo; González 1996, Heizer 1986, Stirling 1941 and 1965: investigations at La Venta; Michael Coe 1968, Grove 1987, Niederberger 1996, Reilly 1991, Sharer and Grove 1989: discussion of Olmec culture and other Mesoamerican regions; Michael Coe 1965 and 1973, Furst 1996, Joralemon 1971 and 1976, Taube 1996: Olmec art style and iconography, including identification of deities and shamanism; Campbell and Kaufman 1976: linguistic identity of the Olmecs.

MESOAMERICAN TRAITS

Kirchhoff: 1943.

Middle Preclassic Period

Blake, et al. 1995, Lee 1989, Sharer 1989: development of Maya culture and Olmec interaction; Sharer and Sheets 1978: Chalchuapa; Hansen 1998: architecture in the lowlands; Rice 1976: settlement patterns in the central lowlands; Hammond 1978: Cuello; Andrews V, Ringle, et al. 1984, Ringle and Andrews V 1988 and 1990: northern lowlands; Barry and McAnany 2000, Mary Pohl, et al. 1996, Turner and Harrison 1983: agriculture.

Late Preclassic Period

Adams 1977, Parsons 1986, Rathje 1971 and 1972, Thompson 1966, Webster 1977: essays on the origins of Maya civilization; Bove 1986: figurine vs. ruler cults; Quirarte 1973: Izapan art; Parsons 1988: Kaminaljuyú and origins of

Maya art; Coe and Kerr 1997, Justeson 1986, Justeson, Norman, et al. 1985: origin of writing; Adams 1991, Kidder, Jennings, and Shook 1946: Kaminaljuyú; Freidel and Schele 1988a and 1988b, Robertson and Freidel 1986: Cerros iconography and ruler insignia; Ringle 1999: ritual politics in the lowlands; Pendergast 1986: Lamanai; Dahlin 1984, Demarest, Sharer, et al. 1984, Hansen 1990 and 1998: El Mirador; Benavides Castillo 1997, Matheny 1978 and 1987: Edzná. Andrews V, Ringle, et al. 1992: Komchén; Ball 1977a: northern region; Dahlin 1983, Sheets 1976a and 1976b: environment and the Late Preclassic hiatus.

Early Classic Period

Adams 1977, Culbert 1991, Willey and Mathews 1985: overview of lowland politics; Reese-Taylor and Walker 2001: rise of Tikal after hiatus; Buikstra, et al. 2000, Coggins 1976, Fash 1997, Schele and Freidel 1990, Schele and Miller 1986, David Stuart 1997 and 1998: Teotihuacan presence in Maya region; Harrison 1999, Christopher Jones 1991: overview of Tikal; Fash 1991, Fash and Stuart 1991: overview of Copán; Chase and Chase 1987 and 1996: Caracol; Folan 1992, Folan, Marcus, et al. 1995, Pincemin et al. 1998: Calakmul; Hansen 1998, Miller 1999: art and architecture.

Late Classic Period

Culbert 1991, Martin and Grube 1995 and 2000: Maya kingdoms and superpowers; Ball 1977, Potter 1977: Chenes and Río Bec region; Ashmore 1981: settlement surveys; Diane and Arlen Chase 1992; Culbert 1991, Fash and Stuart 1991: growth of elite class; Coe 1999, Miller 1999, Schele and Miller 1986: art and the ruler

cult; Fowler, Demarest, et al. 1997: Petexbatún region; Barry and McAnanay 2000: K'axob.

Terminal Classic and Early Postclassic Periods

CLASSIC PERIOD COLLAPSE

Culbert 1973: southern lowland collapse; Andrews and Robles C. 1985, John Graham 1973, Schele and Mathews 1998, Thompson 1970: invasion theories; Brenner 1998, Carr and Hazard 1961, Curtis, et al. 1995, Gill 2000: drought; Abrams and Rue 1988, Culbert and Rice 1990, Dewey, et al. 1979: population and environment; Fash and Stuart 1991, Martin and Grube 2000: warfare and elite power.

NORTHERN LOWLANDS

Andrews 1990, Berlo and Diehl 1989, Koontz 1994, Ringle, et al. 1998: pan-Mesoamerican trade and culture; Miller 1999: art and architecture; Andrews IV 1973, Ball 1974, Prem 1994, Robles C. and Andrews 1986: northern lowlands archaeology; Grube 1994: northern lowland hieroglyphic writing and *multepal*; Andrews V and Sabloff 1986, Kowalski 1994, Schele and Mathews 1998: the Puuc and Uxmal.

CHICHÉN ITZÁ

Kepecs, et al. 1994, Kowalski 1989, Kremer 1994, Lincoln 1986 and 1994, Thompson 1970: chronology and origins; Schele and Mathews 1998, Wren and Schmidt 1991: ballcourt symbolism; Coggins and Shane 1984; Krochock 1998: trade; Graña-Behrens, et al. 1999, Grube 1994, Krochock 1991: hieroglyphs and *k'atun* dates; Ralph Roys 1967, and Edmonson 1982: native chronicles; Andrews and Robles C. 1985, Dahlin 2000, Freidel

1992: warfare in the northern lowlands; Anthony Andrews 1990: collapse.

Late Postclassic Period

Andrews V and Sabloff 1986, Chase and Rice, 1985, Willey 1986: overview of lowland Postclassic; Carmack 1981: overview of highland Postclassic; Alvarado 1972, Edmonson 1982, Recinos, et al. 1967, Ralph Roys 1967, Tedlock 1996, Tozzer 1941: native chronicles and ethnohistoric sources; Pollock, et al. 1962: Mayapán; Pendergast 1986: Belize and Lamanai; Diane Chase 1985, Rice 1986: Petén Lakes; Anthony Andrews 1998, Diane Chase 1986, Freidel and Sabloff 1984, Masson 2000, Sabloff 1977: maritime trade; Carmack 1968, Fox 1987, Schele and Mathews 1998: Quiché origins.

Spanish Conquest to Present

Alvarado 1972, Carmack 1981, Clendenin 1987, Cortés 1986, Díaz del Castillo 1956, Landa 1941, Las Casas 1992, Recinos, et al. 1967, Restall 1992, Ralph Roys 1967: Spanish Conquest; Farriss 1984, Graham, et al. 1995, Grant Jones 1989: frontier Maya kingdoms; Victoria Bricker 1981, Reed 1964: Maya rebellions; Carmack 1981, Farriss 1984, MacLeod and Wassserstrom 1983 conditions for cultural survival; Carlsen 1997, Carmack 1995, Sullivan 1989, Tedlock 1992, Vogt 1993, Watanabe 1992, cultural survival and the living Maya; Menchú 1984, Warren 1998: civil war and pan-Maya movement.

3

GEOGRAPHY OF THE PRE-COLUMBIAN MAYA

The ancient Maya region was larger than modern Italy, a little smaller than France. Extending from the Pacific coast across to the Caribbean Sea and the Gulf of Mexico and covering the land from the Isthmus of Tehuantepec south into western El Salvador and Honduras, the region spanned 390,000 square kilometers (150,540 square miles). Even today, the region is inhabited by millions of Maya. The land is full of contrasting environments, from tropical lowlands to snow-covered mountain peaks, from near desert dryness to drenching wet, and from porous limestone to volcanic ash–enriched soils. The contrast in environment and natural resources between the highlands and the lowlands encouraged trade and cultural exchange.

GREATER MESOAMERICA

The Maya region was only part of the geographically varied world in which the civilization evolved. The Maya were culturally part of Mesoamerica, and the resources of that much larger landscape to the northwest enriched the Maya world, even though the powerful cities of the central Mexican valley were 1,000 kilometers (610 miles) away. The distance was aggravated by a Mesoamerican landscape that was rugged and difficult to traverse. The mountains of Oaxaca, for example, were so difficult to maneuver that they later frustrated the Spaniards because their horses could not find a firm footing; the tangled vegetable growth of the Petén rain forest made directions confusing; and flooding could render the lowlands impassable. The journeys between the highland valleys to the coastal areas exposed travelers to both frigid air in altitudes above 3,000 meters (almost 10,000 feet) and the tropical heat of the seacoast;

after the Spanish Conquest, it was reported that porters died from the climatic extremes experienced on such journeys.

These barriers to communication enabled the Maya to evolve their own distinctive cultural tradition within Mesoamerican civilization. The barriers were not insurmountable, however, and trade goods, domesticated plants, and cultural ideas spread through mountain passes and along the coasts and rivers to reach every Mesoamerican center. The highlands usually had volcanic glass—or obsidian—for tools, volcanic basalt for grinding stones, and volcanic ash for making pottery. The lowlands offered salt, cotton, salted fish, and tropical fruits. These basic resources made the lowlands and highlands dependent on each other. Geographic diversity both unified Mesoamerica and distinguished its peoples, and the cultural exchange gave rise to its civilization.

MAYA GEOGRAPHY AND MYTHOLOGY

Maya geography was incorporated into cosmic and mythological beliefs. The sea bordering much of the Maya world and the caves formed in the limestone of the lowlands were all believed to be portals to the Maya Underworld. The great mountains were ancestral places of origin; when there were no mountains, the Maya replicated them with pyramids. Tropical ceiba trees, their branches reaching high toward the sky, were the center of the cosmos, or the sacred World Tree. Crocodiles floating on water symbolized the earth above the Underworld. Rattlesnakes were vision serpents, conduits to the otherworld. Monkeys were humans from a previous creation. Jaguars, creatures of the night, were the symbols of the sun on its nocturnal passage to dawn. (See

Chapter 6.) Rulers took their names from the natural as well as the supernatural world: For example, Lord First-Dawned-Sky Lightning God (Yax Pas Chan Yoaat) of Copán and Lady Resplendent Quetzal Bird (Sak K'uk') of Palenque were Late Classic Period rulers. Like many rulers of this period, Kan B'alam of Palenque added the sun god title, K'inich, to his name, becoming Lord Sun God Snake Jaguar. The calendar, too, incorporated the flora, fauna, and even earthquakes into symbols of the days and months.

Rainy and Dry Seasons

The Mesoamerican year was divided by the alternation of the rainy and dry seasons, and less so by temperature. The dry season lasts four to five months between November and April. Temperatures vary only moderately, and when they do vary significantly in Mesoamerica, it has more to do with altitude than the season. The highest peaks can be freezing cold; sea-level settlements are hot, averaging 30°C (86°F); and most highland valleys, located somewhere between the two in altitude, have mostly temperate climates that average 20°C (70°F).

The seasonal contrast between rainy months and dry ones had a deep impact on the Maya worldview. These seasons divided the Maya year into all that was verdant and alive and all that was dried or dead. The cycle of rains alternating with periods of drought defined the agricultural season as well, with the rainy season ending around the time of the November harvest and beginning once again in the spring. These alternating seasons were linked with the greater cosmos, the rise and set of Pleiades, and the solstices and the equinoxes, which gave measure to the agricultural year and substance to myths of creation. These perpetual cycles contributed to Maya beliefs that death leads to rebirth and

that renewal follows sacrifice; they shaped the Maya view of world order and underlay Maya rituals of bloodletting and human sacrifice (see Chapters 6 and 9).

MAYA REGIONAL DIVERSITY

The Maya region has culturally been divided into the northern lowlands; the central area, or southern lowlands; and the southern area. This tripartite cultural division does not coincide with the four geologic zones of the region. Three of these zones are in the southern area, two in the highlands alone; the other encompasses all of the lowlands in the central and northern areas. Despite the single lowland geologic category, there is considerable variability within that zone as well.

Pacific Coast and Piedmont

In the southern Maya region, there is a fertile band of land, about 70 kilometers (43 miles) wide along the Pacific coast, that begins in the Soconusco region of Chiapas, Mexico, and continues down the coast into El Salvador. The open terrain has historically encouraged trade through the region as well as attracted foreign interlopers. The Olmec, the Teotihuacanos, and the Aztec from central Mexico all crossed the Isthmus of Tehuantepec from the Gulf of Mexico and heavily influenced the Pacific area. Enriched by volcanic ash from the nearby highlands and alluvial soils from rivers draining into the region, the littoral and piedmont are among the most fertile lands in the Maya region. Moisture from the Pacific is cooled by

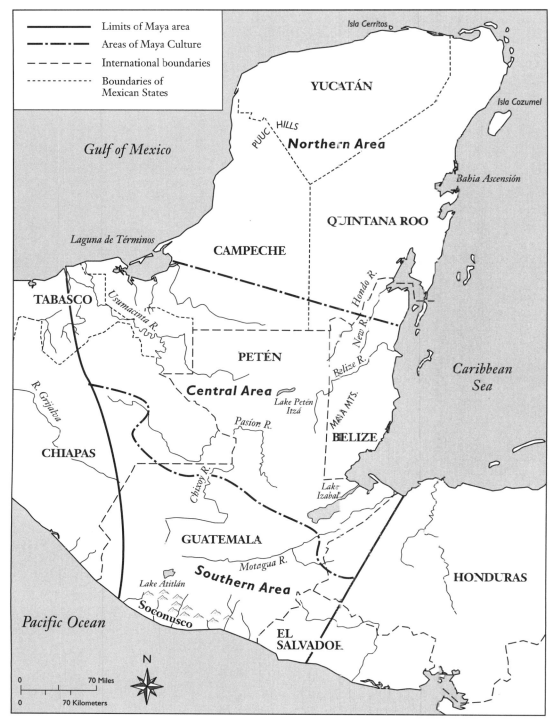

Map 3. *Topographic Map of the Maya Region.*

Legend:
- Limits of Maya area
- Areas of Maya Culture
- International boundaries
- Boundaries of Mexican States

YUCATÁN

Northern Area

Gulf of Mexico

PUUC HILLS

QUINTANA ROO

Isla Cerritos

Isla Cozumel

Bahia Ascensión

Laguna de Términos

CAMPECHE

TABASCO

Usumacinta R.

Hondo R.

New R.

PETÉN

Belize R.

Central Area

Caribbean Sea

R. Grijalva

Lake Petén Itzá

MAYA MTS.

Pasión R.

BELIZE

CHIAPAS

Chixoy R.

Lake Izabal

GUATEMALA

Motagua R.

HONDURAS

Lake Atitlán

Southern Area

Soconusco

Pacific Ocean

EL SALVADOR

N

0 70 Miles

0 70 Kilometers

3.1   Valley of Quetzaltenango in the Guatemala highlands.   (Photo courtesy John Montgomery)

the inland mountains, resulting in heavy annual rainfall. Before being cut for the cultivation of sugarcane during the Spanish colonial period, the area had a high forest canopy and many ferns and was cultivated by the Maya for cacao. The coast, unprotected by reefs, has no natural bays to facilitate maritime trade, but its mangrove swamps were resources for shellfish, sea birds, and alligator-like caimans.

Highlands

VOLCANOES

The highlands provide the most varied terrain, particularly in Guatemala where they are cen-tered between the coasts and contain two geo-logic regions. The first highland zone to appear inland from the Pacific Ocean is a chain of very active volcanoes that thrust their way from Chiapas to El Salvador and down through southern Central America. Nearby are rift valleys created by two clashing tectonic plates that have caused the volcanic eruptions and earthquakes that have periodically devastated the region and continue to do so. Volcán Fuego has erupted more than 50 times since the Spanish Conquest in 1524, and flashes of volcanic fire are a common sight against the Guatemalan night sky. Izalco in El Salvador erupted nearly continuously until a few decades ago. One of the great highland resources, however, was formed by this volcanic activity: obsidian.

CRYSTALLINE MOUNTAINS

The third geologic zone is a more northern mountainous tier bordering the lowlands and spanning from western Guatemala into Honduras. This zone is shaped by the Crystalline Mountains, the oldest rock formation in Central America, more rugged and cut more deeply by gorges than the arc of volcanoes. The highest and coldest elevations in the northern tier are found in the Altos Cuchumatanes—above 3,000 meters (more than 9,900 feet)—in northwestern Guatemala. Other clusters within the Crystalline Mountains, such as the Sierra de Chuacús and the Sierra de las Minas between the Motagua and Polochic Rivers in Guatemala, are rich in mineral resources, including basalt for grinding stones and precious serpentine and jade. In fact, serpentine, which the Maya treasured as a green stone almost as much as jade, and small amounts of gold and copper can be found throughout these venerable mountains.

OAK AND CLOUD FORESTS

The two zones of highland mountains are usually covered with pine and oak forest, but Volcán Tajumulco, rising to 4,220 meters (13,926 feet), the highest peak in Central America, can be covered with snow or frost. Peaks facing the wet winds of the Caribbean receive so much drizzle and rain they form moss-covered cloud forests inhabited by several species of monkeys, parrots, opossums, and the endangered quetzal bird whose blue-green feathers were favored by Mesoamerican kings.

BROAD VALLEYS

The mountains form fertile valleys, some quite extensive such as the Valley of Guatemala, where the modern capital of Guatemala City sprawls over ruins from ancient Kaminaljuyú. These valleys were, and still are, the most densely inhabited regions of the highlands. Ranging in altitude from 750 to 2,000 meters (2,500 to 6,500 feet), the valleys have a temperate, almost year-round springlike climate; they are endowed with volcanic-enriched soils, crossed by rivers and dotted with lakes, such as Lago Amatitlán and Lago Atitlán in Guatemala, that were formed in calderas, or collapsed volcanic cones. With obsidian sources located near the major valleys, the ancient Maya had a valuable trade resource. Connected by rivers to both the Pacific Coast and the lowlands and with mountain passes leading into Chiapas, the highland valleys were well positioned to trade their obsidian and mineral deposits.

Lowlands

Tropical lowlands predominate in the geologic zone that encompasses the central and northern Maya areas. Although free of the volcanic activity of the highlands, the coastal areas are subject to hurricanes and flooding during the rainy season. The forests of hardwoods, covered with parasitic vines and bromeliads, or wild orchids, were more plentifully inhabited in the past by jaguars, white-tailed deer, fer-de-lance, rattlesnakes, and many species of tropical birds and insects. The rivers and swamps were home to crocodiles, alligators, and fish. The landmass is covered with a 3,000-meter (9,900-foot) shelf of limestone, which provided a ready source of building stone and plaster to most Maya cities but resulted in only thin layers of soil. Archaeologists have long been baffled that Maya civilization could flourish for so long in the tropical lowlands. The lowlands were believed to be consistently poor in agricultural potential, capable of producing crops adequate for only small populations. Surveys and analyses of fossil remains and wetlands

3.2   *The northern lowlands spread seamlessly behind the Temple of the Warriors, Chichén Itzá, in the Yucatán.*   (Photo courtesy John Montgomery)

now prove not only their diversity but also the Maya's skill in making their environment productive (see Chapter 11).

FOREST CANOPY TO CACTUS SHRUBS

These lowlands provide a variety of environments. The limestone shelf itself is broken by the Puuc Hills in northern Yucatán, the granite thrust of the Maya Mountains in Belize, and numerous ridges, favored by the ancient Maya for their settlements, located above the floodplains. In western Belize, caves riddle the limestone surface, and in the Vaca Plateau, they form some of the most extensive underground systems in the world. There are savannas as well as forests, cactus, coconut palms, and stands of mahogany trees. The central Petén has lakes and many natural wetlands that are replenished by heavy seasonal rains every year. But traveling north, the land becomes increasingly arid. In the south, there is tropical forest; in the north, thorny scrub forest. Northern Yucatán is almost bare bedrock, but even in the Yucatán, there are fertile areas with deep soils, such as around Oxkutzcab and the Puuc Hills, and shallow lakes, such as those around Cobá.

INTERIOR VS. THE COAST

Contrasts just as great existed between coastal areas and the interior. Coastal regions could trade easily by canoe, but human portage was necessary to bring goods into or across most of the interior. The Caribbean Sea was easy to fish because it has one of the most extensive barrier reefs in the world; coastal lagoons, mangrove swamps, and freshwater springs created extensive wetlands in Belize. The interior, with only a few seasonal streams and few lakes—Lake Petén Itzá being the largest—had less opportunity to supplement its diet with fish and waterfowl; instead, it relied more heavily on the hunting of deer, turkey, and wild peccary.

MAJOR RIVER ROUTES

The central area has major rivers along its edges. The Pasión and Chixoy (Salinas) Rivers join the Usumacinta to form the major communication route through the western Maya world, connecting the Guatemala highlands and the Petén with the Gulf of Mexico. The Motagua River and its many tributaries form the most important riverine route from highland Guatemala to the Caribbean Sea on the east. And the Belize and New Rivers provide transport from the Caribbean partially into the interior.

Rivers are rare, however, and most of the lowlands are landlocked. There is no river that crosses the Petén interior, and the northern lowlands have no rivers at all. The limestone is so porous in the north that rivers cannot form on the surface. In the Yucatán especially, water col-lects in underground rivers; when the limestone surface fractures and collapses over a cave, it forms natural wells called cenotes.

CHANGING ENVIRONMENT

Extreme environmental changes have occurred over the millennia, and reconstructing the environment that the Maya originally exploited has been an archaeological challenge. Fortunately, paleobotanists are now making considerable progress in this area and have corrected some misunderstandings that previously plagued

3.3   Río Pasión, Petén lowlands, Guatemala. (Photo courtesy Peter Selverstone)

archaeologists. The present lack of easily farmed land in the Mirador Basin, for example, had led archaeologists to believe early Maya site selection was unrelated to agriculture; only in the last few years has evidence accumulated that the present claylike soil and seasonable swamps were once permanent lakes and extensively cultivated wetlands.

Volcanic Eruptions

The eruption of Volcán Ilopango c. 250 is an excellent example of the kind of dramatic environmental change the Maya confronted. It destroyed many centers of early Maya culture in the southern Maya area, forcing the abandonment of Chalchuapa in El Salvador for centuries and creating a hiatus in sites on the southeastern Pacific slopes of Guatemala. The eruption deposited enough ash in rivers in the highlands to cause them to change course and flood lowland centers. Such eruptions are known to have occurred periodically in highland Guatemala and El Salvador as well as in other regions of Mesoamerica, including central Mexico.

Drying Trends

Pollen cores from the Petén suggest that the tropical forest did not dominate that region

3.4   *Sacred Cenote, Chichén Itzá.*   (Photo courtesy Peter Selverstone)

until almost the Classic Period and then took over the southern lowlands only after the collapse. Before this change to rain forest, the Petén may have had more oak forests and savannas. Paleoclimatologists suggest that during the formation of Maya civilization in the Middle Preclassic Period, warmer and wetter conditions created wetland swamps in the Petén and small lakes in the Guatemala highlands. These were exploited by the earliest large cities, such as Nakbé and Kaminaljuyú. Drying trends caused by deforestation ushered in vast changes, including a decline in agricultural potential in the Mirador Basin at the end of the Late Preclassic Period. Such drying trends may also have contributed to the collapse of cities in the Petén during the Terminal Classic Period (see Chapter 2).

Deforestation

Deforestation had a great impact on the Maya environment. It reduced rainfall, but it probably also reduced the feasibility of the massive building programs carried out during the Late Preclassic Period. It is estimated that the construction of a simple rural Maya house required 50 small trees. Although Classic Period Maya used more efficient construction techniques (see Chapter 8), they still needed to clear the land for agriculture and to cut trees to make carbon for cooking and lime for plaster. The population density and number of cities from this period must have stripped the lowlands of forest.

The deforestation that occurred during the Classic Period is difficult to imagine today, when the lowlands are covered by tropical forest; for example, archaeologists working at La Milpa in northwestern Belize required special electronic equipment to penetrate the dense forest in order to locate Classic Period buildings in the region of the central pyramid. But with an estimated 8 to 10 million Maya living in the lowlands during the Late Classic Period, the rain forest could not have existed. Such was the extent of deforestation that at La Milpa in 880, the ancient Maya had unobstructed views and actually constructed buildings 4 kilometers (2.5 miles) away to create a quadripartite cosmogram that was visible from the sacred center.

GEOGRAPHY AND CIVILIZATION

The nature of Maya geography has been critical to how their civilization has been viewed. For most of the 20th century, archaeologists thought the heartland of the Petén was geographically invariable and uniformly unsuitable for the rise of civilization or state formation. Tropical rains, it was thought, eliminated the need for massive irrigation systems that gave rise to centralized political states in the ancient Middle East and elsewhere in the world. And thin layers of soil prevented any agriculture other than swidden, a simple system of slash-and-burn farming that cannot support large populations. However, not only are the Maya lowlands more diversified than previously noticed, but the development and exploitation of that environment is now known to have resulted in one of the most densely inhabited regions in the preindustrial world.

Although the southern region does seem to have been the focus of the earliest cultural developments, recent discoveries have revealed surprisingly early developments in the lowlands as well. The archaeological realities have forced scientists to look more closely at the Maya lowlands. They have found many distinctive ecosystems and have discovered agricultural innovations for feeding large populations (see "Early Intensive Agriculture" below and Chapter 11). Areas without rivers, lakes, or other year-round sources of water were forced to create their own supply for the long dry season and for periods of drought. Perhaps it was the need to develop such innovations that led to the rise of the great Classic Period Maya lowland cities. In areas with bountiful rain and food, such as northern Belize, few monumental cities were constructed.

SETTLEMENTS AND AGRICULTURAL BEGINNINGS

The Maya settled in the lowland regions before the introduction of cultivated plants. Swamps, lagoons, and rivers provided an abundance of shellfish and fish. The mangrove swamps and barrier reefs along the Caribbean coast would have made fishing in the shallow waters quite easy, and shrimp, mollusks, and spiny lobsters could also be harvested. The Pacific littoral was also exploited and is where some of the earliest Mesoamerican pottery is found c. 1600 B.C.E. in Chiapas. Although only a few Mesoamerican shell middens have been adequately studied by archaeologists, those few indicate dispersed sedentary settlements from as early as 5000 to 3000 B.C.E. in many lowland areas. Supplementing their fish diet with wild seeds; domesticated squash and avocado; tropical fruits, such as pineapple; and small game, such as Muscovy ducks, wild pig, turkey, and deer, these early hunters and gatherers lived simply but apparently ate quite well. In fact, there is some evidence that many settlements were slow to abandon this lifestyle for farming once domesticated maize (corn) was introduced.

Earliest Maya Settlements

Throughout most of the 20th century, archaeologists thought the central and northern Maya regions were colonized after 1000 B.C.E. by peoples from the southern region. The Maya, they believed, first developed their distinctive culture at known sites along the Pacific coast and in the Guatemalan highlands where they were stimulated by interaction with the Olmecs. At this point, they argued, cultivated maize supported larger populations, and population pressures probably led the Maya—and perhaps Mixe-Zoque people related to the Olmecs—to follow the rivers into the lowlands where farming enabled them to sustain themselves in formerly uninhabited areas.

Human presence in the lowlands is most obviously indicated by pottery: the Xé Ceramic Complex found at a few western Maya sites on the Pasión and Usumacinta Rivers (c. 900–700 B.C.E.) and the Swasey/Eb Ceramic Complex (c. 1000–500 B.C.E.) found from northern Belize to the Petén. Although all these ceramic types derive from the earlier Isthmian tradition, some types form clusters that share more shapes and slips than others. The Xe pottery is most similar to Middle Preclassic ceramics found in Chiapas and the Salamá Valley of highland Guatemala and, therefore, may represent contacts with one or both of these regions; the Río Chixoy and Río Pasión would naturally link them. The Swasey seems related to pottery found in the Guatemalan highlands and western El Salvador. Many archaeologists have argued that these ceramics represent the movement of peoples into the formerly uninhabited lowlands.

LOWLAND SETTLEMENTS

New evidence from botanists and archaeologists has forced revisions in this colonization theory. First, it is unclear that the Guatemalan highlands were so densely populated or culturally leap years ahead of the lowlands around 1000 B.C.E. The highland Salamá and Chixoy Valleys proved amenable to settlement during the Early Preclassic Period, but volcanic activity and thick ash prevented settlement in some of the broader valleys until this time. And second, pollen cores indicate people were growing maize in parts of the lowlands around 2300 B.C.E. In some areas, such as northern Belize, excavations indicate cultural continuity from the time of the earliest lowland settlements forward so that it is reasonable to assume these early lowlanders were ancestors of the Maya. For example, the excavation of Cuello, a Belizean site located on the Bay of Chetumal, demonstrated that the site was occupied by the same ethnic group from before 2500 B.C.E. until the Late Preclassic Period, when it is known to have flourished as a distinctively Maya center. The ethnic identity of villagers in other parts of the lowlands, however, remains controversial. By 1000 B.C.E., population pressures probably encouraged the lowland Maya to expand into interior regions, where the few lakes and lack of rivers made year-round water supply more difficult; many of them probably arrived from more amenable lowland areas, such as the Petén lakes and the Belize wetlands. Maya from the southern region may have added their numbers to the region at this time as well as some Mixe-Zoque, who later were absorbed into the Maya population.

Origin of Maize

There is intense controversy over the origin of the maize plant, but most paleobotanists agree that the domestication process took an exceptionally long time, approximately 5,000 years. The cob on the wild plant is miniscule and contains only a few seeds, or kernels. By contrast, in the ancient Middle East wild wheat was almost as productive as the cultivated plant and was domesticated relatively quickly between 8000 and 6500 B.C.E., leading to farming communities several thousand years before such settlements appeared in the New World. Although theories disagree about the evolution of maize, the most important ones are in basic agreement about the final stages of the biological process: Domesticated maize developed from teosinte, or other wild plants found in the highlands of central Mexico, the Mexican state of Oaxaca, and Guatemala, as well as along the Río Balsas drainage on the Pacific slopes of central Mexico. Around 3000 B.C.E., the modern species of maize first appeared, probably in the highlands of central Mexico or in the Río Balsas drainage (this, too, is hotly disputed) and then diffused to the rest of the Americas where it quickly was adapted to exceptionally diverse environments. It may have been cultivated simultaneously in various regions, because current evidence indicates maize pollen is found by 3000 B.C.E. from the highlands of Mexico to the Maya lowlands. In the small nation of Guatemala, one of the oldest centers of maize cultivation and with many niche environments, there still are more varieties of maize than in the entire United States.

Cultivated Plants

Domesticated maize was incorporated into the Mesoamerican diet late in the Archaic Period, and cultivated plants thereafter became an increasingly important part of the diet. Richard MacNeish's study of Tehuacan caves in highland Mexico indicates that cultivated crops increased from 5 percent of the diet in the mid-Archaic Period to 75 percent by 600 C.E. The introduction of domesticated maize, one of the world's most nutritious and productive cereal crops, into the fertile lowland Mesoamerican environment would have given the villagers a food surplus, albeit a surplus that required some labor in cutting, burning, and exploiting wetlands to achieve. However some wetland areas, such as the precocious settlements on the Pacific littoral that gave rise to the Isthmian tradition, seem to have relied very little on maize initially, as the small cob was not that obvious a nutritious substitute for shellfish and tubers. Archaeologists have suggested that in such instances the small cob of the early cultivar was used to produce beer, not tamales—both would have been good protein sources, but the beer would have provided a special incentive for maize cultivation even in food-rich environments. Eventually, domesticated maize was adapted throughout Mesoamerica, producing food surpluses in wetland areas. This food surplus boosted the New World on the path toward civilization.

In the Maya area, pollen core samples indicate the presence of another cultivar, manioc—a root crop akin to the sweet potato—around 3500 B.C.E., a time when the forest cover was still quite high and dense. Manioc was a valuable supplement to other food resources, particularly because it was drought resistant. Unlike maize it could not sustain sizable populations, but it may have been the primary cultivar of the early Barra Phase villages discovered along the Pacific coast and dated to c. 1600 B.C.E. Thereafter, maize was increasingly cultivated in the rich coastal environment, and as the population grew, these Maya began to exploit the broader and flatter uplands for agriculture. Seasonal ponds and volcanic ash–enriched soils may have enabled the coastal Maya to produce three crops a year, accounting for the luxury items and stratified classes of the

Ocós culture that gave rise to the earliest Pre-classic cities in the southern Maya area.

Early Intensive Agriculture

Although some Maya remained content with their fishing villages, there is evidence for intensive agriculture being practiced in parts of the lowlands at a surprisingly early date. By 1650 B.C.E., maize cultivation had transformed the environment around the New River area of Belize where the forest had been burned and cut, then replaced by house gardens or farms. In this same region, Pulltrouser Swamp was transformed into elaborate field systems as early as 1000 B.C.E.; these systems controlled water through ditches and canals. In addition, there is some evidence the ditches were used to raise and trap fish. By the middle Archaic Period, then, the Maya were living in the lowlands, and by the end of the Early Preclassic, some of them were manipulating wetlands for the intensive cultivation of crops.

Location of Early Maya Villages

Once maize agriculture was adopted throughout the Maya region, by at least 800 B.C.E., nucleated villages and sophisticated pottery became the norm from the Pacific to the Gulf coast, from the southern highlands to the northern lowlands, and from Tabasco, Mexico, to the Motagua Valley in Honduras. Trade, not necessarily migration, could account for the shared ceramics and other artifacts. And trade was essential: Peoples living in the tropical lowlands required large quantities of salt in their diet, and salt was produced primarily in the coastal areas and most especially in northern Yucatán. Obsidian from the highlands and chert, from a variety of areas, also were traded for tools. The first complex settlements were situated to exploit resources and trade routes. By 700 B.C.E., the different early ceramic styles began to merge into the Mamom Ceramic Complex, and, whenever and whoever first settled the earliest lowland villages, the settlement of the entire Maya region and the homogenization of Maya culture was well under way.

PLACE-NAMES OF MAYA CITIES

The following listing includes most of the Maya cities mentioned in the Handbook. For more details regarding the context in which these cities developed, see Chapter 2.

Abaj Takalik

Also known as Piedra Parada and Santa Margarita, this Guatemalan site is located on the Pacific slope, where it developed a system of agricultural terraces. Sculpture indicates close ties with the Olmec culture during the Middle Preclassic Period. During the Late Preclassic Period, the site carved Izapan-style monuments with some of the earliest known Long Count dates.

Aguateca

Aguateca was one of the twin capitals, along with Dos Pilas (see below), of the Petexbatún kingdom that rose to power in the Pasión

River region of the southern lowlands during the Late Classic Period. The fortified city was besieged and destroyed in 790 during some of the most devastating warfare known in Maya history.

Altar de Sacrificios

At the confluence of the Pasión and Usumacinta Rivers, Altar de Sacrificios was one of the earliest settlements in the lowlands; an architectural platform at the site dates from the Middle Preclassic Period. Although it was occupied through the Classic Period when it erected carved and dated monuments, the city had a lot of competitors along this trade route during the Late Classic Period, including the Petexbatún kingdom and Yaxchilán. Like Seibal (see below), the site was occupied for a while during the Terminal Classic Period before being abandoned.

Altun Há

Near the Caribbean coast of northern Belize, this site endured from 1000 B.C.E. until the end of the Late Classic Period, probably because of its fertile agricultural lands and year-round supplies of water. It is best known for the jade caches found in its tombs. Buildings and burials at the site were desecrated during the collapse.

Becán

In southern Campeche, Becán was one of the largest cities during the Late Classic Period in the Chenes–Río Bec region. The city had a long history, reaching back into the Middle Preclassic Period, and probably controlled trade across the Yucatán between its two coasts. During the Late Preclassic Period, it constructed major buildings and fortified itself with ramparts and a moat toward the end of that period, after which it was depopulated. The city revived in the fourth century C.E., perhaps through ties with the trade network forged by the central Mexican city of Teotihuacan (see under "Tikal" below). It is speculated that Becán and other cities in the area may have been under the hegemony of the nearby colossus, Calakmul, during the Late Classic Period, because no dynastic stelae or inscriptions have been recovered for southern Campeche except at Calakmul. Becán continued to function after Calakmul's collapse, but its ceramics indicate ties with northern Yucatán. By the 11th century, however, the city was no longer occupied.

Bilbao   See COTZUMALGUAPA.

Bonampak

A modest-size Classic Period city in the Usumacinta region, Bonampak was alternately dominated by nearby Piedras Negras and Yaxchilán. The site is world famous for its series of narrative murals that cover the walls of three rooms, revealing details about palace life and rituals of warfare in the eighth-century world of the Maya.

Calakmul

Judging from its massive buildings and more than 115 stelae, Calakmul was an important political power from the Late Preclassic Period until early in the ninth century C.E. Located just north of the Petén in the Mexican state of Campeche, Calakmul was surrounded by abundant sources of water, which it converted into reservoirs for irrigation and drinking water to sustain its core population that reached approximately 60,000 in the Late Classic Period. Excavations in the last two decades and the decipherment of hieroglyphs have revealed the ancient city was known as Kaan (snake). In the Late Preclassic, it constructed one of the more massive complexes known for the Maya lowlands of that period, but it probably was one of the several important cities ruled by El Mirador. In the seventh century, Calakmul was probably the most politically powerful city in the central region. Calakmul oversaw the installation of rulers at other large cities such as Dos Pilas, Naranjo, El Perú, and Cancuén, and it developed an elaborate system of alliances, some through marriage. The importance of these marital alliances might be inferred from the frequent depiction of queens in the art of the city. At its apogee, Calakmul ruled over a region with an estimated population of more than 400,000. Its constant warring with Tikal gradually eroded its power, beginning with the defeat of Calakmul's Lord Jaguar Paw Smoke in 695. In 810, the city carved its last dated monument.

Cancuén

On the Río Pasión near the foothills of the Guatemala highlands, Cancuén was well situated for trade between the highlands and Petén region. During the Late Classic Period, the city grew in importance through marriage alliances with Dos Pilas, which was 55 kilometers (34 miles) downstream, and Calakmul. Although the city is known from mentions in the hieroglyphic texts, excavations began at the site only in 2000. The initial clearing and survey work revealed the Classic Period city was 10 times larger than previously believed.

Caracol

Located in western Belize, Caracol constructed some monumental buildings during the Late Preclassic Period, but it was not an important city until the sixth century C.E. It was subjugated by Tikal in the Early Classic Period, but it later formed an alliance with Calakmul and defeated Tikal in 562. In the seventh century, the city center was inhabited by 40,000 Maya, but greater Caracol had an estimated population of more than 120,000. Its substantial satellite centers and agricultural terraces were connected to the center by paved causeways, forming an unusual radial city plan. In 680, the city was attacked but not subjugated by Naranjo; it nonetheless went into a century-long decline. The city revived during the Terminal Classic Period, but its sacred center was burned and abandoned by 900.

Cerén

The so-called Pompeii of the New World, this farming village just north of what is now San Salvador was buried by an eruption of Loma Caldera around 600. The thick layer of volcanic ash preserved materials normally too perishable to be recovered by archaeologists; plaster casts of the ash-entombed gardens and household goods have revealed details about the daily lives of rural farmers in the ancient Maya world. The village was on the periphery of the ancient city of San Andrés.

Cerros

A Late Preclassic site in northern Belize, Cerros was a trading port on the Caribbean. It is especially noteworthy for the stucco masks on the facade of its main ceremonial building. Although it never went through another building phase after c. 250 C.E., artifacts found at the site indicate Cerros was reused during the Terminal Classic Period.

Chalchuapa

These Preclassic Period ruins, located in the Río Paz drainage in western El Salvador, are known also as El Trapiche, and a later occupation is known as Tazumal (see below). Chalchuapa was an important trade center along the Isthmian route, probably because of its control of nearby obsidian sources. By the Middle Preclassic Period, it displayed symbols of considerable power, including Olmec-style boulder carvings and a large pyramid. Before the Maya were forced to abandon Chalchuapa with the eruption of Volcán Ilopango c. 250 C.E., the city had grown quite substantial with nearly 60 large structures and fields of agricultural terraces.

Chichén Itzá

Meaning "the mouth of the well of the Itzá," Chichén Itzá was the most important Postclassic Period Maya city. Located in central Yucatán, the inland city nonetheless controlled ports on the northern tip of the lowlands as well as the Río Lagartos salt flats, the largest in Mesoamerica. The city influenced most cities in northern Yucatán. Its core population has been estimated at 50,000. The last Maya city to carve its history into stone, Chichén Itzá left for posterity the name of its great ruler, K'ak'upakal (Fire-His-Shield). Based on the valuable trade items dredged from its sacred well, the city controlled much of the maritime trade around the Yucatán Peninsula and even into southern Central America, where it obtained the first large quantities of gold found in Mesoamerica. Although the city was abandoned as a political center by c. 1100, for reasons not well understood, the sacred well of the Itzá remained a pilgrimage center until after the Spanish Conquest.

Chunchucmil

This large Classic Period site is estimated to have had a population of 40,000 to 60,000 c. 800, but without the impressive architecture associated with an important political or religious center. It is believed to have been a transshipment center between the Gulf of Mexico and Puuc cities in the Yucatán. Although the poor agricultural potential of its location meant it could not grow enough crops for its population, it was situated next to the second largest salt flats in Mesoamerica. The site was destroyed during the Terminal Classic Period, perhaps by rivals at Chichén Itzá.

Cobá

An important northern lowland city from the Late Preclassic until the Late Postclassic Period, Cobá may have controlled one of the largest Maya territories, based on its 16 paved causeways, one of which was 100 kilometers (62 miles) long and connected it with the city of Yaxuná (see below). Cobá had an unusually wet environment for the northern region and was situated next to five shallow lakes; its agriculture apparently could sustain the city's peak population of 70,000 to 125,000. Cobá's Classic Period architecture and many carved stelae with Long Count dates demonstrate its strong

ties with the southern lowlands, and those ties were probably facilitated by maritime trade from the nearby Caribbean port of Xel Há.

Colhá

On the Río Hondo in northern Belize, the site produced highly sought-after tools from a nearby source of chert. Its control of the valuable commodity led to its early development in the Middle Preclassic Period; occupation of the site continued into the Terminal Classic. Excavators discovered a massive pit burial dating to c. 900 of elite individuals. Whether their violent end was brought about by an invasion or uprising is unknown, but the site was reoccupied during the Early Postclassic.

Copán

Located near the Motagua River valley in Honduras, Copán controlled a fertile valley and nearby sources of jade from Preclassic times. The city grew in importance in the fifth century C.E., after Yax K'uk Mo was installed as the founder of a new dynasty by Tikal and the central Mexican city of Teotihuacan. The major economic and political power on the eastern frontier of the Maya region, Copán controlled Quiriguá and numerous other sites in the Motagua Valley and had close ties with Tazumal and other cities in the broader region of El Salvador and Honduras. Copán was defeated by its dependency and center, Quiriguá, in 738 but revived under later kings. Its last ruler was Yax Pas (Rising Sun), son of a Palenque princess, who acceded to the throne in 763. Its population of 25,000 was the densest for any Maya city. The city was abandoned during the Classic Period collapse, but outlying settlements and farms remained occupied for another century or so.

Cotzumalguapa

Several Terminal Classic sites, Bilbao and El Baúl among them, are scattered around the region of the modern city of Santa Lucía Cotzumalguapa on the Pacific littoral of Guatemala and known under that designation. For many years, many of the sculpted monuments were located on private sugar *fincas* (plantations), but they now have been moved to a museum. The area has only recently been studied more thoroughly as a cultural region. Early examples of Maya writing and art, from the Late Preclassic, are found in this region. Recent studies suggest that in the Terminal Classic Period, the area formed a political state that extended into the central highlands in order to control obsidian sources, when Cotzumalguapa participated in the pan-Mesoamerican trade horizon from 800 to 1000.

Cuello

Located in northern Belize, Cuello is an important site archaeologically because of its early and continuous occupation beginning in the Archaic Period and continuing through the development of Classic Period Maya civilization. Its architecture, including a platform dating to 1000 B.C.E., is some of the earliest and most securely dated in the Maya lowlands.

Dos Pilas

The Late Classic Period city of Dos Pilas was located in the Pasión River area of the southern lowlands. Founded by a disgruntled branch of the Tikal dynasty, the new city allied itself with Tikals enemy, Calakmul, and grew rapidly. Although Dos Pilas, along with Aguateca, became the capital of the large Petexbatún kingdom fused together by war, the mercurial rise of Dos Pilas in the middle of the seventh century was followed by wars of annihilation and total collapse in 761.

Dzibilchaltún

In northwestern Yucatán, this site was continuously occupied from the Late Preclassic Period through the Late Postclassic, probably because of its large cenote, or natural well, and location near the coastal trade route. It was densely populated only during the Late and Terminal Classic Periods, when it had an estimated population of more than 25,000. Although large, its architecture was never especially monumental. Initially, the city had strong ties with the southern lowlands and participated in the stela cult.

Edzná

Located near the modern city of Campeche, Edzná undertook the construction of one of the largest public projects in the ancient Maya world during the Late Preclassic Period: a vast system of canals and artificial fields. The canals were deep and wide enough for canoe transport and must have been a source of fish as well as alluvial fill for intensive agriculture. One canal formed a moat around most of the site. The city participated in the stela cult in the Early Classic Period, but its rulers were most active in erecting stelae in the tradition of the southern lowlands from 633 until 810. After the Classic Period collapse, Edzná remained an important city but its cultural and economic focus shifted to the northern lowlands, where some of its local architectural traits may have influenced the development of the Puuc style. Edzná was wealthy, powerful, and enduring, but its role in the development of the Maya civilization is not well understood. It was abandoned in the Early Postclassic.

Ek Balam

A relatively large site in northern Yucatán that was occupied as early as the Middle Preclassic Period, it flourished during the Late and Terminal Classic Periods. Five causeways linked an area of more than 12 square kilometers (4.6 square miles), and its massive acropolis rose 31 meters (93 feet) high and covered an area almost the size of two football fields—160 meters (528 feet) in length and 70 meters (231 feet) wide. The city shared some cultural traits with the southern lowlands and the Chenes region, including an elaborate carved stucco facade. The last dated inscriptions at the site were in 841, but the city's emblem glyph is mentioned in a ceremony at Chichén Itzá in 870. The city constructed some of the most massive fortifications in the northern lowlands, but it was invaded and defeated by 1000.

El Baúl   See COTZUMALGUAPA.

El Mirador

El Mirador, located in the north central Petén, was probably the greatest political power in the lowlands during the Late Preclassic Period. Raised causeways radiated from the city to some of the other largest cities in the lowlands, including Nakbé, Wakná, and Tintal, all of which may

have been subjugated by El Mirador. The construction of the *sacbeob* would have involved great numbers of laborers: The causeway to Nakbé alone was 13 kilometers (8 miles) long. But these undertakings are diminished by the size of the Danta complex, which was the largest building ever constructed by the ancient Maya (see Chapter 8). And the Danta complex was joined by other massive buildings, such as El Tigre. El Mirador declined in power during the Late Preclassic hiatus (see Chapter 2), and the site was virtually abandoned by c. 400, its power usurped most likely by Tikal and nearby Calakmul. In the Late Classic Period, artisans occupied El Mirador and, along with inhabitants at Nakbé, produced polychrome vases painted with fine black lines in the codex style (see photo 6.8, page 184); many were commissioned by Calakmul.

El Perú

A Classic Period city in the central Petén, El Perú was situated between the two powerful states of Dos Pilas and Calakmul and became part of the struggle between Tikal and Calakmul. The site is known mainly through inscriptions on its monuments, most of which have been looted. The texts suggest El Perú was conquered by Teotihuacan eight days before that central Mexican city took over Tikal in 378. El Perú was probably then integrated into the resulting trade network centered at Tikal during the Early Classic Period. In the Late Classic, however, the city was well integrated into the Calakmul alliance.

El Portón

Set in the north central highlands of Guatemala near the modern town of Rabinal, El Portón straddled the Chixoy River route that led from the highlands into the Río Pasión area of the lowlands. The site has yielded Middle Preclassic treasures, including rich tombs and sculptures carved with some of the earliest examples of Mesoamerican writing (c. 400 B.C.E.). The area was occupied through subsequent periods, and in the Late Postclassic Period, Pokomam Maya who were incorporated into the Quiché kingdom, lived there.

Iximché

A Late Postclassic fortified hill town, Iximché is located in the Guatemala highlands. Once part of the Quiché kingdom, the Cakchiquel Maya founded Iximché as an independent city in 1470. Although the Quiché and Cakchiquel occasionally consulted with each other and jointly performed rituals, competition between the two highland groups persisted until the Spanish Conquest in 1524, when the Cakchiquel allied themselves with the Spaniards in order to defeat their Quiché Maya rivals. Pedro de Alvarado established the first European capital at this city, but when the Cakchiquel rebelled against him and cut off supplies, the city was burned and abandoned. Contemporary Cakchiquel make pilgrimages to the site.

Izapa

A center on the Pacific littoral in Chiapas, Mexico, near the Guatemalan border, Izapa was a participant in the early Isthmian trade and, by the Late Preclassic Period, it was a major cultural center, giving its name to a sculptural style that developed at this time. The style, fluid and naturalistic, was used to depict rulers and mythological scenes alike. The style can be found on stelae in much of the southern region, and a few instances have been found in the northern and southern lowlands as well. Although Izapa was occupied into the Classic Period, it was no longer as important.

Kabah

A Terminal Classic Period site in the Puuc region, Kabah is famous for the building known as the Codz Pop, its facade completely covered with masks of the long-nosed rain god Chak. A dependency of Uxmal (see below), Kabah was connected to Uxmal by a plastered causeway 14.5 kilometers (9 miles) in length. The beginning of the *sacbe* was marked by a freestanding corbeled arch. The name of the Uxmal ruler Lord Chak is inscribed on a Kabah platform.

Kaminaljuyú

One of the most powerful Preclassic cities, Kaminaljuyú occupied the highland valley now occupied by Guatemala City. Situated only 20 kilometers (12 miles) from one of the most important obsidian sources in the Maya region, Kaminaljuyú grew from a small Middle Preclassic Period settlement into the dominant city in the southern region during the Late Preclassic. Its construction included extensive canals and earthen pyramids; its rulers were buried in some of the wealthiest tombs then known; and its art included many stelae in the Izapan style. At the beginning of the Early Classic Period, the city contracted and was depopulated until the central Mexican city of Teotihuacan probably conquered it in the fourth century C.E. and used it as a base for its trade operations in the region. The city was occupied into the Postclassic Period, but after the Early Classic Period, it never rose again to be a major power. It was abandoned by the time of the Spanish Conquest.

Komchén

Controlling the salt flats in northwestern Yucatán, Komchén grew in size and importance in the Late Classic Period when its product was traded to centers in the southern lowlands. It was the largest site in the northern lowlands during the Late Preclassic Period. It was abandoned during the hiatus at the end of the period, replaced by other local powers, particularly Dzibilchaltún, which was expanding nearby.

La Blanca

One of the largest sites on the Pacific slope during the Preclassic Period, La Blanca was situated on the Lower Río Naranjo near salt flats on the coast. In the Middle Preclassic Period, it constructed one of the highest pyramids (25 meters, or 82.5 feet) in Mesoamerica and was almost as large as La Venta. The city was abandoned in the Late Preclassic Period.

Lamanai

From its site in northern Belize, Lamanai participated in the evolution of Maya culture from the Preclassic until the 17th century. By 700 B.C.E., Lamanai had constructed a dock on the easily navigated New River in northern Belize to capitalize on trade from the Caribbean into the Petén. The city also built raised fields in a local lagoon and was agriculturally self-sustaining. It never grew to prominence but had strong ties with the Petén until the ninth century C.E. Unlike its neighbors, it survived the Classic Period collapse and was a vigorous settlement through the Postclassic Period, when it had ties to the northern lowlands and the coastal trade route. The Spaniards built a church at the city in 1570, but the site was too remote for the foreigners to control. In 1670, the Maya were still at Lamanai—some lived in the church and buried their dead there—but the community would soon be disturbed by British loggers in search of mahogany.

La Milpa

In western Belize near the Guatemalan border, La Milpa was a modest site during the Early Classic Period. It nonetheless buried one of its kings, c. 400, with fine jade jewelry. The site was abandoned for about 200 years following c. 500, around the time of the Tikal hiatus, but it was resettled and flourished c. 750–850, when its old and new buildings were combined to create a perfect quadripartite cosmogram and the population reached 50,000.

Mayapán

Meaning "standard of the Maya," Mayapán was the centralized state controlling most of northern Yucatán from c. 1220 to c. 1450. It also was the last monumental Maya city constructed in the lowlands, even though the dimensions of the buildings, some of which were inspired by those at Chichén Itzá, were considerably less impressive than those of its predecessors. The city, with approximately 15,000 inhabitants, was densely packed within a defensive wall that was 8 kilometers (5 miles) in circumference and 2 meters (6.6 feet) high. Ruled by the Cocom, an Itzá lineage, the city forced the nobility of other cities to live within the wall in order to guarantee tribute payments. Before the city was destroyed by a coup led by the rival Xiu lineage, it probably controlled much of the trade around the Yucatán Peninsula.

Mixco Viejo

In the Rabinal region, Mixco Viejo is the best preserved citadel in the Guatemalan highlands that dates to the Late Postclassic Period. The region, inhabited by the Pokomam Maya, was conquered by the Quiché in the 14th century. The fortified town of 120 structures was built on a hilltop surrounded by unusually steep ravines. The Spaniards had considerable difficulty conquering the city because of its naturally defensive location.

Naco

A Late Postclassic Period port, Naco was one of the most thriving Maya cities at the time of the Spanish Conquest, when its population was more than 10,000. Its location on the Río Chalmelcón north of Copán and just south of the Bay of Honduras was strategic for trade in obsidian and cacao and for transshipments from the Caribbean to the Pacific.

Nakbé

In the Mirador Basin region of the Petén, Nakbé was probably occupied by 1400 B.C.E., but between 900 and 500 B.C.E., it constructed the earliest known city in the Maya lowlands. The shape and function of many of its public and ritual buildings became standard at later Maya cities (see Chapter 8), and these buildings were the most monumental in the entire Maya region during the Middle Preclassic Period. Nakbé was overshadowed by nearby El Mirador (see above) in the Late Preclassic Period, but it did erect one of the earliest stelae in the lowlands at that time. It was a minor site during the Classic Period, when it produced codex-style vases, some of which are the best-known Maya polychrome vases from the Late Classic Period (see figures 6.8, page 184, and 6.9, page 186).

Naranjo

A Classic Period city, Naranjo was situated between the Mopán and Holmul Rivers in the Petén, with easy access to trade routes and fertile valleys. It was constantly subjugated by stronger states, Tikal and Caracol among them. But late in the seventh century, under the auspices of yet another important city, Calakmul, Naranjo revived under Lady Six Sky, one of the four known Maya women rulers. Apparently never given the opportunity to enjoy peace, the city nonetheless is well known because of its sculpture and hieroglyphic inscriptions. By 830, its history ended.

Palenque

Because of 20th-century tourism, Palenque is one of the best-known Classic Period cities, but it was neither the largest nor among the most powerful of polities. Yet its exceptionally graceful sculptural and architectural style has come to define the apogee of Maya art and its extensive hieroglyphic texts permitted the first phonetic reading of a Maya king's name, that of Hanab Pakal, whose jade-laden tomb was the first ever discovered within a Maya pyramid (see Chapter 7). The city's inscriptions, perhaps the most thoroughly deciphered for any Maya city, have been critical in recent understandings of ancient Maya civilization. They also name two women rulers. On the edge of the Chiapas highlands and near the Usumacinta drainage, Palenque overlooked the broad, flat plain spreading to the Gulf of Mexico. Palenque's name in the hieroglyphic texts,

Lacamhá (Big Water), derived from the five rivers that coursed through the site and the more than 30 springs that supplied the residences and plazas terraced into the steep hills. Palenque constructed canals, drains, and even underground aqueducts to control and best utilize the water streaming through its city. The beauty of the city disguised much of the wartime bloodshed that perhaps gave the regional state it controlled the name of B'aakal (Bone). Palenque's domain included various cities during its history, among them Pomoná, Tortuguero, and Comalcalco near the Gulf of Mexico. Palenque fought with its powerful Usumacinta neighbors, including Piedras Negras and Toniná, and as an ally of Tikal, it also suffered conflicts with Calakmul. It was abandoned by the early ninth century.

Piedras Negras

The largest city on the Usumacinta River, Piedras Negras was founded in the Early Classic Period and spread over broad terraces set high above the river. Its history, well documented on sculpted monuments, involved see-sawing power struggles with Yaxchilán, located downstream. But in the late seventh century, its domain included Yaxchilán, as well as Bonampak, and the city had diplomatic ties with Calakmul. New excavations at the site in the 21st century should result in a fuller understanding of such an important ancient city. The last monument was erected no later than 810; soon thereafter the city was burned, and its royal throne, smashed.

Quiriguá

Founded as a colony of Copán (see above) in the fourth century, Quiriguá was a modest site with great agricultural and trade potential at its location near the Motagua River. After revolting against Copán, Quiriguá built an impressive sacred center with some of the largest sculptures in the Maya world, including the tallest stela, rising almost 8 meters (26 feet) above ground, anchored 2.5 meters (8 feet) into the ground, and weighing 60 metric tons (66 tons). Quiriguá was abandoned during the Classic Period collapse but was soon reoccupied because of its strategic river location. Items found at the site, especially a *chac mool* sculpture, suggest the city was participating in the new pan-Mesoamerican trade that was dominated by Chichén Itzá.

Río Azul

This northern Petén site was strategically located by a river used for transport from Belize into the interior of the southern lowlands. It also engaged in intensive raised field agriculture. Occupied from 1000 B.C.E. until 1000 C.E., the site's fortunes apparently rose and fell with those of Tikal, flourishing during the Early Classic with public architecture and carved monuments, surviving a hiatus, and then reviving. During the Late Classic Period, it was mostly a small residential site with a population of 3,500.

Santa Rita

On the Bay of Chetumal, Santa Rita was occupied from Middle Preclassic times until 1531, when it was the capital of the province of Chetumal and known for its abundant production of honey and cacao. Most of the site has been lost to the modern town of Corozal, Belize.

Sayil

A Terminal Classic Period city in the Puuc region of Yucatán, Sayil is known for its elegant multi-storied palace (see figure 8.5). In fact, it had many elite residences and was a substantial center, although it probably was a secondary site within the domain of Uxmal. Its population, including the suburbs, was about 17,000. Excavations at the site suggest that around the time of the city's abandonment, the dense population was about to extend beyond the carrying capacity of the land.

Seibal

A lowland city with a long but checkered history, Seibal was located along the Río Pasión. Sparsely inhabited in the Middle Preclassic Period, when it showed signs of Olmec contacts, Seibal also was occupied, and flourishing, after the collapse of other southern lowland cities in the ninth century. Its period of greatest development was the Late Classic, but it was subjugated by Dos Pilas in 735 when one of its rulers was captured by the Petexbatún kingdom. After the collapse of that kingdom, Seibal revived and constructed numerous stelae and buildings between 830 and 930, when it apparently was abandoned. Archaeologists have speculated whether Seibal was occupied by outsiders who then conquered the Maya lowlands, but recent hieroglyphic readings suggest the ninth-century dynasty was installed by another lowland site, that of Ucanal, about which little is known. What is certain is that Terminal Classic Seibal participated in a pan-Mesoamerican trade network that typified those Maya cities that survived the Classic Period collapse.

Tayasal (Tah Itzá)

Tayasal (a Spanish corruption of Tah Itzá) is best known as the Late Postclassic island refuge of the Itzá fleeing from the collapse of Mayapán in northern Yucatán. But there is reason to believe the island capital was occupied earlier, after the fall of Chichén Itzá. Located where Flores is today in the Petén lakes region, Tayasal was the last Maya kingdom to be conquered by the Spaniards. It flourished in the remote but agriculturally fertile area of Lake Petén Itzá and grew into a substantial settlement of 25,000 after the conquest, when other Maya fled the Spaniards. Not until 1697, when Kan Ek', the ruler of Tayasal, was captured by the Spanish, did ancient Maya civilization finally end.

Tazumal

Located on the site of Chalchuapa (see above), Tazumal represents the reoccupation of that city after its Late Preclassic Period devastation by a volcanic eruption. The site had extensive ties with Kaminaljuyú in the fifth century, but it also produced a style of pottery favored by Copán. The city was occupied until the Spanish Conquest, when Pokomam Maya were known to be its residents.

Tikal

Known as Mutul (Hair Knot) or Yax Mutul (First Hair Knot) in hieroglyphic texts, Tikal was one of the largest and most important Maya cities located in the southern lowlands. Tikal was occupied by 900 B.C.E., but its earliest monumental architecture appeared in the Late Preclassic Period. Tikal spread the stela cult through the Petén and was the first city in that region to inscribe a stela with a Long Count date; during its history, it produced more than 200 carved stelae and altars. In the Early Classic Period, Tikal controlled a large kingdom that dominated politics and trade in the central Petén region and influenced events as far away as Copán in Honduras and Palenque in Mexico. In fact, the dynasty that carved out this sphere of influence had been installed by the central Mexican city of Teotihuacan in 378. Tikal was also conquered by Caracol in 562 but revived in the Late Classic Period when it was once again one of the largest and most powerful cities of the lowlands. The population of greater Tikal has been estimated at 70,000, but with it rural residents included, its population approached 125,000 and the region it controlled through alliances may have reached 400,000.

Toniná

Surrounded by the Chiapas foothills, Toniná bordered the lowlands of the Usumacinta region just 65 kilometers (40 miles) from Palenque and participated fully in lowland Maya civilization, erecting stelae that commemorated its dynastic history during the Late Classic Period. One great feat of its dynasty was Lord B'aaknal Chak's capture of Palenque's ruler, K'an Hoy Chitam, in 711. The last known Long Count date of 909 was recorded at Toniná. Broken monuments suggest that the city met with a violent end soon thereafter.

Tulum

Perched above the Caribbean on the Yucatán coast, this Late Postclassic town is one of the best preserved from the period, and remnants of a defensive wall still surround the site on the interior land side. Tulum was one of many petty coastal states that participated in the maritime trade that extended from Central America to central Mexico. Some of the decorative motifs and architectural colonnades recall earlier Chichén Itzá and contemporary Mayapán, but the scale is so small as to be shrinelike rather than imposing. Murals dating to the 15th century indicate two styles: one traditionally Maya and the other in the pan-Mesoamerican Mixteca-Puebla style favored by the Aztecs. One mural was painted late enough to depict a Spanish horse.

Uaxactún

A central Petén city that rivaled Tikal during the Late Preclassic Period, Uaxactún built important ritual structures and carved giant stucco facades. But Uaxactún's future was usurped by its proximity to Tikal, which determined much of its destiny from the fourth century until the eighth. Only toward the end of the Classic Period did Uaxactún once again carve its own monuments and proclaim its independence from Tikal.

Ucanal

A Classic Period city in the eastern Petén, the site remains something of a mystery due to lack of excavations. Nonetheless, its monuments and those at the sites of Caracol, Naranjo, and Seibal suggest that it was an important political power, especially during the Terminal Classic Period when it installed a new dynasty at Seibal.

Utatlán

Originally called K'umarcaaj by the Quiché Maya, the capital was called Utatlán by the

Nahuatl-speaking central Mexicans who accompanied Pedro de Alvarado to Guatemala in 1524. Both names mean "place of the old reeds." In the central highlands of Guatemala, Utatlán was the Late Postclassic citadel of the Quiché ruling elite beginning c. 1400, when it was founded by the legendary ruler K'ucumatz (Feathered Serpent). By the late 15th century, the city ruled a substantial domain that included all of the central highlands of Guatemala and ranged to the Motagua River and down to the Pacific coast. Although the city was burned and evacuated by the Spanish conquistador Pedro de Alvarado, its descendants remained in the region and parts of the ruined site are pilgrimage shrines for many Quiché who inhabit nearby Santa Cruz del Quiché. Chichicastenango, the market town and center for the region, was where the *Popol Vuh*, the famous Quiché manuscript about creation and the founding of the kingdom, was discovered in 1701.

Uxmal

Located in the Puuc Hills of Yucatán, Uxmal was the capital of this region, which flourished during the Terminal Classic Period. The region supported earlier settlements, such as Kiuic (400 B.C.E.) and the city of Chak (Early Classic Period), but it did not rise to prominence before 800 C.E. The region may have developed late, despite its fertile soil, because of the lack of year-round sources of water: the dense populations of the Terminal Classic Period constructed *chultunes*, or artificial underground cisterns. Uxmal is a major tourist destination today, much admired for its exquisite veneer architecture covered with abstract mosaic friezes composed of thousands of finely cut pieces. Its Puuc architectural style spread throughout the region and is found at what are believed to be the secondary sites of Labná, Kabah, and Sayil. Although there are few

hieroglyphic texts or stelae from the site, those that exist celebrate the late ninth-century reign of Lord Chak and mention a political relationship with Chichén Itzá.

Xunatunich

Formerly known as Benque Viejo, the site was occupied by the Late Preclassic Period and survived into the 10th century C.E. One of the largest sites in the Belize River valley, Xunatunich sat on a ridge at the headwaters of the river near the Guatemala border. The city constructed a pyramid-temple 38 meters (127 feet) high and covered its facade with an elaborate stucco frieze, probably around 250 C.E. In the Late Classic Period, the site had an alliance of some sort with Naranjo in the Petén, and it erected its only dated stela in 849, when it is speculated that refugees from Naranjo may have occupied a palace complex. Excavations found evidence of earthquake damage at the site around the time of the Classic Period collapse.

Yaxchilán

This important Classic Period Usumacinta capital is built into the terraces and hills that rise above the river, and judging from remnants of what may have been a bridge crossing the river, the city may have occupied both banks. Its exceptionally fine and numerous sculptural monuments, many of them erected by two rulers best known as Shield Jaguar the Great and Bird Jaguar the Great, depict a militaristic history unusual in its emphasis even for the Late Classic Period. Located 32 kilometers (20 miles) upstream from Piedras Negras, many of the city's vicissitudes resulted from conflicts with its neighbor. To maintain its hegemony, Yaxchilán entered into many marital alliances, such as one with a royal woman from Motul de San José in the Petén. The city was also unusual in the prestige granted some of its queens: These rulers' wives were repeatedly depicted in the art of the city and, in one instance, appeared to have had a separate palace.

Yaxuná

Yaxuná, a moderate-size city in central Yucatán with a long history beginning in the Late Preclassic Period, when it constructed a monumental pyramid 18 meters (60 feet) tall, and shared many characteristics with sites to the south. Early Classic Period burials suggest influences from Teotihuacan. During the Terminal Classic Period, the city was linked to Cobá (see above) by the longest *sacbe* known—100 kilometers (62 miles)—but this did not prevent it from being attacked and destroyed, probably by Chichén Itzá.

READING

Dunning 1996, Sharer 1994, Wallace 1997: environmental diversity and natural resources; Dewey, et al. 1979, Dunning, et al. 2000, Tourtellot and Hammond 2000: changing environment; Adams 1977, Ford 1996, Hansen, et al. 2000: environment and civilization; Andrews V 1990, Ashmore 1981, Hammond 1978, Justeson, Norman, et al. 1985, Leyden 1984, Vaughan, et al. 1985: settlement; Beadle 1972, MacNeish 1970–1974, MacNeish and Eubanks 2000, Mangelsdorf 1974, Pohl, et al. 1996: maize; Dunning, et al. 2000, Culbert, et al. 1990, Fedick 1996, Harrison and Turner 1978, Pohl 1985: early agriculture and resource control; Fedick 1996, Turner and Sanders 1992: gardens and diet.

4

SOCIETY AND GOVERNMENT

The ancient Maya were united by a shared ideology and worldview, but they never were unified into a single political state. There was no Maya empire comparable to ancient Rome, and there was no single centralized authority equivalent to the Egyptian pharaoh. There were, instead, numerous substantial Maya cities, and many of these cities were independent polities. The challenge for the Mayanist has been to understand the sociopolitical nature of these cities and what, if any, relationship they had to one another.

CHIEFDOMS VS. STATES

The issue of whether Maya cities were chiefdoms or more developed states is a question rooted in the complexity of society and the nature of centralized authority necessary to govern that society. (See "Sociopolitical Evolution of the Maya State" below.) Through most of the 20th century, archaeologists believed that a complex state-level government could not have arisen in the tropical lowland environment. Because great public projects such as irrigation networks were not needed in the tropics, it was thought, the centralized political authority necessary for state formation could not have developed. Observations of the living Maya also led them to believe that the pre-Columbian Maya were basically a rural people. The Maya, it was argued, never developed beyond many small, equally empowered centers, or chiefdoms, divided into two social classes of the elite and the commoner. As data accumulated from excavations, settlement surveys, and deciphered texts, however, a deeper appreciation of Maya urban society resulted. Mayanists have learned that

from at least the Late Preclassic Period, Maya society was considerably more complex than previously believed, and that by the end of that period, its political organization had developed into preindustrial states.

In 2000, a palace the size of several football fields was discovered at the Classic Period city of Cancuén, a site previously thought to be only one-tenth the size it is now known to be. At the same time, a mapping project at the well-known site of Palenque demonstrated the city's building and population density was two to three times greater than earlier estimates. Every year there are comparable discoveries proving that there remains much to be learned about the Maya sociopolitical order. The intricate relationships among all cities will never be known of course, but for the Classic Period, the decipherment of hieroglyphic texts has provided a level of understanding that never before was thought possible. Not all sites were equal polities, but rather they were arranged into political hierarchies, with some dependencies of others. Whether these hierarchies resulted in a multitude of city-states, numbering around 60 in the late ninth century, or far fewer regional states, is still being debated.

CITIES VS. CEREMONIAL CENTERS

Ceremonial Centers

Until the 1970s, most archaeologists believed that Maya sites had functioned as ceremonial centers for special festivals or markets, and unlike true cities, they had never had a sizable

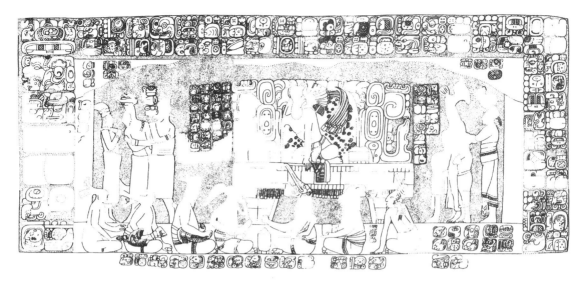

4.1   Piedras Negras Panel 3, eighth century. This badly eroded stone carving demonstrates that Maya nations were organized into a political hierarchy. Ruler 4 of Piedras Negras sits on his throne (center) with kneeling figures below him. The text identifies these subservient individuals as sahals, *or underlords, of various cities and towns in the kingdom of Piedras Negras.*   (Drawing and photo courtesy John Montgomery)

permanent population. The main reason for this misconception was due to inadequate surveying and mapping of Maya sites. Low platforms, especially earthen ones, are hard for surveyors to detect from under centuries of vegetative growth, and the more spectacular architecture of the site core attracted archaeological attention first. Also, Maya cities did not have the street grids or density of modern industrial ones.

The belief in the vacant ceremonial center was compounded by the fact that only the dates and astronomical information of the hieroglyphic texts could be read. This permitted the erroneous impression that the Maya were ruled by priests who lived in the nearly vacant ceremonial centers where they maintained the calendars, observed the movements of stars, and performed rituals that would appease the gods and bring bountiful harvests. The agrarian population, it was thought, would join them in the center for feast days and markets. Under this view, each Maya ceremonial center, surrounded by agricultural land, was a simple independent chiefdom composed of an elite priestly class and a peasantry. Not much centralized authority or bureaucracy was required to administer such theocracies.

Urban Polities

As more evidence accumulated, however, the ceremonial center theory was entirely discredited. Instead of priests concerned only with astrology and ritual, the deciphered texts revealed that Maya rulers, like rulers throughout world history, received tribute, formed alliances, and fought wars. More thorough site surveys demonstrated that Maya sites were far from uninhabited; instead, 80 to 90 percent of all structures were discovered to be residential and crowded enough together to leave no room for

farms anywhere within the city limits. Central Tikal was surrounded by approximately 60 square kilometers (23 square miles) of residential area; Caracol, by 65 square kilometers (25 square miles). And literally thousands of residential structures can still be seen at these cities. The settlement surveys resulted in population estimates for a significant number of cities during the Late Classic Period that were above 20,000 inhabitants, and at least 20 cities had regional populations of 50,000 to more than 125,000. Maya cities were densely populated and intensely engaged in politics.

SOCIOPOLITICAL EVOLUTION OF THE MAYA STATE

Maya sociopolitical organization changed over time, but from the late Archaic Period until the destruction of Maya civilization, society was sharply stratified into at least two classes in which an elite dominated and ruled the majority of Maya. As the population grew in size and number of specialists, so did urbanization and the complexity of the political organization. Development was not always along a forward trajectory, however. There appears to have been a pattern of consolidation into larger kingdoms followed by decentralization. Whether this cycle was due to inherent instability in Maya political organization or to environmental stresses that resulted in periods of population decline and even site abandonment is unclear. The population levels of the Late Preclassic lowland cities were the densest of any period except for the Late Classic. And the powerful centralized states formed during the Late Classic and

Postclassic Periods ended with many petty states.

Under current theories about the functioning of preindustrial states, it appears that the level of social complexity and centralized political authority attained by the Late Preclassic Period and persisting until the Spanish Conquest was, for the most part, that of the political state. The complexity and size of these states was the most impressive, however, from the Late Preclassic through Early Postclassic Periods. These preindustrial states, called archaic states by political scientists, were stratified societies with numerous specialists and a governing central authority capable of controlling great resources of labor, warfare, and tribute. These states controlled territories that involved dependencies and smaller settlements requiring several different tiers of government. Although such sociopolitical characteristics can be difficult to discover archaeologically, both the material remains of Maya civilization and the written record support the view that the ancient Maya lived in such preindustrial states, governed by divine monarchs, not mere chiefs, and a hierarchy of lesser officials.

Chiefdoms

In the Archaic Period and Early Preclassic Periods, Maya settlements on the Pacific coast appear to have become simple chiefdoms in which the shaman-ruler inherited the right to rule. Socially, these chiefdoms were stratified into elite lineages and commoners, as well as specialists, such as potters. There were no large public projects that would require the mobilization of the population. The central and northern areas, meanwhile, were more likely typified by egalitarian fishing villages, not chiefdoms.

In the Middle Preclassic Period, many of these chiefdoms on the Pacific littoral evolved into polities in which the chief ruled over numerous small villages from a capital city. But at the same time, other cities became far more complex urban centers, such as Nakbé in the Petén and Chalchuapa and La Blanca in the southern region. Based on the size of the monumental architecture at such urban centers, the elite class was increasingly wealthy and capable of organizing and directing the large workforce necessary to build masonry complexes (see Chapters 2 and 8). Some of the laborers must have been plaster specialists, stonecutters, and supervisors, suggesting increasing social specialization and political complexity. In the preindustrial world, the rise of complex states was accompanied by the building of such monumental public projects. Some of these cities may have reached the level of incipient state.

Preindustrial States

By the Late Preclassic Period, many Maya sites grew even larger than Nakbé and Chalchuapa. The largest public projects ever undertaken by the ancient Maya—triadic building complexes and canal systems—were constructed during this time period. The Maya elite had solidified their power and wealth in order to build such massive projects: The construction of canals at Kaminaljuyú, for example, may have required 10,000 laborers, and even more at El Mirador (see "Masonry, Architecture, and Labor," Chapter 8). The burials at Kaminaljuyú suggest that sociopolitical position was based on lineage, just as it had been in the early chiefdoms, but the rulers and their elite supporters commanded a far larger and more socially complex territory.

The more powerful cities extended their domains into surrounding areas, and may have ruled over dependencies, substantial in size themselves. Kaminaljuyú is believed to have governed a three-tier political hierarchy of towns and villages in the highlands. It could, and did, call on the labor of surrounding valley towns. El Mirador linked itself with other major lowland cities, including some of the largest in the Late Preclassic Period, such as Nakbé, with raised causeways, and Calakmul, in nearby southern Campeche, seems to have been part of this kingdom as well. Some archaeologists speculate that El Mirador may have been the first Maya regional state. It was the capital of the cities in the Mirador Basin and beyond, and it apparently controlled trade throughout the lowlands. The cultural homogeneity in the lowlands during this period in both Chicanel ceramics and stucco deity facades may be due to El Mirador's influence.

The appearance of hieroglyphic texts and the stela cult suggests that many Late Preclassic cities were being governed by an increasingly centralized authority, but the exact nature of that rulership is presently unclear. It is quite possible that the ruler was selected from any number of elite lineages rather than from a single royal dynasty. El Mirador may have been able to consolidate its authority by including members of the elite class from other cities. At Uaxactún, a *popol nah*, or what was known in the Terminal Classic Period as a council house, has been excavated, suggesting that the elites had an active role in governance at this time, not just the ruler.

The sociopolitical level achieved by the largest cities in the Late Preclassic Period spread through the Maya lowlands during the Early Classic, reaching to the northern point of the Yucatán at Dzibilchaltún. As El Mirador declined, Calakmul expanded; its urban core covered 30 square kilometers (12 square miles), and its surrounding territory encompassed 70 square kilometers (27 square miles). In the Petén, Tikal defined its territory with defensive walls that protected a 120-square-kilometer (46-square-mile) area, and it conquered and allied itself with other major polities. The increased

4.2 Palenque Oval Tablet. Lady Sak K'uk', regent ruler of Palenque, transfers the dynastic crown to her son Hanab Pakal on his accession to the jaguar throne, October 19, 612.   (Photo Alfred P. Maudslay, 1889–1902)

wealth in nonroyal residences suggests increasing social complexity. And it is in the Early Classic Period that the hieroglyphic texts assert that the king belonged to a royal dynasty. As the ruler cult spread throughout the lowlands during this period, it apparently was at the expense of the other elite lineages.

Late Classic Period

In the Late Classic Period, the Maya achieved a new level of sociopolitical complexity; Maya kingdoms included densely populated cities, covered large territories, and encompassed many dependent cities of varying size and importance.

Literally hundreds of cities built stone palaces and temples, and many sites carved monuments depicting semidivine rulers. These rulers governed territories beyond that of the capital city: They ruled over a five-tier hierarchy of dependent cities that ranged from the capital through four other tiers of cities and towns to scattered hamlets. The number of sites graced with at least some monumental construction is stupefying. In the eastern Petén and neighboring Belize River valley, a region not considered to be one of the most densely urbanized regions of the Classic Maya world, there are 28 of these low-level sites that have been mapped by archaeologists but remain unnamed. Some of the secondary, tertiary, and lesser sites may have been places specializing in artisanry, transshipment of trade goods, intensive agriculture, or stone quarrying. Nakbé and El Mirador, for example, were no longer powerful, but their greatly diminished populations specialized in the production of codex-style cylinder vases under the auspices of Calakmul. Throughout the Maya region, these different sites were incorporated into complex political hierarchies (see "City-States, Regional States, and Superpowers" below).

SOCIAL COMPLEXITY

The social structure mirrored the political complexity, with various levels of governors and minor officials ruling the dependencies for the ruler. In the eighth and ninth centuries, the number of palaces and wealthy burials multiplied, suggesting an extensive bureaucracy staffed by the elite class. Names of lesser offices have, in fact, been found in the inscriptions such as "sahal," the title for governors of dependent cities. The elite were patrons of buildings, not the laborers who constructed them. In fact, masonry architecture reflected the labor and tribute labor the elite could demand of the population, and such edifices were monumental testaments to their power in the social and political hierarchy (see Chapter 8).

Elite Class It has been estimated that the elite class constituted 10 percent of the population during this period. The nobility, called *itz'at winik* (wise people) in a text at the city of Tamarindito, were literate and wealthy, and their position in society was based on lineage. Texts indicated that the offices some of these individuals held, whether as scribe or overseer of a secondary site, were often inherited through the lineage as well. Murals and vase paintings depict many kinds of individuals surrounding the king in court scenes: priests, warriors, merchants, tribute payers, scribes, musicians, and painters, some of whom could have been members of the elite or a secondary elite. The most important priests were members of the nobility, and some of the painters of polychrome vases signed their names and titles, demonstrating that they, too, were members of the elite.

Middle Class There may have been a middle class comprising lesser officials, lower ranking priests, artisans, soldiers, and merchants. Based on the different sizes and types of housing excavated—such as those with thatched, not stone, roofs but with relatively rich caches of goods—there were probably many levels of wealth. At the Yucatecan site of Sayil, six different levels of residential construction were identified during excavation. Whether each represented a defined, hereditary class is unknown.

Commoners Although commoners were rarely depicted in art and never mentioned in the writings, they certainly existed: They were farmers, laborers, servants, and slaves. An invaluable insight into their lives was provided by excavations at Cerén, on the outskirts of the site of San Andrés in western El Salvador. The sudden burial of this farming village by a volcanic eruption c. 600 preserved everything down to the rope that tied a duck to a post. The ample adobe homes, well stocked with cooking pots and food, suggest a surprisingly good quality of life. (In fact, the excavators noted that the living conditions of their 20th-century Salvadoran workers were strikingly inferior). Although there are no comparable remains from other sites, contrasts in house construction, burial caches, and skeletal remains at sites such as Tikal and Caracol do not indicate that the gap between Maya commoners and the elite had widened by the Terminal Classic Period.

Early Postclassic Period

The shift from the central area to the northern lowlands resulted in the development of Chichén Itzá, long recognized as a great regional state that endured for well over a century. This city seems to have dominated much of the northern Yucatán during the Early Postclassic Period and controlled a swath of cities along the 100-kilometer (62-mile) path to its Caribbean ports. Although the extent of its political domain is not fully understood, its influence appeared at large cities throughout the area and at ports as far away as Belize. Although Chichén Itzá shared the Yucatán Peninsula with many other powerful states at the beginning of the Terminal Classic Period, by the end of the 10th century, it seems to have had no rival in the Maya world.

Some archaeologists believe that Chichén Itzá developed a new, more stable form of government during its hegemony that was based partly on its military might and partly on better integration of various elite families within a system of *multepal* (or joint rule in Yucatec Mayan). Although this councilor system of government probably functioned in support of the ruler not in place of the ruler, it is unclear that a strong *multepal* system developed before the Late Postclassic Period. (See "Postclassic *Multepal* Government" below.) However, Chichén Itzá did abandon the dynastic ruler cult of the preceding era and apparently legitimized its authority through the glorification of its pan-Mesoamericanism instead.

Late Postclassic Period

The Late Postclassic Period never supported the great complex states of the earlier periods. Although a few major kingdoms temporarily centralized authority over wide areas, they, too, collapsed into smaller, rival states. Some may have declined to a level of complex chiefdom, overseeing kingdoms with fewer tiers in the political hierarchy. However, the northern lowlands and southern highlands remained densely populated and commercially active. Many new trading ports grew up around the peninsula and its islands.

Based on the postconquest native chronicles and ethnohistories describing the final phase of pre-Columbian Maya civilization, the decentralized Maya polities were still governed by elite lineages. The area surrounding Maní, for example, was known as the territory of the Xiu, and that around Chichén Itzá, the territory of the Cupul. In highland Guatemala, the more complex Quiché Maya capital of Utatlán included 24 noble lineages. Numerous offices, especially the highest religious and political ones, were inherited through such lineages. The political organization of each state and, in some instances, chiefdom was organized around a capital city where the most important religious ceremonies were performed, just as they had been since the Archaic Period.

NORTHERN LOWLANDS

Mayapán The city of Mayapán ruled over a confederacy of Maya northern cities that was maintained through military action. The various noble lineage heads of Yucatán lived within the defensive walls of the city. Native documents indicated that Mayapán represented a joint rule, or *multepal*, government. But these same sources also suggest that the joint rule was more symbolic than real. The various Yucatec lineages were forced to support the authority of the city, governed by the Itzá lineage of the Cocom, and the lineage heads lived involuntarily in Mayapán. The city was densely occupied and confined within those walls, but its maritime trade was expansive and included many independent cities, from Tulum in Mexico and Lamanai in Belize to Naco in Honduras. After Mayapán, there never again was a centralized state in the northern lowlands.

Petty States Once Mayapán fell (c. 1450), the Yucatán Peninsula was divided into numerous independent petty states ruled by separate elite lineages. At the time of the Spanish Conquest, cities like Tulum on the Caribbean coast were quite small in architectural scale, and decentralization had resulted in more than 18 separate kingdoms, each with many smaller towns and villages under a capital city, with a hierarchy of officials ruling them. Even the small island of Cozumel had a capital city ruling over 30 smaller towns and villages. This region, still actively involved in sea trade, expanded its reach back into the Petén to the lake region of Tayasal, where cacao was being produced once again.

Ethnohistoric sources mention that rulers usually had a council of nobles to advise them and, at times, special military and foreign advisors. Administrators of the various lesser towns and villages governed through royal appointment or royal permission, and these more local officials acted as judges in hearing legal cases. Only the ruler received tribute, and it was also one of the responsibilities of the lesser officials to collect it.

The Yucatec kingdoms had not yet been forced to pay tribute to the Aztecs, but there is evidence that at the time of the Spanish Conquest, the central Mexican empire was encroaching on trade in the region and plotting to take more control.

SOUTHERN AREA: THE QUICHÉ

In highland Guatemala, the native chronicles and ethnohistoric documents describe an impressive Quiché Maya confederacy. From their highland capital at Utatlán (also known by the Maya name of K'umarcaaj), the Quiché kings demanded tribute from both the west and east, from Soconusco on the Pacific coast to kingdoms situated near the Motagua Valley. The Quiché kings appointed overseers at other major hilltop cities, and their military commanders enforced tribute payments and attempted to quell rebellions. The core area surrounding the Quiché capital may have had a population of 50,000. Its fortified hilltop capital of Utatlán, however, could accommodate fewer than 15,000 people; the sacred center may have been occupied primarily by the ruler and his entourage. Apparently each of the major lineages maintained a palace-style building in the city. By the end of the Late Postclassic Period, even the Quiché capital, the largest at the time, was a greatly diminished version of its Maya predecessors. Before the Spanish Conquest, the Guatemalan kingdom was weakened by warfare and forced to pay tribute to the Aztec Empire.

SOCIETY

The written accounts of 16th-century Spanish observers provide a more detailed glimpse of Maya society as the pre-Columbian civilization neared its end. There were several layers of elite and nonelite classes; only the elite lineages produced territorial rulers, judges, war captains, administrators of towns and villages, and the priesthood. There were many different kinds of administrators, as well as different kinds of priests: The high priests were viewed as oracles for the gods; others maintained the sacred books with their calendrical prophecies; some wielded the knife in sacrificial ceremonies, and some assisted the sacrificer. At the top of the religious hierarchy was the ruler.

For secular offices, there were many functionaries with special titles that ranked under that of the provincial governor. The bureaucratic hierarchy in both religious and civil matters was surprisingly complex, with some offices hereditary, passing from father to son, and others appointed. Some lineages were devoted to the particular offices within the priesthood or military, for example, just as the royal dynasty produced the king.

The Nonelite   Ninety percent of society is estimated to have belonged to the nonelite classes. Although the Spaniards stated that Maya society was divided into three rigid classes, that of the nobility, the commoner, and the slave, excavations have not produced such clear-cut divisions. Even the historic documents suggest that there were wealthy "commoners" and that commoners often had everything the nobility did except for knowledge about rituals. It seems the class of commoners was extremely diverse and probably included a middle class of artisans (unlike during the Classic Period, when some belonged to the nobility), many merchants, lesser priests, and other specialists. Through military action, commoners could rise from foot soldier to more decorated positions within the military, but they could not take on the dress or privileges of the elite.

Nearly everyone owed the ruler tribute, in labor or merchandise. Merchants had a privileged position in society, but even they had to pay tribute just like artisans and farmers. Many farmers owned their land but paid tribute with their harvest; others, like serfs, had no land but worked that of the ruler. Slaves were on the bottom rung of the social ladder, but archaeologists have had trouble identifying "slave" housing or burials. Both commoners and the nobility owned slaves. Enslavement could be temporary: Thieves became the slaves of their victims until they repaid their debt, for example. And slave status was not necessarily inherited, as children of slaves could be redeemed. Orphans became slaves. War captives who were not sacrificed became the property of their captors, and there was considerable trade in slaves for profit. Noble war captives were among the favored sacrificial victims in both the highlands and the northern lowlands, but in Yucatán, families sometimes purchased enslaved orphans to substitute for their own relatives, required by tribute in sacrificial rituals.

Increasing Egalitarianism   Excavations at many of the maritime trading centers that developed during this late period suggest a far more egalitarian society than had previously existed. Lineage and family shrines often competed with those of the state, but one of the powerful remaining roles of the elite was their control over ritual knowledge. Mass produced ceramics reached the lower classes, and imported items of shell and obsidian were widely distributed at many sites, unlike during the Classic Period, when they were considered luxury items for the elite. The Late Postclassic Maya impressed the Spaniards by the neatness of their appearance, the quality of their cotton clothing and gold or copper jewelry, and the size of their cities and towns.

CITY-STATES, REGIONAL STATES, AND SUPERPOWERS

Although the archaeological evidence supports the view that Maya cities developed into com-

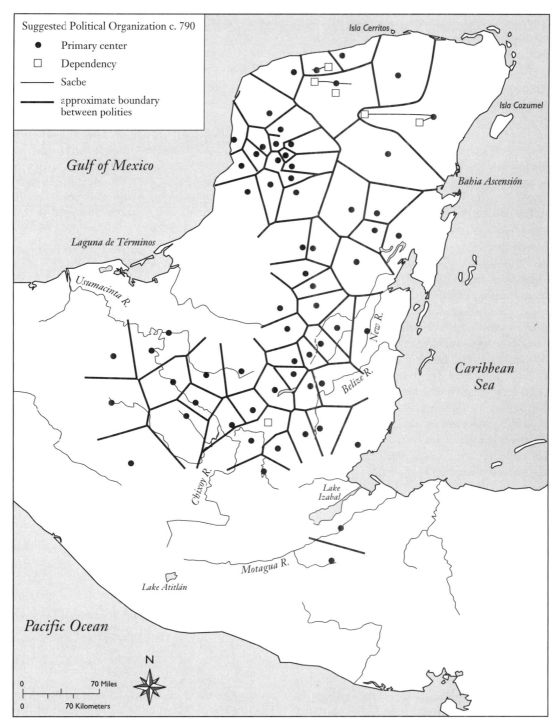

Map 4. *Suggested City-State Political Organization c. 790. This reconstruction of Maya political states used the central place system of Thiessen polygons plotted around sites with Emblem Glyphs.* (Courtesy Peter Mathews 1991)

plex states by the Late Preclassic Period, there have been differences of opinion about how these states carved out their territory within the Maya lowlands. The debate has been fueled until recently by the absence of adequate settlement surveys and thorough site maps, especially for the earlier periods. Also, the Maya hieroglyphic inscriptions do not describe the political boundaries of states, and only in the Late Classic Period are nonmilitary contacts between cities mentioned. Those mentions are disappointingly cryptic.

With no political histories readily available, Mayanists have had to develop techniques for reconstructing the size and number of Maya states and their political relationships. Their efforts have been concentrated on the Late Classic Period, which is the period best known through site excavations, regional surveys, and the decipherment of the hieroglyphic texts.

The resultant political reconstructions have been varied, but all agree that Maya cities were arranged into political hierarchies. Archaeological and epigraphic evidence has convincingly demonstrated that by the Late Classic Period, Maya states were composed of five tiers of settlements. At certain times, for example, Tikal controlled the large city of Uaxactún, as well as the smaller but substantial El Perú and even smaller Nakum and Bejucal. Each city varied in size, wealth, and perhaps function, but all had stone buildings and monuments. At the fifth level, there were farms and hamlets.

Some archaeologists argue that these various levels of cities, towns, and hamlets were forged into many independent Maya polities, called city-states. They were composed of many cities arranged in a political hierarchy under a capital city, but they covered only a small geographic territory. Others argue that the vast majority of Maya cities were integrated into large regional states. The difference is certainly one of size as well as sociopolitical complexity. Under one view of city-states, for example, there were about 24

states in the southern lowlands and a total of approximately 60 in all the Maya lowlands around 790 (see Map 4). Under a reconstruction of regional states, there were eight integrated political states in the northern and southern lowlands combined (see Map 5). A third theory, the recently formulated superstate theory, argues that at times there were two loose confederacies of city-states dominated by the most powerful cities. Which, if any, of these theories survives the test of future excavations and hieroglyphic readings remains to be seen.

Political Hierarchies

From Late Preclassic Kaminaljuyú and El Mirador, archaeologists have recognized that there were capital cities that ruled over other urban settlements. The sheer difference in size between Kaminaljuyú and the smaller settlements in the central Guatemalan highlands suggests that Kaminaljuyú was the political capital of the region. El Mirador, too, was larger than its neighbors, but those neighbors, such as Nakbé, were often sufficiently large to have been considered independent states if paved roads had not radiated from the capital to each of the neighbors in the surrounding territory, making a statement in stone about its central authority.

The ranking of cities under a capital is not usually so clearly delineated in the archaeological record, and in the Late Classic Period, there were so many important cities of similar size that it has been hard to find acceptable measures to differentiate among them. The more careful mapping of both sites and the regions in which they are located, however, has facilitated the ranking of Maya cities. The largest cities in an area are first-rank cities, even if they are smaller than many other Maya cities in other locations. For example, Copán is one-fourth the size of Tikal, but it is by far the largest site in the Motagua River region.

EMBLEM GLYPHS

Epigraphic information has also been used to rank sites. In the 1960s, epigraphers began to identify emblem glyphs, which were then understood to be place-names of cities (see Chapter 10 and figure 10.7, p. 284). Not all cities had emblem glyphs, and in the central area, the most impressive cities seemed to have them and the lesser ones did not. With more subtle readings of the hieroglyphs, it is now known that the emblem glyph is a title held only by a ruler and proclaims the king is the holy lord of a given domain. The hieroglyph actually refers to the state, not just the capital city that was the dynastic seat of the ruler controlling that state. For example, the emblem glyph for Palenque was used by both that city and its dependency at Tortuguero. A separate place-name for the city of Palenque has been identified in its inscriptions. When such dependencies assert their independence, they stopped using the emblem glyph of their former overlord.

Political Boundaries: The Size of Maya States

Site rankings and regional mappings cannot by themselves define the boundaries of the Maya states. More information is needed to create such territorial boundaries and to determine the size and number of Maya political states. With no hieroglyphic inscriptions available for most regions and most periods of Maya civilization, archaeologists have utilized various models about central places to delineate political territories. Assuming that the first-rank cities, such as Tikal, Copán, and Cobá, were at the center of their domains, the boundaries were projected by formulas based on information about the maximum distance for effective communication, transport, and control.

REGIONAL STATES

The world systems theory, for example, argues that a pedestrian society like that of the Maya could cover only 20 kilometers (12.4 miles) in one day and that would be the farthest distance feasible for a secondary center. Such information has recently been used to delineate the Early Postclassic state of Chichén Itzá, and it has successfully explained the carefully spaced towns between that capital city and its port at Isla Cerritos. It could also be used to explain El Mirador's central location amid the series of paved roads to other Late Preclassic Period cities; the paved roads must have expedited travel between the capital and its second-tier cities.

CITY-STATES

For the Classic Period, mathematical models have provoked far more controversy, primarily because there has been less agreement over which cities should be considered capitals. Where emblem glyph information has been available, the advocates of city-states have argued that an emblem glyph indicates an independent polity, regardless of size, unless the hieroglyphic evidence suggests otherwise. For example, the small city of Pomoná, usually considered a dependency of Palenque, had an emblem glyph, and in the eighth century it was independent of Palenque. The size difference between Pomoná and Palenque was no more relevant to their political status in the eighth century, it is argued, than that of Holland and the United States in the 20th century: All are autonomous. The regional states position has tended to elevate only the physically largest of cities with emblem glyphs to the status of a capital and has relied heavily on archaeological evidence as opposed to epigraphic decipherments.

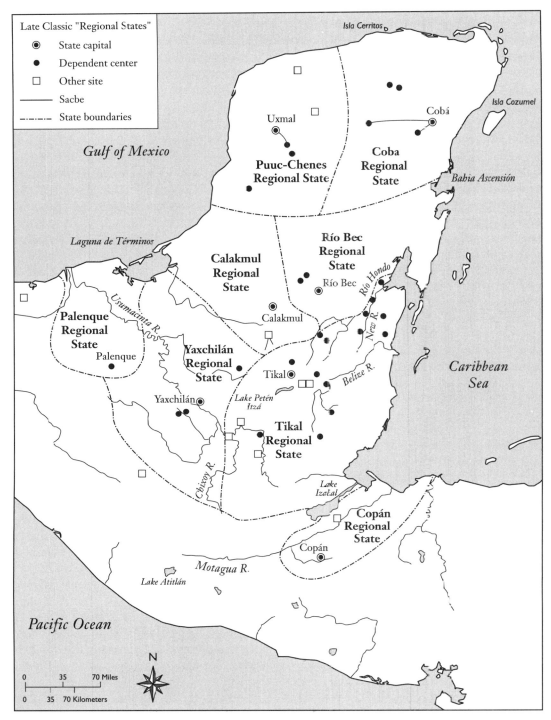

Map 5. *Suggested Late Classic Maya Regional States.* (Courtesy Peter Mathews, 1991, redrawn after Adams, 1986)

DIVERGENT VIEWS

As a result of the profound differences between the two theories, the mathematical models have generated hexagonally-shaped polities, and Thiessen polygrams (see Map 4) have approximated the territory of each Maya state, but the use of different capital cities in the calculations has resulted in wildly divergent views of Maya states. The city-state model identified 60 capitals using emblem glyphs as well as some archaeological information for the period around 790. Based primarily on size rankings, the regional states model identified eight capitals: Uxmal, Cobá, Río Bec, Calakmul, Tikal, Palenque, Yaxchilán, and Copán. For the regional states model, all other cities in the Late Classic Period were dependencies within these states. The contrast between the two positions can best be seen for Tikal. In the regional state model, Tikal was the capital of a vast state that included both the Petén and Belize. In the city-state model, it was just one among many in the Petén, most of which were only 25 kilometers (15.5 miles) in radius.

INTEGRATED VS. FRAGMENTED STATES

Mathematical models and site rankings have not resolved basic issues about the size of Maya political states, and both the regional and city-state theories require some modification to fit more closely with the known archaeological facts. In the case of Chichén Itzá and perhaps even El Mirador, the regional state theory seems to be supported by archaeological evidence. But some archaeologists believe that for most periods of Maya civilization, the Maya political state was inherently unstable and incapable of forming the large unitary states envisioned under the regional state position. Such weak states are called peer polities, or segmentary states, and many argue that the city-state model better captures the fragmentation that results from such instability.

Peer Polities Regardless of their size, segmentary states have the same function. Tikal provided no more benefits to its populace, under this theory, than Nakum did, once it proclaimed its independence from Tikal. If a member of a dynasty were unhappy or if a competing noble lineage became dissatisfied, a splinter state could be formed with no loss. Dos Pilas, it is thought, was founded by just such a disgruntled group from Tikal in 645; within a few decades it became one of the most powerful states in the southern lowlands. In the Terminal Classic Period, many southern lowland cities declared their independence from larger states. Although both city-states and regional states accept the fact that Maya nations were organized into a multitier political hierarchy, the city-state position emphasizes that such states fluctuated constantly in power and influence. Any mapping of states, under this position, must be set within a specific time frame to be accurate. Such fissioning of states typifies peer polities.

Under the peer polity theory, Maya states were incapable of sustaining expansive regional states because the Maya ruler inspired loyalty to local dynasties, not large regional territories (see "Classic Period Maya Rulership" below). Many small, weak states resulted, and their power fluctuated according to whether they had strong, militaristic rulers. According to this view, the Maya political system could not sustain political stability, and the Maya ruler had interest only in protecting his state, not in territorial expansion.

Although there is now considerable evidence that some Maya states were interested in territorial expansion, the peer polity theory has many followers. In fact, supporters of this theory argue that the amount of warfare among the many cities that were allegedly unified into regional states proves they were, in fact, fragmented and not integrated. Tikal was repeatedly attacked and defeated by the very cities it supposedly ruled as a regional state, Caracol being its most notable enemy (562–c. 692). During the Late Classic Period, at least, such political shifts within states, whether city-states or regional states, were not unusual.

SUPERSTATES

By the 1990s, the increasingly refined readings of the hieroglyphic texts enabled Mayanists to understand far more about political relationships than permitted by the emblem glyphs alone. The new information suggests that there may have been immense political territories, as envisioned by proponents of the regional state theory. On the other hand, the texts suggest that such political territories, far from being integrated states, constituted only a confederacy of autonomous city-states. Any city-state's autonomy, however, lasted only as long as the city-state cooperated with the confederacy; autonomy came with a price tag: tribute payments.

The decipherments demonstrate that dynastic rulers of cities with emblem glyphs were sometimes subservient to another. Some were members of the dynastic nobility that had been appointed to govern dependencies. Some rulers were installed under the auspices of a ruler not through dynastic ties but through conquest or marriage alliances. Yet these rulers, apparently subservient to a greater state, continued to fight wars, receive their own tribute to build immense palatial complexes, and take on all the appearances of autonomous city-states. These texts suggest that city-states combined into regional confederations, but the local rulers were permitted to act as if their authority had not been compromised.

The superstate theory is still being refined, but it suggests that the Maya city-states sometimes participated in large territorial confederacies controlled by one of the great military powers Tikal or Calakmul. Tikal and Calakmul were surrounded by extensive territories—at least 120 square kilometers (46 square miles) for Tikal and 70 square kilometers (27 square miles) for Calakmul—in which no other city employed an emblem glyph. Their power may have originated from the vast territorial resources under their direct control, which included many bureaucratic tiers of other cities and towns. As such, they were powerful, independent city-states. The dynasties of these two great military states intermarried with dynasties at other states, conquered yet others and controlled the installation of their rulers, and forged a network of trade and tribute. In the process, these two states created large confederacies, or superstates.

The power of these states was such that smaller ones gained considerable prestige through the association. Also, the inscriptions suggest that the states participating in these confederations did not war with one another. Under this view, there were two different kinds of states in the Late Classic Period: somewhat autonomous city-states and larger superstates that included these semi-independent city-states This might be roughly comparable to the current situation in Europe where many independent nations have joined the European Union mostly for economic reasons, but also for the peace that it insures. In the case of the European Union, however, membership in the confederacy is completely voluntary. For the Maya superstates, military coercion was probably used as often as political persuasion.

A Mesoamerican Model It has been argued that such superstates may be typical of Mesoamerica and are the functional equivalent of the later Aztec Empire. The Aztecs ruled in a triple alliance in which each of the three cities received separate tribute from those territories under their direct control, as well as joint tribute from a broader area. Although there was no doubt that militaristic Tenochtitlan, the Aztec capital, ruled the triple alliance, it clearly permitted considerable autonomy to its allied cities. It also had no interest in governing other Mesoamerican states as long as they paid tribute. Only when tribute was not forthcoming was the army sent in. In the Maya world, the great state of Calakmul shaped a loose confederacy from its network of allies at Dos Pilas, Concuén, Naranjo, and elsewhere. Given the Aztec model, such a confederacy might be called an empire, but the Maya superstates never extended outside the Maya region.

REMAINING ISSUES

The evidence for Classic Period superstates is convincing. But the theory is new, and many details need to be clarified, such as their territorial boundaries and whether they endured longer, and with greater stability, than envisioned under the peer polity theory. It is also unclear to what extent these superstates were integrated. Perhaps they were simply many autonomous states aligned against a common enemy, much like the Cold War alliance during the late 20th century when the so-called free world cooperated with the United States against the common enemy, the Soviet Union and its allies. Proponents of regional states would, no doubt, like to find evidence of a more unified relationship among the city-states under the centralized authority of Tikal or Calakmul.

For the moment, there is no doubt there were Maya political states, and there is no doubt that some of those states were the superpowers of their era. But the nature of these states seems to have varied in different periods and different areas. El Mirador in the Late Preclassic Period and Chichén Itzá and Mayapán in the Postclassic Period endured for centuries and controlled enormous regions. For the latter two, there is little doubt that they were truly centralized superstates. But in the Classic Period, the political reality is just beginning to be understood.

CLASSIC PERIOD MAYA RULERSHIP

Charismatic Leadership

Maya kings ruled at least partially through charisma, legitimizing their authority through their personal ties with both supernatural powers and more earthly political ones. From the earliest evidence of class differentiation in the Archaic Period, there is accompanying evidence of the political leadership of shamans who could intercede with the gods and communicate with deified ancestors. Such charismatic leadership typifies a chiefdom, but by the Late Preclassic Period, Maya cities were developing beyond chiefdoms into more complex political states. The Maya rulers had other means of consolidating their states besides shamanism. Their religious authority was bolstered by claims of direct descent from the creator gods and divinity for themselves (see Chapter 6), and the dynastic ruler cult remained central to governance throughout the Late Classic Period.

The ruler cult appears not to have been a simple one of charismatic rule, however. The Maya ruler performed a variety of functions within the state. The decipherment of some glyphs has revealed the titles of subservient governors and office holders, suggesting a supporting bureaucracy controlled by the Late Classic Period ruler. Based on the existence of reservoirs in the center of many Late Classic Period cities, it seems that Maya rulers frequently controlled the distribution of water, a critical administrative function during the dry season or times of drought. Hieroglyphs and art proclaim the ruler's war victories (see Chapter 5), not just his ritual communication with the gods and performance of religious ceremonies for the state. Royal burials indicate a gradual change from mere dynastic symbolism to more commercial symbolism, suggesting that rulers in the Late Classic Period justified their power, at least in part, with their ability to provide the state with great quantities of exotic trade items. In fact, the ruler's distribution of luxury goods, and the prestige that accompanied them, assured the allegiance of nonroyal elite and administrators at secondary and even tertiary centers. But the ruler's interaction with foreign states, through trade and diplomatic visits, also reinforced his prestige at home.

Legitimacy

Birth into the royal, semidivine lineage was a requirement for rulership. The lineage reached back in mythic time to the creator gods and thus, was sanctioned by the gods to rule. The Maya ruler acceded to office through patrilineal descent, but when the line of succession from father to son was broken, some Maya states permitted royal women to rule. Lady Six Sky of Naranjo (688?–?) and Lady Sak K'uk' of Palenque (612–620?) two of the four known women rulers, were regents for young sons, and took on the leadership role for an undetermined number of years (see figure 4.2, page 123). The Lady of Tikal (511–527?) was installed in office at the age of six, apparently during a crisis in the dynastic secession. Unlike the other queens, she "ruled" with a male military general as her regent.

Although the male line determined position in society, women from powerful cities could add prestige to another city's royal lineage through intermarriage and could also bring better trade connections for exotic goods. The city of Naranjo's dynasty was revived by such a marriage with Lady Six Sky of Dos Pilas. And some cities devoted considerable artistic effort to glorifying their queens: Calakmul paired each king's stela with one of his spouse; often these queens were depicted in warrior stances. Yaxchilán included women with their royal spouses in sculpted panels showing the queens performing acts of self-sacrifice and communicating with the ancestral gods (see figure 6.14, page 193, for example). Although they rarely ruled themselves, women enhanced the authority of the ruling dynasty by their own prestigious familial connections with great powers, some at considerable distance from the state itself.

The Maya belief in the legitimacy of the ruling dynasty and the divinity of the rulers (see Chapters 6 and 7) was capable of imparting stability to the state. For example, when one of Palenque's rulers was captured and kept prisoner by Toniná—a considerable humiliation—the people did not revolt or change allegiance. Instead, they waited more than 10 years for the death of their ruler before installing a new one from the same dynasty. And the same dynasty often ruled a city for centuries: Yax K'uk Mo's lineage governed at Copán for 400 years despite the city's defeat in war.

The Maya worshiped their ancestors (see Chapter 7), and the dynasty represented the state's most powerful ancestors, all of whom were buried in the sacred center of the state capital. The tombs of dynastic founders and revered rulers were often kept accessible for hundreds of years, despite constant urban renewal projects. The ancestors conferred prestige on the city and reinforced local identity in such a way that even conquering states hesitated to usurp the dynasty, though they did sometimes do so. It has been said that the dynasty, not territorial boundaries defined Maya states.

Instability

Although Maya dynasties successfully governed the lowland polities for centuries, the

4.3 Piedras Negras Throne 1. This reconstructed throne was found amid the rubble of the Piedras Negras palace, built by Ruler 7, who became king in 781. The throne back depicts his deified ancestors, who literally support him and legitimize his rule. (Photo courtesy John Montgomery)

stability achieved by the dynastic ruler served only the city nation. Among the cities there were extended periods of continuous warfare, shifting alliances, and, eventually, the collapse of the southern lowland Classic Period cities. This regional instability raises the question of whether the ruler cult was fatally flawed, as peer polity and other theories about the weak Maya state assert (see "Peer Polities," page 132). Maya states, according to these theories, were unstable because they had only the personal charisma of the Maya ruler to maintain social harmony and political boundaries.

The charismatic model is being reexamined because of increasing evidence for a substantial bureaucracy and many-tiered political hierarchy controlled by the ruler. Yet the nature of Maya dynastic rulership did seem to encourage the autonomy of many cities rather than their integration into a single, more powerful, and enduring polity. And the smaller Late Classic cities, with their strong separate identities, shifted alliances from one great power to the next, as proven by Quiriguá's temporary alliance with Calakmul against Copán. Fragmentation, economic competition, and warfare were very often the result of this instability.

The superstate theory has recently challenged this perception of inherently flawed Maya rulership. Although there were, indeed, many small competing states and a Classic Period collapse, it now is argued that the nature of rulership was far more complex than the charismatic model implies. At times, more powerful superstates existed, and such confederacies were capable of maintaining the peace among their own members. The issue remains open as to exactly how enduring these superstates were. Even if the dynastic ruler cult did not constitute purely charismatic rule, the Maya abandoned the cult in the period after the collapse.

Challenges by the Elite

There were many factors in the Classic Period collapse, and the ruler cult may have been one such factor. The growth of the nobility in the Late Classic Period, and apparently a concomitant growth in the bureaucracy, may have challenged the central authority of the ruler. The number of elites participating in public rituals and accumulating wealth suggests that the ruler was forced to appease increasing numbers of them and, perhaps, share power with them. The *popol nah*, or council house, built at Copán in the ninth century, with glyphs for various lineages on its facade, was thought to be proof of *multepal*, or a more council form of gov-

4.4   *Lacamhá Lintel 1, Late Classic. Holding the Maya ceremonial bar of rulership in his hands, this lord presents himself with the trappings of a king, yet the text identifies him as a sahal, or underlord.* (Drawing courtesy John Montgomery)

ernment at this time. However, nonroyal lineages appear to have been consulted by the ruler since the Late Preclassic Period, when a *popol nah* was constructed at Uaxactún. Also, by the end of the Early Classic Period, there are increasing numbers of rich caches in residential compounds outside the sacred center, suggesting increasing power by the nobility at this early date. These potential tensions between the royal dynasty and other elites during earlier periods is still not well understood, however.

The deciphered hieroglyphic texts, such as those at Yaxchilán, imply power struggles among the elite for the rulership, and destroyed stelae and new royal compounds suggest a change in dynasty at various sites. Also, the Late Classic development of centers midway between existing capitals suggests that disgruntled elites were fissioning late in that period. Perhaps one reason the elite were increasingly concentrated in the sacred center was to better control them.

POSTCLASSIC *MULTEPAL* GOVERNMENT

Chichén Itzá

The abandonment of the ruler cult after the Terminal Classic Period has led many archaeologists to believe that a new form of government replaced that of the royal dynasty. The few texts that exist from Chichén Itzá, for example, relate little about dynastic history, and the inscriptions no longer boast of royal achievements but rather of rituals witnessed or attended by numerous members of the elite (see Chapter 10). Having shed the ruler cult, Chichén Itzá may have been governed by a *multepal*, or joint rule. This councilor form of government may have provided legitimacy to the state at a time when dynastic

4.5   North Temple relief carving (detail), Chichén Itzá, Early Postclassic Period. The detail depicts the ruler, standing in the center, amid other members of the nobility. Unlike in the Piedras Negras Lintel 3 (drawing 4.1), the ruler is not above other members of his government, nor is he depicted alone as other rulers were on Classic Period stelae.   (Drawing Linnea Wren after Cohodas 1978)

lineage was looked at suspiciously after the Classic Period collapse.

The success of Chichén Itzá, it is argued, may have partially resulted from its greater incorporation of various groups and lineages into the government. However, ruler accession murals at the city depict only one individual assuming power, yet he was shown surrounded by many individuals. Even if there was a single king, it does seem as if the Early Postclassic city may have integrated nonroyal elite more thoroughly into the government than ever before. Repeated artistic depiction of the elite in bas-reliefs literally overwhelms the ruler himself. The ruler cult was abandoned both in public inscriptions and art.

Late Postclassic Period

Although the exact nature of the government at Chichén Itzá remains undecided, the Late Postclassic Period is better understood, despite the near total absence of hieroglyphic inscriptions in stone. According to 16th-century ethnohistoric descriptions, the abandonment of the architectural and artistic symbols of the venerated ruler was not an abandonment of semidivine rulers or the dynasties legitimizing

their rule. The native documents testify to *multepal* government in the case of the League of Mayapán. Although the league may have originally been formed with the idea that each lineage head would be part of a ruling council, in the end kings from the Cocom dynasty ruled Mayapán and kept other lineage heads captive in that city. Although deprived of their independence, those noblemen were critical to the functioning of the city in that their people provided it with the basic foodstuffs for survival.

TRUE *MULTEPAL*

After the fall of Mayapán, the noble lineages of the league reestablished their own domains based on dynastic rule. These were the most important political kingdoms in the Yucatán Peninsula during this late preconquest period. The ruler, or *halach uinic*, as he was called in the historic documents, was still venerated, but his authority was checked by the *popol nah*, or council house, as well as special military and foreign advisors. Some of the smaller towns apparently did not have a *halach uinic* but instead formed loose alliances; these alliances may have functioned under a true *multepal* government. They also may have functioned for a single purpose, such as religious ceremonies or the working of commonly held lands. In most instances, however, the Maya continued to be governed by dynastic rulers and their advisers.

QUICHÉ COUNCIL

The Quiché Maya king also did not rule alone. His government included the king-elect and two other nobles, as well as representatives from each of the four major lineages. According to native chronicles, decisions of war and other critical matters were made by consultation with allies and the leaders of other elite Quiché lineages. Yet the Spaniards described the Quiché king as powerful and with the right to appoint governors and officials at many important cities throughout the kingdom. Whether the system of consultation amounted to a divergent political practice from what transpired in the earlier Classic Period council houses, or *popol nah*, is unknown, but many archaeologists believe that it strengthened the role of various elite lineages in contrast to the Classic Period ruler cult.

Commercialism

Although the Maya appear to have kept the royal ruler in the highest office, they did reject the ruler cult and may have rejected it for economic as well as political reasons. All evidence points to considerable wealth and population density for the Late Postclassic Period, but the cities are less impressive and the investment in art and architecture far less ambitious, although substantial buildings were constructed in the Guatemalan highlands.

The lack of investment in public projects may have resulted from the commercialization of society, especially in the north. The mercantile elite may have demanded the economy be directed away from massive building projects and elaborate burials for the sake of ruler glorification and invested instead in warehouses and marketable goods. Jade and obsidian were still placed in ritual caches, but they were often chipped or damaged, leading archaeologists to speculate that the finer artifacts were saved for trade and profit.

Commercialism benefited most of the Maya. Archaeologists have discovered traded goods more evenly distributed throughout the different classes of housing compounds. And with fewer monumental public projects, tribute labor was considerably less than during the Classic Period. Under this view of the Maya, the semidivine ruler continued to govern, but the world he ruled had changed. The great Maya achievements in art were abandoned, but at the time of the conquest, it seems the civilization was steering toward a somewhat more egalitarian society.

CONCLUSION

For most of the 20th century, the nature of Maya government and the complexity of its society were obscured by too little archaeological data and a surplus of speculation. Archaeologists now have charted the development of Maya society through settlement patterns, burials and caches, and the monumentality of construction. The accumulated evidence has demonstrated the complexity of Maya political states with their monumental capitals and many tiers of dependent settlements. This assessment has been further confirmed through readings of the inscriptions. Although Maya rulers were semidivine, they were also warriors, traders, and high priests and, when successful, consummate politicians in satisfying the interests of competing elite lineages within their kingdoms. They incorporated advisory councils of the nonroyal nobility into their governments and by the Postclassic Period, these councils apparently assumed far greater power and spread governmental responsibility among various elite lineages in addition to that of the royal dynasty.

Maya polities built vast territorial networks for the purpose of trade, tribute, and mutual defense. Whether these networks amounted to the equivalent of superstates, regional states, or cooperative efforts of totally independent city-states is still a matter of lively debate among Mayanists. Although the size and boundaries of Maya states are not well understood, it is clear that much like contemporary political states, the Maya went through periods of consolidation and fragmentation, from periods of high culture to periods of commercialism. At the time of the Spanish Conquest, the Maya were not only politically decentralized but they were also weakened from the expansion of the Aztec Empire in central Mexico into the Maya region.

READING

See also Chapters 4, 6, 8.

Chiefdoms and Ceremonial Centers

Morley 1946, Thompson 1966 and 1970: ceremonial centers; George Andrews 1975, Culbert 1991, Culbert and Rice 1990: urbanization and population estimates.

Evolution of the Political State

Culbert 1991, Feinman and Marcus 1998, Hansen 1998, Sabloff 1990, Sabloff and Andrews V 1986: development of complex states; Carmean 1991, Diane Chase and Arlen Chase 1992 and 1999, Schele 1991, Schele and Mathews 1998, Sheets 1992, David Stuart 1986, Tourtellot and Sabloff 1992: stratified society and specialization; Lincoln 1994, Sabloff and Andrews V 1986, Schele and Freidel 1990, Wren and Schmidt 1991: Early Postclassic in northern

Yucatán; Arlen Chase 1985, Ralph Roys 1957, Tozzer 1941: Late Postclassic sociopolitical organization; Carmack 1981, John Fox 1987: Quiché empire.

City-States, Regional States, and Superpowers

Adams 1986, Adams and Jones 1981, Bullard 1960, Morley 1946, Trombold 1991: site hierarchies; Flannery 1972, Hammond 1974, Kepecs 1994: mathematical models; Houston and Stuart 1994: place-names; Adams 1986, Culbert 1991, Marcus 1976 and 1993: regional states; Freidel 1986, Hammond 1991, Mathews 1985 and 1991, Mathews and Willey 1991, Palka 1996, Sanders and Webster 1988, Taschek and Ball 1999: city-states and peer polities; Martin and Grube 1995 and 2000: superstates; Mathews 2001: superstates, city-states, and the Cold War.

Classic Period Maya Rulership

Freidel and Schele 1988b, Freidel, Schele, and Parker 1993, Houston and Stuart 1996, Schele and Miller 1986: rulership and ritual power; Fash and Stuart 1991, Grube and Martin 1998, Martin and Grube 2000, Schele and Freidel 1990: Maya dynasties; Freidel 1992, Webster 1998: charismatic rulership; Chase and Chase 1998, Fash and Stuart 1991, Sabloff 1990: elite power.

Postclassic *Multepal*

Fash 1998, Fash and Stuart 1991: council houses, Krochock and Freidel 1994, Lincoln 1994, Sabloff and Andrews V 1986, Schele and Freidel, 1990, Tozzer 1941: *multepal* at Chichén Itzá; Roys 1965: Mayapán; Ralph Roys 1943, Chase 1986: Yucatec kingdoms; Carmack 1981: Quiché state; Sabloff 1990: commercialism.

5

WARFARE

The politically fragmented Maya engaged in many wars against each other, some no more than raids for ritual captives and others for all-out destruction of a rival state. For the most part, however, the Maya probably waged war for economic gain through tribute and the control of trade routes. Despite the frequency of warfare, there is little understanding of the status of the military in the ancient Maya world. Even at the time of the Spanish Conquest, when ethnohistoric sources provide the most detailed observations, it is unclear how armies were trained. Although it is known that there were military offices and most of them were the preserve of the nobility, details about the organization of the military or the logistics of supplying troops in faraway battles remain something of a mystery. Battle scenes are depicted in Maya art, although few murals have survived, and wars and battle victories are mentioned in the Classic Period inscriptions, providing some clues as to Maya warfare and its impact on the Maya world.

RULER AS WARRIOR

The Maya ruler was the supreme war captain. In the Preclassic Period, he was depicted wearing trophy heads, presumably from sacrificed prisoners captured in war. Although the trophy heads later disappeared from the royal belt, the warfare and captive sacrifice that they represented persisted. Classic Period rulers also claimed to capture prisoners, and these prisoners were brought to the victorious city for rituals that most often ended in decapitation. At Chichén Itzá, a sculpted stone *tzompantli*, or skull rack, represents hundreds of such episodes.

Early Classic Period rulers were depicted in sculptures as standing on a captive, and the number of such representations escalated during the Late Classic Period. Rulers boasted of their

5.1   *Terminal Classic* tzompantli, *or stone skull rack,* Chichén Itzá.

war prowess in public art and hieroglyphic texts. Lord Bird Jaguar the Great of eighth-century Yaxchilán, like many other rulers, carried such titles as "He of 20 Captives" and "Captor of Jewel Skull," an enemy who apparently was an important member of another city's nobility. The inscriptions also indicate that before inauguration, prospective rulers had to capture prisoners for sacrifice at the coronation. Warfare was so critical to the prestige of the ruling dynasty that sometimes both the king and queen were depicted standing atop prisoners; even royal ancestral figures, dressed in warrior regalia, could be depicted advising their descendants from the otherworld. At a few sites, the ruler was shown in hand-to-hand combat, grabbing the hair of a captive. The capture of prisoners for sacrifice to the gods was an essential element of Maya rulership. The tradition is documented in Maya art from the Late Preclassic Period into the Postclassic Period, and elite burials suggest it was practiced as early as the Middle Preclassic Period.

Archaeologists have questioned whether Maya rulers actually engaged in warfare themselves. Some suggest the portrayals of warriorrulers were pure propaganda, or no more than symbolic. In this case, they would have been like

5.2 Dos Pilas Stela 2, 736. Ruler 3 of Dos Pilas, attired in a ritual war costume with a jaguar pelt, spear, and shield, stands victoriously on a captive. Many elements of this warrior-ruler costume were adapted during the Early Classic Period from Teotihuacan. The balloon headdress contains trapezoidal symbols of Teotihuacan, and the apron has the goggle eyes of the central Mexican god Tlaloc. (Drawing by Linda Schele, copyright David Schele)

led the Maya troops, but the governors and rulers of cities led their people in fighting, too. In fact, it was the head of the ruling Cupul lineage who attempted single-handedly to assassinate the conquistador Francisco Montejo in the Spanish encampment at Chichén Itzá.

THE MILITARY

In the post–European contact period, it is known that some elite lineages controlled a specific military office. The hereditary office passed from the lineage head upon his death to his son, and if there was no son to inherit, it passed to another family member or lineage member. Such lineages must have preserved and disseminated the specialized knowledge that was necessary for such offices. Some of the training must have involved military strategies, but preparation also involved war dances, music, war banners, and special effigies of the protective gods to be carried into battle. It is these aspects of the battle that are most recorded in the native chronicle *The Annals of Cakchiquels* and they are also depicted in earlier Maya art. (See figures 2.9 and 5.5). Whether commoners were involved as singers, dancers, or standard-bearers in some of these preparations is unclear, but it is known they could advance through the social ranks by proven prowess in warfare. In the highlands, women occasionally fought in battles, according to the native chronicles. Also, mercenaries were hired in Yucatán in the Late Postclassic Period; their social status is unclear.

Officers

BATAB

The *batab* title was held by both rulers and administrators of dependent cities within a state; the title was employed at the time of the

presidents of the United States, who are commanders in chief but not soldiers. According to the art and inscriptions, however, Maya rulers were captured, tortured, and sacrificed. This suggests that they were at least occasionally combatants, if not on the battlefield then within their sacred centers during enemy raids. At the time of the Spanish Conquest, special war captains often

Spanish Conquest in the Yucatán. It covered responsibilities held by officials known as *sahals* in Late Classic Period texts. Sixteenth-century ethnohistories describe the *batab* as both a town governor and a hereditary war captain. According to Spanish observers, they were responsible for leading the local armies into battle under the supreme authority of their ruler.

BATE

The military title *bate* has been deciphered from the Classic Period texts as a title held by rulers and perhaps also elite warriors; at Chichén Itzá, the title is attributed to several men in its inscriptions, including two who most likely were rulers of the city. Based on the full context in the inscriptions, the title may be associated with war captives and their subsequent decapitation in a ball-game ritual ("Purpose of Ritual Performance" and "Ball Games," Chapter 6). At the cities of Calakmul and Yaxchilán, where nonruling noblewomen were prominently portrayed on monuments, they also carried the *bate* title, suggesting it may have been inherited or honorific. Although there is some documentation that Maya women assisted in war, there is none for their functioning as military officers unless they were, in fact, one of the Classic Period female rulers, such as Lady Six Sky of Naranjo (see "Late Classic Period," chapter 2).

NACOM

Postcontact ethnohistoric sources describe a nonhereditary military office that was held for a limited term or just to conduct a particular war. For example, the Quiché council selected a famous war captain to lead them in battle against Pedro de Alvarado. In preparation, this captain, Tecum, was taken to the sacred precinct of Utatlán, adorned with magical mirrors and precious feathers, and carried aloft like an idol during seven days of religious preparation. He organized 10,000 troops from various towns and settlements and led them into battle with four other captains under him. In Yucatán, there also was a military office that was selected, not inherited, and it was so enshrouded in religious preparations that the holder was seated in a temple. This *necom* served as the chief military strategist, but he did not himself lead the troops, unlike his Quiché counterpart.

Conscripts and Mercenaries

The Spaniards claimed they were attacked by thousands of soldiers in a single battle; Alvarado estimated that 30,000 Quiché Maya attacked his troops during the initial battle of the conquest in 1524, but he could have exaggerated. Although there were no standing armies of so many troops, there may have been smaller contingents of trained soldiers kept battle ready, although even that is uncertain. Nonetheless, the Maya seemed ready to fight the Spaniards everywhere the invaders suddenly pulled into port. One ethnohistoric source says that mercenaries were employed but only during wartime; war captains were responsible for paying them a small amount, and citizens housed and fed them. For a full-scale war, commoners must have been conscripted to fight as well, using their hunting weapons to fight, and lacking those, hurling rocks. Serving as a soldier might have been required of adult males as a form of tribute, just as they were forced to labor on other public projects. One advantage of having the nobility as officers was their control over members of the lineages; they could call upon a large human reserve through kinship and tribute relations.

Weapons

The atlatl, or spear-thrower, was a wooden stick, about a half meter (almost 2 feet) long.

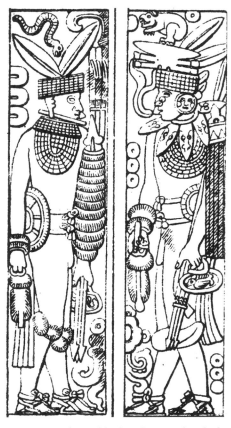

5.3 *Warriors from Chichén Itzá with atlatls, or spear-throwers, Early Postclassic. Atlatls had two finger holes for gripping the shaft and hurling the inserted darts or arrows. The proper grip is shown in these drawings of two warrior reliefs.* (Drawings Alfred P. Maudslay, 1889–1902)

One end was notched for a javelin or dart, the opposite end had two holes. Placing his index and middle fingers through the holes, a warrior launched the chert- or obsidian-pointed weapon at his target about 45 meters (almost 150 feet) away with more than twice as much force and more accuracy than could be accomplished by using his arm alone. The atlatl, introduced into the Maya region by Teotihuacan around the fourth century, represented

thunderbolts hurled by Tlaloc, the central Mexican god of storm and war.

Blowguns were used by commoners in both hunting and war. In the Late Postclassic Period, the bow and arrow was introduced; reed arrows, pointed with flints or sharp fish teeth, were carried in quivers, and the bows, relatively straight, were strung with hemp cord. For hand-to-hand combat, there were razor-sharp obsidian-spiked clubs and spears, axes, and knives with flint or obsidian blades. Even though copper blades were used by the time of Spanish contact, the Maya did not stop using stone and obsidian. In 1502, Christopher Columbus's ship encountered a Maya trading canoe and reported that their wooden swords had flint blades that cut like steel.

Uniforms

The ritual war costume (see figure 5.2, page 144), with symbolic elements borrowed from the formerly powerful central Mexican city of Teotihuacan in the fourth century (see Chapter 2), may have been too unwieldy to wear in combat. Much like today's generals wear their dress uniforms and medals only for ceremonial display, the ruler may have donned this costume for war dances, processions, and displays of war captives in the sacred center of the city. It is documented, however, that the Aztec emperor dressed in full regalia on the battlefield in order to be recognized by his troops—and to inspire them. Perhaps the Maya king did the same. The long apron and layers of clothing would have provided the ruler with some protection against injury. The few surviving sculptures that depict rulers actively capturing prisoners, however, show them wearing lighter clothing more sensible for battle; sometimes they wear a quilted cotton vest for armor (see figure 2.10) and jaguar-pelt leggings for protection. They often wore elaborate jaguar headdresses, and their shields sometimes carried the symbol of the jaguar sun god, a Maya deity of war and the Underworld.

Warriors went into battle with shields. In the Usumacinta River region, flexible shields, folded and carried over the shoulder, were made out of woven mats. Others were shaped of wood and covered with deerskin; they were painted with emblems of lineages or war deities and decorated with feathers. Quilted cotton jackets, sometimes extending to the knees, served as armor. Even the Spanish eventually replaced their own heavy, and unduly hot, metal armor with quilted cotton, which was effective against Mesoamerican weapons.

5.4 *Yaxchilán Stela 15, Late Classic Period. Shield Jaguar the Great, wearing light battle garb, is shown in the act of capturing a war prisoner.* (Photo courtesy Peter Selverstone)

A few Maya, perhaps war captains, wore helmets with various emblems on them; at Chichén Itzá, pillbox helmets with bird insignia were popular. The Classic Period Maya wore more elaborate wooden and cloth headdresses, many of which were animal effigies that might have represented the animal spirit, or way, of the warrior. Rulers, for example, often claimed jaguars as their way. Many Classic Period warriors, however, were depicted with jaguar headdresses, perhaps indicating a specific warrior lineage or even that they were members of a military order. The Aztecs had two such orders: the Jaguar and the Eagle; admission was gained by the number of prisoners a warrior captured. The Late Postclassic highland Maya had an avian military order, and some native documents describe the great warriors as eagles; the Cakchiquel Maya described Quiché warriors as covered with feathers and wearing metal crowns with precious stones. While some warriors may have been resplendent on the battlefield, the common Maya soldier fought with little clothing other than loincloth and body paint, based on battle scenes in the few Maya murals that remain (see figure 2.9, page 54).

KINDS OF WARFARE

The Maya engaged in warfare from as early as the Preclassic Period. Rulers were depicted wearing trophy heads on their royal belts and fortifications are found at many sites. It is believed that the amount of war increased during the Classic Period and became so intense in the Late Classic Period that it contributed to the fragmentation and collapse of the southern lowland region. The Postclassic Period, too, was plagued by considerable warfare. But the appearance of greater militarization in Maya politics from the Terminal Classic Period through the

Spanish Conquest may result from a richness of information for that time span rather than more warfare. Archaeologists certainly have more documentation from the inscribed monuments, native chronicles, and colonial period manuscripts, and these provide the most important clues to understanding the nature of Maya warfare during these later periods.

Ritual Warfare

It was long thought that until the Postclassic Period, Maya warfare was primarily ritual warfare, involving raids on small neighboring settlements to gain sacrificial victims for a ruler's accession or other divinely mandated events requiring human sacrifice. (See "Blood Sacrifices," Chapter 6). Most captives depicted in Maya art were unnamed, suggesting they were not from important places nor were they important political figures.

Rulers were depicted with captives, and their decapitation of those captives was commemorated in stone monuments carved with hieroglyphic texts. Very often, the decapitation ceremony followed a ball-game ceremony that ended with the sacrifice of the captive. At some sites, monuments depict the ball in these "games" as a human skull or the captive's head. The sculptural program around the great ball court at Chichén Itzá is devoted to ruler accession rituals. The ruler-elect is depicted as a warrior, as the captor of a sacrificial victim, and as a ballplayer in a game ending in decapitation. These rituals had mythological and dynastic significance, as the new ruler was identified with the creator gods who triumphed over the Underworld in a ball game (see "Ball Games," Chapter 6). But these rituals also demonstrated the ruler's ability to protect the state.

Ritual warfare did occur, but archaeologists once believed this was the only form of warfare and that the Maya and, indeed, all Mesoamericans, fought only for sacrificial captives, not for victory. Under this view, warfare amounted to no more than raids for captives. This view gained some currency as an explanation of the Mesoamericans' failure to destroy the Spanish conquistadores, whom they far outnumbered. The Maya, however, fought long and hard for victory against the Spaniards, and there is now evidence that they did the same against other Maya.

Territorial Warfare

Wars were fought for political and economic reasons, not just ritual ones. When such territorial warfare began is unclear, but it is well documented beginning in the Classic Period. Some states won their independence from another through warfare, such as Quiriguá from Copán in 738. Other states fought wars to expand their territory within a small region, such as the shifting control between Yaxchilán and Piedras Negras in the upper Usumacinta area. Other wars took place over considerable distance. In the seventh century, Tikal and Naranjo were conquered by the distant state of Caracol in its attempt to control the central Petén area, more than 100 kilometers (62 miles) away. Naranjo sought revenge when it attacked Caracol 50 years later, in 680.

When territorial expansion was the issue, the star wars symbol (see "Star Wars" below), indicating a divinely guided war, often appeared in the hieroglyphic description of the event. This was the case in Tikal's victory over Naranjo, Dos Pilas's conquest of Seibal, and Caracol's subjugation of Tikal. Despite the divine purpose claimed for such warfare, there were very practical consequences. Victorious cities forced defeated ones to pay tribute and took over the trade routes formerly controlled by their enemies. Tribute was paid in both goods and labor, enriching the victorious states and enabling them to build great monuments to their ruling dynasties. Economic power was an integral part of warfare, just as it has been at most places and times in world history.

There were political consequences of conquest, too. The winning state often permitted the conquered dynasty to continue to rule but only as a secondary center that owed fealty, tribute, and wartime assistance to the victor. This was a common practice in the Usumacinta drainage, for example, between Yaxchilán and Piedras Negras. In other instances, the defeated dynasty was humiliated and weakened by the prolonged captivity of its ruler. During the 18 years that Naranjo held Ucanal's ruler captive in the eighth century, no other ruler could accede to the throne, yet the dynasty persisted. At times, the dynasty was usurped by members of the conquering nobility; this apparently happened when Caracol subjugated Tikal, and Dos Pilas defeated Seibal. In the Postclassic Period, Chichén Itzá conquered many states in the Yucatán, and there is some evidence that some of the conquered rulers resided at Chichén Itzá, perhaps in continuation of the southern lowland practice of prolonged captivity or simply as a means of controlling the tribute from the conquered states. This practice may have been followed by Mayapán at the end of its hegemony in the Late Postclassic Period when the heads of Yucatán's ruling lineages were forced to reside within the city walls.

SYMBOLS OF DEFEAT

The Maya subjected defeated cities to numerous indignities. Although capturing a ruler counted as a great military feat, there were other methods of tarnishing the prestige of an enemy state and undermining the confidence of its people. Captured battle banners, effigies of patron gods, and other sacred trophies were so valued that they were carried in processions in the victorious city and depicted on public monuments. Art also served as a form of perpetual humiliation: Caracol forced Naranjo to carve a hieroglyphic staircase in the sacred center as a reminder of its defeat. Representations of important captives were named and sculpted into stone monuments, and it is thought that the defeated city had to carve such monuments for the victor as a kind of tribute. Sometimes the monument is carved in the signature art style of the defeated polity. At other times, when the conquered dynasty was being replaced, its ruler stelae were damaged and ancestral tombs were disturbed.

Wars of Destruction

It is currently believed that most wars were waged for the purpose of controlling large territories for economic purposes as well as political prestige. If so, the destruction of a city would have been wasteful because it would have destroyed the source of tribute, yet there is archaeological evidence that this occurred occasionally. Tamarindito absolutely annihilated Dos Pilas in the eighth century and forced its inhabitants to flee to the allied city of Aguateca, which was also burned and abandoned (see "Fortifications" below). Some state, perhaps Chichén Itzá, did the same to Chunchucmil during the Terminal Classic Period. In both cases, valuable goods were left strewn about the sites, proving their residents departed suddenly and never returned. The reasons for such wars are unclear, but some archaeologists speculate that in the case of Chunchucmil, Chichén Itzá did not want tribute but rather wanted to eliminate an economic rival in the maritime trade of the northern Yucatán. Tamarindito, a dependency of Dos Pilas, may have initiated the destruction of the Petexbatún kingdom as the only route to its own independence.

5.5   *Bonampak mural, Room 2 (detail), c.790. Bonampak warriors present their dying captives on the palace steps at the city. This famous mural suggests that more than just ritual was involved in such ceremonies. In another scene in the throne room, tribute bundles are displayed and marked with hieroglyphs indicating their contents as cacao beans and* Spondylus *shells.*   (Watercolor copy by Antonio Tejada, 1955)

WAR TACTICS

Logistics

Murals at Chichén Itzá demonstrate that canoes were used to attack cities located along coasts or rivers. There is no such information about overland marches, but many archaeologists speculate that the *sacbeob*, or paved causeways, when they existed, would have provided unimpeded and rapid access for armies through scrub jungle and swamps in both the rainy and dry seasons. The terrain was difficult to traverse, as the Spanish conquistadores discovered, and the trees and brush provided ample cover for Maya spies, who reported back to their war captains about the movements of the enemy. Supplies and reinforcements must have followed these overland and maritime routes, but 16th-century sources claim wars were brief because men went to battle only with the food that could be carried on their backs. However, battles are recorded in the Classic Period between cities that were more than 200 kilometers (104 miles) apart, such as Calakmul's attacks on Palenque.

The Battle

The strategies used by the Maya before the 16th century require more speculation than solid understanding, because such matters were rarely depicted in art or discussed in the surviving texts. Yet the art suggests that hand-to-hand combat was common and, in fact, the only way to capture prisoners alive so they could be carried off to the victorious city and sacrificed. (See figures 2.9 and 5.5.) The most common weapons, the obsidian-spiked club and spear, would have required close contact, too. When fighting on open ground, the warriors probably began the battle some distance apart with spear-throwers, slingshots, and, in the Late Postclassic Period, the bow and arrow. Spear-throwers would have been effective in assailing the enemy in a killing alley as well as on the field; bows and arrows increased the distance for effective attacks and may have resulted in the increased reliance on fortifications in the 13th century.

City Raids

Not all battles occurred in open terrain, although judging from the limited number of fortifications in the lowlands, many did, and Alvarado's battles against the Quiché Maya were outside the cities. Raids and battles also occurred inside cities. According to Classic Period inscriptions, the sacred centers of Palenque and Caracol were invaded. And some urban centers show signs of burning and destruction, such as the broken throne at Piedras Negras and the disturbed tombs at Uaxactún. Paintings at Chichén Itzá show vil-

lages being invaded and pole-and-thatch buildings set afire. The presence of barricades also demonstrate that the city itself was sometimes the battleground.

Fortifications

EARLY MOATS AND WALLS

Some of the most impressive Maya fortifications were constructed during the transition from Late Preclassic to the Early Classic Period (see Chapter 2). Agricultural canals apparently were diverted to form moats around walled city centers, like the Campeche site of Becán, where the ditch was 16 meters (53 feet) wide and 6 meters (20 feet) deep and the wall was 11 meters (36 feet) high. Edzná in Campeche is also thought to have had a moated fortress, as is Balberta on the Pacific coast; other sites seem to have less elaborate barriers, such as the great vertical walls at El Mirador and a protective ditch between Tikal and Uaxactún.

While the moats and walls suggest fortifications against political instability and warfare, some archaeologists have challenged whether evidence is totally decisive. Some of the so-called moats may have been reservoirs, and the walls could have delineated elite or ritual space, as they did at Terminal Classic Uxmal. If the moat and wall at Becán were intended for defense, it is hard to explain why as many as seven causeways spanned the moat and entered the city center. The canal at Cuello may have had a defensive function, but it was also used for intensive agriculture. Despite these doubts, these Preclassic defensive structures required a large investment of labor and material, and it does appear that the constructions at Tikal and El Mirador were for no other purpose than to protect those cities from attack.

5.6   Military camp, Upper Temple of the Jaguars, Chichén Itzá, Early Postclassic Period. This detail from a mural in Chichén Itzá's Upper Temple of the Jaguars suggests a military camp with its temporary pole-and-thatch structures and array of battle banners. Warriors on the upper level seem engaged in a war dance and, based on the speech scrolls, singing.   (Drawing by Linda Schele, copyright David Schele)

BARRICADES AND RAMPARTS

Surveys of the Petexbatún region of the southern lowlands and of northern Yucatán have provided some details about the nature of Maya fortifications. The study of the Petexbatún region, destroyed by warfare, revealed that fortifications were more pervasive there than in other areas of the lowlands. In northern Yucatán, there is evidence for perimeter walls and/or barricades around the centers of only 10 sites out of hundreds during the Terminal Classic Period, and they were not nearly as monumental as those found at Becán and other cities in the southern lowlands in earlier periods.

Petexbatún   The greatest investment in fortifications occurred in the Petexbatún region during the eighth and early ninth centuries. At Dos Pilas, barricades were constructed of finely cut stone blocks, ripped from nearby sacred buildings, in an apparently desperate last effort to defend the city (see "Petexbatún Wars," page 57). Two concentric walls were constructed to create a killing zone 20 to 30 meters (66 to 99 feet) wide: Invaders, entering through the gate, found themselves trapped between the walls and easy targets for the defenders behind the inner wall. The numerous projectile points excavated from the alley and burials of decapitated adult males outside the walls prove the effectiveness of this strategy. Nonetheless, the city was defeated. A deep protective ravine and well-constructed perimeter walls 2 meters (almost 7 feet) high and 1.5 meters (5 feet) wide at Aguateca made that site the refuge for the nobility fleeing from Dos Pilas. But even these defenses were breached, and the city set on fire.

Small settlements surrounded by either barricades or palisades sprang up on hillside terraces in the increasingly devastated region, and those at Quimshi Hilan protected intensively cultivated agricultural fields. The best-fortified site in the region and one of the most impregnable citadels in the southern lowlands was the port of Punta de Chimino on Lake Petexbatún. Three ditches were cut into the rocky peninsula surrounding the port; the largest was flooded to create a moat 48 meters (160 feet) long, 30 meters (100 feet) wide, and 9 meters (30 feet) deep. As if that were inadequate protection, post footings were constructed into a perimeter wall to support a wooden palisade 9 meters (30 feet) high. It is thought that palisades would have been plastered to prevent their being set on fire by the enemy. The labor and time required to remove the stone, construct the rampart, and cut the trees with stone axes for the palisade demonstrates this fortress was conceived by leaders of considerable foresight. Yet even Punta de Chimino was destroyed.

Yucatán   In the Terminal Classic Period, the fortifications constructed in the northern lowlands included a few elaborate wall systems, two small forts—such as the one outside Yaxuná to protect it from a rear attack by Chichén Itzá—and some hastily constructed barricades. The barricades are found most frequently; once destroyed and abandoned, the cities, like Chunchucmil, never had a chance to remove what had been intended to be temporary.

Uxmal and Ek Balam constructed impressive perimeter walls, but they would not have been effective for defense; most likely they defined the sanctity of the ritual center. Ek Balam foresaw some danger, however, and complemented the perimeter wall—2 meters (6.6 feet) high and 3 meters (10 feet) wide—with an outer one, creating a killing alley like the one excavated at Dos Pilas. Inside the center, a third wall joined buildings and blocked causeways, forming yet another defensive ring. This elaborate defensive system was planned and carefully constructed in advance, but it must have proved ineffective because a crude rubble barricade was excavated from the great central plaza of the site.

The relative absence of fortifications in the Yucatán Peninsula suggests the Maya did not find them worth the heavy investment of labor; in fact, all the fortified cities identified suffered

defeat. Nonetheless, conditions in the Late Postclassic Period must have changed Maya views on this, and some have suggested the introduction of the bow and arrow at this time may have been the cause. Because the arrow could hit its target from some distance, cities may have responded with greater defensive undertakings. Both Mayapán and Tulum were walled cities, for example, and their ramparts included parapets and interior walkways. Mayapán's fortifications may have helped it endure for more than 200 years, but its policy of forcing the leaders of its potential enemies to live within the walls may actually have had more to do with its success. Tulum was successfully defended until the arrival of the Spaniards.

ISLANDS AND HILLTOPS

Natural defenses always were used by the Maya. Ravines provided a favored defense against approaching armies, and ridges, a protective outlook over the surrounding terrain. Only in the northern Yucatán, where a source for water was perhaps more important than the occasionally defensive location, were such natural defenses not usually employed.

Guatemala Highlands   In the Late Postclassic Period, the Maya in the southern region retreated from their cities on the valley floors to more easily defensible hilltops. The Spaniards tried to seize the citadel of Mixco Viejo, but the steep path up to the city was wide enough for only two soldiers and while they struggled to climb it, the Maya assaulted them with rocks and arrows. The Quiché capital of Utatlán could be entered only at the point where a spit of land joined the citadel with the surrounding terrain. Ditches dug alongside this land bridge created a narrow causeway that was frightening and difficult to ascend by more than one person at a time; at one point, planks were all that crossed the ravines, and they could be removed. Once across the ravine, fortified walls and a guard station reinforced a stone entrance gate. The Quiché province was dotted with many such citadels, and garrisons were stationed at different locations. If one city was besieged, warriors from the others could attack from the rear, as the Spaniards learned. Battles were decided on the valley floor, not in the citadels themselves.

Petén In the Petén, the kingdom of Tayasal was located on and around Lake Petén Itzá. Although the fields and villages surrounded the lake, the sacred center and capital were built on an island in the lake. In times of trouble, the canoes were docked at the island instead of on shore. When Hernán Cortés visited Tayasal in 1525, he had to wait on the lakeshore for an invitation—and a canoe—to visit the ruler. Like the ramparts in northern Yucatán, the lake protected the settlement from surprise attacks by armies employing the bow and arrow. The Spaniards finally conquered Tayasal in 1697; to do so, they built their own ship, carried it to the lake, and reassembled it in order to seize the capital. Even so, if they had not used guns against Maya bows and arrows, they might have been defeated.

Siege

Based on the defeated fortified cities and villages in the Petexbatún region, siege warfare was practiced by at least the Classic Period. In the northern lowlands, it probably was not the preferred tactic given the lack of fortifications. The lack of ramparts in the Yucatán could indicate a relative lack of warfare; it has been suggested that Chichén Itzá, which was not fortified, created a large stable state in the region and perhaps achieved some relative tranquility. On the other hand, the skull rack and murals of warfare at Chichén Itzá suggest otherwise. The relative absence of fortifications may suggest, instead,

the infrequency of siege tactics in that region. No people can survive for long behind their walls without food and water; in the northern Maya lowlands, farms were dispersed and water was a precious resource not necessarily available in the sacred core of the city. While a fortified center was besieged, enemy troops were easily supplied from the surrounding countryside and put the rural farmers, who sustained the city, at risk.

Even if the open battlefield seems to have been preferred in the Yucatán, fortifications obviously were constructed in both the Terminal Classic and Late Postclassic Periods. And according to the Spaniards, the Maya used siege tactics to their advantage. In 1533, the Maya surrounded the camp of conquistadores at Chichén Itzá and cut off their supplies. The Spaniards, unable to get food or water without venturing into surrounding enemy territory, were forced to run for their lives in the middle of the night, and they eventually abandoned the peninsula. They did not return to the Yucatán for more than six years.

Traps

In highland Guatemala, the Quiché Maya invited Alvarado and his troops to a feast to celebrate the peace. The Spaniards had to cross to the ravine-surrounded city of Utatlán on a narrow causeway that led into the fortified capital. Part of the causeway was removable. Once inside, the ramp could have been lifted and the city gate closed. With no means of escape, the Spaniards would have been unable to maneuver their horses or defend themselves in the narrow streets of the citadel. Approaching the entrance gate, Alvarado sensed the danger and retreated. Other traps were reported, including one in the Yucatán in which the Cocom feasted their enemy, the Xiu, before killing them while they slept.

Alliances

The Classic Period inscriptions provide a glimpse into a Maya world of political and military alliances. Postconquest documents state that the Maya willingly formed alliances with their potential enemies in order to defeat better-known ones. In the Yucatán, for example, the Xiu eventually sided with the Spaniards against the Cocom; in highland Guatemala, the Cakchiquel did the same against the Quiché. The Spaniards themselves marched south with many thousands of Indian allies from the central Mexican highlands.

Retreat

The Maya had other strategies, and the most successful one against the Spaniards turned out to be retreat into the wilderness. According to the native chronicles, retreats were standard practice. The Itzá kingdom in the Petén at Tayasal represented just such a tactic after their defeat at Mayapán in the 15th century. Tayasal's population apparently swelled after the conquest to 25,000. Other Maya settlements grew in interior regions too remote for Spanish control in the early days of the colony.

THE SUPERNATURAL IN WAR

The Maya fought their wars under the protection of the gods. Even the strategies for battle were formulated by officers, called *nacoms* in the Yucatán, who were imbued with the magical spirit of the gods. The Quiché claimed these special war captains were shamans, not mere soldiers. War was not hastily decided upon. Sculptured panels at Yaxchilán depict rulers performing acts of autosacrifice in order to conjure the advice of founding ancestors before entering into war. Priestly diviners checked their astronomical charts to see if the time was propitious for war. When it was time for battle, the Maya carried their sacred banners and wooden idols of their patron deities into war for protection. Before beginning a battle, the gods were called forth with dances, accompanied by the cacaphonous music of giant turtle-shell drums struck with deer antlers, conch-shell horns, and shrill stone whistles. The gods were present everywhere in the Maya world and especially on the battlefield.

A 16th-century Quiché Maya description of a battle against Pedro de Alvarado suggests that the Maya did not see war struggles in the same fashion as their European opponents. The Quiché described their war captain Tecum, who had spent weeks being ritually prepared for battle, as an otherworldly spirit soaring like an eagle above the battlefield: "And then Captain Tecum flew up, he came like an eagle full of feathers . . . they were not artificial; he wore wings which also sprang from his body." (Burkhardt and Gasco 1996: 151) Although a great warrior, his effectiveness was destroyed, according to the Quiché version, after Alvarado cast a spell on his weapons. When killed, Captain Tecum was transformed into a beautiful quetzal bird.

Star Wars

Most Maya wars were fought during the dry season, between the final harvest and the spring rains. This period, with all its agricultural and Underworld associations of death, was time for sacrificial rituals that would guarantee renewal through the rains and the new planting cycle. Also, with the harvest completed, most Maya could safely leave their fields untended in order to go into battle. In the 19th century, the Maya nearly succeeded in ridding the Yucatán of all Spaniards in what has been called the Caste War. The Spanish won only because with the first signs of rain, the Maya abandoned the fight in order to plant their cornfields.

Although most wars occurred during the dry season with its Underworld symbolism, the Maya looked to the gods for the exact time to launch a war, and the gods expressed their will by the movements of the stars. The Long Count dates on Classic Period monuments demonstrate that war repeatedly coincided with certain positions of the stars. Priests, consulting their books, could predict the time of eclipses and the first nighttime appearance of planets such as Venus and Mercury; such astronomical events were taken to represent the divine mandate to begin a war.

Venus, considered by the Maya to be the night sun, was the planet most associated with warfare in Mesoamerica. A hieroglyph called the star wars glyph occurred on dates that can be correlated 70 percent of the time to Venus when it is visible as the Evening Star. Warfare was avoided when Venus was invisible during superior conjunction, defined as a 90-day period between the last appearance of the Morning Star and the rise of the Evening Star. In many cases of territorial warfare, the Maya described their actions as a star-war event, which apparently sanctioned it as a divine mission. On these Venus war monuments, the Maya ruler often is depicted in a Tlaloc war costume (see figure 5.2, page 144).

READING

Ruler as Warrior

Miller 1998, Schele and Freidel 1990, Schele and Miller 1986, Stuart 1984: warrior-ruler.

The Military

Alvarado 1972, Carmack 1981, Recinos, et al. 1967: 16th-century descriptions from highland Guatemala; Tozzer 1941: ethnohistoric descriptions from the Yucatán; Hewitt 1999, Pohl and McBride 1991: discussion of military.

Kinds of Warfare

Freidel 1992, Miller 1996, Schele and Miller 1986: ritual warfare; Miller and Houston 1987, Wren and Schmidt 1991: ball game and war sacrifices. Culbert 1991, Grube and Martin 1998, Martin and Grube 2000: territorial warfare; Dahlin 2000, Demarest, et al. 1997, Freidel 1992, Freidel, Schele, and Parker 1993: terminating warfare.

War Tactics

Alvarado 1972, Chamberlain 1948, Folan, Klintz, and Fletcher 1983, Tozzer 1941: ethnohistoric descriptions; Pohl and McBride 1991: weapons; Bey, et al. 1997, Dahlin 2000, Demarest 1993, Demarest, et al. 1997, Webster 1976 and 1993: fortifications.

The Supernatural in Warfare

Burkhart and Gasco 1996, Recinos, et al. 1967: highland Guatemala battles; Freidel, Schele, and Parker 1993, Tozzer 1941: supernatural protection; Aveni and Hotaling 1994, Lounsbury 1982, Milbrath 1999: star wars.

6

RELIGION, COSMOLOGY, AND ART

by Kaylee Spencer-Ahrens
and Linnea H. Wren

In ancient Maya society, cosmological beliefs pervaded all aspects of life and integrated every individual into a unitary worldview and ethos. The Maya understood the relationship between the natural and supernatural spheres to be a constant interplay of dynamic forces. Through their cosmology and art, the Maya conceptualized the structure of cosmic space, the identities of the gods, the unfolding of creation, the significance of the sacred city, the sustenance of life, the defeat of death, the role of nobles and kings, and the purpose of ritual performances.

While conventional Western attitudes separate the secular life from the sacred sphere, Mesoamerican thought fused the material, prosaic world of human beings with the supernatural world of gods, spirits, and ancestors. Through their art, architecture, and artifacts, the Maya materialized the supernatural presence of the gods, the sacred dramas of the cosmos, and the divine roles of rulers and nobles. Art not only depicted religious images but also harbored sacred powers. Maya rulers and elites grasped scepters carved with godly images, held ceramic vessels painted with supernatural scenes, and costumed themselves with divine attributes. In doing so, the rulers and elites became agents in the supernatural sphere. They conjured ancestors, invoked deities, and shaped destiny both for themselves and for the common people whose lives they governed.

THE STRUCTURE OF COSMIC SPACE

Vertical Space: Three Realms

In ancient Maya thought, the universe was suffused with sacredness that resonated from the presence of deities. The ancestors, spirits, and deities not only resided in the Upperworld and the Underworld but also shared the Middleworld, or Earth, with its human and animal populations. In the Middleworld, supernatural beings claimed extraordinary geological features of the natural landscape as their special precincts and magnetized architectural structures that humans constructed for ritual purposes.

The sacred quality that emanated from the gods filled a universe that, the Maya believed, was shaped by logical principles and orderly harmony. In conceptualizing the universe, the Maya constructed a spatial model that organized horizontal and vertical space. Vertical space was divided into three realms consisting of an Upperworld, Middleworld, and Underworld.

Horizontal Space: Quadripartite Order

Horizontal space was divided into four quadrants spreading from a central axis. Oriented to the four cardinal directions, the four quadrants of the Middleworld were associated with the Pawahtun gods. The Pawahtuns were a fourfold version of God N (see under "Major Deities" below), the old god who ruled over the days at the end of the year. Standing at the four corners of the cosmos, the Pawahtuns held the cosmic realms in place. Images of the cosmic world-bearers were incorporated into the architectural sculpture at widely distant Maya sites, including Copán and Chichén Itzá, where the Pawahtuns support thrones, altars, and temple roofs. The four cardinal directions and the central axis of the Middleworld were associated with their own colors, trees, and birds. East was identified as the direction of the rising Sun and was regarded as the primary direction. The color corresponding to east was red. North was regarded as the direction of the ancestors and of death. The color corresponding to north was white. West was identified as the direction of the setting Sun and was regarded as the direction of the Underworld; its corresponding color was black. South was identified as the right hand of the Sun; its color was yellow. The center was regarded as the location of the world axis and had corresponding color of green.

The Center: Quincunx

The conceptualization of horizontal space as a quincunx—a quadripartite world plus its center—was a fundamental theme in Maya cosmology. The central axis of the universe, or axis mundi, was visualized as a great ceiba tree. A celestial bird, called Itzam-Ye by the Maya and sometimes called the Principal Bird Deity by modern scholars, was believed to perch in the branches of the axial tree. With its branches extending into the heavens, its straight trunk piercing the earth, and its roots digging downward, the ceiba tree, at its full height, reached the forest canopy. The supernaturally charged energies of the three vertical cosmic realms flowed along the living axis created by the tree. The cosmological tree, also called the World Tree, provided the channel for the souls of humans, after death, to travel into the Underworld and for the gods, when summoned by human petitioners, to pass into the Middleworld. The central axis was replicated at each of the four cardinal directions by distinct pairings of trees and birds.

SACRED HOMES

The quincunx structure of the Middleworld was replicated on a human scale in vernacular architecture. Constructed by the Maya commoners for their daily living, houses were generally single-room structures. These structures were built with walls consisting of poles and woven branches and with roofs consisting of thatched leaves. The four poles that framed the corners of the houses corresponded to the four trees planted at the four cardinal directions. A fifth pole, erected at the house center, was identified with the ceiba tree that served as the cosmic axis mundi. The cosmic center was further mirrored by the domestic hearth that was often found in the center of the house.

Furthermore, the Maya formed their domestic hearths by placing three stones in a triangular arrangement, mimicking the Cosmic Hearth, which the Maya identified with a triangular configuration of three stars in the nocturnal sky. Just as the three stones of the domestic hearth enclosed a smoky fire that emanated warmth, the three stars of the Cosmic Hearth encompassed a cloudy nebula. Just as their ancestors made metaphorical connections between the celestial hearth of the night sky and the hearths of their dwellings, the modern Maya continue to identify the corner poles and central hearths with cosmic prototypes.

SACRED FIELDS

The quincunx structure of the Middleworld was further replicated on a human scale in the agricultural fields. Four poles were erected at the corners of maize plots cultivated by Maya farmers. The physical boundaries designated by the poles circumscribed a green center consisting of ripening corn. The contemporary Yucatec Maya continue to summon the ancient rain deities into their fields through ch'a chak ceremonies. In these ceremonies, a wooden altar is constructed with four posts that signify the four cosmic supports. Arches formed by saplings bent above the altar top represent the cosmos, while the altar surface represents the earth. Thus the ancient practice of conceptualizing cosmic space within the contexts of commonplace life has survived into modern Maya practice.

The Upperworld

The space in which the Sun and constellations moved across the sky constituted the Upperworld. In the night sky, a path was inscribed by the motion of important celestial bodies including the Sun, Moon, and planets. Called the ecliptic by modern observers, this path of celestial movement was visualized as a double-headed serpent. The metaphorical association between the ecliptic band and the bicephalic serpent was reinforced in Maya speech. Mayan languages use the same words for "sky" and "snake": *kan* in Yucatec, or *chan* in Cholan, for example.

The Upperworld, or heavens, served as a stage upon which the actions of the gods were played out. Many scholars believe that the Maya, like the later Aztecs, divided the Upperworld into 13 ascending levels. The activities of the deities were revealed by the astrological movements of the planets and stars in the Upperworld. As the dead exited the Middleworld, they traveled along the luminous Milky Way. The planet Venus was a bright light that etched a complex pattern in the sky. The Maya associated Venus with war and regarded its presence as powerful and its influence as potentially dangerous. Rulers timed military campaigns according to the appearances of Venus after the planetary inferior or superior conjunctions, and scribes recorded the glyph for Venus in their references to those bellicose campaigns. Warriors who died in battle and women who died in childbirth entered the Upperworld.

Underworld

Like the Upperworld, the Underworld was a sphere associated with supernatural beings. The Maya may have organized the Underworld into nine descending levels. Known as Xibalba in some Maya accounts of the cosmos, the Underworld was a watery place through which two major rivers flowed. Entered through caves or bodies of standing water, such as lakes or natural springs, the Underworld harbored generative powers. At the same time, it was dreaded and believed to be a frightful place of decay and disease. Persons who had died peaceful deaths were consigned to the Underworld.

In addition to conceptualizing cosmic space in terms of a geometric model, cosmic space was also interpreted in metaphors drawn from the natural world. One such metaphor consisted of a great caiman swimming in a pool of water-lilies. The rough back of the caiman represented the surface of the earth, which was worked into furrows by farmers and which was cracked into ridges by solar heat. A second metaphor of cosmic space consisted of a turtle swimming in the primordial sea. Like the back of the caiman, the uneven shell of the turtle offered a parallel to the earth. Some images of Pawahtuns depict a turtle carapace covering the back of the deity, an evident reference to the metaphor of the earth as a turtle. Turtle imagery was also reflected in the night sky where one constellation was identified as a turtle. This constellation, which corresponded to the belt of the Western constellation Orion, could be observed at midnight on the ending of a special cycle of time called a *k'atun*.

Mountains and Caves

As well as considering the Upperworld and Underworld to be realms of supernatural forces, the ancient Maya believed that the natural landscape of the Middleworld was imbued with sacredness. Architectural structures built by the Maya were deliberate replications of geological features that harbored the powers of the divine beings. The Maya were therefore able to utilize both natural landscape formations and their architectural equivalents in order to ensure their continued access to the gods, spirits, and ancestors.

Two natural landscape formations that the Maya re-created in architecture were the mountain and the cave. As houses of the gods, spirits, and ancestors, mountains were identified as especially potent places. Their potency was augmented by the identification of a cosmic mountain as the origin place of maize. Maize not only constituted the most important food source by which the ancient Maya sustained life but also provided the dough from which the gods had created human flesh.

The Maya transferred the power of mountains from the cosmic realm and from the natural landscape into their cities and centers through the construction of pyramids. As access routes into the interiors of sacred mountains, caves were also potent places. Because they were also considered portals to the Underworld, caves were realms of both danger and potential fertility. In the mythology of central Mexico during the Postclassic Period, caves were the natural wombs from which human beings emerged during creation.

Among many contemporary Maya groups, mountains and caves continue to be regarded as sacred places. One such group is the Maya of Zinacantán, a district in the highlands of Chiapas, Mexico. Since ancestral spirits are believed to dwell inside mountains and since those spirits are regarded as having curative powers, the Zinacantecos visit mountain shrines during curing ceremonies for the sick. During a lengthy processional ritual, the patient, family members, and the shaman visit the crosses that are erected at mountain shrines. There, participants attach fresh pine boughs and flowers to the crosses and petition the ancestors for their well-being by lighting candles, offering prayers, and drinking local rum.

Pyramid-Mountains

The modern Maya use the word *witz* to mean a "mountain." The same word was used by the ancient Maya for "pyramid." The temple that normally surmounted a pyramid-mountain was thought to be the place of the gods. Most often called *k'uh nah* (holy, or god, house), such homes for the gods were replicated in temple architecture and incorporated into rituals in virtually all Maya cities.

Because the mountains were considered living entities, the Maya represented mountains as zoomorphic creatures with eyes, muzzles, mouths, and ear ornaments. The stony composition of the *witz* zoomorphs, or monster-mountains, was indicated by inscribed markings resembling bunches of grapes or clusters of small circles. Read as the Maya word *tun*, these markings signify stone and appear on many examples of the *witz* zoomorphs.

A PYRAMID MOUNTAIN AT PALENQUE

One example of the *witz* monster appears at the site of Palenque in the Usumacinta region. The pyramid-temple known as the Temple of the Foliated Cross houses a large tablet carved with a relief image that combines the representation of a historical king, Kan B'alam II, with cosmic symbols (see figure 6.5, page 176). The left side of the relief depicts Kan B'alam standing on top of a zoomorphic head. Foliage, resembling the leaves of corn plants, sprout from the cleft forehead of the creature below the king's feet. Hieroglyphs, inscribed in the creature's eyes, label the zoomorph as a *witz*, or mountain. The Maize Mountain was described in Maya creation mythology and was utilized by Kan B'alam as the cosmic prototype for the Temple of the Foliated Cross. In constructing his pyramid-temple and in commissioning its reliefs, Kan B'alam simultaneously claimed for himself political control over the city he governed and ritual participation in the sacred landscape.

Caves and Temples

Examples of caves constructed within the *witz* pyramid can be identified in at least three architectural practices. In one architectural practice, the *witz* pyramid incorporated a hollow chamber in the center of the structure. At Palenque, the pyramid-temple now known as the Temple of the Inscriptions was built as the tomb of the ruler Hanab Pakal. A cavelike funerary crypt is located beneath the central axis of the architectural structure, while a staircase and a hollow tube provided conduits between the Underworld realm and the human plane.

In a second architectural practice, the *witz* pyramid was constructed above a natural cave. At Chichén Itzá, in northern Yucatán, the pyramid-temple now known as the High Priest's Grave is located above a cave. Steps hollowed out at its edge indicate that the cave had been in ritual use long before its incorporation into an architectural complex. During the construction of the pyramid, a vertical shaft with narrow toeholds was built between the cave roof and the temple above the pyramid. Human remains were deposited in the cave at the bottom of the shaft and were interred within the shaft itself. The practice was Mesoamerican, not just Maya: In central Mexico, the Pyramid of the Sun at Teotihuacan rests atop a lobed cave that represented the cave of human origin.

In a third architectural practice, the *witz* pyramid supported a temple whose interior was metaphorically designated as a cave. At Uxmal in northwestern Yucatán, the exterior temple facade of the Pyramid of the Magicians is ornamented with a *witz* monster mask. By walking through the temple entrance, which is surrounded by the open jaws of the *witz* monster, the human agent in a temple ritual entered a symbolic cave within an architectural mountain.

Other Sacred Architecture

In addition to building architectural equivalents of mountains and caves, the Maya fashioned other sacred spaces in their cities. The combined forces of the cosmic realms and of human sphere were focused in a Maya center. At Chichén Itzá, the grandiose plazas supported many architectural structures, including pyramid-temples, ball courts, and dance platforms that served as loci for human interactions with the supernatural. Raised roads or causeways, called *sacbeob*, radiated from the two most important plazas. Two such causeways led to deep natural wells, or cenotes, that the inhabitants of Chichén Itzá had incorporated into their site. Like caves, cenotes were regarded as providing access to the Underworld and were places of ritual importance. This importance is underscored by the offerings recovered from the muddy bottom of the larger of the cenotes at Chichén Itzá, now known as the Sacred Cenote. Among the offerings thrown by the ancient Maya into Sacred Cenote were gold ornaments, jade objects, and the skeletal remains of men, women, and children. Thus, the *sacbeob* that linked the cenotes to the plazas of Chichén Itzá not only facilitated the movement of people throughout the site precincts but also directed the passage of supernatural powers into the site center.

THE IDENTITIES OF THE GODS

In the Maya cosmos, all things possessed the potential to harbor sacredness. Maya religion was grounded in the abstract concept of sacredness (*k'uhul* in Yucatec Mayan) and in the manifestation of that sacredness in the inanimate forces of nature, in the deified ancestors and lineage founders of Maya families and states, and in supernatural beings or gods. Although more than 250 names of Maya deities have been recorded in sources written during the colonial and modern periods, it is impossible to describe each of these deities as a distinct god. Maya gods cannot be categorized as if they belonged to a Western pantheon in which gods are understood as discrete beings possessing distinctive characteristics, recognizable by individual attributes, and occupying different domains. Instead, Maya gods behaved as fluid beings that manifested sacred qualities in shifting ways. For the Maya, a deity could assume a number of separate aspects of manifestations that could be expressed in a number of different names, appearances, and qualities. Simultaneously, many deities could overlap in their identities, functions, and roles. The most applicable model of the Maya pantheon is one of deity complexes or clusters. Each complex or cluster consisted of multiple deities that shared thematic roles and/or cosmological meanings connected to underlying principles, such as rain, sun, fertility, earth, trade, and war. At the same time, any single deity could belong to multiple complexes and could merge with other deities in terms of their roles and meanings.

Fluidity of Maya Supernaturals

The fluidity of Maya deities can be formulated in a series of principles that activated ancient Maya religion. One principle consists of the widespread Maya belief that a single god could exist in quadriplicity. In quadripartite form, a god manifested four aspects that corresponded to the four world directions and the four world colors. A second principle consists of the widespread Maya belief that a single god could exist in duality. In binary form, a god manifested dual qualities that corresponded to oppositions such as benevolent versus malevolent, young versus old, male versus female. A single god might also occupy opposite realms of the cosmos and be influential during opposite periods of the day. A third principle consists of the widespread Maya belief that a single god could combine aspects of many levels of existence. For example, many images of gods were zoomorphs, combining characteristics of reptiles, jaguars, and other animals. Other deity depictions incorporated animal and supernatural elements into fundamentally anthropomorphic, or human, images. However problematic the Maya conceptualization of deities may seem to Westerners, its complexity undeniably reveals the sophistication of the ancient Maya.

Schellhas Catalog of Deities

At the end of the 19th century, the scholar Paul Schellhas studied the Maya gods as they were depicted in the Maya codices, or screenfold books, which focused on ritual, divination, and prognostication. The most important codex for Schellhas's study was the *Dresden Codex*, which was written in northern Yucatán during the Postclassic Period and is preserved in the library of Dresden, Germany. Schellhas analyzed iconographic elements including costumes worn by the gods and material objects held by them. He further studied physical attributes associated with the gods and the types of activities in which the gods were engaged. As a result Schellhas was able to isolate and describe individual deities. In order to avoid affixing inappropriate names to the gods, Schellhas referred to them by

6.1   *Some gods of the Maya pantheon from Postclassic codices: a) the death god (God A); b) Chak, a rain deity (God B); c) a deity personifying sacredness, or k'uhul (God C); d) Itzamná (God D); e) the maize god (God E); f) the sun god (God G); g) Young Moon Goddess (Goddess I); h) K'awil, a deity embodying rulership (God K); i) merchant god (God M); j) Old Moon Goddess (Goddess O).*   (Drawing by Kaylee Spencer-Ahrens after Coe, 1999)

assigning neutral letters. Except in instances in which the deity name can be identified in ancient Maya texts, this practice continues today. Although it does not represent the entire Maya pantheon, the series of deities cataloged by Schellhas include many deities that are frequently depicted in Maya imagery. With the assistance of Schellhas's catalog, subsequent scholars have been able to ascertain the identities of some deities in Maya imagery of the Classic and Preclassic Periods and have been able to trace the origin of many Maya deities.

Major Deities

GOD D: ITZAMNÁ

Although no single god was worshiped as the supreme deity everywhere in the Maya region throughout the preconquest periods, one god was clearly described as the preeminent deity in the colonial accounts of the Yucatán. This ancient creator god was known as Itzamná, meaning "reptile house" in Yucatec Mayan. Identified by Schellhas as God D, Itzamná is depicted in the codices as an old man whose wrinkled visage is characterized by a toothless lower jaw, sunken cheeks, and a Roman nose. A beaded disk is often depicted upon the brow of Itzamná and is incorporated in the name glyph that identifies him. This disk, which is sometimes inscribed with an *akbal* sign, denoting darkness or blackness, may represent the polished black surface of an obsidian mirror. The polished black surfaces of such mirrors were important devices that allowed shamans to see past and future events. As an attribute of Itzamná, the obsidian mirror suggests an important function of the god.

The importance of God D is further underscored by Itzamná's association with the Ahaw title, which means "great lord" or "king." The association between Itzamná and rulership explains a second function accorded Itzamná as the patron of the day Ahaw in the ritual calendar, or *tzolk'in*.

Attributed by the Maya with the invention of books and writing, Itzamná was fittingly portrayed as a scribe in many images. Identified with curing the sick, Itzamná was invoked as a god of medicine during Sip, a month in the solar calendar, or *haab'*. Ix Chel, the aged goddess of weaving and childbirth and the female companion of Itzamná, also possessed curative powers. As a generative god of creation, Itzamná participated in forming the cosmos by setting the third stone in the Cosmic Hearth. Maya texts of the Classic Period named this stone the Waterlily Throne Stone.

Principal Bird Deity: Vuqub Caquix As Lord of Gods, Itzamná presided over day, night, and the heavens. In one celestial aspect, Itzamná was sometimes manifested as the Principal Bird Deity called Itzam-Ye in Maya texts and Vuqub Caquix in Maya creation mythology of the Postclassic Period. In another celestial aspect, Itzamná was sometimes addressed as K'inich Ahaw Itzamná. This form of address, which indicated the overlapping identities of the Maya deities, combined the name of the aged creator god, Itzamná, with the name of the youthful sun god, K'inich Ahaw.

GOD G: K'INICH AHAW

Designated God G by Schellhas, the principal solar god was called K'inich Ahaw, meaning "the sun-faced lord" or the "sun-eyed lord," by the ancient Maya. The relationship between K'inich Ahaw and Itzamná was visualized in profile images of the sun god, which resemble a younger version of the creator god. Attributes that K'inich Ahaw share with Itzamná include a Roman nose and large square eyes. Attributes that distinguish K'inich Ahaw from Itzamná include a bearded chin, snakelike curves extending from the mouth, and a four-petaled sign decorating the sun god's brow or body. This sign, called the *k'in* sign, represents the Maya words for both the sun and the day. In addition, K'inich Ahaw is shown in frontal view with crossed eyes and with his upper incisors filed into a T shape.

During the day, the sun deity traversed the Upperworld in his manifestation as K'inich Ahaw. During the night, the sun deity journeyed into the Underworld in his transformed manifestation as the fearsome Jaguar God. As K'inich Ahaw, the sun god represented the solar cycle by which farmers based their agricultural activities and the solar heat on which all natural life depended. As the Jaguar God of the Underworld, the sun god functioned as a patron of war. The qualities associated with the sun god led rulers in many Maya centers to assume the identity of the sun god. At Palenque, the Temple of the Sun houses a relief tablet that depicts the birth of war and incorporates imagery of the sun god (see figure 6.6, page 177). The tablet of the Temple of the Sun also intertwines motifs relating to rulership and lineage with symbolism relating to the Sun.

GOD B: CHAK

Chak, labeled God B by Schellhas, was regarded as the most important rain deity by the Maya. In images of the Classic Period, Chak was depicted with many reptilian traits including catfishlike whiskers, a snout, and body scales. The association between Chak and water is further emphasized by the *Spondylus* shells decorating the deity's ears. In codices of the Postclassic Period, Chak retains reptilian features in his face but becomes more human in general appearance. The reptilian snout of Classic Period depictions is metamorphosed into an enormous downward curling nose that, although unnatural in dimension, is recognizably human in form. In the *Madrid Codex*, this deity's name incorporates T-shaped eyes, a feature shared with the central Mexican rain god Tlaloc.

Chak was thought to reside in caves, a moist space where rain-bearing clouds, thunder, and lightning were born. In numerous images, Chak is depicted as if holding a bolt of lightning, a stone ax, or a serpent. Accounts from the colonial period describe Chak as wielding thunder and lightning and as cracking open the rock from which life-giving maize emerged. The inclusion of lightning bolts, stone axes, and serpents in preconquest images of Chak indicate that beliefs about the rain deity were ancient. Because of their dependence on seasonal rains, farmers had appealed to Chak from as early as the Late Preclassic Period at Izapa, and continue to do so today. Generally regarded as a benevolent god, Chak has been continuously worshiped in Mesoamerica for a longer period than almost any other god.

Like many aspects of the cosmos, Chak often assumes a quadripartite form. Each of the four aspects of the quadripartite Chak was linked to a cardinal direction and was associated with its own color. Chak Xib Chak, Red Chak, related to the east; Sak Xib Chak, White Chak, was associated with the north; Ek Xib Chak, Black Chak, corresponded to the west; and Kan Xib Chak, Yellow Chak, was related to the south. Chak Xib Chak was particularly important to Maya rulers, who utilized the associated imagery of this aspect of Chak to denote their own rulership.

GOD K: K'AWIL

Another god who was associated with elite power and status was K'awil. Known in Schellhas's system as God K, K'awil is shown in Classic Period depictions with a serpent foot; a prominent, upturned snout; and his forehead pierced by a smoking torch or ax blade. Full-figure representations of this god were fashioned into handheld scepters, called Manikin Scepters by contemporary scholars. By holding the Manikin Scepter depicting K'awil, a Maya king displayed his emblem of rulership and asserted his position of authority. So significant was this scepter that its bestowal on a lord was a crucial part of accession rituals conducted when a ruler assumed the throne.

GOD E: THE MAIZE GOD

To the ancient Maya, maize was the primary component of the human diet. Its importance was underscored by the cosmic role it played in the creation of humankind. According to Maya myths gods formed the present race of humans from dough made of maize mixed with blood. The maize deity, called God E by Schellhas, incorporated ideas of human, as well as agricultural, fertility. Generally represented as a youthful male with maize plants crowning his head, the maize god evinced two distinct but overlapping aspects. The aspect associated with tender maize sprouts is called the Foliated Maize God by contemporary scholars, while the aspect associated with mature and fertile maize, is called the Tonsured Maize God. The head of the Tonsured Maize God is flattened at the top, resulting in an elongated appearance. In many images, sections of the forehead of the Tonsured Maize God are shown as shaved so that the head of the deity further resembles an ear of corn.

Hun Hunahpu The Tonsured Maize God, or Hun Nal Ye, is the Classic Period prototype of Hun Hunahpu, a supernatural being whose exploits are recorded in postconquest accounts of creation, such as the *Popol Vuh*. Together with his twin brother, Vuqub Hunahpu, Hun Hunahpu is described as entering the Underworld where he is challenged to contests with the lords of Xibalba. Although Hun Hunahpu is defeated and sacrificed, the severed head of Hun Hunahpu retains its potency and begets twin sons, known as the Hero Twins (see below). The twins repeat their father's contests in the Underworld, and retrieve their father's remains. The retrieval of Hun Hunahpu from the Underworld was interpreted by the Maya as a resurrection of life symbolizing the agricultural cycle of growth, decay, and reemergence. Hun Hunahpu is frequently shown as the deity who, like the maize plant he embodies, is resurrected from the cracked earth.

GOD A: THE DEATH GOD

Just as they had special gods associated with fertility and abundance, the Maya also had gods associated with death and decay. The death god resides in the Underworld and patronizes the day Kimi, meaning "death" in Mayan. This god is lettered by Schellhas as God A and is named in the *Madrid Codex* as Kisim, "flatulent one."

The unattractive appearance, as well as the unpleasant name, associated with the death god reflects the undesirability of the deity's Underworld domain. Depictions of the skeletal body and skull of the death god include representations of bare ribs and of the small spiny details of the bones. In some representations, the death god is shown fleshed and bloated. His abdomen is pockmarked by bloody rotting sores, and his skin is covered with dark patches suggesting a state of decomposition. A diagnostic costume element of the death god is a ruff composed of bunches of "death eyes." Literally a wreath of extruded eyeballs, the death-eyes ruff sometimes appears as the hair on the head of the death god, or as cuffs on the deity's wrists and ankles. These attributes emphasize the function of the god in the Underworld realm of death and decay.

The death god has two hieroglyphic names, both of which underscore his associations with death and the Underworld. The first hieroglyphic name represents the head of a corpse with closed eyes, while the second hieroglyphic name depicts the head of the death god himself with a shortened nose, fleshless jaws, and a flint sacrificial knife. Another attribute of the death god is the owl, a bird associated with night, caves, and the deadly capture of prey. In the *Popol Vuh*, owls serve as messengers who fly from the Underworld to the Middleworld.

GOD L: A MERCHANT GOD

Another aged god associated with the Underworld, designated as God L, is frequently shown with a black body. God L typically has square eyes, wears a cape, and smokes a cigar. The most diagnostic attribute of God L is a large brimmed hat on which a bird perches. The bird represented in the headdress of God L is a screech owl, with black-tipped feathers. The screech owl, known as the Muan bird by the Yucatec Maya, sometimes incorporates maize foliage, as well as abstract signs for maize and death. These signs reveal the bird's dual association with rain and maize, as well as with death and the Underworld. In addition to having mortuary connotations, God L serves as the patron of merchants and is sometimes depicted carrying a merchant pack tied with bundles of exotic goods, including cacao and quetzal feathers. On the Classic Period Vase of the Seven Gods, God L is depicted in the company of six other deities (see figure 6.3, page 173). In this scene, the merchant god is shown with three bundles, one at the bottom between the throne and the lower tier of lords, another in front of the upper group of lords, and still another behind him on his throne.

GOD M: A MERCHANT GOD

A second deity who served as a merchant god is known in Schellhas's classification as God M. While he exhibits black-painted skin similar to that of God L, God M also has distinctive attributes including a pendulous lower lip and an extremely long and narrow nose. This deity, who may have been named Ek Chuah, sometimes carries a spear. The military aspect of Ek Chuah reveals the bellicose nature of trade in which attacks on merchants were common and self-defense was essential. During the Postclassic Period, Ek Chuah seems to have eclipsed God L, whose depictions are more frequent in the Classic Period.

GOD N: PAWAHTUN

According to the 16th-century Spanish bishop Diego de Landa, one deity, identified as God N by Schellhas, bears the responsibility of holding up the sky. Glyphically named Pawahtun, this deity exists in four aspects. In its quadripartite form, Pawahtun functions as the four world-bearers who support the corners of the universe at the cardinal directions. When serving as world-bearers, the Pawahtuns are also known as the Bacabs.

On Classic Period painted vessels, God N frequently appears as an old man wearing a turtle shell on his back and a netted cloth headdress. Despite his great responsibility of balancing the cosmos on his shoulders, God N often appears in a state of intoxication accompanied by groups of beautiful young women. In addition to serving as the patron god of scribes, God N also presided over the dangerous five-day period called Wayeb (see Chapter 9).

GODDESS O AND GODDESS I: THE MOON GODDESS

In ancient Maya religion, the Moon was associated with a female deity. The goddess possessed dual aspects of youth and age. In her youthful aspect, the deity is labeled in the Schellhas system as Goddess I, and in her aged aspect, the deity is labeled as Goddess O. Goddess I is depicted as a beautiful young woman whose distinctive attributes are a beaklike nosepiece, the lunar crescent, and a rabbit. Mesoamerican peoples interpreted the shadowed formations on the lunar surface as a rabbit, as opposed to the man on the Moon perceived by Westerners.

At Yaxchilán, in Chiapas, Mexico, the imagery celebrating the parentage of the ruler incorporates paired moon and sun signs. A portrait of the ruler's mother is depicted within the lunar sign, while a portrait of the ruler's father is depicted within the solar sign. The pairing of the signs within the context of the ruler's coupled parents has led scholars to infer that the Moon was the wife of the Sun. The Young Moon Goddess and the Tonsured Maize God sometimes share attributes. In at least one instance, the moon crescent is associated with the Tonsured Maize God. In other examples, the Young Moon Goddess assumes costume features, facial markings, and coiffure that typified the Tonsured Maize God. The overlapping elements reveal the association between the moon goddess and the maize god. Furthermore, Xkik, the wife of Hun Hunahpu and the mother of the Hero Twins, may be an aspect of the moon goddess. Her identification with the Tonsured Maize God may be explained by the widespread use of the lunar cycle for determining times to plant agricultural crops, including maize.

Ix Chel, the Maya name for Goddess O, incorporates the Maya word for rainbow, *chel*. Unlike Westerners, who welcome the rainbow, the Maya dreaded it and described it as the "flatulence of demons." A rainbow was thought to begin in dry wells that the Maya labeled as the anus of the Underworld. Like caves, rainbows were considered sources of disease. The appearance of Ix Chel, with her clawed hands and feet, her fanged mouth, and her skirt decorated with crossed bones, evoked anxieties appropriate to a deity identified with disease, storms, floods, and world destruction.

As well as connoting malevolent qualities, Ix Chel also fulfilled benevolent functions. Through her association with water, the Old Moon Goddess overlapped with Chak, the venerated god of rain. Moreover, Ix Chel was regarded as the great generatrix of creation and was the patron deity of divination, medicine, childbirth, and weaving.

THE HERO TWINS

This set of twins from the Quiché Maya creation narrative the *Popol Vuh* also appeared as a pair of deities in Classic Period art. In the *Popol Vuh*, the Hero Twins, named Hunahpu and Xbalanque, were descended from an older set of twins. The Hero Twins engaged in activities that eventually led to the creation of the current universe and people. Hunahpu was identifiable by the black spot on his cheek and prominent black spots on his body, while Xbalanque's primary attribute included patches of jaguar pelts on his face and body. Some feats undertaken by the Hero Twins mentioned in the *Popol Vuh* included killing the Principal Bird Deity with their blowguns for his arrogance (see figure 6.8, page 184), playing the ball game with Underworld lords, and resurrecting the maize god. As the primary protagonists in bringing the universe into its present order, Maya rulers identified with the actions and responsibilities of the Hero Twins. Many rituals performed by Maya kings sought to reenact their role in world creation.

THE PADDLER GODS

An important pair of deities is the Paddler Gods, so called because they are depicted in some imagery as paddlers in a canoe. One such image is incised on a bone found in Burial 116 at Tikal in the Petén. This image depicts a scene in which the Paddlers transport the maize god in their canoe through the waters of the Underworld. Since some Mayanists have argued that the canoe also served as a visual metaphor for the Milky Way, the Paddler Gods can be understood as journeying across the celestial world until they arrive at the constellation that Westerners call Orion, where creation took place.

The Paddlers are depicted at opposite sides of the canoe. The two gods have been designated by modern scholars as the Old Jaguar Paddler at the front of the boat and the Old Stingray Paddler at the stern. Embodying oppositions, the Paddler Gods represent night and day. The hieroglyphic sign for *akbal*, or "darkness," is associated with the Old Jaguar Paddler, while the hieroglyphic sign for *k'in*, or day, is associated with the Old Stingray Paddler.

In some versions of the creation story, the Paddler Gods participate in establishing the Cosmic Hearth by setting the first of the three hearth stones—the Jaguar Throne Stone—in place at a location called Na-Ho-Chan, or First-Five-Sky. The Old Jaguar Paddler, who shares characteristics with jaguar deities, wears a headdress that is in the shape of a jaguar head covered with black spots. Like other aged deities, he has no teeth.

The Paddlers are often represented in association with serpent imagery. Serpents were used in Maya images as embodiments of the visions by which the Maya manifested their

6.2   *Canoe scene incised on bones from Burial 116, Tikal, Guatemala, Late Classic Period. The top scene shows two paddlers, the maize god, an iguana, a monkey, a parrot, and a dog. The bottom scene, carved on another bone, shows the canoe as it sinks into the primordial sea.*   (Drawing by Linda Schele, copyright David Schele)

ancestors and deities during ritual bloodletting. In some scenes depicting bloodletting rituals, miniature representations of the Paddlers appear within mystical clouds inside the opposite ends of the open jaws of serpents. Other images incorporate miniature representations of the Paddlers emerging from the serpent-headed ends of a ceremonial bar. The association between the Paddlers and bloodletting rituals is underscored by the stingray spines and bones worn in the nasal septum of the Old Stingray Paddler. The same implements were frequently used in sacred rites in which rulers offered their blood to the gods.

THE UNFOLDING OF CREATION

Maya creation stories provided a template for understanding the origin of the cosmos and the role of humankind. Creation stories are described in hieroglyphic texts as well as in Maya art. These myths appear as early as the Late Preclassic Period, when they are represented in monumental stucco facades of buildings and carved into stelae. They persist over the centuries and are incorporated into postconquest native chronicles, such as the *Popol Vuh*, which is invaluable for its elaborate account. A few examples of these creation myths follow, and the fuller story of the *Popol Vuh* is described later in the chapter.

The Tikal Bones

Scenes of the Paddler Gods and the cosmic canoe are incised on four bones interred with Hasaw Chan K'awil, an important king in Tikal Period. In two of the four scenes, the passengers of the canoes include the maize god, an iguana, a monkey, a parrot, and a dog. In one of the scenes depicting these passengers, the canoe sinks into the waters of the Underworld sea. Some art historians and epigraphers have argued that both scenes contain astronomical significance and narrate creation events that preceded the resurrection of the maize god. At midnight on 9.14.11.17.3 (September 16, 743), the date that is inscribed on one of the bones, the Milky Way was stretched across the sky in an east to west orientation. The sinking of the canoe in the scene incised on the Tikal bone corresponds with the rotation of the Milky Way as it brings the three stars of Orion (the Cosmic Hearth) to the nocturnal zenith. The Paddler Gods are shown paddling their canoe across the sky in order to arrive at the belt stars of the constellation known to Westerners as Orion. The triangular space in the nocturnal sky that was marked by the three belt stars was identified by the Maya as the place in which creation occurred. It is at the moment when the three stars reached their zenith that the Paddlers set up the Jaguar Throne Stone, the first stone of the Cosmic Hearth.

Stela C at Quiriguá

According to the Maya calendar, the universe in which humankind currently lives was created on the date 4 Ahaw 8 Kumk'u. The Maya creation date, which corresponds to the Western date August 13, 3114 B.C.E., was inscribed on Maya monuments that recounted how the gods created the universe. One of the most important of these texts is located at the site of Quiriguá.

K'ak' Tiliw Chan Yoaat (better known as Cauac Sky) ruled Quiriguá during the Late Classic Period between 724 and 785 C.E. During his reign, K'ak' Tiliw Chan Yoaat erected a series of magnificent stelae. The text inscribed on Stela C includes references to the events of creation, to the participatory gods, and to the

date on which creation occurred. Creation involved the setting up of the Cosmic Hearth at the place called Na-Ho-Chan (First-Five-Sky). Introducing these actions in the text is the verb *hal*, which means both "to say" and "to make appear." The creation event itself is described not as an esoteric process understandable only to the gods but as a tangible act of the setting and naming three stones, as deciphered by Linda Schele (Freidel, Schele and Parker 1993: 66):

> The Jaguar Paddler and the Stingray Paddler seated a stone.
> It happened at Na-Ho-Chan, the Jaguar-throne-stone.
> The Black-House-Red-God seated a stone.
> It happened at the Earth Partition, the Snake-throne-stone.
> Itzamná set the stone at the Waterlily-throne-stone.

The setting of the three throne stone created a center for the cosmos and allowed the sky to be lifted from the primordial sea. The three celestial stones are mirrored in the three stones forming the hearths in all Maya houses. Just as the three throne stones in the Upperworld delineated the cosmic center, the three stones of domestic hearths marked domiciliary centers. Stela C at Quiriguá also mentions that this creation event took place as a result of the involvement of a deity called Wak Chan Ahaw (Six-Sky-Lord), who has been identified by some Mayanists as the maize god.

Vase of Seven Gods

The creation episode involving the three cosmic stones is illustrated on the elaborately painted Vase of the Seven Gods. On this vessel, six Underworld gods are shown seated in cross-legged poses. One of the six gods is shown with a defleshed face. The six gods face God L, who

6.3 *Vase of the Seven Gods, Late Classic Period. This vase illustrates God L (right) presiding over six deities at the creation of the present universe.* (Photo copyright Justin Kerr, file K2796)

occupies a large throne. Covered by a jaguar pelt, the throne of God L can be identified as the Jaguar Throne Stone named in the creation text of Stela C at Quiriguá. God L smokes a cigar and wears the screech owl headdress that is his typical attribute. Although each of the seven gods depicted on the pot wears a distinctive headdress, every god wears the same costume elements on his torso.

Three bundles, a reference to God L's role as the patron deity of merchants, are included in this scene. Of the three bundles, two are placed in front of God L and are marked with hieroglyphs signifying the phrase Nine-Star-Over-Earth. The third bundle, placed on the Jaguar Throne Stone behind God L is marked with hieroglyphs signifying the word "burden," a possible reference to the Maya concept that the powers of supernaturals and of rulers alike entailed burdensome responsibilities as well as privileges. The extended hieroglyphic text painted in a vertical format on the vessel body reaffirms the creation theme of the imagery. In addition to recording the creation date 4 Ahaw 8 Kumk'u, the text also utilizes the verb *tz'akah*, meaning "to bring into existence" and "to put in order." The verb can be interpreted as a reference to the ordering of the universe. The text also mentions blackness, a quality that is reiterated in the black background of the visual image. Much more than an aesthetic decision on the part of the vessel painter, the background is blackened to represent a sky that has not yet been lifted and an earth that has not yet been lighted.

RELIGION, COSMOLOGY, AND ART

THE SACRED CITY: AN EXAMPLE FROM PALENQUE

By reconstructing the sacred landscape in their architecture, ancient Maya cities proclaimed their ceremonial centers as habitats for the gods. Themes of creation and rulership are intertwined in the sculpture and written texts. Lying at the base of a group of low hills amid the rain forest, Palenque stands as a testament to this Maya fascination with the interstices between the supernatural spheres and the temporal, urban world. The ancient city sits on a flat shelf on a mountain ridge at its midway point; the Maya referred to this natural shelf and the central architectural plaza they constructed on it as Lakamhá (Big Water), perhaps suggesting the birthplace of the cosmos from the primordial sea. Although there are many richly decorated buildings and temples at Palenque that could serve as examples of sacred places, the architectural complex of the Cross Group is particularly representative.

The Cross Group

The Cross Group is located on a large, elevated plaza on the eastern side of the site. (See Map 7, page 227.) The three pyramid-temples in the Cross Group, named by modern scholars as the Temples of the Sun, the Cross, and the Foliated Cross, are constructed with similar plans. The texts associated with the temples record the births of creation deities and reveal the parallel existences of rulers and gods, while the temples themselves symbolize creation.

Each temple in the Cross Group surmounts a stepped pyramid. With their frontal staircases facing the shared plaza, the temples demarcate an enclosed space. The temples were capped with mansard roofs and high roof combs on which *witz* masks were modeled in stucco. These masks mark the temples of the Cross Group as mountains.

Within the temples, smaller sanctuaries house shrines incorporating panels carved in low relief. The panels combine complex figural imagery with hieroglyphic texts. The tablet in each of the three shrines shares similar elements with the other two but also presents a distinctive part of the complete program of meaning. Columns of hieroglyphic texts frame the figural reliefs and amplify the significance of the images. On each tablet, two male figures, shown with a marked difference in height, are represented in profile view as they face a central motif. On the tablets from the Temples of the Cross and the Foliated Cross, the central motif consists of the World Tree, or the axis mundi, that both supports the cosmos and allows interaction between cosmic levels (figs. 6.4 and 6.5). In place of the World Tree, the tablet from the Temple of the Sun depicts an emblem of war consisting of paired, crossed spears and the mask of the Jaguar God of the Underworld.

KAN B'ALAM'S ACCESSION

The inscriptions on the tablets of each of the three temples record the accession of Kan B'alam II to the Palenque throne in 684. The building project of the Cross Group was initiated by Kan B'alam, son of the great ruler Hanab Pakal. Kan B'alam celebrated his kingship not only in texts but also in the images of the tablets. Male figures flank each side of the world trees in the Temple of the Cross and the Temple of the Foliated Cross and of the war emblem in the Temple of the Sun. These figures are paired images of Kan B'alam, who shows himself simultaneously at two life stages. The smaller figure in each pair represents Kan

B'alam as a child, while the larger figure represents Kan B'alam as the adult king.

BIRTHPLACE OF THE GODS

As well as replicating the three Cosmic Hearth stones of creation, the three pyramid temples of the Cross Group also function as symbolic Underworld realms. The interior sanctuary within each temple is labeled as a *pibna*, or "underground building." The inclusion of the Underworld in the temple interiors reaffirms the Maya identification of pyramids as living mountains containing supernatural spaces and reinforces the Maya belief that the lords of the Middleworld interacted directly with the ancestors and deities of the cosmic realms.

A second meaning of the Maya word *pibna*, "sweat bath," expands the significance of the architectural structures in the Cross Group. Among the ancient Maya, sweat baths were places associated with birth, and the sanctuaries in the Temples of the Sun, the Cross, and the Foliated Cross were birthing shrines of the gods. Ethnohistorical accounts document the practice of Maya women purifying themselves in sweat baths both before and after giving birth. The hieroglyphic texts in the tablets of the Temples of the Cross, the Foliated Cross, and the Sun recount the cosmic birth of creation gods as prominent themes.

Temple of the Cross Tablet

On the tablet in the Temple of the Cross, the World Tree is depicted as it rises from the

6.4   Tablet from the Temple of the Cross, Palenque, Late Classic Period. This carved tablet records creation events and the history of Palenque's kings.   (Drawing by Linda Schele, copyright David Schele)

mask of the great earth monster. Principal Bird Deity is perched atop the tree, and a double-headed serpent bar, a symbol of kingship, is intertwined along the stylized branches of the tree. The text that flanks the World Tree begins a mythological chronology of creation by commemorating two events that occurred before the current world began. These two events consist of the births of the progenerative supernatural couple known as First Father (3122 B.C.E.), whose name is Hun Nal Ye, or One Maize Revealed, and First Mother (3121 B.C.E.). The birth of a god, called GI by epigraphers, is recorded as occurring shortly after the creation of the present world. This text continues by recording a historical chronology of the births and accessions of the Palenque kings. Rather than being treated as texts dealing with the births of radically different beings, the mythological and historical chronologies are deliberately paralleled.

Temple of the Foliated Cross Tablet

On the tablet in the Temple of the Foliated Cross, a stylized maize plant symbolically represents the World Tree. The tree rises from a water lily monster, an emblem of the watery Underworld and of the watery fields in which Maya farmers cultivated maize. In

6.5   *Tablet from the Temple of the Foliated Cross, Palenque, Late Classic Period. This tablet celebrates the emergence of maize and the Mountain of Sustenance.*   (Drawing by Linda Schele, copyright David Schele)

6.6   *Tablet from the Temple of the Sun, Palenque, Late Classic Period. This tablet connects warfare themes with ruler accession.*   (Drawing by Linda Schele, copyright David Schele)

this version of the World Tree, the branches are ears of maize seeded with human heads. Kan B'alam, depicted to the left of the World Tree, is dressed in the jade-beaded skirt of the maize god and stands on the cleft of the precious mountain. The eyes of the mountain below Kan B'alam's feet are inscribed with hieroglyphs that read *witz nal*, or "Maize Mountain." The tablet text records the birth of the god labeled GII and the accession of Kan B'alam. The mythological birth of creation and the historical events of kingship are paralleled by the account in the text of a ritual ceremony conducted by Kan B'alam in conjunction with three gods, GI, GII, and GIII (whose birth is recorded in the tablet of the Temple of the Sun), who are described as the ruler's companions.

Temple of the Sun Tablet

On the tablet in the Temple of the Sun, a shield containing the mask of the Jaguar God of the Underworld in front of a pair of crossed spears forms the central motif. Appropriately, this temple is situated on the western side of the group, the same direction that is associated with the setting Sun and death. The shield and darts rest on a thronelike object supported by the two Xibalba lords, posing as captives. This tablet commemorates warfare, captive sacrifice, and the Underworld's jaguar patron. The tablet text records the birth of the god GIII and events in Kan B'alam's life, including his heir designation and various temple dedication ceremonies. The correspondence between the enactment of creation through the actions of gods and the ritual reenactment of creation by the king is evidenced by the textual description of the transformation of Kan B'alam into the Sun in the company of GI.

The Palenque Triad

The deities GI, GII, and GIII, known together as the Palenque Triad, were born within a short range of time, 3000 to 4000 years before the carving of the tablets. Although these deities appear at other sites, their grouping together at Palenque is unique. The Palenque Triad functioned as patrons to the city's rulers and simultaneously were depicted as distinct beings. GI, who may be an aspect of the maize god, appears in anthropomorphic form with square eyes, fish fins on his cheeks, and shell earflares. The mask of this deity was placed on incense burners and was worn by kings in rituals. GI attributes were incorporated into the costumes of Maya kings at Copán and Tikal. GII, also known as God K and K'awil, is associated with rituals involving bloodletting, the summoning of ancestors, and the accession of kings. GIII is characterized by a jaguar ear and a twisted line underneath his eye. Also known as K'inich Ahaw, GIII manifests the sun god in his aspect as the Jaguar God of the Underworld and the Jaguar Night Sun.

THE ROLE OF KINGS AND SHAMANS

The association of the World Tree and Kan B'alam as depicted in the tablets of the Cross Group at Palenque suggests that the Maya believed their rulers could serve as conduits through which supernatural forces were channeled into the human realm. In their function as intercessors, Maya kings, priests, and elites proclaimed their power as shamans.

The idea of shamanism was entrenched within the cosmological views of peoples throughout Mesoamerica. Within this view, the boundaries that separated cosmic levels became permeable in certain circumstances. Shamans were persons with special skills and qualities that allowed them to enter the worlds of the gods. In Maya societies, rulers served as specialists in this cosmic exchange, and their visionary experiences allowed them to communicate directly with deities and ancestors.

Shamanic Travel

Various facets of the cosmic fabric allowed for such interactions to materialize. At the center of the multilayered universe, the axis mundi pierced all tiers of existence. Caves, crevices, wells, and other geological features that pooled water were associated with the axis mundi. Through these portals the gods traveled between the cosmic regions. When positioned at these punctures on the earth's surfaces, shamans could also shift from the realm of the Middleworld into regions of the Underworld and Upperworld. Although some art historians have stated that the Maya believed in shamanic visions, but not in travel, the art in the Lower and Upper Temples of the Jaguars at Chichén Itzá depicts the ruler in a transformed state in both the Middleworld and Upperworld.

Maya shamans readied themselves for spiritual interaction through their ceremonial actions and the energized response of assembled participants. Proper ritual performance manifested a matrix through which shamans entered cosmic portals. These rituals frequently involved the participation of many types of individuals acting toward a common goal. Musicians, dancers, and other participants in ritual processions assisted shamans in engaging with the divine.

Trances and Transformation

Specific actions carried out by shamans placed them in altered states of consciousness. Trances functioned as necessary phases for the embarkation on shamanic journeys to the otherworld. Hallucinogenic plants, fasting, letting blood from the genitals or other body parts, self-hypnosis, and various types of rhythmic activity acted as catalysts and positioned shamans into dreamlike states. Once immersed in altered conditions, the bodies of shamans became hosts for spirits to enter. Trances also provided shamans with another possibility: The souls of shamans could exit their physical bodies and insert themselves into other forms, such as that of the *way*, or spirit companion, that is well documented in Classic Period texts.

During shamanic rituals, the Maya believed that shamans physically and directly encountered gods, spirits, and ancestors. The shamanic ritual did not merely symbolize the negotiations between shamans and otherworld spirits. Instead, these rites provided the atmosphere and energy for these communications to take place in reality. Ethnographic studies of shamanism suggest that shamans, while engaging in trances, were believed to lose their souls. The souls of shamans exited their physical bodies and traveled to the Otherworld. During these expeditions outside of the terrestrial realm, worlds of opportunities opened for shamans. Shamans gained access to deities from the Underworld and Upperworld, ancestors, and other entities. Shaman-rulers confronted celestial forces, engaged in battle, or simply guarded against

malevolent forces. The limitations imposed on humans in the Middleworld were dissolved through shamanic experiences.

Shamanism and Spirit Companions

While engaged in transformation, the souls of shamans could transfer into the bodies of spiritual counterparts. Animals typically served as the spiritual companions of shamans of high status, such as kings and members of the elite. Among high-ranking Maya individuals, the jaguar constituted the most common spirit companion. Because of its great prowess, ferocity, and dominance in the forest, the jaguar became the power animal par excellence. For Maya kings, the jaguar provided an especially fitting power animal since both kings and jaguars presided over the other occupants of their habitats. So ubiquitous was the association between kings and jaguars that jaguar attributes were incorporated into the costumes and implements of kingship. Jaguar pelts, for example, frequently decorate the thrones of rulers.

WAYOB

The Maya called their spiritual alter egos *wayob* (plural of *way*). In Classic Period inscriptions, the hieroglyph signifying the word *way* is comprised of a stylized human face partially covered by a jaguar skin.

Shaman Kings

As the chief shaman of his territory, the Maya ruler engaged in cosmic dialogues with otherworld deities. He thereby protected his subjects from harmful forces, divined the future, petitioned for the success of his state, and maintained the order of the universe. The king therefore acted as a divine transformer. Through kingly participation in shamanic ritual acts, the power of the supernatural merged into the lives of humans and their activities.

The Ruler as Shaman: An Example from Copán

A series of stelae, erected in the Great Plaza at Copán (see Map 6, page 220), provides an excellent example of Classic Period shamanic rulership. Between 695 and 738, the 13th king of Copán, Waxaklahun Ub'ah K'awil, commonly referred to as 18 Rabbit, erected seven stelae in the main plaza and ritual zone of his city. The stelae record the critical rites enacted by 18 Rabbit during a span of 25 years in his 44-year reign.

Through his shamanic participation in these events, the ruler of Copán merged himself and his kingdom with mythological history. Each monument, standing roughly 3.5 meters (12 feet) high, celebrates the position of 18 Rabbit as a transient being, one whose negotiations were not limited to the terrestrial sphere.

By utilizing the upright format of stelae, 18 Rabbit illustrated his axial role as a shaman. The stelae exhibit low-relief carvings on all four sides. The main faces of the stelae present portraits of the ruler himself bedecked in regalia appropriate to a king. Hieroglyphic texts accompany the portraits. Carved on both end sides of the stelae, the texts clarify the identity of the king and of associated ritual participants. The texts also record the dates on which the stelae were erected. The inscriptions on the ruler's stelae are related not as a continuous narrative, but as a group of experiences that established the holiness of the space in which they were erected. The placement of the stelae reinforced this purpose: Located at the cardinal and intercardinal points of the Great Plaza, the stelae define the plaza as part of the sacred cosmic order.

STELA C

The first stela erected by 18 Rabbit reflects the king's interest in representing himself as a shaman-ruler. Stela C at Copán was created to commemorate the date 9.14.0.0.0. (December 5, 711), the first *k'atun* ending following the accession of the ruler. As the only double-portrait stela of this ruler, the main faces of Stela C look to the east and the west. These orientations allowed the ruler to observe the sun's emergence from and return into the Underworld. The same design had been utilized 60 years earlier by Smoke Imix God K, the father of 18 Rabbit to commemorate the 9.11.0.0.0. *k'atun* ending. Both of these *k'atun* endings took place on a day when Venus was first seen in the evening sky.

Ruler as Axis Mundi   Stela C, like the other six stelae in the group, eternalizes the moment when 18 Rabbit became transfixed in his interaction with the otherworld. The ruler is depicted at the center of the universe, within the portal that leads to the farthest reaches of the cosmos. In each of the two portraits on the east and west stela faces, 18 Rabbit used a different set of regalia to claim identity with mythical gods and ancestors. On the west stela face, the king wears a beard and mustache (features quite rare in depictions of the Maya), while on the east stela face, the king is smooth-faced. Inscriptions on the stela do not mention another person, suggesting that it is indeed 18 Rabbit who is represented twice on the same monument. Comparisons between Stela C and other sculptural depictions of this ruler demonstrate that Maya artists at Copán were not concerned with either an exact or a consistent likeness. This variation of physiognomy probably reflected the ruler's desire to portray

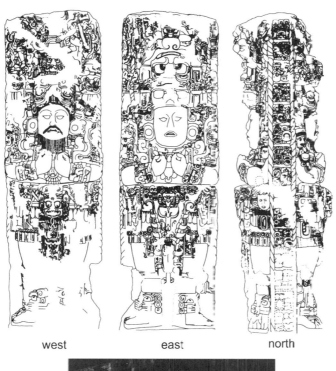

west   east   north

6.7 *Stela C, Copán, Honduras, Late Classic Period: a) west side; b) east side; c) north side. The front and back sides of the stela show Waxaklahun Ub'ah K'awil (18 Rabbit). This ruler commissioned Stela C to commemorate the first* k'atun *ending after his accession to Copán's throne.*   (Drawing of west and east sides by Kaylee Spencer-Ahrens after Barbara Fash; drawing of north side by Linda Schele, copyright David Schele)

RELIGION, COSMOLOGY, AND ART

himself in a fashion most appropriate to the specific kingly ritual commemorated in the monument. Through manipulating his image, 18 Rabbit could adhere to particular details of the rites and could simultaneously present himself as the epitome of shaman-ruler.

Rulership and Spiritual Authority Other aspects of the king's images on Stela C reflect the connection between external costume attributes and the kingly rites, actions, and qualities of 18 Rabbit. Ornate headdresses, backracks, skirts, aprons, and jewels are among the prominent costume components included in the ruler's portraits. These costume elements contain emblems that link the wearer to deities and to mythology. The most overt emblem of temporal and spiritual authority is not worn at all but rather held in the hands of 18 Rabbit. On both faces of Stela C, the ruler grasps double-headed serpent bars. The wide jaws of the serpents extend up to the sides of the ruler's face. From the serpents' maws, ancestors materialize at the outer limits of the stela. On the west side of Stela C, the serpent's breath manifests two aged figures wearing turbans. These figures contrast with those emanating from the jaws of the serpents on the east side of Stela C. The deities on the east face appear to be younger and are shown carrying in their hands the severed heads of the maize god.

Stacks of three headdresses adorn the ruler's head on both sides of Stela C. Although their uppermost extremities are partially destroyed, various elements composing the headdresses can be discerned. On the east side, the Jester God adorns the headdress's front. Like the serpent bar, the Jester God served as an emblem of rulership. In 18 Rabbit's headdress, an ancestral figure sits behind the Jester God. An additional pair of conjured deities emerges from a serpent bar held by the figure. On the west side, the headdress mirrors that on the east. Although damaged, a figure at the top of

the headdress holds a serpent bar with emergent turbaned figures. From the serpent more turbaned figures appear. Twisting ropes, signifying the cosmic umbilicus, hang down from the sides of both headdresses.

Ruler as World Tree The lower portion of the east side of Stela C positions 18 Rabbit as the World Tree that supports the cosmos. The ruler is represented in the form of a crocodile tree emerging from a mountain. His loin apron becomes the trunk of the World Tree while the serpents that extend outward from each side form its branches. The crocodile head, displaying large symmetrically arranged teeth, hangs in front of the ruler's loins. The crocodile head represents a variant of the World Tree, which in other images, such as that from Late Preclassic Izapa, can be shown as a tree trunk rising from a crocodile head. The crocodile tree provided the home for the Principal Bird Deity that plays an important role in cosmic creation.

Costume elements worn by the ruler on the west side of Stela C also illustrate connections between the king and creation. The primordial sea is evoked by the water lily embellishing 18 Rabbit's World Tree loin apron. At the moment of creation, the gods lifted the sky from this body of water. The head of the Jaguar God of the Underworld, identifiable by his jaguar ears and crueller eyes, is affixed to the ruler's belt.

Ruler as Maize God A turtle-shaped altar placed in front of the west side of Stela C reveals another connection to the mythological past. When Stela C is viewed behind its associated altar, the figure of 18 Rabbit appears to emerge from the turtle's carapace. This action re-creates images of the resurrection of the maize god from the clefted surface of the turtle earth.

Ruler as Sacred By costuming himself in attributes of the World Tree on both sides of

Stela C, 18 Rabbit placed himself literally at the center of the universe, or the axis mundi. A multiplicity of deities and ancestors imbued the ruler's costume with sacredness. The plethora of divine images that decorate 18 Rabbit's costume might visualize the supernatural beings with whom the ruler communicated during his shamanic experiences.

Ultimately the sculptures erected by 18 Rabbit at Copán stand as testaments of the ruler's divine engagements. The stelae mark the plaza in which they stand as a sacred space that is manifested though the power of the ruler. 18 Rabbit's sculptural program of stelae reflects beliefs held by the ancient Maya. Among the Maya, kings were thought to be divine shamans who operated in multidimensional ways. Through the power of their ritual performances, shaman-kings ordered and balanced both the worldly and supernatural realms and thereby protected their domains.

THE SUSTENANCE OF LIFE: *POPOL VUH*

An invaluable source for understanding ancient Maya religion and cosmology was written by the Quiché Maya in the highlands of Guatemala during the colonial period. This source, the *Popol Vuh* (see "Postconquest Literature," Chapter 10), is a cosmic epic divided into three main parts. The first part deals with the creation of the world and its inhabitants; the second part continues the story of creation by recounting the story of the Hero Twins; and the third part recounts the founding of the Quiché dynasties. Actions described in the creation story of the *Popol Vuh* can be identified in Preclassic sculptures and Classic Period images painted for centuries on Maya ceramic vessels. Although this native chronicle may diverge in some respects from the ancient versions, the parallels between this postconquest narrative and the scenes depicted in pre-Columbian art demonstrate the antiquity of this Maya creation story.

Creation of the Maya World of Maize

In the *Popol Vuh*, cosmic creation begins through the generative power of dialogue. Before the formation of the earth, the sea and the sky made up a vast, still expanse. The creation dialogue began between the god Tepeu, whose name means "heart of heaven," and the god K'ucumatz, whose shape is that of a serpent plumed with green and blue feathers. Through their godly speech, the earth and mountains emerged from the sea, the landscape was covered by forests, and the sacred cosmos was structured. To shape and order this newly created cosmos, the gods measured its sides and corners with cords, an action parallel to those of Maya farmers when they prepare their maize fields with measuring cords. A poetic description of the divine structuring of the cosmos is recorded in the *Popol Vuh*, as translated by Dennis Tedlock (1996:63–64):

> the fourfold siding, fourfold cornering,
> measuring, fourfold staking,
> halving the cord, stretching the cord
> in the sky, on the earth
> the four sides, the four corners, as it is said,
> by the Maker, Modeler,
> mother-father of life, of humankind . . .

After creating the partitioned universe, the gods filled the forested landscapes of the earth with animals, birds, fish, and reptiles. But these creatures could not fulfill the desire of the gods to be nourished and venerated.

Although undertaken by the gods, the creation of a human race was fraught with difficulty and impeded by initial failures. Efforts to form humans first from clay and then from wood were unsuccessful. Still lacking humans who could sustain them properly with prayer and offerings, the gods paused until the Hero Twins defeated the Underworld forces of death and decay and obtained the appropriate material with which to model human beings; this material turned out to be maize. In a fourth attempt to create a world to their liking, the gods fashioned human beings from a dough made from ground maize and blood, and these people of maize, the Maya, turned out to be appropriately grateful. Thus began the fourth creation of the world, the Maya world of maize. By describing maize and blood as the substance of human flesh, the creation story provided a correspondence between corn, the chief domestic crop grown and eaten by humans, and humans, the primary sacrifice to the gods as tribute payments for agricultural fertility.

The Defeat of Death: The Hero Twins

The actions of the Hero Twins, Hunahpu and Xbalanque, defeated the powers of the Underworld lords and defined the appropriate relationships between humans and gods. The story of the Hero Twins begins with Hun Hunahpu and Vuqub Hunahpu, an earlier generation of twin brothers, renowned gamesters who excelled at dice games and ball games. The noises that resulted from Hun Hunahpu's and Vuqub Hunahpu's energetic exertions on the surface of their masonry ball court reverberated loudly in the Underworld and attracted the attention of the Underworld lords. The gods One Death and Seven Death therefore summoned Hun Hunahpu and Vuqub Hunahpu into their netherworld domain with an overt invitation to play ball, but with the covert intent to put a violent end to the disturbance.

On their journey into the Underworld, Hun Hunahpu and Vuqub Hunahpu are confronted by a series of dangerous obstacles including raging rapids and a river of blood. Once in the

6.8   *Late Classic Maya polychrome cylinder vase, showing the Hero Twin Hunahpu shooting the Principal Bird Deity out of a tree.*   (Photo copyright Justin Kerr, file K1226)

Underworld, Hun Hunahpu and Vuqub Hunahpu are challenged to perform a set of seemingly impossible tasks. Their failure to successfully perform the final task results in the sacrifice of the twin brothers. Hun Hunahpu is to be buried, fittingly, in the Underworld ball court, located beneath the Middleworld ball court, but before his interment, the Underworld gods sever his head and hang it like a trophy in a tree.

Even after death, the severed head possesses potent energy. This energy is manifested by the gourds that flourish on the tree the instant the head is hung from it. This energy is also manifested by the miraculous impregnation of the Underworld maiden Xkik. Attracted by the gourds, Xkik reaches out her hand. Spittle from the head of Hun Hunahpu causes the conception of the Hero Twins.

Enraged by the pregnancy, the father of Xkik orders the maiden to be sacrificed by his owl messengers. However, the merciful owls spare Xkik's life and, instead of returning with her bloody heart, bring back a substitute made of resin. The smell of the burning resin so fascinates the Underworld lords that Xkik is able to escape to the Middleworld.

The maiden Xkik is herself put to a test by Xmucane, the mother of the deceased Hun Hunahpu and Vuqub Hunahpu. The test involves gathering a load of corn from a single maize plant. The nature of the test relates to Hun Hunahpu's identity as a manifestation of the Tonsured Maize God. By passing the test, Xkik proves that she is the wife of Hun Hunahpu.

BIRTH OF THE HERO TWINS

Xkik subsequently gives birth to the Hero Twins, Hunahpu and Xbalanque. The Hero Twins are frequently depicted on Maya vases and are distinguished by the large black spots marking Hunahpu's cheeks and by the patches of jaguar skin displayed on Xbalanque's mouth, torso, and limbs. Like their father, Hun Hunahpu, and their uncle, Vuqub Hunahpu, the Hero Twins revel in sporting events and trickery.

The Hero Twins are avid hunters, killing prey with their blowguns. One event narrated in the *Popol Vuh*, refers to the celestial bird, known as the Principal Bird Deity, whose depiction is a prominent motif in Maya art as seen in the sculpted panels at Palenque (see also figure 6.8, page 184). In the *Popol Vuh*, the celestial bird is named Vuqub Caquix, or Seven Macaw, and is associated with overweening pride. According to the account, the haughty bird fancies himself to be the sun and the moon and, therefore, the lord of the cosmos. Offended by the bird's arrogance, the Hero Twins use their blowguns to shoot the proud bird as he attempts to make his landing in the great ceiba tree. The pellet strikes the tooth of the grand bird, causing it to fall. The twins trick the bird into replacing the missing tooth with a soft maize kernel so that the bird quickly sickens and dies.

The contest between the Hero Twins and the celestial bird is depicted on a polychrome vessel from the Classic Period. On the vase, the Principal Bird Deity appears among the uppermost branches of a tree, which embodies supernatural qualities personified by the deity mask on its trunk. From behind the tree, a jaguar paw can be seen, an indication of the presence of Xbalanque. Hunahpu, identifiable by the black spots that mark his body, crouches on one knee and faces the tree. He wears a costume typical of hunters, complete with a wide-brimmed hat and straw skirt. Placing the end of the blowgun to his mouth, Hunahpu shoots a small black pellet, visible at the edge of the blowgun, directly at the bird. The text that accompanies the scene on the polychrome vessel describes the Principal Bird Deity as "entering or becoming the sky," a verbal metaphor for creation. In the version of creation recounted in the *Popol*

Vuh, defeat of the celestial bird, identified in the Quiché tale as the false sun, was a necessary precursor to the establishment of the authentic sun.

EMERGENCE OF HUMANS AND MAIZE

The successful modeling of humankind requires not only the defeat of Vuqub Caquix but also the subjugation of the powers of the Underworld and the growth of maize. Like Hun Hunahpu and Vuqub Hunahpu, the Hero Twins annoy the lords of the Underworld with the noise from their ball game. When owl messengers deliver a summons from the Under-world lords, Hunahpu and Xbalanque are forced to undergo various trials. Through trickery and wit, however, the Hero Twins not only survive but also overcome the Underworld gods. Their triumph involves playing ball games in the great Underworld court. In one such ball game, the Hero Twins are disadvantaged because Hunahpu's head has been severed the previous night by killer bats; he plays, nonetheless, but with a substitute head fashioned of squash by Xbalanque. The death gods, who are now certain of their victory, have begun the game by throwing out the real head of Hunahpu onto the court to be used as the ball. Aided by sympathetic animals, Xbalanque reverses his and his twin brother's fates. When Xbalanque bounces the real head of Hunahpu out of the court, a rabbit distracts the attention of the death gods while Xbalanque rejoins Hunahpu's head to his body.

The triumph of the Hero Twins involves their performing other magical feats that include dancing, submitting voluntarily to death, being miraculously reembodied, and, finally, decapitating the Underworld gods. After their triumph, the Hero Twins resurrect their father, Hun Hunahpu.

Prior to sacrificing the Underworld gods, the Hero Twins learn that their father's remains were buried beneath the Underworld ball court. Hun Hunahpu is resurrected from the crack in the floor of the ball court. In his resurrected state, Hun Hunahpu takes the form of maize. The resurrection of the maize god is depicted in an image painted on a polychrome codex-style plate. The maize god emerges from the Underworld through the crack in a turtle carapace. On the sides of the maize god, Hunahpu and Xbalanque water the deity as though they are nurturing the new plant. Xbalanque, identifiable by his jaguar patches, uses a vessel marked with an *akbal*, or darkness sign, to pour the water that sustains the growth of maize.

6.9   Codex-style polychrome plate, Late Classic Period. A finely painted scene on the interior of this plate depicts Hun Hunahpu emerging from a turtle carapace. The Hero Twins, Hunahpu (left) and Xbalanque (right), appear on each side of their father. Xbalanque assists in the resurrection of their father as maize by pouring water on the sprouting corn.   (Drawing by Kaylee Spencer-Ahrens after Karl Taube)

The Purpose of Ritual Performance

Ritual performance constituted a central component of Maya cosmology and religion. Texts and images on monuments demonstrate that the rulers were responsible for facilitating communication with ancestral deities and other gods. Ritual performances opened portals of exchange between gods and humans and at the same time legitimized kingly rulership. Rituals were evidently designed to replicate the actions of the creation deities, and performers deliberately assumed the identities of the conjured deities. Of particular importance were dances, blood sacrifices, and ball games.

An array of specific rituals is known from the colonial period. Some of these rituals involved agriculture, economics, hunting, civic and domestic productions, and even beekeeping. The timing of Maya rituals was predicated by the calendar, particularly the 260-day sacred count (see Chapter 9). According to 16th-century descriptions, ritual activity required rigorous preparations. Before certain rites, participants fasted and observed food taboos. Sexual abstinence was rigidly observed. During many rituals, participants felt empowered to petition the gods for their benevolence.

Sacred Substances: *K'uhul*

The Maya word *k'uh* refers to the gods. But this concept was extended by the related word *k'uhul* (also known as *chu'lel*) to encompass the sacred life force and divinity present in the world and called forth in Maya rituals. The appearance in ancient Maya texts of the glyphic compounds for *k'uh* and the symbols for *k'uhul* to mark not only the deities but many other beings and substances demonstrates that these concepts activated Maya religion for at least 1,000 years. Such sacredness could reside in virgin water and the resins from trees, such as that used to make copal incense, both substances used in ancient Maya rituals. But sacredness infused everything: the wind, human blood, plants, the mountains, the sun and sky. Based on their use of these glyphic markers, the ancient Maya apparently believed that their world was animated by a sacred life force emanating from the gods.

Maya shaman-rulers and priests connected with this sacred life force through appropriate rituals facilitated by dancing, bloodletting, and the ingestion of hallucinogens. Scenes depicted in their art indicate that the Maya believed these individuals could transform themselves into gods and communicate directly with the gods on behalf of ritual participants.

Maya Dance

To the ancient Maya, dancing was regarded not as a form of entertainment but rather as an important expression of religious beliefs. Costumed performers impersonated deities and reenacted creation events; in the process, they forged dynamic relationships with deities and ancestors and charged spaces with the *k'uhul* required to facilitate the interactions between worlds. In addition, dance allowed performers to transform themselves into beings from other worlds.

Many images in Maya art depict kings, priests, nobles, and warriors as ritual dancers. Often the action in these scenes is unequivocally identified as dance by the inclusion of the verb *ahk'ot*, "to dance," in hieroglyphic texts associated with images. The different motifs that appear in dance imagery reveal the varied significance that dances assumed. Staffs, scepters, rattles, banners, spears, and even serpents were among the objects that served as critical elements in dances. Costumes often included beads, shells, headdresses with long feathers, and elaborate backracks decorated with deity images. These accoutrements worn and carried by dancers, in turn, were sacred themselves: In the hieroglyphic texts, dances were named after specific items or costumes associated with participants. Among some contemporary Maya groups, dances are still named after such items, which are thought to be so sacred that they are kept in sacrosanct places, including churches.

SNAKE DANCE

One type of dance was presented in the relief sculpture on a lintel from the Yaxchilán area. The dancer on the right stands in frontal pose with outturned feet. He lifts up his foot, bends his body, and turns his head towards his partner. This dancer grasps a four-fanged serpent in front of him. The dancer on the left stands in profile with extended hands. In one hand is a snake, while with the left hand he gestures. The snakes held in the performers' hands and the hieroglyphic inscription on the lintel reveal that the men are performing a snake dance. The hieroglyphic text provides a date and identifies the dancers. The date is the equivalent of October 14, 767; Bird Jaguar IV, depicted on the right, performs with his underlord, a member of the elite who has been appointed to the position of *sahal*.

Both Bird Jaguar IV and his *sahal* wear elaborate costumes. Long quetzal feathers decorate their headdresses, and each dancer wears necklaces, pectorals, wristbands, bead dangles, and elaborate sandals. When set in motion during the dance, the costumes would have swirled through the air and produced jangling noises. Personified wings and bird heads further animate the headdresses. In addition, mat and

reed decorations, symbols of kingship, appear in the top of the headdress of Bird Jaguar IV. The undulating snake held by Bird Jaguar IV is similar to the so-called serpent bars and serpent scepters that also functioned as emblems of rulership throughout the Maya area. The text explains that Bird Jaguar IV is dancing "with the sky snake."

WAYEB DANCE

A complex dance scene involving numerous participants is depicted in the Lower Temple of the Jaguars at Chichén Itzá. Given the prominence of God N in this relief, the dance may have been conducted during Wayeb, the five-day period at the end of the year that was presided over by God N. During this dangerous period of time, the Underworld opened

6.10   *Snake dance represented on a lintel from Site R, near Yaxchilán, Late Classic Period. The bas-relief carving shows Bird Jaguar IV dancing with his* sahal, *or underlord.*   (Drawing by Kaylee Spencer-Ahrens after Nikolai Grube, 1992)

and harmful forces such as disease, death, and political upheaval were released into the mortal level of the universe. To avert disaster, the Maya marshaled together divine energies from as many source as possible. Through the participation of many individuals moving in unison, the dance attracted the gods and brought their divine presence to Chichén Itzá.

During the Wayeb dance, *k'uhul* was summoned by the ruler, as well as an assembly of ritual participants. Every dancer depicted on walls and vaults of the Lower Temple of the Jaguars at Chichén Itzá may have constituted a special individual with unusual access to the divine forces. The most prominent dancer is the semidivine Maya ruler whose cloth throne is placed at his feet. The king's shamanic transformation is indicated by the flames emanating from his body.

The close connections between kings and the supernatural realms are further depicted here by costume attributes associated with the ruler. On his chest the ruler wears a gold disk, while around his eyes the ruler wears gold rings. The reflective surfaces of the gold accoutrements allowed the ruler to see into the supernatural realm, much like the pyrite mirrors did for shaman chiefs as early as in the late Archaic Period.

Most of the other dancers in the reliefs of the Lower Temple of the Jaguars wear the costumes of warriors, as indicated by their spears, shields, and protective padding. Because of their courage, warriors were favored by the gods. Females, too, possessed this special kind of holiness through the association of warfare. The visibly outlined breasts on one warrior in the Lower Temple of the Jaguars clearly identify her as a female. Childbirth and the intense physical effort required by women were regarded as a parallel event to warfare; women who died in childbirth found immediate rebirth in the otherworld, a privilege also granted to warriors.

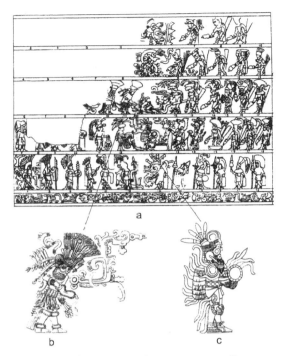

6.11   *Relief depicting a dance procession, Lower Temple of the Jaguars, Chichén Itzá, Early Post-classic Period: a) West Wall; b) detail of a female dancer wearing a snake skirt; c) detail of a possible ruler wearing gold goggles.*   (Drawing by Annie Hunter in Alfred P. Maudslay, 1889–1902)

DANCE OF THE *WAYOB*

Ritual dances also summoned the *wayob*, or the spiritual companions that accompanied humans throughout their life. A polychrome vase from Altar de Sacrificios, in the western Petén, depicts a dance that calls up such spirits. Six beings appear to move around the outside of the painted vase. A tail is appended to a heavy-set man who wears geometric pants and lofts a boa constrictor above his head. A dancer clad in jaguar-patterned pants and mittens lifts his heel to his ankle while raising his arm. A perforator hangs at the groin of the dancer in jaguar-patterned pants, and a red stain indicates that he has let blood from his phallus. Two other beings sit at the feet of the standing dancers. One of these seated figures appears to be cutting off his own head, while the other wears a dragon-deer headdress. Above the seated figures are a pair of floating beings, both of whom hold large objects. The black-caped figure holds a vessel, and the other holds a death head.

The text on this vase indicates that the dancers are not ordinary performers. Instead, the figures represent the special coessences, or companion spirits known as *wayob*. In fact, the individual clad in jaguar pants may be in the act of transforming into his jaguar coessence because ancient Maya men wore kilts and loincloths, not tight-fitting pants. Through ritual acts like dance and bloodletting, shamanic kings, priests, and elites could transform into their *wayob*.

Whether the dancers represented on the Altar de Sacrificios vase were meant to illustrate actual *wayob* or humans impersonating *wayob* is unknown. However, the hieroglyphic text tells us that the *wayob* accompanied specific people. Owners of the *wayob* who are mentioned in the text on the Altar de Sacrificios vase include lords from Tikal and Yaxchilán. The Calendar Round date given in the text probably corresponds to 754.

Blood Sacrifices

Some of the most significant rituals performed by Maya rulers involved the offering of blood, one of the most precious substances known to humans and gods. The offering of blood through autosacrificial rituals was ubiquitous among the ancient Maya and continued through the early colonial period. Condemning the practice as dangerous and heretical, the Spanish friars terminated its practice. Diego de Landa, a

6.12   *Altar de Sacrificios vase, Late Classic Period. This transformation scene depicts the* wayob, *or spiritual companions, of rulers of important Maya cities. The figure in the center appears in a dance pose and has let blood from his penis. The standing figure to the right swings a snake above his head as he participates in the dance. Two other figures, holding ritual objects, float above the scene. A seated figure faces each of the standing dancers. The figure to the left appears to be cutting off his own head.*   (Drawing by Linda Schele, copyright David Schele)

16th-century bishop, described autosacrificial rituals performed by the Yucatec Maya, including rituals in which men cut themselves on the cheeks, lips, tongues, and phalli. Landa further noted that, in some cases, chords or pieces of straw were forced through the incisions, "with horrible suffering." Although Landa explained that only men participated in this gruesome practice, the Maya monuments of the Classic Period prove otherwise; women also participated in ritual bloodletting. Despite the pain, the Maya elite carried out bloodletting rituals for a variety of purposes. They believed they could traverse cosmic boundaries in bloodletting rituals, and Maya rulers could contact deities and ancestors. The importance of these communications encouraged participation in autosacrifice and justified the capture and sacrifice of others.

SUSTENANCE FOR THE GODS

Images depicting bloodletting as a critical ritual act appear with frequency in Maya sculptures, murals, and vessels; hieroglyphic texts both corroborate the importance of the ritual act and provide supplementary details about its significance. During the Classic Period, Maya of elite status performed bloodletting rituals that involved the sacrifice of high-ranking war captives as well as autosacrifice. These bloody acts fulfilled the ancient charter with the gods that obliged humans to nourish the deities with blood drawn from the human body. This obligation had been incurred because the deities, during creation, had willingly spilled their own blood atop maize in order to form human flesh. Through autosacrificial rituals, Maya rulers returned the divine gift of sustenance to the gods.

VISIONS

Ritual bloodletting also allowed participants to engage with divine powers through the achieve-

ment of altered states of consciousness. As a result of blood loss, a Maya ruler was able, probably through the release of endorphins, to produce fantastic visions. Maya art and hieroglyphic texts demonstrate that the Maya believed these visions jumped the thresholds between cosmic layers. Within the charged liminal spaces of their blood sacrifices, elite participants opened channels of communication with deified ancestors and other gods. By engaging in these otherworldly exchanges, Maya rulers expressed their divine heritage and their right to temporal rule. Many visual images illustrate the specific deities conjured through such bloodletting rituals.

Because bloodletting rituals allowed rulers to communicate with ancestors, bloodletting pervades many aspects of Maya existence. Hieroglyphic texts document that the rituals were performed at various times during the lives of Maya lords. Particularly important events that frequently involved autosacrificial rituals were kingly births, accessions, and anniversaries, as well as celebrations of specific periods of the calendar. Through ritual contact on such occasions, the gods could be persuaded to sanction new rulers, to intervene in human events, and to protect the ruler and his people through calendric transitions.

BLOODLETTING IMPLEMENTS

Not just any sharp object sufficed for elite blood offerings. Instead, specific implements, which were regarded as harboring their own powers, were utilized as ritual perforators of human flesh. Stingray spines, obsidian lancets, and carved bone awls served as tools to sever the penis, cheeks, ears, and tongue. Because their spines were naturally angled in one direction, stingray spines forced a ritual participant to complete the act of piercing; once the stingray spine had already begun to sever the flesh, a reversal in direction would have resulted in more severe and drastic cuts than if the stingray spine were pressed all the way through the flesh in the same direction. Models of stingray spines crafted from precious materials such as jade accompanied the burials of elite persons. These models are often personified in the image of the perforator god. A line of three knotted strips of paper or cloth, materials used to catch blood, adorn many bloodletters. Not only do the images of the perforator god and the triple-knot motifs indicate the purpose of the lancets, but these markings also infuse the implements with power and sacredness. The importance of such implements is evidenced by the contexts in which they were unearthed. Found in tombs in the pelvic area of male skeletons, the stingray spines were possibly contained within a pouch placed atop the genitals. Such funerary offerings signified that the person had partaken in bloodletting rituals in the Middleworld and accompanied the soul of the deceased in his journey to the otherworld.

BLOODLETTING RITUAL: A YAXCHILÁN EXAMPLE

Autosacrifice: Lintel 24   Three carved lintels from Structure 23 at Yaxchilán in Chiapas, Mexico, provide depictions of various stages of bloodletting rituals. The first, Lintel 24, depicts an elegantly dressed Maya woman named Lady Xoc kneeling before her husband Itzamná B'alam (known as Shield Jaguar the Great), ruler of Yaxchilán between 681 and 742. Lady Xoc's right hand draws a thorny rope through her pierced tongue, while her left hand pulls the rope end that has already passed through her tongue. On the floor in front of Lady Xoc, a shallow bowl or basket called a *lak* contains a length of rope and strips of paper. The spots on the paper, which represent blood, demonstrate that the precious substance has dripped down from Lady Xoc's wounded tongue. The scrolling lines of small dots

around the mouth and cheeks of Lady Xoc indicate that her face is smeared with blood.

The costume worn by Lady Xoc also indicates that the woman is participating in a bloodletting ritual. She wears a *huipil* that displays the same pattern as on the *huipiles* worn by other women in bloodletting scenes at Yaxchilán. Diamond shapes cover most of the garment, while the edges are trimmed with sky bands and fringe. Around her neck, Lady Xoc wears a special mosaic collar with matching cuffs. Her ornate headdress incorporates symbols indicating that the bloodletting ritual in

6.13   *Lintel 24, Yaxchilán, Late Classic Period. Lady Xoc appears on the right kneeling before her husband Shield Jaguar the Great. The ruler's wife engages in a ritual in which she passes a spiny chord through her tongue to let blood.*   (Drawing courtesy Ian Graham)

which Lady Xoc is involved was associated with war. Affixed to the front of Lady Xoc's headdress and shown in profile is the mask of Tlaloc, a central Mexican deity who symbolized warfare to the Maya. Tlaloc is represented with goggled eyes, the diagnostic trait of the deity. Other components of the headdress, such as the tassels that extend from its band and the Mexican Year sign located behind the Tlaloc head, reinforce the bellicose significance of the scene.

Holding a torch out in front of him, Shield Jaguar illuminates the sacred scene and participates in the ritual. Like his wife, Shield Jaguar wears a distinctive costume, that includes symbols of war and sacrifice. The hair of the ruler is tied in a shape indicative of penitents, and the headband of Shield Jaguar displays the shrunken head of a probable sacrificial victim. According to the inscription, the date on which Lady Xoc and Shield Jaguar, Lord of Yaxchilán, let blood was the equivalent of October 28, 709.

Vision: Lintel 25 The scene carved on Lintel 25 from Yaxchilán may be interpreted as a continuation of the bloodletting ritual depicted on Lintel 24. The hieroglyphic inscription on the lintel indicates that this scene takes place on the day of Shield Jaguar's accession to the throne. Here Lady Xoc appears on the lower right of the scene. With her left hand, she holds the bowl filled with bloodied strips of paper, a stingray spine, and an obsidian lancet. A skull and serpent motif rest on her right hand and wrist. Although Shield Jaguar is absent, his presence is evoked by the woven pattern that has been transferred from the ruler's belt in Lintel 24 to Lady Xoc's *huipil* in Lintel 25.

As a result of Lady Xoc's blood sacrifice, a vision serpent rises from a bowl that rests on the ground. Vision serpents were apparitions of great rearing snakes that became manifested through bloodletting rituals. Ancestors, deities, and nobles were materialized from the mouths

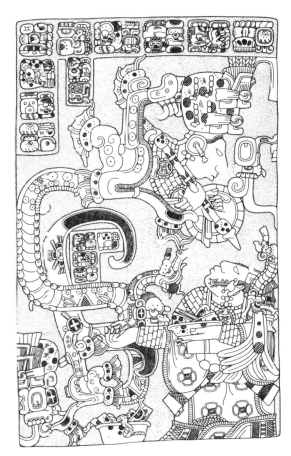

6.14   *Lintel 25, Yaxchilán, Late Classic Period. This lintel depicts an event following the bloodletting rite enacted by Lady Xoc on Lintel 24. Still kneeling while holding a bowl filled with blood-spattered paper, a vision serpent looms before Lady Xoc. From the serpent's mouth, a warrior and a mask of Tlaloc emerge.*   (Drawing courtesy Ian Graham)

of such ethereal serpents. In the scene in Lintel 25, the bloodletting ritual has opened communication with the otherworlds, and the bloodletting bowls function as an *ol*, or portal, through which the vision serpent passes into the Middleworld.

In Lintel 25, the vision serpent has two heads. A warrior wearing a Tlaloc mask and carrying a shield and spear emerges through the mouth of the upper serpent head. A second warrior, wearing a Tlaloc mask with a balloon headdress, emerges through the mouth of the lower serpent head.

Warfare and Captive Sacrifice: Lintel 26
The narrative sequence concerning blood sacrifice related in Lintels 24 and 25 is concluded in Lintel 26. (See figure 2.10, page 57.) In this scene, the autosacrificial acts performed by Lady Xoc are connected to warfare and captive sacrifice. Here Shield Jaguar the Great is dressed in cotton armor. Holding a knife, he appears with his wife, Lady Xoc, who holds his war helmet and shield and helps him prepare for battle. Through successful battle, the ruler will collect captives whose blood will be offered to the gods.

SCATTERING

The scattering ritual comprised a different form of blood offering. Maya imagery indicates that men were the principal ritual performers and that the ritual obligation they discharged was to cast drops of blood from their hands. The scattering ritual appears frequently with period-ending dates, that is, with dates in the Maya calendar that marked the transition from one time period to another. In addition, the scattering ritual could be performed on other important dates and could involve the conjuring of ancestors.

An Example from La Pasadita Lintel 2 from La Pasadita, Guatemala, illustrates a scattering ritual. On this carved lintel, Yaxun B'alam (known as Bird Jaguar IV), ruler of Yaxchilán between 752 and 768, appears as a visitor to the city. Shown on the left side of the relief and wearing much more elaborate costume than his companion, Bird Jaguar participates in a scattering rite. Facing Bird Jaguar is his underlord, or *sahal*, who served the Yax-

6.15 Lintel 2, La Pasadita, El Petén, Guatemala, Late Classic Period. The ruler of Yaxchilán, Bird Jaguar IV appears on the left, opposite his sahal. Bird Jaguar engages in a scattering ritual, involving bloodletting from his penis. (Drawing by Kaylee Spencer-Ahrens after Linda Schele, 1986)

chilán ruler as overseer of La Pasadita. Bird Jaguar may have traveled to this region in order to celebrate the completion of a Maya calendrical cycle (see Chapter 9).

The costume worn by Bird Jaguar during the scattering rite includes a cape, a pectoral, high-backed sandals, numerous ornaments of jade, and a headdress. The heads of two divinities related to creation, Chak Xib Chak and the Principal Bird Deity, are stacked in Bird Jaguar's headdress. The head of Bird Jaguar's dead father, Shield Jaguar the Great, is affixed to the back of Bird Jaguar's belt. The head of Shield Jaguar is topped with a jaguar headdress on which a smoking obsidian mirror is attached. The mirror is marked with signs of darkness, as are the dangling obsidian celts suspended below Shield Jaguar's neck. (The color of obsidian suggests the darkness of the Underworld, while the polished surface of obsidian mirrors serves as scrying devices for shamans to communicate with gods and ancestral beings.) Bird Jaguar's status as king is indicated by the mat motif in his headdress. His jaguar *way*, or spirit companion, is manifested by the jaguar tail, also in his headdress.

The scene carved on Lintel 2 reveals that Bird Jaguar has participated in a penis-perforation rite of bloodletting as well as a hand-scattering rite of autosacrifice. Dot-outlined scrolls, representing blood, spill down from Bird Jaguar's hands and fall onto a bound object, possibly an incense burner or throne. The perforator god hangs in an inverted position over Bird Jaguar's genitals. A glyph in the inscription refers to the hand-scattering rite. This glyph consists of a human hand from which clustered dots are falling.

Ball Games

Throughout Mesoamerica, the most important form of the ball game had religious and cosmological significance. Played in various forms for more than three millennia, ball games could be waged between individuals or between teams of players. Masonry ball courts were sometimes I-shaped with sloping benches and high walls. Although the exact rules of the game are uncertain, the goal evidently was to propel a solid rubber ball through rings suspended high on the walls of the court. Such a goal was made particularly challenging because players were probably not allowed to use their hands to direct the movements of the ball. Instead, players deflected the ball by hitting it with various parts of their body, including their hips and shoulders.

BALL-GAME COSTUME

Depictions of ball games are frequent subjects in the scenes painted on polychrome vases. These scenes reveal that ball-game participants wore padding on their forearms and knees as protection against the hard ball and the even harder masonry surfaces of ball courts. Players also wore special U-shaped belts or yokes, most likely made of leather or wicker. Worn high around the waist, these belts protected the player's ribs and hips from the impact of the hard ball. In public ceremonies, victorious players may have exchanged the leather or wicker yokes for the large, lavishly carved stone yokes that have been found in many parts of Mesoamerica.

Other accoutrements worn by ballplayers included *hachas* and ornate headdresses. *Hachas* were axlike stone implements shaped as animal, bird, or human heads and worn inserted in the belt. *Hachas* that are human in form may have represented trophy heads. Ornate headdresses worn by ball players incorporated components of different animals and gods and were frequently capped with the precious feathers of the quetzal bird.

KINDS OF GAMES

The ball game was played for many reasons, including entertainment and competition. Because the losers were frequently sacrificed, ball games also served as a way to reenact wars with enemy peoples. Among the Classic Period Maya, an enemy captured in war might be bound, used as the ball itself, and bounced down a steep staircase at the conclusion of the game. Additionally, ball games were imbued with cosmological significance. The motions of the ball were thought to parallel the motions of the sun, moon, and Venus as they rose through the sky and sank in the Underworld. The rings through which balls were driven in ball games were sometimes stylized in a quatrefoil design.

This design was recognized by the Maya as the shape of the portals through which the Underworld could be entered.

UNDERWORLD SIGNIFICANCE

The cosmological significance of the ball game also incorporated aspects of Maya creation mythology. The ball game served as a ritual in which participants could reenact the heroic actions of the Hero Twins, who had battled and defeated the lords of Xibalba on the Underworld ball court. The actions of the Hero Twins in the Underworld demonstrate that the ball game was inextricably linked to life, death, and rebirth.

The ball court itself was seen as a point of entry into the Underworld. The hieroglyph for the ball game actually depicts a cross-section of the ball court. This cross-section illustrates the stepped design of the ball-court walls. Some of the hieroglyphs for *ball court* even show the round ball. The stepped shape of the ball-court glyph resembles the crack or crevice that appears on the creation mountain of Maya mythology. In the *Popol Vuh*, the Mayan word *hom*, or "crevice," was also the word for "ball court."

Creation accounts locate the burial of the maize god in the Underworld ball court. Maya creation images depict the resurrection of the maize god through a crevice in the earth's surface. This crevice is sometimes represented as the cracked carapace of a turtle and other times as stepped walls of stone, an allusion to the ball courts built by the Maya. In the *Popol Vuh*, the maize god, Hun Hunahpu, remains in the ball court. It is to the ball court that humans must go in order to properly praise the deity that brought life-sustaining maize through his self-sacrifice. Therefore, the ball court was seen as a locus for interaction with the Underworld. When the Maya played the ball game they re-created the events between the intersections of the third world and the present world.

6.16   Relief (detail), Great Ball Court, Chichén Itzá, Early Postclassic Period. This scene shows the sacrifice of a defeated ball-game player. Blood gushes from the neck of the loser, who is shown kneeling on one knee. A victorious player holds a sacrificial blade in one hand and the severed head of the loser in the other.   (Drawing by Linda Schele, copyright David Schele)

THE GREAT BALL COURT, CHICHÉN ITZÁ

The largest ball court known in Mesoamerica can be found at Chichén Itzá. (See figure 8.6, page 233.) This ball court, which is roughly 156 meters (514 feet) long and 36 meters (118.8 feet) wide, is almost twice the size of a modern football field. The Great Ball Court has vertical walls rather than the more usual slanted walls. Rings mounted 8 meters (26.4 feet) above the ground depict entwined rattlesnakes, and a bench runs along the base of the long alley walls. Temples stand at the north and south ends of the court, while two stacked temples, the Upper Temple of the Jaguar and the Lower Temple of the Jaguar, are incorporated into the east wall of the ball court.

A magnificent carving at Chichén Itzá also tells us a great deal about the ball game. The benches that line part of the alley in the ball court exhibit carvings that show a ball-game scene. This series of six panels shows numerous players engaged in a bloody ball game. Although the costumes are similar, upon examination of the headdresses it becomes clear that there are two teams of players. Each player wears a mirror attached to his back, a single kneepad on one leg, and mismatched shoes. Fringed padding protects the arms of the players, and each player holds a *palma*, or special stone in their hands. *Hachas* extend outward from the players' belts. Some *hachas* seem to terminate in skull-like heads, while others resemble open serpent jaws. All of the players wear nose ornaments. Flurries of feathers swoop from the headdresses and inter-mesh with scrolls of smoke or breath, making visible the soul force involved in the ritual.

The two teams proceed toward the center of the panel where a critical scene from the *Popol Vuh* appears to be taking place. This scene depicts the sacrifice that corresponds with play-ing the ball game. A skull inside a ball marks the center of the panel. The figure on the right kneels in defeat. Spurts of blood shown in the form of six serpents gush from his severed neck, making it clear that his head has just been decap-itated. Six Snake, or Wak Chan, was the name for the axis mundi, or the World Tree, created after the rebirth of the maize god from his skull in the ball court; therefore, sacrifice in the ball court literally created the World Tree. The cen-tral spurt of blood scrolls outward, representing the maize tree itself. The branches begin to bear squash. This panel clearly expresses that the actions of the players in the ball court at Chichén Itzá closely paralleled the actions of the Hero Twins in the ball court of Xibalba. Ritually re-creating these actions paid homage to the great ancestors and provided the deities with the blood sacrifice. These rituals and sacrifices sustained the cosmos.

CONCLUSION

Ancient Maya cosmology not only stimulated the ritual activities of priests within ceremonial precincts but also guided the religious, political, economic, and social behaviors of kings, nobles, and commoners alike. Through their ritual per-formance, the Maya channeled the dynamic forces of the supernatural world into the human sphere. Maya elite opened the thresholds between the cosmic realms during the elaborate ceremonies they conducted in monumental architectural structures such as pyramid-temples and ball courts and in front of altars and shrines. Simultaneously, Maya commoners interacted with deities during ritual ceremonies and ordi-nary activities that they pursued in their homes, their fields, and the surrounding natural habitats.

READING

Structure of Sacred Space

Benson 1985: discussion of cosmological signifi-cance of architecture; Diane Chase 1985: the fashioning of sacred spaces; Gendrop 1980: sym-bolism of architecture; Houston 1998: metaphor and significance of Classic Maya building; Kubler 1992: analysis of Mesoamerican architec-ture; McAnany 1995: involvement of ancestors in space; Ralph Roys 1965: translation of the *Book of Chilam Balam of Chumayel*; Sahagún 1950–71: discussion of central Mexican cosmol-ogy; Schavelzon 1980: symbolism in architec-ture; Schele and Freidel 1990, Schele and Miller 1986, Schele and Mathews 1998, Schele and Vil-lela 1996: descriptions of the universe and cos-mological importance of the natural landscape and built environment; Andrea Stone 1995: sig-nificance of caves and mountains; David Stuart 1987: discussion of *witz* mountains; Taube 1998: cosmological significance of temples and built environment; Thompson 1934, 1970b: discus-sion of Maya spirituality; Tozzer 1941: transla-tion of Landa's *Relación de las Cosas de Yucatán*.

Identities of the Gods

Berlin 1963, Bill 1997: discussion of God M and other deities in the codices; Michael Coe 1973, 1975, 1989, 1999: descriptions of the Maya pantheon and other characters from the *Popol Vuh*; Foster and Wren 1996: discussion of God N; Miller and Taube 1993, Schele and Miller 1986: descriptions of Maya Gods; Schellhas 1904: analysis of gods in the *Dresden Codex*; Sharer 1994: description of Maya gods; Taube 1985, 1988b, 1992: thorough discussion of Maya gods of Yucatán; Thompson 1934, 1939, 1970a and b: Maya gods and religion; Tozzer 1941: translation of Landa's *Relación de las Cosas de Yucatán*; Vail 1997, 1998: analyses of deities in ancient codices.

Unfolding of Creation

Berlin 1963: interpretation of the Palenque Triad; Freidel, Schele, and Parker 1993, Schele and Freidel 1990, Schele and Miller 1986: important sources for discussion of creation; Harris and Stearns 1997: inscriptions on creation vases; Schele and Villela 1996: creation imagery from Copán; Taube 1985, 1988a, 1993: creation mythology; Dennis Tedlock 1996: translation of the *Popol Vuh*; Villela and Schele 1996: discussion of creation iconography and astronomy.

Sacred Cities: An Example from Palenque

Bassie-Sweet 1991, Schele 1981; Sharer 1994: Palenque Cross Group; Baudez 1991, Berlin 1963: discussion of Palenque Triad; Michael Coe 1999; Josserand 1991: inscriptions at Palenque; Merle Robertson 1983, 1985a and b:

building, painting, and sculpture at Palenque; Ruz Lhuillier 1973: Temple of the Inscriptions.

The Role of Kings and Shamans

SHAMANISM

Freidel, Schele, and Parker 1993; Miller and Taube 1993, Newsome 1991, Schele and Freidel 1990: Shamanism; Furst 1996, Furst and Coe 1976, Houston and Stuart 1989: spirit companions and *wayob*.

SHAMANISM AND STELA C, COPÁN

Newsome 1991, 1996, Schele and Mathews 1998: shamans and stelae.

Sustenance of Life: *Popol Vuh*

Michael Coe 1989, 1999: *Popol Vuh* themes in Maya art; Freidel, Schele, and Parker 1993, Schele and Freidel 1990, Schele and Miller 1986: interpretation of creation vases; Taube 1985, 1993: *Popol Vuh* themes in Maya art and discussion of the Hun Hunahpu as the maize god; Dennis Tedlock 1996: translation of the *Popol Vuh*.

The Purpose of Ritual Performance

Diane Chase 1985, Freidel, Schele, and Parker 1993, Schele 1985, Schele and Freidel 1990, Schele and Mathews 1998, Schele and Miller 1986, Taube 1987, Vogt 1969: Maya rituals;

Dennis Tedlock 1996: translation of *Popol Vuh;* Tozzer 1941: translation of Landa's *Relación de las Cosas de Yucatán.*

IMPORTANCE OF ANCESTORS

Arlen Chase and Diane Chase 1994, Diane Chase 1991, Fash 1991, McAnany 1995: ancestor worship.

MAYA DANCE

Bricker 1973, Grube 1992: hieroglyphic and iconographic analysis of Maya dance; Freidel, Schele, and Parker 1993, Reents-Budet 1991, Schele and Miller 1986: Maya dance; Houston 1984, Maudslay 1889–1902: Lower Temple of the Jaguars, Chichén Itzá; Tozzer 1941: translation of Landa's *Relación de las Cosas de Yucatán.*

BLOODLETTING

Diane Chase 1991, Freidel, Schele, and Parker 1993, Ian Graham 1979, Joralemon 1974, Miller and Taube 1993, Schele 1985, Schele and Miller 1986, David Stuart 1984, Thompson 1961, Tozzer 1941: bloodletting ritual.

MAYA BALL GAME

Marquina 1951, Miller and Taube 1993, Schele and Mathews 1998, Wren 1991: the ball game and its significance.

WAYOB

Grube and Nahm 1994, Houston and Stuart 1989: the meaning and function of *wayob.*

7

FUNERARY BELIEFS AND CUSTOMS

Maya funerary practices were determined, in part, by a belief in souls and an afterlife and, more important, by the practice of ancestor worship. Ancestor worship can be traced back to the Olmec horizon, and it is suggested in the earliest burials of lowland Maya culture (c. 1000 B.C.E.). The worship is clearly present through the various developmental stages of Maya civilization, and it continues today in well-known Day of the Dead ceremonies on November 1, when the Maya (and other people inhabiting what was once Mesoamerica) visit the graves of the dead to make offerings to them.

SOULS AND THE AFTERLIFE

Souls

The ancient Maya believed humans had multiple souls, although the details are not well understood. Some of those souls died along with the body. The *way*, or animal companion spirit, was one kind of soul that can be identified in Maya beliefs about shamanism from as early as the Preclassic Periods (see Chapter 6). Such coessences are still believed in by many modern-day Maya, such as the Tzotzil Maya of Zinacantán, in Chiapas. Classic Period rulers often claimed jaguars or the animal spirit of patron deities as their *wayob*, and symbols of these coessences, such as crocodile skins and jaguar pelts, have been found in royal tombs. These coessences could leave the body at death, however, since the spirit of a god did not die with an individual but was reborn in others. There may have been more than one type of soul that could be born in a

7.1 *Dumbarton Oaks Tablet 2. The text of this tablet relates that the soul of the deceased Palenque ruler K'an Hoy Chitam has joined his ancestors at* waybil, *the place of the* wayob, *or souls.* (Drawing courtesy John Montgomery)

new person: Living rulers apparently claimed these spirits were reborn in them when they took on the name of a great ancestor, god, or animal spirit.

Modern ethnographic studies have found that contemporary Maya believe humans have multiple souls, but the number varies from one Maya group to the next. The Maya of Zinacantán, for example, believe there are 13, but their neighbors in Chamula believe in 39. The various types, or divisions, of soul constitute the most important aspects of an individual's life. For the Maya, morality resides in the soul; sickness involves loss of various parts or types of soul; and death is total soul loss. Despite different descriptions of the multiple soul, the various Maya groups maintain that some aspect of the soul is eternal, and burials are often delayed for a few days so that the souls can be released.

Xibalba: The Underworld

Some phrases for death—*och ha'* or *och bih*—in the Classic Period hieroglyphic texts mean "enter the water" or "enter the road." For the Maya, water was a symbol of the Underworld, the place of death, and the road must have been the difficult journey through this frightening world to the afterlife. In the *Popol Vuh*, the Hero Twins descended to Xibalba, the place of death; once they defeated the gods of disease and death, they were reborn as the sun and moon or the sun and Venus (see Chapter 6). Classic Period kings reenacted this same journey on their way to deification. In the eighth-century tomb of Hasaw Chan K'awil of Tikal, a bone finely incised with glyphs mentions the king's Underworld journey. Burials included offerings that may have been considered useful: containers of food and sacrificed attendants to assist in the difficult journey to rebirth.

Maya funerary pyramids often were constructed of nine stepped platforms symbolizing the nine layers of the Underworld; the tomb was built in the bottom level, and the pyramid was constructed around it. Many royal burials were placed on the north side of the main plaza, north also being the Maya direction for the sky above. Skeletal remains were rubbed with red cinnabar or hematite because red was the Maya color associated with the east, the direction of the rising Sun and symbol of rebirth.

FUNERARY MONUMENT: A PALENQUE EXAMPLE

Some of the most elaborate iconography of royal death and resurrection is found in the tomb of Hanab Pakal, the 68-year ruler of Palenque (615–683). Located in the base on the nine-stepped pyramid-temple known as the Temple of the Inscriptions, the tomb was originally reached through a steep series of steps. Five skeletons, probably of individuals sacrificed to accompany Hanab Pakal in the otherworld, were placed at the entrance to the tomb, and the ruler's skeleton was placed inside an immense stone sarcophagus along with considerable jade and shell jewelry. The nine gods of the Underworld were depicted in stucco relief on the walls of Hanab Pakal's tomb; the stone sarcophagus lid depicted him falling into this world of death. In his fall to the Underworld, Pakal wears symbols of the sun god, and like the Sun, he will enter the Underworld but be reborn at dawn. He also wears the skirt of the maize god, who died and was then resurrected. Other symbols of rebirth surround him. In the space between his tomb and the temple above, there were 13 vaults, the number of the layers of the heavens in Maya cosmology. The inscriptions written on the temple panel proclaimed that his rulership would be celebrated thousands of years into the future.

Universal Afterlife

Not all Maya could expect deification after death, but this may not have been the only form of afterlife. There is evidence that for nonroyal individuals, some form of life continued after death. There was a general, but not universal, practice for interments to have the skeleton carefully laid out with the head

7.2 *Hanab Pakal's tomb and carved stone sarcophagus, Palenque. The vaulted tomb measures 9 meters (30 feet) long, 4 meters (13 feet) wide, and 7 meters (23 feet) high.* (Photo courtesy Peter Selverstone)

their dead ancestors. Postconquest documents provide further details about Maya beliefs in that late period, although the Spanish descriptions are distorted by their own Christian beliefs. Nonetheless, it seems that all who died had an afterlife, but some, such as women who died in childbirth and those who committed suicide, did not have to undergo the arduous journey through Xibalba to reach paradise, which was a land of plenty shaded by the sacred ceiba tree. Today, many Maya believe the soul must take an arduous journey across water, and aids for surviving this journey accompany the interment of the body. That the Maya believe some souls make the journey successfully can be seen on November 1, or All Saints' Day, which is celebrated by them, as Day of the Dead, when their offerings and remembrances are said to reach the dead.

Ancestral Deities

Only the most powerful ancestors were transformed into supernaturals who could intervene in earthly events for their descendants. Only these deified ancestors were in a position to help the lineage or community, and only they were worshiped. Even commoners' burials show such distinctions in interment practices: Some are buried around the edges of the house compound; others are centrally placed in the house, which was often reconstructed into a shrine. Whether a great war captain, lineage founder, or the owner of a water hole or fertile strip of land, they were the ancestors the Maya needed to intercede and protect them.

Although not every Maya was promised deification, all Maya lived under the protection of the ancestral gods. In the Guatemala highlands today, these supernaturals are called guardians. By tending to the family's ancestral shrines, providing offerings to the dead, and

directed to nonworldly realms, the north or the west, the direction of the Underworld below. Hollow figurines made into whistles accompanied many burials, their significance suggested by a central Mexican myth that whistles helped the dead find their way through the Underworld. The most famous of these whistle figurines were found on the Campeche island of Jaina, a Late Classic Period cemetery. Shaped into lively dancers, warriors, hunters, elegantly dressed nobles, weavers, and mothers carrying a baby on their back, these whistles may have been portraits of the interred, although some have argued they represented their patron deities who would assist them through their Underworld journey (see figure 12.3, page 338).

Residential compounds outside the ceremonial centers also had temples constructed over tombs, suggesting that many lineages, not just royal ones, worshiped and communicated with

commemorating them, the ancestors of the ancient Maya were properly honored, causing them to look favorably on the living. They would keep the fields fertile, the lineage productive, and the community victorious in war. Without these ancestors, the world would collapse. In pre-Columbian times, ancestors could be conjured through self-sacrifice in which human blood was given as an offering, as so clearly depicted in the famous Yaxchilán panels of Lady Xoc (see figures 6.13, page 192, and 6.14, page 193). After the Spanish Conquest, the Maya continued to revere family shrines and images of their ancestors; they burned copal incense for them, but if blood was offered, it was most often from a chicken.

SKY FIGURES

As early as the Late Preclassic Period, ancestral deities were depicted in sculptures communicating with their descendants. Their disembodied heads, often in a swirl of clouds, were represented in the top register of sculptures with their faces looking down from the sky to their earthbound descendants below (see figure 2.4, page 37). These ancestral figures are depicted throughout Maya civilization. In the Late Classic Period, they sometimes are full bodied and in a quatrefoil or cartouche representing the entrance to the otherworld; both male and female ancestors are represented in these scenes, especially at Yaxchilán in the Usumacinta region, and they appear youthful and vigorous, rebirth having shed them of the ravages of death. By the Late Postclassic Period, Yucatec Maya ancestors are shown on sculpture as the so-called diving gods that adorned temples, such as those at Tulum, and Mayapán-style effigy censers (see figure 1.3, page 11).

SHRINES

Veneration was reserved for the most powerful dynastic founders or lineage heads. Dur-

ing the Late Preclassic and Classic Periods, these acts of worship were most likely performed at the tomb itself or in the temple covering the tomb. Some tombs were repeatedly opened, sometimes to bury another family member in a group crypt, but also for rituals. Excavators have found burn marks on tomb floors, and there is textual evidence that the Maya were burning incense, the smoke of which was food for the gods. Sometimes bones appear to have been removed after burial, perhaps to be used in other commemorative rituals. The place of burial was the location of important, ongoing ancestor rituals. Despite centuries of construction over the tomb of Copán's founder, Yax K'uk Mo, it was commemorated at each level so that rituals honoring him and his dynasty continued until the fall of the city in the ninth century. At Palenque, the stairs to Hanab Pakal's tomb were sealed with rubble after his burial, but a stone duct, 25 meters (80 feet) long, connected the temple with the tomb for continued communication.

In the Late Postclassic Period, the elaborate tombs and monumental temples no longer were constructed; they were replaced by shrines. The royal lineage at Mayapán, that of the Cocom, placed the bones of their dead in shrines, where offerings of incense, flowers, and blood properly honored their memory and gained their intervention for the good of the city. During the 16th century, the Maya continued to maintain household ancestral shrines that included relics from the most elite of the dead. These revered images were most often made from part of the skull and filled with cremated ashes; some of these skulls, the back sawed off and shaped with rubber or a kind of pitch, were painted into an image of the deceased. Ceramic incense burners, shaped into effigies of gods, may have served as ancestor images for the lower classes (see figures 1.3, page 11, and 2.18, page 79). The Spaniards

7.3 *Tikal Altar 5. The hieroglyphic text of this stone monument suggests that this altar commemorated the reinterment of the deceased wife of Lord Hasaw Chan K'awil in 711. The altar was accompanied by a stela portrait of the living king.* (Drawing courtesy John Montgomery)

remarked that many represented women. For the Maya of today, family members are remembered with Day of the Dead altars, which are festooned with pictures and mementos of the dead (see figure 7.5, page 212).

BURIALS

There are many unknown details of ancestor worship, but one aspect is certain: The practice required appropriate burial and commemora-

tive rituals at the place of interment. Sometimes these rituals persisted over centuries at individual Classic Period tombs, and each ritual added to the sanctity of the place and the reverence for the ancestor. Contemporary Maya continue to make pilgrimages to ancestral mountains dating from pre-Columbian times, and they burn candles and incense on ancient monuments believed to represent their ancestors. For the Day of the Dead, they place flowers and burn incense on the graves of more recently deceased family members.

Although large temples and vaulted tombs no longer were constructed in the Late Postclassic Period, the rituals continued at shrines. In fact, smaller household shrines probably existed from earliest times. Small models of houses, believed to have held images of both patron and ancestral deities, have been excavated from the residential areas of Classic Period Copán. In the Postclassic Period, such small shrines were used for royalty as well. From the Late Classic to the period before Spanish contact, royal interments progressed from funerary pyramids to cremated remains placed in an urn.

Commoners

Commoners were buried in the family compound, under the house floor, or on the outside of the building, and this practice persisted from 1000 B.C.E. until the institution of Christian graveyards during the Spanish colony. At the time of the Spanish Conquest, the dead were wrapped in a shroud, and the mouth cavity was filled with ground maize. A standard custom for all burials, regardless of position in the class hierarchy, was to place a jade bead in the mouth to symbolize life, or breath—just such a jade bead was recovered from the jaw of Hanab Pakal in Palenque and from skeletal remains in Preclassic burials at Kaminaljuyú. Wooden or ceramic effigies of gods often were placed with the body, along with objects, such as a figurine and others that identified something about the individual—a farming tool, a spindle whorl, a hunter's sling, and, if a priest, books or divinatory stones.

The Elite

For most of the Classic Period in the southern lowlands, burial practices followed the traditional Maya custom of interring the individual under the floor of the residential compound. It is perhaps not coincidental that the Mayan word *na* means both "house" and "lineage." Skeletal remains often were found intruding into earlier layers of building construction. Many interments were accompanied by luxury possessions—fine polychrome plates or drinking cups, shell and jade ornaments—but there were contrasts among them: Some were simple pit burials, not tombs, placed to the back of the compound, and some were group interments, presumably a family crypt. By the Late Classic Period, some elite burials had become more elaborate, not simply in their grave goods, which sometimes included panels with hieroglyphic texts and artistic symbols, but also in their construction. Vaulted tombs, formerly reserved for royal burials, protected the remains of some of the nobility as well.

However, which members of the elite were buried in residential areas may have become more selective during the Late Classic Period. Cemeteries have been discovered completely outside the residential areas. Although the reason for these burials sites is not known, perhaps they were repositories for those not deemed powerful enough for lineage worship. In the northern lowlands, the island of Jaina, off the coast of Campeche, appears to have been a necropolis. Hundreds of burials, with a wealth of offerings, have been discovered there accompanied by small temples. The site has never been fully excavated, so it is not well understood, but its location on the sea in the direction of the setting sun made it a perfect Maya burial ground, full of Underworld symbolism. Some caves contain hundreds of burials. Caves, Maya entrances to the Underworld, were scenes of pilgrimages and ancestral rituals and those at Naj Tunich in the southeastern Petén were covered with graffiti-style paintings commemorating some of these rituals.

Royal Burials

Funerary practices for royalty changed over time and by region. In many Late Preclassic Period burials, the deceased is wrapped in a flexed position, creating a seated mummy bundle. At Uaxactún, once such interment placed the bundle on a bench, as if the king still ruled from the throne. Later, the shrouded skeletal remains, often carefully defleshed and prepared, were laid out in an extended position, sometimes inside a stone sarcophagus, other times on a stone bench covered with a woven mat, the symbol of rulership. Jade masks, occasionally with shell inlays for eyes and teeth, covered their faces, sometimes replacing cheek bones and other parts of the cranium that had been removed. These burials were accompanied by great riches of jade, exotic shell, obsidian, god effigies, and the finest polychrome pottery. By the Late Postclassic Period, these elaborate royal burial practices had ended. In Yucatán, cremation was more common, and when burials were accompanied by offerings, they included only fragments of obsidian, shell, or jade. But a new offering appeared during this period in the form of copper bells and gold jewelry.

There were other burial variations, the significance of which is not always easily understood. The southern region included sacrificed retainers in crypts from the Preclassic Period, but in the lowlands, the first vaulted tombs included a single person, whether man, woman, or child. As these tombs became more monumental during the Classic Period, they included sacrificed attendants and sometimes other members of the royal family, as is the case in a few Early Classic burials at Uaxactún. But by 400, the individual was once again interred alone, except for sacrificed retainers.

EARLY ROYAL BURIALS

Early royal burials often followed the common Maya practice of home interment, although the temple construction commemorating the burial and the offerings placed in the crypt or tomb were, of course, far more elaborate. In fact, these funerary constructions most often destroyed the residence itself. In the Late Preclassic Period, royal residences were reconstructed upon the king's death and made into triadic temple complexes (see Chapter 8) with accompanying royal tombs. With each burial, these complexes were remodeled, incorporating the old into new, larger funerary monuments. This evolution from residence to clustered funerary complex resulted in some of the largest building complexes of the period. The North Acropolis at Tikal began as one of the earliest settlement areas of the site; by the end of the Early Classic Period, it had become an imposing royal necropolis, containing tombs and temples that spanned 600 years. Such ancestral monuments at the heart of Maya cities must have marked them as sacred places and the center of the Maya cosmos. According to present-day highland Mayas, if the ancestors depart, the world will fall apart.

LATE CLASSIC PERIOD

In the Late Classic Period, the shift away from funerary temples clustered in vast complexes to single pyramid-temples was highly symbolic. The great king, his tomb separated from the palace or royal necropolis, was worshiped not simply as part of the dynasty but as the deified ancestor of the city itself. These funerary pyramids often towered over other buildings at the city (see figure 2.8, page 50). Tikal's six tallest structures were funerary pyramids; the tallest was Yik'in Chan K'awil's Temple IV, which is 70 meters (231 feet) high. These tombs took considerable time to construct, and some rulers initiated the design and construction of their tombs during their own lifetimes. Not all tombs were completed when needed, as proven by the difference in the death dates and burial dates discovered for some rulers, which quite often amounted to more than a year. And not all that were completed were occupied, leaving an open question as to the fate of the ruler.

QUEENS

Some separate and quite elaborate royal tombs were constructed for the ruler's wife. The tombs of a few queens have been excavated, although their identity is often hard to verify due to the lack of accompanying glyphic texts. The tomb of the Red Queen of Palenque, so-called for the cinnabar rubbed on her bones, was placed at the bottom of a small pyramid-temple. Her remains were covered with a 1,200-piece jade necklace and accompanied by two sacrificed retainers. At Copán, a tomb believed to have been constructed for the fifth-century widow of founder Yax K'uk Mo had the richest contents of any known female burial, particularly in the quantity of jade it contained. Her tomb was revisited for decades and new offerings were deposited before it was finally sealed in a rebuilding program. Although no tomb was found for the wife of Tikal's Hasaw Chan K'awil, her portrait was carved on the pyramid-temple that rises so majestically across from that of the ruler's on the main ceremonial plaza of Tikal.

POSTCLASSIC PERIOD

Vaulted tombs have not been discovered yet for the Postclassic Period, but there is some speculation that tombs might exist in the nine-stepped pyramid-temples dating from this period, especially the Castillo at Chichén Itzá (see figure 8.3, page 219). Inscriptions found outside the sacred center of Chichén Itzá indicate that many temples were dedicated to ancestral deities, but burial practices for the site remain confusing. For example, skeletal remains were discovered in a cave under one

7.4 *Quiché funerary urn in the Popol Vuh Museum, Late Postclassic Period.* (Photo courtesy Lawrence Foster)

pyramid at Chichén Itzá, making it difficult to decide whether the bones and accompanying artifacts were offerings to the Underworld or a burial. Archaeologists have uncovered ceramic urns containing cremated ashes, which turns out to have been standard Yucatec practice in later periods.

Although burial customs are not well understood for the Early Postclassic Period, ethnohistoric documents provide insight into Late Postclassic practices, when there was a definite shift away from tomb interments. In the northern lowlands, cremation became a common practice, but only for the elite; their images were worshiped in shrines and their ashes were buried in urns and offerings at temple platforms and temple-pyramids. For the Quiché in the Guatemala highlands, flexed skeletal remains were placed in monumental ceramic urns painted with symbols of the Underworld, but parts of the skeleton were incorporated into enshrined images of the deceased, just as they were for the elite of Yucatán.

Although these changes are quite striking, they also constitute continuations of past practices. Parts of the cranium and skull as well as other bones were sometimes removed from skeletal remains before, and even after, burial during the Classic Period; jade and precious stones often covered parts of the missing face or skull. The Late Postclassic veneration of reconstructed and painted skulls does not seem to be too dissimilar a practice. Heads appear to have had special significance to the Maya. Heads of deified ancestors were often all that were depicted in Late Preclassic vision scenes; in the *Popol Vuh*, it is the skull that is reborn as the maize god (see Chapter 6). In the Late Postclassic Period, skulls were venerated in shrines along with other ancestor images; their spirit was fed with the burning of copal incense and blood, just as it had been in earlier periods. The Maya had foregone the labor of constructing elaborate tombs, but they still had altars and shrines to commemorate their dead.

ANCESTOR WORSHIP AND LEGITIMACY

Maya funerary customs were based on a belief in rebirth and ancestor worship. These two beliefs combined into the foundations of Maya life from the earliest periods to the present. Powerful, semidivine ancestors were reborn as gods and acted for the benefit of descendants—if they were properly propitiated. The proper ancestor rituals occurred in temples atop their tombs at Classic Period Maya cities, which were important places for lineage rituals.

The tomb or shrine not only provided access to the otherworld; it also legitimized inheritance. These tombs were statements that the lineage belonged and had belonged since the distant time of the sacred founders. In Yucatán, the Spaniards reported that the lineage heads could recount hundreds of years of their descent with exceptional details about names and marriages. Such histories were comparable to dynastic lists compiled at Late Classic Period sites; at Palenque, the royal line extended back into mythological time. The land was theirs; they had inherited it from the gods. When the royal tomb became the solitary pyramid-temple, it proclaimed the city itself as the domain of the dynasty.

The Classic Period texts suggest that even though a particular ruler might be removed, the local nobility were permitted to govern under the auspices of the conquering state. When the foreigner Yax K'uk Mo was installed at Copán, for example, he married a woman from the local nobility to legitimize his reign. From the dynasty they founded, 15 male rulers governed Copán, and each accrued the supernatural power of the preceding deified ancestors. Any disruption of such accrued sanctity and legitimacy would be undertaken with considerable risk and subsequent need to reestablish the appearance of legitimacy. In some cases, such as Yaxuná and Uaxactún, this was accomplished not through marriage and the reestablishment of local customs, but rather through the destruction of the dynasty and its ancestral tombs.

7.5 *A Modern Day of the Dead ceremony in highland Guatemala.*

they did not, they would lose their membership and rights within the community.

For the Maya, ancestors linked them to the powers of the otherworld as well as rooted them in their earthly world. The Maya position in the family, in the settlement, and in the cosmos was defined and sanctified by these ancestral associations. Ancestor worship was, and is, such an integral part of the Maya cosmology, that it has survived to this day, despite threats of punishment and even torture from early Christian missionaries and priests. The Day of the Dead is not simply a time of remembrance of the deceased; for the Maya, it is a period of interaction between the earthly and supernatural that reaffirms one's place in the world order.

Property and Position

There is increasing archaeological data that for all Maya, both nobles and commoners, ancestors legitimized property ownership. From the palace down to the simple farmer's home, ancestors were buried under the floors, proof of family ownership. For the dynasty, it meant the right to rule the city. For the peasant family, it meant the right to land; for others, the right to exploit valuable salt pans and the like. Each act honoring the ancestors was also a public reaffirmation of those rights. Today, many Maya continue to claim their rights to certain lands or natural resources through such ancestral claims. The shrines, carefully tended and worshiped for generations, are physical proof of their legal rights. And Maya living in places as distant as the United States return to their communities in order to participate in Day of the Dead rituals; if

READING

See also "Reading" for Chapters 6 and 8.

McAnany 1995 and 1998: overview of ancestor worship; Michael Coe 1975, Freidel, Schele, and Parker 1993, Houston and Stuart 1989, Masson 1999, Schele and Mathews 1998, Tedlock 1996: souls and the afterlife; Freidel and Schele 1989, Houston and Stuart 1996, Schele and Miller 1986, David Stuart 1998: ancestral deities; Chase and Chase 1994, Fash 1998, Harrison 1999, Martin and Grube 2000, Miller 1999: burials; Tozzer 1941, Carmack 1981: ethnohistoric sources; Carlsen 1997, Gossen 1999, Martin and Grube 2000, Barbara Tedlock 1992, Vogt 1990, Watanabe 1992: the living Maya.

8

ARCHITECTURE
AND BUILDING

Archaeologists have argued that civilization requires urban centers and that the measure of a civilization can be made by the architecture of its cities. The more time consuming and sophisticated in construction the architecture, and the more massive the city, the more complex was the society that built them. Although this hypothesis has been challenged in regard to some details, there is little doubt that monumental construction requires the political wherewithal and development to organize labor and material. Based on its architectural remains, Maya civilization ranks as one of the great preindustrial cultures of the world.

The Maya were prodigious builders, leaving an exceptional architectural legacy. Immediately after the Spanish Conquest, for example, the missionary Diego de Landa commented that the glory of Yucatán should have spread through the world based on "the multitude, the grandeur, and the beauty of its buildings" (Tozzer 1941: 171). By 1975, archaeologists had cataloged more than 2,500 Maya locations of varying size and date with some stone construction. Numerous cities with populations in the tens of thousands have left a monumental record of life in the preconquest era. These architectural remains provide some of the best evidence for the evolution of Maya civilization; and the surviving art and hieroglyphic texts that decorate many buildings, as well as the dedicatory caches and burials discovered within them, provide valuable clues to the meaning and function of the ancient buildings. Maya cities and architecture are a testament to Maya cultural and political life.

MASONRY ARCHITECTURE AND LABOR

Maya investment in masonry architecture provides an interesting measure of the complexity of that civilization's political and social order. Masonry architecture required central organization, craft specialization, and the political power to command a large workforce. Experiments in re-creating the tasks of quarrying, transporting materials, and construction indicate just how labor intensive Maya construction was.

Labor Requirements

Stonemasonry requires a considerable amount of labor in contrast to wooden and thatched huts, or even adobe ones, and that labor must be organized and supervised. According to studies by Elliot Abrams, for example, one large elite residence at Copán required an estimated 10,686 person-hours to obtain building materials and to construct; a simple hut required only 67 person-days (a family undertaking, in effect)

8.1 Pyramid of the Magician, Uxmal. This Terminal Classic pyramid rises 35 meters (115 feet) to the roof on the temple at its summit. The monumentality of the pyramid results from at least four different phases of rebuilding earlier and smaller complexes. (Photo courtesy Lawrence Foster)

and a plastered platform for the hut took 125 person-days. An estimated 65 percent of the labor invested in the elite residence was devoted to quarrying, transporting, and preparing the stone and another 24 percent to the preparing and applying of the limestone plaster.

The Maya were able to organize the labor and utilize the expertise of masons, plasterers, and supervising architects to build and maintain their cities of immense stone pyramids, stone palaces, and temples, ball courts, and other ritual buildings. For the single house of the Copán nobleman, it has been estimated that at least 80 to 130 workers would have been employed full time to finish it in two to three months. The densest urban core of a city such as Tikal covered 6 square kilometers (more than 2 square miles), so the numbers of workers involved in construction and reconstruction must have been immense. Studies at the smaller site of Uxmal suggested that the major ceremonial buildings alone required at least 7.5 million person-days of labor and that would not have included site preparation.

Yet the Classic Period cities extended beyond the urban core into the residential suburbs and even into outlying towns, where there were smaller masonry ceremonial centers. Many Maya sites spread over 20 square kilometers (nearly 8 square miles); the defensive moat at Tikal protected an area of 123 square kilometers (47 square miles). At Dzibilchaltún in northern Yucatán, 50,000 structures extended over 50 kilometers (30 miles). Raised and plastered roads often radiated from the center to these suburban areas. Obviously, the pre-Columbian Maya were remarkable builders.

Patrons and Specialists

Maya hieroglyphic texts do not directly name architects and urban planners, but they do suggest that individuals supervised construction and that sometimes these supervisors were from other cities. Texts do, however, often name those who commissioned or dedicated certain buildings, thereby providing some insight into Maya building practices. Although rulers are named as the patrons of buildings—Hanab Pakal of Palenque is referred to as "he of the five-door temple"—other individuals appear in the hieroglyphic texts: Lady Xoc, a queen, commissioned a Late Classic building at Yaxchilán, and members of the elite dedicated buildings outside the main ceremonial center at ninth-century Chichén Itzá. Insofar as these individuals can be associated with Long Count dates, the texts associating them with buildings provide clear temporal sequences for the development of elite sections of the city.

Archaeologists, in attempting to replicate construction techniques, believe that full-time stonemasons and plasterers were necessary by at least the Late Preclassic and that the enormity of many of the projects required the oversight of individuals with the skills of architects and city planners. Some specialized buildings would have also required the collaboration of astronomers and priests, just as stucco decorations and mosaic designs required sculptors and scribes. Despite all this expertise, it is estimated that 90 percent of those involved in construction were general laborers, many of whom were working as a form of tribute payment to a patron or ruler.

ARCHITECTURAL DEVELOPMENT

Classic Period Maya cities have long been respected as the apogee of Maya civilization, but excavations of Preclassic cities at the end of the 20th century have revealed the largest structures ever built by the Maya. These Maya architectural remains provide evidence of rapid population growth and cultural development by 600 B.C.E.—almost a millennium earlier than thought just a few decades ago.

Middle Preclassic Period

The Maya architectural tradition evolved from the simple rectangular or oval-shaped pole-and-thatch huts in the Archaic Period to Middle Preclassic limestone cities consisting of pyramid-temples, palaces, and ritual complexes with plastered roads and stairs connecting the various buildings and areas of the sites. From this early period, Maya buildings and plazas were built according to a plan and often oriented toward the cardinal points. (See Map 6, for example, on page 200.)

Late Preclassic Period

By the Late Preclassic Period, the Maya had already developed the corbeled arch and built the largest complexes in their history. The canal system at Edzná required the movement of so much earth it might constitute the largest engineering undertaking of Maya civilization. Many sites in the southern area, such as the highland city of Kaminaljuyú, also devoted resources to building pyramids and irrigation canals. But the largest building complexes were constructed at the lowland site of El Mirador: Its Danta complex covered 90,000 square meters (968,400 square feet) at its base—the equivalent of almost 200 football fields—and rose in three platform levels to 70 meters (231 feet) at its highest point. Triadic pyramids and

other massive buildings were built on the various levels. El Tigre, within El Mirador, was very small compared to the Danta complex, but it nonetheless could have covered the North Acropolis and the famous pyramid-temples Temples I and II of the great Late Classic phase of Tikal.

From pole-and-thatch structures, the Maya experimented with hard-packed clays and adobe (mud mixed with straw) before using stone construction. In the lowlands, small pebbles or river stones were embedded in earth in the first stone constructions, then by 1000 B.C.E. some regions experimented with layering thin quarried stones in several courses to form platforms and walls. As the Middle Preclassic Period progressed, stone fill was increasingly faced by shaped quarried stone and covered with thick limestone plaster for a smooth facade finish. Large stone blocks were tenoned into the building to make moldings. Eventually rubble fill replaced quarried stones, and facades of large cut limestone blocks were replaced with smaller blocks. In the Late Preclassic tenoned stones also were used for molding stucco decorations on the exterior walls. Toward the end of the period, the corbeled vault was introduced. Plaster covered both interior and exterior surfaces, and sometimes it was tinted to color entire buildings, such as a round platform at Tikal.

Classic Period

During the Classic Period, vaulted masonry construction typified most buildings for the elite; the workmanship of the finished stone became increasingly refined so that less plaster was required to smooth the facade. In fact, the stone mosaic decorations of the Puuc region in Yucatán, like those found at Terminal Classic Period Uxmal, were so finely finished that they were not plastered at all (see figure 8.4, page

225). Also in the Terminal Classic, rounded columns supported doorways in northern Yucatán, and at Chichén Itzá, colonnades, covered with flat roofs, supplemented vaulted buildings. Although the size of individual complexes did not exceed those of previous periods, their number constituted an immense built environment. More than 3,000 structures have been identified in central Tikal, for example, and some of them approached El Tigre of El Mirador in size.

Postclassic Period

Buildings became less monumental after the Terminal Classic Period, even though many of the stylistic innovations of Chichén Itzá persisted throughout the period in the lowlands. This might indicate diminished power of the Maya realm, or it might signify a new political order that was more interested in commerce than in powerful dynastic statements (see Chapter 4). Late Postclassic cities, such as Mayapán, were still substantial in size, but even when buildings were modeled on earlier ones, such as the Castillo at Chichén Itzá, they were smaller and less carefully constructed. By the time of the Spanish Conquest, the size of masonry ceremonial centers had reduced even further at coastal towns like Tulum, where the largest complex was just 7.5 meters (25 feet) in height. Masonry architecture still typified these towns, nonetheless, and the corbeled arch was still occasionally employed (see figure 8.3, page 222). The hilltop citadels of the Guatemala highlands included more substantial buildings, some 18 meters (60 feet) high, but they were constructed most often of plastered adobe, not stone. (See figure 2.18, page 79.)

ARCHITECTURAL TRAITS

Plazas and Interior Spaces

Despite temporal stylistic shifts, regional variations, and differences in royal taste from city to city, many Maya architectural components persisted for 2,000 years. All Maya ceremonial centers were organized around great open plazas with monumental buildings along some or all of the sides. Over time, the buildings incorporated older ones during remodeling projects so that Maya monumental was often achieved through superimposition of one building over others (see figure 8.1, page 215). Although a few causeways linked some sections of Maya cities, a succession of plazas and building complexes rather than a grid of streets organized the city from the center to its outskirts. (See Map 6, page 220; Map 7, page 227.)

The paved open plazas, not building interiors, provided the public spaces for community activities (see figures 2.6, page 45, and 2.8, page 50). The massive walls and facade decorations of buildings that bordered the public plazas were more important than building interiors and provided the backdrop for both political and religious performances, such as dances, ball games, and sacrifices. Medial staircases provided access up to most buildings, but broad ceremonial stairways, such as those found at Copán, may have served as seating for the performances. The size of the buildings and the iconographic themes depicted on them also were meant to impress the populace and foreign visitors with the power of the ruling dynasty and the sacredness of the city.

Interior rooms, however, were quite small and usually could accommodate only a few indi-

8.2   *The Late Postclassic Castillo at Tulum (above) and the Early Postclassic Castillo at Chichén Itzá (below).*   (Photos courtesy John Montgomery)

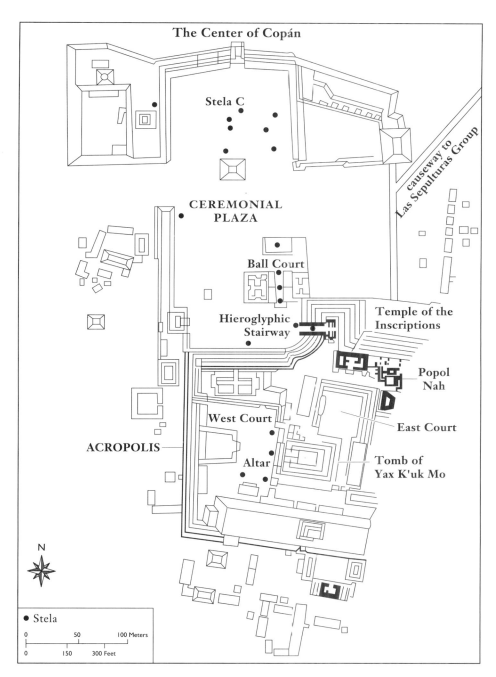

The Center of Copán

Stela C

causeway to
Las Sepulturas Group

CEREMONIAL
PLAZA

Ball Court

Hieroglyphic
Stairway

Temple of the
Inscriptions

Popol
Nah

West Court

East Court

ACROPOLIS

Altar

Tomb of
Yax K'uk Mo

N

• Stela

0   50   100 Meters

0   150   300 Feet

Map 6. *Plan of Central Copán. Oriented to the cardinal directions, Classic Period Copán was constructed on a plateau next to the Copán River. Its buildings were organized around plazas and courtyards, and a causeway led to one of its outlying residential areas.*

viduals at any one time in contrast to one of the plazas at Copán, which could accommodate 3,000 people. Throne rooms and temple interiors were, of necessity, reserved for the elite and priestly classes. At Palenque, intersecting vaults were constructed in order to enhance interior spaces, however, and during the Terminal Classic Period, post-and-lintel construction resulted in larger rooms in northern Yucatán. But even these expanded interior spaces were too small to have served for anything other than elite ceremonies. Residences, for royalty and commoners alike, included courtyards; elite complexes included larger terraces for lineage functions. For the Maya, the most important architectural goal was to create external spaces framed by buildings; in the case of the ceremonial center, those spaces were public, and the buildings were the most monumental in the city.

Specialized Complexes

Complexes of buildings with specialized functions were constructed throughout Mesoamerica, and they were always arranged around open spaces, whether plazas or elevated terraces. The most typical complexes include the pyramid-temple (a temple built on top of a tall, usually stepped pyramidal platform), the ball court, and the palace with internal courtyards, range-style multiroomed buildings, and sometimes even sweat baths. Maya palaces were an aggregate of many buildings that were built on multiple platform levels and became so monumental that they are called acropolises. In addition, the Maya had their own specialized constructions. They often unified building clusters and far-flung areas of the city with paved and elevated roads (*sacbeob*); they favored triadic complexes in which two structures on a platform faced each other while forming a U with a third, larger central one. In addition,

they had other ritual complexes, such as the E-group and Twin Pyramid complexes (see "Types of Construction" below).

Freestanding Monuments

Freestanding monuments were erected on the ceremonial plazas, usually in front of the stairs, or central axis, of royal buildings. This tradition of accompanying buildings with freestanding sculpture, whether altars (perhaps really thrones) and stelae or Postclassic *chac mools* and sacrificial stones, began in the Early Preclassic Period among the Olmec and persisted in all of Mesoamerica until the Spanish Conquest. The Classic Period Maya, however, had a special preference for erecting stelae in front of important buildings and carving them with ruler portraits and hieroglyphic texts. In the Terminal Classic Period, stelae were less common but freestanding sculptures—double-headed jaguar thrones and *chac mool* offertory sculptures—were still aligned with building facades (see figure 2.15, page 70). By the Late Postclassic Period, freestanding sculptures were rare, and when they existed at sites, such as Mayapán, they were crudely made. But plain stone monuments were erected to commemorate calendrical rituals.

Corbeled Vault

The corbeled vault, sometimes known as the false arch in contradistinction to the keystone arch, is prevalent in Mesoamerica only in Maya architecture. Most of Mesoamerica—and the Maya occasionally, as well—constructed stone buildings with thatched roofs or flat ones supported by wooden beams. In the Late Preclassic Period, tombs at the Petén sites of Tikal and Wakná were constructed with crudely formed

Guerrero, where recent excavations have uncovered numerous apparently non-Maya examples, most often in funerary rather than temple contexts. Exactly when the corbeled arch was first used in Guerrero remains uncertain, but a few archaeologists have speculated that the people of Guerrero, not the Maya, were the first to invent the corbeled vault in Mesoamerica, even though vaulted architecture was never typical of that region. Whoever first invented the arch, it was the Maya who utilized it and made it one of the distinguishing characteristics of their architecture.

TEMPORAL STYLISTIC SHIFTS

Architectural fashion and religious cults changed over time. Some of these changes were regional, and others seem temporal, but they were pan-Maya—at least in the lowlands.

Late Preclassic Period

The Late Preclassic Period witnessed the public exhibit of religious and cosmic subject matter that was either carved into stelae in the southern area, such as Izapa on the Pacific coast, or molded onto building facades in the lowlands. Late Preclassic facades in the lowlands were decorated with large stucco masks of deities that flanked the stairways; the stucco sculptures grew into massive art works at sites such as El Mirador and Uaxactún in the Petén, Cerros and Lamanai in Belize, and Yaxuná in the northern lowlands. Stucco masks at El Mirador were 10 meters (34 feet) wide, almost 5 meters (16 feet) high, and 2 to 3 meters

8.3   A corbeled-vault room at Las Monjas, Chichén Itzá, which was used as a camp by Alfred P. Maudslay.   (Photo Alfred P. Maudslay 1889–1902)

stone vaults, the earliest known Maya examples. The corbeled vault became a common Maya building technique by the end of this period and was increasingly used in the construction of stone temples and palaces, not just tombs. By relying on the corbeled arch, the Maya re-created the hip-shaped interiors and roof slopes that characterized their traditional thatched hut. The corbeled vault also limited most Maya buildings to one story and created small interior spaces.

Other Mesoamerican regions so rarely utilized the vault that most instances of the vault outside the Maya region are thought to demonstrate Maya influence. However, the vault is not quite so rare in the Mexican state of

(about 6 to 10 feet) in depth. Some art historians speculate these facades provided the public backdrops to religious celebrations or served as immense idols where people placed offerings.

Classic Period

Most lowland Classic Period buildings limited sculpture to cornice and frieze decorations, as well as pilaster and roof comb designs; some of these continued to be made of stucco, but others were low-relief stone carvings or stone mosaics. Ruler portraits became increasingly common in the Classic Period, but in the Yucatán, geometric motifs were often applied to Late Classic buildings. Deity offerings must have been performed in some other fashion, and art historians have speculated that large ceramic incense burners shaped into effigies of gods might have become more portable substitutes for the Preclassic walls. A ruler cult that began in the southern area during the Late Preclassic gradually replaced some of the earlier religious practices. The erection of stelae carved with individual portraits accompanied by hieroglyphic texts proliferated. By the Late Classic Period, for example, royal tombs were constructed in the ceremonial center and encased in pyramid-temples that were decorated with themes relating to the deified king.

Terminal Classic and Postclassic Periods

During the Terminal Classic and Postclassic Periods, in what many archaeologists and art historians believe signifies the abandonment of dynastic rulership, the stela cult was replaced by other freestanding sculptures, and fewer pyramid-temples were constructed. At Chichén Itzá, for example, roofed colonnades, one of which was as long as 136 meters (450 feet), created a new and impressive form of public space in the main plaza (see figure 3.2, page 96); *chac mools* and jaguar thrones were the most common forms of freestanding sculpture. Monumental feathered serpent columns and the stepped pyramid known as the *castillo* were copied by other Yucatec cities until the Spanish Conquest.

Although many of the architectural forms introduced at Chichén Itzá persisted into the Late Postclassic Period, the building scale and workmanship was greatly reduced. Chichén Itzá's most widespread influence can be found along the Caribbean coast and at Mayapán where buildings with wide doorways supported by columns became the basic architectural form of the period. A new architectural form was introduced, that of the freestanding shrine, or small religious structure. The shrine replaced the grander temples of earlier periods and best exemplifies the diminishing scale of architectural complexes during this final period of pre-Columbian architecture.

REGIONAL VARIATIONS

Maya cities shared common features that distinguished them from the more rectilinearly organized Mesoamerican cities. But the Maya did not have a central ruling authority like the Roman emperor to order the arrangement of their cities. Instead, there is considerable variety in architectural styles and site plans, and this can be seen from as early as the Middle Preclassic Period. In this early period, the town plans and stone constructions found in Chiapas and the Petén, for example, differed from those of the contemporary Olmec site La Venta or the Oaxacan site Monte Albán. And they differed from each other as well, showing both local developments and regional interaction. In the northeastern Petén region of the Mirador Basin, for example, sites were oriented to the east and west as opposed to the north-to-south plan preferred in the Pacific region as well as in the Olmec heartland during the same period.

The availability of different building materials and local preferences resulted in regional styles. The southern region, for example, lacked easily worked stone for masonry construction, resulting in more perishable buildings composed of earthen platforms and adobe or wooden superstructures with thatched roofs. The masonry arch was not used along the Pacific coast or southern highlands, but stone was used for sculptural motifs, stairways, and the like. By contrast, limestone was plentiful in most lowland areas and easily found just below the soil. The southeastern region had more varieties of building stone and greater choice in the kinds of stone to use for both decorative sculpture and stone blocks. It is the masonry architecture of the lowlands that epitomizes Maya civilization.

Topography, climate, building materials, and even ruler preferences created differences among cities. Some of these differences developed into somewhat loosely defined regional styles in the lowlands, especially during the Late Classic Period.

Central Petén Style

The city of Tikal is the archetype for the central Petén style (see figure 2.8, page 50). At Tikal there are six immense and soaring pyramidal platforms, each of which supports a simple temple with one doorway and roof comb. Large masonry block construction is typical of

the style. Examples of this style extend beyond the central Petén to encompass Calakmul to the north and Cobá in the eastern part of the Yucatán Peninsula. Stelae and altar complexes are common accompaniments to buildings, and bas-relief sculptures of rulers and gods adorn lintels, roof combs, and the upper facades of temples and palaces.

Usumacinta Style

Cities in this region of rolling hills and irregular terrain took advantage of their location, lifting their temples by building platforms onto the hills. At Usumacinta sites such as Palenque and Yaxchilán, a more inventive use of vaulting permitted thinner walls and three or more doorways to pierce temple facades (see figure 8.4). Palaces had multiple, arcade-like entrances constructed by the post-and-lintel method rather than vaults. Roof combs were common in the Usumacinta as well as in the Petén. Some sites in the region, such as Palenque, developed exceptional stucco techniques, decorating the piers and upper walls of buildings with finely made sculptures of kings and gods. Most of the sites erected stelae, although Palenque did not, substituting instead elaborately carved panels inside its buildings.

Puuc Style

Uxmal typifies the architectural style that evolved in the Puuc Hills of northwestern Yucatán and spread to other parts of the northern lowlands during the Terminal Classic Period. By utilizing lime concrete instead of rubble as the building core, Puuc masons did not have to rely on thick containing walls to strengthen the structure; the corbeled arch was

8.4   Four Late Classic Period architectural styles: the Puuc style at Uxmal, Yucatán (upper left); the Chenes style at Chicanná, Campeche (upper right); the Río Bec style at Río Bec "B," Campeche (lower left); and the Usumacinta style at Palenque, Chiapas (lower right). (Upper left and right photos courtesy of John Montgomery; lower left and right photos courtesy Peter Selverstone)

similarly strengthened, and freestanding gateways or entrance arches to cities resulted (see figure 8.8, page 242). Finely shaped thin-veneer facade stones were set into the concrete and precut mosaic stones formed the decorative motifs in the upper wall in contrast to an undecorated lower facade. The decorations themselves at times represented Maya deities. For example, long-nosed deity masks once thought to represent the rain god Chak but now believed to also represent an aspect of

Vuqub Caquix, the Principal Bird Deity that was so favored in the art of the Late Preclassic Period, were common adornments (see figure 8.4, upper left). The mosaics also included more abstract symbols than those found elsewhere in the Maya world: crossed bands and lattices, spools, and geometric frets. Some archaeologists believe these geometric mosaics originated outside the Maya area in highland Oaxaca. Roof combs are not as common as in other Maya regions. Multiple doors with columns separating them were common, but single doorways were also utilized. The elegance of the Puuc style inspired Frank Lloyd Wright's Maya revival in the 1930s in the United States.

Chenes and Río Bec Styles

These two Late Classic Period styles are similar to the Puuc style, but they predate the mosaic and veneer technique later used in the Puuc region. Although individual buildings in these styles can be found throughout the northern lowlands, the styles are most prevalent in the southern part of the Yucatán Peninsula. The sites that belong to these two traditions, such as Chicanná and Becán in Campeche, rarely erected stelae or carved hieroglyphic texts into stone, but a few traces of painted texts have survived. Chenes-style buildings, unlike Puuc ones, have mosaic designs on both the upper and lower facades. Mosaic monster masks, representing mountain or sky deities, surround some Chenes building doorways, marking them as entrances into the Maya otherworld. Chenes-style buildings were also built outside the immediate region. For example, a fair number of such buildings were constructed at Calakmul, which may have controlled the smaller Chenes cities; in the northern lowlands, a few examples of the style are found, both Ek Balam and Chichén Itzá, for instance, but these do not typify the entire site. Perhaps the style denoted a particular building function.

The Río Bec style, named after a site in the Mexican state of Quintana Roo and part of the Chenes region, is notable for its palacelike structures surmounted with solid towers, so-called false towers with fake doorways and steep nonfunctional steps and a complete lack of interior rooms. The towers were decorated with deity masks. Río Bec buildings obviously were meant to impress rather than serve any practical function, and unlike Chenes-style buildings, they are not found outside the southern Yucatecan area.

Chichén Itzá Style

The Terminal Classic–Early Postclassic site of Chichén Itzá introduced a number of new building types and construction techniques into the Maya region. Although there are many Puuc temples and acropolis-style buildings at the site, they are mixed with buildings so distinctive in style that controversy still rages over whether they represent a foreign invasion into the Maya region (see Chapters 2 and 4). Archaeologists do agree, however, that the quality and technique of construction is completely Maya. Roofed colonnades and post-and-lintel temple construction with three doorways are utilized as well as the corbeled arch. Puuc-style long-nosed deity masks and Chenes facades are present, but so are massive serpent columns and thousands of carved reliefs of warriors, priests, and other dignitaries. The round structure, found at sites in the Middle Preclassic Period, may be intentionally revived and modified in the Caracol, an astronomical observatory. Many of these innovations persisted into the Postclassic Period at northern lowland sites, such as Mayapán and Tulum.

SITE PLANS

Site locations varied according to whether they were built on the flat limestone plain of northern Yucatán and parts of Campeche or in the

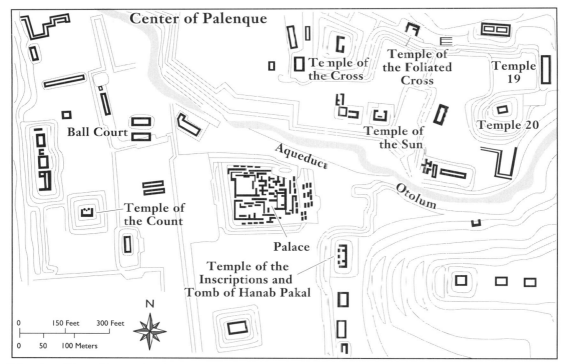

Map 7. *Plan of Central Palenque. The hilly terrain and Otulum River were incorporated into the city of Palenque, resulting in a site plan that is quite distinctive from other Maya cities. (See Map 6 on p. 220, for example.) Palenque's plan is, nonetheless, typically Maya in its organization around plazas, orientation to the cardinal points, and building types, such as the palace, ball court, and pyramid temples.*

hilly and irregular surfaces found elsewhere. Some cities were stretched alongside the rivers of the central and southern Maya regions, and others, on ridges near *bajos* (swamps and depressions that flooded during the rainy season) that may actually have been lakes when the areas were first settled. These different topographies forced the Maya to accommodate natural features into their urban plans and changed the appearance of cities from one region to the next. The ridges in the Petén gave additional height to Tikal's complexes. By contrast, the flat limestone shelf of northern Yucatán permitted Dzibilchaltún to sprawl over vast acreage. The Maya modified hills to incorporate them into a building complex or absorbed caves or cenotes

(naturally formed wells, or sinkholes) as sacred features of their city. Swamps might be crossed by raised *sacbeob* (paved roads) or canalized for irrigation. The Maya response was varied, yet the urban plan that resulted was never gridlike or rigidly symmetrical. Plazas, not streets, organized Maya cities; the occasional causeway provided access between sacred monuments and into the outlying neighborhoods.

Size and Function

Sites varied not just in their topography but also in their size and function. Some were specialized places, developed for agriculture (Nohmul on the Río Hondo), ports of trade (Isla Cerritos, the port of the inland city of Chichén Itzá), trading centers (Chunchucmil in northern Yucatán), or chert manufacture (Colhá). Many specialized centers, such as Colhá and perhaps Quiriguá, also had modest ceremonial and administrative buildings. Others had only a scattering of small buildings. Such was the case with Nohmul, which had a population of only 3,300 for an area of 22 square kilometers (8 square miles), about the geographic size of Palenque, but unlike that great city, Nohmul's land was utilized for intensive agriculture. Chunchucmil was densely populated (40,000 to 60,000 residents) with extensive residential complexes, but its center was devoted more to a large plaza, probably a marketplace, than to impressive pyramids and temples.

Site Hierarchy

There were secondary and tertiary cities and towns, and even smaller settlements, that occupied the terrain between the great capital cities, and although they might have had great stone central plazas or impressive sculptures, they seldom expanded in size, probably because of the power of a nearby capital city. It is suspected, for example, that the lack of inscriptions and true monumental architecture at Río Bec sites was due to their proximity to the great city of Calakmul.

Some tertiary sites appear to have had limited administrative responsibilities, and their architecture reflects their minor importance in the political hierarchy. In the Motagua Valley, there were 14 polities smaller than Quiriguá, and for most of the Classic Period, they were apparently part of the Copán realm. These smaller towns sometimes tried to establish a distinctive identity architecturally by building a temple to a local deity or to enhance their prestige by building a ritual ball court, something not usually found in the smallest communities. Such architectural distinctiveness may also have been an attempt to assert some independence from the regional capital. In contrast, the port of Isla Cerritos was totally under the control of Chichén Itzá, and its architecture was typical of that city.

The Urban Plan

The major Maya cities were organized in a similar fashion, even if their site plans varied in size and geographic detail. The most important governmental and religious buildings were situated around centrally located monumental plazas. Royal palaces, or acropolises, were near or immediately adjacent to these plazas, as were ball courts and other architectural groupings involving state rituals. The palaces of the lesser nobility were further removed and more private, being places that didn't concern the entire populace. Humbler homes were even more removed from the center but often near the more elaborate homes of regional administrators and middle-ranking members of society.

The density of construction in the Maya site core was such that the only foodstuffs grown in town were cultivated in private gardens or orchards. The city, if it was fortunate, was surrounded by a sustaining area of farms and forests for hunting, but it is now known that many cities in the Late Classic Period had to trade for foodstuffs or maintain outlying administrative centers near farmlands in order to feed the populace. A Maya kingdom included suburban towns and secondary and tertiary centers, as well as agricultural hamlets, often connected to the capital by a paved causeway. As the population grew throughout the Late Classic Period, there is evidence that the forest and agricultural land separating settlements disappeared.

Late Postclassic Site Plans

Few Late Postclassic cities survived their occupation following the Spanish Conquest. Pyramids disappeared as cut stone was recycled into mission churches and conquistador homes. Tiho may have been one of the largest cities in northern Yucatán, but it now is covered by the modern city of Mérida; Santa Rita, the preconquest capital of the province of Chetumal, now lies under the Belizean town of Corozal. Many of the cities mentioned by the Spanish conquistadores remain unidentified today. The Quiché capital of Utatlán was burned and dismantled by the conquistadores, but much of its basic plan can be reconstructed. Based on information from surviving cities, defense was foremost in the plan of these cities, and in the northern lowlands, there was little investment in monumental architecture, although sacred centers were created at the most important petty states—and sometimes recycled from earlier cities.

The cities of highland Guatemala were better constructed than in the north, with substantial ritual complexes; they were also hilltop citadels with the sacred center encircled by ramparts and protected by deep ravines. Farms were located on the valley floor along with some settlements. In the Yucatán, some of the largest known cities, Mayapán and Tulum, were enclosed by ramparts. Life behind the walls of Mayapán was congested, and except for the ceremonial core of the city, the site lacked the usual plaza or *sacbe* organization of Maya cities or surrounding sustaining area; foodstuffs had to be imported from other regions of northern Yucatán.

COSMOLOGY, POLITICS, AND ARCHITECTURE

The built environment was more than quarried stone and plaster. The city contrasted with the wilderness for the Maya and symbolized all that was ordered and civilized. The ceremonial center was not just the political heart of the kingdom, it was also the sacred center of the polity and was designed as a cosmogram, recreating the Maya world order.

A simple cruciform site plan at La Milpa in Belize demonstrates this cosmogram most clearly. Four outlying sites, each aligned with one of the cardinal directions, had buildings constructed to face the sacred center in the middle of them, a few kilometers away but easily visible. The Maya world had five directions, the four cardinal ones, each with its special significance, and the center, or axis mundi. At La Milpa, the buildings in the site at the north, the location of the sky and heavens for the Maya, were decorated with the appropriate ancestral symbolism; the buildings at the south, the place of Xibalba, the Maya Underworld, represented this realm; buildings at the sites to the east and west corresponded to the path of the Sun. The sacred center was the portal to the otherworld of the ancestors in the north and the gods of the Underworld in the south, and it was the center of the earthly world marked by the movement of the sun. Symbols of cosmic directions continued to be incorporated into Maya sites until well after the Spanish Conquest. Even when monumental architecture no longer was constructed, stone pillars and caches of sacred materials defined the city as the cosmic center.

The sacred center, often delimited by a low wall to separate it from other parts of the city, recreated the mythological world through architecture, as well as its site plan. As art historians have demonstrated, pyramids with *witz* deity heads (symbols of mountains) on the corners indicated they were sacred ancestral mountains. Chenes-style entrances were carved with monster mouths to represent caves, or entrances to the Underworld. Water symbolism at the bottom of the mountain marked the plaza at its foot as the primordial sea. Other buildings had mythic significance: E-groups may have symbolized the birthplace of the maize god, and ball courts also symbolized the Maya creation by the Hero Twins. (See also Chapter 6).

The sculpted facades of the great ceremonial centers perpetuated processions and rituals in stone and rendered the city all the more sacred. But the sacred ceremonial center also enhanced the power of rulers and legitimized them by placing them in charge of these cities where the earthly rituals facilitated communication with powerful forces in the otherworld. Hieroglyphic texts, sculptures, and paintings glorified rulers and the acts they performed for the benefit of the polity. And not all the actions they commemorated were religious. The Bonampak murals depict a great battle and a dynastic event with exceptional detail. At Chichén Itzá, history is public and carved into each of the four sides of a thousand columns representing priests, warriors, and other dignitaries marching in procession onto the Temple of the Warriors, which probably functioned as the *popol nah*, or council house. Such monumental art could not fail to impress any visitor to the city of the greatness of its rulers.

apsidal in shape, can easily be identified; so, too, can the distinctively shaped ball court, which was in use at the time of the Spanish Conquest. Which buildings were palaces, temples, astronomical observatories, council houses, or specialized ritual complexes has taken some time to sort out, and is still in the process of being sorted out. The purpose of some building complexes, such as what has been termed the E-group, is not yet clearly understood. Murals and narrative scenes on vases have provided some information about the function of different kinds of spaces, for example, platforms for dances. Ethnohistoric sources describe ball games and religious festivals and provide additional information on how the Maya utilized plazas and temples.

Hieroglyphs, murals, and sculpture often help identify the function or symbolic importance of buildings. Mat signs, symbols of rulership, cover the cornice of the council house at Copán, along with what might be symbols of the various lineages residing at that city. Tombs are often named as such in accompanying texts, and ball courts, too, are mentioned in the texts. Houses, clearly elite ones if they are named in hieroglyphic texts, are also mentioned, but even this can be misleading: One ruler's so-called house was actually his throne room. But when a building is not so marked or named in the glyphic texts, identification can be further complicated. Some buildings had names, but they seem to be personal names, unique to a given site. For example, the throne room in the palace at Palenque was called *sak nuk nah*, or the "white big house," a name not found at comparable places in other cities.

TYPES OF CONSTRUCTION

It is not always obvious how various buildings functioned. A simple house, especially when it is

The Basic House

The oval, or apsidal, hut has been found back to the Barra Phase (1600 B.C.E.) on the Pacific coast and in the earliest constructions so far discovered in the Petén (1400 B.C.E.); its enlarged form surely indicates the earliest chief's residences in the pre-Columbian Maya world. Rectangular pole-and-thatch houses were built as well, and most masonry Maya buildings are rectinlinear. The apsidal house form with its hip-shaped and thatched roof was never forgotten by Maya engineers, however: In the Classic Period, it was just as likely to be built of stone or elaborated into rounded corners on pyramidal platforms (see figure 8.1, for example, page 215). These simple structures were even commemorated on masonry buildings; for example, the Labná arch (see figure 8.8, page 242) is decorated with a thatched-hut design on each side of the passageway. The original pole-and-thatch house, whether apsidal or rectilinear, nurtured a preference for the corbeled arch, which created an interior pitch similar to that of a thatched roof. Masonry versions of the basic house form became temples when built on top of pyramidal platforms and palaces when many were built side by side in galleries and around multiple courtyards. The tradition of thatched, apsidal huts is so enduring that many lowland Maya continue to make them their homes today.

The basic Maya residential compound was built for an extended family, however, and included more than one structure. Like the ceremonial center, these buildings were constructed around a courtyard, where house gardens were planted with chiles, fruit trees, and the like (see Chapter 11). Under the hut floors, the Maya were buried, just as kings were buried in the foundation of the palace until at least the Late Preclassic Period. Very often a burial of an important ancestor was covered with an altar or shrine.

Temples

Temples, sometimes called *k'uh nah*, or "god's house" in the hieroglyphic texts, were built on platforms, usually the highest pyramids at a site. Before masonry architecture, temples were simple thatched huts set upon low plat-

forms, and even after their walls were built of stone, they continued to have thatched roofs until the corbeled vault was adopted beginning in the Late Preclassic Period. By the Classic Period, the lower and upper walls were usually separated by molding or sculptural friezes, and the roofs were sometimes topped with roof combs or tall lattice frames that not only added height to the temple but weight to stabilize the vault across the center of the roof. (See figure 8.1, lower right, page 215.) Roof combs also served as a kind of sculptural billboard that could be seen by the populace from considerable distance: The Late Classic roof comb of Tikal's Temple I, dedicated to a deceased ruler, depicted the ruler enthroned for eternity in stone.

Temples usually had from one to three rooms that were dedicated to veneration of important deities, such as the patron gods of a city and powerful, ceified ancestors. Wall niches or small rooms at the rear of the temple were shrines, referred to as *waybil* in the glyphic texts or *pibna* ("birthing" places), where the gods and deified ancestors resided or were conjured through ritual.

Temple decorations often reveal the cult practiced or commemorated within them. Some temples had texts extolling the ruler who was buried at the base of the pyramid; others were dedicated to patron gods, such as the Temple of the Cross at Palenque (see figure 6.4, page 175). At Chichén Itzá, low-relief sculptures depicting autosacrifice may indicate the kind of blood offerings made inside the temple. Hieroglyphic texts indicate rituals that occurred inside the temples, such as the building's dedication or the burning of incense.

Shrines

Shrines replaced pyramid-temples in the Late Postclassic Period in the northern lowlands. Although a single masonry room, like earlier temples, shrines were much smaller and usually built atop a low platform. Instead of having the elaborate sculptural adornments and roof combs of temples, shrines more often contained ceramic vessels shaped like a deity and used for burning incense. Less ambitious, the shrines are more numerous and are found in lineage compounds and other residential areas. Some of these shrines, such as one at Cozumel and another at Santa Rita Corozal, had false back walls. It is believed these were oracle shrines and that a priest hidden behind the wall would speak for the deity. Following the Caste War of 1847 in the Yucatán, the rebel Maya on the Caribbean coast prayed at a similar shrine of the Speaking Cross.

Palaces and Acropolises

Palaces and acropolises are usually found in the center of the site along one side of the most important plazas (see Map 6 and Map 7 on pages 220 and 227). Palaces were range-style, multiroom structures built around a series of courtyards and usually built atop a wide-based, moderately high platform. Although many acropolis structures were in fact royal or elite compounds, the acropolis form refers more generally to a complex in which many buildings are built upon many different levels of platforms. While pyramid-temples are vertical and towering, palace and acropolis complexes are horizontal in plan, and given their residential nature, they often utilized blind entrances to limit access. Some individual structures in Maya acropolises had roof combs.

Archaeologists long speculated about the function of these palaces and other elite residences, which differ in size and location within the city. The conquistador Hernán Cortés described one such compound with five courtyards surrounded by many rooms, with wells

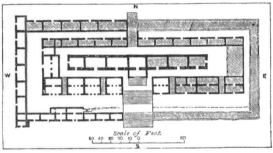

8.5 *Palace and ground-floor plan at the Puuc site of Sayil, Yucatán, Terminal Classic Period. Unlike the palace at Palenque (see figure 1.2, page 9), Sayil is multistoried. Because the vaulting was weak, each story was built upon solid fill, not upon the ceiling of the floor below.*   (After engravings by Frederick Catherwood 1854)

and quarters for servants and slaves. The ruined remains of these buildings further suggest a residential complex because many rooms had stone benches that could be used for sleeping and holes for hanging curtains for privacy. Plumbing was discovered at the Palenque palace, complete with devices that diverted water into the palace and what seem to be three toilets. Sweat baths are commonly placed near palaces or within palaces. The central location, elaborate sculptural adornments, and unusual amenities indicate that these were royal residences.

True palaces, in contrast to a range-style elite residence, should have a throne room, and some have been identified through the decipherment of hieroglyphic texts. At Palenque, an oval tablet set over a carved stone bench clearly established that at least one ruler acceded to office in that room; other texts indicate that some of his successors did as well. A demolished throne, apparently left as a reminder of defeat, was found by archaeologists atop the palace at Piedras Negras. (See figures 4.2 and 4.3, pages 123 and 136.)

Palace scenes are depicted in Maya murals and painted on Late Classic vases. These scenes reveal some of the more perishable items that furnished elite palaces, such as pillows and hanging textiles, as well as the palaces' inhabitants, who are often surrounded by a retinue or appear in scenes of tribute payments or battle victory.

In the Early Classic Period, rulers were buried under the acropolis in vaulted tombs. At Copán, the tomb of the founder of the ruling dynasty was uncovered, nested inside 400 years of later construction. The North Acropolis at Tikal was the site of so many burials during the Late Preclassic and Early Classic Periods that it became a venerated royal necropolis. By the seventh century, rulers often were buried instead in the base of pyramid-temples in the main plazas, but other members of the elite continued to be interred under their house (see Chapter 7).

Ball Courts

Ball courts endured as a Mesoamerican architectural form rather than a specifically Maya one. The earliest known court is from the Soconusco region of Chiapas and dates from 1400 B.C.E., and courts continued to be constructed in Mesoamerica until the Spanish Conquest. Although a Mesoamerican building form, ball courts are not found everywhere; in particular, they are absent at the great central Mexican city of Teotihuacan. The Maya, however, showed a special preference for their construction at sites from the Pacific coast to the northern lowlands.

The basic form consisted of two parallel mounds separated by a playing field, but the ball court evolved and took on an important variation with end zones forming an I shape. Some ball courts had benches along the side or a marker or markers in the center of the court or along the playing walls (so-called benches), all of which may have been sculpted with symbols relating to decapitation and creation myths (see Chapter 6). Because the myths commemorated by ball-game ritual concerned the Maya Underworld, the courts were often constructed at the foot of great vertical constructions or on low land at the site, to indicate the ball court's function as a portal to the Maya otherworld. During the Terminal Classic Period (800–1000), ball courts proliferated at sites. Thirteen have been discovered at Chichén Itzá, and one is the largest known ball court measuring 156 meters (515 feet) in length. In the Late Postclassic Period, ball-court complexes were common at sites in the Guatemala highlands, such as Utatlán and Iximché, but they were absent in the northern lowlands during that period. Being associated with the ruling class and ritual in nature,

8.6 *The Great Ball Court at Chichén Itzá (800–1000) is an I-shaped court with temples enclosing the end zones.* (Photo courtesy Peter Selverstone)

masonry ball-court construction ended with the Spanish Conquest.

Platforms and Pyramids

Platforms vary from simple ones that elevated a humble home above ground level to multilayered, or stepped, ones that were constructed like a wedding cake and, at major sites, commonly soared more than 30 meters (99 feet) high. The tallest, Danta at El Mirador, rose well above 200 feet. Platforms were solid and most often constructed of a rubble fill covered by a cut-stone facade and limestone plaster. Most platforms had medial staircases leading up to the building entrance or elevated terrace; quadripartite platforms had a staircase on each side. Platform facades were decorated with sculpture or stucco masks that related to the function of the superstructure or of the tomb within.

Plazas

Plazas were leveled, paved open areas that were usually rectilinear in shape; buildings were constructed on three or four sides of the plaza, and altars and stelae were erected on those that were the location of royal residences and ritual. Plazas were public ceremonial spaces. Elevated plazas, or terraces, often were more private spaces and part of an elite residential compound or acropolis. As already noted, the major plazas were the location of great public gatherings.

Sacbeob

Sacbe in its singular form, or *sacbeob* in plural, is Yucatec Mayan for "white road," a raised and plastered causeway. This Maya architectural form is occasionally found in other parts of Mesoamerica, but only rarely. Rough stones faced the sides of rubble-filled *sacbeob*, and white lime cement was used on the road surface; these causeways were 0.5 to 2.5 meters (2.5 to 8 feet) in height and varied greatly in width and length. The earliest known Maya *sacbeob* date from the Middle Preclassic at Nakbé. These causeways occasionally delineated a ritual path within the center of the city, such as the one connecting the Castillo and Sacred Well at Chichén Itzá, but they more often connected different areas of a city to the center.

Some causeways connected towns and may indicate alliances among cities or dominance of one city over another. Archaeologists have speculated they may have facilitated rapid deployment of militia through rugged forest to quash rebellions, or they might have been overland routes for the distribution of trade goods. Such roads ran to outlying cities from Late Preclassic El Mirador and Classic Period Caracol. In the Terminal Classic, Cobá was connected to Yaxuná in northern Yucatán by the longest known *sacbe*: more than 100 kilometers (62 miles) long and almost 10 meters (30 feet) wide.

Specialized Buildings and Complexes

TOMBS

Throughout the millennia, the Maya were most often interred in unlined holes in the ground or in the fill of buildings. In the Middle Preclassic Period, however, elite individuals in both the highlands and the lowlands began to be buried in stone-lined crypts. The most sophisticated tomb architecture did not begin until the Late Preclassic, when vaulted masonry rooms for Maya nobles were constructed under temples or beneath houses in the acropolises. In the Late Classic Period, royal tombs were constructed in conjunction with funerary pyramid-temples and named in the hieroglyphic texts as *muk nal*, or "burial place." The vaulted tomb of Hanab Pakal of Palenque (see figure 7.2, page 205) was the first Mesoamerican tomb discovered within a pyramid. The construction of the tomb is known to have been overseen by Hanab Pakal himself, and it was constructed before the pyramid. The pyramidal platform was built into a hill to increase its height and rose in nine levels, as did many such funerary structures, probably to symbolize the nine levels of the Maya Underworld. After Pakal's death in 683 and his subsequent burial in an immense stone sarcophagus, the staircase leading from the temple down to the tomb in the base of the pyramid was blocked with stone rubble. Other tombs, such as a few at Copán and Caracol, were built to be accessible after burial.

COUNCIL HOUSES

Set on platforms, these stone structures have been named in Classic Period texts and identified by decorative mat symbols. Called the *popol nah* (mat house), they were places where the lineage leaders and, perhaps, administrators of secondary sites met with the ruler. One existed in the Late Preclassic Period at Uaxactún.

ASTRONOMICAL OBSERVATORIES

The Maya were excellent astronomers (see Chapter 9), and some buildings seem to have been constructed to allow Maya to observe the planetary and stellar movements. Some buildings were positioned to mark the east-to-west movement of the sun at the equinoxes and solstices (see "E-groups" below). The Caracol at Chichén Itzá was an observatory and actually looked at bit like a modern one, with its conical superstructure and slat windows for marking the movements of Venus. The Caracol had a winding staircase to reach different levels in the interior, and along with towers, it was among the few multilevel buildings in the city. Archaeologists have speculated that towers were also observatories, but only the four-story tower at Palenque still remains standing and archaeoastronomers have yet to find evidence that its windows were used for skywatching.

Observatories, however, were not the only way of marking astronomical events. At Chichén Itzá, the staircase balustrades on the Castillo were carved with feathered serpents in such a manner, and apparently intentionally, that the carved snakes seem to descend the steps to the plaza with the movement of the sun on the days of the equinoxes. The Castillo, as a quadripartite structure (see figure 8.3), might be a Terminal Classic variation of the solar function of the E-group. At Copán, two stelae were aligned to mark the setting sun at the equinoxes. At many sites, astronomical events marked sacred architecture: For example, at Palenque, during the winter solstice, the Sun sets along the line of stairs leading down to the tomb of the great ruler Hanab Pakal.

E-GROUPS

Groups of temples on low platforms, called E-groups, may have been solar observatories. The complex is unvarying in its basic arrangement: On the west side of a plaza, a pyramid, usually with stairways on four sides aligned with the cardinal directions, faces three small temples aligned on the east side of the plaza. The oldest known E-group dates to the Middle Preclassic at Nakbé, but the most studied E-group is from Uaxactún. From the east-facing stairway of the quadripartite structure, the Sun can be observed to align with one of the small temples at sunrise during the solstices and equinoxes. Not all E-groups seem to be properly aligned to work as solar observatories, raising questions as to the function of these complexes. Some archaeologists believe some of the art symbolism on these buildings suggests E-groups represented the place of creation, or the dawning of time. E-groups were built at many sites in the central and southern lowlands for more than a thousand-year time span, indicating they had profound importance in the Maya belief system.

TRIADIC COMPLEXES

Beginning in the Late Preclassic Period, the Maya constructed sets of three temples atop pyramid platforms. These buildings were unlike E-groups in that the two flanking buildings were set at right angles to a larger central one. Triadic complexes were also more common than E-groups: More than 15 were built at El Mirador, and they have been excavated at sites from the southern to northern lowlands. In the Mirador Basin, there were tombs under each of such Late Preclassic temples at the site of Wakná, and in the central Petén, a royal burial was excavated in association with such a triadic complex. In the Classic Period, triadic complexes often were incorporated into acropolises, such as the one at Uaxactún, and covered by later range-style construction. Triadic complexes continued to be built—the Caana complex at Caracol is an example—but royal tombs were more likely to be constructed within a single pyramid-temple. At Late Classic Palenque, the Cross Group was a triadic variant with three temples arranged in the traditional form, but each was set on a separate pyramidal platform. Texts and art that decorate the triad of buildings at Palenque associate them with ruler accession and legitimization. (See "The Sacred City: An Example from Palenque," Chapter 6.) The triadic complex persisted as a Maya architectural form until the conquest, and a 16th-century Spanish document described such a complex in the Lacandón Maya town of Sac Balam.

TWIN PYRAMID GROUPS

These complexes were built at only two sites, Tikal and Yaxhá. They were rigidly symmetrical groups of buildings with two quadripartite platforms on the east and west sides of a plaza, a range structure with nine doorways on the south, and a wall enclosure with a stela and altar on the north. From the hieroglyphic texts on the stelae, it is known that these complexes commemorated *k'atun* period endings, or 20 solar years of 360 days each, an important cycle of time for the Maya.

ROUND STRUCTURES

Round buildings are somewhat rare in Mesoamerica and had been thought to be even rarer in the Maya region. In recent decades archaeologists have uncovered more circular platforms dating from 650 to 300 B.C.E. at sites in the Belize River valley and into the Late Preclassic in all of the lowlands. Quite a number of them were painted red. These early low platforms—none is taller than 2 meters (6 feet)—range in diameter from under 3 meters (about 9 feet) to 11 meters (33 feet), and although many do not appear to have had superstructures, ramps or stairs provided access to the platform top. During the Classic Period, many of these structures were replaced with rectilinear ones, but they continued to be built at some sites in the Petén (Uaxactún) and Belize (Barton Ramie). The round form reappears in the Terminal Classic Period, when circular platforms were built or renovated in Belize (Xunatunich), along the Pasión River (Seibal), and in the Yucatán (Cobá). They were perhaps even elaborated into observatories in northern Yucatán, such as the one at Chichén Itzá (see "Astronomical Observatories" above), which began as a circular platform. The earlier structures, however, do not seem properly situated for an astronomical function and probably had a distinct function. The recovery of burials and burned incense in the Preclassic Period structures suggests a ceremonial function and perhaps even an early form of the ancestral shrine before triadic complexes and pyramid-temples took their place.

SWEAT BATHS

Sweat baths are found inside many palaces and elite residences. Although they sometimes look like regular vaulted rooms, water drains and fire chambers make them easily identifiable. The baths may have been used for ritual purification as well as basic hygiene. Masonry sweat baths are known from the Middle Preclassic Period: one on the outskirts of Komchén in the northern lowlands, dates from the seventh century B.C.E., another at Cuello in Belize dates to 900 B.C.E. Piedras Negras on the Usumacinta River had at least eight sweat baths in the Late Classic Period, an unusually high number. Two were located in the royal palace, and one seems to suggest a communal use. A domed sweat bath with an interior masonry bench was excavated at the farming village of Cerén in El Salvador.

CEREMONIAL STAIRWAYS

Hieroglyphic stairways were quite commonly built and carved to commemorate victory or defeat, and the risers of the stairs, not the treads, were carved. These stairways may have been used to display tribute and captives as well. The most famous one, at Copán, had an exceptionally long text of 2,200 carved glyphs. Recent decipherments at neighboring Quiriguá indicate that Copán's stairway was constructed soon after its defeat by Quiriguá in 738 and was a propagandistic undertaking to extol the greatness of Copán and its ruling dynasty. Some cities were forced to construct punitive monuments in the center of their sites commemorating their defeat. At Naranjo, a ceremonial staircase was carved with hieroglyphs to remind the city of its defeat by Caracol. At both Copán and Yaxchilán broad stairways were associated with a special form of the ball game that involved human sacrifice.

TZOMPANTLI

Tzompantli, meaning "skull racks" in Nahuatl, the language of the Aztecs, were described by the Spanish conquistadores. This Mesoamerican architectural form is found most often in the Postclassic Period in central Mexico where they often were made of real skulls, the result of many human sacrifices. Low platforms, carved with friezes of skulls, are found at a few Maya sites associated with ball courts. There is one at Chichén Itzá and another at Iximché.

WATER-MANAGEMENT STRUCTURES

The Maya invested in major water-control projects. Sloping plaza surfaces, containing walls, drains under plazas, and even aqueducts (at Edzná and Palenque) kept the ceremonial areas from flooding and also redirected the runoff into reservoirs. For intensive agriculture, fields were artificially created in swamps, and canal systems were constructed (see "Agriculture," Chapter 11). By the Late Preclassic Period at Edzná, there was an impressive canal system that included a canal 12 kilometers (8 miles) long; the overall system comprised one of the largest Maya construction projects ever. Water was conserved for the dry season in artificial reservoirs—the largest constructed at Calakmul, had a surface area of 51,304 square meters (551,830 sq. ft.) and *chultunes* (cisterns) cut into the limestone floor. Stairs and ramps were built into caves with underground water sources.

DEFENSIVE AND OTHER ENGINEERING PROJECTS

Defensive moats and ramparts were constructed during various periods in different parts of the Maya region (see Chapter 5). In the

Late Preclassic Period, there was a defensive wall built between Tikal and Uaxactún, and a moat surrounded the site of Becán in the southern Yucatán Peninsula. There also was a perimeter wall built at the site of Calakmul in the Early Classic. Toward the end of the Classic Period, defensive structures appear once again. At the small site of Punta de Chimino, a port for the Petexbatún polity, a deep ditch was mounted by a rampart that was further fortified by wooden palisades. At Dos Pilas, in the southern lowlands, during the Late Classic, concentric perimeter walls formed "killing lanes" in the area between them. In the Postclassic Period, Mayapán and Tulum also constructed encircling ramparts with parapets. There is disagreement over whether all encircling walls were defensive; some were too low to be effective and may have simply demarcated the sacred center of a city, such as the one at Chichén Itzá clearly did.

Other engineering projects included a bridge spanning the Usumacinta River at Yaxchilán and docks at river sites such as Lamanai and the port of Isla Cerritos, just off the eastern tip of the Yucatán Peninsula. A sea wall was also built at Isla Cerritos to create a protected cove. At Chunchucmil, there is some evidence that canals, some 2 kilometers (1.5 miles) in length, were constructed for transporting goods from Punta Canbalam, its port on the Gulf of Mexico, to the city.

MATERIALS AND TECHNIQUES

The Maya constructed cities with complexes that could cover many football fields and pyramidal ones that rose to heights of 70 meters (231 feet), yet they built their cities with Stone Age technology. No steel beams supported pyramids or vaults, no metal tools were available to quarry stone or to carve it. Instead, wooden beams, stone, and lime cement were the structural building blocks; rope-and-water abrasion and stone and obsidian tools provided the basic technology of Maya cities. As far as archaeologists can determine, the wheel was not used, either; heavy loads were carted on barges, carried on litters, or perhaps rolled on logs. The Maya did have rope, so cords and human labor were used to lift stone, but probably without the help of pulleys. Objects that seem to be stone rollers have been found near *sacbeob*, so they may have been used in the construction of causeways. Backbreaking labor, however, built Maya cities.

The hieroglyphic texts do not describe the actual building process, but the epigrapher David Stuart has deciphered the Mayan verbs for "to build," "to dedicate," "to burn," and "to cense" a place; the latter two appear to refer to ceremonies for the dedication of completed buildings. And the texts often mention that objects are made of stone. Archaeologists can determine from the material record that full-time masons and plasterers labored in the construction of Maya cities beginning in the Late Preclassic Period.

Materials

STONE

Limestone was plentiful and soft enough to be worked with stone tools. Only after the limestone was cut and removed from the bed did it harden. The quality of the limestone varied, however, from fine quality in the Usumacinta to relatively poor in the northern lowlands. Other types of stone were available to sites such as Copán and Quiriguá in the Motagua River region. Trachyte, which was used at Copán, is fine grained and good for carving and building, but some nodules were too hard to be worked by stone, so they created blemishes on the surface. Sandstone, marble, and schist were used at Quiriguá.

LIME PLASTER AND CEMENT

Limestone was burned under intense heat to make plaster, or stucco, and cement. To make a small pile of plaster (0.9 meters, or 3 feet, high), 20 trees had to be felled and burned. Plaster on exterior walls weathers poorly, so little is recovered during excavation. There is enough evidence, however, to indicate that some buildings were colored red or cream by the addition of either iron oxide or organic materials to the plaster. Lime cement was used as mortar or fill at many sites, including Palenque and Uxmal.

WOOD AND THATCH

Even after masonry architecture was introduced in the Middle Preclassic Period, wooden pole and thatched houses and temples continued to be constructed. In masonry buildings, wooden lintels over doorways and cross-ties in vaults were sometimes used.

ADOBE

Adobe, or mud reinforced with straw or other binding elements, was applied to a wall surface, usually of woven sticks, to make what is called a basic wattle-and-daub hut. Adobe constructions persisted throughout Maya civilization, in commoners' homes as well as in more monumental buildings in the southern Maya region where easily worked stone was not available.

CLAY-FIRED BRICKS

Only the site of Comalcalco near the Gulf coast used bricks to substitute for its lack of stone

Construction Techniques

The Maya constructed buildings atop platforms that were plastered with limestone or faced with cut stone; the techniques used in such construction, however, varied over time and place. Earthen platforms were used in various kinds of structures throughout the pre-Columbian era, but more elite architecture began to evolve from as early as 1500 B.C.E., when limestone plaster, with earth and pebbles, was utilized in construction at sites along the Pacific coast of Guatemala. Around 1000 B.C.E. in the central lowlands, where stone was more readily available than along the Pacific coast, the Maya stacked flat stones, without mortar, to make walls, and some low platforms reached a half-meter (1.5 feet) in height. By 600 B.C.E. stone was being quarried, cut, and finished for massive building projects in the Mirador Basin. At Nakbé, for example, platforms 8 meters (about 26 feet) high and covering areas of 40,000 square meters (430,400 square feet) were constructed; structures on top of these platforms often rose another 18 meters (59 feet). Floors were laid with plaster or large stones. Moldings and other architectural details were tenoned into walls by this early period, but stucco decorations were molded over projecting stones in the facade.

Some of the early masonry complexes easily collapsed when they were tunneled (as thieves in recent times discovered while looking for burial treasure), but mud cell walls surrounding the fill corrected the problem by the Late Preclassic Period. This latter construction method persisted throughout Maya civilization and was even improved upon in the Classic Period, when various forms of cementlike mortar stabilized masonry walls and vaults.

Quarrying and Masonry Techniques

Techniques in quarrying and shaping stone varied over time and place as well. At a few quarries, the stone naturally flaked into the size used in construction so that little trimming and shaping were necessary. In most areas, the size of the quarried stone was determined by the masons channeling the rock bed with chert or basalt tools and then using wood levers to free the block. A 1997 study at Nakbé reconstructed the quarrying technique, resulting in some of the most detailed information available. During the Middle and Late Preclassic Period, the Maya invested great labor in producing large stone building blocks weighing 246 kilograms (542 pounds) and measuring nearly a meter by half-meter by 39 centimeters thick (about 3 feet by 1.5 feet by 1 foot thick). Small stone axes were used to trim the block, and the resultant debris (as much as 75 percent of the original quarried block) was used for fill and plaster production. The Nakbé quarry experiment demonstrated that an average worker using chert and wood tools would have produced two large blocks a week. Twelve laborers, six of them porters, could transport the block over the 600 meters (less than a half-mile) to the site in a litter in about 30 minutes. The blocks were not finely finished, but thick layers of limestone plaster smoothed over surface irregularities. The quality of the finished stone and the time necessary to quarry it suggest there may have already been

8.7 Examples of Maya stonework: carefully finished facade stones at Copán (top); rougher masonry from Pomoná, Chiapas (bottom). (Top photo courtesy Cherra Wyllie; bottom photo courtesy John Montgomery)

construction specialists as early as the Middle Preclassic Period.

As the Classic Period progressed, the Maya abandoned the large stonemasonry of the Preclassic Period and relied on smaller, thinner stones to cover a rubble fill. The rubble was usually mixed with mortar or mud to stabilize it. Stones were often more finely finished and sometimes beveled. This veneer technique was more efficient because it required less stone as well as less plaster to cover surface irregularities. By the Late Classic Period, Maya in the Puuc region, where the quality of the limestone was not especially good, developed the highest-quality veneer architecture by using lime cement as fill and finely cut stones to create mosaic facades.

Recycling

Maya building techniques incorporated earlier structures into the base of newer ones. At Nakbé, the earlier village—covered with stone—became the fill for monumental Middle Preclassic complexes. Sometimes an entire complex was left completely intact and enshrined, probably in order for the old building to add legitimacy or sanctity to the later one. For example, the inner Castillo at Chichén Itzá, its temple furnished with many items including a jaguar throne, can be visited even today through an entrance at the base of the superimposed pyramid-temple. In other instances, a sacred building was ritually terminated, slightly damaged, or plastered over but basically preserved inside a later construction. Still other times, the older building was substantially or even totally demolished for fill, with the accompanying destruction of the texts and sculpture that decorated the superstructure. Traces of such decorations have occasionally been recovered by archaeologists enabling them to understand the building program of a city. Sometimes the Maya destroyed a building in order to initiate an entirely new type of complex; other times the superimposed building retained the iconographic themes of its predecessor but was improved in size. The savings in labor through recycling were so significant, about 20 percent, and up to 45 percent according to some estimates, that the building programs—and site plans—must have been influenced by the availability of recyclable buildings.

HIDDEN HISTORY

With each new building campaign, the earlier construction became less easily accessible to future archaeologists. The Late Classic Period acropolis at Copán, for example, was only the final stage of superimposed buildings that had accrued for 400 years, and at Tikal, the North Acropolis resulted from 1,500 years of superimposed and modified building projects. For this reason, for many years Maya archaeologists believed the Maya culture began around 300; although earlier materials were found through pits drilled in buildings, they were seen out of context and thought to be isolated. Not until unburied structures from the Preclassic Period were discovered—and, indeed, entire cities from the Middle Preclassic Period—were the engineering accomplishments of the Maya during this early phase properly understood.

POLITICAL BUILDING CAMPAIGNS

It was formerly believed that Mesoamericans rebuilt at the end of every 52-year cycle, or Calendar Round (see Chapter 9), but it is now known that no such renovation cycle was followed. Rebuilding campaigns were usually initiated by a new ruler or dynasty to serve a political purpose rather than a calendrical one. The building campaign might enshrine the ancestors of a new lineage, commemorate a major military victory or military alliance, or incorporate a new architectural fashion that would lend prestige to the ruling dynasty.

REOCCUPIED SITES

It now seems that the Maya sometimes recycled abandoned sites, too. Recent studies indicate that some sites were reoccupied and rededicated, and not necessarily by descendants of the original inhabitants. In Late Postclassic Yucatán, for example, political struggles and land disputes resulted in the displacement of some Maya. These migrant Maya resettled sites and re-created their lineage histories so that they fit into the newly occupied site. Through rituals and dedication ceremonies, earlier buildings became the place of their ancestors and established the right of the migrant Maya to the land and its resources.

Great Petén cities such as Tikal and Nakbé were reoccupied as well; such recycled sites were only modestly changed.

Vaults

As noted above, the corbeled vault was one of the hallmarks of Maya architecture. The inverted V of the corbeled arch differs from the true arch not only in shape but also in that it does not permit great interior spaces. Usually the Maya corbeled vault spanned a space only about 1.5 meters (5 feet) wide, although a few were as wide as 6 meters (20 feet). The corbeled arch results from the layering and overhanging of stones so that each is angled further from the wall than the preceding one. The open space progressively narrows toward the top of the arch, where a stone, set on top of the angled walls, joins them in an almost pointed arch. The result is a high but narrow open space with thick walls to support the vault.

8.8 *Freestanding corbeled arch at Labná, Yucatán. This Puuc-style structure marked the entrance to the palace.* (Photo courtesy Lawrence Foster)

CEMENT AND BOOT STONES

Lime cement strengthened the vault at many sites. The Maya in the Puuc region, however, introduced a technological change in vault construction by using concrete as the building core and capping the vault with a boot stone, which distributed the weight into the walls. The arch was then finished with veneer masonry, though the stones were actually superfluous to the vault. The technique resulted in more stable structures and the construction of some free-standing arches.

KEYSTONE VAULTS

The rounded, or "true," arch in which the central keystone locks all the others into place, is capable of creating great interior spaces and is a more sophisticated architectural tool. Architects at Palenque, however, devised a method of increasing room size by building one high arch perpendicular to a series of parallel ones. Even these rooms, however, were no wider than the vaulting, which rarely spanned even 4.5 meters (15 feet). The Puuc concrete arch was capable of greater interior spans, but the Maya never used it to create them. The keystone arch was occasionally used in the construction of Maya sweat baths, such as one near the so-called Mercado of Chichén Itzá and at Cerén in El Salvador, so at least some Maya apparently understood the principle of construction involved.

ADVANTAGES OF CORBELED VAULT

The Maya probably preferred the corbeled arch because the narrow, peaked rooms it created were like the original thatched huts. The pitch of the roof also permitted easy collection of water runoff, and the interiors maintained a somewhat cool temperature that was agreeable in the tropical lowlands. It was not interior spaces the Maya were seeking, but rather massive constructions that defined open public plazas. And this they accomplished.

POST AND LINTEL

In the Terminal Classic Period, post-and-lintel construction supported flat wooden roofs that could span greater interior spaces. The colonnades at Chichén Itzá are the most remarkable examples of this late style of Maya architecture. But masonry vaulting continued to be used simultaneously, and stone columns sometimes supported the vaulted ceiling. The columns, however, changed only the style, not the size, of the room, which was still determined by the span of the vault. Wooden lintels rotted over time, however, and many more stone vaulted buildings remain intact to this day. Late Post-classic Period cities followed the post-and-lintel tradition; Mayapán and perhaps Tulum were the last Maya cities to construct vaulted buildings.

READING

See also "Reading" in Chapters 2, 4, and 6.

Masonry Architecture and Labor

Abrams 1994 and 1998, Abrams and Freter 1996; Erasmus 1965: labor estimates; Carmean 1991: labor investment and social stratification; Childe 1950, Sanders and Price 1968, Webster 1998: architecture, political complexity, and civilization.

Architectural Development and Styles

George Andrews 1975, Hansen 1998, Kubler 1992, Miller 1999, Proskouriakoff 1963: overview; Matheny 1986: Late Preclassic monumentality; Harrison 1986: Tikal; George Andrews 1994, Kowalski 1986 and 1987, Potter 1977: Chenes, Río Bec, and Puuc styles; Ruppert 1952: Chichén Itzá.

Architectural Traits

Hansen 1998, Miller 1999: traits; Martínez 1994, Reyna 2000, Schmidt 1990: corbeled arch in Guerrero.

Site Plans

Ashmore 2000, Dahlin 2000: specialized sites; Andrews IV 1965, Haviland 1966; Nichols 1996, Sheets 1992, Tourtellot 1993, Vogt and Leventhal 1983, Willey and Bullard 1965: settlement patterns and urbanization; Culbert and Rice 1990: lowland population levels; Looper 1999, Marcus 1976, Mathews 1985: hieroglyphs and site hierarchy; Haviland 1981, Puleston 1974: site hierarchy.

Cosmology and Politics

Ashmore 1991, Fash 1998, Freidel and Schele 1988a and 1988b, Houston 1998: cities as cosmograms and ritual power; Benson 1986, Freidel, Schele, and Parker 1993, Schele and Mathews 1998, Tourtellot and Hammond 2000: cosmograms; Miller 1999: history and politics.

Types of Construction

Stuart 1998: texts and architecture; George Andrews 1975, Hansen 1998: classification of major building types; Schele and Mathews 1998: overview of symbolic meaning and structure of major building types; Freidel and Sabloff 1984: shrines; Cortés 1986, Fash 1998, Kowalski 1987, Miller 1999, Satterthwaite 1935: palaces; Hansen 1998, Hellmuth 1977: triadic complexes; Aveni 1980, Aveni and Hartung 1989: astronomy and E-groups; Aimers, et al. 2000, Pollock 1936: round structures; Satterthwaite 1952: sweat baths at Piedras Negras; Scarborough 1993: water management; Dahlin 2000, Demarest, et al. 1997, Webster 1976: fortifications.

Materials and Technology

Abrams 1994 and 1998, Abrams and Freter 1996, Hansen 1998, Carmean 1991: labor and recycling; Woods and Titmus 1997: quarrying techniques at Nakbé; Lorenzen 1999: recycling sites; George Andrews 1975, Lawrence Roys 1934: engineering and vaults; Stuart 1998: texts and architecture.

9

ARITHMETIC, ASTRONOMY, AND THE CALENDAR

by Kaylee Spencer-Ahrens
and Linnea H. Wren

The Maya were excellent mathematicians and superb astronomers. They invented the concept of zero; they devised innovative methods of measuring and dating time; and they painstakingly tracked the movements of celestial bodies. The sophistication of Maya arithmetic, the exactitude of Maya records of planetary movements, and the orderly logic of the Maya calendar reveal the importance of time in the Maya view of the universe

To the ancient Maya, time was a dynamic concept by which temporal existence was raised to historic importance, meshed with natural rhythms, and was imbued by spiritual significance. When conceived as a rational framework, time allowed the Maya to order the sequence of daily events, to recollect the past, and to anticipate the future. When conceived as an active structure, time permitted the Maya to discern the shapes of physical space, to measure the cycles of the natural world, and to comprehend the meaning of the supernatural realms. As an evocative metaphor, time furnished the Maya with opportunities to encounter other gods and ancestors. By formulating time in an extraordinary creative series of calendrical and astronomical cycles, the Maya intertwined virtually all aspects of existence into a harmonious pattern.

Because time permeated all aspects of life, timekeeping was a primary concern for the peoples of ancient Mesoamerica. Hundreds of dates mark the monuments and objects created by the Maya. The frequency with which dates appear testifies to the importance of expressing time. The arduous and often labor-intensive methods of rendering Maya dates reveal the commitment of the commissioners to define specific moments in universal cycles. The permanent quality of the media that bears calendrical dates suggests that Maya kings intended their monuments to elevate moments of ephemeral existence into commemorations of enduring significance. Through the rendering of dates, the life of the ruler was inscribed into the history of the cosmos.

CYCLICAL HISTORY

The Maya codified the seasons and the planets into many interlocking cycles. Many of these cycles and calendars, ruled over by deities, were used to predict the future and to determine the rituals necessary for survival through times of misfortune. The cycles dominated Maya thought and resulted in a deterministic view in which history repeated itself. If a given day or period resulted in dreadful consequences once, it would do so again when the day returned or when the cycle repeated itself. The intensity in which the Maya believed in these cycles, in contrast to the neutral impact of the Gregorian calendar on the lives of contemporary Westerners cannot be underestimated. The history in the native chronicles that survive from the

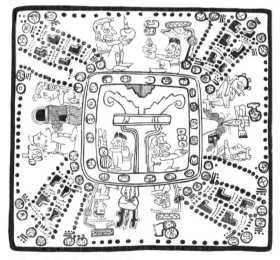

9.1   *Calendar wheel from the* Madrid Codex *combining Maya temporal and spatial order, Late Postclasic Period. The clusters of dots on the wheel mark the 260-day sacred calendar displayed in the quincunx pattern of the spatial order of the Maya cosmos.*   (Drawing by Cyrus Thomas, 1897–98)

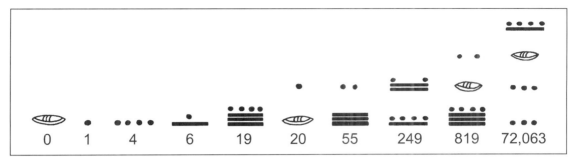

9.2 *Examples of Maya numeration in the vigesimal system.* (Drawing by Kaylee Spencer-Ahrens after Coe, 1999)

postconquest period demonstrate that this belief in repeating cycles affected how the Maya recorded and understood their world. The arrival of the Spanish conquistadores at the end of a major calendrical cycle simply confirmed what the Maya priests already knew: "On that day, a strong man seizes the land; on that day, things fall to ruin" (*Chilam Balam of Chumayel*, Brinton). The event was subsumed into the calendrical category of disaster, mingling and corrupting the many other political catastrophes already recorded there. Maya measurements and Maya cycles were far from casual undertakings or impersonal tools for recording events. Much like their contemporary European counterparts during the 16th century, the Maya were intent on predicting the influence of the planets and stars on terrestrial events. Maya calendars—like European astrology—were a search for the knowledge by which existence is structured.

MAYA ARITHMETIC

A key component of the Maya calendar is the system of conceiving and rendering numbers. The template for this system derives from nature, more specifically from the human body. Motifs resembling a shell, a dot, and a bar constitute the basic symbols for this system. Within this scheme a shell-shaped symbol signifies zero, or, for the Maya, completion. Among the Maya, the completion of cycles was seen as a critical moment in time. A dot or circle indicates the number 1, while a straight bar denotes 5. Combining these symbols allowed Maya scribes to write the numbers 0 through 19. The origin of the dot as a symbol for 1 derives from the human body where the fingers serve as markers for tallying. The symbols of circles, or dots, in the Maya inscriptions represent abstracted human fingertips. The marker for 5 derives from the finger held horizontally. In this sense humans become people full of days, or the embodiment of time itself. Through inscribing a monument with a date, rulers symbolically left the impression of their own hands.

Sacred Numbers

To the Maya, some numbers also had special symbolic value. The reasons that determined the ancient Maya choice of sacred numbers are not always clear to modern Mayanists, but the divisions of the cosmic order seem to explain the selection of at least some numbers as sacred. The number 4, for example, was evidently sacred because it signified the quadripartite order of the Middleworld; the number 9, because it signified the levels of the Underworld; and the number 13, because it signified the levels of the Upperworld. These numbers repeatedly appear in ritual contexts where they are associated with colors and directions, and astronomical cycles or historic events involving multiples of these apparently sacred numbers were noted in Maya writings. The primary use for the Maya system of numeration was, however, found in the Maya calendar, which in its complexity was both practical and sacred.

Positional Values

In addition to modeling their method of counting on the human body, other features of the Maya system of numeration reflect its efficiency and flexibility. Examples of these innovative features include the use of place value and the mathematical concept of zero. The Maya invention of the zero concept was among the earliest in world history. Like the Western system of numeration, the value of a number is determined both by the symbol itself and by its position within the scheme. Instead of adding more symbols to express a large number, the concept of place value allowed scribes to express large numbers with a relatively small corpus of symbols.

Vigesimal System

In conceptualizing quantities, the Maya considered the whole human body. In addition to looking to the five digits on each hand, the Maya mediated 10 toes that connected each human to the earth. The Maya therefore considered both fingers and toes. Unlike our decimal system, with its base of 10, the Maya employed a vigesimal system based on 20. The entire system rests on the number 20 as the basic unit for measurement; consequently, in constructing numbers the positions shift at 20 instead of at 10, where all 20 are required to fill a position within a sequence. Like our system where numbers above nine are expressed by a shift in position, in the Maya system numbers above 19 are expressed on a basis on position. Instead of moving the decimal point left and right to adjust the value by powers of 10 as in our system, in the Maya system the value of the number increases from bottom to top, shifting in vertical columns. Within this vertical scheme, symbols on lowest level have a value of 1. The second level up has a value of 20 times 1, or 20, for each numerical unit. The third level up has a value of 20 times 20, or 400, for each numerical unit. The fourth level up has a value of 20 times 400, or 8000, for each numerical unit. The number 20, for example, would be expressed by placing the nought, or shell motif on the lowest level and a dot on the second. The number 42 would be expressed by placing 2 dots on the lowest level and 2 dots on the second. The number 400 would be expressed by placing the nought on the lowest and second levels and a dot in the third. The number 884 would be expressed by placing 4 dots on the lowest level, 4 dots on the second level and 2 dots on the third level. The vigesimal system could be used to express numbers of enormous size.

EFFICIENCY

This system was far more efficient than the one used by the ancient Romans. To express a large number in the Roman system, one typically had to utilize long sequences of symbols. When using Roman numerals extra symbols placed to the right or left of one another indicates addition or subtraction, causing the system to be cumbersome and inefficient. The vigesimal system employed by the Maya was practical in everyday contexts. For example, colonial accounts tell us that merchants used beans or maize kernels as placeholders. These beans could be easily carried and simply placed on the ground to mark the places. The Maya system of counting therefore provided an efficient system to conceive and render quantities. Based on the human body, this system imprinted human qualities into abstract cosmic concepts.

ORIGINS OF THE CALENDAR

There is no agreement as to the origin of the Maya calendrical system, but its basic components were used by all Mesoamericans. When the calendars were developed is unknown, but some aspects of it were probably already in use during the Early Preclassic Period, given that so-called solar observatories were constructed by the Maya at Nakbé during this period and that day names were carved into stone in Oaxaca by c. 500 B.C.E. Even the Long Count method of dating, normally associated with the Maya, may have been developed first by their Olmec neighbors in the Late Preclassic Period (see Chapter 2).

Of all Mesoamericans, however, the Maya of the Classic Period demonstrated the greatest sophistication as horologists, or students of measured time. They measured the lunar and solar cycles, lunar and solar eclipses, and the movements of Venus and Mars with extraordinary accuracy. They recorded calendrical dates

in elegantly carved and painted texts, on public architecture and ceramic vessels, and in screenfold books, or codices. Ancient scribes exceeded the limits of their own lifespans, recording dates and events that reached far into the mythical past as well as into the future. In many cases the calculations utilized by the Maya were more accurate than those developed by their contemporaries in the Old World: their solar calendar was more exact than the Julian calendar, for example.

Time and the Mapping of Daily Life

The Maya expressed great concern for tracking quantities of time. Equally important, however, was the contemplation of the qualities of time, particularly those qualities that resonated in human affairs. Within the human sphere, the calendar was pivotal in the unraveling of spiritual life. The Maya perceived the calendar to be so important that all ritual acts were dictated by it. Divination practices, the performance of ceremonies, and the observance of feasts linked precisely to specific periods of time. Kings and elites who possessed knowledge of how the calendar operated and understood the timing of such rituals held a special status within Maya communities. Through their knowledge of timekeeping methods, Maya rulers recorded for eternity their participation in rituals, history of conquered peoples, accession to the throne, and ancestral pasts.

Natural Cycles and Agriculture

The calendar also served as a framework for perceiving everyday phenomena. The cyclical nature of time corresponded to the cycles that ordered the natural environment. Through time's periodicity, all things in the universe were ordered and fixed: Day always followed night, the moon waxed and waned, and the sun moved at regular intervals across the sky. The earth rotated on its axis as it revolved around the sun. The life cycles of flora followed the cycles of seasons. As warm summers followed cold winters, plants flourished from the decay of the previous season. These cycles underlay agricultural practices among Maya farmers. Taken into consideration with astronomical events, the natural calendars set the cycles followed by Maya farmers to plant and harvest their crops. Through the framework of time, nature's history necessarily interlaced with the daily lives of the Maya. Kings harnessed time and its natural indicators. Time served as a vehicle through which rulers affirmed their authority among their subjects and within the cosmos. Nature's order was translated into the temporal realm.

CYCLES OF TIME

The Maya codified nature's order through the development of systems to record and express time. The employment of various cycles furnished the Maya with a calendar that reflected the intricacies of the cosmos. The three methods of timekeeping most frequently used by the ancient Maya included a count of 260 days, a 365-day Vague Year, and a 52-year Calendar Round. The roots of these cyclic counts extended deep into the Maya past: The earliest Maya protowriting, c. 400 B.C.E., may record a day in the 260 count. All Mesoamerican peoples shared in this ancient knowledge of situating time and space.

The *Tzolk'in:* A 260-Day Cycle

Although the numbers and units of time in the Maya calendar bear great importance, the most critical aspect of the calendar is how its cycles interlock. The efficacy of time occupies the space within these interrelationships of cyclical points. The 260-day cycle exemplifies the Maya preoccupation with situating themselves within intermeshing cycles. The 260-day calendar, also called the almanac or *tzolk'in*, is the most ancient in Mesoamerica. This *tzolk'in* is known as the sacred calendar because it structured the pattern of ceremonial life and provided the foundations for prophecy.

The base of the *tzolk'in*, composed of overlapping cycles of varying lengths, rests on a cycle of 260 days. This calendar implicates cycles of 20 named days (see figure 10.1, page 276) paired with 13 numbers. The 20 days recur in a set pattern (Imix, Ik', Ak'b'al, K'an, Chikchan, Kimi, Man_k', Lamat, Muluk, Ok, Chuwen, Eb', B'en, Ix, Men, Kib', Kab'an, Etz'nab', Kawak, and Ahaw). The *tzolk'in* begins on the day 1 Imix, continues with 2 Ik', 3 Ak'b'al, until it ends with 13 Ahaw; combining these 20 days with 13 numbers allows for a total of 260 unique days before the cycle repeats again.

The roots of the 260-day cycle draw from the order of the natural world. This cycle exhibits no astronomical or agricultural relations, but some scholars have suggested that it parallels human biorhythms. The average time span between human conception and birth is 266 days. The 266-day gestation period nearly corresponds with the 260 days necessary to complete one *tzolk'in* cycle. Among contemporary Maya, women still associate the *tzolk'in* with the nine-month period of human gestation. Children in various parts of Mexico receive their names based on the day of the *tzolk'in* on which they were born. At the time of birth, children were believed to have already completed one 260-day cycle. Midwives possibly developed this system as a tool to calculate birth dates.

The primary purpose for the sacred calendar was divination. Specific deities served as patrons for all of the 20-day names. When grouped with certain numbers, the day names articulated supernatural messages. Some combinations of days and numbers prophesied fortuitous events, while others served as ominous warnings. On the day of a child's birth, diviners interpreted the position of the cycle in order to foretell the future; for example, a person born on the day 1 Kimi (1 Death) was believed to be prone to drunkenness. In an attempt to avert ruinous futures, parents and diviners were known to shift naming ceremonies to more promising days, according to Spanish documents.

From 16th-century ethnohistoric sources we know that Maya shamans and diviners interpreted the sacred calendar to aid members within their communities. Trained in reading the *tzolk'in* and believed to possess the ability to converse with gods and other supernatural forces, shaman priests provided insights into the future. The Maya codices (see Chapter 10) contain almanacs with suggested divinations associated with the days of the *tzolk'in*, and Maya diviners used such almanacs to guide rulers and commoners in making important political, economic, and religious decisions. For example, the Maya ruler consulted priestly diviners and astronomers before undertaking a military attack or burying a predecessor, and the calendrical anniversaries and astronomical reasons for such actions are sometimes recorded on Classic Period monuments. Among the modern Quiché Maya, special "daykeepers," or shamans, still shoulder the responsibility of interpreting the calendar for the right day for religious ceremonies, marriages, or even undertaking a business journey.

The *Haab'*: A 365-Day Cycle

The Maya employed another count of days that operated in conjunction with the 260-day calendar. In the Maya region, the grouping of 365 days into a cycle constituted the calendar known as the *haab'*. This cycle nearly corresponded to the length of one complete solar year. Because the *haab'* did not contain exactly 365 days, modern scholars often refer to it as the Vague Year. Eighteen periods, or months, of 20 days each composed the main portion of the calendar (see figure 10.1, page 276). In the *haab'*, the names of these months were Pohp, Wo, Sip, Sotz', Tzek, Xul, Yaxk'in, Mol, Ch'en, Yax, Sak, Keh, Mak, K'ank'in, Muwan, Pax, K'ayab', and Kumk'u. Supernatural patrons oversaw each month and imbued each period of time with otherworldly significance. Numbers ranging from 1 to 20 (or 0 to 19 in some regions) represented each day of the month. The *haab'* calendar began with 1 Pohp, the next day being 2 Pohp, etc. The last day of the month did not carry the coefficient 20, but a symbol meaning the "seating" of the month to follow. Because the Maya did not use leap days, the system was not exact. To compensate for the undocumented time, the Maya added five days to the end of the year. This short five-day time period at the end of the cycle is known as Wayeb.

AGRICULTURE AND THE *HAAB'*

Despite its slight inaccuracies, the *haab'* still functioned as a seasonal indicator. This 365-day calendar formed the basis of an agrarian calendar. Within the sequence, the names of the months and their groupings suggest agricultural underpinnings. The names of the months relating to water are grouped together. Months with names relating to the earth are also clustered together in the sequence. After the earth months, months believed to symbolize the maize seed immediately follow. Months associated with the dry season complete the cycle.

The Calendar Round: Interlocking Cycles

The 260-day *tzolk'in* and 365-day *haab'* functioned simultaneously. Although each calendar had a different purpose, both presented units of days and numbers thought to be the embodiments of deities. In recording dates, scribes intermeshed the cycles by including the *tzolk'in* date, consisting of its number and day name followed by the *haab'* date, consisting of its day number and month name. For example, dates recorded in Maya monumental texts and associated with Waxaklahun Ub'ah K'awil, the Copanec ruler also known as 18 Rabbit (see Chapter 6), include *tzolk'in* and *haab'* dates. Waxaklahun Ub'ah K'awil acceded to the throne of Copán on a day that is reckoned in the Gregorian calendar as July 8, 695. In the Maya calendrical system, this date includes the *tzolk'in* date, 7 Lamat, followed by the *haab'* date, 1 Mol. The Maya calendrical record of the day on which Waxaklahun Ub'ah K'awil died, May 1, 738, includes the *tzolk'in* and *haab'* dates, 6 Kimi 4 Sak.

The naming of a specific year depended on the position in which the two cycles met. Most Maya cultures named the year for the first day of the New Year in the 260-day cycle. When the two calendars operated simultaneously, 52 years or 18,980 days would pass before the entire round would be completed. This 52-year period is called a Calendar Round.

The advantages of Calendar Round dating can be illustrated by a date recorded in the texts of the Maya site of Seibal. According to the texts, Ahaw B'ot, the king of Seibal, acceded to the throne on January 22, 771. The Calendar Round date for this day is 13 Ahaw 18 Kumk'u, which is also the Calendar Round date of cosmic creation. Ahaw B'ot may well have timed his accession to correspond to the Calendar Round date of mythological creation in order to associate his actions with the deeds of the gods during creation. But the disadvantages of Calendar Round dating can also be inferred from the same date. 13 Ahaw 18 Kumk'u, like every other Calendar Round date, recurs every 52 years. The Maya considered creation to have occurred thousands of years earlier in linear time than the accession of Ahaw B'ot. The resultant ambiguities are similar to those in a Western calendrical date such as June 8, '52, which does not specify whether June 8, 1442, June 8, 1952, or another of many other possible dates is intended. Unless further calendrical information had been recorded, the absolute date of Ahaw B'ot's accession, or of any other event recorded in the Calendar Round, would have remained unknown.

Wayeb

The five nameless days at the end of the calendrical cycle incited great fear throughout Mesoamerica. This brief but dangerous time was called Wayeb. During Wayeb, portals between the mortal realm and the Underworld dissolved. No boundaries prevented ill-intending deities from causing disasters. If the gods desired, they could travel to the Middleworld and spread sickness, death, or decay. During Wayeb, the destruction of the universe loomed in the minds of the Maya who feared the New Year cycle might not begin without special rituals.

Rites involving Wayeb appear in the *Dresden, Paris,* and *Madrid Codices.* Within these codices, the hieroglyph for Wayeb reveals its frightening nature. The hieroglyph that symbolized Wayeb was rendered as the sign for *tun,* or "stone," with a U-shaped skeletal maw on its top. The skeletal maw characterizes many of the denizens occupying the Underworld. During Wayeb, these evil Underworld forces might manifest themselves in the realm of humans through cosmic portals such as caves.

Early contact-period sources provide us with some information regarding Wayeb. Among the Maya of Yucatán, the most important rituals were enacted during this frightful period of time. Bishop Diego de Landa, a Spanish missionary, chronicled many of the ritual activities of the Maya living in Yucatán. Writing during the early colonial period, Landa indicated that rites celebrating the New Year began some days before the arrival of the New Year itself and were enacted during the five-day Wayeb period.

NEW YEAR'S RITUALS

Only four of the 20 *tzolk'in* days could begin a New Year. Known as "year-bearers," these days included K'an, Muluk, Ix, and Kawak at the time of the Spanish invasion. Each year-bearer day had both directional and color associations that determined where the ceremonies were performed and the color of some of the items used in the rituals. Four basic types of ceremonies corresponded to each of the year-bearers. The four ceremonies contained unique components, but all of the ceremonies shared a basic framework of events. One common component of the ceremonies involved the construction of a clay idol. Through ritual processions, the idol oscillated between the town center and spaces at the community's periphery. Another component of the New Year's festivals involved counterclockwise shifting of the idols at the beginning of each festival. These idols were placed at the south, east, north, and west entrances of the city. Blood offerings, from either humans or animals, constitute another critical component of New Year's rituals.

The basic features of these ceremonies are illustrated in the rites celebrating the New Year's beginning on K'an days. Bishop Landa tells us that before the advent of the New Year, participants fashioned a hollow clay idol called Kan u Uayeyab, which was erected atop a stone altar at the southern entrance of the town. A second statue representing the deity Bolon Dzacab was set up in the home of the ceremony's sponsor. The processional route leading from the sponsor's home to the outward-lying shrine was cleared and decorated for the occasion. The idol of Kan u Uayeyab was censed with ground corn and offered a headless chicken. The idol was then transported to the home of the sponsor where it was positioned opposite the statue of Bolon Dzacab. The Maya offered both idols food and prayers. Blood from the pierced ears of the participants served as another offering. The human blood was then ritually smeared on a stone called a *kanal acantun*. At the end of the Wayeb period, the Maya removed the image of Bolon Dzacab and transported it to the temple. The idol of Kan u Uayeyab was set on the eastern side of the town where it stood for one year. At the ceremony's termination, a final sacrifice was offered to the gods. Priests killed a victim and from the top of the temple, hurled the victim's body over the edge of the platform, where it landed on a pile of rocks.

The contemporary Maya of Zinacantán still enact New Year's ceremonies. Many features of these ceremonies recall the events described by Landa. A central component of the Zinacantán ritual involves a sacred pilgrimage to each of the town's sacred shrines. Cross-shaped shrines constructed of cedar are erected at the tops and bases of mountains, in churches, and at other places harboring holiness. Boughs of pine, candles, and flowers adorn each of the crosses for the celebration. After days of ritual feasting, musical performances, and offering prayers, shamans proceed from the ceremonial center to visit the sacred shrines. This pilgrimage always takes place on a Tuesday, because it is believed that the gods are the most attentive on this day and likely to respond to prayers and offerings. When all of the sacred mountains, caves, and temples have been visited, the shamans gather to enact the final component of the ritual. Chanting in unison, the shamans offer additional prayers. At timed intervals, the kneeling shamans shift in counterclockwise movements to address the four cardinal directions.

A time-period similar to the Maya Wayeb concerned other Mesoamericans as well. The Aztecs believed that destructive supernatural forces also attacked the earth at the end of the 52-year cycle. The ancient Aztecs greatly feared the arrival of the celestial demons, called *tzitzimme*, thought to dive down from heaven. These malevolent swooping creatures wielded great claws, inflicting great harm to humans. In order to secure the continuation of time and guard against such demons, the Aztecs fashioned special rituals. As part of these rites, the Aztecs destroyed all pots and household utensils, confined pregnant women indoors, and extinguished all fires, leaving the community in complete darkness. At midnight on the day preceding the New Year, the Aztecs drilled a new fire within the open chest cavity of a sacrificial victim whose heart had been excised. Within the cavity that once held the heart, flames were ignited. Priests spread the new fire using bundles of 52 sticks, which symbolized the 52 years of the Calendar Round. From this new fire, the priests carried the flaming torches through Tenochtitlan relighting the rest of the city's hearths.

THE LONG COUNT

By the second century, the Maya had become experts in cultivating land, expanding their states, building cities, and erecting monumental architecture. At this time rulers introduced

a significant change to the existing calendar. Hundreds of years after the first appearance of the *tzolk'in*, a new dating system evolved that eliminated ambiguity in dates (see "Origin of Writing and Long Count," page 38.) Because specific dates within 52-year periods risked becoming confused with one other, the Maya began using another method of tracking time. This new method of recording time is now referred to as the Long Count.

The Long Count recorded a continuous and chronological record of the passing of individual days from a fixed moment in time. For the Maya, the date 13.0.0.0.0 4 Ahaw 8 Kumk'u (August 11, 3114 B.C.E. when correlated with the Gregorian calendar) marked the beginning of time. This date corresponds to the moment that the universe was created and subsequently forms the base date of the Long Count. Events occurring before this date could also be expressed, and the Maya understood them to refer to episodes before the fourth creation, the world in which they lived.

Stela 2 at Chiapa de Corzo records the date 36 B.C.E. This example is the earliest known recording of a Long Count date in Mesoamerica. In subsequent periods of Maya history, Long Count dates mark vast numbers of monuments. A plethora of Long Count dates appears on Classic Period monuments. These dates provide useful information, because they frequently appear in texts that record the histories of Maya kings. With knowledge of secure dates and corresponding history, scholars are now able to reconstruct many aspects of Mesoamerican chronology and culture. By the 10th century however, the Maya abandoned this convention and expressed dates in a modified format.

Initial Series

Long Count dates typically introduce Classic Maya inscriptions. Because Long Count dates

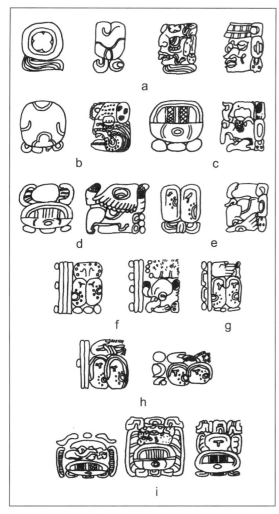

9.3 *Hieroglyphs denoting time periods:*
a) k'in; *b)* winal; *c)* tun; *d)* k'atun; *e)* bak'tun;
f) piktun; *g)* calabtun; *h)* k'inchitun; *and*
i) alautun *or Long Count introductory glyphs.*
(Drawing by Kaylee Spencer-Ahrens after Morley
and Brainerd, 1956)

appear at the beginning of hieroglyphic texts,
19th century scholars refer to them as the Initial Series. Specific hieroglyphs, termed introductory hieroglyphs, mark the beginning of

such dates. These glyphs indicate that those
that follow express a Long Count date.
Within the sequence of glyphs that follow the
introductory hieroglyph, the largest units of
time appear at the top. The first unit is usually
the *bak'tun*, or period of 144,000 days. As one
reads from left to right downward, the periods
of time decrease in size. Each unit of time can
also be identified by its hieroglyphic symbol.
The immediate glyph to the right of a *bak'tun*
is *k'atun.* On the level directly below these
two glyphs, the next unit in the sequence on
the left is a *tun*, followed by a *winal* and then a
k'in. The Calendar Round, or position where
the *tzolk'in* and *haab'* conjoin, completes the
Long Count date. Numbers expressed with
the bar-and-dot system indicate how many
glyphs of each time period are represented.
The current shorthand convention for writing
these dates without hieroglyphs, such as
13.0.0.0.0 4 Ahaw 8 Kumk'u begins with the
bak'tun (13), followed by the *k'atun* (0), the
tun (0), the *winal* (0), the *k'in* (0), and then the
Calendar Round date.

K'in: The Day

How the Maya organized units of time is critical to understanding how the Long Count
operates. To the Maya, the *k'in*, equaling one
day, was the most basic unit of time. Not only
were single days referred to as *k'ins*, but the
Maya used the same term to name the sun. The
meaning of *k'in*, therefore, extended beyond
qualifying a quantity; for the Maya, it embod-
ied the sun's horizontal movement from east to
west, and the sun's vertical movement between
up (north) and down (south). The hieroglyph
for *k'in* reveals its role as a signifier of time and
as a descriptor of space. Each *k'in* hieroglyph,
with four petal-like lobes, also represents the
four world directions.

Winal and *Tun:* Month and Year

Within the Maya calendar, *k'ins* were combined into groups of 20. This group of 20 *k'ins*, or days, equaled one *winal*, similar to a month in the Gregorian calendar. In a pure vigesimal system, the next largest unit should be composed of 400 *k'ins*, but the Maya deviated from the system at this point. Instead of 400, the next largest unit of time was a period of 360 days, a better approximation to the solar year. This 360-day time unit was called a *tun.* Eighteen *winals* (rather than 20) equaled one *tun*, or a period of 360 days. In other words, with the exception of the third position of the *tun*, each place in a number series contained 20 times the quantity of the previous unit. The term naming the third position functions in a polyvalent manner. In Mayan, the word *tun* also means "stone." In most examples of carved stone sculptures, the Maya fixed their position within the cosmos by inscribing their dates and histories.

K'atun: The Decade

After the *tun*, the system returned once again to the vigesimal system based on the number 20. Continuing in this fashion, 20 *tuns* equaled one *k'atun*, or 7,200 days. The Maya considered the *k'atun* a particularly important unit of time. A host of deities served as patrons of the *k'atuns.* Like the days of the *tzolk'in*, each *k'atun* expressed a prophecy of the future while at the same time embodying the historical past. When a *k'atun* was completed, the Maya enacted rituals and celebrations. As part of these celebrations kings erected monuments that exhibit *k'atun*-ending dates. At Copán, for example, the king Waxaklahun Ub'ah K'awil, also known as 18 Rabbit, erected stelae to commemorate the endings of various *k'atuns.* Stela C, for example, records the date 9.12.0.0.0 (December 5, 711), or the end of the first *k'atun* following the king's accession to the throne. These larger-than-life-sized carved sculptures depict the ruler engaged in shamanic trances as he celebrates the completion of the cycle. At Tikal, the termination of the *k'atun* prompted the construction of monumental sculpture and architecture. The architectural complex called the Twin Pyramid Group (see "Types of Construction," Chapter 8) was erected at Tikal specifically for this occasion. Because the completion of a *k'atun* inspired the creation of sculpted monuments, inscriptions recording *k'atun* endings appear with great frequency.

Bak'tun and Higher

Maya scribes utilized even larger units of time to express Long Count dates. Twenty *k'atuns* equaled one *bak'tun*, or 144,000 days. Although rarely used, units of time longer than the *bak'tun* were available to Maya scribes. For example, 20 *bak'tuns* equaled one *piktun*, or 2,880,000 days; 20 *calabtuns* equaled one *k'inchiltun*, or 1,152,000,000 days; and 20 *k'inchiltuns* equaled one *alautun*, or 23,040,000,000 days. Each of these units of time can be identified by particular hieroglyphs. Numbers, expressed through bars and dots affixed to the hieroglyphs, indicate how many times each unit should be counted. These units constitute the building blocks through which the Maya expressed periods of time.

Long Count Date: An Example

The east side of Monument 6 from Quiriguá, Guatemala, exhibits a Long Count date. The top of the inscriptions begins with an introductory glyph. Within the inscription this glyph is easily identifiable because of its large size; the introductory glyph normally appears four times as large as the glyphs that follow it. The portrait represented in the center of the introductory glyph constitutes a variable component. This portrait head corresponds with the patron of the months of the *haab'*, or vague year. In the center of the Quiriguá example, a deity serving as the patron of the month Pax is depicted.

Directly below the introductory glyph, the Long Count date begins. One reads the hieroglyphs in rows from left to right, top to bottom. In this case, the head variant on the upper left signifies *bak'tuns*. The bar and four dots attached to the left of the symbol express the number 9. Their combination signifies nine *bak'tuns* (9 × 144,000 days). The second glyph appears directly to the right of the *bak'tun* glyph. This symbol expresses 17 *k'atuns*, or 17 periods of 7,200 days. The next three glyphs exhibit trilobed motifs affixed to their left sides. Like the stylized shell, the trilobed glyphs indicate the concept of zero, or completion, signaling that no *tuns* (periods of 360 days), *winals* (periods of 20 days), or *k'ins* (single days) are to be considered. The presence of the zero sign with these hieroglyphs simply holds these places.

The hieroglyph occupying the sixth position expresses the Calendar Round date. In this case, the number 13 appears with the hieroglyph for Ahaw. Skipping down to the last glyph of the sequence, the hieroglyph on the extreme right represents 18 Kumk'u. When added together, all of the days contained in the first five hieroglyphs of the inscription indicate the number of days elapsed since the beginning

9.4 Example of a Maya Long Count date, from the east side of Monument 6, Quiriguá.
(Drawing by Kaylee Spencer-Ahrens after Morley and Brainerd, 1956)

of time. Expressed in the notation used by modern scholars, this Long Count date is therefore read as 9.17.0.0.0 13 Ahaw 18 Kumk'u (January 22, 771, in the Gregorian calendar). The same Long Count date was used at Seibal where it recorded the accession of the king Ahaw B'ot. By using the Long Count as well as the *tzolk'in* and *haab'* dates, the scribes of Seibal clearly fixed Ahaw B'ots accession to a single moment in linear time while simultaneously providing a metaphorical connection to mythological and cyclical time.

The Supplementary Series

The remaining glyphs on Monument 6 from Quiriguá include the Supplementary Series. Also called the Lunar Series, these glyphs give information regarding the moon. Because their exact names are uncertain, scholars have applied letter names to these glyphs for the purpose of discussion. Examples of some of the types of counts represented in the Supplementary Series include the count of the Lords of the Night, the age of the current moon, and the number of moons completed in a given half year. The final glyph in the series expresses the position of the *haab'*. The Supplementary Series, therefore, provides cosmological context for the date.

LORDS OF THE NIGHT

Within the Supplementary Series, Long Count dates give information regarding the Lords of the Night. Nine Lords of the Night constitute yet another dynamic count that operated in conjunction with the other cycles. Known as the G series of the Supplementary Series, few of the lords have been correlated with other better-known gods from the Maya pantheon. For example a jaguar-pawed deity may have served as the patron for the month Pax. The Lord of the Night termed G9 represents Pawahtun, the aged quadripartite god who supports the cosmos at its corners and thereby allows the universe to retain its shape. Each of the nine Lords of the Night was a

patron of a day of the Maya calendar, and it was believed that these gods moved incessantly in cycles throughout time. Although their exact names are uncertain, the Lords of the Night constituted an important group of Maya deities.

OTHER CYCLES

Short Count: *K'atun* Endings

During the Late Classic Period, Long Count dates began to be replaced with abbreviated methods of expressing time. These shortened and less specific dates are called period-ending dates. In examples that exhibit the period-ending dates, the inscriptions include only a particular *k'atun* and the name of the day that the *k'atun* ended. Because the 7,200 days that formed a *k'atun* could be evenly divided by the 20 day names, the *k'atun* was always named Ahaw. This dating system was represented most monumentally in the *k'atun* inscriptions commemorated by the Twin Pyramid Group at Tikal, but it was also recorded on so-called Ahaw altars during the Late Classic Period.

This abbreviation of the Long Count, termed the Short Count, became widely used during the Terminal Classic Period at Chichén Itzá in the Yucatán and well into the colonial period as reflected in the postconquest literature from that region, specifically in the *Books of the Chilam Balam* (see Chapter 10). The Short Count drastically reduced the accuracy of the calendric expressions by eliminating all information except the *k'atun* ending of the Long Count and the day name. This meant that a Short Count date repeated approximately every 256 years, or 260 Maya *tuns*.

The 819-Day Count

The Maya reflected their view of the universe in yet another method of grouping days into cycles. One such cycle is the 819-day count. This system typically operates independently of the other cycles but occasionally appears in the Supplementary Series. The roots of this cycle are unknown, but it utilizes elements common to all Maya cultures. The numbers 7, 9, and 13 bore spiritual significance among the ancient Maya. When multiplied together, they produce 819, the number of days counted in a never-ending cycle. The days are counted backward from the Initial Series in order to reach the last date on which the cycle was completed. This count of days was associated with each of the four quadrants of the universe, where one of the four color and directional aspects of God K (see "The Identities of the Gods," Chapter 6) presided over each direction. The red aspect was paired with the east, black with the west, white with the north, and yellow with the south. This cycle, therefore, addressed the issue of time as it meshed with space.

ASTRONOMY

The Maya were excellent astronomers: They could calculate the 584-day Venus cycle with only a two-hour margin of error. They were highly motivated to follow with precision planets' paths because from their sky charts, they believed they could divine propitious times for coronations and war and could pre-

dict dangerous times requiring special ritual watchfulness.

Maya astronomers charted cycles of celestial bodies and incorporated them into their calendars, refining them and infusing them with greater significance. Five Venus cycles, for example, coincided with eight *haab'* cycles, and these long periods leading to cyclic completion and overlap were recorded in Maya codices. The Maya marked the position of other planets, such as Mars, Mercury, and Jupiter, and they developed a zodiac (see Chapter 10) of the constellations that interested them, such as Scorpio, but these aspects of their astronomy are not well understood or agreed upon by Mayanists.

The movements of the stars for the Maya had mythological and divine significance as well as earthly importance. The rise of Venus as the morning star, for example, announced the dawning of a new creation brought on by the Hero Twins after their labors in the Underworld, for the twins were reborn, according to Maya creation texts, as aspects of Venus and the Sun. Some Mayanists believe the Milky Way was an essential part of the Maya zodiac. As the celestial representation of the cosmic center, or World Tree, the Milky Way represented human access to the otherworld. In the southern sky, the Milky Way appeared as a head that resembled a crocodile. This crocodile's head formed the roots of the World Tree, while its body merged with the trunk; such representations of the World Tree existed in ancient Maya art. The trunk of the World Tree, some Mayanists have theorized, was the road along which dead souls walked into the Underworld. Walking on this path, the constellation Scorpio was seen as the ecliptic, or the path that the Sun, Moon, and planets moved on.

However the Maya interpreted the Milky Way and celestial constellations, there is no doubt that sky watching for Maya priestly astronomers involved a deep understanding of the Maya cosmos, the periods in which different deities were ascendant, and the significance of such stellar behavior on the Middleworld. Much like modern astrologers, the Maya studied the celestial bodies to make their prognoses for the future and to incorporate such prophecies into the calendrical almanacs. They did so with unusual skill.

Naked-Eye Astronomy

Maya astronomers did not have telescopes or other powerful tools for observing the tropical night sky, but they found ways to enhance their naked-eye observations. Archaeoastronomers studying Maya architecture have come to know the innovations employed by the Maya in tracking the stars. Some images from ancient screenfold codices illustrate devices employed as tools to observe the skies. Although no observatories appear in these manuscripts, in some examples from central Mexico a man sitting atop a temple looks through a pair of crossed sticks. In another example, star symbols are centered in the crosslike device. Using crossed sticks as a sighting device, the Maya probably collected a vast corpus of information regarding celestial bodies.

The Maya also constructed architectural complexes for marking the movements of celestial bodies. The E-group complexes (see "Types of Construction," Chapter 8) sometimes functioned as solar monuments marking the solstices and equinoxes. Other buildings had doorways and windows specifically aligned to observe certain celestial bodies, particularly Venus. An example of this function-specific architecture can be found at Uxmal where all buildings were aligned in the same direction except for a building called the House of the Governor. The central doorway of this building provides a sight line on a single mound about 5 kilometers (3 miles) away to the southeast. Venus would have risen exactly above the mound when the planet reached is southerly extreme. One unusual, conical tower at Chichén Itzá appears so specifically constructed for astronomy that it is called an observatory by Mayanists; this Caracol complex has been proven to align with the northerly extremes of Venus. Diagonal sight lines in one of the windows of the tower align with the northern extremes of Venus, while another diagonal sight line matched the planet's setting position when it attained its maximum southerly declination.

Venus

Venus was the most closely observed and important of all celestial bodies for the Maya. From the Early Classic Period onward, Maya astronomers charted this planet's cycle and correlated it with other systems for tracking time Pre-Columbian codices include intricate charts mapping the position of Venus. Some of these codices, such as the *Dresden* and *Grolier* (see "The Maya Codices," Chapter 10), depict the destruction that occurs under the auspices of the Venus gods. These upheavals frequently occur at the planet's heliacal rising. Understanding the cycles dictating such movements, therefore, became paramount to Maya astronomers.

VENUS CYCLE

The Maya noticed that Venus, the brightest of all "stars," rose in the morning. The planet journeyed on its path from the Underworld while leading the Sun. When Venus rose as the evening star, it entered the sky after sunset and then followed the Sun back into the dark

Underworld. Because Venus orbits nearer to the Sun than Earth, its path is shorter, but seen from Earth, it takes 584 days for the two planets and the Sun to align. Specific points of Venus's orbit are known as inferior conjunction and superior conjunction. Modern astronomers have labeled the position of Venus as it travels directly in front of the Sun inferior conjunction. At this point Venus typically is invisible and cannot be observed for eight days before its heliacal rising. Afterward, it rises as the morning star for 263 days. When Venus orbits behind the Sun, it is known as superior conjunction. This position lasts 55 to 60 days. During this period, Venus cannot be perceived. When Venus makes its first appearance as the evening star, it remains in this position for 263 days before becoming invisible in front of the Sun again. The entire cycle requires 584 days to play out.

VENUS AND WARFARE

The study of Venus was particularly important among the Maya because this planet was closely associated with war. To the Maya, the movements of this planet could warn of bellicose disasters. The very hieroglyph for *war* incorporates a Venus sign over separate variable elements, usually glyphs serving to name the parties engaged in the war. Classic Maya inscriptions also record "star wars," or battles that coincided with the movements of Venus. Maya rulers specially planned for wars to occur on the days when Venus rose for the first time in its inferior or superior conjunction. For example, the first sighting of Venus as the evening star on December 3, 735, coincided with the attack on Seibal by Dos Pilas. Dos Pilas captured the ruler of Seibal but kept the king alive for 12 years. Finally, the prisoner king was sacrificed at a ritual ball game. This latter event transpired during an inferior conjunction of Venus.

Eclipses

Dreaded throughout Mesoamerica, eclipses were believed to be extremely dangerous and threatening. Information provided in the Supplementary Series probably assisted in predicting eclipses, based on almanacs maintained by Maya astronomer priests. Eclipses were seen as the biting of the Sun or of the Moon. To the Maya, solar eclipses imported more danger than lunar eclipses. Predicting both solar and lunar eclipses was essential, because such knowledge allowed the Maya to engage in rituals to avert crises. Solar eclipses occur only during the dark of the Moon and within 18 days of the crossing of the Moon's path with the Sun. Taking this into account, lunar tables, such as those in the *Dresden Codex*, sought to standardize such events in order to generate eclipse warning tables. In the *Dresden Codex*, a solar eclipse is pictured as the eating of the *k'in* glyph by a sky serpent.

SUMMARY

To the ancient Maya, the measured cycles of the calendars and the planets were seen as a cosmic pattern that pervaded all aspects of existence. Within this pattern, cycles of smaller networks overlapped and were interwoven with textile-like intricacy where the threads of one cycle become dependent on the looping of another. These patterns shaped the Maya universe within which all things had to fit. The Maya recognized these patterns and actively sought to define their space within the cosmos and the supernatural realm. Knowledge of time and its efficacy allowed the Maya to replicate the sacred networks in their daily life. With this cosmic participation, time allowed the ancient Maya to engage with the supernaturals. The intervals timing the movements of celestial bodies, therefore, paralleled the activities of humans within Maya societies.

READING

Cyclical History

Aveni 1989; Brinton 1982, Michael Coe 1999: cycles in history.

Maya Arithmetic

Michael Coe 1999: example of Maya vigesimal numeration; Lounsbury 1978, Morley 1915; Satterthwaite 1947, 1965: Sharer 1994; Thompson 1941, 1971: general Maya arithmetic.

Origins of the Calendar

Aveni and Hartung 1986, Justeson and Mathews 1983, Kelley 1976, Lounsbury 1976, 1978, Miller 1996, Miller and Taube 1993, Morley 1915, Sharer 1994, Thompson 1971: Maya calendar.

Cycles of Time

Aveni 1989, Bill, et al. 2000, Michael Coe 1999, Justeson and Mathews 1983, Kelley 1976, Lounsbury 1978, Miller 1996, Miller and Taube 1993, Morley 1915, Morley & Brainard 1956, Satterthwaite 1965, Schele and Miller 1986, Sharer 1994, Spinden 1913, 1924, Barbara Tedlock 1992, Thompson 1971, Vogt 1969: cycles in time.

The Long Count

Aveni 1989, Kelley 1976, Miller and Taube 1993, Morley 1915, Morley and Brainard 1956, Satterthwaite 1947, 1965, Schele and Miller 1986, Taube 1988a, Teeple 1931, Thompson 1941, 1950, 1971, Tozzer 1941: Maya Long Count; Sharer 1994: discussion of Monument 6 Long Count date from Quiriguá.

Other Cycles

Diane Chase 1985, Michael Coe 1999, Coggins 1979, Miller and Taube 1993, Satterthwaite 1965, Sharer 1994, Taube 1988b, Tozzer 1941: other Maya count cycles.

Astronomy

Aveni 1975, 1979, Freidel, Schele, and Parker 1993, Harvey Bricker and Victoria Bricker 1983. Arlen Chase 1991, Michael Coe 1975, Dütting 1985, Fox and Justeson 1978, Aveni, Gibbs and Hartung 1975, Hartung 1975, Kelley 1975, 1976, Kelley and Kerr 1973, Lounsbury 1978, 1982, Milbrath 1999, Miller and Taube 1993, Ricketson and Ricketson 1937, Schele and Miller 1986, Tate 1986, Teeple 1926 1931, Thompson 1972: Maya astronomy.

10

WRITTEN EVIDENCE

by Ruth J. Krochock

Our current understanding of ancient Maya civilization has been greatly enhanced by recent advances in our ability to understand Mayan languages and read Maya hieroglyphic texts, but this understanding has been long in coming and is by no means complete. We are fortunate to live at a time when vigorous and productive decipherment is taking place at an ever-increasing speed. Even so, we may never completely understand all that has been written by the ancient Maya.

HISTORY OF MAYA HIEROGLYPHIC DECIPHERMENT

Diego de Landa

The earliest Europeans to encounter hieroglyphic writing were the Spanish soldiers and missionaries who arrived in Mexico and Guatemala in the 16th century. At that time, there were only a few Maya who could still read hieroglyphs. In a desire to expunge pagan beliefs from the lives of the Maya, Spanish missionaries such as Bishop Diego de Landa, Antonio de Ciudad de Real, and Friar Luis de Villalpando burned many of the native manuscripts. Three Maya hieroglyphic books, however, found their way to Europe, possibly as part of the New World treasures presented to the Holy Roman Emperor Charles V, King of Spain. Eventually, they would be deposited in the libraries of Dresden (Germany), Madrid (Spain) and Paris (France) where the scholars of the early 19th century would begin the work of decipherment. Fortunately, in about 1566, before all native knowledge of hieroglyphic writing was lost forever, Landa recorded invaluable information about Maya culture shortly after the conquest. This document also included information about the Maya calendrical signs and "alphabet" used in hieroglyphic writing. Landa's manuscript work would eventually prove to be a valuable key to decipherment, but not before it remained buried in European libraries for some 300 years.

Nineteenth-Century Travelers

Early scholars in the 19th-century were becoming fascinated with the accounts of the travels of writer John Lloyd Stephens and artist Frederick Catherwood to Mexico and Central America in which they gave reports of a mysterious ancient civilization left in ruins in the rain forests. The explorers went on two expeditions in 1839 and 1842, and the books they wrote, complete with vivid and colorful descriptions and illustrations of Maya ruins, quickly became some of the most popular reading of the day. Stephens speculated that the monuments carved with hieroglyphs were records of Maya history, but it would take almost 120 years before scholars could confirm his idea.

First Decipherments

Finally in 1863, Landa's work, *Relación de las Cosas de Yucatán* (Account of the Things of Yucatán), was rediscovered by the French cleric Charles Etienne Brasseur de Bourbourg and brought to the attention of contemporary scholars who were interested in understanding the Maya script. Brasseur was also responsible for rediscovering other important documents that would aid in decipherment, including a colonial Maya dictionary, part of the *Madrid Codex*, and the *Paris Codex* (see "The Maya Codices" below). Brasseur provided some important contributions to decipherment, although much of his work, which focused on the lost city of Atlantis, did nothing to further our understanding of Maya hieroglyphics. His more valuable contributions include the correct interpretation of Maya bar-and-dot numbers, his verification of the meanings of the day signs, the identification of the *k'in*, or "day," sign and the *tun* sign for periods of 360 days, and finally, his identification of the personal pronoun *u*, meaning "he, she, and it."

Léon de Rosny, a contemporary of Brasseur de Bourbourg, brought us the first publications of the *Paris Codex* in 1887 and 1888. He also produced accurate decipherments of the glyphs for the world directions. In 1876 and 1883, he published the first general work on Maya hieroglyphic writing that might be considered contributions to decipherments. In 1884, his work was published in Spanish, and this version contained the first complete and accurate transcription of Landa's *Relación*.

Pioneer Epigraphers

From the work of the early scholars, it became evident that the Maya codices and the inscribed monuments at the ruined cities of the Maya were based on the same writing system subject to many of the same rules. This inspired explorers to visit ruins in order to record more hieroglyphic texts. The enlarged corpus of hieroglyphs facilitated decipherment.

ERNST FÖRSTEMANN: THE CALENDAR

Between 1880 and 1900, Ernst Förstemann was the royal librarian at Dresden, and therefore had first-hand access to the *Dresden Codex*.

He concentrated his efforts on understanding the month and day signs and the system of bar-and-dot numbers that appear in the codex. At this time, there was really no way to understand the noncalendrical or nonnumerical glyphs. Förstemann is credited with elucidating the workings of the Maya calendar system, mathematics, and much of Maya astronomy. A major contribution was his observation that the calendar was based on two cycles of time: the 260-day *tzolk'in* and the 360-day *haab'*, also called the vague year. Förstemann also explained the Maya Long Count system and found that the Maya beginning of time was placed at the date 4 Ahaw 8 Kumk'u. In the process of his discoveries, he found that the Maya used a base 20, or vigesimal, number system in contrast to our base 10, or decimal, system. By 1894, Förstemann turned to understanding the monumental inscriptions and successfully read a Long Count date from a Copán stela. In the meantime, in 1882, Cyrus Thomas (see below) had discovered the correct reading order for the glyphs: left to right, top to bottom in pairs of columns. His discovery surely aided the work of Förstemann.

ALFRED PERCIVAL MAUDSLAY

The English traveler and scientist Alfred Percival Maudslay began his investigations of the Maya area in 1882. During Maudslay's scientific expeditions to Maya centers such as Copán, Quiriguá, Palenque, Yaxchilán, Chichén Itzá, and Tikal, he meticulously recorded site plans and hieroglyphic inscriptions present at the sites with drawings, moulds, and glass-plate photography. Over the next 13 years, he produced four large tomes of work that were published as volumes 55 to 59 of the *Bilogia Central-Americani*, a compendium of natural history published between 1879 and 1915. Maudslay was ably assisted by artist Annie Hunter and photographer Henry Sweet. The superb efforts of Maudslay, Hunter, and Sweet set the scholarly standard for such work for many years to come.

DANIEL BRINTON

Daniel Garrison Brinton, who was originally a physician but later became a professor of American archaeology and linguistics at the University of Pennsylvania, contributed much to our understanding of Native American languages and literature. His work *A Primer of Mayan Hieroglyphics* was intended by the author as a summary of what was known about the Maya script at that time. One great contribution of his work was his insistence that little progress could be made toward understanding Maya hieroglyphic writing without first understanding more about the Mayan languages in which they were written.

CYRUS THOMAS

Cyrus Thomas of the Bureau of American Ethnology of the Smithsonian Institution of Washington D.C., first contributed to Maya studies with his work on the *Codex Troano*, published in 1882. Here he demonstrated with careful structural comparisons of passages from the codices and those carved in stone the basic reading order of Maya texts, that is, left to right, top to bottom in pairs of columns. In his work he also stressed the idea that the Maya script was mainly phonetic, but unfortunately he was unable to establish a phonetic key.

EDUARD SELER

The work of Eduard Seler has contributed significantly to our understanding of Mesoamerican studies, especially in his demonstration that all of Mesoamerica shared a cultural unity. His works addressed a great many topics including the interpretation of the *Borgia Codex*

and other Mexican manuscripts, Maya codices, and the ruins of Chichén Itzá, Palenque, and Uxmal. Among his many notable contributions he identified the color signs in the glyphs, as well as other glyphs for "dog," "fire," and "capture."

JOSEPH GOODMAN

Joseph Goodman contributed significant decipherments to Maya glyph studies. Most important, he identified the correlation between the Maya calendar and the Gregorian calendar we use today; that is, he determined the linkage between the two systems, thus allowing us to match a Maya Long Count date to an absolute date in our system. In addition, he identified the head variants for numerals in the inscriptions.

First Excavations: Carnegie Institution

SYLVANUS GRISWOLD MORLEY

Sylvanus Griswold Morley was an energetic scholar who spent much of his life recording the epigraphic record. Morley convinced the Carnegie Institution of Washington, D.C., to support an ambitious program of archaeological research at the sites of Copán, Quiriguá, Chichén Itzá, Uaxactún, and many other smaller Maya sites. These undertakings not only represented among the first excavations at Maya sites, but they contributed to the collection of more hieroglyphic inscriptions and their decipherment. Morley's largest and most impressive published work about the hieroglyphs, *Inscriptions of Petén*, includes drawings of inscriptions, especially ones focused on the Initial Series dates, from sites throughout the Maya area.

JOHN TEEPLE

The Carnegie Institution also supported some of the research of John Teeple in the area of Maya astronomy. Teeple's primary contribution was his discovery that many of the additional glyphs that appear after the Initial Series dates in monumental inscriptions referred to the lunar calendar.

HERMANN BEYER

The work of Hermann Beyer has proven to be incredibly valuable because he developed a method of structural analysis that makes the noncalendrical portion of the hieroglyphic record more accessible to study. His method of identifying parallel phrases in the inscriptions of Chichén Itzá allows one to more easily see the linguistic patterns, identify equivalent signs, and demonstrate the structure of the texts. His method of structural analysis is central to modern epigraphic analysis and methodology.

J. ERIC S. THOMPSON

The British scholar J. Eric S. Thompson was perhaps the most influential and productive Mayanist of his time. He virtually dominated the field between 1930 and 1960. During his career, Thompson published between 250 and 300 papers on archaeology, ethnology, ethnohistory, and linguistics. Among his contributions is his 1937 groundbreaking study on Yucatecan dating, the so-called Short Count (see Chapter 9), in which he demonstrated how to read the unusual system of dates employed in the inscriptions of several sites in northern Yucatán. This work finally allowed scholars to understand the epigraphic chronology of Chichén Itzá. Although some of his conclusions are now outdated, his *Maya Hieroglyphic Writing: An Introduction* (1950) and *A Catalog of Maya Hieroglyphs* (1962) are still used today as basic texts and references.

Phoneticism

Thompson suggested that certain signs in the Maya script could represent sounds, such as in rebus writing, but could also function as independent speech particles. Thompson, however, strongly opposed the notion that signs in the Maya script could convey purely phonetic syllables. Thompson believed that the Maya used hundreds of symbols for different words rather than a few phonetic signs; as a result, he argued there would be no alphabet and no Rosetta Stone to permit wholesale decipherments. Instead, he thought the Maya texts would remain largely unreadable, except for calendrical information, as translations could proceed in only a piecemeal fashion.

Then in 1952, a young Soviet scholar named Yuri Knorosov published several papers that promoted the view that the Maya script was phonetic, in spite of Thompson's opinion. The great influence Thompson had on the field effectively dissuaded many scholars of the time from pursuing the matter any further. Thompson held steadfast to his view until his death in 1975. Although Thompson's incredible contributions to Maya studies will never be forgotten, his firm rejection of phoneticism in the Maya script would eventually push his work out of the spotlight.

YURI KNOROSOV

In 1956, Michael and Sophie Coe found themselves in Mérida, Mexico, staying at the same hotel as Tatiana Proskouriakoff, who would make the first breakthrough in deciphering Maya history (see below). In a Mérida bookstore, the three came across a Spanish translation of one of Knorosov's papers promoting the notion of phoneticism in the Maya script and found his ideas intriguing. The Coes decided that Knorosov's work should be translated into English, and in 1958, Sophie Coe translated one of Knorosov's papers. Proskouriakoff was reluctant to oppose Thompson's opinion on this matter; in 1967, however, she edited a volume in which Sophie Coe translated selected chapters from Knorosov's work.

DAVID H. KELLEY

Fortunately, other scholars such as David H. Kelley also found the merit of Knorosov's phonetic arguments and in the 1960s began promoting them to the rest of the scholarly community. In 1962, he published a paper on phoneticism in the Maya script in which he defended Knorosov's phonetic readings against Thompson's attacks on Knorosov's work. In 1968, he was the first to use Knorosov's ideas to decipher a name in the hieroglyphic inscriptions of Chichén Itzá, the name of a person known in ethnohistoric documents as K'ak'u-pakal. He found evidence that the name was spelled out phonetically as *k'a-k'u-pa'-ka-la*. When Kelley's 1976 work *Deciphering the Maya Script* was published one year after Eric Thompson's death, it was clear to most Mayanists that Knorosov's ideas concerning phoneticism must be accepted in spite of Thompson's earlier objections.

Historical Texts

Until the mid-20th century, progress in the decipherment of the hieroglyphs had been made only in calendrical and astronomical readings. This had led Thompson to believe that the hieroglyphic inscriptions were written by Maya priests and astronomers with no political interest or militant purpose, and that the texts, even if they could be deciphered, would not contain the history of the Maya. Once again, he would be proven terribly wrong.

BERLIN AND LOUNSBURY: EMBLEM GLYPHS

In 1958, Heinrich Berlin published a groundbreaking paper in which he identified emblem glyphs in the Maya inscriptions. These emblem glyphs, according to Berlin, referred to specific sites either by identifying them with certain places or with specific lineage or family names. In his 1973 paper on the decipherment of the so-called *ben-ich* prefix, Floyd Lounsbury presented linguistic data and ethnohistoric sources as supporting evidence for Berlin's proposed glyphic reading. Lounsbury's demonstration of the interdisciplinary approach set a standard for analytical methodology for all future epigraphers to follow.

One of the implications of Berlin's discovery was that the Maya hieroglyphic inscriptions discussed matters that were historical in nature, a theme that continues to be productive today. In 1959, Berlin had the opportunity to analyze a hieroglyphic text on Hanab Pakal's sarcophagus at Palenque and determined that the portraits of the individuals on the sides of the sarcophagus were named in the accompanying hieroglyphic texts, an analysis that reinforced his historical hypothesis.

TATIANA PROSKOURIAKOFF: MAYA KINGS

Among Tatiana Proskouriakoff's important contributions to Maya studies and hieroglyphic decipherment is her 1960 seminal work on the inscriptions of Piedras Negras. She discovered a pattern of dates and other glyphs on a series of stelae at that site which suggested the monuments were recording the births and accessions of various rulers. Her historical hypothesis was the first study of its kind to clearly demonstrate that actual historical information was recorded in hieroglyphic inscriptions. This breakthrough, readily accepted by Thompson and others in the field, started a chain reaction of investigations focused on documenting the dynastic sequences of rulers at a number of Maya sites. Early examples include Kelley's 1962 work on the site of Quiriguá and Proskouriakoff's 1963 and 1964 papers on the site of Yaxchilán.

New Era of Decipherment

By 1970, Maya scholars understood that many Maya symbols were phonetic and that the texts contained history of the ancient cities. Once linguists, Maya scholars, and art historians joined together to read the inscriptions, decipherment progressed at an astonishing rate. As Maya archaeologists recovered yet more samples of texts, the corpus grew, and epigraphers could more easily find patterns of symbols to decipher. Meanwhile computer technology increasingly enabled Mayanists to share information with unusual accuracy and speed. Phonetic syllabaries were developed and continued to be refined; understanding of the Maya script grew exponentially, each decipherment giving rise to yet others.

MATHEWS AND SCHELE: THE PALENQUE DYNASTY

A conference that became known as the Palenque Round Table was first held by Merle Greene Robertson and Lawrence W. (Bob) Robertson at their home in Chiapas, Mexico, in 1973. Scholars in attendance included many who would be influential in the future decipherment, especially Michael Coe, Floyd Lounsbury, Linda Schele, and Peter Mathews. During this meeting, Mathews and Schele, with the help of Lounsbury, presented the first dynastic sequence from the hieroglyphic texts of Palenque. Their work was a significant advancement in decipherment: It not only indicated that extensive texts could be read, revealing the history of an ancient Maya city, but also successfully employed David Kelley's identification of *Pakal*, the first phonetic reading of the real name of a Maya ruler, that of the great Hanab Pakal. These collaborative forums continued, in Palenque, Austin, Texas, and many other locations, and they created a groundswell of interest in the problems of decipherment.

LINDA SCHELE: MAYA WORKSHOP

In 1984, Schele published her dissertation *Maya Glyphs: The Verbs* in which she presented thorough documentation and analysis on this grammatical category in the Maya script. Schele published many papers on the hieroglyphic decipherment and political history of Palenque and Copán, and wrote several more general texts with scholars David Freidel and Mathews. Schele became one of the most energetic and beloved Mayanists in recent history. With the encouragement and assistance of the scholar Nancy Troike in the late 1970s, she began an annual workshop on Maya hieroglyphic writing at the University of Texas at Austin that attracted professional scholars from the fields of linguistics, art history, and anthropology from all over the world. Many would become the most famous epigraphers of the Maya script, such as Mathews, Nikolai Grube, Stephen Houston, Simon Martin, David Stuart, and, of course, Schele herself. In addition to academicians, the workshop attracted hundreds of amateur enthusiasts who found the decipherment of Maya hieroglyphic writing an irresistible obsession that brought them back to Austin year after year. Schele continued to hold this workshop annually until her death in 1998, and it now continues under the direction of Grube.

CORPUS OF HIEROGLYPHS

Long-term documentation programs such as the Corpus of Maya Hieroglyphic Inscriptions Project directed by Ian Graham at the Peabody Museum at Harvard University began in the 1970s and continue to provide superb line drawings and photographs of all the known Maya inscriptions, facilitating decipherment. Anyone who has gone to the Maya lowlands looking for hieroglyphic monuments in the rain forest can appreciate the huge contribution the Harvard corpus project offers scholars of Maya script. Now researchers can simply open the pages of a book to see a particular monument instead of trudging through the brush or wading through museum collections. Of course, archaeologists continue to devote themselves to such fieldwork, so there will never be any shortage of new material to be recorded and analyzed.

Databases   Another project called the Maya Hieroglyphic Database Project, directed by Martha Macri at the University of California at Davis, has taken on the task of recording every known glyph from both Maya artifacts and the codices. The database is organized by region, site, and monuments within sites. Each text is fully annotated with provenence, a glyph-by-glyph reading, grammatical coding, and scanned line drawings of the inscriptions in full textual context and separately so that when this information is finally completed and available, researchers can access information quickly and easily.

Macri also assisted Merle Greene Robertson to produce a series of CD-ROMs on which she recorded her vast corpus of rubbings of Maya art and hieroglyphic inscriptions from carved monuments. Like the Harvard corpus project and the database project, Greene Robertson's rubbings provide a wealth of information that was not previously accessible to scholars.

Current Research

The last decade of work on the decipherment of hieroglyphic writing has been particularly productive. Epigraphers have advanced their knowledge of Mayan languages to the point where they are able to propose complex arguments on language variability in the Maya script, analyze grammatical constructions, track the variability and evolution of various glyphic signs through time and distribution throughout the region, and offer hypotheses on the origin of certain signs in the writing system. Huge archaeological projects are currently in progress or have recently been completed at major Maya cities such as Copán, Palenque, Caracol, Cancuén, Calakmul, Chichén Itzá, Tikal, and others. These projects continue to provide invaluable contributions to our understanding of the ancient Maya world and written history recorded in the inscriptions. New archaeological projects at poorly understood Maya sites are beginning every year that offer the promise of new hieroglyphic texts to record and decipher.

MAYAN LANGUAGES AND WRITING

One advantage we have in the decipherment of the Mayan writing system is that 31 Mayan languages are still spoken today. We can reconstruct the workings of the ancient Maya script not only internally from the structure of the texts themselves but also externally by comparing the modern spoken languages of today with the structure of the written ancient texts. Dictionaries of Mayan languages, especially those first compiled during the colonial period, also aid epigraphers in decipherment by providing a way to look up terms for words that may not be used in modern spoken language but would have been relevant to the ancient spoken and written languages. Some writing systems such as cuneiform or Hittite hieroglyphics were written by speakers of languages that have long been dead. Epigraphers working to decipher such scripts have had to reconstruct them in large part from patterns evident in the ancient written texts alone.

The 31 existing Mayan languages are distinct from each other, and most are mutually unintelligible. Some of these languages are still spoken by hundreds of thousands of modern speakers, while others survive with only a few hundred native speakers. Due to years of civil war in Guatemala, some indigenous populations and their languages have become nearly extinct.

Splintering from Proto-Mayan

Before 2000 B.C.E., a single Mayan language that linguists term proto-Mayan was spoken. The Huastec and Yucatec languages split off from proto-Mayan, with Huastec speakers settling along the Gulf coast in northern Veracruz and Tamaulipas in Mexico. Yucatec speakers spread throughout the Yucatán Peninsula and parts of the central area. Later, proto-Mayan split off into two other major groups: Eastern Mayan and Western Mayan.

In general, Yucatecan languages are spoken in the northern lowlands, and Cholan languages are spoken in the southern lowlands. In between these two areas is an area where both Yucatecan and Cholan languages are spoken. Southwest of the southern lowlands are the highlands of Guatemala, and this is where those who speak the Eastern Mayan languages live.

Western Mayan split into Greater Cholan and Greater Kanjobalan. Greater Cholan then split into Cholan and Tzeltalan. Cholan divided into Chol, Chontal, Chorti, and Cholti. Speakers of Chontal and Chol can now be found in the northwest near the site of Palenque and northward to the Gulf coast. Chorti is now spoken in a region near the sites of Quiriguá, in Guatemala, and Copán, in Honduras. In ancient times, Cholan languages probably dominated a band across the base of the Yucatán Peninsula from the Gulf coast to far-western Honduras. The Tzeltalan language split into Tzotzil and Tzeltal, languages spoken mainly in the Chiapas highlands near San Cristól de las Casas.

Greater Kanjobalan split off into Kanjobalan and another group. The Kanjobalan later divided into Motozintlec, Jacaltec, Acatec, and Kanjobal. The other group split into Tojolobal and Chuj. The speakers of these languages seem to have stayed in the western Guatemalan highlands.

Eastern Mayan, meanwhile, split into Mamean and Greater Quichean. Among the Eastern Mayan languages, Mamean split off into Mam, Ixil, Teco, and Agautepec. Mam speakers mostly settled along the Pacific coast, while Ixil speakers concentrated around the town of Nebaj. Greater Quichean split into two groups that subdivide into Kekchi (also spelled K'eq'chi), Uspantec, and Pokom, which later broke into Pokomchi and Pokomam. The other subgroup includes Quichean, which broke down into Quiché (also spelled K'ich'e), Sipakapa, Sacapultec, Cakchiquel (also spelled Kaqchikel), and Tzutujil, whose speakers live around Guatemala's Lake Atitlán.

Mayan Languages and Decipherment

The two main Mayan language groups that are most relevant to the decipherment of the ancient writing system are Yucatecan and Cholan. The Yucatecan languages include Yucatec, spoken throughout the Yucatán Peninsula, parts of the Petén, and northern Belize, and several branch languages that splintered from it by the 13th century: Itzá, spoken in the Petén lakes region; Mopán, centered in southern Belize, and Lacandón, spoken in the central area. The major Cholan languages include Chol, Chontal, Chorti, and Cholti. Today these languages are spoken in parts of Mexico, Guatemala, El Salvador, Honduras, and Belize where we find the ancient Maya sites containing hieroglyphic texts.

The Tzeltalan languages may be of more importance at some Maya sites located in the far southwest Maya area. The highland Mayan languages that are still spoken in the Guatemalan highlands and Chiapas may have had more influence in the initial stages of development of Maya hieroglyphic writing. These language groups may have had more contact with the innovators of the Isthmian texts, which seem to predate the Mayan script (see page 38).

Languages of Ancient Texts

Recently new theories have been proposed concerning the nature of the languages used to write the hieroglyphic texts. Some have suggested that Maya inscriptions are written in a specialized elite language based in the Cholan languages rather than in Yucatec, as has been assumed by some for many years. One reason this problem is still an issue in Maya studies is that the language used to write Maya hieroglyphs is no longer spoken in the same form by modern speakers. Also, linguists who have studied the grammar of the ancient Maya script find evidence that more than one language is reflected in the script in terms of verbal affixes and vocabulary. As yet, there is no unanimous acceptance of the new theory concerning the use of a specialized elite language in the writing of Maya hieroglyphic writing. Many linguists will want to rigorously test the hypothesis before it is generally accepted among the scholarly community.

Orthography and Pronunciation

Various systems of transcription were devised in colonial times by the Spanish friars so that the Mayan languages could be written using our alphabetic writing system. Over the years, modern linguists have made changes to the early transcriptions that reflect the nuances of the various Mayan languages reflected in the script. Some sounds exist in Mayan languages that are not used in European languages. For example, the sound *sh* that exists in Mayan languages was transcribed by the Spanish friars as *x* and is still used in modern orthographies, as seen in the word *yax*, meaning "first" or "blue-green." Other consonants in Mayan languages are differentiated with the use of a glottal stop, a sudden constriction in the back of the throat or a sudden explosive burst of air accentuated at the lips or with the tongue just behind the front teeth. In modern orthography, these glottalized sounds are marked with an apostrophe after the letter. The consonants that appear as glottalized and nonglottalized pairs are *k'* and *k*, *tz'* and *tz*, *b'* and *b*, *p'* and *p*, *t'* and *t*, and *ch'* and *ch*. The Yucatecan languages use five vowels—*a*, *e*, *i*, *o*, and *u*—which are pronounced as they are in Spanish. The Cholan languages add a sixth vowel—*ä*—pronounced like the *u* in *cut*.

Recently, some Mayanists agreed that the various systems of orthography in use, especially in Guatemala, should be standardized in order to avoid confusion. Contemporary Maya, many of whom are linguists themselves, have

DAY NAMES					MONTH NAMES				
1		Imix / Imix	11		Chuwen / Chuen	1		Pohp / Pop	11		Sak / Zac
2		Ik' / Ik	12		Eb' / Eb	2		Wo / Uo	12		K'ank'in / Kankin
3		Ak'b'al / Akbal	13		B'en / Ben	3		Sip / Zip	13		Mak / Mac
4		K'an / Kan	14		Ix / Ix	4		Sotz' / Zotz'	14		Keh / Ceh
5		Chikchan / Chicchan	15		Men / Men	5		Tzek / Tzec	15		Muwan / Muan
6		Kimi / Cimi	16		Kib' / Cib	6		Xul / Xul	16		Pax / Pax
7		Manik' / Manik	17		Kab'an / Caban	7		Yaxk'in / Yaxkin	17		K'ayab' / Kayab
8		Lamat / Lamat	18		Etz'nab' / Etz'nab	8		Mol / Mol	18		Kumk'u / Cumku
9		Muluk / Muluc	19		Kawak / Cauac	9		Ch'en / Ch'en			(Wayeb) / (Uayeb)
10		Ok / Oc	20		Ahaw / Ahau	10		Yax / Yax			

10.1   The 20 Maya day glyphs and the 18 Maya month glyphs, with their names both in the new orthography (above) and in 16th-century Yucatec Mayan.   (Drawings by Ruth Krochock after Coe 1992 and Mathews 1990)

been instrumental in helping the Guatemalan Ministry of Culture develop the new system. One feature that has changed is the spelling of the day, month, and period names, although many Mayanists believe the old spelling system is more appropriate for Yucatecan Mayan languages. Today both systems are used. But as linguists gain a more sophisticated understanding of Mayan languages, even these spelling conventions may change. In 2000, for example, Simon Martin and Nikolai Grube argued that *ah* and *aw* should be replaced by *aj*. In this system, *ahaw* would be spelled *ajaw*, and Hanab Pakal's name, *Janab Pakal*.

DECIPHERMENT OF HIEROGLYPHS

Early Maya Writing

The origin of the Maya writing system seems to have been inspired by some dramatic political changes that began to take place in the Maya lowlands about 300 or 400 B.C.E. At this time, Maya society was subjected to greater centralized authority (see Chapter 2). This political change was accompanied by the development of a writing system by those more elite members of Maya society; this change gradually evolved into the Maya ruler cult. The use of writing was one way to document the elevated status of those who became the rulers.

Isolated Glyphs in Art

Although there are a few instances of pro-towriting in the Guatemala highlands c. 400 B.C.E., the first readily recognizable symbols from the Classic Period Maya writing system appear around 50 B.C.E. as isolated glyphs for *ahaw* (lord), *yax* (first) and *k'in* (Sun) and are incorporated into the art on public monuments such as the huge stucco masks on Structure 5C-2nd at Cerros, Belize.

RULERSHIP

Following this, short hieroglyphic texts are found incised on small portable objects. One of the first readable texts appears on the reused Olmec jade that is now part of the permanent collection at Dumbarton Oaks in Washington, D.C. On this jade, we find the portrait of a ruler who is depicted with objects that symbolize Maya rulership. The ruler's name appears as a glyph next to his portrait. A short hieroglyphic text, which can be read only partially at this time, appears on the back of the object and includes the name of the ruler and his accession to office. Other examples of early texts include one that is inscribed on the sides of a cliff in San Diego, Guatemala, and another that is carved on a miniature stela called the Hauberg Stela. In both of these examples we find depictions of the rulers associated with symbols of power and rulership. The texts that accompany the portraits include partial records of the dates the monuments were dedicated and a few events such as bloodletting ceremonies and the ruler's accession on to office. In these early examples, the writing system is still in a developmental stage before the Long Count (see Chapter 9, pages 255ff.) was fully developed and standardized the way it appears on later Maya monuments.

Where Glyphs Are Found

Hieroglyphs, which have been either carved or painted, can be found in many kinds of places and on numerous types of surfaces. They are often carved on stone, and sometimes wooden, monuments such as stelae, lintels, door jambs, altars, wall panels, columns, benches, and stairways. Glyphs are also carved on small portable objects such as ear spools, stone tools such as celts, jade plaques, shells, bones, and some ceramic vessels. Many of the Maya ceramics that have been found in royal tombs are decorated with painted hieroglyphic texts just below the rim of the vessel. The hieroglyphic texts that appear in the bark-paper books known as codices are painted in red and black paint. It is likely that other objects made of wood and other perishable materials such as leather and cloth were also decorated with hieroglyphic texts but simply have not survived the elements to the present day. Glyphic texts were sometimes painted on cave walls such as at Naj Tunich Cave in Belize or in royal tombs, such one at Río Azul. Hieroglyphic texts also appear on painted murals such as those found in three rooms of a ruined building at Bonampak, in Chiapas, México. Some of the gold discs recovered from the Sacred Cenote at Chichén Itzá were decorated with hieroglyphic texts that were embossed into the metal.

Scribes

Not very much is known about Maya scribes, but in recent years, some of their names, painted on ceramics and carved on stone monuments, have been identified. Based on information from the texts on painted ceramics, it is known that at least some of the scribes were members of elite society, such as one who belonged to the royal family of Naranjo, in Guatemala. The ceramic vessels were usually signed by only one artist, whereas as many as eight sculptors' signatures have been found on a single stela at the site of Piedras Negras in the Usumacinta region. This suggests that single artists decorated the ceramics while a number of sculptors worked together to create the huge stone monuments. Despite the exciting discovery of scribal signatures, most monuments and ceramic vessels remain unsigned and anonymous.

The Writing System

PHONETIC SYLLABLES AND LOGOGRAPHS

Maya hieroglyphic writing is a mixed phonetic and logographic script. Phonetic signs represent syllables consisting of a consonant and vowel (for example, *la*, *ba*, and *tu*) that are combined to spell out words. Logographs, sometimes called word signs, represent entire words. Some of the logographs are pictographic in that they resemble the words they represent. Both phonetic signs and logographs can be used in a variety of combinations depending on the whim of the scribe writing the texts. A Maya scribe, therefore, could decide to write the glyph for "jaguar," or *b'alam*, in several different ways. He might use a logograph, that is, he might draw or carve a picture of a jaguar. There could be any number of variations in the rendering of this jaguar glyph, depending on the discretion of the scribe, and all variations would be viable substitutions for each other. Instead of using a logograph, the scribe might choose to spell out the word using only the phonetic signs *ba-la-ma* for the word *b'alam*. Yet another possibility is a combination of a logograph and phonetic signs used as complements to give clues to the reader as to how he should pronounce the glyph. To do this, the logograph is the main sign, and the phonetic complements are affixed above, below, or alongside the main sign.

LANDA'S ALPHABET

Decipherment of the Maya hieroglyphic writing system would surely have taken much longer if not for a document recorded by Bishop Diego de Landa around the time of the Spanish Conquest—the *Relación de las cosas de Yucatán*. In this manuscript, Landa recorded what happened when he asked a literate Maya man named Gaspar Antonio Chi to explain hieroglyphic writing. Without ever considering that the Maya writing system might be different from the European writing system, Landa asked him to explain and write down the Maya alphabet. Because Maya writing, when it is phonetically spelled, is syllabic but not alphabetic (for example, *la* but never just *l*), the "alphabet" that Gaspar Antonio Chi gave

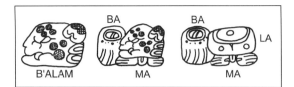

10.2 Various ways to write b'alam (jaguar) in Mayan script: logographic (left); logographic with phonetic complements (center); and purely phonetic (right). (Drawings by Ruth Krochock after Harris and Sterns, 1997)

Landa is actually a partial list of Maya syllabic signs. It took centuries before anyone understood the information recorded by Landa and realized that this Maya syllabary was an important key to decipherment, as the Rosetta Stone was in the decipherment of Egyptian hiero-

glyphics. Landa also recorded the names of the months and days, which eventually lead to the decipherment of calendric glyphs.

READING ORDER

Maya hieroglyphic texts can be arranged in a variety of ways. The standard way to write a text is in vertical pairs of columns to be read from left to right, top to bottom. When the reader reaches the bottom of a pair of columns, he proceeds to the top of the next pair of columns. For convenience in reading and referring to specific glyphs, a standard way to annotate text has been developed: Columns are labeled with letters, while rows are labeled with numbers. So, for example, in a text of four columns consisting of three glyphs each, the four columns would be

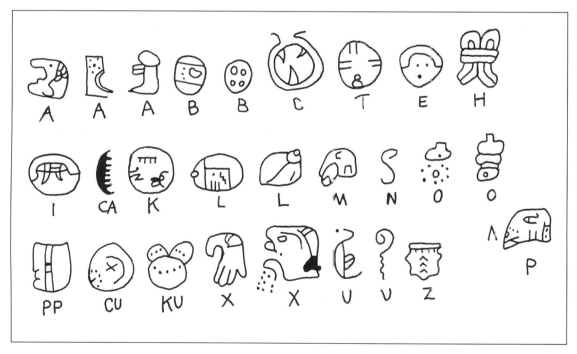

10.3 Landa's "alphabet." (Drawing by Ruth Krochock after Tozzer, 1941)

labeled A, B, C, and D, and the three rows of glyphs would be labeled 1, 2, and 3. Reading would begin with glyph A1 and would progress to B1, then A2, B2, and A3, B3. From here, the text would continue at the top of columns C and D with C1 and D1, followed by C2, D2, C3, and D3.

Texts can also be arranged in single horizontal bands that are read left to right, single vertical bands read top to bottom, circular arrangements around the tops or sides of disks, or any number of other configurations that are created by the scribe at the time of writing. At the site of Copán, Honduras,

Stela J is covered with a hieroglyphic text that appears in a woven pattern. At Chichén Itzá, we find a variety of unusual reading orders, such as those on the Monjas lintels, which are carved in a square at the edge of the stone, or those on the Temple of the Three Lintels, which start out reading in pairs of columns but then suddenly switch to vertical single columns of glyphs. At the site of Yaxchilán, a text on Lintel 25 is written in mirror image, thus requiring the reader to read from right to left. In the case of texts with unusual reading orders, it is assumed that the scribes exercised a certain amount of artistic license with the understanding that the educated reader would be able to figure out the proper reading order.

WORD ORDER IN GLYPHIC TEXTS

In English, word order tends to be subject-verb when the verb is intransitive (for example, "She laughs"). The word order is subject-verb-object in situations that involve a transitive verb (for example, "He feeds the baby"). In Maya hieroglyphic texts, the word order in phrases with intransitive verbs tends to be verb-subject.

For phrases with transitive verbs, the word order in hieroglyphic texts tends to be verb-object-subject. An example from Yaxchilán relates that a person named Jeweled Skull was captured and that he is the prisoner of the ruler named Bird Jaguar (see Figure 10.5). The phrase reads, *chukah* Jeweled Skull *u bak* Bird Jaguar or "was captured Jeweled Skull his prisoner Bird Jaguar." In this case, the verb *chukah* comes first. This is followed by the object of the verb, a person named Jeweled Skull. Jeweled Skull is then further identified as Bird Jaguar's captive (*u bak*). Bird Jaguar acts as the subject of the verb. Following Bird Jaguar's name is a title phrase, *u chan Ah Uk*, or "his guardian Ah Uk." This title further identifies

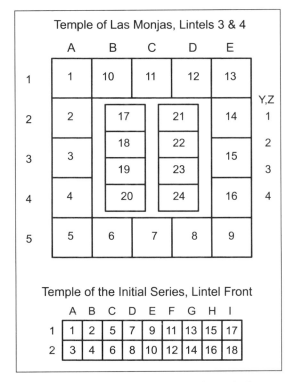

10.4 *Examples of reading orders from the hieroglyphic texts of Chichén Itzá: an unusual reading order (above) and the standard reading order (below).* (Drawings by Ruth Krochock, 1998)

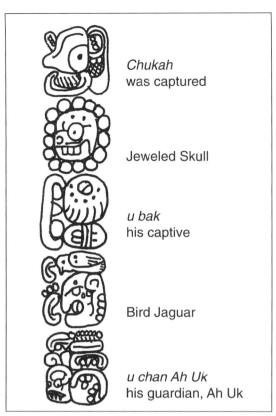

Chukah
was captured

Jeweled Skull

u bak
his captive

Bird Jaguar

u chan Ah Uk
his guardian, Ah Uk

10.5 Example of verb-object-subject word order in the Mayan Script from Yaxchilán Lintel 41, C1–C4. (Drawing by Ruth Krochock after Ian Graham, 1979)

Bird Jaguar as the guardian of yet another prisoner named Ah Uk.

The Correlation Problem

The so-called correlation problem refers to the efforts of many scholars to reconcile the Maya Long Count calendar with our present day Gregorian calendar. The correlation that became accepted as the standard was developed in 1905 by Joseph Goodman (see above). Later refine-

ments were supplied in 1927 by J. Eric Thompson and his collaborator, Juan Martínez Hernández, thus giving it the name the Goodman-Martínez-Thompson (or GMT) correlation. The Maya placed the beginning of their calendar at the date 4 Ahaw 8 Kumk'u, and the GMT correlation equates this date with August 13, 3114 B.C.E. In more recent years, the accuracy of the correlation has been questioned and tested by various means, including radiocarbon dating of samples taken from carved hieroglyphic lintels. In 1982, Floyd Lounsbury discovered that the Maya timed the dates of certain warfare events recorded in the inscriptions with a specific astronomical event involving the position of Venus in the night sky (see Chapter 5). From this information, he was able to confirm the accuracy of the GMT correlation.

DECIPHERED HIEROGLYPHS

Some Verbs

BIRTH

One of the most common verbs found in the hieroglyphic inscriptions is "to be born" because Maya rulers felt it important to document the important events of their lives. As with most glyphs, there are several variants that are literally read in different ways but convey similar meanings. Three such examples are of the so-called up-ended frog, which can be read *sih*, or "birth." Verbal suffixes such as *hi* and *ya* are added to the glyphs in order to make the verb in past tense, so, for example, while *sih* means "birth," *sihi* means "was born." Another way to say that a person was born is to declare that "he (or she) has arrived," as in the expression read *huli*, or "he arrived." A third way to say a person was born is an idiomatic expression in Maya that can be roughly translated as "to touch the earth."

ACCESSION

Accession to rulership is another event frequently expressed in public hieroglyphic inscriptions. This action can be expressed in a number of ways. The *ch'am* glyph means "to receive" or "to display." This is drawn as an open hand ready to receive the *k'awil* scepter, which is a symbol of Maya rulership. Another way to express the action of taking office is to use the glyph *chum*, meaning "to be seated," or *chumwan ti ahawlel*, "he was seated as lord." Yet another accession expression is read *hok'ah*, or "he tied" or "he came out." The meaning of this reading may seem obscure, but it has to do with a headband that is tied around the forehead of a ruler as he accedes to office. This expression is often found in the phrase *hok'ah ti ahawlel*, meaning "he came out (or was tied) in the rulership."

SACRIFICE, CONJURING, AND SCATTERING

Once, scholars believed that the Maya were a peaceful people who did not have any interest in war. Now we know that warfare was extremely common in ancient Maya times and that the competition over the control of various places was of great importance to the ruling elite. Several glyphs express the concept of bloodletting, some concerned with the sacrifice of captives and some concerned with a personal ritual letting of blood from one's own body in order to honor the ancestors.

The glyph *ch'am* or *ch'ab*, "to sacrifice" or "to harvest," is usually used in the context of sacrifice of a prisoner of war. The Maya devised several gruesome methods of torture and sacrifice including, but not limited to, rip-ping out the fingernails, cutting open the body so the entrails fell out, cutting off the head, and removing the heart.

Less grisly versions of bloodletting are the self-inflicted rites meant to honor the ancestors. These might include piercing certain body parts with sharp object such as stingray spines or thorns. One glyph that may refer to this act is read *chok*, "to scatter," as in *u chok ch'ah*, "he scattered drops." This may refer to the scattering of one's own drops of blood as an offering and may also refer to the act of scattering incense into the fire.

The Maya believed personal bloodletting induced visions, so self-sacrifice seems to have been done by the ancient Maya in order to gain contact with their ancestors. A glyph for this reads *tzak*, "to make manifest" or "to conjure." Sometimes epigraphers find the phrase *u tzak k'uh*, "he conjured the gods."

WAR AND CAPTURE

Warfare was a common occurrence in ancient Maya times. One glyph that expresses war is a sign of a star over the sign for earth. The origin of this glyphic compound may reflect an ancient Maya practice of timing war with certain astronomical events in the evening sky. Mayanists do not know how to read this glyph, however in the literature on the Maya, one will find references to the star-over-earth glyph or a star-war event. A glyph that certainly and specifically refers to the taking of a war captive is read *chukah*, or "was captured."

DEATH AND BURIAL

Often when a ruler died, this information was recorded in the texts as a natural historic event. There are several ways to express death. One glyph reads *kimi*, "died." Others are more metaphorical, such as *och bih*, "entered the road," and *och ha'*, "entered the water." Another rather beautiful metaphorical expres-

Birth

Sihahi
was born

U ? kab
he touched
the earth

Huli
He arrived

Death

Kimi
He died

Och bi
He entered
the road

Och ha'
he entered
the water

U k'ay u sak niiknal
it died, his white
maize flower

Accession

Ch'am
To receive,
display

?? Ahaw
was seated
as Ahaw

Chumwan ti Ahawlel
was seated as Ahaw

Hok'ah
He tied,
He exted

Hok'ah ti Ahawlel
He came out in
the rulership

Sacrifice, Scattering, Conjuring, War, and Capture

Ch'ab/ch'am
To harvest,
to sacrifice

Chok
To scatter
drops

U chok ch'ah
He scattered

Tzak
To make
manifest,
conjure up

tzak k'uh
He conjured
the gods

"Star-over-Shell"
warfare

Chukah
was
captured

Titles

Bakab
"stood-up
one"

Ah K'una
He of the
books

Ch'ahom
"scatterer"

Y'ahaw K'ak'
Lord of the fire

Yahaw Te'
Lord of the
tree

Ahaw
Lord

Sahal
Secondary
Lord

Relationship Expressions

Yal
child of
mother

U nikil
child of
father

Yunen
he is the
child of

Yitz'in
His younger
brother

Suku winik
older brother
person

Yatan
his wife

10.6   *Examples of some known glyphs.*   (Drawings by Ruth Krochock after Harris and Sterns, 1997)

sion for death reads *u k'ay u sak nik nal*, "it died, his white maize flower."

OTHER VERBS

Many other activities are recorded in hieroglyphic inscriptions. Some of these include *ak'ot*, "to dance"; *hom*, "to complete"; *u k'al*, "was closed"; *tz'ap*, "to set up" or "to erect" a monument, such as a stela; *yilah*, "he witnessed" or "he saw"; and *hoch' k'ak'*, "to drill fire."

Emblem Glyphs

In 1958, Heinrich Berlin found the first key to understanding Classic Maya historical politics. He discovered certain glyphic compounds, which he called emblem glyphs, recorded in hieroglyphic texts. He hypothesized that these glyphs served as place-names associated with specific sites or as the names of lineages or families at those sites. We now know that they function as royal titles linking rulers or other high-ranking persons to a specific site. The glyphic compound consists of three major parts: a prefix to the main sign that reads, *k'uhul*, or "divine"; another element that reads, *ahaw*, or "lord"; and then a main, variable element that represents the name of a particular site. In other words, an emblem glyph would read *k'uhul X ahaw*, or "divine X lord," X representing the name of the site. There are now more than 50 emblem glyphs that have been identified in hieroglyphic inscriptions and on painted ceramics.

Titles

When rulers and other important people are mentioned in hieroglyphic texts, their names

Bonampak Calakmul Copán Naranjo Palenque

Piedras Negras Quiriguá Seibal Yaxchilán

10.7 A carved emblem glyph of the site of Dos Pilas and, below, other examples of emblem glyphs. (Photo courtesy Peter Selverstone; drawings by Ruth Krochock after Harris and Sterns, 1997)

are often followed by additional titles. The titles help to further identify the person or to accentuate his important accomplishments. These titles include *ahaw*, "lord"; *sahal*, a title for secondary lord; *chok*, literally "sprout," used to describe a young person; *bakab*, "stood-up one"; *k'inich*, "sun-faced"; *ch'ahom*, literally "dripper," perhaps referring to one who throws incense into the fire; *y'ahaw k'ak*, "lord of the fire"; *y'ahawte*, "lord of the tree"; *u chan*, "the guardian of," invariably identifying a person as the guard of a captive; *ah k'al bak*, "he of 20 captives"; *ah k'u hun*, "he of the sacred books"; *ah tzi'b*, "he the scribe"; and *itz'at*, "artist" or "sage."

Relationship Glyphs

An important part of justifying one's right to rule as king of a Maya city is having the correct parents. Nearly all Maya rulers who recorded their history on public monuments wanted others to see that they had been born of royal blood. The way we see this in inscriptions is with a device known as a parentage statement. In short, this phrase is constructed as follows: Person *X* is the child of the mother *Y* and the father *Z*. Glyphs that are used to express the idea that someone is the child of his mother include *u huntan*, "her cherished one," and *yal*, "her child." A glyph whose reading is not known but whose meaning is known to be "mother of" appears in phrases constructed as follows: Person *X* is the "mother of" child *Y*. A similar compound that works in reverse and whose precise reading is also unknown but has the meaning "child of mother" appears in the following construction: Child *X* is "the child of mother" *Y*. A variant of this glyph is the image of a baby bird inside the open mouth of an adult bird. Glyphs that are used to express a father-child relationship include one that reads *u nikil*, "he is the flower of," and another that reads, *yunen*, "he is the child of." Other relationships are also expressed in the inscriptions, such as *yitz'in*, "his younger brother"; *suku winik*, "older brother person"; *yatan*, "his wife"; *yichan*, "mother's brother"; *mam*, "maternal grandfather"; and *mim*, "grandmother."

Objects Mentioned in Glyphs

Countless objects are mentioned throughout Maya texts. Just a few of these include *u tz'ib*, "his/her writing"; *tun*, "stone"; *pakal*, "shield"; *pibnah*, "underground sweat bath"; *eb*, "stair"; *u wohol*, "his/her glyphs"; *yotot*, "his/her house"; *paka'*, "lintel"; and *lakam tun*, "stela."

Directions and Colors

Glyphs exist for the four cardinal directions and several different colors. The direction glyphs are *xaman*, "north"; *nohol*, "south"; *lak'in*, "east"; and *chik'in*, "west." The known color glyphs include *chak*, "red"; *sak*, "white"; *yax*, "blue-green"; *kan*, "yellow"; and *ek*, "black."

Place-Names

As more advances are made in decipherment, many new toponyms, or place-names, are being identified. Some of these include a glyph that reads *nal*, or "place"; for example, *hem nal*, meaning "valley place," and *chan nal*, for "sky place." Other place-names include *ox witik* and *mo' witz*, both meaning "macaw mountain" and referring to two places at the site of Copán; *sak ha' witznal*, meaning "clear water mountain place"; and *lakam ha'*, or "great water" place.

INSCRIPTIONS ON PUBLIC MONUMENTS

The range of information that appears on public monuments is limited in scope. The topics that dominate the texts are those deemed politically and historically important for the documentation of legitimacy of the ruler and other members of the royal family and court.

The Ideal Text

DATE

The ideal text will begin with a Long Count date that is the dedication date of the monument. This is followed by supplementary information about the phase of the moon and other cycles the Maya used to further anchor the dedication date in time. Alternatively, a shorter version of the date may be used, which includes only the day and month (see Chapter 9 for a discussion of Maya dates).

VERBS

The date is then followed by a series of events, or verbs, that can be thought of as a biography of the ruler. These may include birth, accession, taking of war captives, observance of various ceremonies and rituals, visits with foreign dignitaries, documentation of parentage, the birth of heirs to the throne, involvement of various patron deities who oversee the events and provide protection or additional legitimization to the ruler, the ruler's death and burial, and the accession of the next successor to the throne. Several events may be mentioned in a single text separated by glyphs known as distance numbers, which identify how much time has elapsed between the events, so that most can be dated with the exactitude of the original Long Count date.

SUBJECT

The name of the protagonist, with his or her various titles, follows the date and verbal phrases.

Reconstructing a Dynasty

Of course, most texts are far from ideal; the date is corrupted, the name is eroded, or the inscription is too brief to be useful. Even when the texts are not ideal, the entire set of them at a site can provide enough information for epigraphers to reconstruct the dynastic sequence, that is, the list of kings and queens who ruled at a particular site. Information from other sites can also be useful.

Throughout the course of Maya history from the Early Classic to the Terminal Classic Periods, there were hundreds of rulers and their successors who held political office. The site of Tikal, which can boast the longest known historical record on Maya public monuments, had a dynastic sequence that included at least 33 rulers who reigned from c. 90 to c. 889. Other sites were occupied for a much shorter period of time. For example, the site of Dos Pilas was established around 650 and fell shortly after 800; it was ruled by only nine different rulers or so.

YAXCHILÁN: A SAMPLE DYNASTIC HISTORY

Since it would be impossible to review all the dynastic sequences in Maya history in this chapter, a more detailed view of the history of royal succession of just one site, Yaxchilán, will serve as the primary example.

Early Yaxchilán Rulers   The earliest rulers of Yaxchilán appear in the Early Classic Period during the mid-sixth century. A series of four lintels that were carved in approximately 550 (Lintels 11, 49, 37, and 35) provides us with the beginning of Yaxchilán's dynastic history by listing the accession of its first 10 rulers. At the beginning of Lintel 11, the first ruler, or founder, named Yoaat B'alam I, is identified as *u nah tal chum ahaw*, or "the first seated lord." His reign began in c. 359. He was succeeded by nine other rulers who reigned until approximately 537. Each ruler's name is preceded by a similar expression stating the position he held

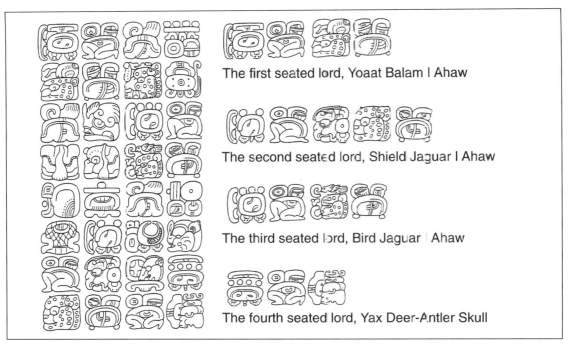

The first seated lord, Yoaat Balam I Ahaw

The second seated lord, Shield Jaguar I Ahaw

The third seated lord, Bird Jaguar I Ahaw

The fourth seated lord, Yax Deer-Antler Skull

10.8   Reconstructing the Yaxchilán dynastic sequence: Lintel 11 lists the first four rulers of Yaxchilán.
(Drawing by Nikolai Grube)

in the dynastic sequence; for example, the second ruler, Shield Jaguar I, is introduced with the phrase *u ka' tal chum ahaw*, or "the second seated lord." The third ruler, Bird Jaguar I, ruled from 378 to 389. The succession continued with Yax Deer-Antler Skull I, ruling from approximately 389 to 402, and then Ruler 5 for whom no more detailed information is available. The sixth ruler was named K'inich Tatb'u Skull I, and the seventh ruler, Moon Skull, who ruled from c. 454 to 467. The eighth ruler, Bird Jaguar II, took office in about 467. We have a bit more information about him than we have for some of the earlier rulers. Bird Jaguar II's wife was named Lady Chuwen, and together they had two sons, Knot-Eye Jaguar I and K'inich Tatb'u Skull II, who would become the ninth and 10th rulers, respectively. Knot-Eye Jaguar I ruled from c. 508 to 518, and his brother, K'inich Tatb'u Skull II, held office from 526 to 537.

Following the tidy listing of the first 10 rulers, the existing hieroglyphic record is not as easily read due to its weather-worn condition. Epigraphers have determined that four rulers held office between 537 and 629; however, only one, Knot-Eye Jaguar II, can be identified with certainty.

The next ruler, Bird Jaguar III, was in office from approximately 629 to 669. He is known primarily through the monuments later erected by his son, Shield Jaguar II, and grandson, Bird Jaguar IV. One such reference is on Hieroglyphic Stairway 3 (Step IV, B6) in front of Structure 44, a building devoted to the recording of Shield Jaguar II's military exploits and those of his royal ancestors. Other references appear on Stelae 3 and 6, which were commissioned by Bird Jaguar IV. In addition to his personal name, Bird Jaguar III carried the title *ah wak tun*, or "he of six *tuns.*" He is also called the 15th ruler and is said to be the guardian of the captive named Chakhal Te'.

Shield Jaguar the Great   The next ruler in the dynastic sequence is Itzamná B'alam, better known as Shield Jaguar II, who held office for 61 years, from 681 to 742. His father was Bird Jaguar III, and his mother, Lady Pakal, lived to be at least 98 years old. The majority of public monuments at Yaxchilán date to the reigns of Shield Jaguar II and his son, Bird Jaguar IV. Shield Jaguar II, known as Shield Jaguar the Great, significantly changed the appearance of Yaxchilán during his reign by erecting an impressive series of buildings adorned with hieroglyphic stairways, lintels, and associated stelae. Shield Jaguar's energetic building program may have begun in reaction to military conflicts with Piedras Negras, which resulted in the capture of a Yaxchilán lord. In reaction to this humiliation, Shield Jaguar drastically changed Yaxchilán's appearance to enhance his city's prestige and proclaim its independence. Many of the monuments erected at this time by Shield Jaguar II boast of his prowess as a warrior and his taking of numerous captives: Ah Nik from the site called Maan, Ah K'an Usha from B'uktuun, Popol Chay from Lancanhá, another captive named Ah Sak Ichiy Pat, and finally a lord from the site of Hix Witz. Three of the most brilliantly carved lintels ever produced (Yaxchilán Lintels 24, 25, and 26) appear above the doorways of Structure 23, which is identified as the house of Shield Jaguar's principal wife, Lady K'abaal Xook, better known as Lady Xoc (see figures 2.10, page 57; 6.13, page 192; and 6.14, page 193).

Accession Text of Bird Jaguar the Great
Yaxchilán Stela 12 is a good example of a public inscription, and it provides specific infor-mation about the transfer of power from Shield Jaguar II to the next ruler, his son, Yaxun B'alam or Bird Jaguar IV. The inscription opens with a date of 6 Ix 12 Yaxk'in, which translates to June 19, 742, in our calendar. We next learn that on this date someone has died. The death expression used is the metaphor *k'ayi u sak nik nal*, or "died his white maize flower." After the verb we find out who has died: It is a person named with the titles *ch'ahom*, or "incense offerer," and 5 K'atun Ahaw, indicating that the person is a noble lord, or *ahaw*, who lived into his fifth *k'atun* of life, making him over 78 years old. This phrase is followed by the personal name of the ruler known as Shield Jaguar II. He is then named as the *u chan* (guardian) of a prisoner named Ah Nik (He of Flowers). In summary, the text states that on June 19, 742, the ruler, Shield Jaguar II died. He was the incense offerer and was more than 78 years old. He was the guardian of the captive Ah Nik.

The text continues with a distance number, an expression that announces a change in dates (*u tz'akah*, or "its change"). In this instance, the new date occurs after Shield Jaguar's death, and it is determined by counting forward 6 *k'ins* and 10 *tuns* (6 days plus 10 periods of 360 days, or 3,606 days) to the next event. The new phrase begins with an expression that is read *iwai ut*, or "and then it happened," followed by the date 11 Ahaw 8 Sek (May 3, 752). On this date we find the verbal phrase, *chumwan ti ahaw*, or "he was seated in office as lord." The person being installed is named with an expression that likens him to the sky god and another expression that names him as the guardian of the captive named Ah Uk. Following is the personal name of Shield Jaguar II's son, Bird Jaguar IV, also called Bird Jaguar the Great. As he is succeeding his father as ruler, he is now named *k'ul ahaw*, or "holy lord," of Yaxchilán and is additionally called *bakab*, or "the stood-up one." In free translation the last half of this

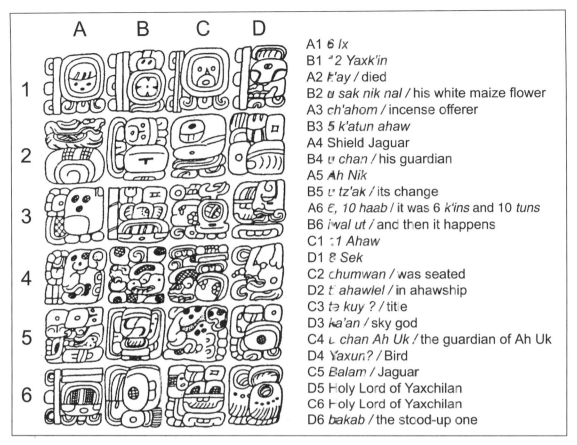

A1 6 *Ix*
B1 2 *Yax'kin*
A2 *t'ay* / died
B2 *u sak nik nal* / his white maize flower
A3 *ch'ahom* / incense offerer
B3 5 *k'atun ahaw*
A4 Shield Jaguar
B4 *u chan* / his guardian
A5 *Ah Nik*
B5 *u tz'ak* / its change
A6 *6, 10 haab* / it was 6 *k'ins* and 10 *tuns*
B6 *iwal ut* / and then it happens
C1 11 *Ahaw*
D1 8 *Sek*
C2 *chumwan* / was seated
D2 *t' ahawlel* / in ahawship
C3 *ta kuy ?* / title
D3 *ka'an* / sky god
C4 *u chan Ah Uk* / the guardian of Ah Uk
D4 *Yaxun?* / Bird
C5 *Balam* / Jaguar
D5 Holy Lord of Yaxchilan
C6 Holy Lord of Yaxchilan
D6 *bakab* / the stood-up one

10.9 A decipherment of the text from Yaxchilán Stela 12. (Drawing by Linda Schele, copyright David Schele)

text is, "The date changed 3,606 days forward to reach the date May 3, 752, when Bird Jaguar IV (Shield Jaguar's son) was seated as lord. He is the guardian of Ah Uk. He is like the sky god. He is the holy lord of Yaxchilán. He is the stood-up one."

Political Intrigue The Stela 12 text poses an interesting problem in the royal succession at Yaxchilán, because it reveals that 10 years lapsed between the death of Shield Jaguar II and the accession of Bird Jaguar IV. Until recently, epigraphers could only speculate on the answer to the question of royal succession. Some suggested that a serious power struggle took place that prevented anyone from officially taking the throne. A new reading of a panel from Piedras Negras by Simon Martin and Nikolai Grube, however, may have solved the mystery. The panel asserts that a "holy lord of Yaxchilán" was present at a celebration for Ruler 4 of Piedras Negras in the year 749, in the middle of the so-called interregnum (742–752) at Yaxchilán. Martin and Grube now suggest that this person, Yoaat B'alam II, may have been the ruler of

Yaxchilán at this time, perhaps under the control of Piedras Negras. This interpretation is still open to debate, however, since no monuments that discuss Yoaat B'alam II's reign survive at Yaxchilán. If they had ever been there, they have been removed or intentionally deleted from history.

Bird Jaguar's Reign   Bird Jaguar IV took office in 752, about two months after the birth of his son Shield Jaguar III. Some epigraphers have suggested that for political reasons that are still not well understood, Bird Jaguar IV had to produce an heir before he could rightfully take office. It is worth noting that Bird Jaguar's mother, Lady Ik'Skull from Calakmul, one of Shield Jaguar II's lesser wives, was never mentioned in any of Shield Jaguar II's monuments. The lower status of Bird Jaguar's mother in comparison to Lady Xoc may have also contributed to the long delay before Bird Jaguar IV acceded to the throne. After his 10-year wait to take office, he was extremely anxious to justify his position. Like his father, he continued to add to the architectural splendor of the site with approximately 12 new buildings and at least 33 public monuments carved with hieroglyphic inscriptions. In the inscriptions, Bird Jaguar IV glorified his royal status and promoted that of his mother and his son. Again, like his father, he celebrated his prowess as a warrior by proudly listing his captives. Eventually, he took the title *ah k'al bak*, or "he of 20 captives," as though there were simply too many to count.

Shield Jaguar III   Bird Jaguar IV's last monument, Lintel 9, was dated four months before his death in October 768. Probably aware that death would soon come, he wanted to ensure a smooth transition of power to his son. On Lintel 9, Bird Jaguar IV recorded a ceremony he performed with his brother-in-law, Great Skull, entrusting him with Shield Jaguar III's

installation as the next ruler of Yaxchilán. Great Skull apparently carried out Bird Jaguar IV's wishes because within four months after the death of his father, Shield Jaguar III acceded to office.

Shield Jaguar III ruled from c. 769 to 800. Like his father and grandfather, he boasted of his accomplishments in war and eventually was credited with taking 16 captives. He also attempted to continue a building program for the site. At the beginning of his reign, he was relatively successful, but as time went on, building efforts declined and the quality of the carved monuments suffered. During his reign, he was responsible for erecting Structure 20, perhaps his finest architectural accomplishment. This structure was decorated with three hieroglyphic lintels (Lintels 12, 13, and 14) and Hieroglyphic Stairway 5, whose inscription extended in a single band running across the full length of the monument. Also associated with Structure 20 are altars and the stelae 3, 4, 5, 6, 7, and 33. With Lady Ch'ab Ahaw, Shield Jaguar III produced a son, K'inich Tatb'u Skull III, who would be his successor to the throne.

The Last Ruler   K'inch Tatb'u Skull III, Yaxchilán's last ruler, took office shortly after his father's reign ended in c. 800. Unlike his ancestors, he erected only one hieroglyphic lintel, Lintel 10, which was poorly executed. The lintel was set in Structure 3 and proclaimed at the end of the text that he had captured Ruler 7 of Piedras Negras. But any success he may have experienced in war was not able to save Yaxchilán from its ultimate decline.

DYNASTIC HISTORIES AND RULER BIAS

The reconstructed dynastic sequence at Yaxchilán is typical of the kind of public record found at any given Classic or Late Classic

Maya site. The rulers of the major Maya cities had similar concerns regarding the messages they put on public display for the entire community to view and read. While each Maya site had its own unique style and design, many themes were common to all, including the ruler's desire to govern successfully and win wars.

Some archaeologists have argued that Maya hieroglyphic writing is too filled with propaganda to be useful history. While it is certainly true that Maya rulers promoted their legitimacy or sometimes glorified their elite status with exaggerated claims, this kind of bias is common in any written history. For this reason, Mayanists need to evaluate history for its point of view and accuracy and epigraphers need to analyze hieroglyphic texts by taking into account the many factors that may have influenced the content of the text. The careful epigrapher will consider the archaeological history of the site, the political stability of the site at the time of writing, and whether the ruler is in a position where he must scramble to convince his public that he is fit to rule before the epigrapher decides how to interpret the contents of the text in question. Inscriptions from other sites, whether allies or enemies, also provide corrections to the accounts of individual rulers.

When trying to evaluate the validity of hieroglyphic inscriptions, it may be useful to reflect on our own political policies and behaviors at election time, for example, or when attempting to inspire public acceptance of a king or queen. Recent investigations about the modern-day issue of "truth in advertising" may be applied to the ancient Maya; in other words, while a Maya ruler may omit the fact that he has been humiliated or defeated in war, no false claims to war victories have yet been discovered. This suggests that on the whole, the fabric of historical information tends to be truthful.

Terminal Classic Inscriptions

While Yaxchilán tended to adhere to all the expected patterns regarding the production of hieroglyphic texts and architecture, the Terminal Classic site of Chichén Itzá presents a unique pattern. The collapse of the southern lowland cities basically ended public inscriptions of the kind of dynastic history exemplified by Yaxchilán. Public inscriptions and the ancient Maya history they contained would soon die out completely, but initially, the city of Chichén Itzá continued carving inscriptions into monuments.

At the end of the Classic Period, a time when the great Maya centers of the southern lowlands were collapsing, Chichén Itzá in northern Yucatán grew and prospered. One key to Chichén Itzá's success may have been its rejection of the dynastic ruler cult and its control of a pan-Mesoamerican long-distance trade network (see Chapter 2). From the founding of the city, the rulers of Chichén Itzá established a new program of political rhetoric.

The hieroglyphic inscriptions of Chichén Itzá appear on the lintels and panels of at least 17 major structures. These texts comprise one of the largest bodies of extant texts in northern Yucatán, although the corpus of inscriptions is continually growing as more archaeological investigations are accomplished. Chichén Itzá's use of public hieroglyphic writing covers a period of 166 years, between 832 and 998. As some scholars suggest, the tradition of public writing in the southern kingdoms no longer sustained the political system, and, in fact, it was too central to the institution of dynastic kingship to survive the collapse. In contrast, hieroglyphic inscriptions at Chichén Itzá remained important, especially in elite residences and palaces. But their content conveyed a different message.

The inscriptions at Chichén Itzá document the collective participation of the nobility in rituals such as house dedications, the drilling of fires, ball-court-related activities, bloodletting, and family or lineage affiliation. The elite at Chichén Itzá still used hieroglyphic writing and iconography to disseminate political information, but they changed the style of presentation to accommodate their involvement in pan-Mesoamerican trade. Writing was used primarily in elite residences, whereas elaborate programs of narrative art without hieroglyphic texts were displayed in the central plaza. Chichén Itzá had become a great cosmopolitan center that could accommodate multiethnic and multilingual visitors from distant regions of Mesoamerica.

It has been suggested that a system of joint, rather than dynastic, rule existed at Chichén Itzá (see Chapter 3). The inscriptions at Chichén Itzá mention many individuals with numerous titles, and no great dynasty is described. In contrast to the 33 generations of rulers found at Tikal, for example, only the mothers and grandmothers of Chichén Itzá's nobility are mentioned. This pattern clearly diverges from what Mayanists have found in southern lowland texts, in which a political hierarchy is made obvious.

A difficulty in identifying the primary ruler at Chichén Itzá comes from the fact that there is no known emblem glyph for that city or most other nearby sites. Identification of a contemporary ruler in the southern lowlands inscriptions is usually made simpler because he or she will be called the *k'ul ahaw* (divine lord) of a particular site. Without this information at Chichén Itzá, identification of a primary ruler has been challenging.

More recent readings of the inscriptions, however, have led many to believe that the person known as K'ak'upakal (Fire-His-Shield) should be considered the primary leader at Chichén Itzá and should perhaps be thought of as the "first speaker" in a ruling council. Evidence for this idea comes from a reading of the phrase *u tahal*, meaning "his words" or "he speaks," which appears several times in the texts of the Temple of the Four Lintels. The *u tahal* expression seems to be associated primarily with K'ak'upakal supporting the notion that he was identified as "first speaker" and thus ranks higher in status than his associates. Although the political structure at Chichén Itzá was distinctive from that of the southern lowland cities, its exact nature remains unclear.

Relationship expressions in the inscriptions of Chichén Itzá also differ from examples in the southern Classic Period texts in that descent from women, rather than both men and women, is emphasized. This emphasis on female descent may indicate, as it does in the Classic inscriptions from the southern lowlands, that there was likely some problem with the legitimacy of male descent for the purposes of rulership. Whether this emphasis on female descent at Chichén Itzá is an indication of the abandonment of the system of patrilineal dynastic descent found previously in southern lowland cities or indicates that the male Itzá rulers of Chichén Itzá came to the city from elsewhere, as some believe (see Chapter 2), and married into prestigious local families is debatable. It does however suggest that prominent women could legitimatize power and heritage, even though they were not emphasized in the hieroglyphic texts.

Diversity in Public Inscriptions

The contrasts in the public inscriptions of Chichén Itzá and Yaxchilán demonstrate that public pronouncements were tailor-made for and by the elite who lived at the cities. Many basic similarities existed from city to city, but each expressed itself in its own way and defined itself by what the people who wrote the texts chose to put on public display.

Maya Vase Writing

Late Classic Period polychrome vases were sometimes painted with hieroglyphic texts that contained elaborate information, such as kings' lists and creation myths (see figure 6.3, page 173). But most were painted with a band of glyphs around the rim that were so mysterious that some art historians argued they were pseudoglyphs. Pseudoglyphs are signs that only resemble hieroglyphic characters but do not express a coherent message. Some artists did decorate ceramic vessels and stone monuments with these pseudoglyphs, perhaps because they wanted the object to appear that it carried a hieroglyphic text but did not know how to write using true Maya hieroglyphics. In 1973, Michael Coe published *The Maya Scribe and his World* in which he illustrated Classic Maya ceramics and related works of art. In this study, he recognized that the hieroglyphic texts painted around the rim of the ceramics were organized in formulaic and repeating patterns that he termed the Primary Standard Sequence (PSS). At that time, he hypothesized that the texts were funerary chants because many of these ceramics had been recovered from tombs.

While Coe's initial hypothesis eventually proved to be incorrect, his careful analysis inspired other epigraphers to forge ahead with new decipherments. From the work of these epigraphers, the structure of these texts is now understood. The texts include hieroglyphs describing various types of pottery and their uses, as well as the names and titles of their owners and even the names of the scribes who painted the texts and accompanying art.

The Primary Standard Sequence

No two vessel texts are exactly the same, but most include similar or substituting elements that can be separated into five different sections. First comes the presentation section of the text, which includes an introductory statement announcing that the vessel came into being, was presented, and was blessed by the gods.

The second section describes the surface treatment of the vessel. A text might describe whether the vessel was painted or carved, or it might say that the surface of the vessel was blessed to receive its writing.

Third is a section that names the type of ceramic vessel on which the text appears. In some cases the vessel is in the form of a vase, described as *yuch'ab*, or "his/her drinking vessel." Other examples include the phrases *u lak*, or "his/her plate," or *u hawte'*, "his/her tripod plate."

The fourth section records the intended contents of the vessel. The most common content is a chocolate beverage made from the fruit of the cacao tree. Cacao is spelled out phonetically in the glyphs as *ka-ka-wa*. Sometimes the *kakaw* glyph is preceded by an expression that reads *ta yutal*, meaning "for food of . . . ," other times by the phrase *yuch'ab ta yutal kakaw*, or "his drinking vessel for his food cacao." Another food that is sometimes indicated in the text is a corn beverage known in Spanish as *atole* and in Mayan as *sa'* or *ul*. Atole, which is still a daily part of the Maya diet, is made from cooked corn mixed with water. It can be made either thin enough to drink or thick as a gruel and is usually sweetened with honey or sugar.

Not surprisingly, certain vessel types are better for certain foods. The tall, cylindrical vases are usually meant for drinking liquid foods such as beverages made from cacao, while bowls are designated to be used for thicker foods such as *ul* or *atole*. In the hiero-

here	was wrapped	its surface	their drinking vessel
alay	*k'ahl-aj*	*y-ich*	*(y)-uk'ab*

here
alay

was wrapped
k'ahl-aj

Maize Lord
Aj-Ik'

10.10   Above and right: Rollout photograph of a Maya cylinder vase and a translation of its hieroglyphic text.   (Photo copyright Justin Kerr, file K1183; drawing by Barbara MacLeod from Reents-Budet, 1994, translation by Barbara MacLeod, 2001)

glyphic texts on plates, however, the food intended for its use is rarely indicated. When plates are illustrated in the art, they are usually filled with solid foods such as *wah*, literally "maize bread," or tamales.

The fifth and last section of formulaic text is the closure. This section includes descriptive characteristics and the name and titles of the individual who owns the vessel. Examples of these phrases might be *chak ch'ok*, or "great lineage member," or *k'ul chahtan winik*, "sacred person of the dark place." In some cases, the person's profession might be mentioned, such as *itz'at*, "artist." In other cases, the person's political affiliation, such as *k'ul ahaw*, meaning "holy lord" of a specific site, might appear.

Codex-Style Vessels

In addition to ceramic vessels that contain a formal Primary Standard Sequence text around the rim, there are other vessels called codex-style pottery that seem to have been used among a broad segment of society. (See figure 6.9, page 186.) In general, the execution of the construction and decoration tends to be poor in comparison to those vessels that definitely come from elite contexts. Usually the same type of information is included in the text, but some codex-style vessels are adorned with hieroglyphic texts over a large portion of the surface of the vessel. One exceptional vessel contains a long hieroglyphic text that records a king list from the site of Calakmul.

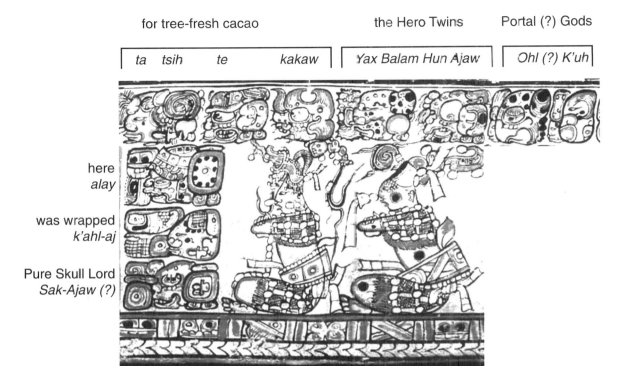

for tree-fresh cacao   the Hero Twins   Portal (?) Gods

ta tsih te kakaw   *Yax Balam Hun Ajaw*   *Ohl (?) K'uh*

here
alay

was wrapped
k'ahl-aj

Pure Skull Lord
Sak-Ajaw (?)

Chocholá

Not all Maya ceramics that bear hieroglyphic texts are painted. A type of ceramic known as Chocholá, generally found in northern Yucatán, is carved rather than painted. These vessels also contain Primary Standard Sequence texts around the rims, and they tend to follow the same pattern as the painted texts.

NAME-TAGGING AND OWNERSHIP OF OBJECTS

Before much was known about the content of Maya inscriptions, many scholars speculated that they always contained esoteric, even mystical information. As decipherment has progressed in recent years, epigraphers have found that inscriptions were often used for ordinary purposes. An example of this is what has been termed name-tagging, that is, the labeling of personal possessions with the owner's name.

Portable Objects

The first example of name-tagging was recognized by Peter Mathews on a pair of ear spools, large ear ornaments that were worn like earrings, from a Classic Maya royal tomb at the site of Altun Há in Belize. An inscription that extended from one ear spool to the next, with three glyphs on each, simply read *u tup*, or "his ear spools," followed by the name of the owner.

Other examples have been seen from vase writing in which the inscriptions contain a phrase such as *u lak*, or "his plate," followed by the owner's and/or artist's name.

Public Monuments

Name-tagging did not only appear on small portable objects. Phrases, such as *u kohow*, or "his helmet," and *u hal*, "his necklace," appear in the monumental inscriptions of Palenque. On monuments at Yaxchilán, expressions like *u bak*, meaning "his prisoner," identify the name of individuals who have been taken captive in war. An example of this is the phrase *Ah Nik u bak Itzam B'alam*, or "Ah Nik is the prisoner of Shield Jaguar." At the site of Chichén Itzá, it is evident on Lintel 1 of the Temple of the Four Lintels, which declares the building to be the house of a sky god known in literature as Yax T'ul. The phrase reads *yotot*, or "his house," followed by the owner's name. On Lintel 3 of the same building, the doorway where the lintel is located is tagged as belonging to another sky god known as Double Jawbone by the phrase *u k'al*, roughly meaning "his enclosure," followed by the name of the god. At Copán, inscriptions identify individual stelae as belonging to a person in an expression that reads *u te tun*, or "his stone tree." Some of the stone monuments from the site of Piedras Negras contain the name phrases of the artists who helped produce the carvings, tagging them as *their* work.

THE MAYA CODICES

Among the treasures that were taken from the people of Yucatán in 1519 by the conqueror Hernán Cortés and his soldiers were some screenfold books, most likely Maya codices.

Shortly after these books and other items were brought back to Europe, they began to attract attention. Giovanni Ruffo da Forlì, archbishop of Cosenza and papal nuncio at the Spanish court, described the codices in a letter he wrote on March 7, 1520, in the town of Valladolid, Yucatán. He noted that the painted manuscripts were folded into books measuring less than a handspan in width and were decorated with figures and signs similar to Arabic or Egyptian letters.

Screenfold Books

Peter Martyr, historiographer to the Spanish court, secretary of the Council of the Indies, and friend of Ruffo, also described the codices in one of his works dating between 1520 and 1526. He recounted that the books were made of the thin inner bark of a tree, now known to be the fig tree, fashioned into long sheets (see Chapter 11). The sheets were covered with a lime wash to create a smooth, white surface, folded accordian fashion, and painted on one or both sides. The books are made to be viewed two pages at a time, with the other pages folded underneath. Martyr correctly speculated that the books contained information pertaining to laws, ceremonies, agriculture, computations, and astronomy. When not in use, the documents were folded up and protected with outer covers made of wood, making them resemble modern books. On painted Maya ceramics, there are depictions of screenfold books that appear to be covered with jaguar pelt covers.

Destruction of Codices

The humid environmental conditions of the Maya lowlands are not conducive to the preservation of organic materials such as Maya bark-paper manuscripts, and for this reason, these documents were not destined to survive the elements. Even though books were written by Maya living in the more temperate Guatemalan highlands, these have not survived in their original hieroglyphic codex form.

The Spanish priests who were stationed in the New World as missionaries believed that the books represented pagan beliefs that were contrary to the teachings of the Catholic Church. Individuals such as Friar Diego de Landa, Antonio de Ciudad de Real, and Friar Luis de Villalpando were responsible for the destruction and burning of the hieroglyphic texts. The most famous of these was Landa, who burned dozens of hieroglyphic books in bonfires in a 1562 auto-da-fé in the town of Maní, Yucatán. Landa was chastised by the Spanish Crown for his harsh actions and was called back to Spain where he remained for 11 years. During this time, he was put on trial for his crimes, accused of oppressing the customs, culture, and the antiquities of the people of Yucatán. As part of his defense, he prepared his manuscript *Relación de las cosas de Yucatán*. Landa's document recorded a wealth of information about Maya culture and society, including knowledge about the hieroglyphic texts that he had destroyed. Ironically, it was this information about the Maya "alphabet" that ultimately led to the decipherment of the Maya hieroglyphic script. Landa was acquitted and allowed to return as bishop to Yucatán in 1573, but the burned books were gone forever. Landa recorded that their loss afflicted the Maya to a surprising degree.

Surviving Codices

Only four Maya codices are known to remain from the contact period. Three of them were removed from Yucatán at the time of the conquest and brought to Europe. These codices, known today as the *Dresden, Paris,* and *Madrid Codices,* were named for the libraries in Europe

in which they were kept. A fourth codex, the *Grolier,* apparently never left Mexico until the 20th century. After being exhibited at the Grolier Club in New York City in 1971, it became known as the *Grolier Codex.*

DRESDEN CODEX

The *Dresden Codex* may be one of the documents that was taken by Cortés from Mexico in 1519 to Europe. From then onward, the whereabouts of the manuscript were unknown until it was acquired in Vienna in 1739 by Johann Christian Götze, director of the Saxon Royal Library in Dresden, from a private owner. It took quite some time before the codices became known and accessible to the public. In 1810, the scientist Alexander von Humboldt first published five pages from the *Dresden Codex.* In 1829 and 1830, Edward King, Viscount Kingsborough began the publication of his *Antiquities of Mexico* in which Mexican manuscripts were illustrated. In Volume 3 of the series, he included the first reproduction of all 74 pages (39 pages painted on both sides) of the *Dresden Codex.* This publication of the *Dresden Codex,* illustrated by the Italian artist Augustine Aglio, is especially precious for it reflects the original well-preserved state of the codex before it sustained water damage in the Dresden fire storm during World War II.

The *Dresden Codex* is arranged in a series of almanacs that provide instruction for the timing of various religious rituals. The almanacs contain information about the Moon Goddess and diseases, the astronomical cycles of the planet Venus and the Moon, *k'atun* prophecies, and the New Year ceremonies. Some scholars believe that the *Dresden Codex* includes a major source of astronomical information, containing tables for the synodical revolutions of Jupiter, Mars, Saturn, and Mercury. Others maintain that this information in the codex pertains only to the cycles of Venus and the predictions of lunar eclipses. The hieroglyphic texts, which include names, actions, and dates, are painted with red and black paint. These are accompanied by painted illustrations in blue, yellow, red, and black of the persons, deities, and objects discussed in the texts.

PARIS CODEX

It is not known for certain how or when another codex, now known as the *Paris Codex*, arrived in Europe. The manuscript, also called the *Codex Pérez* or *Codez Peresianus*, was bought by the Bibliothèque Impériale of Paris, France, in 1832. The *Paris Codex* was first drawn in 1835 by Augustine Aglio and was to appear in Volume 10 of the Kingsborough *Antiquities of Mexico*, however, due to Kingsborough's death, it was never published. In 1849, Joseph M. A. Aubin published a reference to the *Paris Codex*. In 1855, the Mexican scholar José F. Ramírez noted the similarity of the *Paris Codex* to the *Dresden Codex*, which he had seen in the Kingsborough publication, although his commentary would not be published for almost a century. In 1859, José Pérez published two descriptions of the *Paris Codex*, one with an illustration. In spite of this publication, the *Paris Codex* remained, for the most part, unknown to the general public. Shortly after Pérez worked with the manuscript, the 22-page fragment (11 pages painted on both sides) was found by Léon de Rosny. The manuscript was wrapped in a piece of paper labeled "Perez," and for this reason Rosny named the manuscript *Codex Pérez* or *Codex Peresianus*. It became known as the *Paris Codex*, however, to avoid confusion with the colonial period documents named after Juan Pio Pérez. In the early 1860s, Rosny finally brought the *Paris Codex* to the attention of the world.

) The first half of the *Paris Codex* records a sequence of *k'atuns* with their respective ceremonies and rituals. The Maya of Yucatán recorded various historical events, naming them for *k'atuns* and *tuns* within the *k'atuns*. The Maya priest would consult this table of events in order to determine the omens for the *tuns*, and this would aid him in making important decisions.

Pages 19 and 20 of the codex deal with the year-bearers, or days. These pages illustrate a 52-year sequence of year-bearers that begin the Maya 365-day year. Because of the mathematics involved in calculating time in the Maya calendar, with all of its interconnected cycles, only four of the 20 day names ever land on the first day of the Maya month Pohp. These four days are known as the year-bearers; in the *Paris Codex* they are Lamat, B'en, Etz'nab', and Ak'b'al.

There are some pages that deal with the arrangement of spirit forces the Maya thought to be present in both the Upperworld and the Underworld. Here, supernatural beings known as Pawahtuns are associated with sky, while the gods of death are thought to reign in the Underworld.

The codex also contains a zodiac of 13 animal signs that represent constellations in the night sky. The animals include two species of birds, a turtle, a bat, a scorpion, a rattlesnake, and other unidentified creatures that carry the sun glyph between their teeth or in their beak. Constellations in the form of these animals are thought to rule the night sky during successive periods of 28 days. There is a 28-day interval between the 13 signs, totaling a 364-day approximation of the solar year. Five zodiacs translate into seven rounds of the 260-day calendar, or *tzolk'in*. The zodiacs were used to predict certain astronomical events and to calculate when to perform certain activities.

Some consider the *Paris Codex* to be a handbook for Maya priests. The information recorded in its pages was intended to be used for divinatory purposes and allowed the priest to clearly see the workings of the universe.

MADRID CODEX

In 1866, Charles Etienne Brasseur de Bourbourg discovered the third Maya codex—actually a 70-page codex fragment—which he named the *Codex Troano* after its owner don Juan Tro y Ortolano, a professor of Spanish paleography in Madrid. In 1875, another 42-

page codex fragment was acquired by the Museo Arqueológico of Madrid, Spain. This fragment was named the *Codex Cortesianus* because it was thought to have been brought to Europe by Hernán Cortés. In 1880, Léon de Rosny photographed the fragment and found that it was a missing part of the *Codex Troano*. The two portions of the codex were reunited, and the manuscript became known as the *Codex Tro-Cortesianus* or *Madrid Codex*.

The *Madrid Codex* contains a series of almanacs based on the 260-day period of time known as the *tzolk'in*. This cycle interconnected with the 365-day cycle known as the *haab'*. As we have seen above, only four out of the 20 days could fall on the first day of the year: These days are known as the year-bearers. There are three different systems of year-bearers that were used during the Classic and Postclassic Periods. The first was used during the Classic Period and is called the Tikal calendar. The Tikal system year-bearers are Ik', Manik', Eb', and Kab'an. The Campeche calendar uses Ak'b'al, Lamat, Ben, and Etz'nab' as the year-bearers, as we saw in the *Paris Codex*. The Mayapán calendar year-bearers are K'an, Muluk, Ix, and Kawak. The *Madrid Codex* uses two of these calendars: the Tikal and the Mayapán.

The almanacs in the *Madrid Codex* cover a variety of themes including deer hunting, deer trapping, astronomical information, and information concerning certain deities. Other themes as marriage, beekeeping, weaving, rites to bring rain, and agriculture are also discussed and presented in the form of predictive or repeating almanacs.

GROLIER CODEX

Although the discovery location of the *Grolier Codex* is not entirely clear, it is thought to have been found in a dry cave near Tortuguero, in Chiapas, Mexico, within the last 30 years. The codex was acquired in 1965 by a Mexican collector at a flea market in Mexico City and was subsequently presented to the Grolier Club of New York for an art exhibition of Maya hieroglyphic art in 1971. In 1973, Michael Coe published a catalog for this exhibition, which included an illustration of this 11-page fragment of a Maya hieroglyphic book that once had an estimated 20 pages. The manuscript was initially the source of considerable debate because some thought it to be a forgery. It is now generally accepted as a legitimate Maya artifact, based on its hieroglyphic writing style and a radiocarbon date of 1230. The *Grolier Codex* is an astronomical table concerned with the cycles of the planet Venus.

POSTCONQUEST LITERATURE

Shortly after the Spanish arrived in the New World, the Maya of Mexico and Guatemala were forced to discontinue their use of hieroglyphic writing. Books and manuscripts written in hieroglyphs were considered to contain pagan and idolatrous beliefs that needed to be eradicated in order to make way for the introduction of Christianity. Missionaries learned to speak the Mayan languages and developed ways to write them using the Spanish alphabet so that they might bring Christian teachings to the Maya.

In time, the Maya adapted to this change and began to record native manuscripts using the Spanish alphabet. Some of these native chronicles may have been transcribed directly from original hieroglyphic books in attempts to save these sources of native history and knowledge from being forever lost to a rapidly changing world. The lyrical style of the writing in some of these documents suggests that they were originally meant to be recited aloud and performed for audiences rather than read as books. Several of these transcriptions have survived to the present day because they were cared for, copied and recopied over the years as they became worn, and eventually placed in libraries where they were protected from the elements. These documents record a wealth of information including native history, medicine, legends, poetry, drama, music, customs, beliefs, and other knowledge that had been passed down from generation to generation.

Popol Vuh

The *Popol Vuh* (Council Book) is a narrative that relates the Maya story of creation (see Chapter 6) and the history of the noble lords of the three ruling lineages of the Quiché: the Cauec, the Greathouses, and the Lords Quiché. Much like the ancient dynastic kings at Palenque, the Quiché lords related their rule to the creation gods: "This is the Beginning of the Ancient Word, here in this place called Quiché. Here we shall inscribe the Ancient Word, the potential and source for everything done in the citadel of Quiché, in the nation of the Quiché people" (Tedlock 1996: 71).

During the mid-16th century, the document was transcribed into the Quiché language using the Spanish alphabet by various Quiché nobles, who mostly remain anonymous. The authors stated that they were writing "amid the preaching of God, in Christendom now," perhaps to protect themselves against punishment for reviving pagan texts. In 1524, when Pedro de Alvarado conquered the Quiché capital of Utatlán, the ruling Quiché lords were burned at the stake. Those nobles who escaped fled about 25 kilometers (15 miles) south to what is now known as Chichicastenango, which is where the *Popol Vuh* was discovered in 1701. The Quiché transcription of the *Popol Vuh* was lost, but fortunately not before it was translated into Spanish between 1701 and 1703 by Francisco Ximénez, a Dominican priest who served at that time as the curate of Chichicastenango.

The Spanish version is now in the Newberry Library in Chicago.

The first two parts of the *Popol Vuh* consist of mythology, including the story of creation. The story begins with there being only sky and sea: "Whatever might be is simply not there: only murmurs, ripples, in the dark, in the night" (Tedlock 1996: 72). It then launches into the story of the sacrifice of the first twins, Hun Hunahpu and Vuqub Hunahpu by the lords of Xibalba, the Underworld lords of death. The second part recounts the adventures of the Hero Twins, the sons of Hun Hunahpu, who are named Hunahpu and Xbalanque. They eventually defeat the lords of Xibalba, preparing for the creation of the Maya world with the rebirth of the maize god. These stories are found in Maya art from Preclassic times and persist in the beliefs of the living Maya.

The third part of the manuscript is composed of historical chronicles written in a style similar to the historical sections of the Old Testament. It includes a list of all the noble titles held by the various segments of the ruling lineages for about 13 generations. This section provides a list of the Quiché lords who were living during the writing of the transcription. From this, scholars have determined that the manuscript had to have been written between 1554 and 1558, the same decade that witnessed the writing of several other Quiché documents, including *Title of the Lords of Totonicapán*.

Title of the Lords of Totonicapán

This document, written in the year 1554, was also transcribed into the Quiché language using European script. This historical contribution is considered very important because it helps to clarify some of the ambiguities presented in other documents of the time. Because the manuscript was signed by the kings and nobles of the Quiché court, some believe it was written in the kingdom's capital of Utatlán. The names of the authors remain unknown, although some believe that it was written in part by Diego Reynoso because of the following passage from the fourth chapter of the work (Recinos, Chonay, and Goetz 1967: 177): "Hear what I am going to relate, what I am going to declare, I, Diego Reynoso, Popol Vinak, son of Lahuh-Noh"

Title of the Lords of Totonicapán provides a historical record that begins in the legendary past and continues up to the time of King Quikab, who was in office during the latter part of the 15th century. Some of the historical and legendary information recorded in this manuscript is very similar to that found in the *Popol Vuh*. The last part of the document records an expedition made by King Quikab to the Pacific coast, during which the land boundaries assigned to each tribe were settled.

The Annals of the Cakchiquels

The Annals of the Cakchiquels, also known as *Memorial de Solalá*, was written at the end of the 16th century in the town of Solalá, near Lake Atitlán in Guatemala, by several authors who were members of the ancient family of the Xahil. The document, which was written in the Cakchiquel language using the Spanish alphabet, can be roughly divided into three parts. The only existing copy of *The Annals of the Cakchiquels* was probably recopied from older versions of the document in the middle of the 17th century by a professional scribe.

The first part, which was probably written by Francisco Hernández Arana, grandson of King Hunyg, contains primarily mythical and legendary information that had been passed down by word of mouth for generations. Some

of this information concerns the creation of man such as is also recorded in the *Popol Vuh*. The second section is considered important for its contribution to history. Here we find a year-by-year narrative of events (for this reason the document is known as *The Annals*) about kings, warriors, the founding of villages, and the succession of rulers until the conquest. Part of this section seems to have been written by Francisco Díaz between 1581 and 1604. The third section, which focuses on the end of the chronological narrative, becomes a sort of diary including entries by various members of the community who had access to the manuscript. This section provides a view of native life that includes a record of births and deaths, land disputes, natural occurrences such as earthquakes and eclipses, upkeep and maintenance of the local church, charities, expenditures, the arrival of visitors, the capture of criminals, and the burning of plantations.

The Ritual of the Bacabs

The document called *The Ritual of the Bacabs* was found in the Yucatán during the winter of 1914–15 by Frederic J. Smith. Its current name derives from the frequent mention of the Bacabs, the Maya deities associated with holding up the four corners of the sky (see Chapter 6). The manuscript primarily consists of medical incantations intended for use in curing illnesses. Some examples of these incantations include the words a shaman would say to cure various types of seizures, fevers, breathing difficulties, parasites, toothaches, burns, insect and snake bites, rashes and skin eruptions, gout, ulcers, and broken bones and to induce the emergence of the placenta after childbirth. These incantations are not easily understood today, as can be seen in the excerpt from one for a tooth infection: "I stand ready to take his fire. I roast him in the heart of the food, in the tooth of the green wooden man, the green/stone man. Red is my breath, white is my breath, black is my breath, yellow is my breath" (Roys 1965: 55). Some nonmedical incantations also appear in the manuscript, such as the words to say for the cooling of a pit oven or to call deer. *The Ritual of the Bacabs* manuscript was probably once the property of a Maya shaman who used it as a handbook for his curing ceremonies and other rituals.

Books of the Chilam Balam

The *Books of the Chilam Balam* are important 18th-century chronicles written in the Yucatán, in Mexico. Like some of the other documents discussed in this section, the *Books of the Chilam Balam* may have been originally transcribed from hieroglyphic texts into a Mayan language, in this case Yucatec Mayan, written with Spanish characters. These native chronicles record information about Maya history, religious beliefs and ceremonies, customs, and prophecies.

One of the most important aspects of these manuscripts is the Count of the K'atuns, a divinatory almanac based on the cycle of k'atuns, or 20-year periods. When trying to understand a document such as a *Chilam Balam* book, the cyclical nature of the Maya concept of time (see Chapter 9) is a serious obstacle to developing a clear chronology of events. In the *Books of the Chilam Balam*, all dates in the Short Count, or *k'atun* cycle, such as K'atun 4 Ahaw, recur many times throughout Maya history. As a result, archaeologists and epigraphers have sometimes found it impossible to satisfactorily correlate dates mentioned in the native chronicles with our Gregorian calendar and have found what appear to be contradictions or errors in the native texts. Because the European concept of time is linear, it is safer to assume that not all the nuances of Maya time are understood than to assume that some kind of error has been made by the scribe.

The name of these documents comes from their containing sermons or prophecies thought to have been delivered by priests known as the Chilam Balam (Spokesmen of the Jaguar). Each of the books full names includes the town in which it was found. At least 14 books are named *Chilam Balam* even though only five of these, the *Books of the Chilam Balam of Chumayel, of Tizimin, of Maní, of Chan Cah,* and *of Kaua,* contain the prophecies of the jaguar priest. Four of the books, those from Chumayel, Maní, Tizimin, and Kaua, also have in common the series of *k'atun* histories. The *Chilam Balam of Tusik* contains the mysterious and poorly understood "language of Zuyua." Medical information is recorded in the *Chilam Balam of Ixil*, while the *Chilam Balam* books from Tekax and Nah (modern Teabo) contain calendrical information. The *Books of the Chilam Balam of Hocabá, of Nabula, of Telchac, of Tihosuco,* and *of Tixkokob* are now lost.

BOOK OF THE CHILAM BALAM OF CHUMAYEL

The *Book of the Chilam Balam of Chumayel* may be the most accessible, as it has been translated more than once and has been given much scholarly attention. It is written in a poetic style and is composed almost entirely in couplets. In general, these couplets consist of two juxtaposed phrases where both contain the same information but each is expressed in a slightly different way. Sometimes, the second phrase will function to clarify the first phrase, as is exemplified in this simple couplet from the *Chilam Balam of Chumayel: Hulom kuk; Ulom yaxun,* or "Come the quetzal; come the blue bird." The poetry of the *Chilam Balam of Chumayel* also contains puns, metaphors, and various plays on words in the Yucatec Mayan language. Similar couplet constructions and poetic devices can also be found in ancient hieroglyphic inscriptions. This reinforces the idea that these documents represent a continuation of an ancient literary tradition that originated in hieroglyphic texts. Some of the textual similarities shared by these native chronicles and the ancient hieroglyphic texts have aided epigraphers in decipherment.

In the *Chilam Balam of Chumayel*, many references are made to agriculture, animals, plants, food, medicine, gods, Christian sacraments and rites, Maya ceremonials such as those concerning the various cycles of time (the *bak'tun, k'atun, tun, winal, tzolk'in, tun, and haab'*), divination, curing, sacrifice, land, requests, examinations, migrations of people, legends, military orders, the histories of various cities, and prophecies of things to come.

Rabinal Achí

The dance drama known as *Rabinal Achí* (The Warrior of Rabinal) was not recorded in writing until the middle of the 19th century. It is one of many ritual dances that had been performed by the Maya of Guatemala since before the Spanish Conquest. The *Rabinal Achí* is the only transcription of a complete dance drama that has survived in the Americas. Throughout the elaborate oration and acting out of the story, the play is accompanied by music and dancing.

According to researcher Carol Edward Mace, 18 ritual dances from Rabinal survived into the 1970s, including eight in Spanish, six in Quiché, two in both Quiché and Spanish, and two without dialogue, but none are as complete or elaborate as the *Rabinal Achí*. Mace attributes the survival of the dances to the presence of the Dominicans who founded the town of Rabinal c. 1540. In contrast to other religious orders that considered these dances too pagan, the Dominicans encouraged the continuation of the traditional dances and encouraged the learning of new ones.

In 1855, Bartolo Ziz, a Maya, dictated the drama to Brasseur de Bourbourg who transcribed it in Quiché and translated it into French. He gave the manuscript the appearance of a play script written in three acts including a cast of characters, modest stage directions, and a musical score for the final scene. Brasseur, who already had a deep interest in Mayan languages and manuscripts, had taken charge of the Rabinal parish so that he might learn the Quiché language. The play had not been performed for a couple of decades by the time Brasseur arrived in Rabinal, partly because of the prohibitive cost of the costumes and scenery. Another reason this play was not performed often was that the Spanish clergy was highly opposed to the pagan theme of human sacrifice that dominates the story.

THE DANCE DRAMA

The dance drama is the story of two warriors, one from Rabinal and the other from Quiché. While the Rabinal warrior was away on business, the Quiché warrior kidnapped his father, the aged king Hobtoh, and several other men of Rabinal. Upon his return, the captives were released but the Rabinal warrior swore to bring the Quiché warrior to justice for his crimes.

The play opens with the two warriors meeting in the woods near the Palace of Cakyug. The Rabinal warrior captures the Quiché warrior and brings him back to the king to receive his punishment, which was death by sacrifice. Old King Hobtoh grants the Quiché warrior several last requests, including drinking fancy liquors, dancing with the king's daughter, sparring with the king's guards, and allowing him to take a few moments to collect his thoughts, make peace with himself, and say farewell to his home. Finally the Quiché warrior allows the guards to surround him, lay him over a sacrificial altar, and cut out his heart. The drama ends with more music and dancing.

READING

History of Decipherment

Michael Coe 1989, Tozzer 1941: colonial period observations of Maya writing; Stephens 1841, 1843: early accounts of travel in the Maya area; Michael Coe 1992, Houston 1989, Kelley 1962a, George Stuart 1992: history of decipherment; Justeson and Campbell 1984, Kelley 1968, Knorosov 1958, 1967: phoneticism in hieroglyphic writing; Berlin 1958, 1959, Kelley 1962b, Lounsbury 1973, Proskouriakoff 1960, 1963, 1964: important early decipherments.

Mayan Languages and Writing

Bricker 1986, Schele 1982: grammatical studies; Justeson, Norman, et al. 1985: Mayan language and hieroglyphic writing.

Maya Hieroglyphic Writing

Coe and Kerr 1997, Harris and Stearns 1997, Houston 1989, Kelley 1976, Thompson 1971: decipherment of hieroglyphic writing.

Inscriptions on Public Monuments: Dynastic Histories

Martin and Grube 2000: Classic Maya dynasties; Houston 1993, Jones and Satterthwaite 1982, Tate 1992: studies of individual sites; Culbert 1991, Schele and Freidel 1990: Maya political history.

Maya Vase Writing

Michael Coe 1973, Kerr 1989–2000, Reents-Budet 1994: Maya ceramics and writing.

Tagging—Personal Possessions

Michael Coe 1999, Houston and Taube 1987, Matheny 1979: name-tagging.

The Maya Codices

Lee 1985: facsimile of the four Maya codices; Bricker and Vail 1997, Vail 1994: *Madrid Codex*; Love 1994: *Paris Codex*; Thompson 1972: *Dresden Codex*.

Postconquest Literature

Edmonson 1982: *Book of the Chilam Balam of Tizimin*; Edmonson 1986, Ralph Roys 1967: *Book of the Chilam Balam of Chumayel*; Craine and Reindorp 1979: *Codex Pérez* and the *Book of the Chilam Balam of Maní*; Ralph Roys 1965: *The Ritual of the Bacabs*; Dennis Tedlock 1996: *Popul Vuh*; Recinos, et al. 1967: *The Annals of the Cakchiquels* and *Title of the Lords of Totonicapán*; Irving 1985: selections from *Popul Vuh*, *Rabinal Achí*, *The Annals of the Cakchiquels*, *Title of the Lords of Totonicapán*, and the *Book of the Chilam Balam of Chumayel*; Mace 1970: Spanish-Quiché dance dramas of Rabinal; Tozzer 1941: Landa's *Relación de las cosas de Yucatán*; Taube 1993: Maya mythology.

11

ECONOMY, INDUSTRY, AND TRADE

Maya civilization flourished with a Stone Age technology and thrived in areas considered to have low agricultural potential. The preindustrial economy was primarily founded on agriculture and partially on craft production; the method of exchange was through tribute and trade. Agriculture produced foodstuffs for the eight to 10 million Maya living in the lowlands during the eighth century, and it produced valuable trade items as well, such as cacao and cotton. Artisans produced household tools as well as exotic trade goods, and industry produced salt, honey, and dyes. Regional and long-distance trade was fueled by both utilitarian products and luxury items that added prestige to members of the elite class and to the sacred cities themselves.

AGRICULTURE

The greatest population density occurred in the Maya tropical lowlands, an environment that archaeologists usually consider inhospitable for prolonged or intensive farming. Unlike the highlands where volcanic-enriched soils and lakes made agriculture very productive, the thin soils of the lowlands were less fertile and easily washed away without the protection of the forest canopy. Also the Maya lowlands had few rivers and lakes for year-round water supply (see Chapter 3), making farming and survival all the more difficult during the dry season or times of drought. The strategies developed by the Maya to exploit the lowland environment were varied and inventive.

Water-Resource Management

By 700 B.C.E., Kaminaljuyú had constructed an irrigation canal fed by a nearby lake. In the rainier tropical lowlands, however, massive irrigation systems were not usually necessary, although arid northern Yucatán could have used them, if only they had had the water to do so. Small-scale systems of ditches and drains have been identified at many sites in the southern lowlands; canals sometimes encircled sacred centers such as that at Cerros, serving perhaps both agricultural and defensive purposes. The canal system at Edzná was the largest system of water control identified for the Maya world. This canal-and-reservoir system, constructed by 100 C.E., covered almost 23 kilometers (14 miles). The canals were wide enough for canoe traffic and held more than 2 million cubic meters (more than 7 million cubic feet) of water, creating vast farmlands that could be cultivated during the dry season. The canals probably were used to raise fish as well.

More common water-management strategies in the lowlands included wells and clay-lined *aguadas*, or "reservoirs." The reservoirs sometimes were made from quarry pits, created during major construction projects. The pit was subsequently shaped and paved for better water retention. These usually sufficed to get a population through the dry season, even one prolonged by drought. The *aguada* system at Tikal was adequate to supply 70,000 people for a dry period of 120 days, and runoff systems at the city directed water back into the reservoirs once the rains started, so they refilled quickly. Similar elaborate systems existed at many sites in the southern lowlands, including Calakmul and El Mirador. In areas where clay was unavailable to line reservoirs or the water too far below the surface for wells—as is the case in much of northern Yucatán—subterranean cisterns called *chultunes* were carved into the limestone bedrock in order to collect water during the rainy season. Natural water-retaining depressions, or *bajos*, existed, but water evaporated too quickly from them to last through the dry season; in order to slow down the rate of evaporation in these seasonal swamps, the Maya cultivated water lilies on the water's surface and dug wells and *chultunes* into the murky bottom to expand their capacity. It has been suggested that the shallow lakes that still exist at Cobá may have originally been just such extended *bajos*.

Soil Conservation and Intensive Cultivation

Seasonal flooding, not drought, was the greater problem in much of the lowlands for much of the duration of Maya civilization. It was a problem for settlements along the Pacific littoral, where rains were the heaviest in the Maya region, and also in the swampy areas of the New and Hondo Rivers in northern Belize and southern Quintana Roo; inundations were common along the Candelaria River area of Campeche, and the Usumacinta and Pasión drainage of the southern lowlands. A solution to flooding was practiced in these Maya areas: drained and raised fields. Drainage ditches were cut into fields, and the earth from these was often piled up in the same fields, thereby raising the system of fields artificially above the floodplain or swamp; the ditches formed a system of canals. These agricultural field systems efficiently controlled water while preserving fertile soils—but at a considerable investment of labor. They also permitted intensive year-round planting, with the topsoil replenished from the bottom of the canals. Such intensive farming produced not just subsistence crops but also ones for export, especially cacao. Some canals were 25 meters wide (almost 83 feet), and a single large raised field was typically 200 square meters (2,152 square feet) in size. There currently are intense debates among paleobotanists and archaeologists over exactly where artificial fields were utilized by the Maya and in

which time periods they practiced such intensive agriculture. That such systems existed, however, has been convincingly demonstrated.

Heavy rains damaged more than river floodplains. They also carried off topsoil from fields cultivated on rolling hills and sloping terrain from the Yucatán to the central Petén and the Maya Mountains as well as in the highlands of the southern region. Stone terraces and meter-high platforms were constructed to prevent erosion and control water runoff. Thousands of such terraces have been detected from the Pacific slopes to the uplands of the Río Bec region.

Farming Strategies

The Maya cleverly exploited the land according to their needs and environmental setting, using a variety of techniques for intensifying production when population pressures or trade opportunities required them. Perhaps more surprising than the variety of farming techniques utilized is the fact that the Maya introduced intensive agricultural systems as early as the Preclassic Period, beginning in 1000 B.C.E. Farming on optimal lands, such as the alluvial soils of the Copán Valley or the volcanic ash–enriched lands in El Salvador and along the Pacific littoral, did not require as much manipulation of the environment as in wetlands or regions with no sources of year-round water. There is evidence that optimal lands were planted continuously, which suggests that crop rotation and fertilizer, made from household refuse, were employed to replenish the soil. The traditional planting of nitrogen-rich beans next to maize also had the practical effect of replacing the nitrogen extracted by the growing maize. In areas without population pressure, swidden agriculture—that is, the simple clearing and burning of fields followed by long fallow periods (two to four years) after one year of planting—served the Maya just fine.

Until the 1970s, archaeologists thought that all pre-Hispanic agriculture was the same as the swidden agriculture observed in modern Maya villages. It is now known, however, that pre-Columbian practices were far more complex. Without the innovative water- and soil-management systems described above, the ancient Maya could not have settled the interior lowlands or other marginal lands, nor could they have sustained the large urban populations of ancient Maya civilization (see Chapter 4) or exported great quantities of export crops. Swidden agriculture can sustain 77 persons per square kilometer (199 per square mile), but not the levels of Late Classic Maya society, which could range as high as 700 persons per square kilometer (1,813 per square mile) around the largest cities.

FIELD PREPARATION AND PLANTING

Maya farming technology required backbreaking labor and patience. There were no steel axes for felling trees, no oxen to plow the fields. In the Late Postclassic Period, the Maya did have copper axes, but before then Maya stone tools would have made clearing the forest an unusually time-consuming process. Clearing and weeding usually occurred toward the end of the dry season (January through March or April), when the brittle plants could be more easily cut without metal tools. Many details of Maya farming practices are difficult to reconstruct, but some insights are offered by 16th-century ethnohistoric documents and rituals performed by contemporary Maya. In addition, nature itself, in the form of volcanic eruptions, has occasionally contributed to scientific understanding. A New World Pompeii was discovered at the Salvadoran site of Cerén, where lava and ash preserved perishable materials from c. 600 to such a remarkable degree that archaeologists could reconstruct many details of Maya farming practices.

Once the land was cleared, the Maya weeded and worked the soil into furrowed rows that were about 1 meter (3.3 feet) apart. After the first rains in the late spring, in April or May, they walked along the rows with a seed bag on their shoulders and a pointed stick to make holes for planting the seeds, much as they still do today. At Cerén, maize was sowed in the ridges and the squash and beans in the furrows between them. As the plants grew, they were staked when necessary. At Cerén archaeologists could reconstruct the rope that tied maize plants to stakes. The first yields began in August, when a second crop was seeded in areas of plentiful rainfall, such as the Pacific slope. Once the maize matured, the stalks were doubled over, a common practice in the tropics to speed up the drying process and protect the ears of corn from pest and fungus attacks until harvest; it also was used as a form of maize storage in some areas.

Religious Rites For the Maya, maize was the foundation of their existence and the maize god was the father of world creation (see Chapter 6). Field preparation and planting must have required the appropriate rituals to honor the gods, just as they do among many modern Maya. The ordering and preparation of the quadripartite Maya world that gave birth to the maize god is replicated in the Maya cornfield today. Land is likewise measured and oriented to the cardinal directions, and boundaries are marked with standing stones. After nightlong rituals, the first corn is planted in the center of the plot with a Maya cross, completing the quincunx shape of the world ruled by the maize god. Incense burning and prayers must have been as essential as tilling the soil was for ancient Maya. Propitious times for preparing fields and sowing seeds were decided by prophecies based on priestly readings of the sacred 260-day calendar. When drought threatened crops, *ch'a chak* ceremonies must have been undertaken to bring the rains through prayers and offerings, just as they are today in the Yucatán. The 16th-century Spaniards remarked that the Maya were so devoted to their plots that it seemed corn itself was a god. And it was.

Kitchen Gardens and Orchards

The earliest domesticated plants were probably cultivated in small household gardens. Conveniently close to the kitchen, the plants could be more carefully watered and tended year-round than those in distant fields. Fossil remains from city plazas indicate they often were used as gardens, and household gardens and orchards were created on the stone plazas of Middle Preclassic stone buildings at Nakbé, where soil was hauled along a paved causeway from nearby wetlands to elite residences. They are found at Cerén, and they continue as a Maya practice in modern times.

These kitchen gardens typically included tomatoes, chili peppers, herbs—many of them used in cures for stomach ailments—gourd trees for containers, and agave plants for hemp rope (see below). The orchards sometimes had a few cacao trees along with avocado, pineapple, papaya, guava, and other tropical fruit trees. These gardens also were used to grow foods useful in times of drought, such as root plants like manioc and sweet potatoes, as well as ramon trees for the breadnuts that could be ground into a flour. In addition to these home plots, it is also believed that groves of valued trees may have been cultivated in the forest for more commercial harvesting. Various species of palm trees have been detected in unusually dense concentrations on the islands and coast of the Caribbean; their fruit was not only nutritious but it also produced palm oil, and the fronds were used to thatch homes. The copal tree may also have been planted: The resin produced precious incense, the food of the gods. The bark of wild fig trees was commercially exploited as well, soaked and pounded into cloth and paper.

Crops

The subsistence crops of Mesoamerica were maize, beans, and squashes. By the Late Classic Period, these cultivated crops constituted most of the Mesoamerican diet, yet the Maya utilized many plants, some grown in the house garden and others gathered in the forest. At Cerén, many foods were found stored in homes on that late August day when the volcano erupted: maize, two kinds of beans, chili peppers, and wild berries. Tropical fruits and tomatoes were growing just outside the door. Cotton seeds were recovered from a *metate*, or "grinding stone," perhaps to be made into cooking oil.

EXPORT CROPS

Cotton and Cacao Cacao beans and cotton were the major export crops of the Maya, but vanilla and other niche crops were produced. Cacao beans were among the most valued of pre-Columbian products; they were used to make chocolate beverages for the elite class, and they also functioned as currency (see under "Trade" below). Although originally cultivated by the Olmec, much of the cacao was later produced in the Maya tropics where there were rich soils, heavy rain, and hot temperatures: The Soconusco region along the Pacific produced the best cacao in Mesoamerica. Pollen analyses also demonstrate that cacao was intensively cultivated in the raised fields of the Belize wetlands.

Cotton was a particularly suitable crop for the arid Yucatán and was especially abundant there, but it also was grown in other parts of the Maya region. Two species of cotton were cultivated, one naturally brown and the other whiter. Cotton was spun into thread, dyed, and woven into more valuable textiles before being exported. The trading canoe encountered by Christopher Columbus on his fourth voyage contained many woven and embroidered cotton textiles.

Hemp   The agave plant, particularly the species known as henequen, was also cultivated to make textiles and sandals. Hemp fiber was used to make inexpensive clothing, often worn by commoners, as the finest cotton was almost exclusively worn by the elite class and used to pay tribute. The agave leaves, depulped with obsidian scrapers, were also used to make a particularly strong rope. The cordage was of export quality not only in the pre-Columbian world but also in modern times; synthetics did not replace it in the global market until after World War I. Although a species of agave produced fermented drinks in central Mexico (and is used today to make tequila and *mezcal*), its use for this purpose has not been identified in the Maya region.

Foodstuffs   Foodstuffs were grown primarily for local consumption, but they were also exported to neighboring areas that had inadequate supplies. The distance over which it was feasible to transport foodstuffs, however, was limited by the means of transport. Overland carriers, it has been argued, would consume as much maize as they could deliver if distances exceeded 150 to 275 kilometers (93 to 171 miles); canoe transport, however, permitted larger cargoes per person and made export feasible over longer distances. There is no doubt that imported staple crops were critical to overpopulated and agriculturally unproductive Maya regions, from Komchén in northern Yucatán during the Middle Preclassic Period to cities in the Petén heartland in the Terminal Classic Period. Such efficiency problems did not affect most other trade items.

STORAGE

Diego de Landa, the 16th-century bishop of Yucatán, reported that there were underground granaries. He apparently was referring to *chultunes*, the cisterns dug out of the limestone earth. *Chultunes* are believed to have been employed for water storage, but they may also have been used to store maize, as confirmed by traces of the grain recovered from some of them. Archaeologists discovered warehouses in excavations on the island of Cozumel, although these may have stored long-distance trade items, not local grains. However, thatched and adobe storehouses have been excavated at Cerén, and each was associated with a home, suggesting household use. The storerooms contained bins for ears of maize, as well as baskets, ceramic pots, and gourds for storing maize kernels, beans, chili peppers, and other items. All these storage containers were kept off the floor to keep them dry; stones elevated pots, and baskets were hung from thatched roofs. Chili peppers, strung together in what today are called *ristras*, hung from kitchen rafters. In some regions today, grains often are stored in wooden lattice bins built into trees, where they are kept dry and out of reach of many animals. Such storage bins would not survive from preconquest times.

OTHER FOOD PRODUCTION

Domesticated Animals

Unlike Europe, Mesoamerica had no herds of cattle, sheep, or goats. Animal husbandry clearly involved only the dog, which was domesticated by 3000 B.C.E. But the Muscovy duck probably was domesticated by the Late Postclassic Period. The ocellated turkey cannot really be domesticated, but it was caught in the wild, penned, and fattened. Sometimes turkeys were semidomesticated, attracted to a rural house by the scattering of maize seeds. These three animals were raised for food, although dogs often were kept for hunting as well as for pets. There is some evidence that the Maya also fed deer to keep them within house range. Bishop Landa apparently saw a woman breast-feeding a deer. In some instances deer may have been penned and fed, just like turkeys.

Hunting

The Maya hunted a great variety of animals. Both white-tailed and brocket deer were snared, but these larger animals as well as peccary also were rounded up in drives led by packs of dogs. Spears and, in the Late Postclassic Period, bows and arrows were used to kill prey, including crocodiles and manatees, but these animals may have been trapped in nets first. Blowguns killed birds, like quail and partridge, and other arboreal animals, such as spider and howler monkeys. Spiked pits and dead fall traps were employed to capture a wide variety of animals, including tapirs and armadillos. Traps were used to capture turtles and iguanas, both favored for their eggs as well as their flesh. Birds, such as macaws and quetzals, and animals like the jaguar were hunted for their feathers and pelts, not their meat. Some animals were kept as pets, coatimundi and parrots among them.

Fishing

Nets with ceramic weights were used to harvest spiny lobsters, shrimp, conch, and other shellfish from the Caribbean, and fish were caught with both nets and hooks made of bone and in the Late Postclassic Period of copper, too. Maya living on the coast had enough fish to salt and trade it to interior regions where it was more of a delicacy; the salted fish could last four years. The skeletal remains of a noble couple buried at Lamanai demonstrated that only the male ate seafood, so even salted fish must have been a luxury item. However, the Maya did fish interior lakes and the rivers as well for fish, frogs, mollusks, and snails, and it is possible that the canals draining artificial field systems may have been stocked with fish.

Foraging

Wild herbs and roots were gathered from forests and ravines. Epazote, a green herb akin to cilantro, was a favorite addition to tamales; annatto seeds colored food red; and allspice and oregano flavored dishes. There were medicinal herbs, berries such as the cherimoya, and the sap of the sapodilla, which was chewed, used today in the manufacture of commercial chewing gum. Greens were also gathered, especially *chaya*, which tastes a bit like cabbage. A variety of mushrooms, some of them hallucinogenic, were plentiful during the rainy season; and, in times of drought, there were root vegetables, including the jicama, much like a large white radish in appearance. Maya exploitation of the forest sometimes involved the actual cultivation of plants, such as vanilla orchid vines that grew in tropical rain forests and along the Pacific coast of the southern Maya region. These vines were carefully tended for their seeds, which once fermented produced the distinct fragrance and flavor so valuable in both perfumes and foods.

Salt Production

In the Middle Preclassic Period, Komchén in northern Yucatán existed in the most marginal agricultural lands simply in order to produce and export salt. In fact, the salt flats in northern Yucatán, from modern Celestún, around the peninsula, to Río Lagartos, yielded the most valued salt in Mesoamerica through all periods of ancient Maya civilization. Other regions, such as the Pacific coast, some highland springs, and even the nearby Belizean coast, produced salt, but Yucatán's so-called white salt was worthy of the nobility as far away as central Mexico. To produce the salt, seawater was usually boiled in pots until only the salt residue remained, but in Yucatán, shallow salt pans were constructed along the coast so the seawater would evaporate under the bright sun, leaving great quantities of salt. It is estimated that the ancient Maya produced 3,000 to 5,000 metric tons (3,300 to 5,500 tons) of salt from the flats at Río Lagartos on the most eastern tip of the peninsula.

Honey

Honey, the only sweetener known from the Maya region, was produced in many tropical areas for local consumption, but the honey of Yucatán was also produced for long-distance trade and was so important in the economy that myths and offerings were often made to a local bee divinity. Some Late Postclassic cities, such as Santa Rita, were known for its manufacture. The tiny Maya bees were stingless, so the honeycomb was easily removed. In the Yucatán, hives were made from artificially hollowed tree trunks that were plugged on the ends; a small hole was bored into the trunk for the bees to enter. The hives were stacked into a pyramid against a wall so that many honey-combs could be harvested at once. The Spanish colonists found the system so productive that they made considerable profits selling the cakes of honey themselves.

Alcoholic Beverages

The Maya fermented many fruits to make alcoholic beverages; most were consumed during ceremonial feasts and rituals. The *Rabinal Achí* states that there were 12 such beverages in the Guatemala highlands, and some were reserved for the elite. The two favorite drinks of the Maya were *balché*, made from the fermented bark of the tree of the same name and mixed with water and honey, and *chicha*, made of fermented maize and tasting much like beer. The earliest maize plants produced such minuscule ears of corn that archeologists believe the plant may not have been very useful as food but was cultivated instead for *chicha*. Fermented maize was still being produced at the time of the conquest, and Ferdinand Columbus, the great explorer's son, drank some from a Maya trading canoe off the Honduran coast and found it quite tasty.

Tobacco

Uncut tobacco is a potent plant, not something for routine consumption. It was rolled into cigars or placed in a clay pipe and smoked—but probably as a hallucinogen in religious ceremonies. Underworld gods are depicted smoking it as well. Sixteenth-century sources describe it as an offering given to the gods during ceremonies. It is possible that like incense, the smoke was considered appropriate food for supernaturals. Ethnohistoric documents suggest it was also used as a cure for various ailments.

CRAFT PRODUCTION

Artisans and artists were the workers in the preindustrial Maya economy. Many of them were exceptionally skilled, such as vase painters, weavers, stonecutters, and jade carvers, and in the Classic Period, a period of exceptional artistry, some were members of the nobility. The crafts produced ranged from ceramic spindle whorls numbering in the thousands to jewels for royalty; some were produced for local consumption and others for long-distance trade and probably even tribute. The technology employed was Paleolithic until metallurgy was introduced in the Late Postclassic Period, when a few copper tools were introduced. The Maya understood the rotation principle of the wheel—they used it in spinning thread and drilling stone—and they actually made wheeled toys. They rolled quarried stone over logs and used rope and wooden levers to lift heavy objects. But the Maya never built wheeled transport or employed pulleys. (For building techniques and more detail on quarrying stone, see Chapter 8.)

Ceramics

Maya pottery evolved over the millennia, changing shape and surface treatment, from simple red clay slipped cooking pots to polished ones punched and pinched into effigies and incised ones rubbed with red cinnabar (mercuric sulfide). They could be painted or covered with stucco and then painted. The variety of shapes produced is impressive as well. Throughout their civilization, the Maya showed a preference for the rimless *tecomate*—or gourd-shaped shallow bowls—water jugs, and tripod pots, but at various periods they experimented with different forms, such as the Late Preclassic "cream

11.1　*Classic Period ceramic pots displayed at the Lamanai site museum.*　(Photo courtesy Peter Selverstone)

pitcher" and the Classic Period cylinders with screw-on lids. The artistic masterpieces, however, were the polychrome cylinder vases and plates of the Late Classic Period (see figures 2.11, page 58; 6.3, page 173; and 6.9, page 186) produced for the elite classes. The workshops for some of these ceramics have been found in the palace compounds themselves.

Whatever their form, function, or surface treatment, Maya ceramics were made without the potter's wheel, and the clays were tempered with volcanic ash and fired into hard durable containers. Ceramic vessels were formed out of coils or slabs of clay that were pinched and pulled into shape, then smoothed. They were never glazed, but a resin rubbed onto the post-fired surface created a glossy appearance. Mass-produced ceramics were made from molds, such as the Plumbate pots, or assembled from molded parts, such as Late Postclassic deity censers. Puuc slateware and other ceramics were modeled or produced by molded designs pressed into the wet clay (see figure 1.3, page 11). Even some of the finest Late Classic figurines, such as those from the island of Jaina (see figure 12.3, page 338), were often made from molds, but they were often individualized by handmade additions.

PAINTS AND PAINT IMPLEMENTS

Chemical analyses of Maya ceramics suggest the paints, mixed with a resin such as copal to make them viscous, were derived from special clays (yellow, blue, white kaolin), charcoal (black), and iron oxides such as hematite (red) and limonite (yellows and browns). The implements used by Maya artists and scribes to apply these paints are often depicted on the vases themselves. The artist is usually shown holding a paintbrush in one hand and a paint pot, made from a halved conch shell, in the other. The hard, smooth interior surface of the conch shell was a practical choice for mixing paint, and the nonabsorbent shell meant the paint would not be contaminated with water, which would have dried it out.

A variety of brush types were used. One type was fashioned from a hollow tube with fine human hair or animal bristles attached to one end and closely resembled a Chinese calligraphy brush. This type of brush would hold a large amount of paint while allowing the scribe to create the delicate, flowing lines needed to paint hieroglyphic texts. Another type of brush had a stiff handle with a flexible point end and may have been made out of yucca fibers. Fine yucca brushes allowed artists to create thin, precise lines even when using thick pigments. Broad brushes were useful for painting large surfaces, such as the interior of a bowl. A tool resembling a stylus, such as those used by scribes in the ancient Near East, is also depicted in Maya art. This stiff implement may have been made of wood and without bristles.

Tools

Chipped and flaked chert and obsidian were the primary materials for sharp weapons and tools, but bone was made into needles and

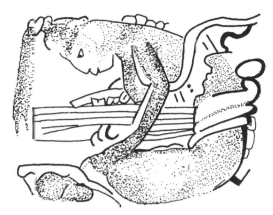

11.2 *A Maya scribe, detail from a Late Classic Period cylinder vase in the Museum of the American Indian, New York. The scribe, holding what appears to be a stylus and with a conch-shell inkpot on the floor, leans over a stack of screen-folded paper.* (Drawing by Cherra Wyllie after Persis Clarkson)

fishing hooks. Wood was shaped into weaving battens, handles, levers, and bows. By the 13th century, copper was used to make axes, tweezers, and fishing hooks as well. Basalt was most often used for heavier work tools, such as scrapers, chisels, axes, and grinding stones (*manos* and *metates*, the pestles and mortars of Mesoamerica) for maize, squash seeds, and nuts. General work tools, whether made out of stone or obsidian, are found in many urban contexts and rural settlements. But specialized tools for precision work, such as the microdrills used for the finest lapidary work, have been found only in elite residential complexes, suggesting that the artists who created these objects themselves belonged to the upper class or at least held a special position in Late Classic Period society. In the Early Postclassic Period, such specialized tools, a few covered in gold, were found as sacred offerings in the well at Chichén Itzá.

Stone and Ceramic Carving

Both ceramics and stone monuments were carved with designs, narrative scenes, and hieroglyphic texts. For monuments, the stone was first quarried and transported (see Chapter 8). Stone axes would have been used to shape the rough block, and then smooth sanding stones would have finished the preparation. Small stone tools of shell, bone, or obsidian with curved, sharpened ends were used to actually carve the monuments, incise the pots, and make the sculptural details. Archaeologists have uncovered stone monuments that were in the process of being carved but never finished. From one such example, the scribes first planned the monument by painting a grid on the surface and marking the location of the design elements, such as the hieroglyphs.

Lapidary, Bone, and Shell

Jades, serpentine, and other hard green stones as well as bone and red spiny oyster shells were gauged, drilled, incised, perforated, and polished into exquisite works: tubular beads, carved pendants and ear spools, mosaic death masks, and alabaster bowls. Cut turquoise and pyrite were attached to round discs and made into precious items for throne rooms, the pyrite ones being used as divining mirrors.

Multipurpose stone tools were used first to saw and shape the general form out of a larger stone or shell. In the case of jade, which is exceptionally hard, harder than steel, in fact, it is remarkable the Maya could work it without metal tools. The preliminary saw cuts were made by abrasion: A cord was pulled back and forth over an obsidian incision in the jade; sand and water increased this abrasive movement, deepening and widening the incisions. Such cuts were made into both sides of the material and then hammered to make the final break. Once the material was shaped, a variety of specialized tools, including microdrills and bifacial blades made of the finest-grade chert and hafted into a wooden socket for precision, were used to perform the more refined tasks. Some have suggested hollow bird bones were even used as tubular drills. Tubular beads were drilled from both ends, but given the average finger length of these beads, unusual skill in rotating the drill was required. Obsidian blades were used for fine incised designs and the final flawless polish was probably accomplished by rubbing the artifact with leftover powdered fragments.

Textiles and Basketry

Textiles, baskets, and mats, all made of perishable materials, rarely survive from the pre-Columbian period. Yet these materials often left their imprint in the earth and are identified by chemical analyses. Hemp fiber was commonly used for clothing, but pounded bark cloth (see below) also was worn, although perhaps only for ritual occasions. Homespun cotton was found in humble homes in Cerén, El Salvador, but more finely woven cotton textiles were apparently restricted to the noble few. The best-known fabrics from the ancient Maya are the clothing of the elite class because they were depicted in paintings and sculptures. Lintel 24 from Yaxchilán (see figure 6.13, page 192) shows the royal couple wearing elaborate brocaded clothing, and set between them is a fine basket, woven in chevron and other geometric designs called step frets.

DESIGNS

Many of the woven designs on the Yaxchilán lintel and in other works of art are still woven and worn today in the Maya highlands. Although geometric in form, they have cosmological sig-

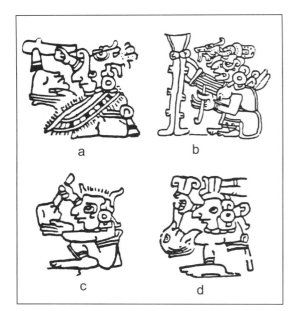

11.3   Examples of tools from the Madrid Codex: *a) deity as sculptor with a carving ax; b) deity as weaver wearing a backstrap loom tied to a stake; c) deity sculpting with a knife; and d) deity sculpting details with a perforator.*   (Drawing by Villacorta 1933)

Maya women and, in fact, many indigenous women from what used to be Mesoamerica. A wooden rod at each end stretches the warp wide, and as the cloth is woven, it is wrapped around one rod, freeing the warp. One rod is tied to a tree or other tall stationary object; the other rod is placed on the woman's lap, and is made taut by tying it around her waist. The loom produces cloth that is usually only 1 meter (3.3 feet) wide, so pieces are sewn together when wider textiles are desired. Expert weavers employed a variety of complicated techniques, producing gauzes, tapestries, and brocades. Feathers were occasionally woven into fabrics, yet other design details were embroidered. The finest textiles must have been reserved as tribute payments or gifts to royalty.

nificance: The designs on Lady Xoc's sleeve are abstracted snakes, symbolizing the sky; the diamond on her *huipil*, or dress, stands for the quadripartite universe. The entire process of spinning and weaving was a metaphor for creation and the Maya life cycle, from procreation to childbirth. The patron of weaving was the moon goddess Ix Chel, who was often depicted with tufts of cotton in her headdress.

WEAVING COTTON

Cotton was carded of seeds with a wooden stick and, then, spun into thread. Spinning involved rotating a wooden spindle stick that was placed into the center hole of a ceramic whorl, or disc. The thread was dyed and then woven on a backstrap loom. Backstrap looms are still used by

DYES

There were a great variety of natural dyes exploited by the Maya. The indigo plant produces a dark blue dye, and cochineal, a tiny insect that feeds on the prickly pear cactus, produces a fine red. Both dyes were later commercially exploited by the Spaniards, and cochineal was especially valued in Europe (the red coats of the British militia were made using it) until aniline dyes replaced it in the 19th century. A sea snail from the Pacific produces a purple dye. Brazilwood, when chopped fine and put in water, turns red, and logwood, later exploited by the British in Belize, makes a purple-black dye.

BASKETRY

Palm fiber and vines were the most usual materials to be woven into baskets, mats, and fans. From Maya art it is clear that baskets were used to receive offerings in rituals, and some have survived from the cenote at Chichén Itzá. These few remnants of ceremonial baskets indicate that leaves were coiled and plaited, then shaped into cylindrical baskets with contrasting colors and decorative stitching; there is evidence for wickerwork as well. Baskets also served as simple storage containers and large seats for palanquins, or litters. Mats, used today for sleeping and kneeling on dirt floors, symbolized the ruler, and their imprint can be found under burial remains. The woven mat symbol decorated Puuc buildings and royal garments.

Metalwork

The Maya region was not an important area of metallurgy. Although gold was panned in the Guatemala highlands, it was not produced in great quantity. For the most part, the Maya traded for their copper, gold, tumbago (a copper-and-gold alloy), and silver. The largest cache of precious metals found in the Maya region was dredged from the sacred well at Chichén Itzá; dating to the ninth century, this cache may also represent the first significant trade in gold in Mesoamerica. (Only a few gold figurines have been found in earlier Maya burials.) The gold in the sacred well contained hammered discs with mythohistoric scenes of warfare and human sacrifice, done in the art style of the local Maya. Perhaps the Maya themselves created the repoussé, or raised designs hammered into the gold, or perhaps they directed more experienced goldsmiths from Central America to make them. Other metal pieces from the well, mostly figurines cast in the lost wax process, were clearly imports, not just in their composition but also in the manner and style in which they were made; they came from various areas of Mexico, Honduras, Costa Rica, Panama, and probably Colombia. A cache of copper bells discovered at Quiriguá may date from the same period; the copper was imported, but there is reason to believe the bells were locally cast.

Paper

Mesoamerican bark paper was less processed than true paper. Unlike the Chinese, the bark was never made into a pulp that changed its original fibrous texture. Based on 20th-century papermaking techniques in a few villages in central Mexico, the Maya probably harvested inner layers of bark from the wild fig tree, soaked and boiled it in maize water (treated with lime or ash), and rinsed it. The pliable strips of bark were then laid out on a wooden board, first a layer lengthwise and then one crosswise, and pounded with a hafted stone bark beater into a sheet of paper. After it was dried in the sun, the paper was peeled off the wooden board and then smoothed with a stone. It still was not smooth enough, however, for Maya scribes, so they covered the paper with a thin layer of plaster before writing.

Although the exact nature of papermaking before the conquest is unknown, there is evidence that it was being made more than 2,000 years ago. The earliest known bark beaters are found in the Maya region along the Pacific coast and date to the Middle Preclassic Period. The Maya codices were made from a continuous piece of double-ply paper that was folded into leafs, accordian style; the sheets must have been glued together for added thickness and the appropriate length. The source of the glue is not currently known.

Clothes were made of bark as well, but bark cloth would not have been as refined as codical paper; the bark may simply have been soaked, dried, and then pounded. Paper held ritual significance for the ancient Maya. The prophetic books were written on it; strips of papers, placed in sacrificial bowls, absorbed blood offerings; gods and sacrificial victims were depicted with paper capes and ear ornaments in ancient art. Most likely, any clothing made of bark also had a ceremonial function rather than utilitarian one. Even today, bark paper is made for curing and cleansing ceremonies.

TRADE

Maya cities traded both raw materials—feathers, salt, pottery temper, or ash, and obsidian, for example—and manufactured goods—cotton textiles, polychrome vases, and jade jewelry. They traded across the Maya region with each other, exchanging lowland salt and cacao for highland obsidian and jade, and they exchanged goods with other Mesoamerican cities, especially in central Mexico and along the Gulf coast, as well as with regions beyond the Mesoamerican frontier. The Early Postclassic city of Chichén Itzá, for example, was key to one of the most extensive trade routes, receiving turquoise from what is now Cerillos, New Mexico, in the United States, to the north and hammered gold discs from Panama and Colombia to the south. The Maya traded with various regions during the Olmec horizon of the Preclassic Period, and they were still trading after the Spanish Conquest.

Trade and Maya Civilization

Trade was an integral part of the Maya economy, and it was a vital factor in the development of Maya civilization. The most important cities often controlled commodities or portage routes. The great cities of the highlands, for example, controlled obsidian sources during different periods: Chalchuapa, Kaminaljuyú, Cotzumalguapa, and Utatlán. The great cities of the northern lowlands controlled the salt flats: Komchén, Dzibilchaltún, Chunchucmil, Chichén Itzá, and Mayapán.

The rise and fall of some the greatest Maya cities occurred with apparent shifts in the control of trade routes. Such shifts were accompanied by major cultural and geographic changes in Maya civilization. Trade shifts can be discerned in the demise of Olmec cities and the rise of Preclassic Maya ones; in the transition to the Early Classic Period, when the Maya lowlands replaced the southern region in importance; and during the Classic Period collapse of the southern lowland Maya cities and the rise of northern ones (see Chapter 2).

Long-Distance Trade

ROYAL CONTROL

Long-distance trade has been of particular interest to archaeologists, because it probably created a wealthy class that evolved into the centralized political authority of the Maya states. Royal families probably controlled both the utilitarian and luxury goods involved in such trade. The Maya traded the great wealth of commodities from within their region, but they also exploited their strategic middle position between Central American cultures to the south and Mexican ones to the north.

The exotic items exchanged on such routes were used to glorify kings, associating them with distant and powerful places and permitting them to preside over rituals of state: the sacred ball game, for example, required rubber balls imported from either Veracruz or Central America. Foreign goods also enabled rulers to solidify their relationships with other powerful members of society through gifts of feathers, shells, and fine pottery and through feasts in which chocolate beverages—cacao had to be imported into most Petén cities—were consumed as a symbol of privilege.

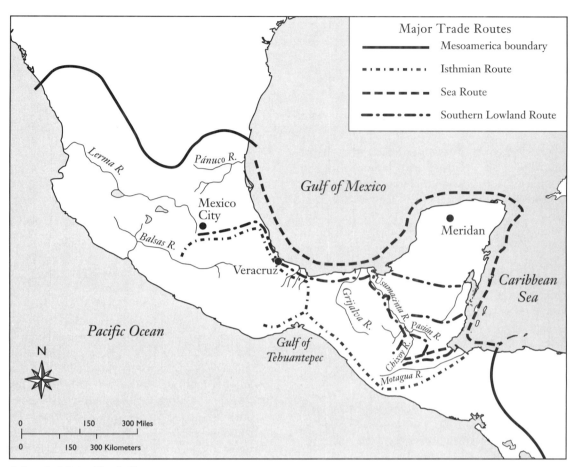

Map 8. *Major Trade Routes*

MERCHANTS

Rulers may have controlled trade, but they were not merchants themselves. Unfortunately, little is known about Maya merchants. Some must have belonged to the nobility because they are occasionally depicted on polychrome vases, elaborately dressed in a manner permitted only to the nobility and named in the accompanying hieroglyphic texts. Some carry what may be canoe paddles, and most hold a small wicker fan. Ethnohistoric documents provide support for the elite status of some merchants as well: A member of the powerful Cocom lineage was described as being on a trading trip between Yucatán and Honduras during the conquest period. Most merchants seemed to have belonged to the middle class, however, and they probably were primarily involved in local and regional trade.

When merchants traveled outside their native city, they were understood to be travel-

Trade Goods from Maya Region

Product	Primary Export Area
Amber	Chiapas
Bark paper	Pacific coast, lowlands
Cacao	Pacific coast, Belize and Honduran wetlands
Chert, or flint	Lowlands, especially Colhá
Cinnabar	Guatemala highlands
Copal incense	Lowlands
Cotton	Yucatán and Pacific coast
Dyes	Pacific coast, lowlands
Feathers	Highlands, rain forest lowlands
Fish, salted	Coastal and lake areas
Gold	Highlands (limited)
Grinding stone	Highlands
Hematite	Highlands
Hemp rope	Northern Yucatán
Honey	Caribbean coast of Yucatán
Jade	Highland Motagua Valley
Jaguar Pelts	Southern lowlands
Maize	Belize wetlands, El Salvador
Obsidian	Highlands: Ixtopeque, San Martín Jilotepeque, El Chayal
Pottery	Many areas
Pottery ash	Highlands
Pyrite	Highlands
Salt	Northern Yucatán
Serpentine	Highlands
Shells	Coastal areas
Stingray spines	Coastal areas
Textiles	Bark from Pacific; hemp from Yucatán; cotton, many areas
Tobacco	Lowlands
Vanilla	Pacific coast

Imported or Transshipped Goods[*]

Product	Primary Producing Area
Alabaster	Central Mexico
Cacao	Central America
Cochineal	Oaxaca
Copper	Western Mexico, Central America
Cotton	Central America
Feathers	Central America
Gold artifacts	Colombia, Costa Rica, Oaxaca, and Panama
Kaolin	Veracruz
Obsidian	Central and western Mexico
Pearls	Pacific coast Nicaragua and Costa Rica
Pottery	Mexico, Central America, possibly Ecuador
Rubber	Veracruz and Central America
Semiprecious stones	Central America
Shells	Coastal Central America, northwestern Pacific, and perhaps Ecuador
Silver	Central America
Tobacco	Mexico
Turquoise	Southwestern United States

Source: *Robert J. Sharer 1994, pages 454–55.*

[*]In addition to these products, there was considerable trade for slaves from Central America, according to the Spaniards.

ing in a dangerous, foreign world comparable to the Underworld. For this reason, their patron deities were two Underworld gods that were frequently shown carrying backpacks and with their skin painted black (see "The Identities of the Gods," Chapter 6). Merchants also were painted black to signify their journey through darkness and carried weapons of warfare to protect themselves.

The actual distances Maya merchants traveled can be partially but not totally reconstructed. Maya trade enclaves have been identified at Early Classic Teotihuacan, 1,600 kilometers (1,000 miles) from the Maya region. There is some evidence of their physical presence at other central Mexican sites, such as Cacaxtla, Puebla, and Tula, in subsequent periods. In the early period of Spanish contact, native chronicles suggest that diplomatic missions, and probably trade missions, were sent from highland Guatemalan cities to the Aztec capital of Tenochtitlan.

Whether Maya merchants traveled to other distant places is not easily determined. From the perspective of archaeology, the presence of nonlocally produced items at a site raises many questions. The primary one is whether the items arrived through direct contact or were passed along through intermediaries. In the case of Chichén Itzá, for example, it is unknown whether Maya merchants actually traveled to New Mexico for turquoise, but archaeologists believe they did not. Instead, there is evidence that a series of northern and western Mexican cities stretched along the route to what is now the United States. These cities probably passed the turquoise from one to the next until it reached central Mexico, and from there to Yucatán. The Itzá merchants may have obtained Central American gold directly, however, although this, too, is uncertain. They could have followed their own Caribbean maritime route to Honduras. They could have continued on to Costa Rica or the north coast of Panama, although this is not known. It is unlikely, however, that these sea traders traveled overland from the Caribbean to the Pacific coast of Panama for Coclé cast gold figurines; instead, these figurines may have been traded by either the Coclé or their intermediaries at the Costa Rican or Honduran ports. Some art historians have proposed that Panamanian goldsmiths traveled to Chichén Itzá with blank gold discs that were worked there with the designs and hieroglyphs chosen by the Maya. For the moment, these issues cannot be resolved nor can such details be determined for many periods of the ancient Maya past.

Tribute

Archaeologists often have difficulty deciding whether the presence of artifacts at a site represents trade or tribute. Such objects could also represent diplomatic gifts or religious offerings rather than commercial transactions or the discharge of political obligations. These distinctions are not easily made without other kinds of information, such as distribution of goods across a region or inscriptions describing political alliances and subservience, but this information has increasingly become available.

Although tribute goods can be difficult to discern in the record, they existed, just as tribute labor constructed most Maya cities. Sixteenth-century documents mention tribute payments to the rulers of Mayapán, as well as Quiché tribute payment to the Aztecs, and the Spaniards observed that the Maya constructed buildings for the elite at their own expense. The Spaniards themselves continued the tribute system: The 1549 census in Yucatán required each Maya married couple to pay taxes of cotton textiles, turkey, corn, wax, and personal service.

Despite all the evidence that tribute must have existed, it is only recently that archaeologists have confidently identified such tribute payments in earlier Maya art, supported by translations of texts about "cargo" being presented to kings and gifts being delivered. In numerous palace scenes painted on Late Classic Period vases, the Maya king sits on his throne, receiving sacks of tribute delivered by individuals from dependent and conquered states; usually only the vassels' position, not their names, is given. A recently discovered carved panel from Palenque is believed to depict one of the last rulers of that city lifting a tribute sack, perhaps to be delivered to Toniná after that city's victory over Palenque. The tribute sacks are sometimes labeled or the goods protrude from them, revealing their contents of cacao beans, red *Spondylus* shells, quetzal feathers, and other precious items.

Transport

OVERLAND

Without pack animals, the wheeled cart was not useful and never employed by the Maya. Maya overland trade was cumbersome as a result. Yet such portage routes existed, based on the important cities that are found inland from the maritime and river routes used for canoe transport. When they existed, *sacbeob* between cities would have facilitated transport over wetlands and rugged terrain, although there is no evidence that this is how the paved causeways were actually used. The steep mountain terrain and swampy wetlands probably would have rendered heavy carts and pack animals impractical, even if they had been available.

Porters Whether by *sacbeob* or trail, the goods were carried by humans. Human carriers

11.4 *Tribute scene on a Late Classic Period polychrome cylinder vase from Dos Pilas. This vase detail depicts an exchange of tribute items between Tikal or Dos Pilas and Calakmul. A scribe, mentioned in the hieroglyphic text, may be represented seated on the bench, recording the delivery of goods from the kneeling figure who carries a bundle of offerings in his jaguar pelt backpack. The stack of items next to the scribe could be a codex, but it more likely represents tribute in the form of textiles topped with a handful of exotic feathers. Under the bench a tribute bundle is marked 3 pi, which David Stuart has interpreted to be a standard measure for cacao beans. One pi equaled 8,000 beans.* (Drawing Linda Schele, copyright David Schele)

are depicted in Mesoamerican art and reported by the Spaniards, who continued to use them for centuries. Today, poor Maya often do not have the money for donkeys or bicycles to transport water or goods; buses and roads often do not serve their remote farms. They survive by carrying their firewood and other materials in the same fashion as in pre-Columbian times. Carried on the porter's back, the pack is secured by a tumpline across the forehead that distributes the weight and frees the hands. The ancient porters also carried kings and other members of the nobility on litters, with the poles on the shoulders of two porters, one in front and one behind.

The Aztecs regulated the size of burdens, the length of a porter's journey, and his pay, but such detailed information is not available for the Maya. Estimates however, have been made based on colonial documents and modern practices. Cargo carried by an individual porter working a 10-hour day averaged from 35 to 68 kilograms (80 to 150 pounds), and, with rest periods, the distance covered averaged 2.2 kilometers (1.3 miles) per hour over difficult mountainous terrain to 4.5 kilometers (2.8 miles) per hour over the flat terrain of Yucatán. Porters carrying heavy cargoes, such as human beings, were frequently relieved by relay teams. Communication along trade routes was greatly facilitated by relay runners.

WATERBORNE

From as early as the Archaic Period, there is evidence of waterborne exchanges over considerable distances. One distribution route of Olmec-style goods from the Gulf of Mexico to the Pacific, for example, follows the course of the Grijalva River. The earliest settlements in the lowlands are along rivers and coasts, areas that were made easily accessible by canoe; one of the earliest masonry constructions known to archaeologists is the Lamanai river dock (700 B.C.E.). Waterborne transport increased in importance in the Terminal Classic Period, when canoes were depicted in murals at Chichén Itzá (see figure 2.13, p. 65); and by the Late Postclassic Period, there were more than 150 ports involved in the circumpeninsular trade of the Yucatán.

A Maya Canoe A Maya canoe was encountered in the Bay of Honduras on Christopher Columbus's fourth voyage in 1502. His son, Ferdinand, described the canoe as much like a Venetian gondola. The canoe was made out of a single hollowed tree trunk, and it had a palm canopy against the sun to shelter the women and children; it was 2.5 meters (8 feet) wide and long enough to accommodate 25 rowers. A substantial vessel, the canoe carried cacao beans, obsidian clubs, copper bells and axes, pottery, and woven cotton textiles; it also contained food and even *chicha*, maize beer, for the crew.

Portage and Ports

There is some archaeological evidence of special redistribution sites for trade. At Chunchucmil in northern Yucatán, for example, a very large central plaza has few ceremonial buildings in contrast to other sites of its size. Given its strategic location near salt flats and Puuc cities, it is believed that Chunchucmil was a commercial site, not a sacred or capital city, involved in the circumpeninsular sea trade in the Late and Terminal Classic Periods. Isla Cerritos, the port for the Early Postclassic city of Chichén Itzá, was another such specialized site. During the Late Classic Period, sacred sites may have served a dual purpose as neutral trade zones where even warring groups could conduct their business in peace due to the sanctity of the location. The warehouses at Cozumel, where there was a pilgrimage site for the goddess Ix Chel, have been thought to identify that island as such a port of trade. Classic Period sites also functioned as transshipment centers: Lamanai on the New River was at the crossroads between the Caribbean and the Petén interior. And some of the greatest Maya cities— El Mirador, Tikal, and Calakmul—probably controlled the portage across the southern lowlands between the Caribbean and Gulf of Mexico.

Markets and Distributive Networks

Once trade goods reached their destination, they were then distributed through the political state. From the capital city, they gradually reached the subsidiary centers, probably working their way through secondary towns to tertiary ones, and so forth. Archaeologists believe the elite controlled the distribution of many exotic trade items, and rulers in capital cities would provide such items to other elite residents of the capital and subsidiary towns in order to maintain a network of mutual support and obligation. Sumptuary laws most likely controlled who could wear luxury items and consume exotic drinks and foods. Under such a model of elite control, luxury items would not have been available to most of the people.

Most other items probably were bartered or sold in markets. There is ample evidence that such markets existed in Mesoamerica: The Spanish soldier Bernal Díaz del Castillo described the principal Aztec market at Tlatelolco in extraordinary detail, and the Spaniards mention them, more cryptically, in the Yucatán and the Guatemala highlands. Today, such markets are favorite tourist destinations. Yet specialized buildings for markets have not been definitively identified archaeologically. They may have been temporarily set up on plazas in the center of cities, much as they are today.

Currency

Cacao beans were not simply ground, toasted, and whipped into a frothy chocolate drink or reduced to cocoa butter. Cacao beans were money. Christopher Columbus reported they were so valuable that when some spilled while he was investigating a trading canoe, the Maya scrambled to collect them as if they had lost their eyeballs. An average cacao tree yielded 1,000 to 2,500 beans annually, but the beans did not survive storage, so their value was short lived. It is unknown whether currency controls were implemented when there was an unusually plentiful crop, devaluing the currency; perhaps more beans than usual were taken out of circulation and consumed as chocolate instead. The value of cacao varied with its distance from the source: At the time of the Spanish Conquest, a load of cacao (defined as 24,000 beans, or in the Maya numerical system 3 *pi*) was worth twice as much in the Aztec capital of Tenochtitlan as it was along the Gulf coast. Counterfeiting was a recognized practice: The flesh was removed—and consumed—and replaced with avocado rind or earth. Cacao beans continued to be used as currency in the Spanish colony when 650 beans equaled about 25 cents; a Yucatec Maya porter was typically paid 20 cacao beans for a trip, and in Nicaragua, a rabbit cost 10.

OTHER FORMS OF PAYMENT

In the 16th century, the Spanish observed that other goods such as gold, copper bells, and beads made of jade or thorny oyster shell (*Spondylus*), seemed to have set market values for commercial exchanges. Except for the metals, which were not introduced into Mesoamerica until the Postclassic Period, these same items are identified on Classic Period tribute sacks. Barter was quite common, so currency was not necessary for market transactions. Tribute payments also involved specific goods, particularly textiles, as well as labor, instead of monetary sums. Barter was also employed for work in the form of reciprocal labor: Maya women helped one another with weaving and Maya men built homes for one another.

LOANS AND CONTRACTS

Contractual transactions are mentioned in ethnohistoric documents and early colonial histories. Apparently contracts were sealed by public drinking, and they were employed most often in the sale of slaves and cacao plantations. The Spaniards observed that the Maya were honorable in their business dealings, and usury did not exist.

READING

See also Chapters 2, 3, 4, and 8.

Agriculture

Carr and Hazard 1961, Culbert Levy, and Cruz 1990, Culbert and Rice 1990, Fedick 1996, Harrison 1990, Matheny 1978, Mary Pohl, et al. 1996, Rice and Puleston 1981, Scarborough 1993 and 1998: water management, soil conservation, and farming strategies; Folan, Fletcher, and Kintz 1979, Hansen, et al. 2000, Sheets 1992: kitchen gardens; Freidel, Schele, and Parker 1993, Landa 1941, Schele and Freidel, 1990, Sheets 1992, Thompson 1966: field preparation; Drennan 1985, Sanders and Santley 1983: transport of foodstuffs; Anthony Andrews 1983, Sophie Coe 1994, Foster and Cordell 1992, Gómez-Pompa, et al. 1990, McBryde 1947, McKillop 1994: other agricultural products.

Craft Production

Coggins 1992, Coggins and Shane 1984: examination of many types of artifacts; Aldenderfer 1991, Hester and Shafer 1991, Sheets, Ladd, and Bathgate 1992: tools; Miller 1999, Reents-Budet 1994, Rice and Sharer 1987: pottery; Coe and Kerr 1997, Reents-Budet 1994: pottery painting and stonecarving implements; Digby 1972, Proskouriakoff 1974: jade; Anawalt 1981, Cordry and Cordry 1968, Morris 1987: textiles; Bray 1977, Mark Graham 1996, Samuel Lothrop 1952: metalwork; Christensen and Marti 1971, Coe and Kerr 1997, Hagen 1999, Tolstoy 1991: paper; Landa 1941, Sahagún 1950–71: ethnohistoric descriptions.

Trade

Anthony Andrews 1990, Brumfiel and Earl 1987, Rathje 1971 and 1972, Sharer and Grove 1989, Tourtellot and Sabloff 1972, Voorhies 1989: civilization and trade; Gillespie and Joyce 1998, Mark Graham 1996, Miller 1999: merchants; Kelly 1966: Mesoamerica and the U.S. Southwest; Miller 1997, Reents-Budet 1994, Schele and Miller 1986, David Stuart 1998: tribute and gifts; Krochock and Looper 2000: tribute scene on Late Classic Period vase; Columbus 1963, Hassig 1985, Trombold 1991: transport; Rathje and Sabloff 1978: ports of trade; Tozzer 1941, Díaz del Castillo 1956: markets; Coe and Coe 1996, Thompson 1966: currency.

12

DAILY LIFE

Sixteenth-century Spanish observations provide the greatest detail about daily life among the Maya. Unless there is additional evidence, however, these observations must be accepted with some caution in regard to Maya lifestyles during earlier periods. Fortunately, archaeologists have provided supporting evidence for understanding earlier periods of Maya civilization. They have identified the foods eaten by Classic Period Maya and can sometimes determine how the food was cooked, and they have excavated simple Maya residential compounds, such as the well preserved ones at Cerén, as well as palaces. Art historians and epigraphers have also revealed many aspects about kinship and the concepts of personal beauty. Despite these understood aspects of Maya existence before the Spanish invasion, many other details are unknown, and they may have been very different from those that existed in the 16th century.

DIVERSITY OF POPULATION

All Maya regulated their lives by the sacred calendar and the prognostications of diviners. They shared a basic diet and a common belief in the origin of the world, and they followed similar patterns of residential living and family and lineage associations. But many aspects of everyday life, from the clothing worn to the foods consumed, were largely determined by one's position in the social hierarchy and the region in which one lived, whether coastal or highland (see Chapter 3).

Archaeologists estimate that Maya society required 75 percent of its population to be engaged in food production. Men worked the fields and hunted, women maintained the kitchen gardens, foraged in forests, and prepared the food, and some Maya maintained the raised fields and terraces for intensive agricultural production. Most Maya did not farm on a year-round basis, however. The dry season permitted other activities, and farmers were also part-time weavers and tool makers, soldiers, and construction laborers. The remaining 25 percent of the population, their basic food needs provided by the majority, led very different lives. They included the elite classes, estimated at 10 percent of the population, as well as the full-time specialists and professionals: shaman priests, merchants, potters, painters, sculptors, stonecutters, and many others. According to the Spaniards, the work of slaves was not very different from that of the vast majority, but their legal status left them few rights against abusive treatment by their owners.

Other Ethnic Groups

There were relatively few Mayan languages spoken during the Classic Period, so the Maya could have understood one another over relatively large regional areas. Yucatec, for example, was the language of Tikal in the Petén as well as the northern lowlands. The several 16th-century Mayan languages spoken in the Guatemala highlands were recent branches of Quiché, the single language spoken by these groups during the Classic Period. Even when the Maya did not speak the same language, as was the case between Palenque and Uxmal, for example, some epigraphers believe the elite class may have shared a court language that was the basis of the writing system. Whether these differences in ethnic identity, based on language, affected the course of Maya civilization is unknown. Perhaps they caused wars or perhaps they limited trade initiatives. Most Maya, however, were probably never in contact with people different from themselves.

There is little doubt that some Maya encountered not only other Maya, but also other Central Americans, such as the Lenca in western El Salvador, and other Mesoamericans. Mayan languages show many borrowed rituals words from Mixe-Zoquean, the language of the Olmecs and other neighbors to the west. The Maya, however, culturally absorbed these contacts into their own civilization. For example, it is unknown whether the Classic Period residents of Cerén, located on the southeastern Maya frontier, were Mayan speakers or not, but they were culturally Maya in every way.

There also were enclaves of Nahuatl speakers, originating from central Mexico in the Postclassic Period, living along the Pacific coast at the time of the Spanish Conquest. And central Mexicans had invaded the Maya region in the Early Classic Period as well. Yet most Maya probably saw such foreigners only at regional markets or on feast days in the great capital cities, if then. Only the rulers and merchants involved in diplomatic exchanges and long-distance trade were frequently exposed to foreigners. Such cultural and economic exchanges contributed to the development of a common Mesoamerican culture (see Chapter 2). At the time of the Spanish Conquest, when numerous Maya spoke Nahuatl as the lingua franca of trade, such ethnic exchanges were still affecting the course and development of Mesoamerican civilization.

THE FAMILY

Marriage and Divorce

Most marriages were arranged by a third party who determined whether the union of a couple would satisfy certain basic societal rules. The bride and groom could not have the same surname, thereby increasing the likelihood that they were not from the same lineage; it was preferred, however, that they were from the same town and same class. Once the choice of spouse was decided, a shaman priest performed the marriage ceremony, usually in the home of the bride's father. The bride kept the surnames of her father and mother, and the groom his, suggesting just how important descent remained 700 years after the Classic Period rulers carved their dynastic lists in stone.

For the first several years of marriage, the couple resided with the wife's parents, and the young husband worked with the family as a form of payment for his wife. Afterward, he built a permanent home next to that of his parents and lived in the family residence until death, where even burial was within, or near, the residence (see Chapter 7). The husband, as a son, inherited land and rights through his father; the wife had no legal right to inheritance.

Except for the wealthiest individuals, the Maya were basically monogamous, and in the case of the elite class, multiple marriages such as those recorded at Late Classic Period cities like Yaxchilán represented political alliances. In the 16th century, divorce was arranged by the repudiation of one spouse by the other. Families could also banish men who did not do their share of work. To remarry involved just as little ceremony as divorce: A couple living together was considered married. Adultery with a married woman was severely punished (see below); married men, however, appear to have had more latitude as long as their adulterous relations were with unmarried women. Some legally kept their slaves as concubines.

Children

The Maya started having children as soon as they were married, around the age of 20, and they liked to have many children. Women prayed and made offerings to the goddess Ix Chel for fertility and easy childbirth. A child's fate was determined by the sacred calendar, and in the highlands, children were named after their birth date; in Yucatán, they were named by a priest, based on his divination for the infant. All Mesoamericans were apparently willing to manipulate fate and changed the official birth dates of their children to a more auspicious day, if necessary. Babies were nursed as long as possible, usually for two to five years, and according to Bishop Landa of Yucatán, they were wonderfully plump and cheerful. They were left naked until they were approximately five years old, when a ceremony was performed: Skirts were put on girls, a loincloth and cloak on boys. The parents were responsible for the proper upbringing, and as the children became old enough, they gradually assumed responsibilities within the household. Children carried the surnames of both their parents, even though inheritance was only through the male line. The importance of family cannot be underestimated. Orphans were often enslaved and offered for human sacrifice.

Adolescence

Adolescence was the transition between puberty and marriage. The young could be married only after they had gone through public puberty rituals signifying they were adults. The timing of these rituals was partially determined by the sacred calendar, as interpreted by the local priest. After these ceremonies, youths awaited for their marriages to be arranged. The women lived at home and were expected to conduct themselves modestly in the presence of men, stepping aside to let them pass and remaining chaste. The young men, how-ever, lived apart from their families in a community dormitory but worked with their fathers during the day. Unlike the chastity restrictions placed on young women, the male youths lived in dormitories that were the favored haunts of prostitutes.

Trades and Education

Kinship relationships determined position in society, the offices one could hold in the community, and one's trade or profession. Paternal descent was the deciding factor in all inheritance (see Chapter 7), and there is considerable evidence that lineages controlled certain professions and civic offices, from priestly to scribal ones. Classic Period residential compounds, based on lineage, were devoted to scribes and artists, for example, and 16th-century documents state that priestly and military duties could also be inherited. Farmers inherited their work and their land as well, but usually little else other than tribute obligations to the community.

In many ways, these kinship arrangements also made education quite easy: The Maya inherited their occupation and were basically apprenticed to their extended family in order to learn their trade. Parents were in charge of morally educating their children and teaching them traditional household tasks and farming techniques, which were divided according to gender (see below). But specialized trade skills, such as stonecutting or flute playing, could be learned from other members of the lineage. Most Maya were illiterate, so a more formal education was not normally necessary except for the elite who were able to read and write. It is unknown whether all members of the nobility were literate, but at least some women were, because they are depicted in the art as scribes.

12.1 *Cakchiquel Maya girl in her mother's kitchen,* learning to grind maize with the tradi-tional *mano* and *metate.* (Photo courtesy Cherra Wyllie)

The more esoteric knowledge of astronomy, mythohistory, religious rituals, medicine, and priestly divination required more intensive education. However, there may have been schools of a sort: One Classic Period text suggests that a young man was sent from a satellite town to a nearby capital city for training as a scribe. Ethnohistoric documents state that the high-ranking priests in the cities were involved in the training and examination of provincial priests and diviners in their knowledge of the books and sciences. The sons of other priests and nobles were brought to them for training, sometimes from infancy. Also, male youths lived separately from their families in community dormitories, perhaps so they could receive training in matters of communal concern, such as ceremonial dances and warfare.

CRIMES AND PUNISHMENT

Class status determined more than wealth and privilege; it also determined crimes and punishments. Sumptuary laws probably prohibited commoners in the Classic Period from wearing the exotic feathers and shell jewelry that were highly valued by the nobility, and the murder of a slave was not treated with the seriousness of most homicide cases. On the other hand, punishments for the elite were often distinctive from those for commoners: A thief usually had to pay restitution or be enslaved until the debt was paid, but a nobleman was forced to have his entire face tattooed as a symbol of his crime. And women were often were given a different punishment from men: Public disgrace was considered sufficient punishment for an adulterous woman, but her paramour could be sentenced to death.

Accusations of crimes were brought before leading town officials who then acted as judges, listening to the evidence presented by all the concerned parties. Although no one appeared before such high-ranking members of the nobility without bringing gifts, however small, the judges acted impartially, according to the Maya, and their judgments were accepted. If the concerned parties were found guilty, they were sentenced. Death by stoning, arrow shots, or dismemberment was a common punishment for violent crimes. Murderers could be sacrificed or suffer death in the same manner as their victims, but families of the victims could demand money instead. Adulterers could be pardoned by the injured husband, but otherwise death was considered the appropriate punishment, just as it was for arsonists and rapists. Punishment for property crimes most often involved restitution, and if that could not be paid, it was worked off through temporary enslavement. In highland Guatemala, death was the punishment for killing valuable quetzal birds.

THE MAYA HOUSEHOLD

All Maya lived and worked in residential compounds that were composed of several buildings arranged around patios and courtyards, and just as often several generations and various relatives lived together as an extended family. This pattern of residence was followed whether in the royal palace, where many buildings were arranged around multiple courtyards, or in the households of commoners.

Masonry Palaces

Archaeologists have tried to reconstruct how the Maya utilized elite residences, looking for clues as to the function of various rooms. Workshops for the production of elite goods have been identified by debris; throne rooms and public meeting halls, by the hieroglyphs and wide benches; sleeping quarters, by the ring holes for curtains and benches for beds; and steam baths, by heating and draining mechanisms. Special lineage shrines, tombs, and ritual spaces have also been identified in these very large complexes. The artifacts found in these residences have been among the best studied of ancient Maya civilization (see Chapters 2, 7, and 8).

Common Households

MULTIPLE BUILDINGS

The adobe and thatched-roof homes of commoners have been more difficult to find in a state of preservation that would be as revealing as the masonry palaces. However, the excavations at Cerén, perfectly preserved by volcanic ash c. 600. have vividly revealed the nature of residential compounds in a farming community and the functions of the various buildings constructed around an informal patio. The Maya at Cerén constructed separate adobe structures for living and storage; a thatched work area for tool working, traditionally male work; and a pole-and-thatched kitchen, traditionally female work. One residential complex even had a steam bath. Each of these structures was constructed atop a raised adobe platform. Excavations at Copán and other sites also found numerous buildings comprising a residential unit, although they were not always as well constructed atop raised platforms. Modern Maya in both the lowlands and highlands continue to live in such residential complexes, with separate kitchens and covered work areas in the courtyards. (See figure 12.2, page 334.)

At Cerén, the main house was a large room divided into different functional areas: the living room, dining room, sleeping area, and some storage space. A large adobe bench probably served many functions, including seating, dining, and with mats laid over it, sleeping. Sixteenth-century accounts state that women ate apart from the men, usually sitting on a mat on the floor. The multifunctional mats were rolled up and stored in the rafters to make more room during the day. The dining area, identified from a pot of beans, contained imported pottery: large fragments from broken pots were apparently used as plates. A covered porch was used for many activities: Spindle whorls and balls of clay suggest the area was used by women for weaving and making common

12.2   Modern Maya residential compound on the Pasión River.   (Photo courtesy Peter Selverstone)

household pottery while they watched over their children playing nearby.

HOUSEHOLD ARTIFACTS

Most homes that have been excavated were exposed to the elements for centuries, and in the process they lost all their household contents. The suddenness of the volcanic eruption at Cerén meant these goods were left in place as the occupants fled, and they were subsequently preserved under deep layers of lava and ash. The well-preserved artifacts at these residences have revealed a surprisingly comfortable lifestyle, with plentiful food (see pages 310–311) and ample, well-built living spaces. A smattering of goods once thought to be reserved for the elite were also excavated: decorated pottery and finely painted gourds, many razor-sharp obsidian blades (all stored in roof rafters out of the reach of children, several jade beads and exotic shell fragments that may have once made a fine necklace, and cotton cloth.

Work Areas

FOR WOMEN

Storage containers and debris found in work areas indicated the wide range of activities performed by the various residents. Because extended families often shared residential compounds, women could share some of their work and socialize while performing their tasks. Women spun thread and wove cloth, they made common household pots, and at one Cerén house, several jars of red paint and numerous gourds suggested they produced the finely painted gourds that were used for serving food. Shelling, drying, and grinding activities probably were done in the shared courtyard or kitchen, as was the raising of domesticated and semidomesticated animals. The women probably tended the kitchen gardens as well. Spanish documents state the women took such barnyard animals and produce to the market and bartered it for other household goods. The women had separate, well-ventilated pole-and-thatch kitchens with earthen floors. The open-lattice walls permitted the smoke from burning charcoal to escape to some degree and kept such contamination outside the more enclosed house.

FOR MEN

The men joined together to build their houses and repair the residential complex. Most of their fields were some distance away, and the men spent their days preparing and harvesting them, returning home in the evening for the main meal. In their spare time, the men chipped and sharpened tools in a special thatched-roof work area near the house and chopped firewood.

FOOD AND DRINK

The Maya had a great variety of foods to choose among (see Chapter 11), but most days they consumed simple meals of maize, beans, and squash. Women were in charge of food preparation in the Maya household, from the softening of maize kernels and the grinding of their own flour to the cooking for the daily meals. They also foraged for wild plants and fruits.

Nutrition

Skeletal analyses indicate that the ancient Maya, even commoners, were usually well fed. There were variations within the population according to class and location, but generally the Maya were a robust people, just as the Spaniards described them. The basic subsistence diet was a nutritious one. Beans combined with maize provided a complete chain of the amino acids necessary for good health. Squashes, chili peppers, and fruits provided variety and a complement of vitamins, except for niacin (vitamin B). The Maya boiled their maize with *cal* (white lime) or snail shells, however, and this simple technique of softening the kernels also released niacin. Without this process, the Maya would have been subject to pellagra, a disease marked by skin eruptions and stomach disorders. On special feast days, even commoners supplemented this diet with venison, turkey, or shellfish, depending on where they lived.

Atole and Tamales

Bishop Landa described many cooking routines for the 16th-century Maya. Maize was consumed in a variety of ways. Ground three times, the maize flour was thinned with water to make various drinks, including the fermented drink *chiche*. The most important form of maize, however, was *atole*, a gruel drunk warm as the morning meal and consumed cold for lunch. The nobility favored their *atole* mixed with chocolate, but for the farmer, *atole* was more often flavored with chili peppers, toasted and ground squash seeds, honey, or herbs. It was an extremely practical way of consuming maize because it was easily carried in a gourd to the fields and required no implements to drink. In death, the Maya were buried with containers of *atole* for their trip through the Underworld.

The main meal of the day was more substantial, either tamales or a stew. When the maize dough was wrapped in avocado leaves or maize husks and steamed in a clay pot, it was transformed into tamales. The simplest meal of tamales was mixed with a ground chili sauce, but usually whole or mashed beans—black beans were the most popular—were also added. Spices like epazote, green vegetables like *chaya*, iguana eggs, or strips of meat or poultry, were added, too, especially for festive occasions. Sauces made of ground seeds and chili peppers could be added as a condiment. Elaborate versions were given as religious offerings, some of them with 13 layers of maize representing the levels of the heavens; Classic and Early Postclassic Period sculptures and paintings depict tamales in offertory bowls. The flat, thin crepe known as tortillas may have been more of a central Mexican tradition, introduced in the Maya region in the Postclassic Period. Ceramic griddles, or *comales*, for making tortillas are rarely found at Maya sites, but it is possible tortillas were made without the traditional *comal*.

Cooking Methods

THE HEARTH

The Maya cooked over a three-stone hearth, representing the traditional three-stone birthplace of the maize god in creation myths. Food, such as sweet potatoes, was placed on the stones, in the embers, or in ceramic pots to cook. Excavated bone and shell remains suggest that turtles and iguanas were grilled over the fire. Fish and poultry were often boiled, perhaps in the making of a stew in which the meat would be cooked with tomato, chili peppers, and spices, for example. For steaming, a little water was placed in a ceramic pot and boiled, then food was placed on a lattice of sticks above the water and steamed. Food was also smoked and toasted over the hearth or simply cooked in a ceramic pot.

STEAMING AND BARBECUING

Barbecuing was a favorite method for cooking dog, peccary, venison, and poultry: The meat was skewered and placed on wooden spit frame over an open fire. But pit roasting also was a specialty, especially for festivals when large quantities of food were consumed. The meat or poultry was prepared, perhaps covered with maize dough or rubbed with herbs, then wrapped in leaves or a palm mat before being placed in a pit oven, called a *pib*, that was dug out of the ground. A fire was lit under stones placed in the *pib*, and once the stones were hot, the meat was placed on top; the *pib* was sealed with earth or leaves until the meat was ready.

MEDICINE AND HEALTH

Cleanliness, herbal cures, and curing rituals formed the basis of Maya medicine. Maya homes and courtyards were swept clean, and the Maya themselves bathed often in cold water, evoking much comment from the Spaniards, who did not. After eating, they washed their hands and mouths. They also took steam baths, but less often; these were apparently part of a curing ceremony or in preparation of a religious one. Masonry steam baths have been excavated at many Maya sites. Personal hygiene, however, could not prevent the spells that Maya believed caused illness.

Shaman priests performed cures using herbal remedies and religious incantations, following the accumulated knowledge recorded in their books on the causes of disease and the remedies. Based on the native books that have survived from the colonial period, such as *The Ritual of the Bacabs,* disease involved disharmony in a part of the soul or an affront to the gods. The cure, facilitated through divination, brought the soul back into harmony through offerings to the gods and the bleeding of the diseased part of the body, such as the forehead for a headache. Of course, divination did not always provide a cure but instead indicated the patient was going to die. There were also elderly female shamans who specialized in childbirth, praying and assisting in the birth. Today venerated priests who are both diviners and healers are found in both lowland and highland Maya communities; women also are healers and midwives.

While the shamans' spells attacked the spiritual cause of disease, the herbal cures provided their own beneficial results: A natural diuretic, called *kanlol* in Yucatec Mayan, would have relieved heart conditions, and modern penicillin was discovered through just such an herbal cure. Tobacco, however, was mistakenly considered a cure for asthma and other ailments. Ethnobotanists continue to sort through herbal remedies used by traditional cultures, such as that of the Maya, in the hope of finding the key to new medicines. The Maya also had their home remedies: They grew plants in their kitchen gardens to cure stomach upset and diarrhea; they believed getting drunk on *balché* and vomiting was a cure, too, purging the body of worms. Ointments made from tree barks and resins were used to prevent mosquito bites.

PERSONAL APPEARANCE

Maya Beauty

The Maya concept of beauty did not change very much over the centuries, judging from Classic Period portraits of the nobility and 16th-century Spanish observations. The Maya preferred their foreheads sloped back; their noses in a very Roman profile; their eyes slightly crossed; their ears, noses, and lips pierced; their teeth filed into patterns and, in the Classic Period, inlaid with jade; and their bodies tattooed and painted. These marks of beauty could be as painful to achieve as a modern facelift.

The perfect nose could be achieved by a removable artificial nose bridge. Eyes could be crossed by tying soft tiny balls to strands of a child's hair and letting them dangle between the eyes. The head was artificially shaped in a process called trepanning, when the cranium was still malleable after birth. The baby's head was deformed into the desired shape by two boards tied to the head, one in the back and the other against the forehead. Within a few days, the forehead was successfully flattened for a lifetime of beauty. (See figure 12.4 on p. 339, for example.) Recent skeletal analyses from 94 Maya sites prove that approximately 90 percent of the Maya artificially shaped their heads and that the practice began in the Preclassic Period and continued until the colonial period. Far from being a symbol of nobility, it seems to have been instead a sign of being Maya. It is speculated that this profile was meant to look like an ear of maize.

TATTOOS

Both men and women pierced their ears and tattooed parts of their bodies. To tattoo, the design was painted on the body, which was then cut into. The paint and scar formed a tattoo. The process was said to be extremely painful, and for this reason tattoos were signs of personal bravery; the process caused infection and temporary illness. Some individuals were depicted with tattoos in Maya art, but most did not have them. Tattooing may have become more prevalent by the 16th century, when the Catholic priests complained of it and banned it. Men were not tattooed until their marriage, after which they would tattoo their bodies and parts of their faces. Women tattooed more delicate designs into the upper part of their bodies, but not on their breasts.

BODY PAINTING

Body painting was a common Maya practice. Classic Period murals and polychrome vases depict warriors covered with red or black paint; sometimes their bodies were striped with red paint. Paint was also used around the eyes and nose to give a fierce expression. In the 16th century, these practices continued. Women also applied red paint to their faces and bodies, but presumably to make themselves look beautiful, not fierce. Small paint jars of red hematite mixed with mica were found in the houses at Cerén, and these may have been for cosmetic use. Unmarried young men painted their bodies black, and so did those who were undergoing periods of ritual purification and fasting. Priests often wore blue body paint.

HAIRSTYLES

Long hair was stylish for all Maya, according to the Spaniards. The men may have cut the sides short, but they left a long thin strand down the back, occasionally braiding it with feathers or ribbon. Women were said to wear their hair long but arranged into an elegant headdress or in braids. Despite the many artistic representations from the earlier periods, it is frequently

12.3 *Ceramic burial whistle from the Usumacinta region depicting one Maya woman's dress and hairstyle in the Late Classic Period.* (Photo J. Eric S. Thompson, 1927)

hard to determine particular hairstyles because men usually wore headdresses, and women, turbans. In war scenes, however, male captives appear stripped of their finery, and their hair hangs down, shoulder length or longer, or is tied back in a ponytail. The front of the head often appears shaved, but this may have been only an artistic device to emphasize the flattened forehead. (See figure 5.5 on p. 150) A few portraits do show hair as part of the headdress, as a hank pulled forward or cut into an elaborate stepped sideburn. When a woman's hair can be discerned, it appears at least shoulder length. Despite the length, it seems the style of headdress for men and women was at least as important as the hair itself.

BEARDS

The Maya, like all Native Americans, do not have much facial hair, but many men can grow beards and mustaches. They do not seem to have been fashionable, however. In the 16th century, mothers rubbed hot cloths on the faces of their sons to burn off any peach fuzz; tweezers were also used to pluck out facial hair, both men's beards and women's eyebrows. In earlier periods, however, there are a few instances of rulers depicted with beards, goatees, or mustaches (see figures 2.13 on p. 65 and 6.7 on p. 181); in some instances, they seem to have been artificial and worn like other elements of the costume.

PERFUMES

The Maya applied various ointments and fragrances on themselves. Vanilla is one perfume that has been identified, but fragrances were also made from flowers as well herbs.

Clothing and Jewelry

The Maya wove beautiful garments and embellished them with feathers and animal skins, but they rarely tailored clothing to fit their limbs. Cloth was draped into cloaks or tied into scarflike jackets, wrapped around the chest into a sarong, around the hips for a skirt or male kilt, and between the legs for a breechclout. Such clothing was secured with a knot or woven belt with long tassels. Head holes were cut into cloth to permit a loose-fitting shirt, or

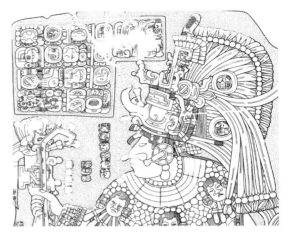

12.4 El Perú Stela 34 (detail), Late Classic Period. This ruler epitomizes the Classic Period Maya ideal of beauty with his sloping forehead, jade nose beads and ear plugs, and elaborate jade necklaces. (Drawing courtesy John Montgomery)

huipil, a woman's blouse. These items were often layered: a jacket over a sarong, a long skirt covered by a hip wrap, or a kilt over a breechclout, for example.

Women wore their hair wrapped into turbans or elaborate styles interwoven with cloth. Men also wore turbans, but their headdresses were more varied and occasionally looked oddly like bowlers or pillbox hats; more often, they were elaborate constructions of animal heads, hides, feathers, deity figures, and jewels. Sandals were made of untanned deerskin or hemp, and in preconquest art they are shown as ornamented with jaguar skin, pompoms, and other adornments.

Ancient Maya art depicts many of these costumes worn by rulers and their spouses as well as other members of the court. But there is no information about how the vast majority of the population dressed. The 16th-century Spaniards, however, described similar dress for the Maya. All men wore breechclouts, and most also had capes; all women wore skirts, although not all covered their breasts with sarongs or scarf jackets. In the Classic Period, the only women who did not cover their breasts appear to have been goddesses or characters in mythological scenes painted on vases. This difference, however, may have more to do with the fact that portraiture was restricted to noblewomen.

Jewelry

Men and women basically wore the same kind of jewelry, but women did not wear lip or nose plugs; in fact, nose plugs seem to have symbolized special status among elite men during the Terminal Classic Period. Even beyond facial ornaments, men usually wore more jewelry than women: many-stranded bead collars as well as single-strand bead necklaces with pendants, heavy ritual belts, and ornate ear plugs. Ear plugs were two-piece earrings in which a ring would be secured in the ear by a thick plug, usually of semiprecious stone. The ear plugs were so heavy, they distorted the ear lobe.

In the Classic Period, jade and exotic shells were the most valued materials for ear and lip plugs, necklaces, wristlets, and ritual belts worn by rulers and other members of the nobility. The weight of all the jade and serpentine jewelry depicted on royalty must have restricted their movements to some extent. By the Early Postclassic Period, the jade source was mostly exhausted, and turquoise and serpentine continued to be used along with shells; at Chichén Itzá, gold was introduced. By the Late Postclassic Period, gold, copper, and tumbago (a copper-and-gold alloy) became increasingly popular for bracelets and nose plugs, and the Spaniards mentioned amber stones set in metal for nose plugs. The gold, in fact, attracted the attention of the Spaniards in their early explorations around the Yucatán Peninsula and increased their resolve to return.

ENTERTAINMENT

The religious and seasonal cycles must have provided the most elaborate entertainment for the Maya. The Spaniards said that people traveled great distances to attend important ceremonies, and at times 15,000 Maya were gathered at one place to watch a ceremonial dance. But there were more secular forms of entertainment as well, although not much is known about them. The equivalent of board games may be depicted in the graffiti painted on ancient walls, and gambling with dice may have been known as well. There also seemed to have been ball games that did not have state or ritual significance that were played on dirt fields with rubber balls. The most that is known, however, concerns public ceremonies and private banquets.

Music and Dance

The Maya used music in many different contexts. There were court musicians, judging from the Classic Period murals there were bands that led funerary processions, and musicians who accompanied warriors into battle. Funerary whistles (see figure 12.3 on p. 338) were crafted to call the gods' attention to the dead's journey through the Underworld. Music also accompanied ceremonial dances. On an entrance pier to the Lower Temple of the Jaguars at Chichén Itzá, a god holds a rattle, perhaps a depiction of a Wayeb dance (see pages 188–189). Inside the temple a figure, the first in a long procession of carved figures, has his heel raised in the traditional dance position. Low platforms may have functioned as dance stages in the middle of large plazas at Maya cities where the populace gathered for public ceremonies.

DRUMS

Maya instruments were depicted in art, buried in royal tombs and elite necropolises, and left among household debris later excavated by archaeologists. They were also described by the early Spaniards. There existed many kinds of drums: Turtle carapaces struck with the palm of the hand made doleful sounds; hollow wooden drums called *tunkul* were immense and when struck with long wood sticks tipped with rubber, made noises that could be heard over a considerable distance; and other drums, including small kettledrums, were used.

RATTLES AND FLUTES

The wooden or ceramic maraca, a rattle decorated with plumes, was a common accompaniment in processions; ceramic pellets or seeds made the desired noise when rattled. There were many kinds of trumpets; some were long and wooden with twisted gourds at the end, others were conch shells. Figurine whistles, called *ocarinas* when they had more than one stop, were common in burials. Other flutes were made of reed, wood, ceramic, or the leg bone of a deer; the number of notes they played was determined by the number of stops, usually one to four. At the Belizean site of Pacbitún, male and female *ocarinas* were still playable when they were excavated; they made a sound like a piccolo, and the male figurines were deeper in pitch.

SONGS AND PERFORMANCES

The Maya sang as well as danced, and they sang well enough for the Spanish to relieve them of any further tribute payment if they agreed to sing in the church choir. When they sang about their fables and ancient lore, they were led by an honored priest. Ethnographers believe that Maya books were often read or performed in public ceremonies, and even the *Popol Vuh* was probably used in this fashion; the *Rabinal Achí* was written as a theatrical work and performed in historic times.

There are not many dances that were carefully recorded by the early Spaniards, but there were many different ones depicted in Maya art (see pages 187 ff.). Some were performed by a single dancer; there are stelae of Maya rulers, with one foot raised, in what appear to be solitary dances. The Spaniards described 16th-century dances that were performed by many men, and at least one of these was a war dance; another was performed by elderly women; and yet another, performed by both men and women, was considered erotic by the Catholic priests.

Banquets

The Maya probably feasted from the earliest times, and archaeologists suspect that the first use of maize was to make beer for such occasions. In the Classic Period, chocolate drinks were known to be part of such banquets among the nobility, and some painted scenes on vases suggest that there were parties devoted to inebriation through enema (enemas, because they bypass the digestive tract, have a more immediate impact than drinking). The Maya made several kinds of alcoholic drinks (see page 313), and although these were often consumed at religious ceremonies, the Spanish priests described their excessive consumption at upper-class banquets as well.

The most lavish banquets included musicians, dancers, and jesters, some of whom in the Postconquest Period, mimicked the Spaniards, apparently with great wit. There were also chocolate drinks, roasted fowl, tamales, and other delicacies as well as tubfuls of alcoholic *balché* consumed by the men. At the end of such feasts, the men were so drunk that their wives would have to come to help them home. These banquets involved a system of elite reciprocity in which those who attended had to invite the host

12.5   Bonampak mural, Room 1 (detail), 790. Musicians play the drum and feathered rattles, called maracas.   (Watercolor copy by Antonio Tejada, 1955)

to their own banquets. There were parties for family occasions, too, such as weddings and ancestor anniversaries, and these were celebrated by all classes, not just the nobility.

READING

Tozzer 1941: ethnohistoric overview of family, crimes, and customs; Chao 1986, Sanders and Santley 1983: division of labor; Coe 1999: overview of Mayan languages; Justeson, Norman 1985, Schortman 1986, Doris Stone 1966: languages and ethnicity; Farriss 1984, Redfield 1941, Ralph Roys 1957: family; Grove and Joyce 1999, Johnston and Gonlin 1998, Schele and Mathews 1998, Sheets 1992, Webster, et al. 1997: Maya household; Sophie Coe 1994, Danforth, et al. 1997, Landa 1941, Love 1989: food and drink; Gubler 1996, Ralph Roys 1965 and 1976, Thompson 1970, Tozzer 1941: medicine and health; Anawalt 1981, Cordry and Cordry 1968, Kerr 1989–2000: personal appearance; Healy 1988, Kerr 2000, Kurath 1967: entertainment.

CHRONOLOGICAL CHART* _____

	Southern Area	Central Area	Northern Area
B.C.E.			
2400–1700	———————— Fishing and incipient farming villages near water sources ————————		
1600	Barra ceramics		
1400–1000	———————————— Agricultural settlements ————————————		
1400	Isthmian horizon (Locona Phase)		
1200	Ocós Phase Olmec influences	traces of ceramics	
1000–700	Planned urban centers Olmec interaction	Eb, Swasey, Xe ceramics Earliest plastered buildings	
700–400	———————— Mamom horizon and Olmec interaction ————————		
	Chalchuapa, Kaminaljuyú	Nakbé	Komchén
	———————— Monumental architecture and public works ————————		
400	Protowriting at El Portón	———————— Spread of masonry architecture ————————	
	———————————— Olmec decline ————————————		
300	———————————— Chicanel horizon ————————————		
	———————— Growth in number and size of urban centers ————————		
	Izapa/Epi-Olmec stelae	———————— Giant stucco facades ————————	
	Kaminaljuyú, Abaj Takalik, Chalchuapa, and La Blanca	Mirador Basin sites Uaxactún and Cerros	Kohunlich, Dzibilchaltún, Edzná, and Becán
	Hieroglyphic texts	Corbeled tombs	
C.E.			
250	Hiatus; sites abandoned; eruption of Ilopango	———————— Tzakol ceramic horizon ———————— Tikal and Calakmul	Cobá and Yaxuná

* Only a few of the known Classic Period dated events are represented on this chart.

	Southern Area	Central Area	Northern Area
292		Maya Long Count, Tikal	
378		Teotihuacan installs dynasty at Tikal and Uaxactún	Becán, Oxkintok, and other sites
		———————— Spread of stela cult ————————	
400	Teotihuacan at Kaminaljuyú and Pacific coast sites		
420		Yax K'uk Mo begins new dynasty at Copán	
426		Copán founds Quiriguá	
534		Caracol rises to power	
553		Tikal oversees installation of Caracol king	
556–562		War between Caracol and Tikal	
562		Caracol defeats Tikal	
562–692		Hiatus at Tikal	
599	Cerén buried by volcanic eruption	Calakmul attacks Palenque	
		———————— End of Teotihuacan Influence ————————	
		———————— Tepeu ceramic horizon ————————	
619	Tazumal and other sites revive	Calakmul and Caracol allies	
631		Caracol defeats Naranjo; hiatus begins at Naranjo	Stelae at Edzná, Cobá, Dzibilchaltún, and
645		First ruler installed at Dos Pilas	other sites
648		Calakmul is overlord of Dos Pilas	
652–672		Calakmul flourishes; 40 stelae erected	
656		Calakmul oversees installation of ruler at Cancuén	
672		A century of Maya artistic apogee begins	
682		Naranjo revives under marriage alliance with Dos Pilas	
690		Naranjo raids Caracol; Caracol hiatus until 800	
695		Tikal defeats ruler of Calakmul; continued wars between these superpowers	
700		Tikal controls Motul de San José	
735		Petexbatún kingdom expands; defeats Seibal	
738		Quiriguá revolts against Copán	
743–744		Tikal defeats El Perú and Naranjo	
768		Tamarindito attacks Dos Pilas	
771		Fragmentation of states; small kingdoms, such as at Pomoná, erect monuments with emblem glyphs	
		Peak population levels	

	Southern Area	Central Area	Northern Area
780		Increasing elite class; Carved texts in nonroyal buildings	
790–810		Last dated monuments at Aguateca, Palenque, Bonampak, Yaxchilán, Piedras Negras, Calakmul, Naranjo, and Quiriguá	
c. 800	Kaminaljuyú abandoned Pan-Mesoamerican trade	Petexbatún kingdom completely collapsed	Cobá, Edzná, and Dzibilchaltún persist Maritime and pan-Mesoamerican trade
800–1000	Cotzumalguapa and other southern cities flourish		Rise of Puuc cities and Chichén Itzá
820		Last dated monument at Naranjo	
822		Last dated monument at Copán	
830		New dynasty at Seibal installed by Ucanal	
832			Inscriptions begin at Chichén Itzá and continue at Ek Balam
849		Seibal stelae of "foreigners"; last dated monument at Caracol	
869		Last inscription at Tikal	
869–881			Many inscriptions at Chichén Itzá
889		Last inscription at Seibal	
c. 890		Caracol sacred center abandoned	
907			Last inscription at Uxmal
909		Last Long Count date	
998			Last dated monument at Chichén Itzá

———————————————— End of inscriptions on stone monuments ————————————————

	Southern Area	Central Area	Northern Area
1000		Petén sites totally abandoned; only rivers and coast of Belize remain populated	
1100–1200	Decline of Cotzumalguapa		Decline of Chichén Itzá
1220	Small kingdoms; fortifications	Lake districts reoccupied	Rise of Mayapán; fortifications
1375	Quiché empire; Utatlán		

	Southern Area	Central Area	Northern Area
1450			Destruction of Mayapán
1470	Cakchiquel rebellion; Iximché founded		Small kingdoms; maritime trade; Tulum and Santa Rita
1510	Quiché pay tribute to Aztecs		Aztec artistic and trade influence
1519	————— Spaniards land in Veracruz; conquest of Mesoamerica begins —————		
1521	Plague kills 1/3 of highland population		
1524	Spanish conquest of Utatlán		
1525		Hernán Cortés at Tayasal	
1527			Failed Spanish attempt to conquer Yucatán
1530	Cakchiquel Maya surrender to Spaniards		
1531–35			Another failed attempt to conquer Yucatán
1542			Spaniards conquer Yucatán
1697		Conquest of Tayasal	

BIBLIOGRAPHY

Abrams, Elliot M. *How the Maya Built Their World: Energetics and Ancient Architecture.* Austin: University of Texas Press, 1994.

———. "Structures as Sites: The Construction Process and Maya Architecture." In Houston 1998.

Abrams, Elliot M., and Ann Corinne Freter. "A Late Classic Lime Plaster Kiln from the Maya Centre of Copan, Honduras." *American Antiquity* 60 (1996): 422–28.

Abrams, Elliot M., and D. Rue. "The Causes and Consequences of Deforestation Among the Prehistoric Maya." *Human Ecology* 16 (1988): 377–95.

Adams, Richard E. W., ed. *The Origins of Maya Civilization.* Albuquerque: University of New Mexico Press, 1977.

———. "Rio Azul." *National Geographic* 169 (1986): 420–25.

———. Prehistoric Mesoamerica. Rev. ed. Norman: University of Oklahoma, 1991.

Adams, Richard E. W., and R. C. Jones. "Spatial Patterns and Regional Growth Among Classic Maya Cities." *American Antiquity* 46 (1981): 301–22.

Aimers, James J., Terry G. Powis, and Jaime J. Awe. "Preclassic Round Structures of the Upper Belize River Valley." *Latin American Antiquity* 11, no. 1 (2000): 71–86.

Aldenderfer, Mark. "Functional Evidence for Lapidary and Carpentry Craft Specialties in the Late Classic of the Central Peten Lakes Region." *Ancient Mesoamerica* 2, no. 1 (1991): 205–14.

Alvarado, Pedro de. *An Account of the Conquest of Guatemala in 1524.* Trans. by Sidley J. Mackie. Boston: Milford House, 1972.

Anawalt, Patricia Rieff. *Indian Clothing Before Cortes: Mesoamerican Costumes from the Codices.* Norman: University of Oklahoma Press, 1981.

Andrews, Anthony P. *Maya Salt Production and Trade.* Tucson: University of Arizona Press, 1983.

———. "The Fall of Chichen Itza: A Preliminary Hypothesis." *Latin American Antiquity* 1 (1990): 259–67.

———. "The Role of Trading Ports." In Clancy and Harrison 1990.

———. "El comercio marítimo de los mayas del posclásico." *Arqueología mexicana* 6, no. 33 (1998): 16–23.

Andrews, Anthony P., and Fernando Robles C. "Chichén Itzá and Cobá: An Itza-Maya Standoff in Early Postclassic Yucatan." In Chase and Rice 1985.

Andrews, E. Wyllys, IV. "Progress Report on the 1960–64 Field Seasons National Geographic Society–Tulane University Dzibilchaltun Program." Publication 31. New Orleans: Middle American Research Institute, 1965.

———. "The Development of Maya Civilization after the Abandonment of the Southern Cities." In Culbert 1973.

Andrews, E. Wyllys, V. "The Early Ceramic History of the Maya Lowlands." In Clancy and Harrison 1990.

Andrews, E. Wyllys, V., William M. Ringle, et al. "Komchén: An Early Maya Community in Northwest Yucatán." *Investigaciones recientes en el area Maya* 1 (1984): 73–92.

Andrews, E. Wyllys, V., and Jeremy A. Sabloff. "Classic to Postclassic: A Summary Discussion." In Sabloff and Andrews V 1986.

Andrews, George F. *Maya Cities: Placemaking and Urbanization.* Norman: University of Oklahoma Press, 1975.

———. "Architectural Survey of the Río Bec, Chenes, and Puuc Regions: Progress and Problems." In Prem 1994.

Ashmore, Wendy, ed. *Lowland Maya Settlement Patterns.* Albuquerque: University of New Mexico Press, 1981.

———. "Site-Planning Principles and the Concept of Directionality among the Ancient Maya." *Latin American Antiquity* 2 (1991): 199–226.

———. "Thoughts on Settlement and Society at Quirigua." Paper presented at the 65th Annual Meeting of the Society for American Archaeology. Philadelphia, 2000.

Aveni, Anthony F. *Archaeoastronomy in Precolumbian America.* Austin: University of Texas Press, 1975.

———. "Venus and the Maya." *American Scientist* 67 (1979): 274–85.

———. *Skywatchers of Ancient Mexico.* Austin: University of Texas Press, 1980.

———, ed. *Archaeoastronomy in the New World.* Cambridge, England: Cambridge University Press, 1982.

———. *Empires of Time: Calendars, Clocks, and Cultures.* New York: Basic Books, 1989.

Aveni, Anthony F., Sharon L. Gibbs, and Horst Hartung. "The Caracol Tower at Chichen Itza: An Ancient Astronomical Observatory?" *Science* 188 (1975): 977–85.

Aveni, Anthony F., and Horst Hartung. "Maya City Planning and the Calendar." *Transactions of the American Philosophical Society* 67, no. 7 (1986).

———. "Uaxactun, Guatemala, Group E and Similar Assemblages: An Archaeoastronomical Reconsideration." In *World Archaeo-astronomy,* ed. by Anthony F. Aveni. Cambridge: Cambridge University Press, 1989.

Aveni, Anthony F., and Lorren D. Hotaling. "Monumental Inscriptions and the Observational Basis of Mayan Planetary Astronomy." In *Archaeoastronomy* 19 (1994): S21–S54.

Ball, Joseph W. "A Coordinate Approach to Northern Maya Prehistory: A.D. 700–1200." *American Antiquity* 39, no. 1 (1974): 85–93.

———. "The Archaeological Ceramics of Becan, Campeche, Mexico." Publication 43. New Orleans: Middle American Research Institute, 1977.

———. "The Rise of Northern Maya Chiefdoms: A Socioprocessual Analysis." In Adams 1977.

Bardsley, Sandra Noble. "Rewriting History at Yaxchilan: Inaugural Art of Bird Jaguar IV." In Fields 1994.

Barry, Kimberly A., and Patricia McAnanay. "Feeding and Clothing K'axob. Evidence for Wetland Cultivation at a Maya Settlement." Paper presented at the 65th Annual Meeting of the Society for American Archaeology. Philadelphia, 2000.

Bassie-Sweet, Karen. *From the Mouth of the Dark Cave.* Norman: University of Oklahoma Press, 1991.

Baudez, Claude F. "The Cross Pattern at Copán: Forms, Rituals, and Meanings." In *Sixth Palenque Round Table, 1986,* ed. by Merle Greene Robertson. Norman: University of Oklahoma Press, 1991.

Beadle, George W. "The Mystery of Maize." *Field Museum of Natural History Bulletin* 43, no. 10 (1972): 2–11.

Benavides Castillo, Antonio. *Edzná: Una ciudad prehispánica de Campeche/Edzná: A Pre-Columbian City in Campeche.* Pittsburgh: University of Pittsburgh, 1997.

Benson, Elizabeth P. "Architecture as Metaphor." In Fields 1985.

———, ed. *City-States of the Maya—Art and Architecture.* Denver: Rocky Mountain Institute for Pre-Columbian Studies, 1986.

Berlin, Heinrich. "El glifo 'emblema' en las inscripciones mayas." *Journal de la Société des Américanistes* 47 (1958): 111–19.

———. "Glifos nominales en el sarcófago de Palenque." *Humanidades* 2, no. 10 (1959): 1–8.

———. "The Palenque Triad." *Journal de la Société des Américanistes* 52 (1963): 91–99.

Berlo, Janet, and Richard A. Diehl, eds. *Mesoamerica After the Decline of Teotihuacan A.D. 700–900.* Washington, D.C.: Dumbarton Oaks, 1989.

Berlin, Heinrich and David Kelley. "The 819-Day Count and Color-Direction Symbolism Among the Classic Maya." *Archaeological Studies in Middle America.* Tulane University, Middle American Research Institute, Publication 26. (1961).

Bey, George, C. A. Hanson, and William M. Ringle. "Classic to Postclassic at Ek Balam, Yucatan." *American Antiquity* 8 (1997): 237–54.

Beyer, Hermann. "The True Zero Date of the Maya." *Maya Research* 3 (1936): 202–4.

———. *Studies on the Inscriptions of Chichén Itzá.* Contributions to American Archaeology, no. 21. Publication 483. Washington, D.C.: Carnegie Institution of Washington, 1937.

Bill, Cassandra R. "The Roles and Relationships of God M and Other Black Gods in the Codices with Specific Reference to Pages 50–56 of the Madrid Codex." In Bricker and Vail 1997.

Bill, Cassandra R., Christine L. Hernández, and Victoria R. Bricker. "The Relationship Between Early Colonial Maya New Year's Ceremonies and Some Almanacs in the Madrid Codex." *Ancient Mesoamerica* 11 (2000): 149–68.

Blake, Michael, John E. Clark, Barbara Voorhies, et al. "Radiocarbon Chronology for the Late Archaic and Formative Period of the Pacific Coast of Southeastern Mesoamerica." *Ancient Mesoamerica* 6, no. 2 (1995): 161–83.

Bove, Frederick J. "The Teotihuacán-Kaminaljuyu-Tikal Connection: A View from the South Coast of Guatemala." In *The Sixth Palenque Round Table, 1986,* ed. by Merle Greene Robertson. Norman: University of Oklahoma, 1986.

Bray, Warwick. "Maya Metalwork and Its External Connections." In *Social Process in Maya Prehistory: Essays in Honor of Sir J. Eric S. Thompson,* ed. by Norman Hammond. New York: Academic Press, 1977.

Brenner, Mark. "Climate and Culture in Precolumbian America." *American Quarternary Asso-*

ciation Program and Abstracts of the 15th Biennial Meeting, Puerto Vallarta, Mexico (1998).

Bricker, Harvey M., and Victoria R. Bricker. "Classic Maya Prediction of Solar Eclipses." *Current Anthropology* 24 (1983): 1–24.

Bricker, Victoria R. *Ritual Humor in Highland Chiapas.* Austin: University of Texas Press, 1973.

———. *The Indian Christ, the Indian King: The Historical Substrate of Maya Myth and Ritual.* Austin: University of Texas Press, 1981.

———. *A Grammar of Mayan Hieroglyphs.* Publication 56. New Orleans: Middle American Research Institute, 1986.

Bricker, Victoria R., and Harvey M. Bricker. "Archaeoastronomical Implications of an Agricultural Almanac in the Dresden Codex." *Mexicon* 8, no. 2 (1986): 29–35.

Bricker, Victoria, and Gabrielle Vail, eds. *Papers on the Madrid Codex.* New Orleans: Middle American Research Institute, 1997.

Brinton, Daniel G. *The Maya Chronicles.* No. 1. Philadelphia: Brinton's Library of Aboriginal American Literature, 1982.

———. *A Primer of Mayan Hieroglyphics.* Vol. 3, no. 2. Philadelphia: University of Pennsylvania Series in Philology, Literature, and Archaeology, 1985.

Bruhns, Karen Olsen, and Karen E. Stothert. *Women in Ancient America.* Norman: University of Oklahoma Press, 1999.

Brumfield, F., and T. Earl, eds. *Specialization, Exchange, and Complex Societies.* Cambridge, England: Cambridge University Press, 1987.

Buikstra, Jane, et al. "The Early Classic Royal Burials at Copan: A Bioarchaeological Perspective." Paper presented at the 65th Annual Meeting of the Society for American Archaeology. Philadelphia, 2000.

Bullard, William R., Jr. "Maya Settlement Pattern in Northeastern Peten, Guatemala." *American Antiquity* 25 (1960): 355–72.

Burkhart, Louise M., and Janine Gasco. "Mesoamerica and Spain: The Conquest." In *The Legacy of Mesoamerica: History and Culture of a Native American Civilization,* ed. by Robert M. Carmack, Janine Gasco, and Gary H. Gossen. Upper Saddle River, N.J.: Prentice Hall, 1996.

Campbell, Lyle R., and Terrence S. Kaufman. "A Linguistic Look at the Olmecs." *American Antiquity* 41 (1976): 80–89.

Carlsen, Robert S. *The War for the Heart and Soul of a Maya Highland Town.* Austin: University of Texas Press, 1997.

Carmack, Robert M. "Toltec Influence on the Postclassic Cultural History of Highland Guatemala." Middle American Research Institute, Publication 26 (1968): 50–92.

————. *The Quiché Mayas of Utatlán: The Evolution of a Highland Guatemalan Kingdom.* Norman: University of Oklahoma Press, 1981.

————. *Rebels of Highland Guatemala: The Quiche Mayas of Momostenango.* Norman: University of Oklahoma Press, 1995.

Carmean, Kelli. "Architectural Labor Investment and Social Stratification at Sayil, Yucatan, Mexico." *Latin American Antiquity* 2 (1991): 151–65.

Carr, R. F., and J. E. Hazard. "Map of the Ruins of Tikal, El Peten, Guatemala." *Tikal Reports 11.* Philadelphia: University Museum, 1961.

Castellanos, Jeanette, and Antonia E. Foias. "Fine Paste Wares and the Terminal Classic in the Southwest Lowlands." Paper presented at the 65th Annual Meeting of the Society for American Archaeology. Philadelphia, 2000.

Catherwood, Frederick. *View of Ancient Monuments in Central America, Chiapas, and Yucatan.* New York: 1844.

Chamberlain, Robert S. *The Conquest and Colonialization of Yucatan.* Washington, D.C.: Carnegie Institution of Washington, 1948.

Chao, Kang. *Man and Land in China.* Stanford: Stanford University Press, 1986.

Chase, Arlen F. "Postclassic Peten Interaction Spheres: The View from Tayasal." In Chase and Rice 1985.

————. "Cycles of Time: Caracol in the Maya Realm." In *Eighth Palenque Round Table,* ed. by Merle Greene Robertson. Norman: University of Oklahoma Press, 1991.

Chase, Arlen F., and Diane Z. Chase. *Investigations at the Classic Maya City of Caracol, Belize, 1985–1987.* Monograph 3. San Francisco: Pre-Columbian Art Research Institute, 1987.

————. "Maya Veneration of the Dead at Caracol, Belize." In *Seventh Palenque Round Table,* ed. by

Virginia M. Fields. San Francisco: Pre-Columbian Art Institute, 1994.

————. "A Mighty Maya Nation." *Archaeology* September/October 1996: 66–76.

Chase, Arlen F., and Prudence M. Rice, eds. *The Lowland Maya Postclassic.* Austin: University of Texas Press, 1985.

Chase, Diane Z. "Between Earth and Sky: Idols, Images and Postclassic Cosmology." In Fields 1985.

————. "Social and Political Organization in the Land of Cacao and Honey: Correlating the Archaeology and Ethnohistory of the Postclassic Lowland Maya." In Sabloff and Andrews V. 1986.

————. "Lifeline to the Gods: Ritual Bloodletting at Santa Rita Corozal." In *Sixth Palenque Round Table, 1986,* vol. 8, ed. Merle Greene Robertson. Norman: University of Oklahoma Press, 1991.

Chase, Diane Z., and Arlen F. Chase. *Mesoamerican Elites.* Norman: University of Oklahoma Press, 1992.

————. "The Architectural Context of Caches, Burials and Other Ritual Activities for the Classic Period Maya as Reflected at Caracol, Belize." In Houston 1998.

Childe, C. Vernon. "The Urban Revolution." *Town Planning Review* 21 (1950): 3–17.

Christensen, Bodil, and Samuel Marti. *Witchcraft and Pre-Columbian Paper.* Mexico: Ediciones Euroamericanas Klaus Thiele, 1971.

Clancy, Flora S., and Peter D. Harrison. *Vision and Revision in Maya Studies.* Albuquerque: University of New Mexico Press, 1990.

Clark, John E. "The Beginnings of Mesoamerica: Apologia for the Soconusco Early Formative." In *The Formation of Complex Society in Southeastern Mesoamerica,* ed. by William R. Fowler, Jr. Boca Raton, Fla.: CRC Press, 1991.

Clendenin, Inga. *Ambivalent Conquests: Maya and Spaniard in Yucatán, 1517–1570.* Cambridge, England: Cambridge University Press, 1987.

Cloos, Michael. "Venus in the Maya World: Glyphs, Gods, and Associated Astronomical Phenomena." In *Tercera Mesa Redonda de Palenque,* vol. 4. Edited by Merle Greene Robertson. San Francisco: Pre-Columbian Art Institute, 1979.

Coates, Anthony G., ed. *Central America: A Natural and Cultural History*. New Haven, Conn.: Yale University Press, 1997.

Coe, Michael D. "The Olmec Style and Its Distribution." In *Handbook of Middle American Indians*, vol. 3. Austin: University of Texas Press, 1965.

———. *America's First Civilization: Discovering the Olmec*. New York: American Heritage, 1968.

———. *The Maya Scribe and His World*. New York: Grolier Club, 1973.

———. "Death and the Ancient Maya." In *Death and the Afterlife in Pre-Columbian America*, ed. by Elizabeth P. Benson. Washington, D.C.: Dumbarton Oaks, 1975.

———. "Native Astronomy in Mesoamerica." In Aveni 1975.

———, "The Hero Twins: Myth and Image." In *The Maya Vase Book*, vol. 1, ed. by Justin Kerr. New York: Kerr Associates, 1989.

———. "The Royal Fifth: Earliest Notices of Maya Writing." *Research Reports on Ancient Maya Writing*. Washington, D.C.: Center for Maya Research, 1989.

———. *Breaking the Maya Code*. New York: Thames and Hudson, 1992.

———. *The Maya*. 6th edition. New York: Thames and Hudson, 1999.

Coe, Michael D., and Richard A. Diehl. *In the Land of the Olmec: San Lorenzo Tenochtitlan*. 2 vols. Austin: University of Texas Press, 1980.

Coe, Michael D., and Justin Kerr. *The Art of the Maya Scribe*. London: Thames and Hudson, 1997.

Coe, Sophie D. *America's First Cuisines*. Austin: University of Texas Press, 1994.

Coe, Sophie D., and Michael D. Coe. *The True History of Chocolate*. London: Thames and Hudson, 1996.

Coggins, Clemency C. "Teotihuacan at Tikal in the Early Classic Period." *Actes de XIII Congrés International des Américanistes* 8 (1976): 251–69.

———. "A New Order and the Role of the Calendar: Some Characteristics of the Middle Classic Period at Tikal." In *Maya Archaeology and Ethnohistory*, ed. by Norman Hammond and Gordon Willey. Austin: University of Texas Press, 1979.

———, ed. *Artifacts from the Cenote of Sacrifice, Chichén Itzá, Yucatan*. Peabody Museum of Archaeology and Ethnology Papers, vol. 10. Cambridge, Mass.: Harvard University, 1992.

Coggins, Clemency C., and Orrin C. Shane, eds. *Cenote of Sacrifice: Maya Treasures from the Sacred Well of Chichén Itzá*. Austin: University of Texas Press, 1984.

Cogolludo, Diego López. *Historía de Yucatán*. Madrid: 1688.

Cohodas, Marvin. *The Great Ball Court at Chichén Itzá, Yucatan*. New York: Garland Publishing, 1978.

Columbus, Ferdinand. *Journals and Other Documents on the Life of Christopher Columbus*. Ed. by Samuel Eliot Morrison. New York: Heritage, 1963.

Cordry, Donald, and Dorothy Cordry. *Mexican Indian Costumes*. Austin: University of Texas Press, 1968.

Cortés, Hernán. *Letters from Mexico*. Trans. and ed. by Anthony Pagden. New Haven, Conn.: Yale University Press, 1986.

Craine, Eugene R., and Reginald C. Reindrop. *The Codex Pérez and the Book of Chilam Balam of Maní*. Norman: University of Oklahoma Press, 1979.

Culbert, Patrick T., ed. *The Classic Maya Collapse*. Albuquerque: University of New Mexico Press, 1973.

———. *Classic Maya Political History: Hieroglyphic and Archaeological Evidence*. Cambridge, England: Cambridge University Press, 1991.

———. "The New Maya." *Archaeology* September/October 1998: 48–52.

Culbert, Patrick T., Laura J. Levi, and Luis Cruz. "Lowland Maya Wetland Agriculture: The Rio Azul Agronomy Program." In Clancy and Harrison 1990.

Culbert, Patrick T., and Don S. Rice, eds. *Precolumbian Population History in the Maya Lowlands*. Albuquerque: University of New Mexico Press, 1990.

Curtis, J. H., D. A. Hodell, and M. Brenner. "Possible Role of Climate in the Collapse of Classic Maya Civilization." *Science* 375 (1995): 391–94.

Cyphers, Ann. "Reconstructing Olmec Life at San Lorenzo." In *Olmec Art of Ancient Mexico*, ed. by Elizabeth P. Benson and Beatriz de la Fuente. Washington, D.C.: National Gallery of Art, 1996.

Dahlin, Bruce H. "Climate and Prehistory on the Yucatan Peninsula." *Climatic Change* 5 (1983): 245–63.

————. "A Colossus in Guatemala: The Preclassic City of El Mirador." *Archaeology* 37, no. 5 (1984): 18–25.

————. "The Barricade and Abandonment of Chunchucmil: Implications for Northern Maya Warfare." *Latin American Antiquity* 11, no. 3 (2000): 283–98.

————. "Climate as a Variable in the Collapse of Maya Civilization." Paper presented at the 65th Annual Meeting of the Society for American Archaeology. Philadelphia, 2000.

Danforth, Marie Elaine, Keith P. Jacobi, and Mark N. Cohen. "Gender and Health Among the Colonial Maya of Tipu, Belize." *Ancient Mesoamerica* 8, no. 1 (1997): 13–22.

Demarest, Arthur A. "The Archaeology of Santa Leticia and the Rise of Maya Civilization." Publication 56. New Orleans: Middle American Research Institute, 1986.

————. "The Olmecs and the Rise of Civilization in Eastern Mesoamerica." In Sharer and Grove 1989.

————. "Violent Saga of a Maya Kingdom." *National Geographic* 183, no. 2 (1993): 95–111.

Demarest, Arthur A., M. Mansky, C. Wolley, et al. "Classic Maya Defensive Systems and Warfare in the Petexbatun Region: Archaeological Evidence and Interpretation." *Ancient Mesoamerica* 8, no. 1 (1997): 229–54.

Demarest, Arthur A., Robert J. Sharer, William Fowler, et al. "Las excavaciones: El Mirador." *Mesoamerica* 7 (1984): 14–15.

Deuel, Leo. *Conquistadors Without Swords: Archaeologists in the Americas.* New York: Schocken Books, 1974.

Dewey, E. D., Donald S. Rice, Prudence P. Rice, et al. "Maya Urbanism: Impact on a Tropical Karst Environment." *Science* 206 (1979): 298–306.

Díaz del Castillo, Bernal. *The Discovery and Conquest of Mexico.* Ed. and trans. by A. P. Maudslay. New York: Farrar, Straus, & Giroux, 1956.

Digby, Adrian. *Maya Jades.* London: British Museum, 1972.

Dixon, E. James. *Bones, Boats, and Bison.* Albuquerque: University of New Mexico Press, 2000.

Drennan, Robert D. "Long-Distance Transport Costs in Pre-Hispanic Mesoamerica." *American Anthropologist* 86 (1984): 105–112.

Drew, David. *The Lost Chronicles of the Maya Kings.* Berkeley: University of California Press, 1999.

Drucker, P., Robert Heizer, and R. J. Squier. *Excavations at La Venta, Tabasco.* Bulletin 170. Washington, D.C.: Bureau of American Ethnology, 1955.

Dunning, Nicholas P. "A Reexamination of Regional Variability in the Prehistoric Agricultural Landscape." In Fedick 1996.

Dunning, Nicholas P., Vernon Scarborough, T. Patrick Culbert, et al. "The Rise of the Bajos and the Rise of Maya Civilization." Paper presented at the 65th Annual Meeting of the Society for American Archaeology. Philadelphia, 2000.

Dütting, Dieter. "The Astronomical Background of Mayan Historical Events." In Fields 1985.

Edmonson, Munro S. *The Ancient Future of the Itza: The Book of Chilam Balam of Tizimin.* Austin: University of Texas Press, 1982.

————. *Heaven-Born Merida and Its Destiny, The Book of Chilam Balam of Chumayel.* Austin: University of Texas Press, 1986.

Erasmus, C. J. "Monument Building: Some Field Experiments." *Southwestern Journal of Anthropology* 21, no. 4 (1965): 277–301.

Farriss, Nancy M. *Maya Society Under Colonial Rule: The Collective Enterprise of Survival.* Princeton, N.J.: Princeton University Press, 1984.

Fash, Barbara W., and William L. Fash. "Copan Temple 20 and the House of Bats." In Fields 1994.

Fash, William L. "Lineage Patrons and Ancestor Worship Among the Classic Maya Nobility: The Case of Copán Structure 9N-82." In *Sixth Palenque Round Table, 1986,* vol. 8, ed. by Merle Greene Robertson. Norman: University of Oklahoma Press, 1991.

————. *Scribes, Warriors, and Kings: The City of Copán and the Ancient Maya.* New York: Thames and Hudson, 1991.

————. "Official Histories and Archaeological Data in the Interpretation of the Teotihuacan-Copan Relationship." A paper presented at Symposium on Tale of Two Cities: Copan and Teotihuacan. Harvard University, 1997.

————. "Dynastic Architectural Programs: Intention and Design in Classic Maya Buildings at Copan and Other Sites." In Houston 1998.

Fash, William L., and David S. Stuart. "Dynastic History and Cultural Evolution at Copán, Honduras." In Culbert 1991.

Fedick, Scott L., ed. *Managed Mosaic: Ancient Maya Agriculture and Resource Use.* Salt Lake City: University of Utah Press, 1996.

Feinman, Gary M., and Joyce Marcus, eds. *Scale and Complexity in Archaic States.* Santa Fe, N.M.: School of American Research Press, 1998.

Fields, Virginia M., ed. *Fifth Palenque Round Table, 1983.* Vol. 7. San Francisco: Pre-Columbian Art Research Institute, 1985.

———, ed. *Seventh Palenque Round Table.* San Francisco: Pre-Columbian Art Research Institute, 1994.

Flannery, Kent V. "The Cultural Evolution of Civilization." *Annual Review of Ecology and Systematics* 3 (1972): 399–426.

Folan, William J. "Calakmul, Campeche: A Centralized Urban Administrative Center in the Northern Peten." *World Archaeology* 24 (1992): 158–68.

Folan, William J., Laraine A. Fletcher, and Ellen R. Kintz. "Fruit, Fiber, Bark, and Resin: Social Organization of a Maya Urban Center." *Science* 204 (1979): 697–701.

Folan, William J., Ellen R. Kintz, and Laraine A. Fletcher. *Coba: A Maya Metropolis.* New York: Academic Press, 1983.

Folan, William J., Joyce Marcus, Sophia Pincemin, et al. "Calakmul: New Data from an Ancient Maya Capital in Campeche, Mexico." *Latin American Antiquity* 6 (1995): 310–34.

Ford, Anabel. "Critical Resource Control and the Rise of the Classic Period Maya." In Fedick 1996.

Foster, Lynn V., and Linnea Wren. "World Creator and World Sustainer: God N at Chichén Itzá." In *Eighth Palenque Round Table, 1993*, vol. 10, ed. by Martha J. Macri and Jan McHargue. San Francisco: Pre-Columbian Art Research Institute, 1996.

Foster, Nelson, and Linda S. Cordell, eds. *Chilis to Chocolate: Food the Americas Gave the World.* Tucson: University of Arizona Press, 1992.

Fowler, William R., Jr., and Arthur A. Demarest, et al. "The Vanderbilt Petexbatun Regional Archaeology Project, 1989–1994." *Ancient Mesoamerica* 8, no. 2 (1997): 207–363.

Fox, James A., and John S. Justeson. "A Mayan Planetary Observation." *Contributions of the University of California Archaeological Research Facility,* 36 (1978): 55–59.

Fox, John W. *Maya Postclassic State Formation: Segmentary Lineage Migration in Advancing Frontiers.* Cambridge, England: Cambridge University Press, 1987.

Freidel, David A. "Maya Warfare: An Example of Peer Polity Interaction." In *Peer Polity Interaction and the Development of Sociopolitical Complexity*, ed. by Colin Renfrew and J. F. Cherry. Cambridge, England: Cambridge University Press, 1986.

———. "Children of First Father's Skull: Terminal Classic Warfare in the Northern Maya Lowlands and the Transformation of Kingship and Elite Hierarchies." In Chase and Chase 1992.

Freidel, David A., and Jeremy A. Sabloff. *Cozumel: Late Maya Settlement Patterns.* New York: Academic Press, 1984.

Freidel, David A. and Linda Schele. "Kingship in the Late Pre-Classic Maya Lowland: The Instruments and Places of Ritual Power." *American Anthropology* 90 (1988): 547–67.

———. "Symbol and Power: A History of the Lowland Maya Cosmogram." In *Maya Iconography*, ed. by Elizabeth Benson and Gillett Griffin. Princeton, N.J.: Princeton University Press, 1988.

———. "Dead Kings and Living Temples: Dedication and Termination Rituals Among the Ancient Maya." In *Word and Image in Maya Culture*, ed. by W. C. Hank and D. S. Rice. Salt Lake City: University of Utah Press, 1989.

Freidel, David, Linda Schele, and Joy Parker. *Maya Cosmos: Three Thousand Years on the Shaman's Path.* New York: William Morrow, 1993.

Furst, Peter T. "Shamanism, Transformation, and Olmec Art." In *The Olmec World: Ritual and Rulership*, ed. by Princeton, N.J.: Princeton University Press, 1995.

Furst, Peter T., and Michael D. Coe. *Hallucinogens and Culture.* San Francisco: Chandler and Sharp, 1976.

———. "Ritual Enemas." *Natural History* 86, no. 3 (1977): 88–91.

Gann, Thomas. "Mounds in Northern Honduras." *Annual Report of the Bureau of American Ethnology* 19 (1900), Washington, D.C.

Gendrop, Paul. "Dragon-Mouth Entrances: Zoomorphic Portals in the Architecture of Central Yucatan." In *Third Palenque Round Table, 1978 Part II*, vol. 5, ed. by Merle Greene Robertson. Austin: University of Texas Press, 1980.

Gill, Richard B. *The Great Maya Droughts: Water, Life and Death.* Albuquerque: University of New Mexico Press, 2000.

Gillespie, Susan D., and Rosemary A. Joyce. "Deity Relationships in Mesoamerican Cosmologies." *Ancient Mesoamerica* 9, no. 2 (1998): 279–96.

Gómez-Pompa, Arturo, José Salvador Flors, and Mario Aliphat Fernández. "The Sacred Cacao Groves of the Maya." *Latin American Antiquity* 1 (1990): 247–57.

González Lauck, Rebecca. "La Venta: An Olmec Capital." In *Olmec Art and Ancient Mexico*, ed. by Elizabeth P. Benson and Beatriz de la Fuente. Washington, D.C.: National Gallery of Art, 1996.

Gossen, Gary. "Death and Immortality in the Modern Maya World." Paper presented at the 25th Texas Symposium of the Maya Meetings. University of Texas, 1999.

Graham, Elizabeth A., Grant D. Jones, and Robert R. Kautz. "Archaeology and Ethnohistory on a Spanish Colonial Frontier: An Interim Report on the Macal-Tipu Project in Western Belize." In Chase and Rice 1985.

Graham, Ian. *Corpus of Maya Hieroglyphic Inscriptions.* Vol. 3, part 2: Yaxchilan. Cambridge, Mass.: Peabody Museum of Archaeology, 1979.

Graham, John A. "Aspects of Non-Classic Presences in the Inscriptions and Sculptural Art of Seibal." In Culbert 1973.

Graham, Mark Miller. "Merchants and Metalwork in Middle America." In *Paths to Central American Prehistory*, ed. by Frederick W. Lange. Boulder: University of Colorado Press, 1996.

Graña-Behrens, Daniel, Christian Prager, and Elisabeth Wagner. "The Hieroglyphic Inscription of the 'High Priest's Grave' at Chichén Itzá, Yucatán, Mexico." *Mexicon* 21 (1999): 4–6.

Greene Robertson, Merle. *Merle Greene Robertson's Rubbings of Maya Sculpture.* CD-ROM, vols. 1–11. San Francisco: Pre-Columbian Art Research Institute, 1998.

Grove, David C., ed. *Ancient Chalcatzingo.* Austin: University of Texas Press, 1987.

Grove, David C., and Rosemary A. Joyce, eds. *Social Patterns in Pre-Classic Mesoamerica.* Washington, D.C.: Dumbarton Oaks, 1999.

Grube, Nikolai. "Classic Maya Dance: Evidence from Hieroglyphs and Iconography." *Ancient Mesoamerica* 3 (1992): 201–18.

———. "Hieroglyphic Sources for the History of Northwest Yucatan." In Prem 1994.

Grube, Nikolai, and Simon Martin. "Deciphering Maya Politics." *Notebook for the 22nd Maya Hieroglyphic Forum at Texas, Maya Meetings.* University of Texas, 1998.

Grube, Nikolai, and Werner Nahm. "A Census of Xibalba: A Complete Inventory of Way Characters on Maya Ceramics." In *The Maya Vase Book: A Corpus of Rollout Photographs of Maya Vases*, vol. 4, ed. by Barbara Kerr and Justin Kerr. New York: Kerr Associates, 1994.

Gubler, Ruth. "Traditional Medicine in Yucatan: What of Its Future?" In *The Fragmented Present*, ed. by Ruth Gubler and E. Hostettler. Mockmuhl, Germany: Verlag Anton Saurwein, 1996.

Hagen, Victor W. Von. *The Aztec and Maya Papermakers.* Reprint of 1944 edition. New York: Dover Publications, 1999.

Hammond, Norman. "The Distribution of Late Classic Maya Major Ceremonial Centers in the Central Area." In *Mesoamerican Archaeology: New Approaches*, ed. by Norman Hammond. Austin: University of Texas Press, 1974.

———. "Cuello Project 1978: Interim Report." Publication 1. New Brunswick, N.J.: Rutgers University, 1978.

———. *Ancient Maya Civilization.* New Brunswick, N.J.: Rutgers University Press, 1982.

———. "Inside the Black Box: Defining Maya Polity." In Culbert 1991.

Hansen, Richard D. "Excavations in the Tigre Complex, El Mirador, Peten, Guatemala." *Paper 62, El Mirador Series, Part 3.* Provo, Utah: New World Archaeological Foundation, 1990.

———. "The Road to Nakbé." *Natural History* 5 (1991): 8–14.

———. "Continuity and Disjunction: The Preclassic Antecedents of Classic Maya Architecture." In Houston 1998.

Hansen, Richard D., Ronald L. Bishop, and Federico Fahsen. "Notes on Maya Codex-Style

Ceramics from Nakbé, Petén, Guatemala." *Ancient Mesoamerica* 2, no. 2 (1991): 225–44.

Hansen, Richard D., et al. "Climactic and Environmental Variability in the Rise of Maya Civilization: A Perspective from the Northern Peten." Paper presented at the 65th Annual Meeting for the Society for American Archaeology. Philadelphia, 2000.

Harris, John F., and Stephen K. Stearns. *Understanding Maya Inscriptions: A Hieroglyph Handbook.* 2nd rev. ed. Philadelphia: University Museum, 1997.

Harrison, Peter D. "Tikal: Selected Topics." In Benson 1986.

———. "The Revolution in Ancient Maya Subsistence." In Clancy and Harrison 1990.

———. *The Lords of Tikal: Rulers of an Ancient Maya City.* London: Thames and Hudson, 1999.

Harrison, Peter D., and B. L. Turner III. *Pre-Hispanic Maya Agriculture.* Albuquerque: University of New Mexico Press, 1978.

Hartung, Horst. "A Scheme of Probable Astronomical Projections in Mesoamerican Architecture." In Aveni, 1975.

Hassig, Ross. *Trade, Tribute, and Transportation: The Sixteenth-Century Political Economy in the Valley of Mexico.* Norman: University of Oklahoma Press, 1985.

Haviland, William A. "Maya Settlement Patterns: A Critical Review." Middle American Research Institute, Publication 36 (1966): 21–47.

———. "Dower Houses and Minor Centers at Tikal, Guatemala." In Ashmore 1981.

Healy, Paul F. "Music of the Maya." *Archaeology* January/February 1988: 24–31.

Heizer, Robert F. "New Observations on La Venta." In *Dumbarton Oaks Conference on the Olmec,* ed. by Elizabeth P. Benson. Washington, D.C.: Dumbarton Oaks, 1968.

Hellmuth, Nicholas. "Cholti-Lacandon (Chiapas) and Peten-Ytza Agriculture, Settlement Pattern, and Population." In *Social Process in Maya Prehistory,* ed. by Norman Hammond. New York: Academic Press, 1977.

Hendon, Julia A. "The Pre-Classic Maya Compound as the Focus of Social Identity." In Grove and Joyce 1999.

Hester, Thomas R., and Harry Shafer, eds. *Stone Tools and Maya Civilization.* Madison, Wisc.: Prehistory Press, 1991.

Hewitt, Erika A. "What's in a Name: Gender, Power and Classic Maya Women Rulers." *Ancient Mesoamerica* 10, no. 2 (1999): 251–62.

Houston, Stephen D. "A Quetzal Feather Dance at Bonampak, Chiapas, Mexico." *Journal de la Société des Américanistes de Paris* 70 (1984): 127–38.

———. *Maya Glyphs.* Berkeley: University of California Press, 1989.

———. *Hieroglyphs and History at Dos Pilas: Dynastic Politics of the Classic Maya.* Austin: University of Texas Press, 1993.

———, ed. *Function and Meaning in Classic Maya Architecture.* Washington, D.C.: Dumbarton Oaks, 1998.

Houston, Stephen D., and David Stuart. "The Way Glyph: Evidence for 'Co-essences' Among the Classic Maya." *Research Reports on Ancient Maya Writing* 30 (1989).

———. "Of Gods, Glyphs, and Kings: Divinity and Rulership Among the Classic Maya." *Antiquity* (1996): 289–312.

Houston, Stephen D., and Karl A. Taube. "'Name-Tagging' in Classic Mayan Script: Implications for Native Classifications of Ceramics and Jade Ornaments." *Mexicon* 9, no. 2 (1987): 38–41.

Irving, Thomas Ballantine. *The Maya's Own Words.* Culver City, Calif.: Labyrinthos, 1985.

Johnston, Kevin J., and Nancy Gonlin. "What Do Houses Mean? Approaches to the Analysis of Classic Maya Commoner Residences." In Houston 1998.

Jones, Christopher. "Cycles of Growth at Tikal." In Culbert 1991.

Jones, Christopher, and L. Satterthwaite. "The Monuments and Inscriptions of Tikal: The Carved Monuments, Tikal." Report 33A. Philadelphia: University Museum, 1982.

Jones, Grant D. "The Last Maya Frontier of Colonial Yucatán." In *Spaniards and Indians in Southeastern Mesoamerica,* ed. by Murdo J. MacLeod and Robert Wasserstrom. Lincoln: University of Nebraska Press, 1983.

———. *Maya Resistance to Spanish Rule: Time and History on a Colonial Frontier.* Albuquerque: University of New Mexico Press, 1989.

Joralemon, David. *A Study of Olmec Iconography.* Washington, D.C.: Dumbarton Oaks, 1971.

———. "Ritual Blood Sacrifice Among the Ancient Maya: Part I." In *Primera mesa redonda de Palenque*, part 2, ed. by Merle Greene Robertson. Pebble Beach, Calif.: Robert Louis Stevenson School, 1974.

———. "The Olmec Dragon: A Study in Pre-Columbian Iconography." In *Origins of Religious Art and Iconography in Preclassic Mesoamerica*, ed. by H. B. Nicholson. Los Angeles: University of California Press: 1976.

Josserand, J. Kathryn. "The Narrative Structure of Hieroglyphic Texts at Palenque." In *Sixth Palenque Round Table*, 1986, vol. 8, ed. by Merle Greene Robertson. Norman: University of Oklahoma Press, 1991.

Joyce, Rosemary and John S. Henderson. "Beginnings of Village Life in Eastern Mesoamerica." *Latin American Antiquity* 12, 1 (2001): 5–24.

Justeson, John S. "The Origin of Writing Systems: Preclassic Mesoamerica." *World Archaeology* 17 (1986): 437–58.

Justeson, John S., and Lyle Campbell, eds. *Phoneticism in Mayan Hieroglyphic Writing*. Albany, N.Y.: Institute for Mesoamerican Studies, 1984.

Justeson, John S., and Peter Mathews. "The Seating of the Tun: Further Evidence Concerning a Late Preclassic Lowland Maya Stela Cult." *American Antiquity* 48 (1983): 586–93.

Justeson, John S., William M. Norman, et al. "The Foreign Impact on Lowland Mayan Language and Script." Publication 53. New Orleans: Middle American Research Institute, 1985.

Kelley, David H. "Glyphic Evidence for a Dynastic Sequence at Quiriguá, Guatemala." *American Antiquity* 27 (1962): 323–35.

———. "A History of the Decipherment of Maya Script." *Anthropological Linguistics* 4, no. 8 (1962): 1–48.

———. "Kakupacal and the Itzas." *Estudios de cultura maya* 7 (1968): 255–68.

———. "Planetary Data on Caracol Stela 3." In Aveni 1975.

———. *Deciphering the Maya Inscriptions*. Austin: University of Texas Press, 1976.

Kelley, David H., and K. Ann Kerr. "Mayan Astronomy and Astronomical Glyphs." In *Mesoamerican Writing Systems*, ed. by Elizabeth Benson. Washington, D.C.: Dumbarton Oaks, 1973.

Kelly, J. Charles. "Mesoamerican Studies and the Southwestern United States." In *Handbook of the Middle American Indians*, vol. 4, ed. by Gordon F. Ekholm and Gordon R. Willey. Austin: University of Texas Press, 1966.

Kepecs, Susan, Gary Feinman, and Sylviane Boucher. "Chichén Itzá and Its Hinterland: A World-Systems Perspective." *Ancient Mesoamerica* 5, no. 2 (1994): 141–58.

Kerr, Justin. *The Maya Vase Book: A Corpus of Rollout Photographs of Maya Vases*. Vols. 1–6. New York: Kerr Associates, 1989–2000.

———. "A Good Time Was Had by All: Fun and Games Among the Ancient Maya." Paper presented at the Symposium on Fun in Ancient America. Pre-Columbian Society of Washington, D.C.: 2000.

Kidder, Alfred V., Jesse Jennings, and Edwin Shook. *Excavations at Kaminaljuyú, Guatemala*. Publication 561. Washington, D.C.: Carnegie Institution, 1946.

Kirchhoff, Paul. "Mesoamerica." *Acta Americana* 1 (1943): 92–107.

Knorosov, Yuri V. "The Problem of the Study of the Maya Hieroglyphic Writing." *American Antiquity* 23 (1958): 248–91.

———. *Selected Chapters from the "Writing of the Maya Indians."* Trans. by Sophie D. Coe, ed. by Tatiana Proskouriakoff. Russian Translation Series 4, Peabody Museum of Archaeology and Ethnology, Harvard University, 1967.

Koontz, Rex. *The Iconography of El Tajín, Veracruz, Mexico*. Ph.D. dissertation. Austin: University of Texas, 1994.

Kowalski, Jeff Karl. "Uxmal: A Terminal Classic City in Northern Yucatan." In Benson 1986.

———. *The House of the Governor: A Maya Palace at Uxmal, Yucatán, Mexico*. Norman: University of Oklahoma Press, 1987.

———. "Who Am I Among the Itzá? Links Between Northern Yucatán and the Western Maya Lowlands and Highlands." In Berlo and Diehl 1989.

———. "The Puuc as Seen from Uxmal." In Prem 1994.

Kremer, Jurgen. "The Putun Hypothesis Reconsidered." In Prem 1994.

Krochock, Ruth. *The Development of Political Rhetoric at Chichén Itzá, Yucatán, Mexico*. Ph.D. dissertation. Dallas: Southern Methodist University, 1998.

———. "Dedication Ceremonies at Chichén Itzá: The Glyphic Evidence." *Sixth Palenque Round Table*, ed. by Merle Greene Robertson. Norman: University of Oklahoma Press, 1991.

Krochock, Ruth, and David Freidel. "Ballcourts and the Evolution of Political Rhetoric at Chichén Itzá." In Prem 1994.

Krochock, Ruth, and Mathew Looper. Personal communication, 2000.

Kubler, George. *The Art and Architecture of Ancient America: The Mexican, Maya, and Andean Peoples*. 4th edition. Baltimore: Pelican History of Art, 1992.

Kurath, Gertrude Prokosch. "Drama, Dance, and Music." In *Handbook of the Middle American Indian*, vol. 6, ed. by Manning Nash. Austin: University of Texas Press, 1967.

Landa, Diego de. *Relación de las cosas de Yucatán*. Trans. and annotated by Alfred M. Tozzer. Papers of the Peabody Museum of Archaeology and Ethnology, vol. 18. Cambridge, Mass.: Harvard University Press, 1941.

Las Casas, Bartolomé de. *A Short Account of the Destruction of the Indies*. Ed. and trans. by Nigel Griffin. London: Penguin Books, 1992.

Lee, Thomas A. *Los códices mayas*. Fundacíon Arqueológica Nuevo Mundo, A.C., San Cristóbal de las Casas, Chiapas, y Brigham Young University, Provo, Utah. Edición Conmemorativa X Aniversario. San Cristobal de las Casas, Mexico: Universidad Autónoma de Chiapas, 1985.

———. "Chiapas and the Olmec." In Sharer and Grove 1989.

Leyden, Barbara S. "Man and Climate in the Maya Lowlands." *Quarternary Research* 28 (1984): 407–14.

Lincoln, Charles E. "The Chronology of the Itza: A Review of the Literature." In Sabloff and Andrews V 1986.

———. "Structural and Philological Evidence for Divine Kingship at Chichén Itzá, Yucatán, Mexico." In Prem 1994.

Looper, Matthew G. "New Perspectives on the Late Classic Political History of Quirigua, Guatemala." *Ancient Mesoamerica* 10 (1999): 263–80.

Lorenzen, Karl James. "New Discoveries at Tumben-Naranjal: Late Postclassic Reuse and the Ritual Recycling of Cultural Geography." *Mexicon* 21 (1999): 98–107.

Lothrop, Jay Mahler. "Textiles." In Coggins 1992.

Lothrop, Samuel K. *Metals from the Cenote of Sacrifice, Chichén Itzá, Yucatan*. Memoirs of the Peabody Museum of Anthropology and Ethnography, vol. 10, no. 2. Cambridge, Mass.: Harvard University Press, 1952.

Lounsbury, Floyd G. "On the Derivation and Reading of the 'Ben-Ich' Prefix." In *Mesoamerican Writing Systems*, ed. E. P. Benson. Washington, D.C.: Dumbarton Oaks, 1973.

———. "A Rationale for the Initial Date of the Temple of the Cross at Palenque." In *Segunda mesa redonda de Palenque, 1974*, ed. by Merle Greene Robertson. Pebble Beach, Calif.: Robert Louis Stevenson School, 1976.

———. "Maya Numeration, Computation, and Calendrical Astronomy." In *Dictionary of Scientific Biography*, vol. 15, ed. by Charles C. Gillespie. New York: Charles Scribner's Sons, 1978.

———. "Astronomical Knowledge and Its Uses at Bonampak, Mexico." In Aveni 1982.

———. "The Identities of the Mythological Figures in the Cross Group Inscriptions of Palenque." In *Fourth Palenque Round Table, 1980*, vol. 6, ed. by Elizabeth Benson. San Francisco: Pre-Columbian Art Institute, 1985.

Love, Bruce. "The Hieroglyphic Lintels of Yula, Yucatan, Mexico." *Research Reports on Ancient Maya Writing*, no. 24. Washington, D.C.: Center for Maya Research, 1989.

———. *The Paris Codex: Handbook for a Maya Priest*. Austin: University of Texas Press, 1994.

Lowe, Gareth. "The Mixe-Zoque as Competing Neighbors of the Early Lowland Maya." In *Origins of Maya Civilization*, ed. by Richard E. W. Adams. Albuquerque: University of New Mexico Press, 1977.

Mace, Carol Edward. "Two Spanish-Quiché Dance-Dramas of Rabinal." *Tulane Studies in Romance Languages and Literature* 3 (1970).

MacLeod, Barbara, and Dorie Reents-Budet. "The Art of Caligraphy: Image and Meaning." In *Painting the Maya Universe: Royal Ceramics of the Classic Period*. Durham, N.C.: Duke University Press, 1994.

MacLeod, Murdo J., and Robert Wasserstrom, eds. *Spaniards and Indians in Southeastern Mesoamerica.* Lincoln: University of Nebraska Press, 1983.

MacNeish, Richard S., ed. *The Prehistory of the Tehuacan Valley.* Vol. 1. Austin: University of Texas Press, 1967.

———. *The Prehistory of the Tehuacan Valley.* 4 vols. Austin: University of Texas, 1970–74.

MacNeish, Richard S., and Mary W. Eubanks. "Comparative Analysis of the Río Balsas and Tehuacan Models for the Origin of Maize." *Latin American Antiquity* 2 (2000): 3–20.

MacNeish, Richard S., and A. Nelken-Terner. "The Preceramic of Mesoamerica." *Journal of Field Archaeology* 10 (1983): 71–84.

Mangelsdorf, Paul C. *Corn: Its Origin, Evolution, and Improvement.* Cambridge: Belknap Press, 1974.

Marcus, Joyce. "The Territorial Organization of the Lowland Maya." *Science* 180 (1973): 911–16.

———. *Emblem Glyph and State in the Classic Maya Lowlands.* Washington, D.C.: Dumbarton Oaks, 1976.

———. "Ancient Maya Political Organization." In *Lowland Maya Civilization in the Eighth Century,* ed. by Jeremy A. Sabloff and John S. Henderson. Washington, D.C.: Dumbarton Oaks, 1993.

Marquina, Ignacio. *Arquitectura prehispánica.* Mexico: Instituto Nacional Autónoma de México, 1951.

Martin, Simon, and Nikolai Grube. "Maya Superstates." *Archaeology* November/December 1995: 41–45.

———. *Chronicle of the Maya Kings and Queens: Deciphering the Dynasties of the Ancient Maya.* London: Thames and Hudson, 2000.

Martínez, Donjuán Guadalupe. "Los olmecas en el estado de Guerrero." In *Los Olmecas en Mesoamerica,* ed. by John E. Clark. Mexico: El Equilibrista, 1994.

Masson, Marilyn. "From the Jaws of the Sky: Yucatec and Zapotec Ancestor Deification." Paper presented at the 25th Texas Symposium of the Maya Meetings. Austin: University of Texas, 1999.

———. "Peripheral No More: Long-Term Trends of Postclassic Maya Economic Growth and Social Change as Reflected in Household Assemblages of Northern Belize." Paper presented at the 65th Annual Meeting of the Society for American Archaeology. Philadelphia, 2000.

Matheny, Ray T. "Northern Maya Lowland Water-Control Systems." In Harrison and Turner 1978.

———. "Early States in the Maya Lowlands During the Late Preclassic Period: Edzna and El Mirador." In Benson 1986.

Mathews, Peter. The Glyphs on the Ear Ornaments from Tomb A-1/1. In *Excavation at Altún Ha, Belize, 1964–1970,* vol. I, edited by David Pendergast. Toronto: Royal Ontario Museum, 1979.

———. "Maya Early Classic Monuments and Inscriptions." In Willey and Mathews 1985.

———. *The Proceedings of the Maya Hieroglyphic Weekend, October 27–28, 1990.* Transcribed and ed. by Phil Wanyerka. Cleveland, Ohio, 1990.

———. "Classic Maya Emblem Glyphs." In Culbert 1991.

———. Personal communication, 2000.

Mathews, Peter, and Merle Greene Robertson. "Notes on the Olvidado, Palenque, Chiapas, Mexico." In Fields 1985.

Mathews, Peter, and Linda Schele. "Lords of Palenque: The Glyphic Evidence." In *Primera mesa redonda de Palenque, Part I,* ed. by Merle Greene Robertson. Pebble Beach, Calif.: Robert Louis Stevenson School, 1974.

Mathews, Peter, and Gordon Willey. "Prehistoric Politics in the Pasion Region: Hieroglyphic Texts and Their Archaeological Settings." In Culbert 1991.

Maudslay, Alfred P. *Archaeology: Biologia Centrali-Americani.* London: R. H. Porter and Dulau. 1889–1902.

McAnany, Patricia. *Living with the Ancestors: Kinship and Kingship in Ancient Maya Society.* Austin: University of Texas Press, 1995.

———. "Ancestors and the Classic Maya Built Environment." In Houston 1998.

McBryde, Felix Webster. "Cultural and Historical Geography of Southwestern Guatemala." *Institute of Social Anthropology Publication 4.* Washington, D.C.: Smithsonian Institution, 1947.

McKillop, Heather. "Ancient Maya Tree Cropping." *Ancient Mesoamerica* 5, no. 2 (1994): 129–40.

Meltzer, David S., and Jeremy A. Sabloff, ed. *Search for the First Americans*. Washington, D.C.: Smithsonian Institution, 1995.

Menchú, Rigoberta. *I, Rigoberta Menchú: An Indian Woman in Guatemala*. London: Verso, 1984.

Milbrath, Susan. "Astronomical Images and Orientations in Architecture of Chichen Itza." In *New Directions in American Archaeoastronomy*, ed. by Anthony F. Aveni. Oxford, England: BAR International Series 454, 1988.

———. *Star Gods and the Maya: Astronomy in Art, Folklore, and Calendars*. Austin: University of Texas Press, 1999.

Miller, Mary Ellen. "A Re-examination of Mesoamerican Chacmool." *Art Bulletin* 67 (1985): 7–17.

———. *The Art of Mesoamerica: From Olmec to Aztec*. Rev. ed. New York: Thames and Hudson, 1996.

———. "Imaging Maya Art." *Archaeology* May/June 1997: 34–40.

———. "A Design for Meaning in Maya Architecture." In Houston 1998.

———. *Maya Art and Architecture*. New York: Thames and Hudson, 1999.

Miller, Mary Ellen, and Stephen D. Houston. "The Classic Maya Ballgame and Its Architectural Setting: A Study in Relations Between Text and Image." *RES* (1987): 47–66.

Miller, Mary, and Karl Taube. *The Gods and Symbols of Ancient Mexico and the Maya*. New York: Thames and Hudson, 1993.

Morley, Sylvanus G. *An Introduction to the Study of Maya Hieroglyphs*. Bulletin 57. Washington, D.C.: Smithsonian Institution, Bureau of American Ethnology, 1915.

———. *Inscriptions of Peten*. 5 vols. Publication 437. Washington, D.C.: Carnegie Institution, 1937–38.

———. *The Ancient Maya*. Stanford, Calif.: Stanford University Press, 1946.

Morley, Sylvanus G., and George W. Brainard. *The Ancient Maya*. 3rd ed. Stanford, Calif.: Stanford University Press, 1956.

Morris, Earl H., Jean Charlot, and Ann Axtell Morris. *Temple of the Warriors at Chichén Itzá, Yucatan*. Vols. 1–2. Washington, D.C.: Carnegie Institution, 1931.

Morris, Walter F., Jr. *Living Maya*. New York: Harry N. Abrams, 1987.

Newsome, Elizabeth A. *Trees of Paradise and Pillars of the World: Vision Quest and Creation in the Stelae Cycle of 18 Rabbit–God K, Copan, Honduras*. Ph.D. dissertation. Austin: University of Texas, 1991.

———. "Precious Stones of Grace: A Theory of the Origin and Meaning of the Classic Maya Stela Cult." In *Eighth Palenque Round Table, 1993, vol. 10*, ed. by Martha J. Macri and Jan McHargue. San Francisco: Pre-Columbian Research Institute, 1996.

Nichols, Deborah. "An Overview of Regional Settlement Pattern Survey in Mesoamerica 1060–1995." In *Arqueología mesoamérica: Homenaje a William T. Sanders*, ed. by Alba Guadalupe Mastache, et al. Mexico: Instituto Nacional de Antropología e Historia, 1996.

Niederberger, Christine. "Olmec Horizon Guerrero." In *Olmec Art of Ancient Mexico*, ed. by Elizabeth P. Benson and Beatrize de la Fuente. Washington, D.C.: National Gallery of Art, 1996.

Palka, Joel W. "Sociopolitical Implications of a New Emblem Glyph and Place Names in Classic Maya Inscriptions." *Latin American Antiquity* 7, no. 3 (1996): 211–27.

Parsons, Lee. *The Origins of Maya Art: Monumental Stone Sculpture of Kaminaljuyú, Guatemala and the Southern Pacific Coast*. Washington, D.C.: Dumbarton Oaks, 1986

———. "Proto-Maya Aspects of Miraflores-Arenal Monumental Stone Sculpture from Kaminaljuyú and the Southern Pacific Coast." In *Maya Iconography*, ed. by Elizabeth Benson and Gillett Griffin. Princeton, N.J.: Princeton University Press, 1988.

Pendergast, David M. "Lamanai, Belize: Summary of Excavation Results, 1974–1980." *Journal of Field Archaeology* 8 (1981): 29–53.

———. "Stability Through Change: Lamanai, Belize, from the Ninth to the Seventeenth Century." In Sabloff and Andrews V 1986.

Pielou, E. C. *After the Ice Age*. Chicago: University of Chicago Press, 1992.

Pincemin, Sophia, Joyce Marcus, et al. "Extending the Calakmul Dynasty Back in Time: A New Stela from the Maya Capital in Campeche." *Latin American Antiquity* 9, no. 4 (1998): 310–27.

Pohl, John, M.D., and Angus McBride. *Aztec, Mixtec, and Zapotec Armies*. Great Britain: Osprey Publishing, 1991.

Pohl, Mary D., ed. *Prehistoric Lowland Maya Environment and Subsistence Economy*. Papers of the Peabody Museum of Archaeology and Ethnology 77. Cambridge, Mass.: Harvard University Press, 1985.

Pohl, Mary D., et al. "Early Agriculture in the Maya Lowlands." *Latin American Antiquity* 7, no. 4 (1996): 355–72.

Pollock, H. E. D. *Round Structures of Aboriginal Middle America*. Publication 471. Washington, D.C.: Carnegie Institution, 1936.

Pollock, H. E. D., Ralph C. Roys, et al. *Mayapán, Yucatán, Mexico*. Publication 619. Washington, D.C.: Carnegie Institution, 1962.

Potter, David F. *Maya Architecture of the Central Yucatan Peninsula, Mexico*. Publication 44. New Orleans: Middle American Research Institute, 1977.

Prem, Hanns J., ed. *Hidden Among the Hills: Maya Archaeology of the Northwest Yucatan Peninsula*. Mockmuhl, Germany: Verlag Von Flemming, 1994.

Proskouriakoff, Tatiana. "Historical Implications of a Pattern of Dates at Piedras Negras, Guatemala." *American Antiquity* 25, no. 4 (1960): 454–75.

———. *An Album of Maya Architecture*. Reprint of 1946 edition. Norman: University of Oklahoma Press, 1963.

———. "Historical Data in the Inscriptions of Yaxchilán." *Estudios de cultura maya* 3 (1963): 149–67.

———. "Historical Data in the Inscriptions of Yaxchilán." Part 2. *Estudios de cultura maya* 4 (1964): 177–202.

———. *Jades from the Cenote of Sacrifices, Chichén Itzá*. Memoirs of the Peabody Museum of Anthropology and Ethnology, vol. 10, no. 1. Cambridge, Mass.: Harvard University Press, 1974.

Puleston, Dennis E. "Intersite Areas in the Vicinity of Tikal and Uaxactún." In *Mesoamerican Archaeology: New Approaches*, ed. by Norman Hammond. Austin: University of Texas Press, 1974.

Quirarte, Jacinto. *Izapan-Style Art: A Study of Its Form and Meaning*. Washington, D.C.: Dumbarton Oaks, 1973.

Rathje, William L. "The Origin and Development of Lowland Classic Maya Civilization." *American Antiquity* 36 (1971): 275–85.

———. "Praise the Gods and Pass the Metates: A Hypothesis of the Development of Lowland Rainforest Civilization in Middle America." In *Contemporary Archaeology*, ed. by M. P. Leone. Carbondale: Southern Illinois University Press, 1972.

Rathje, William L., and Jeremy A. Sabloff. "A Model of Ports-of-Trade." *Estudios de cultura maya* 10 (1978): 81–90.

Recinos, Adrián, Dionisio José Chonay, and Delia Goetz. *The Annals of the Cakchiquels and Title of the Lords of Totonicapán*. Norman: University of Oklahoma Press, 1967.

Redfield, Robert. *The Folk Culture of Yucatán*. Chicago: University of Chicago Press, 1941.

Reed, Nelson. *The Caste War of Yucatan*. Stanford, Calif.: Stanford University Press, 1964.

Reents-Budet, Dorie. "The 'Homul Dancer' Theme in Maya Art." In *Sixth Palenque Round Table, 1986*, ed. by Merle Greene Robertson. Norman: University of Oklahoma Press, 1991.

———. *Painting the Maya Universe: Royal Ceramics of the Classic Period*. Durham: Duke University Press, 1994.

Reese-Taylor, Katherine and Debra S. Walker. "Boom and Bust: Interaction between Northern Belize and the Central Petén during the Late Formative to Early Classic Transition. "Paper presented at the 65th Annual Meeting of the Society for American Archaeology. Philadelphia, 2000.

Reilly, Kent, III. "Olmec Iconographic Influences on the Symbols of Maya Rulership." In *Sixth Palenque Round Table, 1986*, ed. by Merle Greene Robertson. Norman: University of Oklahoma Press, 1991.

Restall, Matthew. *Maya Conquistador*. Boston: Beacon Press, 1992.

Reyna, Rosa María. "Guerrero y la cultura arquelógica mezcala." In *Arqueología Mexicana* 7, no. 41 (2000): 68–73.

Rice, Don S. "Middle Pre-Classic Maya Settlement in the Central Maya Lowlands." *Journal of Field Archaeology* 3 (1976): 425–445.

Rice, Don S., and Dennis E. Puleston. "Ancient Maya Settlement Patterns in the Peten, Guatemala." In Ashmore 1981.

Rice, Prudence M. "The Peten Postclassic: Perspectives from the Central Peten Lakes." In Sabloff and Andrews 1986.

———. "Economic Change in the Lowland Maya Late Classic Period." In *Specialization, Exchange, and Complex Societies,* ed. by Elizabeth M. Brumfiel and Timothy K. Earle. Cambridge, England: Cambridge University Press, 1987.

Rice, Prudence M., and Robert J. Sharer, eds. *Maya Ceramics: Papers from the 1985 Maya Ceramic Conference.* 2 vols. British Archaeological Reports 345 (1987).

Ricketson, Oliver G., and Edith B. Ricketson. *Uaxactun, Guatemala, Group E, 1926–1937.* Publication 477. Washington, D.C.: Carnegie Institution, 1937.

Ringle, William M. "Pre-Classic Cityscapes: Ritual Politics among the Early Lowland Maya." In Grove and Joyce, 1999.

Ringle, William M., and E. Wyllys Andrews V. "Formative Residences at Komchen, Yucatan, Mexico." In *Household and Community in the Mesoamerican Past,* ed. by R. R. Wilk and Wendy Ashmore. Albuquerque: University of New Mexico Press, 1988.

———. "The Demography of Komchen: An Early Maya Town in Northern Yucatan." In Culbert and Rice 1990.

Ringle, William M., Tomás Gallareta Negón, and George Bey III. "The Return of Quetzalcoatl: Evidence for the Spread of a World Religion During the Epiclassic Period." *Ancient Mesoamerica* 9, no. 2 (1998): 183–232.

Robertson, Merle Greene. *The Temple of the Inscriptions.* Vol. 1 of *The Sculpture of Palenque.* Princeton, N.J.: Princeton University Press, 1983.

———. *The Early Buildings of the Palace and the Wall Paintings.* Vol. 2 of *The Sculpture of Palenque.* Princeton, N.J.: Princeton University Press, 1985.

———. *The Late Buildings of the Palace.* Vol. 3 of *The Sculpture of Palenque.* Princeton, N.J.: Princeton University Press, 1985.

Robertson, Robin A., and David A. Freidel, ed. *Archaeology at Cerros, Belize, Central America.* Vol. 1. Dallas: Southern Methodist University, 1986.

Robles C. Fernando, and Anthony P. Andrews. "A Review and Synthesis of Recent Postclassic Archaeology in Northern Yucatan." In Sabloff and Andrews 1986.

Rosny, Léon de. *Essai sur le déchiffrement de l'écriture hiératique de l'Amérique Centrale.* Paris: Maisonneuve, 1867.

Roys, Lawrence. *The Engineering Knowledge of the Maya.* Publication 436. Washington, D.C.: Carnegie Institution, 1934.

Roys, Ralph L. *The Indian Background of Colonial Yucatan.* Publication 548. Washington, D.C.: Carnegie Institution, 1943.

———. "Personal Names of the Maya." In *Contributions to American Anthropology and History* 6 (1957): 31–48.

———. *The Political Geography of the Yucatec Maya.* Publication 613. Washington, D.C.: Carnegie Institution, 1957.

———. "Lowland Maya Native Society at Spanish Contact." In *Handbook of Middle American Indians,* vol. 3, ed. by Gordon R. Willey. Austin: University of Texas Press, 1965.

———. *The Ritual of the Bacabs.* Norman: University of Oklahoma Press, 1965.

———. *The Book of Chilam Balam of Chumayel.* Reprint of 1933 edition. Norman: University of Oklahoma Press, 1967.

———. *The Ethnobotany of the Maya.* Reprint. Philadelphia: Institute for the Study of Human Issues, 1976.

Ruppert, Karl J. *Chichén Itzá: Architectural Notes.* Publication 595. Washington, D.C.: Carnegie Institution, 1952.

Ruz Lhuillier, Alberto. *El Templo de las Inscripciones, Palenque.* Mexico City: Instituto Nacional de Arqueología e Historia, 1973.

Sabloff, Jeremy A. "Old Myths, New Myths: The Role of Sea Trader in the Development of Ancient Maya Civilization." In *The Sea and the Precolumbian World,* ed. by Elizabeth P. Benson. Washington, D.C.: Dumbarton Oaks, 1977.

———. *The New Archaeology and the Ancient Maya.* New York: Scientific American Library, 1990.

Sabloff, Jeremy A., and E. Wyllys Andrews V, eds. *Late Lowland Maya Civilization: Classic to Postclassic.* Albuquerque: University of New Mexico Press, 1986.

Sabloff, Jeremy A., and John Henderson, eds. *Lowland Maya Civilization in the Eighth Century A.D.* Washington, D.C.: Dumbarton Oaks, 1993.

Sahagún, Fray Bernardino. *Florentine Codex: General History of the Things of New Spain*. Trans. by J. O. Anderson and C. E. Dibble. Santa Fe, N.M.: School of American Research, 1950–71.

Sanders, William T., and Barbara J. Price. *Mesoamerica: The Evolution of Civilization*. New York: Random House, 1968.

Sanders, William T., and Robert S. Santley. "A Tale of Three Cities: Energies and Urbanization in Prehispanic Central Mexico." In *Prehistoric Settlement Pattern Studies*, ed. by Evon Z. Vogt. Albuquerque: University of New Mexico Press, 1983.

Sanders, William T., and David Webster. "The Mesoamerican Urban Tradition." *American Anthropologist* 90 (1988): 521–46.

Satterthwaite, Linton, Jr. "Palace Structures J-2 and J-6." *Piedras Negras Papers, No. 6*. Philadelphia: University Museum, 1935.

———. Calendrical Arithmetics. *Joint Publications, University of Pennsylvania Museum, Philadelphia Anthropological Society*, no. 3. Philadelphia, 1947.

———. *Piedras Negras Archaeology Architecture, Part V: Sweathouses*. Philadelphia: University Museum, 1952.

———. "Calendrics of the Maya Lowlands." In *Handbook of Middle American Indians*, vol. 3, ed. by Gordon R. Willey. Austin: University of Texas Press, 1965.

Scarborough, Vernon L. "Water Management in the Southern Lowlands: An Accretive Model for the Engineered Landscape." In *Economic Aspects of Water Management in the Prehispanic New World*, ed. by Vernon L. Scarborough and Barry Isaacs. Greenwich, Conn.: JAI Press, 1993.

———. "Ecology and Ritual: Water Management and the Maya." *Latin American Antiquity* 9, no. 2 (1998): 135–59.

Scarre, Chris. "High-Tech Digging." *Archaeology* September/October 1999: 50–55.

Schavelzon, Daniel. "Temples, Caves, or Monsters? Notes on Zoomorphic Facades in Pre-Hispanic Architecture." In *Third Palenque Round Table, 1978*, vol. 5, ed. by Merle Greene Robertson. Austin: University of Texas Press, 1980.

Schele, Linda. "Sacred Site and World-View at Palenque." In *Mesoamerican Sites and World-Views*, ed. by Elizabeth Benson. Washington, D.C.: Dumbarton Oaks, 1981.

———. *Maya Glyphs: The Verbs*. Austin: University of Texas Press, 1982.

———. "The Hauberg Stela: Bloodletting and the Mythos of Maya Rulership." In Fields 1985.

———. "An Epigraphic History of the Western Maya Region." In Culbert 1991.

Schele, Linda, and David Freidel. *A Forest of Kings*. New York: William Morrow, 1990.

Schele, Linda, and Peter Mathews. *The Code of Kings, The Language of Seven Sacred Maya Temples and Tombs*. New York: Scribner, 1998.

Schele, Linda, and Mary Ellen Miller. *Blood of Kings: Dynasty and Ritual in Maya Art*. New York: George Braziller, 1986.

Schele, Linda, and Khristaan D. Villela. "Creation, Cosmos, and the Imagery of Palenque and Copan." In *Eighth Palenque Round Table, 1993*, vol. 10, ed. by Martha J. Marci and Jan McHargue. San Francisco: Pre-Columbian Art Research Institute, 1996.

Schellhas, Paul. *Representations of Deities of the Maya Manuscript*. Cambridge, Mass.: Peabody Museum of Archaeology and Ethnology, 1904.

Schmidt, Paul. *Arqueología de Xochipala, Guerrero*. Mexico: Universidad Nacional Autónoma de México, 1990.

Schortman, Edward M. "Interaction Between the Maya and Non-Maya Along the Late Classic Southeast Maya Periphery: The View from the Lower Motagua Valley, Guatemala." In *The Southeast Maya Periphery*, ed. by Patricia A. Urban and Edward M. Schortman. Austin: University of Texas Press, 1986.

Schroeder, Susan, Stephanie Wood, and Robert Haskett. *Indian Women of Early Mexico*. Norman: University of Oklahoma Press, 1997.

Sharer, Robert J. "The Olmec and the Southeast Periphery of Mesoamerica." In Sharer and Grove 1989.

———. *Ancient Maya*. 5th ed. Stanford, Calif.: Stanford University Press, 1994.

Sharer, Robert J., and David C. Grove, eds. *Regional Perspectives on the Olmec*. Cambridge, England: Cambridge University Press, 1989.

Sharer, Robert J., and Payson D. Sheets. *The Prehistory of Chalchuapa, El Salvador*. Vol. 1. Philadelphia: University of Pennsylvania Press, 1978.

Sheets, Payson D. "Environmental and Cultural Effects of the Ilopango Eruption in Central America." In *Volcanic Activity and Human Ecology*, ed. by Payson D. Sheets and Donald Grayson. New York: Academic Press, 1976.

———. *The Ilopango Volcanic Eruption and the Maya Protoclassic*. University Museum Studies, no. 9. Carbondale: Southern Illinois University Press, 1976.

———. *The Ceren Site: A Prehistoric Village Buried by Volcanic Ash in Central America*. Fort Worth, Tex.: Harcourt, Brace, Javonovich, 1992.

Sheets, Payson D., John M. Ladd, and David Bathgate. "Chipped Stone Artifacts." In Coggins 1992.

Smith, A. Ledyard. "The Corbeled Arch in the New World." In *The Maya and Their Neighbors*, ed. by C. L. Hays, et al. New York: Appleton-Century, 1940.

Smyth, Michael P. "Before the Florescence: Chronological Reconstructions at Chac II, Yucatan, Mexico." *Ancient Mesoamerica* 9, no. 1 (1998): 137–50.

Spinden, Herbert J. *A Study of Maya Art, Its Subject Matter and Historical Development*. Cambridge, Mass.: Peabody Museum of Archaeology and Ethnology, 1913.

———. *The Reduction of Maya Dates*. Cambridge, Mass.: Peabody Museum of Archaeology and Ethnology, 1924.

Stephens, J. L., and Frederick Catherwood. *Incidents of Travel in Central America, Chiapas, and Yucatan*. 2 vol. Harper and Brothers, New York, 1841. Reprint edition by Dover, 1962.

———. *Incidents of Travel in Yucatan*. 2 vol. Harper and Brothers, New York, 1843. Reprint edition by Dover, 1963.

Stirling, Matthew. "Expedition Unearths Buried Masterpieces of Carved Jade." *National Geographic* 80 (1941): 277–302.

———. "Monumental Sculpture in Southern Veracruz and Tabasco." In *Handbook of Middle American Indians*, vol. 3, ed. by Gordon R. Willey. Austin: University of Texas Press, 1965.

Stone, Andrea. *Images from the Underworld: Naj Tunich and the Tradition of Maya Cave Painting*. Austin: University of Texas Press, 1995.

Stone, Doris. "Synthesis of Lower Central American Ethnohistory." In *Handbook of Middle American Indians*, vol. 4, ed. by Gordon F. Ekholm and Gordon R. Willey. Austin: University of Texas Press, 1966.

Stuart, David. "Blood Symbolism in Classic Maya Iconography." *RES: Anthropology and Aesthetics* 7, no. 8 (1984): 6–20.

———. "The Classic Maya Social Structure: Titles, Rank, and Professionals as Seen from the Inscriptions." Paper presented at the Symposium on Maya Art and Civilization: The New Dynamics. Kimbell Art Museum, Fort Worth, Texas, 1986.

———. *Ten Phonetic Syllables*. Research Reports on Ancient Maya Writing, no. 14. Washington, D.C. 1987.

———. "Smoking Frog, K'inch Yax K'uk' Mo, and the Epigraphic Evidence for Ties Between Teotihuacan and the Classic Maya." Paper presented at the Symposium: A Tale of Two Cities: Copan and Teotihuacan. Harvard University, 1997.

———. "The Fire Enters His House: Architecture and Ritual in Classic Maya Texts." In Houston 1998.

———. "The New Inscriptions of Temple XIX." Paper presented at the Tenth Palenque Round Table. Chetumal, Mexico, 1999.

———. "The Arrival of Strangers: Teotihuacan and Tollan in Classic Maya History." In *Mesoamerica's Classic Heritage*, ed. by David Carraseo, Scott Sessions, and Lindsay Jones. Boulder: University Press of Colorado, 1999b.

Stuart, David and Stephen Houston. *Classic Maya Place Names*. Washington, D.C.: Dumbarton Oaks, 1994.

Stuart, George. "Quest for Decipherment: A Historical and Biographical Survey of Maya Hieroglyphic Investigation." In *New Theories on the Ancient Maya*, University Museum Monograph 77 University Museum Symposium Series, vol. 3. Philadelphia: University Museum, 1992.

Sullivan, Paul. *Unfinished Conversations: Mayas and Foreigners Between Two Wars*. Berkeley: University of California Press, 1989.

Taschek, Jennifer T., and Joseph W. Ball. "Las ruinas de Arenal: Preliminary Report on a Subregional Major Center in the Western Belize Valley." *Ancient Mesoamerica* 10, no. 2 (1999): 215–36.

Tate, Carolyn. "Maya Astronomical Rituals Recorded on Yaxchilan Structure 23." *Rutgers Art Review* 7 (1986): 1–20.

———. *Yaxchilán, The Design of a Maya Ceremonial City.* Austin: University of Texas Press, 1992.

Taube, Karl A. "The Classic Maize God: A Reappraisal." In Fields 1985.

———. *A Representation of the Principal Bird Deity in the Paris Codex.* Research Reports on Ancient Maya Writing, no. 6. Washington, D.C., 1987.

———. *The Ancient Yucatec New Year Festival: The Liminal Period in Maya Ritual and Cosmology.* Ph.D. dissertation. New Haven, Conn.: Yale University, 1988.

———. "A Prehispanic Maya Katun Wheel." *Journal of Anthropological Research* 44, no. 2 (1988): 183–201.

———. *Major Gods of Ancient Yucatán: Schellhas Revisited.* Studies in Pre-Columbian Art and Archaeology, no. 32. Washington, D.C.: Dumbarton Oaks, 1992.

———. *Aztec and Maya Myths.* Austin: University of Texas Press, 1993.

———. "The Iconography of Toltec Period Chichén Itzá." In Prem 1994.

———. "The Rainmakers: The Olmec and Their Contributions to Mesoamerican Belief and Ritual." In *The Olmec World: Ritual and Rulership, ed. by Princeton: Art Museum, 1996.*

———. "The Jade Hearth: Centrality, Rulership and the Classic Maya Temple." In Houston 1998.

Tedlock, Barbara. *Time and the Highland Maya.* Rev. ed. Albuquerque: University of New Mexico Press, 1992.

Tedlock, Dennis. *Popol Vuh: The Definitive Edition of the Mayan Book of the Dawn of Life and the Glories of God and Kings.* Rev. ed. New York: Simon & Schuster, 1996.

Teeple, John E. "Maya Inscriptions: The Venus Calendar and Another Correlation." *American Anthropologist* 28 (1926): 402–8.

———. *Maya Astronomy.* Publication 403. Washington, D.C.: Carnegie Institution, 1931.

Tejada, Antonio Fonseca. *Ancient Maya Paintings of Bonampak, Mexico.* Washington, D.C.: Carnegie Institution, 1955.

Thomas, Cyrus. "A Study of the Manuscript Troano." *Contributions to North American Ethnol-ogy,* vol. 5. Washington, D.C.: Government Printing Office, 1882.

———. "Notes on Certain Maya and Mexican Manuscripts." *Annual Report of the Bureau of American Ethnology* 3. Washington, D.C., 1884.

———. "Mayan Calendar Systems." *Annual Report of the Bureau of American Ethnology* 19. Washington, D.C., 1900.

Thompson, J. Eric S. *The Civilization of the Mayas.* Chicago: Chicago Natural History Museum, 1927.

———. "Sky Bearers, Colors and Directions in Maya and Mexican Religion." *Contributions to American Archaeology,* Publication 436, no. 10. Washington, D.C.: Carnegie Institution, 1934.

———. *A New System for Deciphering Yucatecan Dates with Special Reference to Chichén Itzá.* Publication 483, no. 22. Washington, D.C.: Carnegie Institution, 1937.

———. "A Blood-Drawing Ceremony Painted on a Maya Vase." *Estudios de Cultura Maya* 1 (1961): 13–20.

———. "The Moon Goddess in Middle America with Notes on Related Deities." *Contributions to American Anthropology and History,* vol. 5. Publication 509, no. 29. Washington, D.C.: Carnegie Institution, 1939.

———. *Maya Arithmetic.* Publication 528. Washington, D.C.: Carnegie Institution, 1941.

———. *A Catalog of Maya Hieroglyphs.* Norman: University of Oklahoma Press, 1962.

———. *Rise and Fall of Maya Civilization.* Norman: University of Oklahoma Press, 1966.

———. "The Bacabs: Their Portraits and Their Glyphs." In *Monographs and Papers in Maya Archaeology,* ed. by William R. Bullard Jr. Papers of the Peabody Museum of Archaeology and Ethnology, vol. 61. Cambridge, Mass.: Harvard University, 1970.

———. *Maya History and Religion.* Norman: University of Oklahoma Press, 1970.

———. *Maya Hieroglyphic Writing: An Introduction.* Reprint of 1950 ed. Norman: University of Oklahoma Press, 1971.

———. *A Commentary on the Dresden Codex.* American Philosophical Society Memoir 93. Philadelphia, 1972.

Tiesler, Vera. "Head Shaping and Dental Decoration Among the Ancient Maya: Archaeological and Cultural Aspects." Paper presented at the 64th Annual Meeting of the Society for American Archaeology. Chicago, 1999.

Tolstoy, Paul. "Paper Route." *Natural History* June 1991: 7–14.

Tourtellot, Gair. "A View of Ancient Maya Settlement in the Eighth Century." In Sabloff and Henderson 1993.

Tourtellot, Gair, and Norman Hammond. "The City Plan of Late Classic La Milpa, Belize." Paper presented at the 65th Annual Meeting of the Society for American Archaeology. Philadelphia, 2000.

Tourtellot, Gair, and Jeremy A. Sabloff. "Exchange Systems Among the Ancient Maya." *American Antiquity* 37 (1972): 126–135.

———. "Will the Real Elites Please Stand Up? An Archaeological Assessment of Maya Elite Behavior in the Terminal Classic Period." In Chase and Chase 1992.

———. "Community and Structure at Sayil: A Case Study of Puuc Settlement." In Prem 1994.

Tozzer, Alfred M., trans. and ed. *Landa's Relación de las Cosas de Yucatán*. Papers of the Peabody Museum of Archaeology and Ethnology, vol. 13. Cambridge, Mass.: Harvard University Press, 1941.

———. "Chichen Itza and Its Cenote of Sacrifice: A Comparative Study of Contemporaneous Maya and Toltec." *Memoirs of the Peabody Museum of American Archaeology and Ethnology*. Cambridge, Mass.: Harvard University Press, 1957.

Trombold, Charles D., ed. *Ancient Road Networks and Settlement Hierarchies in the New World*. Cambridge, England: Cambridge University Press, 1991.

Turner, Bruce L., and Peter D. Harrison, eds. *Pulltrouser Swamp: Ancient Maya Habitat, Agriculture and Settlement in Northern Belize*. Austin: University of Texas Press, 1983.

Turner, Bruce L., and William T. Sanders. "Summary and Critique." In *Gardens and Prehistory: The Archaeology of Settlement Agriculture in Greater Mesoamerica*, ed. by Thomas W. Killion. Tuscaloosa: University of Alabama Press, 1992

Vail, Gabrielle. "A Commentary on the Bee Almanacs in Codex Madrid." In *Códices y documentos sobre México, primer simposio*, ed. by Constanza Vega Sosa. Mexico City: Instituto Nacional de Antropología e Historia, 1994.

———. *The Gods in the Madrid Codex: An Iconographic and Glyphic Analysis*. Ph.D. dissertation. New Orleans: Tulane University, 1996.

———. "The Yearbearer Gods in the Madrid Codex." In *Códices y documentos sobre México*, segundo simposio, vol. 1, ed. by Salvador Rueda Smithers, et al. Mexico: Instituto Nacional de Antropología e Historia and Dirrección General de Publicaciones del Consego Nacional para la Cultura y las Artes, 1997.

———. "Kisin and the Underworld Gods of the Maya." *Latin American Indian Literatures Journal* 14 (1998): 167–87.

———. "Pre-Hispanic Maya Religion: Conceptions of Divinity in the Postclassic in Maya Codices." *Ancient Mesoamerica* 11 (2000): 123–47.

Vaughn, H. H., Edward S. Dewey Jr., and S. E. Garnett-Jones. "Pollen Stratigraphy of Two Cores from the Peten Lake District." In Pohl 1985.

Villacorta C., José A., and Carlos Villacorta C. *Códices mayas*. Guatemala City: Tipografía Nacional, 1933.

Villela, Khristaan D., and Linda Schele. "Astronomy and the Iconography of Creation Among the Classic and Colonial Period Maya." In *Eighth Palenque Round Table, 1993*, vol. 10, ed. by Martha J. Macri and Jan McHargue. San Francisco: Pre-Columbian Research Institute, 1996.

Vogt, Evon Z. *Zinacantan. A Maya Community in the Highlands of Chiapas*. Cambridge, Mass.: Harvard University Press, 1969

———. *The Zinacantecos of Mexico: A Modern Maya Way of Life*. New York: Holt, Rinehart & Winston, 1990.

———. *Tortillas for the Gods: A Symbolic Analysis of Zinacanteco Rituals*. Norman: University of Oklahoma Press, 1993.

Vogt, Evon Z., and Richard M. Leventhal, eds. *Prehistoric Settlement Patterns: Essays in Honor of Gordon R. Willey*. Albuquerque: University of New Mexico Press, 1983.

Voorhies, Barbara, ed. *Ancient Trade and Tribute: Economies of the Soconusco Region of Mesoamerica.* Salt Lake City: University of Utah Press, 1989.

Wallace, David Rains. "Central American Landscapes." In Coates 1997.

Warren, Kay B. *Indigenous Movements and Their Critics: Pan-Maya Activism in Guatemala.* Princeton, N.J.: Princeton University Press, 1998.

Watanabe, John. *Maya Saints and Souls in a Changing World.* Austin: University of Texas Press, 1992.

Webster, David L. *Defensive Earthworks of Becan, Campeche, Mexico: Implications for Maya Warfare.* Publication 41. New Orleans: Middle American Research Institute, 1976.

———. "Warfare and the Evolution of Maya Civilization." In Adams 1977.

———. "The Study of Maya Warfare: What It Tells Us About the Maya and What It Tells Us About Maya Archaeology." In Sabloff and Henderson 1993.

———. "Classic Maya Architecture: Implications and Comparisons." In Houston 1998.

Webster, David L., Nancy Gonlin, and Payson Sheets. "Copan and Cerén: Two Perspectives on Ancient Mesoamerican Households." *Ancient Mesoamerica* 8, no. 1 (1997): 43–62.

Willey, Gordon R. "The Postclassic in the Maya Lowlands: A Preliminary Overview." In Sabloff and Andrews 1986.

Willey, Gordon R., and W. R. Bullard. "Prehistoric Settlement Patters in the Maya Lowlands." In *Handbook of Middle American Indians*, vol. 2, ed. by Gordon R. Willey. Austin: University of Texas Press, 1965.

Willey, Gordon R., and Peter Mathews, eds. *Consideration of the Early Classic Period in the Maya Lowlands.* Publication 10. Albany, N.Y.: Institute for Mesoamerican Studies, 1985.

Willey, Gordon R., and Jeremy A. Sabloff. *A History of American Archaeology.* San Francisco: W. H. Freeman, 1974.

Willey, Gordon R., and Demitri B. Shimkin. "The Maya Collapse: A Summary View." In Culbert 1973.

Woods, James C., and Gene L. Titmus. *Ancient Limestone Quarries of Nakbé, Guatemala.* RAINPEG Project, 1997.

Wren, Linnea. "The Great Ballcourt Stone at Chichen Itza." In *Sixth Palenque Round Table, 1986*, vol. 8, ed. by Merle Greene Robertson. Norman: University of Oklahoma Press, 1991.

Wren, Linnea, and Peter Schmidt. "Elite Interaction During the Terminal Classic Period of the Northern Maya Lowlands: Evidence from the Reliefs of the North Temple of the Great Ball Court." In Culbert 1991.

Zeuner, Frederick E. *Dating the Past: An Introduction to Geo-chronology.* 4th ed. New York: Haftner Publisher, 1970.

INDEX

Boldface page numbers indicate major treatment of a subject. Page numbers in italics with suffix *f* denote a figure; suffix *m* denotes a map; and suffix *t* denotes a table.

A

AAS (atomic absorption spectronomy) 11
Abaj Takalik 29, 37, **103**
Abrams, Elliot 215
abstinence, sexual 187
Acatec 274
accession, ruler 177*f*, 178, 191, 193–194, 236, 250, 257, 259, 271, **282**, 283*f*, 285, 286, 288–289, 290. *See also* throne(s)
Account of the Things of Yucatán, An (Landa) ix
acropolises 60, 108, 209, 217, 221, 228, **232–233**, 234, 235, 236, 241
administrators, administration 126, 135, 144–145, 228
adobe 215, 217, 218, 224, **239**, 311, 333
adolescence **331**
adultery 330, 332–333
afterlife **203–207**
Agautepec 274
agave 310, 311
Aglio, Augustine 297, 298
agriculture **307–311**. *See also* farmers, farming; fields; plants
    at Abaj Takalik 103
    at Altun Há 103
    Archaic Period 17, 19, 21, 100, 102
    books on 296, 299, 303
    canals and reservoirs for 9

Classic Period 7, 82, 99, 106
    cycles of 92, 170, 250–251, 252–253
    Early Classic Period 105, 112
    Early Colonial Period 187
    Early Postclassic Period 71, 72
    Hun Hunahpu and 168
    intensive 308, 329
    at Lake Petén Itzá 113
    Late Classic Period 43, 49, 52, 59, 103, 106, 124, 152, 229
    Late Postclassic Period 113
    Late Preclassic 42
    Late Preclassic Period 39, 99, 107, 151
    Lithic Period 19
    in lowlands 31, 95
    Middle Preclassic Period 32, 110
    at Nohmul 228
    Olmec 27, 28
    paleobotanical studies of xi
    Preclassic Period 45, 308
    at Quiriguá 112
    sun god and 166
    swidden 99, 102, 308–309
    Terminal Classic Period 60
    warfare and 155
    wetland 98, 237
aguadas 307
Aguateca 53, 54, 57, **103**, 107, 149, 152
Ah Abnal 70

Ahaw 166
Ahaw B'ot 253
Ah-Bolon-Abte 62*f*
Ah K'an Usha 288
Ah Ne Ol Mat 51*t*
Ah Nik 288, 296
Ah Sak Ichiy Pat 288
Ah Uk 281, 288, 289
akbal 166, 170, 186
Aké 80
Akul Anab I 51*t*
Akul Anab II 51*t*
Akul Anab III 51*t*
alabaster 316, 321*t*
alautun 256*f*, 257
alliances, political 121
    building campaigns and 241
    causeways and 234
    Classic Period 112, 134, **155**, 211
    Early Classic Period 105, 123
    Early Postclassic Period 71, 72
    Late Classic Period **52–53**, 54, 55, 56, 57, 59, 104, 107, 108, 112, 114, 115–116, 133, 136, 330
    Late Postclassic Period 76, 77, 133–134, 138, 139
    Late Preclassic Period 123
    in Mexico 62*f*
    Postclassic Period 78
    at Spanish Conquest 81, 109

elite(s) *(continued)*
    Terminal Classic Period 123,
      221, 340
    tools of 315
    trade and 307, 325
    vessels of 294
    writing system of 277
El Manatí 25
El Mirador **41, 108**
    Cerros and 39
    Danta Complex at 39, 45–46,
      108, 217, 234
    defensive wall at 42
    Early Classic Period 43, 44,
      123
    El Tigre Complex at 39, 108,
      217, 218
    Late Classic Period 124, 132
    Late Preclassic Period 34, 104,
      122, 123, 129, 130, 134, 151,
      217, 222–223, 234, 236
    Nakbé and 111
    Preclassic Period 45
    stelae at 37
    trade at 324
    triadic complexes at 236
    water management at 307
El Perú 53, 55, 104, **108**, 129, 339*f*
El Portón 11, **31, 108–109**
El Salvador 3
    cotton fabric in 316
    Early Classic Period 46, 106
    farming in 308
    geography of 91
    keystone arch in 243
    languages of 275
    Late Classic Period 59,
      124–125
    Late Postclassic Period 77
    Late Preclassic Period 34–35,
      37, 42
    Lenca in 330
    Locona culture in 22
    Middle Preclassic Period 100
    Olmec culture in 25, 29, 30,
      92, 105
    sweat baths in 237
    Terminal Classic Period 66
    volcanoes in 94, 98, 309
El Tajín 65, 67, 68, 72
El Tigre Complex 39, 108, 217, 218
El Trapiche 30, 105
Emal 66, 71
emblem glyphs 49–50, 52, 53, 57,
    58, 108, **130**, 132, 133, **271, 284**
embroidery 311, 317
employment 84
enemas 341

entertainment **340–342**
environment viii, x, 7, 42, 59, 63, 64,
    72, 91, **97–99**, 106, 121
epazote 312, 336
epigraphers, epigraphy **7–8**, 85,
    268–274, 286, 287, 289, 290, 291,
    293, 295, 302, 329
Epi-Olmec culture 17, 35
equinoxes 92, 235, 261
ethnic groups, non-Maya **329–330**
ethnologies **13**
Evening Star 156
examinations 303
excavations vii, **6–7, 269–270**
explorers, early **5–6**
exports 32, 39, 308, **310–311**, 321*t*
eyebrows 339
eyes 144*f*, 337, 338

F

fabric 10
facades 218
    Classic Period 217
    cosmology of 230
    of cut stone 239
    at Ek Balam 108
    in Guerrero 24
    hieroglyphic texts on 9
    at Kabah 109
    Late Classic Period 56, 136,
      224, 226, 240
    Late Postclassic Period 74
    Late Preclassic Period 34, 36,
      39, 40, 105, 114, 115, 123,
      171, 222–223
    Middle Preclassic Period 217,
      239
    of platforms 234
    Terminal Classic Period 221,
      225
    at Uaxactún 114
    at Xunantunich 115
family 212, **330–332**, 333, 335
fans 317, 320
farmers, farming **308–310**. *See also*
    agriculture; plants
    agricultural cycles and 251
    burials of 212
    Classic Period 154
    contemporary 84
    dry season and 329
    food of 335–336
    Late Classic Period 124, 129,
      228
    Late Postclassic Period 78,
      127, 229
    Late Preclassic Period 167
    lineage and 331

in Middle East 101
Olmec 27
residential compounds of 333
settlement surveys and 7
sun god and 166
fasting 179, 187, 338
feasts, feasting 59, 121, 154, 250,
    254, 313, 319, 330, 335, 336,
    341–342
Feathered Serpent 67, 69, 71, 77,
    84, 115, 183
feathers, exotic bird
    in ball games 195, 197
    on clothing 339
    commoners and 332
    in dances 188
    Early Classic Period 44
    gifts of 319
    God L and 169
    in hairstyles and headdresses 9,
      338, 339
    Kucamatz and 183
    Late Classic Period 188
    Late Postclassic Period 74, 145
    on rattles 341, 342*f*
    from Salamá Valley 31
    for trade 28, 42, 46, 95, 319,
      321*t*
    as tribute 323
    in warfare 147, 155
    in weavings 317
fer-de-lance 95
ferns 94
fertility 162, 164, 167, 184, 206, 331
fertilizer 308
festivals 13, 45, 84, 119, 121, 230,
    254, 336
fields 31, 32, 42, 107, **160**, 197, 206,
    237, **308–310**, 312, 329, 335, 336
figurines 22, 23, 30, 34, 205, 208,
    314, 318, 322, 338*f*, 340, 341
fill, in construction 7, 24, 217, 234,
    235, 239, 240, 241
fire, firewood 237, 255, 292, 323,
    335, 336
Fire-His-Shield 69, 105, 292
First Crocodile 44
First-Dawned-Sky Lightning God
    92
First Father 176
First-Five-Sky 170, 172
First Hair Knot 113–114
First Mother 176
fish, fishing 3, 95, 96, 100
    cooking of 336
    creation of 183
    Early Preclassic Period 102
    as export 321*t*

painting(s) *(continued)*
   of mythological scenes 159, 340
   Olmec 28
   of palace scenes 10, 233
   of ruler cult 230
   of shields 147
   at shrines 206
   on skulls 211
   on vases 10, 172–173, 189, 293
paints, paint implements **315**, 335,
   338
Pakal 272
palace(s) 9, 221, **232–233**
   at Bonampak 56
   burials in 212, 231
   at Cancuén 119
   ceramic workshops in 314
   at Chichén Itzá 291–292
   Classic Period 104, 119
   construction of 216
   corbeled arch and 242*f*
   at Dos Pilas 57
   Early Classic Period 45
   Early Colonial Period 82
   Early Postclassic Period 69
   excavations of 329
   Late Classic Period 56, 57,
     115, 124, 133, 209, 224, 323
   Late Postclassic Period 78, 126
   Late Preclassic Period 38, 222
   location of 228
   masonry 333
   Middle Preclassic Period 217
   Olmec 27
   paintings of 10, 233
   at Palenque 227*m*, 233
   at Piedras Negras 233
   residences in 333
   at Sayil 113
   sweat baths in 237
   Terminal Classic Period 64,
     113, 232*f*
Palenque **111–112**, 119, 135, 205*f*,
   227*m*, 273
   aqueduct at 237
   Berlin at 271
   building materials at 239
   Calakmul and 53
   Classic Period 70, 130,
     150–151, 221
   collapse of 60
   creation myths and 300
   Early Classic Period 114
   emblem glyph of 130, 284*f*
   funerary monuments at 203*f*,
     204
   Hanab Pakal at 206, 208, 216,
     235

   languages of 274, 329
   Late Classic Period 49, 51*t*,
     106, 114, 132, 135, 175*f*,
     204, 210, 211, 224, 225*f*, 236
   Maudslay at 6, 268
   name-tagging at 296
   Oval Tablet at 123*f*
   palaces at xi, 9*f*, 232, 233
   panels at 185
   panels from 323
   Pomoná and 52, 57
   pyramid-mountain at 162–163
   Red Queen of 210
   rulers of 51*t*, 92, 233, **272**, 323
   as sacred city **174–178**
   Schele on 272
   Seler on 269
   stucco portraiture at 55
   Temple of the Cross at 175*f*,
     231
   Temple of the Foliated Cross at
     176*f*
   Temple of the Sun at 166, 177*f*
   throne at 230
   Tikal and 114
   tomb at 206, 235
   Toniná and 56
   tower at 235
   Usumacinta style at 224, 225*f*
   vaulting at 221, 243
Palenque Round Table **272**
Palenque Triad **178**
palisades 57, 152, 153, 238
palma 197
palm oil 310
Panama 66, 70, 74, 79, 318, 319, 322
panels, carved 155, 224, 277, 291, 323
pan-Mesoamerican culture. *See*
   Mesoamerica, pan-Mesoamerican
   culture
papaya 310
paper 310, 315*f*, **318–319**, 321*t*
paradise 205
parapets 238
parentage statement 285, 286
parents 331
Paris Codex 6, 253, 267, 268, 297, **298**
parrots 95, 312
partridge 312
Pasión River 54, 63, 97*f*, 100, 103,
   104, 107, 109, 113, 236, 308
Paso de la Amada 22, 23, 24
patios 333
Pawahtun 159, 161, **169**, 259, 298
Peabody Museum 6, 273
pearls 10, 321*t*
peccary 96, 336
Pechtún Há 59

   pectorals 188, 194
peer polities 132–133, 134, 136
pendants, carved 316, 340
penicillin 337
penis 28, 190*f*, 191, 194*f*, 195. *See
   also* genitals; phallus
Pérez, José 298
Pérez, Juan Pio 298
perforator 189, 317*f*
perfumes **339**
personality cult 43
pestles 315
Petén 3, 5
   Archaic 230
   architectural style of **224**
   burials in 170
   cave paintings in 10
   Classic Period 17, 18, 111,
     114, 236, 329
   collapse of 8
   contemporary 84
   Early Classic Period 43, 44, 48,
     108, 112, 114, 123
   Early Colonial Period 82
   Early Postclassic Period 69, 72
   environment of 98–99
   excavations at 6, 7
   fortifications in 154
   geography of 96, 97, 98–99
   jade in 31
   languages of 275
   Late Classic Period 49, 53, 59,
     104, 115, 116, 124, 132, 148,
     189–190, 208
   Late Postclassic Period 76,
     113, 126, 154, 155
   Late Preclassic Period 34, 38,
     41, 42, 104, 108, 113–114,
     221–222, 236
   Middle Preclassic Period 32,
     33, 100, 101, 110, 111, 122,
     223–224
   overpopulation in 63
   rain, rain forest in 91, 308
   reoccupied sites in 242
   round structures in 236
   rulers of 58*f*
   scattering rituals in 194*f*
   site location in 227
   stucco deity masks in 40
   Terminal Classic Period 60, 63,
     311
   tourism in 8
   trade in 319, 324
Petén Itzá 76, 82, 96, 113, 154
Petexbatún 49, **54**, **57**, 58, 61, 62,
   63, 103, 107, 113, 149, **152–153**,
   154, 238

Popol Vuh ix, 12–13, 28, 35, 36, 77, 83, 115, 168, 170, 171, **183–186,** 196, 197, 204, 211, **300,** 341
Popol Vuh Museum 210*f*
population(s) 124, 215
    agriculture and 100, 228, 308, 309
    Archaic Period 19, 21, 22, 102
    of Calakmul 104
    of Chichén Itzá 105
    of Chunchucmil 106, 228
    Classic Period 7, 99
    of Cobá 106
    contemporary 84, 85, 91
    diversity of **329–330**
    of Dzibilchaltún 107
    Early Classic Period 42, 44, 46, 48, 105
    Early Postclassic Period 70, 71, 72, 105
    Early Preclassic Period 24
    imports for 311
    at La Milpa 110
    Late Classic 104, 121, 123
    Late Classic Period 18, 49, 50, 51, 52, 53, 59, 121
    Late Postclassic Period 74, 77, 78, 110, 125, 126, 139
    Late Preclassic Period 34, 38, 39, 41, 42, 104, 121
    in lowlands 307
    of Mayapán 110
    Middle Preclassic Period 32, 101
    of Mixco Viejo 111
    of Naco 111
    of Nohmul 228
    Preclassic Period 217
    of Río Azul 112
    at Sayil 113
    slash-and-burn farming and 99
    at Spanish Conquest 81
    of Tayasal 113
    Terminal Classic Period 60, 63, 64, 107, 113, 115
    of Tikal 114
    of Utatlán 126
porch, covered 333
portable objects **295–296**
porters **323,** 325
portraiture, ruler 3, 24, 26*f*, 43, 45, 55, 56, 180–183, 207*f*, 210, 221, 223, 271, **277,** 340
ports, portage 32, 39, 44, 49, 65, 110, 228, **324**
Postclassic Period
    burials in **210–211**
    Chichén Itzá in 13

construction in **218, 223**
Dresden Codex from 12*f*
excavations on 6
government in **137–140**
northern area in 74
Toltecs in 77
Yucatán in 17
post-conquest period 18*t*. *See also* Spanish Conquest
postindependence **83**
pots 11*f*, 255, 311, 314, 316, 335, 336
potters, pottery 6, **10,** 329. *See also* ceramic(s); *specific kinds of pottery*
    Archaic Period 17, 19, 21–22, 23, 100, 122
    in burials 32
    codex-style 294–295
    decorated 334
    Early Classic Period 46, 48, 113
    Early Preclassic Period 122
    gifts of 319
    hieroglyphic texts about 293
    Late Classic Period 57
    Late Preclassic Period 36, 209
    Lithic Period 3, 5
    in lowlands 31
    making 333
    Middle Preclassic Period 100, 102–103
    Olmec 27
    painting on 11
    in residences 333
    temper 319
    Terminal Classic Period 60, 61
    for trade 321*t*
    transport of 324
    volcanic ash in 91, 314
    women as 335
poultry 336, 341
poverty 84
prayers 162, 254–255, 309, 310, 331, 337
Preclassic Period 7, 11, 22, 65, 67, 69, 77
pride, mythological 185
priests, Catholic 12, 82, 83, 212, 338, 341
priests, shaman. *See* shamans
Primary Standard Sequence (PSS) 293–294
Primer of Mayan Hieroglyphics, A (Brinton) 269
Principal Bird Deity 36, 40, 160, **166,** 170, 176, 182, 184*f*, 185–186, 194, 225

professions, professionals 329, 331. *See also specific professions and professionals*
pronunciation **275–276**
property **212,** 333. *See also* land
prophecies. *See also* divination
    astrology and 261
    in *Books of the Chilam Balam* 302, 303
    in *Dresden Codex* 297
    farming 309
    k'atun and 257
    260-day cycle and 251
Proskouriakoff, Tatiana 270–272
prostitutes 331
proto-Mayan 23, **274**
protowriting 24, **31,** 37, 251, 277
pseudoglyphs 293
public works **32,** 38, 39
Puebla 322
Pulltrouser Swamp 59, 102
punishments **332–333**
Punta Canbalam 65, 238
Punta de Chimino 57, 152–153, 238
purification, ritual 237, 338
Putún 61, 69, 77
Puuc Hills region
    architectural style of 56, 108, 115, **224–226,** 242*f*, 243, 318
    cities in 109, 324
    Classic Period 217
    Early Postclassic Period 71, 72
    geography of 96
    Late Classic Period 64, 106, 240
    slateware from 11*f*, 314
    Terminal Classic Period 68, 113, 115, 232*f*
pyramid-mountains 91, **162–163**
Pyramid of the Magicians 163
Pyramid of the Sun 163
pyramids, pyramid-temples. *See* temple-pyramid(s)
pyrite 316, 321*t*

Q

Qik'ab 77
quadripartite order 84, 110, 159–160, 164, 167, 169, 249, 259, 309, 317
quail 312
quarrying, stone 124, 215, 216, 217, **240,** 307, 314, 316
quartz crystals 38
quatrefoil 195–196, 206
queens. *See* ruler(s)
quetzal 28, **31,** 74, 95, 155, 169, 188, 195, 312, 323, 333